Why Do You Need This New Edition?

If you're wondering why you should buy this new edition of *The Prentice Hall Guide for College Writers*, here are a few great reasons!

1 A completely revised and updated chapter on doing research explains the wide variety of current sources, from books to Web 2.0 sources like wikis and blogs, so that you can do library and Internet research effectively.

2 New Source Evaluation Charts for print, online database, and Web sources show you how to tell whether research sources are credible as well as useful for what you are writing.

3 New sections based on the latest MLA and APA style manuals give you the most up-to-date and accurate citation examples to help you cite and document your sources properly.

4 New student essays provide you with models for writing visual analyses, film reviews, problem-solution papers, explanatory essays, and literary analysis essays.

5 New Techniques Charts highlight key techniques and procedures for different types of writing in a handy, at-a-glance format.

6 New Writing Assignment Charts help you choose an appropriate type of writing—for example, a blog, essay, or letter to the editor—depending on whether you are writing for a personal, academic, or public audience.

7 25 new readings bring you up-to-date perspectives on a wide range of interesting topics—including Web 2.0, Facebook and its founder, Wikipedia, Twitter, U2's Bono, white collar crime, citizen journalism, plagiarism detection, and climate change—and provide ideas for your own writing.

PEARSON

BRIEF NINTH EDITION

The Prentice Hall Guide for College Writers

STEPHEN REID
Colorado State University

Prentice Hall

Boston Columbus Indianapolis New York San Francisco Upper Saddle River
Amsterdam Cape Town Dubai London Madrid Milan Munich Paris Montreal Toronto
Delhi Mexico City Sao Paulo Sydney Hong Kong Seoul Singapore Taipei Tokyo

Senior Acquisitions Editor: *Brad Potthoff*
Senior Development Editor: *Marion Castellucci*
Senior Marketing Manager: *Sandra McGuire*
Senior Media Producer: *Stefanie Liebman*
Project Coordination, Text Design, and Electronic Page Makeup: *Nesbitt Graphics, Inc.*
Senior Art Director: *Anne Nieglos*
Cover Designer: *Laura Gardner*
Image Permission Coordinator: *Angelique Sharps*
Photo Researcher: *Pearson Image Resource Center/ Teri Stratford*
Operations Specialist: *Mary Ann Gloriande*
Printer and Binder: *Courier Corporation*
Cover Printer: *Coral Graphic Services, Inc.*

For permission to use copyrighted material, grateful acknowledgment is made to the copyright holders on pages C–C-2, which are hereby made part of this copyright page.

Library of Congress Cataloging-in-Publication Data
Reid, Stephen
The Prentice Hall guide for college writers / Stephen Reid.— Brief 9th ed.
p. cm.
Includes bibliographical references and index.
ISBN 978-0-205-75207-2
Complete CIP data is on file at the Library of Congress.

Prentice Hall
is an imprint of

www.pearsonhighered.com

1 2 3 4 5 6 7 8 9 10—CRK—13 12 11 10

Brief Edition ISBN-13: 978-0-205-75207-2
Brief Edition ISBN-10:   0-205-75207-1

Contents

Thematic Contents   xii

Preface   xvii

1 WRITING MYTHS AND RITUALS   3

Writing Fitness: Rituals and Practice   5

Place, Time, and Tools   6

Energy and Attitude   7

Keeping a Journal   9

Reading Entries • Write-to-Learn Entries • Writing Entries

WARMING UP Journal Exercises   10

"On Keeping a Journal" by Roy Hoffman   11

2 SITUATIONS, PURPOSES, AND PROCESSES FOR WRITING   15

The Rhetorical Situation   16

Elements of the Rhetorical Situation   16

The Writer • The Occasion • Purpose • Audience • Genre • Context

Why the Rhetorical Situation Is Important   18

Purposes for Writing   19

Writer-Based Purposes   19

Subject- and Audience-Based Purposes   20

Combinations of Purposes   20

Subject, Purpose, and Thesis   21

Purpose and Audience   22

Audience Analysis   22

Purpose, Audience, and Genre   24

Analyzing the Rhetorical Situation   25

Purpose, Audience, and Context in Two Essays   26

"The Struggle to Be an All-American Girl" by Elizabeth Wong   27

"I'm OK, but You're Not" by Robert Zoellner   28

Dimensions of the Writing Process   30

Collecting   31

Shaping   31

Drafting   31

Revising   32

The Whole Process   32

WARMING UP Journal Exercises   33

A Writing Process at Work: Collecting and Shaping   34

"Athletes and Education" by Neil H. Petrie   34

"On Writing 'Athletes and Education'" by Neil H. Petrie   38

A Writing Process at Work: Drafting and Revising   41

"From the Rough Draft of 'The Declaration of Independence'" by Thomas Jefferson   41

3 OBSERVING   45

Techniques for Writing About Observations   48

Observing People   49

Observing Places   50

Observing Objects   51

WARMING UP Journal Exercises   52

"Take This Fish and Look at It" by Samuel H. Scudder   53

"Trailing History" by Scott Vogel   58

Observing: The Writing Process   63

ASSIGNMENT FOR OBSERVING   63

Choosing a Subject   63

Collecting   65

Sketching • Taking Double-Entry Notes • Answering Questions • Freewriting

Shaping   66

Spatial Order • Chronological Order • Comparison/Contrast • Definition • Simile, Metaphor, and Analogy • Title, Introduction, and Conclusion

Drafting   72

Reread Journal Entries and Notes • Reobserve Your Subject • Reexamine Purpose, Audience, Dominant Idea, and Shape • Create a Draft

Revising   72

Gaining Distance and Objectivity

Peer Response   73

Rereading and Responding to Your Readers • Guidelines for Revision

POSTSCRIPT ON THE WRITING PROCESS   75

"Permanent Tracings" by Jennifer Macke (student)   76

"Empty Windows" by Stephen White (student)   82

4   REMEMBERING   87

Techniques for Writing About Memories   88

Remembering People   91

Remembering Places   92

Remembering Events   92

WARMING UP Journal Exercises   94

"Beauty: When the Other Dancer Is the Self" by Alice Walker   94

"César Chávez Saved My Life" by Daniel "Nene" Alejandrez   102

Remembering: The Writing Process   106

ASSIGNMENT FOR REMEMBERING   106

Choosing a Subject   107

Collecting   108

Brainstorming • Looping • Clustering

Shaping   109

Genre • Chronological Order • Comparison/Contrast • Image • Voice and Tone • Persona • Dialogue • Title, Introduction, and Conclusion

Drafting   114

Revising   115

Guidelines for Revision

Peer Response   116

POSTSCRIPT ON THE WRITING PROCESS   117

"The Wind Catcher" by Todd Petry (student)   118

"The Red Chevy" by Juli Bovard (student)   121

5   READING   127

Techniques for Analyzing and Responding to Texts   129

Critical Reading Strategies   130

Double-Entry Log • Critical Rereading Guide

Guidelines for Class Discussion   132

Summarizing and Responding to an Essay   133

"Teach Diversity—with a Smile" by Barbara Ehrenreich   134

Summarizing   137

Summary of "Teach Diversity—with a Smile"   137

Responding   138

Types of Responses • Kinds of Evidence

Response to "Teach Diversity—with a Smile"   139

WARMING UP Journal Exercises   141

"Letter to America" by Margaret Atwood   142

Casebook on Responses to Climate Change   145

"The IPCC Fourth Assessment" by Jerald L. Schnoor   146

"A Climate Repair Manual" by Gary Stix   148

"The Rise of Renewable Energy" by Daniel M. Kammen   150

"50 Things You Can Do"   155

Reading and Writing Processes 159

ASSIGNMENT FOR READING/WRITING 159

Choosing a Subject 159

"Teaching Tolerance in America" by Dudley Erskine Devlin 159

Collecting 162

Text Annotation • Reading Log

Shaping 164

Summary Shaping 164

Description • Paraphrase • Direct Quotation • Avoiding Plagiarism

Sample Summaries 166

Response Shaping 167

Analyzing • Agreeing/Disagreeing • Interpreting and Reflecting

Outlines for Summary/Response Essays 169

Drafting 170

Revising 171

Guidelines for Revision

Peer Response 172

POSTSCRIPT ON THE WRITING PROCESS 173

"Letter to Margaret Atwood" by Dean C. Swift (student) 173

"Two Responses to Deborah Tannen" by Jennifer Koester and Sonja H. Browe (students) 176

6 ANALYZING AND DESIGNING VISUALS 183

Techniques for Analyzing Visuals 185

Analyzing Visuals 186

Composition • Focal Point • Narrative • Themes

Analyzing Visuals with Text 189

Analyzing Visuals in Context 191

"Progress or Not" by Jonathan Alter 192

"Who's a Looter?" by Tania Ralli 194

Analyzing the Genre of the Visual 194

Rhetorical Appeals to the Audience 197

Appeal to Reason • Appeal to Emotion • Appeal to Character and Credibility • Combined Appeals in an Ad

Techniques for Designing Visuals 199

WARMING UP Journal Exercises 201

"Analysis of Rosetta Stone Ad" by Sarah Kay Hurst (student) 204

"Miss Clairol's 'Does She . . . or Doesn't She?': How to Advertise a Dangerous Product" by James B. Twitchell 205

Processes for Analyzing and Designing Visuals 211

ASSIGNMENT FOR ANALYZING VISUALS 211

ASSIGNMENT FOR DESIGNING VISUALS 212

Choosing a Subject 212

Collecting 213

Shaping 214

Analysis Focused on the Visual

"Triple Self-Portrait" by Charles Rosen and Henri Zerner 214

Analysis Focused on the Social Context

"Out of the Picture on the Abortion Ban" by Ellen Goodman 215

Analysis Focused on the Story

"Coming Home" by Carolyn Kleiner Butler 218

Drafting 220

Revising 220

Guidelines for Revision

Peer Response 221

POSTSCRIPT ON THE WRITING PROCESS 222

"Some Don't Like Their Blues at All" by Karyn M. Lewis (student) 223

"Weight Loss 101 for the Adult Fitness Program" by Lawrence Fletcher (student) 226

7 INVESTIGATING 237

Techniques for Investigative Writing 238

Report on a Research Study 239

"Drivers on Cell Phones Are as Bad as Drunks" by David Strayer, et al. 240

Brief Report with Graphics 242

"Gimme an A (I Insist!)" by Abigail Sullivan Moore 242

Profile of a Person 243

"Face to Face" by David Kushner   243

Interview   246

"Henry Louis Gates Jr. Will Now Take Your Questions"   246

WARMING UP Journal Exercises   248

"Surfin' the Louvre" by Elizabeth Larsen   249

"The Homeless and Their Children" by Jonathan Kozol   251

Investigating: The Writing Process   258

ASSIGNMENT FOR INVESTIGATING   258

Choosing a Subject   259

Community Service Learning   260

Collecting   261

Asking Questions

Research Tips   263

Summarizing • Citing Sources in Your Text

Doing Field Research   264

Interviewing • Writing Questionnaires

Shaping   267

Inverted Pyramid • Chronological Order • Comparison and Contrast • Additional Shaping Strategies • Title, Introduction, and Conclusion

Drafting   269

Revising   270

Guidelines for Revision

Peer Response   271

POSTSCRIPT ON THE WRITING PROCESS   272

"The Hollywood Indian" by Lauren Strain (student)   272

"My Friend Michelle, an Alcoholic" by Bridgid Stone (student)   280

8 EXPLAINING   285

Techniques for Explaining   287

Explaining *What*: Definition   288

Explaining *How*: Process Analysis   290

Explaining *Why*: Causal Analysis   292

WARMING UP Journal Exercises   294

"Multiracialness" by LaMer Steptoe (student)   295

"How to Take Control of Your Credit Cards" by Suze Orman   296

"How Male and Female Students Use Language Differently" by Deborah Tannen   302

Explaining: The Writing Process   308

ASSIGNMENT FOR EXPLAINING   308

Choosing a Subject   309

Collecting   310

Questions • Branching • Observing • Remembering • Reading • Investigating

Shaping   312

Audience and Genre • Definition and Classification

Research Tips   313

Example • Voice and Tone • Chronological Order and Process Analysis • Causal Analysis

Tips for Integrating Images   316

Introduction and Lead-In • Lead-In, Thesis, and Essay Map • Paragraph Transitions and Hooks • Body Paragraphs

Drafting   321

Revising   321

Peer Response   322

Guidelines for Revision

POSTSCRIPT ON THE WRITING PROCESS   324

"White Lies: White-Collar Crime in America" by Chris Blakely (student)   325

"Anorexia Nervosa" by Nancie Brosseau (student)   334

9 EVALUATING   339

Techniques for Writing Evaluations   340

"Hunan Dynasty" by Phyllis C. Richman   342

Evaluating Commercial Products or Services   343

"Cell-phone Face-off" by Consumer Reports   344

Evaluating Works of Art   344

"'American Gothic,' Pitchfork Perfect" by Paul Richard   345

Evaluating Performances   347

"Slumdog Millionaire" by Manohla Dargis   348

WARMING UP Journal Exercises   350

"Evaluating a Web Site" by Robin Williams and John Tollett   351

"All's Not Well in Land of 'The Lion King'" by Margaret Lazarus   355

"Today's Special" by David Sedaris   356

Evaluating: The Writing Process   360

ASSIGNMENT FOR EVALUATING   360

Choosing a Subject   361

Collecting   362

Observing • Remembering • Reading • Investigating

Shaping   364

Audience and Genre • Analysis by Criteria • Comparison and Contrast • Chronological Order • Causal Analysis • Title, Introduction, and Conclusion

Research Tips   367

Peer Response   367

Drafting   368

Revising   369

Guidelines for Revision

POSTSCRIPT ON THE WRITING PROCESS   370

"Borrowers Can Be Choosy" by Linda Meininger (student)   370

"Vulgar Propriety" by Courtney Klockeman (student)   379

10 PROBLEM SOLVING   385

Techniques for Problem Solving   386

Demonstrating That a Problem Exists   388

Proposing a Solution and Convincing Your Readers   389

WARMING UP Journal Exercises   391

"Should Educators Use Commercial Services to Combat Plagiarism?" by Rebecca Moore Howard   393

"One Thing to Do About Food" by Eric Schlosser, Marion Nestle, Michael Pollan, Troy Duster and Elizabeth Ransom, Peter Singer, and Jim Hightower   395

"The Argument Culture" by Deborah Tannen   403

Problem Solving: The Writing Process   409

ASSIGNMENT FOR PROBLEM SOLVING   409

Choosing a Subject   410

Collecting   411

Identify and Focus on the Specific Problem • Demonstrate That the Problem Needs a Solution • Discover Possible Solutions • Evaluate Possible Solutions • Convince Your Readers • Answer Possible Objections to Your Proposal • List Possible Steps for Implementation • Observing • Remembering

Research Tips   415

Reading and Investigating

Shaping   415

Genres for Problem Solving • Outlines for Problem Solving • Causal Analysis • Criteria Analysis • Chronological Order

Drafting   418

Peer Response   418

Revising   419

Guidelines for Revision

POSTSCRIPT ON THE WRITING PROCESS   421

"Can Citizen Journalism Pick Up the Pieces?" by Adam Richman (student)   422

"New Regulations and You" by Jessica Cook (student)   429

11 ARGUING   439

Techniques for Writing Arguments   440

Claims for Written Argument   442

Claims of Fact or Definition • Claims About Cause and Effect • Claims About Value • Claims About Solutions or Policies

Appeals for Written Argument   446

Appeal to Reason • Appeal to Character • Appeal to Emotion • Combined Appeals

Rogerian Argument   450

The Toulmin Method of Argument   453

Example of a Toulmin Analysis • Using the Toulmin Model

WARMING UP Journal Exercises 454

"The Internet: A Clear and Present Danger?" by
Cathleen A. Cleaver 456

Multigenre Casebook on Web 2.0 462

"You Have No Friends" by Farhad Manjoo 464

". . . And Why I Hate It" by Sarah Kliff 467

"Facebook U.S. Audience Growth" 469

"Say Everything" by Emily Nussbaum 470

"Teens Feel Safe on MySpace" by Larry D. Rosen 473

"Protect the Willfully Ignorant" by Lily Huang 474

"Think Before You Post" AdCouncil 476

"Wikipedia and the Meaning of Truth" by Simson L.
Garfinkel 477

"Can Wikipedia Handle Stephen Colbert's
Truthiness?" by James Montgomery 480

"Why You Can't Cite Wikipedia in My Class" by Neil
L. Waters 481

"Professors Should Embrace Wikipedia" by Mark
Wilson 484

"Twitter on the Barricades in Iran: Six Lessons
Learned" by Noam Cohen 487

Arguing: The Writing Process 491

ASSIGNMENT FOR ARGUING 491

Choosing a Subject 491

Collecting 492

Narrowing and Focusing Your Claim •
Remembering

Analyzing Statistics 494

Observing • Investigating

Shaping 494

List "Pro" and "Con" Arguments • Draw Circle
of Alternative Positions • Outlines for
Arguments • Developing Arguments

Research Tips 499

Drafting 499

Peer Response 500

Revising 501

Revision Guidelines • Revising Fallacies in Logic

POSTSCRIPT ON THE WRITING PROCESS 505

"Welfare Is Still Necessary for Women and Children
in the U.S." by Crystal Sabatke (student) 505

"Standardized Tests: Shouldn't We Be Helping Our
Students?" by Eric Boese (student) 513

12 RESPONDING TO LITERATURE 523

RESPONDING TO A SHORT STORY 526

"The Story of an Hour" by Kate Chopin 526

RESPONDING TO A POEM 529

"Musée des Beaux Arts" by W. H. Auden 529

Techniques for Responding to Literature 531

WARMING UP Journal Exercises 532

Purposes for Responding to Literature 533

Responding to Short Fiction 534

Character • Plot • Narrative Point of View •
Setting • Style • Theme

"The Lesson" by Toni Cade Bambara 537

Responding to Poetry 544

Voice and Tone • Word Choice • Figures of
Speech • Sound, Rhyme, and Rhythm

Five Contemporary Poems by Aurora Levins
Morales, Gary Soto, Joy Harjo, Wislawa
Szymborska, and Yusef Komunyakaa 546

Responding to Literature: The Writing Process 552

ASSIGNMENT FOR RESPONDING TO LITERATURE 552

Collecting 553

Shaping 556

Explaining Relationships • Evaluating •
Arguing • Investigating Changes in
Interpretation

Drafting 558

Revising 558

Guidelines for Revision

POSTSCRIPT ON THE WRITING PROCESS 559

"Facing It: Reflections on War" by Grace Rexroth (student) 560

"Death: The Final Freedom" by Pat Russell (student) 563

 RESEARCHING 567

Techniques for Researching 569

Using Purpose, Audience, and Genre as Guides 570

Know Your Purpose • Accommodate Your Audience • Consider Your Genre

Finding the Best Sources: Currency, Reliability, and Relevance 572

Planning Your Research 572

WARMING UP Journal Exercise 573

Maintaining Your Voice and Purpose: Effectively Incorporating Sources 574

Documenting Your Sources 575

Research Processes 576

ASSIGNMENT FOR RESEARCHING 576

Choosing a Subject 577

Narrowing and Focusing Your Subject

WARMING UP Journal Exercise 580

Developing a Research Strategy 582

Collecting and Notetaking 583

Record Bibliographic Information • Note the Source's Relevance, Reliability, and Currency • Summarize Pertinent Source Material • Note Key Quotations • Synthesize Sources in Your Notes • Rethink and Revise Your Hypothesis or Working Thesis

Choosing and Evaluating Sources 589

Primary and Secondary Sources • Background Information and General Reference • The 21st Century Library: Physical and Online Sources • Online Database Sources • Open Web Sources

Writing Processes 603

Shaping 604

Plan • Working Outline

Drafting 607

What Sources to Cite • Avoiding Plagiarism • How to Cite Sources in Your Text

Revising 612

Guidelines for Revision

Documenting Sources 613

In-Text Documentation: MLA Style • Works Cited List: MLA Style • In-Text Documentation: APA Style • References List: APA Style

"Foreign Language Study: An American Necessity" by Kate McNerny (student) (MLA Format Research Paper) 634

APPENDIX: WRITING UNDER PRESSURE A-1

Know Your Audience A-3

Analyze Key Terms A-3

Make a Sketch Outline A-4

Know the Material A-6

Practice Writing A-7

Proofread and Edit A-8

Sample Essay Questions and Responses A-8

Credits C

Index I-1

Thematic Contents

The Prentice Hall Guide for College Writers, ninth edition, contains selections from over 100 writers, artists, poets, and photographers. Thematic clusters of essays, articles, editorials, Web sites, cartoons, poems, short fiction, and images are indicated below. An asterisk (*) indicates a complete essay.

WEB 2.0 LITERACIES

- AdCouncil, "Think Before You Post"   476
- *Rebecca Moore Howard, "Should Educators Use Commercial Services to Combat Plagiarism?"   393
- *Simson L. Garfinkel, "Wikipedia and the Meaning of Truth"   477
- *Lily Huang, "Protect the Willfully Ignorant"   474
- *Sarah Kliff, " . . . And Why I Hate It"   467
- *David Kushner, "Face to Face"   243
- *Farhad Manjoo, "You Have No Friends"   464
- James Montgomery, "Can Wikipedia Handle Stephen Colbert's Truthiness?"   480
- *Noam Cohen, "Twitter on the Barricades in Iran: Six Lessons Learned"   487
- *Adam Richman, "Can Citizen Journalism Pick Up the Pieces?"   422
- Larry D. Rosen, "Teens Feel Safe on MySpace"   473
- *Neil L. Waters, "Why You Can't Cite Wikipedia in My Class"   481
- *Mark A. Wilson, "Professors Should Embrace Wikipedia"   484

TECHNOLOGY AND THE INTERNET

- *Rebecca Moore Howard, "Should Educators Use Commercial Services to Combat Plagiarism?   393
- *Cathleen A. Cleaver. "The Internet: A Clear and Present Danger?"   456
- Consumer Reports "Cell-phone Face-off"   344
- *David Kushner, "Face to Face"   243
- *Elizabeth Larsen, "Surfin' the Louvre"   249
- Tania Ralli, "Who's a Looter?"   194
- *Adam Richman, "Can Citizen Journalism Pick Up the Pieces?"   422
- *David Strayer, et al., "Drivers on Cell Phones Are as Bad as Drunks"   240
- *Robin Williams and John Tollett, "Evaluating a Website"   351
- *Noam Cohen, "Twitter on the Barricades in Iran: Six Lessons Learned"   487

ADVERTISING AND THE MEDIA

- *Jonathan Alter, "Progress or Not"   192
- *Carolyn Kleiner Butler, "Coming Home"   218
- Sarah Kay Hurst, "Analysis of Rosetta Stone Ad"   204
- *Courtney Klockeman, "Vulgar Propriety"   379
- *Margaret Lazarus, "All's Not Well in Land of 'The Lion King'"   355
- *Karyn Lewis, "Some Don't Like Their Blues at All"   223
- *Suze Orman, "How to Take Control of Your Credit Cards"   296
- Tania Ralli, "Who's a Looter?"   194
- *Lauren J. Strain, "The Hollywood Indian"   272
- *James B. Twitchell, "Miss Clairol's 'Does She ... Or Doesn't She?': How to Advertise a Dangerous Product"   205
- *Robin Williams and John Tollett, "Evaluating a Website"   351
- Marie Winn, from *The Plug-In Drug*   444

CLIMATE CHANGE

- *Daniel M. Kammen, "The Rise of Renewable Energy"   150
- Oregon State University, "50 Things You Can Do"   155
- *Jerald L. Schnoor, "The IPCC Fourth Assessment"   146
- *Gary Stix, "A Climate Repair Manual"   148

EDUCATIONAL ISSUES

- Toni Cade Bambara, "The Lesson" [Fiction]   537
- Caroline Bird, from "College Is a Waste of Time and Money"   444
- *Eric Boese, "Standardized Tests: Shouldn't We Be Helping Our Students?"   513
- *Dudley Erskine Devlin, "Teaching Tolerance in America"   159
- *Elizabeth Larsen, "Surfin' the Louvre"   249
- *Jonathan Kozol, "The Homeless and Their Children"   251
- *Kate McNerny, "Foreign Language Study: An American Necessity"   634
- *Abigail Sullivan Moore, "Gimme an A (I Insist!)"   242
- *Suze Orman, "How to Take Control of Your Credit Cards"   296
- *Neil H. Petrie, "Athletes and Education"   34
- *Samuel H. Scudder, "Take This Fish and Look at It"   53
- James Thurber, from "University Days"   112
- Scott Vogel, "Trailing History"   58

LITERACY AND LANGUAGE

- *Cathleen A. Cleaver. "The Internet: A Clear and Present Danger?"   456

- *Roy Hoffmann, "On Keeping a Journal" 11
- Jonathan Kozol, from *Illiterate America* 293
- *Jonathan Kozol, "The Homeless and Their Children" 251
- *David Kushner, "Face to Face" 243
- Abigail Sullivan Moore, "Gimme an A (I Insist!)" 242
- *Suze Orman, "How to Take Control of Your Credit Cards" 296
- *Neil H. Petrie, "On Writing 'Athletes and Education'" 38
- *Noam Cohen, "Twitter on the Barricades in Iran: Six Lessons Learned" 487
- *Adam Richman, "Can Citizen Journalism Pick Up the Pieces?" 422
- *Deborah Tannen, "The Argument Culture" 403
- * James B. Twitchell, "Miss Clairol's 'Does She . . . Or Doesn't She?': How to Advertise a Dangerous Product" 205
- *Scott Vogel, "Trailing History" 58
- *Robin Williams and John Tollett, "Evaluating a Website" 351

RACE AND CULTURAL DIVERSITY

- *Daniel "Nene" Alejandrez, "César Chávez Saved My Life" 102
- Toni Cade Bambara, "The Lesson" [Fiction] 537
- Geoffrey Canada, from "Peace in the Streets" 389
- *Manohla Dargis, "Slumdog Millionaire" 348
- *Dudley Erskine Devlin, "Teaching Tolerance in America" 159
- *Barbara Ehrenreich, "Teach Diversity—with a Smile" 134
- *"Henry Louis Gates Jr. Will Now Take Your Questions" 246
- Jeanne Wakatsuke Houston, from "Farewell to Mansanar" 92
- Martin Luther King, Jr., from "Letter from Birmingham Jail" 449
- *Margaret Lazarus, "All's Not Well in Land of 'The Lion King'" 355
- Paul Merideth, "Man Touching Vietnam Veterans Memorial" [Image] 522
- N. Scott Momaday, from *The Way to Rainy Mountain* 91
- Tania Ralli, "Who's a Looter?" 194
- *LaMer Steptoe, "Multiracialness" 295
- *Lauren J. Strain, "The Hollywood Indian" 272
- *Alice Walker, "Beauty: When the Other Dancer Is the Self" 94
- *Stephen White, "Empty Windows" 82
- *Elizabeth Wong, "The Struggle to Be an All-American Girl" 27
- *Scott Vogel, "Trailing History" 58
- *Robert Zoellner, "I'm OK, but You're Not" 28

GENDER ROLES

- *Juli Bovard, "The Red Chevy"   121
- *Nancie Brosseau, "Anorexia Nervosa"   334
- *Sonja H. Browe and Jennifer Koester, "Two Responses to Deborah Tannen"   176
- Kate Chopin, "The Story of an Hour" [Fiction]   526
- *James B. Twitchell, "Miss Clairol's 'Does She . . . Or Doesn't She?': How to Advertise a Dangerous Product"   205
- Joy Harjo, "Perhaps the World Ends Here" [Poem]   548
- Dorothea Lange, "Migrant Agricultural Worker's Family" [Image]   188
- *Margaret Lazarus, "All's Not Well in Land of 'The Lion King'"   355
- *Karyn Lewis, "Some Don't Like Their Blues at All"   223
- Richard Rodriguez, "The Boy's Desire"   92
- *Crystal Sabatke, "Welfare Is Still Necessary for Women and Children in the U.S."   505
- *Deborah Tannen, "How Male and Female Students Use Language Differently"   302
- *Elizabeth Wong, "The Struggle to Be an All-American Girl"   27

SOCIAL ISSUES

- *Daniel "Nene" Alejandrez, "César Chávez Saved My Life"   102
- *Jonathan Alter, "Progress or Not"   192
- *Margaret Atwood, "Letter to America"   142
- *Chris Blakely, "White Lies: White-Collar Crime in America"   325
- *Carolyn Kleiner Butler, "Coming Home"   218
- Yusef Komunyakaa, "Facing It" [Poem]   550
- *Jonathan Kozol, "The Homeless and Their Children"   251
- Dorothea Lange, "Migrant Agricultural Worker's Family" [Image]   188
- The Library of Congress, "Manzanar War Relocation Center" [Image]   47
- "Man at the Vietnam Veterans Memorial" [Image]   522
- *Suze Orman, "How to Take Control of Your Credit Cards"   296
- Tania Ralli, "Who's a Looter?"   194
- *Grace Rexroth, "Facing It"   560
- *Crystal Sabatke, "Welfare Is Still Necessary for Women and Children in the U.S."   505
- *Eric Schlosser, Marion Nestle, Michael Pollan, Troy Duster and Elizabeth Ransom, Peter Singer, and Jim Hightower, "One Thing to Do About Food"   395
- *LaMer Steptoe, "Multiracialness"   295
- Wislawa Szymborska "End and Beginning" [Poem]   549

- *Bridgid Stone, "My Friend, Michelle, an Alcoholic" 280
- *Deborah Tannen, "The Argument Culture" 403
- UNICEF, "Children and Work in Factories and Mines" [Image] 392
- *Scott Vogel, "Trailing History" 58

CULTURAL ISSUES

- *Margaret Atwood, "Letter to America" 142
- W. H. Auden, "Musée des Beaux Arts" [Poem] 529
- Toni Cade Bambara, "The Lesson" [Fiction] 537
- *Manohla Dargis, "Slumdog Millionaire" 348
- *Dudley Erskine Devlin, "Teaching Tolerance in America" 159
- Joy Harjo, "Perhaps the World Ends Here" [Poem] 548
- *Courtney Klockeman, "Vulgar Propriety" 379
- Dorothea Lange, "Migrant Agricultural Worker's Family" [Image] 188
- *Karyn Lewis, "Some Don't Like Their Blues at All" 223
- Aurora Levins Morales, "Child of the Americas" [Poem] 546
- Tania Ralli, "Who's a Looter?" 194
- *Grace Rexroth, "Facing It" 560
- *Paul Richard, "American Gothic" 345
- Norman Rockwell, "Triple Self-Portrait" [Image] 213
- Charles Rosen and Henri Zerner, from "Scenes from the American Dream" 214
- *David Sedaris, "Today's Special" 356
- Gary Soto, "Black Hair" [Poem] 547
- *LaMer Steptoe, "Multiracialness" 295
- *Deborah Tannen, "The Argument Culture" 403
- *James B. Twitchell, "Miss Clairol's 'Does She . . . Or Doesn't She?': How to Advertise a Dangerous Product" 205

ENVIRONMENTAL ISSUES

- *Jessica Cook, "New Regulations and You" 429
- Isak Dinesen, "The Iguana" 49
- John Muir, from "Yosemite" 50
- *Eric Schlosser, Marion Nestle, Michael Pollan, Troy Duster and Elizabeth Ransom, Peter Singer, and Jim Hightower, "One Thing to Do About Food" 395
- *Robert Zoellner, "I'm OK, but You're Not" 28

Preface

Ready or not, teachers of writing today find themselves ushered or perhaps even beamed into a New Media world. In some cases, we have a technological head start on our students; in other cases, we are scrambling to catch up with our students' knowledge of and facility with hybrid texts. The Internet, with its proliferation of Web sites, databases, blogs, tweets, YouTube videos, and Facebook pages, is quickly becoming the dominant medium, and it features an amazing array of genres, images, photographs, video clips, sound bites, and other forms of digitized communication.

Thus a major goal of teaching writing in the twenty-first century is, in fact, to teach students traditional critical reading and writing skills while adapting to these rapidly evolving digital media. One of the most crucial challenges is helping students find and evaluate a variety of media sources in a Web 2.0 world dominated by Google and Wikipedia. Students need to be familiar not just with databases, visuals, videos, Powerpoint presentations, and Web sites, but also with how to analyze these media so they can employ them in an effective rhetorical manner for a variety of audiences, purposes, and genres. Our students may be digital natives, but they are often rhetorical novices.

Providing students with a firm grounding in rhetorical matters is still the best way to teach students to write in twenty-first century electronic environments. The WPA Outcomes Statement for First-Year Composition (available at the WPA Council Web site) outlines five key goals: building students' *rhetorical knowledge* of purpose, audience, genre, cultural context, voice, and tone; improving students' *critical thinking, reading,* and *writing* skills; developing students' strategies for *writing processes;* helping students develop their *knowledge of conventions;* and helping students learn how to *compose in electronic environments.* Clearly, the first of these goals—building rhetorical knowledge of purpose, audience, genre, and cultural context—is crucial to the last goal—helping students learn how to analyze electronic texts so that they can compose effectively in electronic environments. Therefore, a major goal of the ninth edition of *The Prentice Hall Guide for College Writers* is to teach students how to integrate traditional rhetorical skills into a digital world—in particular into the Web 2.0 world where students currently live, work, and play.

WHAT'S NEW IN THE NINTH EDITION?

The most important revisions of the ninth edition of *The Prentice Hall Guide for College Writers* relate to the challenges of digital literacy that students and teachers face in the twenty-first century. These revisions are designed to help students assess, evaluate, and respond to a wide variety of texts and contexts.

- **In keeping with the emphasis on *information literacy* and *critical reading and evaluation of texts,* Chapter 13, Researching, has been completely revised** to demonstrate contemporary strategies students need while selecting and focusing their research projects, collecting and evaluating sources, integrating sources into their projects, and documenting their sources while avoiding plagiarism.

  - **New Source Evaluation Charts for print, online database, and open Web sources** (such as blogs), sample research plans, and updated strategies for taking notes on sources help students with their research as they write for a variety of personal, public, and academic audiences.

  - **A "behind the scenes" examination of Wikipedia** shows students how entries are edited and why there are risks involved in using Wikipedia as a source.

  - **Updated documentation instruction and examples based on the 2009 *MLA Handbook for Writers of Research Papers* and the 2009 *Publication Manual of the American Psychological Association*** provide students with the latest models of correct MLA and APA style.

- **A new *Multigenre Casebook on Web 2.0* in Chapter 11, Arguing, features eleven essays, images, and blogs about Facebook, Wikipedia, and Twitter.** These pieces engage students in critical reading about accuracy and reliability issues on Wikipedia, privacy concerns about Facebook, and the varied public and personal uses of Twitter.

- **More coverage of digital literacy issues appears in Chapters 7 and 10.** Chapter 7, Investigating, features a profile of Mark Zuckerberg, creator of Facebook, as well as an essay on driving while using cell phones. Chapter 10, Problem Solving, contains a debate on whether teachers should use plagiarism detection devices such as Turnitin.com to combat plagiarism. Other multigenre selections throughout the ninth edition provide support for a key theme of the text, Web 2.0 literacies.

- **Twenty new professional pieces and five new student essays** are included on topics often related to new media literacy, ranging from cell phones, ad analysis, and plagiarism detection programs to climate change, citizen journalism, and white collar crime. Featured professional writers include Scott Vogel, Gary Stix, Daniel Kammen, Henry Louis Gates, Jr., Manohla Dargis, Rebecca Moore Howard, Farhad Manjoo, Sarah Kliff, Lily Huang, and Noam Cohen.

- **New chapter-opening images give visible focus to contemporary literacies.** Google street views, Wikipedia graphics, Web pages, climate change graphics, and modern and pop art introduce ideas and images that are picked up in the essays, visuals, and journal ideas in every chapter.

- An updated *Multigenre Casebook on Climate Change* in Chapter 5, Reading, has been refocused to reflect the shift from arguments about the causes of climate change to arguments over responding to climate change. It includes essays on reversing climate change and using renewable energy sources, and a Web site on changing personal lifestyles to reduce our carbon footprint.
- New at-a-glance graphics in Chapters 3 through 13 highlight key content for students. Techniques Charts summarize techniques and procedures for different types of writing, and Writing Assignment Charts show the genres appropriate for writing to personal, academic, and public audiences.

Overall, these new features of the ninth edition of *The Prentice Hall Guide for College Writers* are designed to give teachers the resources they need to help students develop the information literacy skills they need for learning and working in our twenty-first century world.

CONTINUING KEY FEATURES

Annotated Instructor's Edition

The Annotated Instructor's Edition contains additional guidelines for teaching each chapter, including instructional tips on critical reading, critical thinking, responding to assignments, peer group activities, and ESL teaching tips designed to alert teachers to possible problems and solutions for ESL writers.

Alternate Thematic Table of Contents

The essays, stories, poems, and images in the ninth edition combine to create thematic clusters of topics that recur throughout the text: Web 2.0 Literacies, Race and Cultural Diversity, Gender Roles, Technology and the Internet, Environmental Issues, Education, Literacy and Language, Advertising and the Media, Social Issues, and Cultural Explorations.

Emphasis on Student Writing

The ninth edition continues to showcase student writing, featuring the work of more than forty student writers from several colleges and universities. The ninth edition contains *twenty-five full-length student essays* and eleven essays with sample prewriting materials, rough drafts, peer response sheets, and postscripts.

Logical Sequence of Purpose-Based Chapters

Within the rhetorical situation, aims and purposes help guide the reader to select appropriate genres, organizational strategies, appeals to audience, and styles. Early chapters in *The Prentice Hall Guide for College Writers* focus on observing, remembering, critical reading, analyzing visuals, and investigating, while later chapters emphasize exposition and argumentation (explaining, evaluating, problem solving, arguing, and researching).

Focus on Writing Processes

Every major chapter contains guidelines for writing, journal exercises, reading and writing activities, collaborative activities, peer response guidelines, revision suggestions, and professional and student samples to assist students with their work-in-progress within their rhetorical situation.

Journal Writing

Throughout the text, write-to-learn activities help writers improve their critical reading skills, warm up for each assignment, and practice a variety of invention and shaping strategies appropriate for understanding their purpose, audience, genre, and social context.

Marginal Quotations

Nearly a hundred short quotations by composition teachers, researchers, essayists, novelists, and poets personalize for the inexperienced writer a larger community of writers still struggling with the same problems that each student faces.

STRUCTURE OF *THE PRENTICE HALL GUIDE FOR COLLEGE WRITERS*

The text contains thirteen sequenced chapters that gradually build students' rhetorical knowledge and skills. Initial chapters focus on writing process and rhetorical situations; middle chapters give students practice and facility with invention, descriptive and narrative writing, critical reading skills, and basic skills for analyzing images and visuals. The next group of chapters focuses on argument skills for personal, academic, and public audiences. The final chapters help students with writing about literature and conducting research for a variety of purposes and audiences.

Chapter 1: An Introduction to Myths and Rituals for Writing

Chapter 1, "Writing Myths and Rituals," discounts some common myths about college writing courses, introduces the notion of writing rituals, and outlines the variety of journal writing used throughout the text. Writing process rituals are crucial for all writers but especially so for novice writers. Illustrating a variety of possible writing rituals are testimonies from a dozen professional writers on the nature of writing. These quotations continue throughout the book, reminding students that writing is not some magical process, but rather a madness that has a method to it, a process born of reading, thinking, observing, remembering, discussing, and writing.

Chapter 2: An Orientation to Rhetorical Situation and to Writing Processes

Chapter 2, "Situations, Purposes, and Processes for Writing," grounds the writing process in the rhetorical situation. It shows how audience, genre, subject, and context work together with the writer's purpose to achieve a rhetorical end. It demonstrates how meaning evolves from a variety of recursive, multidimensional, and hierarchical activities that we call the *writing process*. Finally, it reassures students that, because individual writing and learning styles differ, they will be encouraged to discover and articulate their own processes from a range of appropriate possibilities.

Chapters 3 to 11: Aims and Purposes for Writing

The text then turns to specific purposes and assignments for writing. Chapters 3 through 7 ("Observing," "Remembering," "Reading," "Analyzing and Designing Visuals," and "Investigating") focus on invention and critical reading strategies. These chapters introduce genres and situations for writing that build students' rhetorical repertoires: observing people, places, objects, and images; remembering people, places, and events; developing critical reading and responding strategies; developing critical reading strategies for visuals and rhetorical principles for designing visuals; and investigating and reporting through genres such as interviews, profiles, and multiple-source articles.

Chapters 8 through 11 ("Explaining," "Evaluating," "Problem Solving," and "Arguing") emphasize subject- and audience-based purposes and occasions for writing. The sequence in these chapters moves the student smoothly from exposition to argumentation (acknowledging the obvious overlapping), building on the strategies and repertoires of the previous chapters. The teacher may, in fact, use Chapters 8 through 11 as a minicourse in argument, teaching students how to develop and argue claims of fact and definition, claims of cause and effect, claims about values, and claims about solutions or policies.

Chapter 12: Responding to Literature

Chapter 12, "Responding to Literature," guides students through the process of reading and responding to poetry and short fiction, using many of the critical reading strategies, invention techniques, and shaping strategies practiced in earlier chapters.

Chapter 13: Researching

Chapter 13, "Researching," draws on all the reading, writing, and researching strategies presented in the first twelve chapters. Research papers are written for specific purposes, audiences, and contexts, but the invention, drafting, and revising processes are more extended. This chapter helps students select and plan their projects, find and critically evaluate print, online database, and open Web documents, record key content and bibliographic information, and document their sources using MLA or APA style.

Appendix: Writing Under Pressure

The appendix provides students with advice about taking timed essay exams, including analyzing the prompt, making a sketch outline, and drafting and proofreading. It also provides sample essay questions and responses.

SUPPLEMENTS FOR INSTRUCTORS AND STUDENTS

Annotated Instructor's Edition

The Annotated Instructor's Edition contains the entire student text with additional guidelines for each chapter, including teaching tips on critical reading, critical thinking, responding to assignments, and peer group activities. The AIE also offers teaching tips designed to alert instructors to problems commonly experienced by ESL writers and suggests solutions to those problems.

Instructor's Manual: Teaching Composition with *The Prentice Hall Guide for College Writers*

This instructor's manual, written by Stephen Reid, is designed to complement the AIE with additional classroom activities and ideas, as well as detailed discussion of effective strategies for the teaching of written expression skills. The manual also includes chapter commentaries, answers to discussion questions, and sections on composition theory, policy statements, lesson plans, collaborative writing, writing in a computer classroom, teaching ESL writers, small group learning, write-to-learn exercises, reading/writing exercises, journal assignments, suggestions for student conferences, and ideas for responding to and evaluating writing.

mycomplab MyCompLab™

MyCompLab empowers student writers and facilitates writing instruction by uniquely integrating a composing space and assessment tools with market-leading instruction, multimedia tutorials, and exercises for writing, grammar, and research.

Students can use MyCompLab on their own, benefiting from self-paced diagnostics and a personal study plan that recommends the instruction and practice each student needs to improve her writing skills. The composing space and its integrated resources, tools, and services (such as online tutoring) are also available to each student as he writes.

MyCompLab is an eminently flexible application that instructors can use in ways that best complement their courses and teaching styles. They can recommend it to students for self-study, set up courses to track student progress, or leverage the power of administrative features to be more effective and save time. The assignment builder and commenting tools, developed specifically for writing instruction, bring instructors closer to their student writers, make managing assignments and evaluating papers more efficient, and put powerful assessment within reach. Students receive feedback within the context of their own writing, which encourages critical thinking and revision and helps them to develop skills based on their individual needs.

Learn more at www.mycomplab.com.

Interactive Pearson eText

An e-book version of *The Prentice Hall Guide for College Writers* is also available in MyCompLab. This dynamic, online version of the text is integrated throughout MyCompLab to create an enriched, interactive learning experience for writing students.

CourseSmart eTextbook

The Prentice Hall Guide for College Writers is also available as a CourseSmart etextbook. This is an exciting new choice for students, who can subscribe to the same content online and search the text, make notes online, print out reading assignments that incorporate lecture notes, and bookmark important passages for later review. For more information, or to subscribe to the CourseSmart etextbook, visit www.coursesmart.com.

Other Supplements

Pearson English has a wide array of other supplementary items—some at no additional cost, some deeply discounted—that are available for packaging with this text. Please contact your local Pearson representative to find out more.

ACKNOWLEDGMENTS

Because teaching writing is always a situated enterprise, I would like to thank the members of the composition faculty and staff at Colorado State University whose teaching expertise and enthusiasm have improved every page of the text: Kate Kiefer, Sarah Sloane, Lisa Langstraat, Tobi Jacobi, Carrie Lamanna, and Sue Doe. Many of the innovative teaching strategies, resources, and syllabi developed by Colorado State University composition faculty members are available at http://writing.colostate.edu.

In addition, I wish gratefully to acknowledge Dominic DelliCarpini, Writing Program Administrator at York College of Pennsylvania, who expertly revised and updated the research strategies in Chapter 13, "Researching," and materially contributed to the new focus on Web 2.0 materials throughout the book.

Many of the other key suggestions for improvement came from the following teachers who offered excellent advice about changes and additions for the ninth edition: Jeanette Adkins, Tarrant County College; Young Eui Choi, Richland College; Joseph Rocky Colavito, Butler University; Jennifer Pooler Courtney, University of North Carolina Charlotte; Kevin R. Martin, Cochise College; LeRoy H. Miller, Northern Kentucky University; Missy Nieveen Phegley, Southeast Missouri State University; Coretta Pittman, Baylor University; and Chrishawn Speller, Seminole Community College. I wish to thank them for their thorough, honest, constructive, and professional advice.

For the expert crew at Pearson Education, I am especially grateful. Phil Miller, a fine editor and friend, has enthusiastically supported this text from the first edition. Brad Potthoff provided an excellent vision for this revision as well as continuing support, while Marion Castellucci did a wonderfully thorough and professional job as development editor.

Finally, I wish to thank my family for their continued personal and professional support.

—STEPHEN REID
Colorado State University

The
Prentice Hall
Guide for
College Writers

Beach Reader was painted by award-winning artist, actor, and author Mark Shasha. In this chapter, Journal Exercise 7 on page 11 invites you to analyze this painting and relate it to places where you like to read or write.

Writing Myths and Rituals

For me, the most effective writing ritual is to gather up all of my stuff—legal pad and pencil, notes, and dictionary—and get on my bike, ride to campus, and set myself up in the art lounge in the student center. During the week, I'll do this in the evening after dinner. On a weekend, I go any time from 10 A.M. to midnight. I don't write effectively at home because there are always distractions. Some people will be moving around and I'll go see who they are and what they're doing, or I'll go get a cup of coffee or a piece of toast, or I'll snap on the TV, ignoring that tiny voice inside saying, "Get busy—you have to get this done!" So what makes the art lounge better? Simple—no distractions. I can lay out all of my stuff, get a cup of coffee, and go to work. All around me people are doing the same thing, and somehow all of those hardworking people are an encouragement. The art lounge is always quiet, too—quieter than the library—and it doesn't smell like the library.

One myth about writing I have believed my whole life is that "good writers are born, not made." My attitude when beginning this writing course was one of apprehension and dread. I wondered if I *could* improve my writing, or if I was destined to receive B's and C's on every essay for the rest of my life. This writing class has given me concrete examples and suggestions for improvement—not just grammar or essay maps. The freewriting is such a great help that whenever I'm stuck, I immediately turn to my ten-minute freewriting to open up blocked passages. Once I get past my writer's block, I see that I can be a good writer.

> A writer is someone who writes, that's all.
> —GORE VIDAL, NOVELIST AND SOCIAL COMMENTATOR

> I've always disliked words like *inspiration*. Writing is probably like a scientist thinking about some scientific problem or an engineer about an engineering problem.
> —DORIS LESSING, AUTHOR OF ESSAYS AND FICTION, INCLUDING *THE GOLDEN NOTEBOOK*

> I always worked until I had something done and I always stopped when I knew what was going to happen next. That way I could be sure of going on the next day.
> —ERNEST HEMINGWAY, JOURNALIST AND NOVELIST, AUTHOR OF *THE OLD MAN AND THE SEA*

As you begin a college writing course, you need to get rid of some myths about writing that you may have been packing around for some time. Don't allow misconceptions to ruin a good experience. Here are a few common myths about writing, followed by some facts compiled from the experiences of working writers.

MYTH: "Good writers are born, not made. A writing course really won't help my writing."

FACT: *Writers acquire their skills the same way athletes do—through practice and hard work.* There are very few "born" writers. Most writers—even professional writers and journalists—are not continually inspired to write. In fact, they often experience "writer's block," the stressful experience of staring helplessly at a piece of paper, unable to think or to put words down on paper. A writing course will teach you how to cope with your procrastination, anxiety, lack of "inspiration," and false starts by focusing directly on solving the problems that occur during the writing process.

MYTH: "Writing courses are just a review of boring grammar and punctuation. When teachers read your writing, the only thing they mark is that stuff, anyway."

FACT: *Learning and communicating—not grammar and punctuation—come first in college writing courses.* Knowledge of grammar, spelling, punctuation, and usage is essential to editing, but it is secondary to discovering ideas, thinking, learning, and communicating. In a writing course, students learn to revise and improve the content and organization of each other's writing. *Then* they help each other edit for grammar, punctuation, or spelling errors.

MYTH: "College writing courses are really 'creative writing,' which is not what my major requires. If I wanted to be another Shakespeare and write poetry, I'd change my major."

FACT: *Writing courses emphasize rhetoric, not poetry.* Rhetoric involves practicing the most effective means or strategies for informing or persuading an audience. All writing—even technical or business writing—is "creative." Deciding what to write, how to write it, how best to get your reader's attention, and how to inform or persuade your reader requires creativity and imagination. Every major requires the skills that writing courses teach: exploring new ideas, learning concepts and processes, communicating with others, and finding fresh or creative solutions to problems.

MYTH: "Writing courses are not important in college or the real world. I'll never have to write, anyway."

FACT: *Writing courses do have a significant effect on your success in college, on the job, and in life.* Even if you don't have frequent, formal writing assignments in other courses, writing improves your note-taking, reading comprehension, and thinking skills. When you do have other written tasks or assignments, a writing course teaches you to adapt your writing to a variety of different purposes and audiences—whether you are writing a lab report in biology, a letter to an editor, a complaint to the Better Business Bureau, or a memorandum to your boss. Taking a writing course helps you express yourself more clearly, confidently, and persuasively—a skill that comes in handy whether you're writing a philosophy essay, a job application, or a love letter.

The most important fact about writing is that you are already a writer. You have been writing for years. A writer is someone who writes, not someone who writes a nationally syndicated newspaper column, publishes a bestseller, or wins a Pulitzer Prize. To be an effective writer, you don't have to earn a million dollars; you just have to practice writing often enough to get acquainted with its personal benefits for you and its value for others.

WARMING UP   Freewriting

Put this book aside—right now—and take out pencil or pen and a piece of paper. Use this free exercise (private, unjudged, ungraded) to remind yourself that you are already a writer. Time yourself for five minutes. Write on the first thing that comes to mind—*anything whatsoever*. Write nonstop. Keep writing even if you have to write, "I can't think of anything to say. This feels stupid!" When you get an idea, pursue it.

When five minutes are up, stop writing and read what you have written. Whether you write about a genuinely interesting topic or about the weather, freewriting is an excellent way to warm up, to get into the habit of writing, and to establish a writing ritual.

Writing Fitness: Rituals and Practice

Writing is no more magic or inspiration than any other human activity that you admire: figure skating at the Olympics, rebuilding a car engine, cooking a gourmet meal, or acting in a play. Behind every human achievement are many unglamorous hours of practice—working and sweating, falling flat on your face, and picking yourself up again. You can't learn to write just by reading some chapters in a textbook or by memorizing other people's advice. You need help and advice, but you also need practice. Consider the following parable about a Chinese painter.

> A rich patron once gave money to the painter Chu Ta, asking him to paint a picture of a fish. Three years later, when he still had not received the painting, the patron went to Chu Ta's house to ask why the picture was not done. Chu Ta did not answer but dipped a brush in ink and with a few strokes drew a splendid fish. "If it is so easy," asked the patron, "why didn't you give me the picture three years ago?" Again, Chu Ta did not answer. Instead, he opened the door of a large cabinet. Thousands of pictures of fish tumbled out.

Most writers develop little rituals that help them practice their writing. A ritual is a *repeated pattern of behavior* that provides structure, security, and a sense of

66 My idea of a prewriting ritual is getting the kids on the bus and sitting down. 99
—BARBARA KINGSOLVER
AUTHOR OF *PRODIGAL SUMMER*

> 66 Writing is [like] making a table. With both you are working with reality, a material just as hard as wood. Both are full of tricks and techniques. Basically very little magic and a lot of hard work are involved. . . . What is a privilege, however, is to do a job to your own satisfaction. 99
>
> —GABRIEL GARCÍA MÁRQUEZ,
> NOBEL PRIZE-WINNING AUTHOR OF *ONE HUNDRED YEARS OF SOLITUDE*

progress to the one who practices it. Creating your own writing rituals and making them part of your regular routine will help reduce that dreaded initial panic and enable you to call upon your writing process with confidence when you need it.

PLACE, TIME, AND TOOLS

Some writers work best in pen and ink, sprawled on their beds in the afternoon while pets snooze on nearby blankets. Others are most comfortable with their keyboards and word processors at their desks or in the computer lab. Legal-sized pads help some writers produce, while others feel motivated by spiral notebooks with pictures of mountain streams on the covers. Only you can determine which place, time, and tools give you the best support as a writer.

The place where you write is also extremely important. If you are writing in a computer lab, you have to adapt to that place, but if you write a draft in longhand or on your own laptop, you can choose the place yourself. In selecting a place, keep the following tips in mind.

- **Keep distractions minimal.** Some people simply can't write in the kitchen, where the refrigerator is distractingly close, or in a room that has a TV in it. On the other hand, a public place—a library, an empty classroom, a cafeteria—can be fine as long as the surrounding activity does not disturb them.

- **Control interruptions.** If you can close the door to your room and work without interruptions, fine. But even then, other people often assume that you want to take a break when they do. Choose a place where you can decide when it's time to take a break.

- **Have access to notes, journal, textbooks, sources, and other materials.** If the place is totally quiet but you don't have room to work or access to important notes or sources, you still may not make much progress. Whatever you need—a desk to spread your work out on, access to notes and sources, extra pens, or computer supplies—make sure your place has it.

The time of day you write and the tools you write with can also affect your attitude and efficiency. Some people like to write early in the morning, before their busy days start; others like to write in the evening, after classes or work. Whatever time you choose, try to write regularly—at least three days a week—at about the same time. If you're trying to get in shape by jogging, swimming, or doing aerobics, you wouldn't exercise for five straight hours on Monday and then take four days off. Like exercise, writing requires regular practice and conditioning.

Your writing tools—pen, pencil, paper, legal pads, four-by-six-inch notecards, notebooks, computer—should also be comfortable for you. Some writers like to make notes with pencil and paper and write drafts on computers; some like to do all composing on computers. As you try different combinations of tools, be aware of how you feel and whether your tools make you more effective. If you feel comfortable, it will be easier to establish rituals that lead to regular practice.

> 66 Writers are notorious for using any reason to keep from working: overresearching, retyping, going to meetings, waxing the floors—anything. 99
>
> —GLORIA STEINEM,
> FORMER EDITOR OF
> *MS. MAGAZINE*

Rituals are important because they help you with the most difficult part of writing: getting started. So use your familiar place, time, and tools to trick yourself into getting some words down on paper. Your mind will devise clever schemes to avoid writing those first ten words—watching TV, texting a friend, drinking some more coffee, or calling a classmate and whining together about all the writing you have to do. But if your body has been through the ritual before, it will walk calmly to your favorite place, where all your tools are ready (perhaps bringing the mind kicking and screaming all the way). Then, after you get the first ten words down, the mind will say, "Hey, this isn't so bad— I've got something to say about that!" And off you'll go.

FRANK AND ERNEST ®by Bob Thaves

Copyright © 1987 by Bob Thaves. Reprinted with the permission of Bob Thaves.

Each time you perform your writing ritual, the *next* time you write will be that much easier. Soon, your ritual will let you know: *"This is where you write. This is when you write. This is what you write with."* No fooling around. Just writing.

ENERGY AND ATTITUDE

Once you've tricked yourself into the first ten words, you need to keep your attitude positive and your energy high. When you see an intimidating wall starting to form in front of you, don't ram your head into it; figure out a way to sneak around it. Try these few tricks and techniques.

- **Start anywhere, quickly.** No law says that when you sit down to write a draft, you have to "begin at the beginning." If the first sentence is hard to write, begin with the first thoughts that come to mind. Or begin with a good example from your experience. Use that to get you going; then come back and rewrite your beginning after you've figured out what you want to say.
- **Write the easiest parts first.** Forcing yourself to start a piece of writing by working on the hardest part first is a sure way to make yourself hate writing. Take the path of least resistance. If you can't get your thesis to come out right, jot down more examples. If you can't think of examples, go back to brainstorming.
- **Keep moving.** Once you've plunged in, write as fast as you can—whether you are scribbling ideas out with a pencil or hitting the keys of a computer. Maintain your momentum. Reread if you need to, but then plunge ahead.
- **Quit when you know what comes next.** When you do have to quit for the day, stop at a place where you know what comes next. Don't drain

❝I am by nature lazy, sluggish and of low energy. It constantly amazes me that I do anything at all. **❞**
—MARGARET ATWOOD, WHO HAS MANAGED TO PRODUCE NUMEROUS BOOKS OF FICTION AND POETRY

❝Since I began writing I have always played games. . . . I have a playful nature; I have never been able to do things because it is my duty to do them. If I can find a way to do my duty by playing a game, then I can manage. ❞

—MARIA IRENE FORNES, OBIE AWARD-WINNING PLAYWRIGHT

❝I carry a journal with me almost all the time. . . . ❞

—NTOZAKE SHANGE, AUTHOR OF THE PLAY *FOR COLORED GIRLS WHO HAVE CONSIDERED SUICIDE WHEN THE RAINBOW IS ENUF*

the well dry; stop in the middle of something you know how to finish. Make a few notes about what you need to do next and circle them. Leave yourself an easy place to get started next time.

One of the most important strategies for every writer is to *give yourself a break from the past and begin with a fresh image.* In many fields—mathematics, athletics, art, engineering—some people are late bloomers. Don't let that C or D you got in English back in tenth grade hold you back now like a ball and chain. Imagine yourself cutting the chain and watching the ball roll away for good. Now you are free to start fresh with a clean slate. Your writing rituals should include only positive images about the writer you are right now and realistic expectations about what you can accomplish.

- **Visualize yourself writing.** Successful athletes know how to visualize a successful tennis swing, a basketball free throw, or a baseball swing. When you are planning your activities for the day, visualize yourself writing at your favorite place. Seeing yourself doing your writing will enable you to start writing more quickly and maintain a positive attitude.
- **Discover and emphasize the aspects of writing that are fun for you.** Emphasize whatever is enjoyable for you—discovering an idea, getting the organization of a paragraph to come out right, clearing the unnecessary words and junk out of your writing. Concentrating on the parts you enjoy will help you make it through the tougher parts.
- **Set modest goals for yourself.** Don't aim for the stars; just work on a sentence. Don't measure yourself against some great writer; be your own yardstick. Compare what you write to what *you* have written before.
- **Congratulate yourself for the writing you do.** Writing is hard work; you're using words to create ideas and meanings literally out of nothing. So pat yourself on the back occasionally. Keep in mind the immortal words of comedian and playwright Steve Martin: "I think I did pretty well, considering I started out with nothing but a bunch of blank paper."

KEEPING A JOURNAL

Many writers keep some kind of notebook in which they write down their thoughts, ideas, plans, and important events. Some writers use a journal, a private place for their day-to-day thoughts. Other writers create weblogs, or "blogs," a more public place for their ideas. Both journals and blogs can be a "place for daily writing." If you choose a private, written journal, you can later select what you want others to read; if you use your blog, your thoughts and ideas are there for others to read and respond to. Whatever medium you choose, use it as part of your daily writing ritual. In it can go notes and ideas, bits and pieces of experience, or responses to essays or books you're reading. Sometimes journals or blogs are assigned as part of your class work. In that case, you may do in-class, write-to-learn entries, plans for your essays, postscripts for an essay, or reflections on a portfolio.

Your journal or blog can be a place for formal assignments or just a place to practice, a room where all your "fish paintings" go.

As the following list indicates, there are many kinds of journal entries. They fall into three categories: *reading entries, write-to-learn entries,* and *writing entries.*

1. Reading entries help you understand and actively respond to student or professional writing.
2. Write-to-learn entries help you summarize, react to, or question ideas or essays discussed in class.
3. Writing entries help you warm up, test ideas, make writing plans, practice rhetorical strategies, or solve specific writing problems.

All three kinds of journal writing, however, take advantage of the unique relationship between thinking, writing, and learning. Simply put, writing helps you learn what you know (and don't know) by shaping your thoughts into language.

READING ENTRIES

- **Prereading journal entries.** Before you read an essay, read the headnote and write for five minutes on the topic of the essay—what you know about the subject, what related experiences you have had, and what opinions you hold. After you write your entry, the class can discuss the topic before you read the essay. The result? Your reading will be more active, engaged, and responsive.
- **Double-entry logs.** Draw a line vertically down a sheet of paper. On the left-hand side, summarize key ideas as you reread an essay. On the right-hand side, write down your reactions, responses, and questions. Writing while you read helps you understand and respond more thoroughly.
- **Essay annotations.** Writing your comments in the margin as you read is sometimes more efficient than writing separate journal entries. Check out the author on Google and look up any unfamiliar terms or references. Also, in a small group in class, you can share your annotations and collaboratively annotate a copy of the essay.
- **Vocabulary entries.** Looking up unfamiliar words in a dictionary and writing out definitions in your journal will make you a much more accurate reader. Often an essay's thesis, meaning, or tone hinges on the meanings of a few key words.
- **Summary/response entries.** Double-entry logs help you understand while you reread, but a short one-paragraph summary and one-paragraph response after you finish your rereading helps you focus on both the main ideas of a passage and your own key responses.

WRITE-TO-LEARN ENTRIES

- **Lecture/discussion entries.** At key points in a class lecture or discussion, your teacher may ask you to write for five minutes by responding to a few questions: What is the main idea of the discussion? What one question would you like to ask? How does the topic of discussion relate to the essay that you are currently writing?

> 66 The most valuable writing tool I have is my daybook. . . . I write in my lap, in the living room or on the porch, in the car or an airplane, in meetings at the university, in bed, or sitting down on a rock wall during a walk. . . . It is always a form of talking to myself, a way of thinking on paper. 99
>
> —DONALD MURRAY, JOURNALIST, AUTHOR OF BOOKS AND ESSAYS ABOUT WRITING

- **Responses to essays.** Before discussing an essay, write for a few minutes to respond to the following questions: What is the main idea of this essay? What do you like best about the essay? What is confusing, misleading, or wrong in this essay? What strategies illustrated in this essay will help you with your own writing?
- **Time-out responses.** During a controversial discussion or argument about an essay, your teacher may stop the class, take time out, and ask you to write for five minutes to respond to several questions: What key issue is the class debating? What are the main points of disagreement? What is your opinion? What evidence, either in the essay or in your experience, supports your opinion?

WRITING ENTRIES

- **Warming up.** Writing, like any other kind of activity, improves when you loosen up, stretch, get the kinks out, practice a few lines. Any daybook or journal entry gives you a chance to warm up.
- **Collecting and shaping exercises.** Some journal entries will help you collect information by observing, remembering, or investigating people, places, events, or objects. You can also record quotations or startling statistics for future writing topics. Other journal entries suggested in each chapter of this book will help you practice organizing your information. Strategies of development, such as comparison/contrast, definition, classification, or process analysis will help you discover and shape ideas.
- **Writing for a specific audience.** In some journal entries, you need to play a role, imagining that you are in a specific situation and writing for a defined audience. For example, you might write a letter of application for a job or a letter to a friend explaining why you've chosen a certain major.
- **Revision plans and postscripts.** Your journal is also the place to keep a log—a running account of your writing plans, revision plans, problems, and solutions. Include your research notes, peer responses, and postscripts on your writing process in this log.
- **Imitating styles of writers.** Use your journal to copy passages from writers you like. Practice imitating their styles on different topics. Also, try simply transcribing a few paragraphs. Even copying effective writers' words will reveal some of their secrets for successful writing.
- **Writing free journal entries.** Use your journal to record ideas, reactions to people on campus, events in the news, reactions to controversial articles in the campus newspaper, conversations after class or work, or just your private thoughts.

> **WARMING UP**   Journal Exercises

Choose three of the exercises below and write for ten minutes on each. Date and number each entry.

1. Make an "authority" list of activities, subjects, ideas, places, people, or events that you already know something about. List as many topics as you can. If your reaction is "I'm not really an *authority* on anything," then imagine you've met someone from another school, state, country, or historical period. With that person as your audience, what are you an "authority" on?

2. Choose one activity, sport, or hobby that you do well and that others might admire you for. In the form of a letter to a friend, describe the steps or stages of the process through which you acquired that skill or ability.

3. In two or three sentences, complete the following thought: "I have trouble writing because . . . "

4. In a few sentences, complete the following thought: "In my previous classes and from my own writing experience, I've learned that the three most important rules about writing are . . . "

5. Describe your own writing rituals. *When, where,* and *how* do you write best?

6. Write an open journal entry. Describe events from your day, images, impressions, bits of conversation—anything that catches your interest. For possible ideas for open journal entries, read the essay by Roy Hoffman reprinted here.

7. Look again at the chapter opening work of art, *Beach Reader,* by Mark Shasha. Mark Shasha is an award-winning artist, author, and actor who travels much of the year to talk to children about the world of reading, writing, and drawing. Describe how Shasha uses color, light, balance, and focus in his painting to create an inviting place for reading, writing, or just relaxing.

PROFESSIONAL WRITING

On Keeping a Journal

Roy Hoffman

In a Newsweek On Campus *essay, Roy Hoffman describes his own experience, recording events and trying out ideas just as an artist doodles on a sketch pad. Your own journal entries about events, images, descriptions of people, and bits of conversation will not only improve your writing but also become your own personal time capsule, to dig up and reread in the year 2030.*

Wherever I go I carry a small notebook in my coat or back pocket for thoughts, observations and impressions. As a writer I use this notebook as an artist would a sketch pad, for stories and essays, and as a sporadic journal of my comings and goings. When I first started keeping notebooks, though, I was not yet a professional writer. I was still in college.

I made my first notebook entries . . . just after my freshman year, in what was actually a travel log. A buddy and I were setting out to trek from our Al-

...continued On Keeping a Journal, **Roy Hoffman**

abama hometown to the distant tundra of Alaska. With unbounded enthusiasm I began: "Wild, crazy ecstasy wants to wrench my head from my body." The log, written in a university composition book, goes on to chronicle our adventures in the land where the sun never sets, the bars never close and the prepipeline employment prospects were so bleak we ended up taking jobs as night janitors.

When I returned to college that fall I had a small revelation: the *3* world around me of libraries, quadrangles, Frisbees and professors was as rich with material for my journals and notebooks as galumphing moose and garrulous fishermen.

These college notebooks, which built to a pitch my senior year, are gold *4* mines to me now. Classrooms, girlfriends, cups of coffee and lines of poetry—from mine to John Keats's—float by like clouds. As I lie beneath these clouds again, they take on familiar and distinctive shapes.

Though I can remember the campus's main quadrangle, I see it more *5* vividly when I read my description of school on a visit during summer break: "the muggy, lassitudinal air . . . the bird noises that cannot be pointed to, the summer emptiness that grows emptier with a few students squeaking by the library on poorly oiled bicycles." An economics professor I fondly remember returns with less fondness in my notebooks, "staring down at the class with his equine face." And a girl I had a crush on senior year, whom I now recall mistily, reappears with far more vitality as "the ample, slightly-gawky, whole-wheat, fractured object of my want gangling down the hall in spring heat today."

When, in reading over my notebooks, I am not peering out at quadran- *6* gles, midterm exams, professors or girlfriends, I see a portrait of my parents and hometown during holidays and occasional weekend breaks. Like a wheel, home revolves, each turn regarded differently depending on the novel or political essay I'd been most influenced by the previous semester.

Mostly, though, in wandering back through my notebooks, I meet *7* someone who could be my younger brother: the younger version of myself. The younger me seems moodier, more inquisitive, more fun-loving and surprisingly eager to stay up all night partying or figuring out electron orbitals for a 9 a.m. exam. The younger me wanders through a hall of mirrors of the self, writes of "seeing two or three of myself on every corner," and pens long meditations on God and society before scribbling in the margin, "what a child I am." The younger me also finds humor in trying to keep track of this hall of mirrors, commenting in ragged verse.

> I hope that one day
> Some grandson or cousin
> Will read these books,
> And know that I was
> Once a youth
> Sitting in drugstores with

Anguished looks.
And poring over coffee,
And should have poured
The coffee
Over these lines.

I believe that every college student should attempt to keep some 8
form of notebook, journal or diary. A notebook is a secret garden in
which to dance, sing, muse, wander, perform handstands, even cry. In the
privacy of this little book, you can make faces, curse, turn somersaults
and ask yourself if you're really in love. A notebook or journal is one of
the few places you can call just your own.

. . . Journal writing suffers when you let someone, in your mind, look 9
over your shoulder. Honesty wilts when a parent, teacher or friend looms
up in your imagination to discourage you from putting your true thoughts
on the page. Journal writing also runs a related hazard: the dizzying suspicion that one day your private thoughts, like those of Samuel Pepys or Virginia Woolf, will be published in several volumes and land up required
reading for English 401. How can you write comfortably when the eyes of
all future readers are upon you? Keep your notebooks with the abandon of
one who knows his words will go up in smoke. Then you might really strike
fire a hundred years or so from now if anyone cares to pry.

By keeping notebooks, you improve your writing ability, increasing 10
your capacity to communicate both with yourself and others. By keeping
notebooks, you discover patterns in yourself, whether lazy ones that need
to be broken or healthy ones that can use some nurturing. By keeping
notebooks, you heighten some moments and give substance to others:
even a journey to the washateria offers potential for some off-beat journal observations. And by keeping notebooks while still in college, you
chart a terrain that, for many, is more dynamically charged with ideas
and discussions than the practical, workaday world just beyond. Notebooks, I believe, not only help us remember this dynamic charge, but also
help us sustain it.

Not long ago, while traveling with a friend in Yorktown, Va., I passed 11
by a time capsule buried in the ground in 1976, intended to be dug up in
2076. Keeping notebooks and journals is rather like burying time capsules into one's own life. There's no telling what old rock song, love note,
philosophical complaint or rosy Saturday morning you'll unearth when
you dig up these personal time capsules. You'll be able to piece together
a remarkable picture of where you've come from, and may well get some
important glimmers about where you're going.

Mona Lisa Barn
Dennis Wiemer
Layne Kennedy,
Photographer

The picture above, taken by photographer Layne Kennedy, shows a famous Mona Lisa barn painting on a farm near Cornell, Wisconsin. Mona Lisa's shirt has been repainted to celebrate Wisconsin's victory in the 1994 Rose Bowl. A freewriting assignment on page 25 invites you to describe the purpose, audience, and genre of this image.

Situations, Purposes, and Processes for Writing

As a veteran smoker, you have become increasingly irritated at the nonsmoking regulations that have appeared in restaurants, businesses, and other public places. And it's not just the laws that are irritating, but the holier-than-thou attitude of people who presume that what's good for them should be good for you. Non-smoking laws seem to give people license to censure your behavior while totally ignoring their own offensive behavior: polluting the atmosphere with hydrocarbons, fouling the aquifers with fertilizers, and generally corrupting the social air with odors of false superiority. So after one particularly memorable experience, you write a letter to the editor of the local paper, intending not only to express your own frustration but also to satirize all those smug do-gooders.

As a Chinese-American woman growing up in America, you decide to write about the difficulty of living in two cultures. You recall how, during your childhood, you rebelled against your mother when she insisted that you learn about your Chinese heritage. You remember how much you hated your Chinese school and how embarrassed you were that your mother could not speak English properly. As you grew older, however, you realized the price you paid for your assimilation into American culture. After discussing this conflict with your friends, you decide to describe your experiences to others who share them or who may want to know what you learned. At that point, you write an autobiographical account of your experiences and post it on the Web.

> " First and foremost I write for myself. Writing has been for a long time my major tool for self-instruction and self-development. "
> —TONI CADE BAMBARA, AUTHOR OF *THE SALT EATERS*

> " How do I know what I think until I see what I say? "
> —E. M. FORSTER, AUTHOR OF *A PASSAGE TO INDIA*

T HE WRITING FOR THIS COURSE (AND THE STRUCTURE OF THIS TEXTBOOK) ASSUMES THAT WRITING IS VALUABLE FOR TWO RELATED REASONS. FIRST, WRITING ENABLES YOU TO LEARN ABOUT SOMETHING, TO HELP YOU OBSERVE YOUR SURROUNDINGS, TO REMEMBER IMPORTANT IDEAS AND events, and to record and analyze what you see and read. Second, writing is an important means to communicate with your readers, to explain or evaluate an idea, to offer a solution, or to argue your point of view. These two reasons for writing are usually related. If you want to persuade others to agree with your point of view, you'll be more effective if you reflect on how your personal observations, memories, experiences, and things you've read and heard might help you convince your readers. Whatever you write, however, you are always writing in a particular situation or context. Understanding how your goals as a writer relate to the writing situation and to your own processes for writing is the focus of this chapter.

The Rhetorical Situation

As you begin this writing course, consider how you and your writing fit into a larger context. Anytime you write an e-mail response, a letter to your friends, a posting on your Facebook page, an essay for your English or history class, an application for a job, a letter to the editor, or an entry in your journal, you are in the middle of a rhetorical situation. If rhetoric is the "art of using language effectively or persuasively," then the rhetorical situation is the overall context in which your writing occurs.

ELEMENTS OF THE RHETORICAL SITUATION

The key parts of the rhetorical situation are you, the writer; the immediate occasion that prompts you to write; your intended purpose and audience; your genre or type of writing; and the larger social context in which you are writing. Because these key terms are used repeatedly in this course, you need to know exactly what each term means and how it will help guide your writing.

● **THE WRITER**   You are the writer. Sometimes you write in response to an assignment, but at other times, you choose to write because of something that happened or something that made you think or react. In college or on the job, you often have writing assignments, but in your life, you are often the one who decides to write when you need to remember something, plan, remind others, express your feelings, or solve a problem.

● **THE OCCASION**   The occasion is whatever motivates you to write. Often you are motivated by an assignment that a teacher or a boss gives you. Sometimes, however, a particular event or incident makes you want to write. The cause may be a conversation you had with a friend, an article you read, or something that happened to you recently. The occasion is simply the immediate cause or the pressing need to write, whether assigned to you by someone else or just determined by you to be the reason for your desire to write.

● **PURPOSE**   Your purpose in writing is the effect you wish to have on your intended audience. Major purposes for writing include **expressing** your feelings; investigating a subject and **reporting** your findings; **explaining** an idea or concept; **evaluating** some object, performance, or image; **proposing a solution** to a problem; and **arguing** for your position and responding to alternative or opposing positions.

● **AUDIENCE**   Your knowledge about your intended audience should always guide and shape your writing. If you are writing for yourself, you can just list ideas, express your thoughts, or make informal notes. If you are writing to explain an idea or concept, you should think about who needs or wants to know about your idea. To whom do you want to explain this idea? Are they likely to be novices or experts on the topic? Similarly, if you are arguing your position, you need to consider the thoughts and feelings of readers who may have several different points of view. What do they believe about your topic? Do they agree or disagree with your position, or are they undecided?

● **GENRE**   The genre you choose is simply the kind, type, or form of writing you select. Everyone is familiar with genres in literature, such as poems, novels, and plays. In nonfiction, typical genres are essays, memoirs, magazine articles, and editorials. In college, you may write in a variety of genres, including e-mail, personal essays, lab reports, summaries, reviews of research, analytical essays, argumentative essays, and even scientific or business reports. Sometimes, you may need to write multigenre or multimedia reports with graphic images or pictures. For community service learning or on the job, you may write reports, analyses, brochures, or flyers. As a citizen of the community, you may write letters to the editor, responses to an online discussion forum, or letters to your representative.

The genre you choose helps create the intellectual, social, or cultural relationship between you and your reader. It helps you communicate your purpose to your reader or makes possible the social action you wish to achieve. If your purpose is to analyze or critique material you are reading in a class, an essay is a genre suitable to your purpose and your intended audience (your teacher and your peers in class). A lab report is a different genre, requiring your notes, observations, and hypothesis about your experiment, presented for members of a scientific community. Finally, the purpose of a one-page brochure for your

❝Every genre positions those who participate in a text of that kind: as interviewer or interviewee, as listener or storyteller, as a reader or a writer, as a person interested in political matters, as someone to be instructed or as someone who instructs; each of these positionings implies different possibilities for response and for action.❞

—GUNTHER KRESS, AUTHOR OF *LITERACY IN THE NEW MEDIA AGE*

66A rhetorically sound definition of genre must be centered not on the substance or form of discourse but on the action it is used to accomplish. 99

—CAROLYN MILLER, TEACHER AND AUTHOR OF *GENRE AS SOCIAL ACTION*

community crisis center, for example, may be to advertise its services to a wide audience that includes college students and members of the community. The point is to learn what readers expect of each genre and then choose—or modify— a genre that is appropriate for your purpose and audience. Learning which genres are appropriate for each writing situation and learning about the formal features of each genre (such as introduction, presentation of information, paragraphing, and vocabulary) is a key part of each writing task. Remember, however, that genres have rules but are not rulebound. Every text should have recognizable features of a genre but also individual variation appropriate for that particular occasion.

● **CONTEXT**   As both a reader and a writer, you must consider the rhetorical and social context. When you read an essay or other text, think about the **author**, the **place of publication**, the **ongoing conversation** about this topic, and the larger **social or cultural context**. First, consider who wrote an essay and where it appeared. Was the essay a citizen's editorial in the *New York Times,* a journalist's feature article in *Vogue,* a scientist's research report in the *New England Journal of Medicine,* or a personal essay on an individual's Web site? Often, who wrote the article, what his or her potential bias or point of view was, and the place of publication can be just as important as what the article says. Next, consider the ongoing conversation to which this essay contributes. What different viewpoints exist on this topic? Which perspectives does this essay address? Finally, the larger sense of culture, politics, and history in which the article appears may be crucial to your understanding.

Similarly, when you write an essay, think about where it might be read or published and what conversation already exists on the topic. What cultural or political points of view are represented in the conversation? How does that ongoing conversation affect what you think? How does your own cultural, political, ethnic, or personal background affect what you believe? Understanding and analyzing the larger rhetorical and social context helps you become a better reader and writer.

WHY THE RHETORICAL SITUATION IS IMPORTANT

So, you understand each of the elements of the rhetorical situation, and you see how they are interconnected. But how does that knowledge help you as a writer? The answer is both easy and difficult. The easy part is that every decision you make as a writer—how to begin, how much evidence you include, how you organize, whether you can use "I" in your writing, what style or tone you should use— depends on the rhetorical situation. The style and organization of a lab report is different from an essay, which is different from a brochure. If you've ever asked your teacher, "Won't you just tell me what you want?" the answer to that question always is, "Well, it depends." It depends on what is appropriate for the purpose, audience, genre, and context. And that is where the difficult part of writing be-gins: learning which genres, styles, and methods of organization are appropriate for each writing situation. To learn the various approaches to writing and how they are most effectively used is the reason that you continually read and practice writing the major genres taught in your composition class.

FREEWRITING: INVENTORY OF YOUR WRITING

Before you read further in this chapter, take out a pen or open a computer file and make a list of what you have written in the last year or two. Brain-storm a list of all the genres you can think of: shopping lists for a trip, let-ters to family or friends, applications for jobs, school essays, personal or professional Web sites, science projects, or memos for your boss. Then, for one of your longer writing projects, jot down several sentences de-scribing the situation that called for that piece of writing—what was the occasion, purpose, and audience? What form or genre did your writing take? How did that genre help define a relationship between you and your reader? Where did you write it, and what was your writing process?

Purposes for Writing

Getting a good grade, sharing experiences with a friend, or contributing to so-ciety may be among your motives for writing. However, as a writer, you also have more specific rhetorical purposes for writing. These purposes help you make key decisions related to your audience and genre. When your main purpose is to express your feelings, you may write a private entry in your journal. When your main purpose is to explain how your sales promotion increased the number of your company's customers, you may write a formal sales report to your boss. When your main purpose is to persuade others to see a movie that you like, you may write a review for the local newspaper. In each case, the intended rhetorical purpose—your desire to create a certain effect on your audience—helps deter-mine what you write and how you say it.

WRITER-BASED PURPOSES

Because writing is, or should be, for yourself first of all, everything you write in-volves at least some purpose that benefits you. Of course, expressing yourself is a fundamental purpose of all writing. Without the satisfaction of expressing

> 66 The writer may write to inform, to ex-plain, to entertain, to persuade, but whatever the purpose there should be first of all, the satisfaction of the writer's own learning. 99
> —DONALD MURRAY, TEACHER AND PULITZER PRIZE-WINNING JOURNALIST

your thoughts, feelings, reactions, knowledge, or questions, you might not make the effort to write in the first place.

A closely related purpose is learning: Writing helps you discover what you think or feel, simply by using language to identify and compose your thoughts. Writing not only helps you form ideas but actually promotes observing and remembering. If you write down what you observe about people, places, or things, you can actually "see" them more clearly. Similarly, if you write down facts, ideas, experiences, or reactions to your readings, you will remember them longer. Writing and rewriting facts, dates, definitions, impressions, or personal experiences will improve your powers of recall on such important occasions as examinations and job interviews.

SUBJECT- AND AUDIENCE-BASED PURPOSES

Although some writing is intended only for yourself—such as entries in a diary, lists, class notes, reminders—much of your writing will be read by others, by those readers who constitute your "audience."

- You may write to *inform* others about a particular subject—to tell them about the key facts, data, feelings, people, places, or events.
- You may write to *explain* to your readers what something means, how it works, or why it happens.
- You may write to *persuade* others to believe or do something—to convince others to agree with your judgment about a book, record, or restaurant, or to persuade them to take a certain class, vote for a certain candidate, or buy some product you are advertising.
- You may write to *explore* ideas and "truths," to examine how your ideas have changed, to ask questions that have no easy answers, and then to share your thoughts and reflections with others.
- You may write to *entertain*—as a primary purpose in itself or as a purpose combined with informing, explaining, persuading, or exploring. Whatever your purposes may be, good writing both teaches and pleases. Remember, too, that your readers will learn more, remember more, or be more convinced when your writing contains humor, wit, or imaginative language.

COMBINATIONS OF PURPOSES

In many cases, you write with more than one purpose in mind. Purposes may appear in combinations, connected in a sequence, or actually overlapping. Initially, you may take notes about a subject to learn and remember, but later you

> 66 I think writing is really a process of communication. . . . It's the sense of being in contact with people who are part of a particular audience that really makes a difference to me in writing. 99
> —SHERLEY ANNE WILLIAMS,
> POET, CRITIC, AND NOVELIST

> 66 Writing, as a rhetorical act, is carried out within a web of purpose. 99
> —LINDA FLOWER,
> TEACHER AND RESEARCHER IN COMPOSITION

may want to inform others about what you have discovered. Similarly, you may begin by writing to express your feelings about a movie that you loved or that upset you; later, you may wish to persuade others to see it—or not to see it.

Purposes can also contain each other, like Chinese boxes, or overlap, blurring the distinctions. An explanation of how an automobile works will contain information about that vehicle. An attempt to persuade someone to buy an automobile may contain an explanation of how it handles and information about its body style or engine. Usually, writing to persuade others will contain explanations and basic information, but the reverse is not necessarily true; you can write simply to give information, without trying to persuade anyone to do anything.

SUBJECT, PURPOSE, AND THESIS

The *thesis, claim,* or *main idea* in a piece of writing is related to your purpose. As a writer, you usually have a purpose in mind that serves as a guide while you gather information about your subject and think about your audience. However, as you collect and record information, impressions, and ideas you gradually narrow your subject to a specific topic and thus clarify your purpose. You bring your purpose into sharper and sharper focus—as if progressing on a target from the outer circles to the bull's-eye—until you have narrowed your purpose down to a central thesis. The thesis is the dominant idea, explanation, evaluation, or recommendation that you want to impress upon your readers.

The following examples illustrate how a writer moves from a general subject, guided by purpose, to a specific thesis or claim.

Subject	Purpose	Thesis, Claim, or Main Idea
Childhood experiences	To express your feelings and explain how one childhood experience was important	The relentless competition between my sisters and me changed my easygoing personality.
Social networking sites	To inform readers about how to set privacy settings on MySpace and Facebook	The default settings on MySpace and Facebook will not always protect your online privacy.
Carbon footprint	To persuade readers to reduce their carbon footprint	Americans should take ten important steps to reduce their carbon footprint when they are at home, when they shop, and when they travel.

Purpose and Audience

Writing for yourself is relatively easy; after all, you already know your audience and can make spontaneous judgments about what is essential and what is not. However, when your purpose is to communicate to other readers, you need to analyze your audience. Your writing will be more effective if you can anticipate what your readers know and need to know, what they are interested in, and what their beliefs or attitudes are. As you write for different readers, you will select different kinds of information, organize it in different ways, or write in a more formal or less formal style.

FREEWRITING: Writing for Different Audiences

Before you read further, get a pen or pencil and several sheets of paper and do the following exercise.

1.   For your eyes only, write about what you did at a recent party. Write for four minutes.
2.   On a second sheet of paper, describe for the members of your writing class what you did at this party; you will read this aloud to the class. Stop after four minutes.
3.   On a third sheet of paper, write a letter to one of your parents or a relative describing what you did at the party. Stop after four minutes.

AUDIENCE ANALYSIS

If you are writing to communicate to other readers, analyzing your probable audience will help you answer some basic questions.

- What genre should I choose? What genre—or combination of genres— would best enable me to communicate with my audience?
- How much information or evidence is enough? What should I assume my audience already knows? What should I not tell them? What do they believe? Will they readily agree with me, or will they be antagonistic?
- How should I organize my writing? How can I get my readers' attention? Can I just describe my subject and tell a story, or should I analyze everything in a logical order? Should I put my best examples or arguments first or last?

- Should I write informally, with simple sentences and easy vocabulary, or should I write in a more elaborate or specialized style, with technical vocabulary?

Analyze your audience by considering the following questions. As you learn more about your audience, the possibilities for your own role as a writer will become clearer.

1. **Audience profile.** How narrow or broad is your audience? Is it a narrow and defined audience—a single person, such as your Aunt Mary, or a group with clear common interests, such as the zoning board in your city or the readers of *Organic Gardening?* Is it a broad and diverse audience: educated readers who wish to be informed on current events, American voters as a whole, or residents of your state? Do your readers have identifiable roles? Can you determine their age, sex, economic status, ethnic background, or occupational category?

2. **Audience–subject relationship.** Consider what your readers know about your subject. If they know very little about it, you'll need to explain the basics; if they already know quite a bit, you can go straight to more difficult or complex issues. Also estimate their probable attitude toward this subject. Are they likely to be sympathetic or hostile?

3. **Audience–writer relationship.** What is your relationship with your readers? Do you know each other personally? Do you have anything in common? Will your audience be likely to trust what you say, or will they be skeptical about your judgments? Are you the expert on this particular subject and the readers the novices? Or are you the novice and your readers the experts?

4. **Writer's role.** To communicate effectively with your audience, you should also consider your own role or perspective. Of the many roles that you could play (friend, big sister or brother, student of psychology, music fan, employee of a fast-food restaurant, and so on), choose one that will be effective for your purpose and audience. If, for example, you are writing to sixth-graders about nutrition, you could choose the perspective of a concerned older brother or sister. Your writing might be more effective, however, if you assume the role of a person who has worked in fast-food restaurants for three years and knows what goes into hamburgers, french fries, and milkshakes.

Writers may write to real audiences, or they may create audiences. Sometimes the relationship between writer and reader is real (sister writing to brother), so the writer starts with a known audience and writes accordingly. Sometimes, however, writers begin and gradually discover or create an audience in the process of writing. Knowing the audience guides the writing, but the writing may construct an audience as well.

Purpose, Audience, and Genre

In addition to considering your purpose and audience, think also about the possible forms or genres your writing might take. If you are writing to observe or remember something, you may want to write an informal essay, a letter, a memoir, or even an e-mail to reach your audience. If you are writing to inform your readers or explain some idea, you may write an article, essay, letter, report, or pamphlet to best achieve your purpose and address your audience. Argumentative writing—writing to evaluate, persuade, or recommend some position or course of action—takes place in many different genres, from e-mails, blogs, and letters, to reviews and editorials, to proposals and researched documents. As you select a topic, consider which genre would most effectively accomplish your purpose for your intended audience.

Below are some of the common genres that you will read or write while in college, on the job, or as a member of your community. Each genre has certain organization and style features that readers of this genre expect. Knowing the genre that you are writing or reading helps answer questions about how to write or how to respond to a piece of writing.

Genre	Conventions of Organization and Style
Personal essay	Some narrative and descriptive passages Informal; uses first-person "I" Applies personal experience to larger social question
Research review	Uses concise, accurate summary May be an annotated bibliography or part of a larger thesis Adheres to MLA, APA, Chicago styles
Argumentative essay	Makes a claim about a controversial topic Responds to alternative or opposing positions Carefully considers audience Supports claims with evidence and examples Uses reasonable tone Has formal paragraphing
Laboratory report	May be informal description of materials, procedures, and results May be formal organization with title, abstract, introduction, method, results, and discussion

Brochure	Mixes graphics, text, visuals Visually arresting and appealing layout Concise information and language
Letter to the editor	Refers to issue or topic States opinion, point of view, or recommendation Usually concise to fit into editorial page
Posting to an electronic forum	Connects to specific thread in discussion May be informal style Flaming and trolling occur, but are often censured

E-mail, text message or tweet	Usually short
	Informal and personal style
	Often without salutation, caps, or punctuation
	May use emoticons such as :-), :-(, :-.) (Cindy
	    Crawford), or 8(:-) (Mickey Mouse), or
	    acronyms such as BTW, LOL, FYI, or THX

FREEWRITING: PURPOSE, AUDIENCE, GENRE, AND CONTEXT IN AN IMAGE

Before you read further in this chapter, analyze the rhetorical elements in the photograph by Layne Kennedy that appears at the beginning of this chapter. What is the purpose of this barn painting? Who was the intended audience? How would you describe this genre of art? What was the social and cultural context in which this painting appeared? (Use Yahoo!, Google, or your favorite search engine to discover background information.) Overall, how effective is this painting at achieving its rhetorical purpose for its audience and context? Explain.

Analyzing the Rhetorical Situation

To review, the rhetorical situation consists of the writer, the occasion, the purpose and audience, the genre and the context. Sometimes several of these are assigned to the writer, but at other times, the writer chooses a purpose, audience, and genre. The key point to remember is that these terms are all interrelated and interconnected. Your overall purpose often depends on your selected audience. Deciding on a particular audience may mean choosing a particular genre. Thinking about the context and conversation surrounding a particular topic may help you be more persuasive for your selected audience. Writing and revising require reconsidering and revising each of these elements to make them work harmoniously to achieve your rhetorical goal.

The following scenarios illustrate how the writer's purpose, the occasion, the audience, genre, and context work together to define the rhetorical situation. In the following descriptions, identify each of the key parts of the rhetorical situation.

> A student who transferred from a community college to a 4-year school had to give up her well-paying job and move 75 miles to attend a state institution. The cost of getting her degree ballooned to nearly $10,000 per year. She decides to write a letter to send to her state senator arguing that some 2-year schools in her state should be able to grant bachelor's degrees for high-achieving students. She cites precedents in several states, including California and Florida. Although she acknowledges that such a policy would change the mission of community colleges, she tries to persuade her senator that in these difficult economic times, students need options for getting a degree that do not leave them with thousands of dollars of debt to repay.

> In response to a request by an editor of a college recruiting pamphlet, a student decides to write an essay explaining the advantages of the social and academic life at his university. According to the editor, the account needs to be realistic but should also promote the university. It shouldn't be too academic and stuffy—the college catalog itself contains all the basic information—but it should give high school seniors a flavor of college life. The student decides to write a narrative account of his most interesting experiences during his first week at college.

PURPOSE, AUDIENCE, AND CONTEXT IN TWO ESSAYS

The two short essays that follow appeared as columns in newspapers. Both relate the writers' own experiences. They are similar in genre but have different purposes, they appeal to different readers, and they have different social and cultural contexts. First, read each essay just to understand each writer's point of view. Then reread each essay, thinking particularly about each writer's main purpose, his or her intended audience, and the social and cultural context surrounding each topic.

The Struggle to Be an All-American Girl

Elizabeth Wong

It's still there, the Chinese school on Yale Street where my brother and I 1
used to go. Despite the new coat of paint and the high wire fence, the
school I knew 10 years ago remains remarkably, stoically the same.

Every day at 5 p.m., instead of playing with our fourth- and fifth- 2
grade friends or sneaking out to the empty lot to hunt ghosts and animal
bones, my brother and I had to go to Chinese school. No amount of kicking, screaming, or pleading could dissuade my mother, who was solidly
determined to have us learn the language of our heritage.

Forcibly, she walked us the seven long, hilly blocks from our home to 3
school, depositing our defiant tearful faces before the stern principal. My
only memory of him is that he swayed on his heels like a palm tree, and
he always clasped his impatient twitching hands behind his back. I recognized him as a repressed maniacal child killer, and knew that if we ever
saw his hands we'd be in big trouble.

We all sat in little chairs in an empty auditorium. The room smelled 4
like Chinese medicine, and imported faraway mustiness. Like ancient
mothballs or dirty closets. I hated that smell. I favored crisp new scents.
Like the soft French perfume that my American teacher wore in public
school.

Although the emphasis at the school was mainly language—speak- 5
ing, reading, writing—the lessons always began with an exercise in po-
liteness. With the entrance of the teacher, the best student would tap a
bell and everyone would get up, kowtow, and chant, "sing san ho," the
phonetic for "How are you, teacher?"

Being ten years old, I had better things to learn than ideographs 6
copied painstakingly in lines that ran right to left from the tip of a *moc
but,* a real ink pen that had to be held in an awkward way if blotches were
to be avoided. After all, I could do the multiplication tables, name the
satellites of Mars, and write reports on "Little Women" and "Black
Beauty." Nancy Drew, my favorite book heroine, never spoke Chinese.

The language was a source of embarrassment. More times than not, 7
I had tried to disassociate myself from the nagging loud voice that followed me wherever I wandered in the nearby American supermarket
outside Chinatown. The voice belonged to my grandmother, a fragile
woman in her seventies who could outshout the best of the street ven-
dors. Her humor was raunchy, her Chinese rhythmless, patternless. It was
quick, it was loud, it was unbeautiful. It was not like the quiet, lilting romance of French or the gentle refinement of the American South. Chinese sounded pedestrian. Public.

...continued The Struggle to Be an All-American Girl, **Elizabeth Wong**

In Chinatown, the comings and goings of hundreds of Chinese on 8
their daily tasks sounded chaotic and frenzied. I did not want to be
thought of as mad, as talking gibberish. When I spoke English, people
nodded at me, smiled sweetly, said encouraging words. Even the people
in my culture would cluck and say that I'd do well in life. "My, doesn't she
move her lips fast," they would say, meaning that I'd be able to keep up
with the world outside Chinatown.

My brother was even more fanatical than I about speaking English. He 9
was especially hard on my mother, criticizing her, often cruelly, for her pid-
gin speech—smatterings of Chinese scattered like chop suey in her conversation. "It's not 'What it is,' Mom," he'd say in exasperation. "It's 'What is it,
what is it, what is it!'" Sometimes Mom might leave out an occasional "the"
or "a," or perhaps a verb of being. He would stop her in mid-sentence: "Say
it again, Mom. Say it right." When he tripped over his own tongue, he'd
blame it on her: "See, Mom, it's all your fault. You set a bad example."

After two years of writing with a *moc but* and reciting words with 10
multiples of meanings, I finally was granted a cultural divorce. I was permitted to stop Chinese school.

I thought of myself as multicultural. I preferred tacos to egg rolls; I 11
enjoyed Cinco de Mayo more than Chinese New Year.

At last, I was one of you; I wasn't one of them.   12

Sadly, I still am.   13

PROFESSIONAL WRITING

I'm O.K., but You're Not

Robert Zoellner

The American novelist John Barth, in his early novel, *The Floating Opera,* 1
remarks that ordinary, day-to-day life often presents us with embarrassingly obvious, totally unsubtle patterns of symbolism and meaning—life
in the midst of death, innocence vindicated, youth versus age, etc.

The truth of Barth's insight was brought home to me recently while 2
having breakfast in a lawn-bordered restaurant on College Avenue near
the Colorado State University campus. I had asked to be seated in the
smoking section of the restaurant—I have happily gone through three or
four packs a day for the past 40 years.

As it happened, the hostess seated me—I was by myself—at a little 3
two-person table on the dividing line between the smoking and non-
smoking sections. Presently, a well-dressed couple of advanced years, his
hair a magisterial white and hers an electric blue, were seated in the non-
smoking section five feet away from me.

It was apparent within a minute that my cigarette smoke was bugging *4* them badly, and soon the husband leaned over and asked me if I would please stop smoking. As a chronic smokestack, I normally comply, out of simple courtesy, with such requests. Even an addict such as myself can quit for as long as 20 minutes.

But his manner was so self-righteous and peremptory—he re- *5* minded me of Lee Iacocca boasting about Chrysler—that the prompt-ings of original sin, always a problem with me, took over. I quietly pointed out that I was in the smoking section—if only by five feet—and that that fact meant that I had met my social obligation to non-smokers. Besides, the idea of morning coffee without a cigarette was simply incon-ceivable to me—might as well ask me to vote Republican.

The two of them ate their eggs-over-easy in hurried and sullen si- *6* lence, while I chain-smoked over my coffee. As well as be hung for a sheep as a lamb, I reasoned. Presently they got up, paid their bill, and stalked out in an ambiance of affronted righteousness and affluent propriety.

And this is where John Barth comes in. They had parked their car— *7* a diesel Mercedes—where it could be seen from my table. And in the car, waiting impatiently, was a splendidly matched pair of pedigreed poodles, male and female.

Both dogs were clearly in extremis, and when the back door of the *8* car was opened, they made for the restaurant lawn in considerable haste. Without ado (no pun intended), the male did a doo-doo that would have done credit to an animal twice his size, and finished off with a leisurely, ruminative wee-wee. The bitch of the pair, as might be expected of any well-brought-up female of Republican proclivities, confined herself to a modest wee-wee, fastidious, diffident, and quickly executed.

Having thus polluted the restaurant lawn, the four of them mar- *9* shalled their collective dignity and drove off in a dense cloud of blue smoke—that lovely white Mercedes was urgently in need of a valve-and-ring job, its emission sticker an obvious exercise in creative writing.

As I regretfully watched them go—after all, the four of them had *10* made my day—it seemed to me that they were in something of a hurry, and I uncharitably wondered if the husband was not anxious to get home in order to light the first Fall fire in his moss-rock fireplace, or apply the Fall ration of chemical fertilizer to his doubtlessly impeccable lawn, thus adding another half-pound of particulates to the local atmosphere and another 10 pounds of nitrates and other poisons to the regional aquifers. But that, of course, is pure and unkindly speculation.

In any case, the point of this real-life vignette, as John Barth would *11* insist, is obvious. The current controversy over public smoking in Fort Collins is a clear instance of selective virtue at work, coming under the rubric of, what I do is perfectly OK, but what you do is perfectly awful.

? QUESTIONS FOR WRITING AND DISCUSSION

❶ Choosing only one adjective to describe your main reaction to each essay, answer the following question: "When I finished the _____ [Wong, Zoellner] essay, I was _____ [intrigued, bored, amused, irritated, curious, confused, or _____] because _____. Explain your choice of adjectives in one or two sentences.

❷ Referring to specific passages, explain the purpose and state the thesis or main point of each essay.

❸ What personality or role does each writer project? Drawing from evidence in the essay, describe what you think both writers would be like if you met them.

❹ Both of these essays appeared in newspapers. What kind of reader would find each essay interesting? What kind of reader would not enjoy each essay? For each essay, find examples of specific sentences, word choices, vocabulary, experiences, or references to culture or politics that would appeal to one reader but perhaps irritate another.

❺ These two essays are similar in genre—they are both informal essays narrating personal experiences and explaining what each writer discovered or learned. There are differences, however, in structure and style. What differences do you notice in the way each essay begins and concludes, in the order of the paragraphs, and in vocabulary or style of the sentences?

❻ Each essay has a particular social, cultural, and political context. Describe this context for both essays. Then identify at least three other viewpoints that exist in the cultural, social, or political conversations that surround each of these topics. (For example, what are different points of view about multicultural or bilingual education? What arguments exist both for and against smoking in privately owned business establishments?) How effective is each writer in responding to the ongoing cultural, social, or political context or conversation?

Dimensions of the Writing Process

Processes for writing vary from one writer to the next and from one writing situation to the next. Most writers, however, can identify four basic stages, or dimensions, of their writing process: collecting, shaping, drafting, and revising. The writing situation may precede these stages—particularly if you are assigned a subject, purpose, audience, and form. Usually, however, you continue to narrow your subject, clarify your purpose, meet the needs of your audience, and modify your form as you work through the dimensions of your writing process.

COLLECTING

Mark Twain, author of *The Adventures of Huckleberry Finn,* once observed that if you attempt to carry a cat around the block by its tail, you'll gain a whole lot of information about cats that you'll never forget. You may collect such firsthand information, or you may rely on the data, experience, or expertise of others. In any case, writers constantly collect facts, impressions, opinions, and ideas that are relevant to their subjects, purposes, and audiences. Collecting involves observing, remembering, imagining, thinking, reading, listening, writing, investigating, talking, taking notes, and experimenting. Collecting also involves thinking about the relationships among the bits of information that you have collected.

> **I don't see writing as communication of something already discovered, as "truths" already known. Rather, I see writing as a job of experiment. It's like any discovery job; you don't know what's going to happen until you try it.**
>
> —WILLIAM STAFFORD, TEACHER, POET, AND ESSAYIST

SHAPING

Writers focus and organize the facts, examples, and ideas that they have collected into the recorded, linear form that is written language. When a hurricane hits the Gulf Coast, for example, residents of Texas, Louisiana, Mississippi, Alabama, and Florida are likely to collect an enormous amount of data in just a few hours. Rain, floods, tree limbs snapping in the wind, unboarded windows shattering, sirens blaring—all of these events occur nearly simultaneously. If you try to write about such devastation, you need to narrow your focus (you can't describe everything that happened) and organize your information (you can't describe all of your experiences at the same time).

The genre of the personal essay, weaving description in a chronological order, is just one of the shapes that a writer may choose to develop and organize experience. Such shaping strategies also help writers collect additional information and ideas. Reconstructing a chronological order, for example, may suggest some additional details—perhaps a wet, miserable-looking dog running through the heavy downpour—that you might not otherwise have remembered.

> **The writing process is not linear, moving smoothly in one direction from start to finish. It is messy, recursive, convoluted, and uneven. Writers write, plan, revise, anticipate, and review throughout the writing process.**
>
> —MAXINE HAIRSTON, TEACHER AND AUTHOR OF ARTICLES AND TEXTBOOKS ON WRITING

DRAFTING

At some point, writers actually write down a rough version of what will evolve into the finished piece of writing. Drafting processes vary widely from one writer to the next. Some writers prefer to reread their collecting and shaping notes, find a starting point, and launch themselves—figuring out what they want to say as they write it. Other writers start with a plan—a mental strategy, a

> **We must and do write each our own way.**
>
> —EUDORA WELTY, NOVELIST AND ESSAYIST

short list, or an outline—of how they wish to proceed. Whatever approach you use in your draft, write down as much as possible: You want to see whether the information is clear, whether your overall shape expresses and clarifies your purpose, and whether your content and organization meet the needs and expectations of your audience.

REVISING

When writers revise rough drafts, they literally "resee" their subjects—and then modify drafts to fit new visions. Revision is more than just tinkering with a word here and there; revision leads to larger changes—new examples or details, a different organization, or a new perspective. You accomplish these changes by adding, deleting, substituting, or reordering words, sentences, and paragraphs. Although revision begins the moment you get your first idea, most revisions are based on the reactions—or anticipated reactions—of the audience to your draft. You often play the role of audience yourself by putting the draft aside and rereading it later when you have some distance from your writing. Wherever you feel readers might not get your point, you revise to make it clearer. You may also get feedback from readers in a class workshop, suggesting that you collect more or different information, alter the shape of your draft to improve the flow of ideas, or clarify your terminology. As a result of your rereading and your readers' suggestions, you may change your thesis or write for an entirely different audience.

Editing—in contrast to revising—focuses on the minor changes that you make to improve the accuracy and readability of your language. You usually edit your essay to improve word choice, grammar, usage, or punctuation. You also use a computer spell-check program and proofread to catch typos and other surface errors.

THE WHOLE PROCESS

In practice, a writer's process rarely follows the simple, consecutive order that these four stages or dimensions suggest. The writing process is actually recursive: It begins at one point, goes on to another, comes back to the first, jumps to the third, and so forth. A stage may last hours or only a second or two. While writing a letter to a friend, you may collect, shape, revise, and edit in one quick draft; a research paper may require repeated shaping over a two-week period. As writers draft, they may correct a few mistakes or typos, but they may not proofread until many days later. In the middle of reorganizing an essay, writers often reread drafts, go back and ask more questions, and collect more data. Even while editing, writers may throw out several paragraphs, collect some additional information, and draft new sections.

In addition to the recursive nature of the writing process, keep in mind that writing often occurs during every stage, not just during drafting and revising. During collecting, you will be recording information and jotting down ideas. During shaping, you will be writing out trial versions that you may use later when you draft or revise. Throughout the writing process, you use your writing to modify your subject, purpose, audience, and form.

The most important point to keep in mind is that the writing process is unique to each writer and to each writing situation. What works for one writer may be absolutely wrong for you. Some writers compose nearly everything in their heads. Others write only after discussing the subject with friends or drawing diagrams and pictures.

During the writing process, you need to experiment with several collecting, shaping, and drafting strategies to see what works best for you and for a particular piece of writing. As long as your process works, however, it's legitimate—no matter how many times you backtrack and repeat stages. When you are struggling with a piece of writing, remember that numerous revisions are a normal part of the writing process—even for most professionals.

Circling back over what you have already written—to sharpen your thesis, improve the organization, tighten up a paragraph, or add specific details to your examples—is likely to be the most time-consuming, yet worthwhile, part of your writing process. Most professional writers testify to the necessity and value of writing numerous drafts. When you are reworking a piece of writing, scrawling revisions over what you had hoped would be your finished product, remember what Nobel laureate Isaac Bashevis Singer once pointed out: "The wastepaper basket is the writer's best friend."

WARMING UP   Journal Exercises

The following exercises will help you review and practice the topics covered in this chapter. In addition, you may discover a subject for your own writing. Choose three of the following entries, and write for ten minutes on each.

1 Reread your "authority" list from Chapter 1. Choose one of those topics and then explain your purpose, identify a possible audience, and select a genre you would use.

2 From the resources available to you at home or on your computer, find examples of four different genres, such as advertisements, pamphlets, letters, articles, letters to the editor, and so forth. For each sample genre, identify the purpose, audience, and context. Bring these samples to class and be prepared to explain the rhetorical situation for each genre and why each sample is or is not effective.

3 **Writing Across the Curriculum.** If you have already been given a writing assignment in another course, explain the purpose, the intended audience,

and the genre for that assignment. Be prepared to explain in class (or in a discussion forum) how you plan to complete that assignment.

④ During the first week of the term, one of your friends, Mark Lindstrom, is in an accident and is hospitalized. While still under the effects of anesthesia, he scribbles the following note for you to mail to his parents.

> Dear Mom and Dad,
>
> I arrived here last week. The trip was terrible. Dr. Stevens says that my leg will be better soon. My roommate is very strange. The police say my money is gone forever.
>
> Please send $1,500 to my new address right away.
>
> Thanks!
>
> Your loving son
>
> Mark

Because you were at the accident and can fill in the details, Mark asks you to explain everything to his parents. Write a short letter to them. Next, write a paragraph to your best friend that describes what happened to Mark.

⑤ Read Neil Petrie's essay and postscript at the end of this chapter. Then find the best paper you've written during the past year or two and write a "postscript" for it. Describe (a) the rhetorical situation, (b) your purpose, and (c) the process you used to write it.

A Writing Process at Work: Collecting and Shaping

PROFESSIONAL WRITING

Athletes and Education

Neil H. Petrie

In the following essay, which appeared in The Chronicle of Higher Education, *Neil H. Petrie argues that colleges have a hypocritical attitude toward student athletes. Although most universities claim that their athletes—both male and female—are in college to get a good education, in reality the pressures on athletes compromise their academic careers. The problem, Petrie argues, is not the old cliché that jocks are dumb, but the endless hours devoted to practice or spent on road trips, which drain even the good student-athlete's physical and mental energies. Colleges point with pride to a tiny number of athletes who become professionals, but much more frequently the collegiate system encourages athletes to set-tle for lower grades and incomplete programs. In far too many cases, ath-letes never graduate. These are the students whom, as Petrie says, "the system uses and then discards after the final buzzer."*

I have spent all my adult life in academe, first as a student and then as a   *1* professor. During that time I have seen many variations in the role of in-tercollegiate athletics in the university, and I've developed sharply split opinions on the subject. On one hand, I despise the system, clinging as it does to the academic body like a parasite. On the other hand, I feel sym-pathy and admiration for most of the young athletes struggling to bal-ance the task of getting an education with the need to devote most of their energies to the excessive demands of the gym and the field.

My earliest experiences with the intrusion of athletics into the class-   *2* room came while I was still a freshman at the University of Colorado. While I was in my English professor's office one day, a colleague of hers came by for a chat. Their talk turned to the football coach's efforts to court the favor of the teachers responsible for his gladiators by treating them to dinner and a solicitous discussion of the academic progress of the players. I vividly recall my professor saying, "He can take me out to dinner if he wants, but if he thinks I'll pass his knuckleheads just because of that, he'd better think again."

Later, as a graduate teaching fellow, a lecturer, and then an assistant   *3* professor of English, I had ample opportunity to observe a Division I uni-versity's athletics program. I soon discovered that the prevailing stereo-types did not always apply. Athletes turned out to be as diverse as any other group of students in their habits, tastes, and abilities, and they showed a wide range of strategies for coping with the stress of their dual roles.

Some of them were poor students. An extreme example was the   *4* All-American football player (later a successful pro) who saw college only as a step to a six-figure contract and openly showed his disdain for the educational process. Others did such marginal work in my courses that I got the feeling they were daring me to give them D's or F's. One woman cross-country star, who almost never attended my composition class, used to push nearly illiterate essays under my office door at odd hours.

Yet many athletes were among the brightest students I had. Not so   *5* surprising, when you consider that, in addition to physical prowess, suc-cess in athletics requires intelligence, competitive drive, and dedica-tion—all qualities that can translate into success in the classroom as well as on the field. The trouble is that the grinding hours of practice and road trips rob student athletes of precious study time and deplete their

...continued Athletes and Education, **Neil H. Petrie**

reserves of mental and physical energy. A few top athletes have earned A's; most are content to settle for B's or C's, even if they are capable of better.

The athletes' educational experience can't help being marred by their 6 numerous absences and divided loyalties. In this respect, they are little different from the students who attempt to go to college while caring for a family or working long hours at an outside job. The athletes, however, get extra help in juggling their responsibilities. Although I have never been bribed or threatened and have never received a dinner invitation from a coach, I am expected to provide extra time and consideration for athletes, far beyond what I give other students.

Take the midterm grade reports, for example. At my university, the 7 athletic department's academic counselor sends progress questionnaires to every teacher of varsity athletes. While the procedure shows admirable concern for the academic performance of athletes, it also amounts to preferential treatment. It requires teachers to take time from other teaching duties to fill out and return the forms for the athletes. (No other students get such progress reports.) If I were a cynic it would occur to me that the athletic department might actually be more concerned with athletes' eligibility than with their academic work.

Special attendance policies for athletes are another example of pref- 8 erential treatment. Athletes miss a lot of classes. In fact, I think the road trip is one of the main reasons that athletes receive a deficient education. You simply can't learn as much away from the classroom and the library as on the campus. Nevertheless, professors continue to provide make-up tests, alternative assignments, and special tutoring sessions to accommodate athletes. Any other student would have to have been very sick or the victim of a serious accident to get such dispensations.

It is sad to see bright young athletes knowingly compromise their 9 potential and settle for much less education than they deserve. It is infuriating, though, to see the ones less gifted academically exploited by a system that they do not comprehend and robbed of any possible chance to grow intellectually and to explore other opportunities.

One specific incident illustrates for me the worst aspects of college 10 athletics. It wasn't unusual or extraordinary—just the all-too-ordinary case of an athlete not quite good enough to make a living from athletics and blind to the opportunity afforded by the classroom.

I was sitting in my office near the beginning of a term, talking to a 11 parade of new advisees. I glanced up to see my entire doorway filled with the bulk of a large young man, whom I recognized as one of our basketball stars from several seasons ago who had left for the pros and now apparently come back.

Over the next hour I got an intensive course on what it's like to be a 12 college athlete. In high school, John had never been interested in much outside of basketball, and, like many other indifferent students, he went on to junior college on an athletic scholarship. After graduating, he came to the university, where he played for two more years, finishing out his eligibility. He was picked in a late round of the N.B.A. draft and left college, but in the end he turned out to be a step too slow for the pros. By that time he had a family to support, and when he realized he could never make a career of basketball, he decided to return to college.

We both knew that his previous academic career hadn't been particularly focused, and that because of transferring and taking minimum course loads during the basketball season, he wouldn't be close to a degree. But I don't think either one of us was prepared for what actually emerged from our examination of his transcripts. It was almost as if he had never gone beyond high school. His junior-college transcript was filled with remedial and nonacademic courses.   13

Credit for those had not transferred to the university. Over the next two years he had taken a hodgepodge of courses, mostly in physical education. He had never received any advice about putting together a coherent program leading to a degree. In short, the academic side of his college experience had been completely neglected by coaches, advisers, and, of course, John himself.   14

By the time we had evaluated his transcripts and worked out a tentative course of study, John was in shock and I was angry. It was going to take him at least three years of full-time study to complete a degree. He thanked me politely for my time, picked up the planning sheets, and left. I was ashamed to be a part of the university that day. Why hadn't anyone in the athletic department ever told him what it would take to earn a degree? Or at least been honest enough to say, "Listen, we can keep you eligible and give you a chance to play ball, but don't kid yourself into thinking you'll be getting an education, too."   15

I saw John several more times during the year. He tried for a while. He took classes, worked, supported his family, and then he left again. I lost track of him after that. I can only hope that he found a satisfying job or completed his education at some other institution. I know people say the situation has improved in the last few years, but when I read about the shockingly low percentages of athletes who graduate, I think of John.   16

Colleges give student athletes preferential treatment. We let them cut classes. We let them slide through. We protect them from harsh realities. We applaud them for entertaining us and wink when they compromise themselves intellectually. We give them special dorms, special meals, special tutors, and a specially reprehensible form of hypocrisy.   17

I can live with the thought of the athletes who knowingly use the college-athletics system to get their pro contracts or their devalued degrees. But I have trouble living with the thought of the ones whom the system uses and then discards after the final buzzer.   18

On Writing "Athletes and Education"

Neil H. Petrie

In the following postscript on his writing process, Neil Petrie describes why he wanted to write the paper, how he collected material to support his argument, and how he shaped and focused his ideas as he wrote. His comments illustrate how his purpose—to expose the hypocrisies of collegiate athletics—guided his writing of the essay. In addition, Petrie explains that other key questions affected the shape of his essay: how he should begin, where he should use his best example, and what words he should choose.

This essay has its origin, as all persuasive writing should, in a strongly 1 held opinion. I'm always more comfortable if I care deeply about my subject matter. As a teacher, I hold some powerful convictions about the uneasy marriage of big-time athletics and higher education, and so I wanted to write an essay that would expose what I think are the dangers and hypocrisies of that system.

At the beginning of my essay, I wanted to establish some author- 2 ity to lend credibility to my argument. Rather than gather statistics on drop-out rates of student athletes or collect the opinions of experts, I planned to rely on my own experiences as both a student and teacher. I hoped to convince my readers that my opinions were based on the authority of firsthand knowledge. In this introduction I was also aware of the need to avoid turning off readers who might dismiss me as a "jock hater." I had to project my negative feelings about the athletic system while maintaining my sympathy with the individual student athletes involved in that system. The thesis, then, would emerge gradually as I accumulated the evidence; it would be more implied than explicitly stated.

Gathering the material was easy. I selected a series of examples from 3 my personal experiences as a college student and instructor, as well as anecdotes I'd heard from other instructors. Most of these stories were ones that I had shared before, either in private discussions with friends or in classrooms with students.

Shaping the material was a little tougher. As I began thinking about 4 my examples and how to order them, I saw that I really wanted to make two main points. The first was that most colleges give preferential treatment to athletes. The second point was that, despite the extra attention, the success of the athlete's academic career is often ignored by all parties involved. Many of my examples, I realized, illustrated the varieties of pressures put upon both athletes and instructors to make sure that the students at least get by in class and remain eligible. These examples seemed to cluster together because they showed the frustrations of teachers and the reactions of athletes trying to juggle sports and academics. This group would make a good introduction to my general exposé of the system. But I had one more example I wanted to use that seemed to go beyond the cynicism of some athletes or the hypocrisy of the educators. This was the case of John, an athlete who illustrated what I thought were the most exploitative aspects of varsity athletics. I originally planned on devoting the bulk of my essay to this story and decided to place it near the end where it would make my second point with maximum emotional effect.

A two-part structure for the essay now emerged. In the first segment 5 following my introductory paragraph, I gave a series of shorter examples, choosing to order them in roughly chronological order (paragraphs 2–4). I then moved from these specific details to a more general discussion of the demands placed upon both students and teachers, such as lengthy practice time, grade reports, road trips, and special attendance policies. This concluded my description of the way the system operates (paragraphs 5–8).

Then it was time to shift gears, to provide a transition to the next part 6 of my essay, to what I thought was my strongest example. I wanted the story of John to show how the system destroyed human potential. To do this, I needed to increase the seriousness of the tone in order to persuade the reader that I was dealing in more than a little bureaucratic boondoggling. I tried to set the tone by my word choice: I moved from words such as "sad," "compromise," and "settle" to words with much stronger emotional connotations such as "infuriating," "exploited," and "robbed," all in a single short transitional paragraph (paragraph 9).

I then introduced my final extended example in equally strong lan- 7 guage, identifying it as a worst-case illustration (paragraph 10). I elaborated on John's story, letting the details and my reactions to his situation carry the more intense outrage that I was trying to convey in this second part of the essay (paragraphs 10–16). The first version that I tried was a rambling narrative that had an overly long recounting of John's high school and college careers. So I tightened this section by eliminating such items as his progress through the ranks of professional basketball and his dreams of million-dollar contracts. I also cut down on a discussion of the various courses of study he was considering as options. The result was a sharper focus on the central issue of John's dilemma: the lack of adequate degree counseling for athletes.

After my extended example, all that was left was the conclusion. As I 8 wrote, I was very conscious of using certain devices, such as the repetition of key words and sentence patterns in paragraph seventeen ("We let them . . . We let them . . . We protect them . . . We applaud them . . . We give them . . .") to maintain the heightened emotional tone. I was also

...continued On Writing "Athletes and Education", **Neil H. Petrie**

conscious of repeating the two-part structure of the essay in the last two paragraphs. I moved from general preferential treatment (paragraph 17) to the concluding and more disturbing idea of devastating exploitation (paragraph 18).

On the whole, I believe that this essay effectively conveys its point 9 through the force of accumulated detail. My personal experience was the primary source of evidence, and that experience led naturally to the order of the paragraphs and to the argument I wished to make: that while some athletes knowingly use the system, others are used and exploited by it.

QUESTIONS FOR WRITING AND DISCUSSION

1 In your journal, describe how your extracurricular activities (athletics, jobs, clubs, or family obligations) have or have not interfered with your education. Recall one specific incident that illustrates how these activities affected your classwork—either positively or negatively.

2 Describe Petrie's audience and purpose for this essay. What sentences reveal his intended audience? What sentences reveal his purpose? What sentences contain his thesis, claim, or main idea? Do you agree with that thesis? Why or why not?

3 Reread Petrie's postscript. Based on his comments and on your reading of the essay, how does Petrie describe or label each of the following sections of his essay:

paragraphs 1–4
paragraphs 5–8
paragraph 9
paragraphs 10–16
paragraphs 17–18

4 Who do you think is most to blame for the situation that Petrie describes: The athletes themselves? The colleges for paying their scholarships and then ignoring them when they drop out? The students and alumni who pay to see their teams win?

5 Petrie does not explicitly suggest a solution to the problem that he describes. Assume, however, that he has been asked by the president of his university to propose a solution. Write the letter that you think Petrie would send to the president.

A Writing Process at Work: Drafting and Revising

While drafting and revising, writers frequently make crucial changes in their ideas and language. The first scribbled sentences, written primarily for ourselves, are often totally different from what we later present to other people in final, polished versions. Take, for example, the final version of Abraham Lincoln's Gettysburg Address. It begins with the famous lines "Four score and seven years ago our fathers brought forth on this continent a new nation . . . . " But his first draft might well have begun, "Eighty-seven years ago, several politicians and other powerful men in the American Colonies got together and decided to start a new country . . . . " It is difficult to imagine that language ingrained in our consciousness was once drafted, revised, drafted again, and edited, as the author or authors added, deleted, reordered, and otherwise altered words, sentences, and ideas. In fact, it usually was.

Carl Becker's study of the American Declaration of Independence assembles the early drafts of that famous document and compares them with the final version. Shown below is Thomas Jefferson's first draft, with revisions made by Benjamin Franklin, John Adams, and other members of the Committee of Five that was charged with developing the new document.

Rough Draft of the Opening Sentences
of the Declaration of Independence
Thomas Jefferson

When in the course of human events it becomes necessary for a [one] people to dissolve the political bands which have connected them with another, and to ~~advance from that subordination in which they have hitherto remained, & to~~ assume among the powers of the earth the ~~equal & independent~~ [separate and equal] station to which

the laws of nature & of nature's god entitle them, a decent respect to the opinions

of mankind requires that they should declare the causes which impel them to the separation. ~~the change.~~

We hold these truths *to be* ~~sacred & undeniable; that~~ [self-evident] all men are created equal ~~& independent~~; that ~~from that equal creation they derive in rights~~ [they are endowed by their creator with] inherent

_{rights; that} _{these}
& inalienable among ~~which~~ are ~~the preservation of~~ life, ~~&~~ liberty, & the pursuit

of happiness. . . .

The Final Draft of the Opening Sentences of the Declaration of Independence, as Approved on July 4, 1776

When in the Course of human events, it becomes necessary for one people

to dissolve the political bands which have connected them with another, and to

assume among the powers of the earth, the separate and equal station to which

the Laws of Nature and of Nature's God entitle them, a decent respect to the

opinions of mankind requires that they should declare the causes which impel

them to the separation.

We hold these truths to be self-evident, that all men are created equal, that

they are endowed by their Creator with certain inalienable Rights, that among

these are Life, Liberty and the pursuit of Happiness.

? QUESTIONS FOR WRITING AND DISCUSSION

1. Select one change in a sentence that most improved the final version of the Declaration of Independence. Explain how the revised wording is more effective.

2. Find one change in a word or phrase that constitutes an alteration in meaning rather than just a choice of "smoother" or more appropriate language. How does this change affect the meaning?

3. Upon rereading this passage from the Declaration of Independence, one reader wrote, "I was really irritated by that 'all men are created equal' remark. The writers were white, free, well-to-do, Anglo-Saxon, mostly Protestant males discussing their own 'inalienable rights.' They sure weren't discussing the 'inalienable rights' of female Americans or of a million slaves or of

nonwhite free Americans!" Revise the passage from the Declaration of Independence using this person as your audience.

4 On the Internet, visit the National Archives at http://www.nara.gov to see a photograph of the original Declaration of Independence and learn how the Dunlap Broadside of the Declaration was read aloud to troops. What does this historical context add to what you know about the Declaration of Independence? Do the revisions help make the document more revolutionary or propagandistic? In addition, this site has other treasures from the National Archives including the police blotter listing Abraham Lincoln's assassination, the first report of the *Titanic*'s collision with an iceberg, and Rosa Parks's arrest records. Do you think these documents are as important to our history and culture as the Declaration itself? Explain.

PEARSON
mycomplab

For additional writing, reading, and research resources,
go to http://www.mycomplab.com

This street painting was completed in 2008 by art students in Weilheim, Germany, to replicate a painting of the same square done 99 years earlier by artist Vassily Kandinsky. After observing the details of the painting in this photograph, respond to journal entry 5 on page 53.

Observing

3

I n the far corner of a friend's living room is a lighted aquarium. Instead of water, the aquarium has a few inches of white sand, a dish of water, and a small piece of pottery. When you ask about the aquarium, your friend excitedly says, "You mean you haven't met Nino?" In a matter of seconds, you have a small, tannish-brown snake practically in your lap, and your friend is saying, "This is Nino. She—or he—is an African sand boa." You imagined that all boa constrictors were huge snakes that suffocated and then swallowed babies. "Actually," replies your friend, "Nino is very shy. She prefers to burrow in the sand." The snake is fascinating. It is only fifteen inches long, with a strong, compact body and a stub tail. Before it burrows into your coat pocket, you observe it closely so you can describe it to your younger brother, who loves all kinds of snakes.

In the physics laboratory, you're doing an experiment on light refraction. You need to observe how light rays bend as they go through water, so you take notes describing the procedure and the results. During each phase of the experiment, you observe and record the angles of refraction. The data and your notes will help you write up the lab report that is due next Monday.

> ❝ My task . . . is, by the power of the written word, to make you hear, to make you feel—it is, before all, to make you see. ❞
> —JOSEPH CONRAD, AUTHOR OF *HEART OF DARKNESS* AND OTHER NOVELS

> ❝ Seeing is of course very much a matter of verbalization. Unless I call my attention to what passes before my eyes, I simply won't see it. ❞
> —ANNIE DILLARD, NATURALIST AND AUTHOR OF *PILGRIM AT TINKER CREEK*

O BSERVING IS ESSENTIAL TO GOOD WRITING. WHETHER YOU ARE WRITING IN A JOURNAL, DOING A LABORATORY REPORT FOR A SCIENCE CLASS, OR WRITING A LETTER TO THE EDITOR OF A NEWSPAPER, KEEN OBSERVATION IS ESSENTIAL. WRITING OR VERBALIZING what you see helps you discover and learn more about your environment. Sometimes your purpose is limited to yourself: you observe and record to help you understand your world or yourself better. At other times, your purpose extends to a wider audience: you want to share what you have learned with others to help them learn as well. No matter who your audience is or what your subject may be, however, your task is to see and to help your readers see.

Of course, observing involves more than just "seeing." Good writers draw on all their senses: sight, smell, touch, taste, hearing. In addition, however, experienced writers also notice what is *not* there. The smell of food that should be coming from the kitchen but isn't. A friend who usually is present but now is absent. The absolute quiet in the air that precedes an impending storm. Writers should also look for *changes* in their subjects—from light to dark, from rough to smooth, from bitter to sweet, from noise to sudden silence. Good writers learn to use their previous *experiences* and their *imaginations* to draw comparisons and create images. Does a sea urchin look and feel like a pincushion with the pins stuck in the wrong way? Does the room feel as cramped and airless as the inside of a microwave oven? Finally, good writers write from a specific point of view or role: a student describing basic laws of physics or an experienced worker in a mental health clinic describing the clientele.

The key to effective observing is to *show* your reader the person, place, object, or image through *specific detail.* Good description follows the advice of experienced writers: *Show, don't tell.* Showing through vivid detail allows the reader to reach the conclusions that you may be tempted to just tell them. If your reader is going to learn from your observations, you must give the *exact details that you learned from,* not just your conclusions or generalizations. Even in writing, experience is the best teacher, so use specific details to communicate the look, the feel, the weight, the sights and sounds and smells.

Although effective description depends on detailed observation, what we already know about the subject—and what we can learn during our observations—can be crucial. The people, places, objects, or images that we observe are often difficult, complex, or contested. They do not give up their meaning in our first glance. If we look at an Impressionist painting, are we seeing pretty colors in shimmering light or just careless, undisciplined brushwork? If we see workers in a field planting or harvesting crops, is it a natural agricultural scene or the exploitation of Japanese internment workers? A key part, then, of effective observation is learning and reading about what we see. An observant eye requires a critical, inquiring mind.

Claude Monet, *Impression: Sunrise*, 1872. This painting gave the Impressionists their name.

Ansel Adams, farm, farm workers, Mount Williamson in background, 1943. Photograph of Japanese-American Internment, Manzanar Relocation Center, California.

Whether you are a tourist describing the cliff dwellings at Mesa Verde, a student in a chemistry class writing up your laboratory experiment, a social worker observing working and housing conditions of agricultural workers, or a volunteer observing at a community crisis center, your task is to critically observe and then describe your subject—to show your readers, to make them *see*.

❝The real voyage of discovery consists not in seeking new landscapes but in having new eyes. ❞

—MARCEL PROUST, AUTHOR OF *REMEMBRANCE OF THINGS PAST*

Techniques for Writing About Observations

The short passages on the following pages use specific techniques for observing people, places, objects, or images that are described here. In all of the passages, the writer *narrows* or *limits* the scope of the observation and selects specific details that support the *dominant idea* of the passage. The dominant idea reflects the writer's purpose for that particular audience. As you read each passage, notice how the authors use the techniques listed below for making their writing more vivid and effective.

Techniques for Writing About Observations

Technique	Tips on How to Do It
Giving sensory details (sight, sound, smell, touch, taste)	Use *sensory descriptions, comparisons,* and *images.* "Zoom in" on crucial details. Also include *actual dialogue* and *names of things* where appropriate.
Describing what is *not* there	Sometimes keen observation requires stepping back and noticing what is *absent,* what is *not* happening, or who is *not* present.
Noting changes in the subject's form or condition	Even when the subject appears static—a land-scape, a flower, a building—look for evidence of changes: a tree being enveloped by tent worms, a six-inch purple-and-white iris that eight hours earlier was just a green bud, a sandstone exterior of a church being eroded by acid rain.
Learning about your subject	An observant eye requires a critical, inquiring mind. Read about your subject. Google key ideas or terms. Ask other people or experts on the subject. Probe to find what is *unusual, surprising,* or *controversial* about your subject.
Writing from a distinct point of view	Good writers assume a distinct role. A lover and a botanist, for example, see entirely different things in the same red rose. *What* is seen depends on *who* is doing the seeing.

Focusing on a dominant idea	Focus on those details and images that clarify the main ideas or discoveries. Discovery often depends on the *contrast* between the writer's expectations and the reality.

These techniques for observing are illustrated in the following two paragraphs by Karen Blixen, who wrote *Out of Africa* under the pen name Isak Dinesen. A Danish woman who moved to Kenya to start a coffee plantation, Blixen knew little about the animals in Kenya Reserve. In this excerpt from her journals, she describes a startling change that occurred when she shot a large iguana. (The annotations in the margin identify all six observing techniques.)

In the Reserve I have sometimes come upon the Iguana, the big lizards, as they were sunning themselves upon a flat stone in a riverbed. They are not pretty in shape, but nothing can be imagined more beautiful than their coloring. **They shine like a heap of precious stones or like a pane cut out of an old church window. When, as you approach, they swish away, there is a flash of azure, green and purple over the stones, the color seems to be standing behind them in the air, like a comet's luminous tail.**

Role: A newcomer to the Reserve

Comparisons, images, and sensory details

Once I shot an Iguana. I thought that I should be able to make some pretty things from his skin. A strange thing happened then, that I have never afterwards forgotten. As I went up to him, where he was lying dead upon his stone, and actually while I was walking the few steps, he faded and grew pale, all color died out of him as in one long sigh, and by the time that I touched him he was grey and dull like a lump of concrete. It was the live impetuous blood pulsating within the animal, which had radiated out all that glow and splendor. Now that the flame was put out, and the soul had flown, the Iguana was as dead as a sandbag.

Changes in condition

Learning about the subject

What is not there

Dominant idea: Now colorless and dead

OBSERVING PEOPLE

Observing people—their dress, body language, facial features, behavior, eating habits, and conversation—is a pastime that we all share. In a *Rolling Stone* article, for example, Brian Hiatt describes U2 lead singer Bono in his native Dublin. Notice how the descriptive details and images work together to create the dominant impression of Bono as a famous, high-energy rock star, conversationalist, and global philanthropist.

Bono rounds a corner onto a narrow Dublin street, boots crunching on old cobblestone, sleek, black double-breasted overcoat flapping in the January breeze. . . . He's running late for his next appointment, which is not unusual in what must be one of the most overstuffed lives on the planet: "part-time" rock stardom; global advocacy for Africa's poor that's won him nominations for the Nobel Peace Prize; various multinational business and charitable ventures; an op-ed column for the *New York Times*; and four kids with Ali Hewson, his wife of 26 years. "I find it very hard to leave home," he says, "because my house is full of laughter and songs and kids."

Interviewing Bono is like taking an Alaskan husky for a walk—you can only suggest a general direction, and then hold on for dear life. Over an 80-minute lunch at a favorite Dublin restaurant, Eden, he repeatedly goes off on wild, entertaining tangents, which tend to include names such as Bill Clinton, Microsoft co-founder Paul Allen, genomic researcher Craig Venter and Archbishop Desmond Tutu (Bono calls him "the Arch"). He tosses out one killer sound bite after another, blue eyes moving like tropical fish behind today's pinkish-purple shades.

He eats his chicken breast in big bites, avoiding the potatoes, talking with his mouth full—and when the chicken is gone, he dips a finger into the sauce and licks it off, more than once. "We began this decade well—I think we'll end it better," he says, sitting on a white chair at a white table in a restaurant that's otherwise empty— apparently because management has cleared it out for him. "Wouldn't it be great if, after all these years, U2 has their heyday? That could be true of a painter or a filmmaker at this stage."

OBSERVING PLACES

In the following passage, John Muir describes California and the Yosemite Valley as it looked over 130 years ago. John Muir, of course, was the founder of the Sierra Club, whose first mission was to preserve the vision of Yosemite that Muir paints in the following paragraphs. Notice how Muir uses all of the key techniques for observing as he vividly describes the California Sierra.

Arriving by the Panama steamer, I stopped one day in San Francisco and then inquired for the nearest way out of town. "But where do you want to go?" asked the man to whom I had applied for this important information. "To any place that is wild," I said. This reply startled him. He seemed to fear I might be crazy and therefore the sooner I was out of town the better, so he directed me to the Oakland ferry.

So on the first of April, 1868, I set out afoot for Yosemite. It was the bloom-time of the year over the lowlands and coast ranges; the land-scapes of the Santa Clara Valley were fairly drenched with sunshine, all the air was quivering with the songs of the meadow-larks, and the hills were so covered with flowers that they seemed to be painted. Slow indeed was my progress through these glorious gardens, the first of the California flora I had seen. Cattle and cultivation were making few scars as yet, and I wandered enchanted in long wavering curves, knowing by my pocket map that Yosemite Valley lay to the east and that I should surely find it.

Looking eastward from the summit of the Pacheco Pass one shining morning, a landscape was displayed that after all my wanderings still appears as the most beautiful I have ever beheld. At my feet lay the Great Central Valley of California, level and flowery, like a lake of pure sunshine, forty or fifty miles wide, five hundred miles long, one rich furred garden of yellow *Compositae*. And from the eastern boundary of this vast golden flower-bed rose the mighty Sierra, miles in height, and so gloriously colored and so radiant, it seemed not clothed with light, but wholly composed of it, like the wall of some celestial city. Along the top and extending a good way down, was a rich pearl-gray belt of snow; below it a belt of blue and dark purple, marking the extension of the forests; and stretching along the base of the range a broad belt of rose-purple; all these colors, from the blue sky to the yellow valley smoothly blending as they do in a rainbow, making a wall of light ineffably fine. Then it seemed to me that the Sierra should be called, not the Nevada or Snowy Range, but the Range of Light.

In general views no mark of man is visible upon it, nor anything to suggest the wonderful depth and grandeur of its sculpture. None of its magnificent forest-crowned ridges seems to rise much above the general level to publish its wealth. No great valley or river is seen, or group of well-marked features of any kind standing out as distinct pictures. Even the summit peaks, marshaled in glorious array so high in the sky, seem comparatively regular in form. Nevertheless the whole range five hundred miles long is furrowed with canyons 2,000 to 5,000 feet deep, in which once flowed majestic glaciers, and in which now flow and sing the bright rejoicing rivers.

OBSERVING OBJECTS

In observing an inanimate object such as a cookie, Paul Goldberger—architecture critic for *The New York Times*—brings his special point of view to his description. He totally ignores the cookie's taste, ingredients, and calories, focusing instead on the architectural relationships of function and form. Goldberger's architectural perspective helps focus his observations, creating a dominant idea for each passage.

Sugar Wafer (Nabisco)

There is no attempt to imitate the ancient forms of traditional, individually baked cookies here—this is a modern cookie through and through. Its simple rectangular form, clean and pure, just reeks of mass production and modern technological methods. The two

wafers, held together by the sugar-cream filling, appear to float . . . this is a machine-age object.

Fig Newton (Nabisco)

This, too, is a sandwich but different in every way from the Sugar Wafer. Here the imagery is more traditional, more sensual even; a rounded form of cookie dough arcs over the fig concoction inside, and the whole is soft and pliable. Like all good pieces of design, it has an appropriate form for its use, since the insides of Fig Newtons can ooze and

would not be held in place by a more rigid form. The thing could have had a somewhat different shape, but the rounded tip is a comfortable, familiar image, and it's easy to hold. Not a revolutionary object but an intelligent one.

> ❝For Godsake, keep your eyes open. Notice what's going on around you. ❞
> —WILLIAM BURROUGHS, NOVELIST

WARMING UP   Journal Exercises

The following topics will help you practice close, detailed observation and may possibly suggest a subject for your assignment on observing. Read the exercises and then write on the two or three that interest you the most.

1. Go to a public place (library, bar, restaurant, hospital emergency room, gas station, laundromat, park, shopping mall, hotel lobby, police station, beach, skating rink, beauty salon, city dump, tennis court, church, etc.). Sit and observe everything around you. Use your pencil to help you see, both by drawing sketches and by recording sensory details in words. What do you see that you haven't noticed before? Then *narrow* your attention to a single person, *focus* on a restricted place, or *zoom* in on a single object. What do you see that you haven't noticed before?

2. In one of your classes, use your repeated observations of the total learning environment (the room, the seating arrangements, the blackboards, the audiovisual or computer equipment, the teacher, the daily teaching or learning rituals, and the students) to speculate on who has authority, how knowledge is created or communicated, and what the learning goals are for this course.

3 If you are working on a community-service learning project, for your first assignment, go and observe the place, people, and setting for the agency. Start by taking double-entry notes in your journal. On the left-hand side, record visual and sensory details; on the right-hand side, record your reactions and impressions. Use these notes for a description of your agency that will go in your final portfolio for your learning project.

4 Go to a gallery, studio, or museum where you can observe sculpture, paintings, or other works of art. Choose one work of art and draw it. Then describe it as fully as possible. Return to the gallery the next day, reread your first description, observe the work again, and add details that you didn't notice the first time.

5 Study the chapter-opening photograph of the Weilheim, Germany, street painting on page 44. Then go to Google images and enter "Vassily Kandinsky Weilheim" and examine the original painting of the buildings in that square. How accurately has the street painting on page 44 captured the original Kandinsky image? Because the street painting is not an exact replication, what are the differences between the image on the street and the original Kandinsky painting you found on Google? Consider the details, the color saturation, the use of rectangular blocks, and the overall style. Explain these differences, citing specific details from both the original Kandinsky painting and the photograph of the street art.

PROFESSIONAL WRITING

Take This Fish and Look at It

Samuel H. Scudder

In this essay, Samuel H. Scudder (1837–1911), an American entomologist, narrates his early attempts at scientific observation. Scudder recalls how a famous Swiss naturalist, Louis Agassiz, taught him the skills of observation by having him examine a fish—a haemulon or snapper—closely, carefully, and repeatedly. Agassiz, a professor of natural history at Harvard, taught his students that both factual details and general laws are important. "Facts are stupid things," he said, "until brought into connection with some general law." Scudder, writing about his studies under Agassiz, suggests that repeated observation can help us connect facts or specific details with general laws. The essay shows us an important lesson that Scudder learned: To help us see, describe, and connect, "A pencil is one of the best of eyes."

It was more than fifteen years ago that I entered the laboratory of *1* Professor Agassiz, and told him I had enrolled my name in the Scientific School as a student of natural history. He asked me a few questions about my object in coming, my antecedents generally, the mode in which I afterwards proposed to use the knowledge I might acquire, and, finally, whether I wished to study any special branch. To the latter I replied that, while I wished to be well grounded in all departments of zoology, I purposed to devote myself specially to insects.

"When do you wish to begin?" he asked.   *2*

"Now," I replied.   *3*

This seemed to please him, and with an energetic "Very well!" he *4* reached from a shelf a huge jar of specimens in yellow alcohol. "Take this fish," he said, "and look at it; we call it a haemulon; by and by I will ask what you have seen."

With that he left me, but in a moment returned with explicit instruc- *5* tions as to the care of the object entrusted to me.

"No man is fit to be a naturalist," said he, "who does not know how *6* to take care of specimens."

I was to keep the fish before me in a tin tray, and occasionally mois- *7* ten the surface with alcohol from the jar, always taking care to replace the stopper tightly. Those were not the days of ground-glass stoppers and elegantly shaped exhibition jars; all the old students will recall the huge neckless glass bottles with their leaky, wax-besmeared corks, half eaten by insects, and begrimed with cellar dust. Entomology was a cleaner science than ichthyology, but the example of the Professor, who had unhesitatingly plunged to the bottom of the jar to produce the fish, was infectious; and though this alcohol had a "very ancient and fishlike smell," I really dared not show any aversion within these sacred precincts, and treated the alcohol as though it were pure water. Still I was conscious of a passing feeling of disappointment, for gazing at a fish did not commend itself to an ardent entomologist. My friends at home, too, were annoyed when they discovered that no amount of eau-de-Cologne would drown the perfume which haunted me like a shadow.

In ten minutes I had seen all that could be seen in that fish, and *8* started in search of the Professor—who had, however, left the Museum; and when I returned, after lingering over some of the odd animals stored in the upper apartment, my specimen was dry all over. I dashed the fluid over the fish as if to resuscitate the beast from a fainting fit, and looked with anxiety for a return of the normal sloppy appearance. This little excitement over, nothing was to be done but to return to a steadfast gaze at my mute companion. Half an hour passed—an hour—another hour; the fish began to look loathsome. I turned it over and around; looked it in the face—ghastly; from behind, beneath, above, sideways, at three-quarter's view—just as ghastly, I was in despair; at an early hour I concluded that lunch was necessary; so, with infinite relief, the fish was carefully replaced in the jar, and for an hour I was free.

On my return, I learned that Professor Agassiz had been at the Museum, but had gone, and would not return for several hours. My fellow-students were too busy to be disturbed by continued conversation. Slowly I drew forth that hideous fish, and with a feeling of desperation again looked at it. I might not use a magnifying-glass; instruments of all kinds were interdicted. My two hands, my two eyes, and the fish: it seemed a most limited field. I pushed my finger down its throat to feel how sharp the teeth were. I began to count the scales in the different rows, until I was convinced that was nonsense. At last a happy thought struck me—I would draw the fish; and now with surprise I began to discover new features in the creature. Just then the Professor returned.   9

"That is right," said he; "a pencil is one of the best of eyes. I am glad   10 to notice, too, that you keep your specimen wet, and your bottle corked."

With these encouraging words, he added: "Well, what is it like?"   11

He listened attentively to my brief rehearsal of the structure of parts   12 whose names were still unknown to me: the fringed gill-arches and movable operculum; the pores of the head, fleshy lips and lidless eyes; the lateral line, the spinous fins and forked tail; the compressed and arched body. When I finished, he waited as if expecting more, and then, with an air of disappointment:

"You have not looked very carefully; why," he continued more   13 earnestly, "you haven't even seen one of the most conspicuous features of the animal, which is plainly before your eyes as the fish itself; look again, look again!" and he left me to my misery.

I was piqued; I was mortified. Still more of that wretched fish! But   14 now I set myself to my task with a will, and discovered one new thing after another, until I saw how just the Professor's criticism had been. The afternoon passed quickly; and when, towards its close, the Professor inquired:

"Do you see it yet?"   15

"No," I replied, "I am certain I do not, but I see how little I saw   16 before."

"That is next best," said he, earnestly, "but I won't hear you now; put   17 away your fish and go home; perhaps you will be ready with a better answer in the morning. I will examine you before you look at the fish."

This was disconcerting. Not only must I think of my fish all night,   18 studying, without the object before me, what this unknown but most visible feature might be; but also, without reviewing my discoveries, I must give an exact account of them the next day. I had a bad memory; so I walked home by Charles River in a distracted state, with my two perplexities.

The cordial greeting from the Professor the next morning was reas-   19 suring; here was a man who seemed to be quite as anxious as I that I should see for myself what he saw.

"Do you perhaps mean," I asked, "that the fish has symmetrical sides   20 with paired organs?"

...continued Take This Fish and Look at It, **Samuel H. Scudder**

His thoroughly pleased "Of course! Of course!" repaid the wakeful 21 hours of the previous night. After he had discoursed most happily and enthusiastically—as he always did—upon the importance of this point, I ventured to ask what I should do next.

"Oh, look at your fish!" he said, and left me again to my own devices. 22 In a little more than an hour he returned, and heard my new catalogue.

"That is good, that is good!" he repeated; "but that is not all; go on"; 23 and so for three long days he placed that fish before my eyes, forbidding me to look at anything else, or to use any artificial aid. "Look, look, look," was his repeated injunction.

This was the best entomological lesson I ever had—a lesson whose 24 influence has extended to the details of every subsequent study; a legacy the Professor had left to me, as he has left it to so many others, of inestimable value, which we could not buy, with which we cannot part.

A year afterward, some of us were amusing ourselves with chalk- 25 ing outlandish beasts on the Museum blackboard. We drew prancing star fishes; frogs in mortal combat; hydra-headed worms, stately craw-fishes with gaping mouths and staring eyes. The Professor came in shortly after, and was as amused as any at our experiments. He looked at the fishes.

"Haemulons, every one of them," he said; "Mr. _____ drew them." 26

True; and to this day, if I attempt a fish, I can draw nothing but 27 haemulons.

The fourth day, a second fish of the same group was placed beside 28 the first, and I was bidden to point out the resemblances and differences between the two; another and another followed, until the entire family lay before me, and a whole legion of jars covered the table and surround-ing shelves; the odor had become a pleasant perfume; and even now, the sight of an old, six-inch worm-eaten cork brings fragrant memories.

The whole group of haemulons was thus brought in review; and 29 whether engaged upon the dissection of the internal organs, the prepa-ration and examination of the bony framework, or the description of the various parts, Agassiz's training in the method of observing facts and their orderly arrangement was ever accompanied by the urgent exhorta-tion not to be content with them.

"Facts are stupid things," he would say, "until brought into connec- 30 tion with some general law."

At the end of eight months, it was almost with reluctance that I left 31 these friends and turned to insects; but what I had gained by this outside experience has been of greater value than years of later investigation in my favorite groups.

vo·cab·u·lar·y

In your journal, write down the meanings of the italicized words in the following phrases.

- my *antecedents* generally (**1**)
- *Entomology* was a cleaner science than *ichthyology* (**7**)
- dared not show any *aversion* (**7**)
- to *resuscitate* the beast (**8**)
- instruments of all kinds were *interdicted* (**9**)

- movable *operculum* (**12**)
- I was *piqued* (**14**)
- with my two *perplexities* (**18**)
- his repeated *injunction* (**23**)
- *hydra-headed* worms (**25**)
- the urgent *exhortation* (**29**)

? QUESTIONS FOR WRITING AND DISCUSSION

1. If you have taken any science classes with laboratory sections, describe any observing techniques you used while completing the lab assignments. What were you asked to observe? What were you asked to record? How were these sessions similar to or different from Scudder's experience? Explain.

2. Follow Professor Agassiz's advice about observing: Without looking again at the essay, record in writing what you found to be the most memorable parts of the essay. What parts seemed most vivid? Explain.

3. Apply Scudder's technique of *repeated observation* to his own essay. Read the essay a second time, carefully, looking for techniques for recording observations. Use a pencil to help you read, by underlining or making brief notes. What do you notice on the second reading that you did not see in the first?

4. What is the purpose of this essay? To inform us about fish? To explain how to learn about fish? To persuade us to follow Professor Agassiz's method? To entertain us with college stories? In your estimation, what is the primary purpose?

5. Describe the genre and intended audience for this essay. Review the list of genres on pages 24–25. What features of the essay (such as content, dialogue, paragraphing, narrative voice) help indicate the genre of this piece? Who is the intended audience? Which sentences most clearly address the intended audience?

6. "Facts are stupid things," Agassiz says, "until brought into connection with some general law." Reread paragraph 8. What is the "general law" about scientific observation—or, in this case, the *dominant idea*—created by the specific details describing Scudder's first session with his fish? Explain.

Trailing History

Scott Vogel

Shortly after the inauguration of President Barack Obama, Washington Post *travel writer and editor Scott Vogel travelled to Birmingham, Alabama, to rediscover the civil rights country made legendary by Martin Luther King, Jr., Rosa Parks, the Freedom Riders, and legions of civil rights marchers. During his stay, Vogel visited with women such as Yvonne Williams at the Birmingham Civil Rights Institute and Shirley Cherry at the Dexter Parsonage Museum, who thought that they would never live to see the day that an African American would be elected president of the United States. In this article, Vogel combines profiles of people he interviewed in Birmingham with vivid descriptions of historical events and places where King endured harassing phone calls, firebombs, and moments of self-doubt and despair.*

You need to get to the rain forests before they're all gone, and the polar ice caps may have melted by the time you try to see them, but it's Alabama that demands your immediate attention. And by Alabama I mean that place where elegant black ladies of a certain age stand sentinel over the trails through civil rights country. 1

Really. They're lit from within, these women; they glow as only people can who never thought they'd live to see the day but then live to see the day. And as they gaze out on the landscape of a country facing agonizing choices and certain pain, they haven't a doubt in the world that we'll get through this. After all, we've gotten through far worse. 2

The day I landed in Birmingham a few weeks back, there was every reason to believe that the rain and icy temperatures would soon end and the city would return to the 60-degree weather to which it's accustomed in February. Instead, it began to rain harder, and then it began to pour. Pedestrians with mangled umbrellas raced through Kelly Ingram Park, a standard-issue urban green space where pansies now grow in dainty rows but where thousands once gathered to demand an end to segregation and police retaliated by siccing attack dogs on children and aiming at them with fire hoses powerful enough to strip the bark off trees. 3

Across the street at the Birmingham Civil Rights Institute, a museum and research center, five massive picture windows overlook the park in a room devoted to the Kelly Ingram chapter of the story. The institute also houses a charred Greyhound bus, a replica of one that a group of Freedom Riders rode through Alabama before it was firebombed; and the pale green bars of the cell where the Rev. Martin Luther King Jr. wrote his famous "Letter From Birmingham Jail." And when you get to the end of a long se- 4 ries of hallways (a gut-wrenching trip that begins with sharecropper mannequins and ends with a quote from then-Sen. Barack Obama: "We are the ones we've been waiting for"), you get to Yvonne Williams's desk. Before coming to the institute, Williams spent all of 31 years teaching fourth grade in Birmingham public schools. And still she retired too soon.

"We used to have that poster with all the presidents, you know?" 5 Williams says. "And I distinctly remember this little boy coming up to me one day and saying, 'Mrs. Williams, where is the black one?' I thought, Lord, give the words to say it." She stops for a moment, collects herself.

"I just said to him, 'Maybe in your lifetime.'"   6

Williams has worked in the institute's research division for five years 7 now "and will be here till God sends me home." She worries about the younger generation, for whom nonviolent resistance is a quaint notion, and she wonders if they've already forgotten how rocky the road to Inauguration Day really was. They're up against a lot these days, she says, and toughness in the face of such trials is the only thing that's going to work.

"We just have to keep fighting. That's what I tell them. That's what 8 America's all about. Don't stop."

On the other end of Dexter Avenue, just a few blocks away, sits what was 9 once the home of the Montgomery Fair department store. In 1955 it was the place where Rosa Parks worked as an assistant tailor, spending endless hours on her feet before boarding the bus for home at Montgomery and Lee streets a few blocks away. Now at that corner sits the Rosa Parks Library and Museum, a powerful testament to the woman who famously wouldn't give up her seat.

It's an oft-told story, of course, but one that the museum manages to 10 make fascinating all over again. I watch a short film about Parks's life with a class of local students, after which we're all ushered into a room whose major feature is a cutaway replica of a yellow Montgomery Transit Authority bus. Using projected video, the museum provides a riveting, moment-by-moment dramatization of a bus ride that at least initially seems unremarkable: Passengers board, Parks among them, make small talk, settle into their papers. Even Parks's famous reply when the police threaten arrest—"You may do that"—sounds less like an act of defiance than the weary cry of a woman who has been standing on her feet all day. You see the reactions of fellow bus riders, some of whom are annoyed, some who can't believe what they're seeing and some who can't be bothered to look up from their papers and see history unfolding before their eyes.

The film continues. Parks is at last forcibly removed from the bus, 11 but there's no melodramatic music or fanfare of any kind. No, her seat is immediately taken by a white passenger, and the bus simply pulls off. The final sections of the presentation proceed like the first; it's just an ordinary day again. If you blinked, you might have missed the meeting of the moment and the spark, the beginning of things never being the same.

"If people hadn't stuck together, it would never have worked."   12

That's Shirley Cherry, yet another lambent Alabama sentinel I meet 13 on my travels. Cherry runs tours of the Dexter Parsonage Museum on Centennial Hill, King's home while he was a pastor in town. As a girl she worked in a cleaners in Tuskegee and was regularly charged with the task of washing the white robes of Ku Klux Klansmen. ("I always say that the Klan put me through school," she says with a wry smile.) The sun has come out, but there's a bitter wind blowing up from downtown Montgomery. Cherry walks slowly but steadily from an adjacent building to the parsonage, a proud 1912 relic of what was once an upscale African American neighborhood but is now spiraling downward.

"People have to stick together," Cherry says, shaking her head and 14 gazing down South Jackson Street.

We flee the cold and enter the house, and just like that it's the '50s 15 again. On the coffee table in the parlor, there's a dish of pecans gathered from the trees out back, crocheted doilies and a few loose cigarettes scattered here and there. ("Dr. King was a private smoker," Cherry confides. "Some people say he smoked Winstons. Most people say he smoked OPBs—other people's brands. I mean, who's not going to give Martin Luther King a cigarette?")

In the living room, afternoon sunlight is falling on an upright piano. 16 Through the window I see the front porch, the one with the sizable gash in its floor, a vivid reminder of the night of Jan. 30, 1956, when the parsonage was firebombed. King's wife and a friend were in the parlor with the pecans and doilies, his 10-week-old daughter asleep in a crib in the next room. If you look at the house now, with all its cozy, homey details, at first it's almost impossible to imagine a bomb blowing a hole in the living room, the family within barely escaping death. But then you remember that this is Alabama, a place where history has a way of happening anywhere.

"This is not the actual phone where they received the harassing 17 phone calls," Cherry explains, "but it would have looked just like this." On a table in the hallway, a black Bell rotary phone just like this one used to receive 30 to 40 threatening calls a day, so many that an extra line had to be added in King's study. There I see a desk, a hat rack and a record player with jazz albums King loved and shelves full of books. (Well, not full exactly. "Write in your article that we need pre-1960-copyright books to put on display," Cherry tells me. "They can send them to me.")

And then we come to the kitchen. Cherry sighs. "This is the room 18 you have to see," she says softly, her eyes wandering from the Maytag hand-cranked washing machine in the corner to the Hot Shot bug spray in the pantry to the vintage canisters to King's own teakettle on the stove, at last settling on the modest kitchen table in the center of the room.

"Nobody's teaching the young people about how they got to where 19 they are," she says, staring at the four settings of blue Melmac dishes. "It's

A young girl poses beside Eric Blome's sculpture of Rosa Parks at the library and museum honoring the Montgomery woman who refused to give up her seat on a bus. (Alabama Tourism Department)

not just history. It's a way of saying, 'You can do anything if you try.' I've had my share of trials, but then I think of Dr. King and those harassing phone calls."

Cherry embarks on a story about a January evening just a few days 20 before the parsonage was bombed. "That night he got a particularly troubling phone call. He was called names I won't repeat."

Although it was late and he was exhausted, King found himself un- 21 able to sleep. "He came in this kitchen and made a cup of coffee and sat right here."

Cherry pulls out the chair at the head of the table and sits down her- 22 self. "He put his head in his hands like this and said, 'God, fears are creeping up my soul.'" She looks up from her hands. "Fears of the body are one thing, but these were fears of the soul."

As he recounted in his autobiography, King, alone in this kitchen, 23 confessed that he was losing his courage. "I am at the end of my powers," he remembered praying. "I have nothing left. I've come to the point where I can't face it alone."

And then, as Cherry puts it, King had "an epiphany. God came to 24 him and said, 'Martin Luther, I'll be with you.'"

The sun is now low in the sky, and the ancient hot water heater is 25 making clicking sounds from somewhere. Cherry stands up and carefully pushes the chair into the table.

"If Dr. King could go on," she says, "so can I."   26

vo·cab·u·lar·y

Write down the meanings of the italicized words in the following phrases.

- stand *sentinel* (**1**)
- *sharecropper mannequins* (**4**)
- is a *quaint* notion (**7**)
- a powerful *testament* (**9**)
- a cutaway *replica* (**10**)

- no *melodramatic* music (**11**)
- yet another *lambent* Alabama sentinel (**13**)
- the *vintage* canisters (**18**)
- King had an *epiphany* (**24**)

? QUESTIONS FOR WRITING AND DISCUSSION

1 List a few things you know about the Civil Rights Movement and Martin Luther King, Jr. Then cite examples from Vogel's article that presented information or events with which you were unfamiliar. Explain which pieces of information or description most caught your attention.

2 One of the most important techniques for writing about observations is to include details that evoke the senses of sight, sound, smell, touch, or taste. In paragraph 3, for example, Vogel describes the "rain and icy temperatures" on the day he landed in Birmingham. Find at least three other examples of Vogel's use of sensory detail in his descriptions.

3 In addition to sensory descriptions, Vogel uses images and comparisons to make the people and places more vivid. In the second paragraph, Vogel says that the women he interviews "glow as only people can who never thought they'd live to see the day" that an African American was elected president. Find at least three other examples of effective images or comparisons.

4 In his article, Vogel includes pictures of the civil rights marches and historical figures such as Rosa Parks. Go to the Library of Congress site (at http://www.loc.gov/exhibits/civilrights/) and look at other photographs and images from the civil rights era. At that site, or others that you locate on the Internet, find at least three other pictures that could accompany Vogel's article. Explain why each image would be appropriate.

5 For your own essay, think about an historical site near your own home. Visit this site, take a tour, talk to officials at the site, and do some research at your library and on the Internet. Then write a description of what you saw and what you learned. Assume that your audience will be readers of a local magazine or newspaper who might not have recently visited this site.

Observing: The Writing Process

ASSIGNMENT FOR OBSERVING

Do a piece of writing in which you observe a specific person, place, object, and/or image. Your goal is to show how specific, observed details create a dominant impression about the person, place, object, image, or overall scene. For this assignment, remember that *repeated observation* is essential. Choose a specific place, scene, environment, group of people, or recurring event that *you can observe several times* during your writing process.

Though your initial purpose is to observe, you also need to think about a possible audience and genre. The chart below will help you choose a genre that will be appropriate and effective for your purpose and audience:

- A personal audience includes yourself, family, and close friends.
- An academic audience includes teachers, students, and anyone connected to an academic setting.
- A public audience includes people who are typically addressed through newspapers, magazines, newsletters, online articles or blogs, advertisements, and business publications.

Audience	Possible Genres for Descriptive Writing
Personal Audience	Journal, letter, blog, social networking site, email, scrapbook, multigenre documents
Academic Audience	Academic essay, science lab report, essay exam, business observation, technical report, online essay, class forum posting, multigenre documents.
Public Audience	Newspaper, magazine, or Internet article, editorial, newsletter, pamphlet, flyer, public blog, wiki posting, multigenre documents

CHOOSING A SUBJECT

If one of your journal entries suggested an interesting subject, try the collecting and shaping strategies. If none of those exercises caught your interest, consider the following ideas.

- **Think about your current classes.** Do you have a class with a laboratory—chemistry, physics, biology, engineering, animal science, horticulture, industrial sciences, physical education, social work, drawing, pottery—in which you have to make detailed observations? Use this assignment to help you in one of those classes: Write about what you observe and learn during one of your lab sessions.

- **Seek out a new place on campus that is off your usual track.** Check the college catalog for ideas about places you haven't yet seen—a theater where actors are rehearsing, a greenhouse, a physical education class in the martial arts, a studio where artists are working, a computer laboratory, or an animal research center. Or visit a class you wouldn't take for credit. Observe, write, and learn about what's there.

- **From a magazine that you read, choose an advertisement or an image to describe.** Start by observing the composition or arrangement of the

"Write about dogs!"

figures and the use of color, lines, balance, and contrast in the advertisement or work of art. *Your goals are to describe this image in detail and to analyze the effectiveness of this image in its rhetorical context.* As part of the rhetorical context, consider the artist or sponsor, the occasion, the purpose and intended audience, the genre, and the cultural context of this image. (See Chapter 6 for additional help.)

As you write on your subject, consider a tentative audience and purpose. Who might want to know what you learn from your observations? What do you need to explain? What will readers already know? Jot down tentative ideas about your subject, audience, and purpose. Remember, however, that these are not cast in concrete: You may discover some new idea, focus, or angle as you write.

COLLECTING

Once you have chosen a subject from your journal or elsewhere, begin collecting information. Depending on your purpose, your topic, or even your personal learning preferences, some activities will work better than others. However, you should *practice* all of these activities to determine which is most successful for you and most appropriate to your topic. During these collecting activities, go back and *reobserve your subject.* The second or third time you go back, you may see additional details or more actively understand what you're seeing.

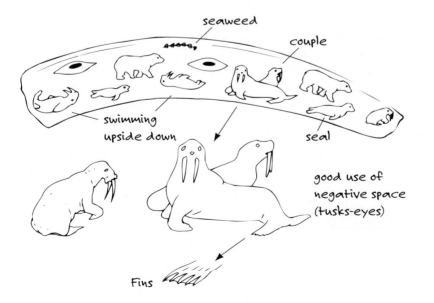

seaweed

couple

swimming
upside down

seal

good use of
negative space
(tusks-eyes)

Fins

66 We don't take in the world like a camera or a set of recording devices. The mind is an agent, not a passive receiver. . . . The active mind is a composer and everything we respond to, we compose. 99
—ANN BERTHOFF,
AUTHOR AND TEACHER

● **SKETCHING**   Begin by *drawing* what you see. The essayist Samuel Scudder says that pen or pencil can be "the best of eyes." Your drawing doesn't have to be great art to suggest other details, questions, or relationships that may be important. Instead of trying to cover a wide range of objects, try to focus on one limited subject and draw it in detail.

Here's an example. Writing student Brad Parks decided to visit an Eskimo art display at a local gallery. As part of his observing notes, he drew these sketches of Eskimo paintings. As he drew, he made notes in the margins of his sketches and zoomed in for more detail on one pair of walruses.

● **TAKING DOUBLE-ENTRY NOTES**   Taking notes in a double-entry format is a simple but effective system for recording observed details. At the top of the page, write the place and time of your observation and your perspective, role, or point of view. Place a vertical line down the middle of a page in your journal. On the left-hand side, write down description and sensory details. On the right-hand side, record your reactions, thoughts, ideas, and questions.

● **ANSWERING QUESTIONS**   To help you describe the person, place, object, or image, write a short response in your journal to each of the following questions.

- What exactly is it? Can you *define* this person, place, object, or image? If it's an object, are its parts related? Who needs it, uses it, or produces it?
- How much could it change and still be recognizable?
- Compare and contrast it. How is it similar to or different from other comparable people, places, things, or images?
- From what points of view is it usually seen? From what point of view is it rarely seen?

● **FREEWRITING**   *Freewriting* means exactly what it says. Write about your subject, nonstop, for five to ten minutes. Sometimes you may have to write, "I can't think of anything" or "This is really stupid," but keep on writing. Let your words and ideas suggest other thoughts and ideas. For observing, the purpose of freewriting is to let your imagination work on the subject, usually *after* you have observed and recorded specific details. Freewriting on your subject will also develop more *associations* or *comparisons* for the right-hand side of your double-entry log. It should also help you to identify a dominant idea for your details.

SHAPING

To focus once again on the shaping process, consider your subject, purpose, and audience. Has your purpose changed? Can you narrow your subject to a specific topic? You may know the answers to some questions immediately; others you may not know until after you complete your first draft. Jot down your current responses to the following questions.

- **Subject:** What is your general subject?
- **Specific topic:** What aspect of your subject interests you? Try to narrow your field or limit your focus.
- **Purpose:** Why is this topic interesting or important to you or to others? From what point of view will you be writing? What is the *dominant idea* you are trying to convey?
- **Audience:** Who are your readers? Are you aiming for a personal, an academic, or a public audience? What are these readers like, and why might they be interested in your topic?
- **Genre:** What specific genre might best serve your purpose and reach your intended audience? Experiment with a couple of genres to see which one might be most effective.
- **Context:** What is the cultural, political, social, or personal context in which this person, object, or image appears? How does that context affect your subject? How does the context affect you?

> 66 Your audience is one single reader. I have found that sometimes it helps to pick out one person—a real person you know, or an imagined person—and write to that one. 99
>
> —JOHN STEINBECK, NOVELIST

With answers to these questions in mind, you should experiment with several of the following genre possibilities and organization strategies. These genres and strategies not only will organize your specific examples but also may suggest related ideas to improve your description.

As you practice these strategies, try to *focus* on your subject. In a profile of a person, for example, focus on key facial features or revealing habits or mannerisms. If you're writing about a place or an event, narrow the subject. Describe, for instance, the street at night, a spider spinning a web in a windowsill, a man in a laundromat banging on a change machine, a bird hovering in midair, a photograph, a fish. Write in depth and detail about a *limited* subject.

With a limited subject, a shaping strategy such as spatial order, chronological order, or comparison/contrast will organize all the specific details for your audience. Shaping strategies give you ways of seeing relationships among the many bits of your description and of presenting them in an organized manner for your reader. Seeing these relationships will also help you discover and communicate the dominant idea to your reader.

● **SPATIAL ORDER** Spatial order is a simple way to organize your descriptive details. Choose some sequence—left to right, right to left, bottom to top—and describe your observed details in that sequence. In the following description of his "trashed" dorm room, Dale Furnish, a student who was the victim of a prank, uses spatial order. The italicized words illustrate the spatial order.

As I walked in the door, I could hardly believe that this scene of destruction used to be my room. *Along the left-hand wall,* nearly hiding my desk and mirror, was a pile of beer cans and bottles, paper cups, and old crumpled newspapers. The small window *on the far wall* was now covered with the mattress of the bed, and the frame of the bunk bed stood on end. The clothes closet, *to the right of the window,* looked as though it were a giant washing machine which had just gone through spin cycle—clothes were plastered all over, and only four hangers remained, dangling uselessly on the pole. *On the right wall,* where the bed had been, was the real surprise. Tied to the heating pipe was a mangy looking sheep. I swear. It was a real sheep. As I looked at it, it turned to face me and loudly and plaintively said, "Baaaa." *Behind me,* in the hall, everyone began laughing. I didn't know whether to laugh or cry.

● **CHRONOLOGICAL ORDER**   Chronological order is simply the time sequence of your observation. In the following passage, Gregory Allen, writing from his point of view as a five-foot-six-inch guard on a basketball team, describes sights, sounds, and his feelings during a pickup game. The italicized words emphasize the chronological order.

The game *begins.* The guy checking me is about 6'1", red hair, freckles, and has no business on the court. He looks slow, so I decide to run him to tire him. I dribble twice, pump fake, and the guy goes for it, thinking that he's going to block this much smaller guy's shot. *Then* I leap, flick my wrist, and the ball glides through the air and flows through the net with a swish as the net turns upside down. I come down and realize that I have been scratched. *Suddenly,* I feel a sharp pain as sweat runs into the small red cut. I wipe the blood on my shorts and *continue playing* the game. *After* that first play, I begin to hear the common song of the game. There's the squeak of the high-top Nike sneakers, the bouncing ball, the shuffle of feet. *Occasionally,* I hear "I'm open!" "Pass the ball!" "Aught!" And *then,* "Nice play, man!"

● **COMPARISON/CONTRAST**   If what you've observed and written about your subject so far involves seeing similarities or differences, you may be able to use comparison/contrast as a shaping strategy—either for a single paragraph or for a series of paragraphs. The following two paragraphs, for example, are taken from Albert Goldman's biography of Elvis Presley, titled *Elvis.* In these paragraphs, Goldman's dominant idea depends on the striking contrast between what he finds on the front lawn of Graceland, the rock star's mansion in Memphis, and what he notices when he steps through the front door.

Prominently displayed on the front lawn is an elaborate creche. The stable is a full-scale adobe house strewn with straw. Life-sized are the figures of Joseph and Mary, the kneeling shepherds and Magi, the lambs and ewes, as well as the winged annunciatory angel hovering over the roof beam. Real, too, is the cradle in which the infant Jesus sleeps.

When you step through the ten-foot oak door and enter the house, you stop and stare in amazement. Having just come from the contemplation of the tenderest scene in the Holy Bible, imagine the shock of finding yourself in a *whorehouse!* Yet there is no other way to describe the drawing room of Graceland except to say that it appears to have been lifted from some turn-of-the-century bordello down in the French Quarter of New Orleans. . . . The room is a gaudy melange of red velour and gilded tassels, Louis XV furniture and porcelain bric-a-brac, all informed by the kind of taste that delights in a ceramic temple d'amour housing a miniature Venus de Milo with an electrically simulated waterfall cascading over her naked shoulders.

Examine once again your collecting notes about your subject. If there are striking similarities or differences between the two parts or between various aspects of your subject, perhaps a comparison or contrast structure will organize your details.

● **DEFINITION**   Definition is the essence of observation. Defining a person, place, or object requires stating its exact meaning and describing its basic qualities. Literally, a definition sets the boundaries, indicating, for example, how an apple is distinct from an orange or how a canary is different from a sparrow. *Definition,* however, is a catchall term for a variety of strategies. It uses classification and comparison as well as description. It often describes a thing by negation—by saying what it is not. For example, Sidney Harris, a columnist for many years for the *Chicago Daily News,* once defined a "jerk" by referring to several types of people ("boob," "fool," "dope," "bore," "egotist," "nice person," "clever person") and then compared or contrasted these terms to show where "jerk" leaves off and "egotist" begins. In the following excerpt, Harris also defines by negation, saying that a jerk has no grace and is tactless. The result, when combined with a description of qualities he has observed in jerks, is definition.

Thinking it over, I decided that a jerk is basically a person without insight. He is not necessarily a fool or a dope, because some extremely clever persons can be jerks. In fact, it has little to do with intelligence as we commonly think of it; it is, rather, a kind of subtle but persuasive aroma emanating from the inner part of the personality.

I know a college president who can be described only as a jerk. He is not an unintelligent man, or unlearned, nor even unschooled in the social amenities. Yet he is a jerk *cum laude,* because of a fatal flaw in his nature—he is totally incapable of looking into the mirror of his soul and shuddering at what he sees there.

A jerk, then, is a man (or woman) who is utterly unable to see himself as he appears to others. He has no grace, he is tactless without meaning to be, he is a bore even to his best friends, he is an egotist without charm. All of us are egotists to some extent, but most of us—unlike the jerk—are perfectly and horribly aware of it when we make asses of ourselves. The jerk never knows.

At this stage in the writing process, you have already been defining your subject simply by describing it. But you may want to use a deliberately structured definition, as Harris does, to shape your observations.

● **SIMILE, METAPHOR, AND ANALOGY**   Simile, metaphor, and analogy create vivid word pictures or *images* by making *comparisons*. These images may take up only a sentence or two, or they may shape several paragraphs.

- A *simile* is a comparison using *like* or *as:* A is like B. "George eats his food like a vacuum cleaner."
- A *metaphor* is a direct or implied comparison suggesting that A is B. "At the dinner table, George is a vacuum cleaner."
- An *analogy* is an extended simile or metaphor that builds a point-by-point comparison into several sentences, a whole paragraph, or even a series of paragraphs. Writers use analogy to explain a difficult concept, idea, or process by comparing it with something more familiar or easier to understand. If the audience, for example, knows about engines but has never seen a human heart, a writer might use an analogy to explain that a heart is like a simple engine, complete with chambers or cylinders, intake and exhaust valves, and hoses to carry fuel and exhaust.

As an illustration of simile and metaphor, notice how Joseph Conrad, in the following brief passage from *Heart of Darkness,* begins with a simile and then continues to build on his images throughout the paragraph. Rather than creating a rigid structural shape for his details (as classification or comparison/contrast would do), the images combine and flow like the river he is describing.

> Going up that river was like travelling back to the earliest beginnings of the world, when vegetation rioted on the earth and the big trees were kings. An empty stream, a great silence, an impenetrable forest. The air was warm, thick, heavy, sluggish. There was no joy in the brilliance of sunshine. The long stretches of the waterway ran on, deserted, into the gloom of overshadowed distances. On silvery sand-banks hippos and alligators sunned themselves side by side. The broadening waters flowed through a mob of wooded islands; you lost your way on that river as you would in a desert, and butted all day long against shoals, trying to find the channel, till you thought yourself bewitched and cut off forever from everything you had known once—somewhere—far away—in another existence perhaps.

An analogy helps shape the following paragraph by Carl Sagan, author of *The Dragons of Eden* and *Cosmos.* To help us understand a difficult concept, the immense age of the Earth (and, by comparison, the relatively tiny span of human history), Sagan compares the lifetime of the universe to something simple and familiar: the calendar of a single year.

> The most instructive way I know to express this cosmic chronology is to imagine the fifteen-billion year lifetime of the universe . . . compressed into the span of a single year. . . . It is disconcerting to find that in such a cosmic year the Earth does not condense out of interstellar matter until early September; dinosaurs emerge on Christmas Eve; flowers arise on December 28th; and men and women originate at 10:30 P.M. on New Year's Eve. All of recorded history occupies the last ten seconds of December 31; and the time from the waning of the Middle Ages to the present occupies little more than one second.

Consider whether a good analogy would help you shape one or more paragraphs in your essay. Ask yourself, "What is the most difficult concept or idea I'm trying to describe?" Is there an extended point-by-point comparison—an analogy—that would clarify it?

● **TITLE, INTRODUCTION, AND CONCLUSION**   Depending on your purpose and audience, you may want a title for what you're writing. At the minimum, titles—like labels—should accurately indicate the contents in the package. In addition, however, good titles capture the reader's interest with some catchy phrasing or imaginative language—something to make the reader want to "buy" the package. Samuel H. Scudder's title is a good label (the essay is about looking at fish) and uses catchy phrasing: "Take This Fish and Look at It." If a title is appropriate for your observation, write out several possibilities in your journal.

The introduction should set up the context for the reader—*who, what, when, where,* and *why*—so that readers can orient themselves. Depending on your audience and purpose, introductions can be very brief, pushing the reader quickly into the scene, or they can take more time, easing readers into the setting. Stephen White, in his essay about Mesa Verde at the end of this chapter, begins mysteriously: "It is difficult for me to say exactly what it was that drew me to this solitary place." White doesn't tell his reader that he's talking about Mesa Verde until the second paragraph.

Conclusions should wrap up the observation, providing a sense of completeness. Conclusions vary, depending upon a writer's purpose and audience, but they tend to be of two types or have two components: a *summary* and a *reference* to the introduction. Scudder uses both components when he refers to his eight months of study and to Agassiz's "urgent exhortations" not to be content with hasty observations. The clincher to the conclusion is the parting quotation from Agassiz: "Facts are stupid things until brought into connection with some general law."

As you work on shaping strategies and drafting, make notes about possible titles, appropriate introductions, or effective conclusions for your written observations.

DRAFTING

> **66** The idea is to get the pencil moving quickly. **99**
> —BERNARD MALAMUD, NOVELIST

● **REREAD JOURNAL ENTRIES AND NOTES**   Before you start drafting, review your material so you aren't writing cold. Stop and reread everything you've written on your subject. You're not trying to memorize particular sentences or phrases; you're just getting it all fresh in your mind, seeing what you still like and discarding details that are no longer relevant.

● **REOBSERVE YOUR SUBJECT**   If necessary, go back and observe your subject again. One more session may suggest an important detail or idea that will help you get started writing.

● **REEXAMINE PURPOSE, AUDIENCE, DOMINANT IDEA, AND SHAPE**   After all your writing and rereading, you may have some new ideas about your purpose, audience, or dominant idea. Take a minute to jot these down in your journal. Remember that your specific details should show the main point or dominant idea, whether you state it explicitly or not.

Next, if the shaping strategies suggested an order for your essay, use it to guide your draft. You may, however, have only your specific details or a general notion of the dominant idea you're trying to communicate to your reader. In that case, you may want to begin writing and work out a shape or outline as you write.

● **CREATE A DRAFT**   With the above notes as a guide, you are ready to start drafting. Work on establishing your ritual: Choose a comfortable, familiar place with the writing tools you like. Make sure you'll have no interruptions. Try to write nonstop. If you can't think of a word, substitute a dash. If you can't remember how to spell a word, don't stop to look it up now—keep writing. Write until you reach what feels like the end. If you do get stuck, reread your last few lines or some of your writing process materials. Then go back and pick up the thread. Don't stop to count words or pages. You should shoot for more material than you need because it's usually easier to cut material later, when you're revising, than to add more if you're short.

REVISING

> **66** All the stuff you see back there on the floor is writing I did last week that I have to rewrite this week. **99**
> —ERNEST J. GAINES, AUTHOR OF *THE AUTOBIOGRAPHY OF MISS JANE PITTMAN*

● **GAINING DISTANCE AND OBJECTIVITY**   Revising, of course, has been going on since you put your first sentence down on paper. You've changed ideas, thought through your subject again, and observed your person, place, object, or image. After your rough draft is finished, your next step is to revise again to resee the whole thing. But before you do, you need to let it sit at least twenty-four hours, to get away from it for a while, to gain some distance and perspective. Relax. Congratulate yourself.

PEER RESPONSE

The instructions below will help you give and receive constructive advice about the rough draft of your observing essay. You may use these guidelines for an in-class workshop, a take-home review, or a computer response.

Writer: Before you exchange drafts with another reader, write out the following information about your rough draft.

1. What is the dominant impression that you want your description to make? What overall idea or impression do you want your reader to have?
2. What paragraph(s) contain(s) your best and most vivid description? What paragraph(s) still need(s) some revision?
3. Explain one or two things you would like your reader to comment on as he or she responds to your draft.

Reader: First, without making any marks, read the entire draft from start to finish. As you reread the draft, answer the following questions.

1. What *dominant impression* does the draft create? Does the dominant impression you received agree with the writer's own idea? If not, how might the writer better achieve that overall impression?
2. Look at the writer's responses to question 2. Does the writer, in fact, use vivid description in his or her best paragraph(s)? How might the paragraphs that the writer says need revision be improved? Review the six techniques for descriptive writing at the beginning of this chapter. Where or how might the writer improve the *sensory details, images,* descriptions of what is not there, changes in the subject, or *point of view?* Offer specific suggestions.
3. Reread the assignment for this essay. Explain how this essay should be revised to more clearly meet the assignment. Does the writer understand the *rhetorical situation?* What changes in purpose, audience, genre, or style would help the essay meet the assignment?
4. List the *two most important things* this writer should work on as he or she revises this draft. Explain why these are important.

About the time you try to relax, however, you may get a sudden temptation—even an overwhelming urge—to have someone else read it—immediately! Usually, it's better to resist that urge. Chances are, you want to have someone else read it either because you're bubbling with enthusiasm and you want to share it or because you're certain that it's all garbage and you want to hear the bad news right away. Most readers will not find it either as great as you hope *or* as awful as you fear. As a result, their offhand remarks may seem terribly insensitive or condescending. In a day or so, however, you'll be able to see your writing more objectively: Perhaps it's not great yet, but it's not hopeless, either. At that point, you're ready to get some feedback and start your revisions.

● **REREADING AND RESPONDING TO YOUR READERS**   When you've been away from the draft for a while, you are better able to see the whole piece of writing. Start by rereading your own draft and making marginal notes. Don't be distracted by spelling errors or typos; concentrate on the quality of the details and the flow of the sentences. Focus on the overall effect you're creating, see if your organization still makes sense, and check to make sure that all the details support the dominant idea. Now you're ready to get some peer feedback. Depending on the reactions of your readers, you may need to change the point of view, add a few specific examples or some comparisons or images, fix the organization of a paragraph, reorder some details, delete some sentences, or do several of the above. Be prepared, however, to rewrite several paragraphs to help your readers really see what you are describing.

GUIDELINES FOR REVISION

As you revise your essay, keep the following tips and checklist questions in mind.

* **Reexamine your purpose and audience.** Are you doing what you intended? If your purpose or audience has changed, what other changes do you need to make as you revise?
* **Pay attention to the advice your readers give you, but don't necessarily make all the changes they suggest.** Ask them *why* something should be changed. Ask them specifically *where* something should be changed.
* **Consider your genre.** Does your chosen genre still work for your purpose, audience, and context? Would including pictures, visuals, graphics, poetry, or quotations in a multigenre format be more effective?
* **Consider your point of view.** Would changing to another point of view clarify what you are describing?
* **Consider your vantage point.** Do you have a bird's-eye view, or are you observing from a low angle? Do you zoom in for a close-up of a person or object? Would a different vantage point fit your purpose and audience?
* **Make sure you are using sensory details where appropriate.** Remember, you must *show* your reader the details you observe. If necessary, *reobserve* your subject.
* **Do all your details and examples support your dominant idea?** Reread your draft and omit any irrelevant details.

- **What is *not* present in your subject that might be important to mention?**
- **What changes occur in the form or function of your subject?** Where can you describe those changes more vividly?
- **Make comparisons if they will help you or your reader understand your subject better.** Similes, metaphors, or analogies may describe your subject more vividly.
- **Does what you are observing belong to a class of similar objects?** Would classification organize your writing?
- **Be sure to cue or signal your reader with appropriate transition words.** Transitions will improve the coherence or flow of your writing.
  - **Spatial order:** on the left, on the right, next, above, below, higher, lower, farther, next, beyond
  - **Chronological order.** before, earlier, after, afterward, thereafter, then, from then on, the next day, shortly, by that time, immediately, slowly, while, meanwhile, until, now, soon, within an hour, first, later, finally, at last
  - **Comparison/contrast:** on one hand, on the other hand, also, similarly, in addition, likewise, however, but, yet, still, although, even so, nonetheless, in contrast
- **Revise sentences for clarity, conciseness, emphasis, and variety.**
- **When you have revised your essay, edit your writing for correct spelling and appropriate word choice, punctuation, usage, and grammar.**

> ❝I went for years not finishing anything. Because, of course, when you finish something you can be judged. ❞
> —ERICA JONG,
> AUTHOR OF *FEAR OF FLYING*

POSTSCRIPT ON THE WRITING PROCESS

When you've finished writing this assignment, do one final journal entry. Briefly, answer the following questions.

1. What was the hardest part of this writing assignment for you?
2. Put brackets ([ ]) around the paragraph containing your most vivid sensory details. Explain what makes this paragraph so vivid.
3. What exercise, practice, strategy, or workshop was the "breakthrough" for you? What led you to your discovery or dominant idea?
4. State in one sentence your discovery or the dominant idea of your essay.
5. What did you learn about your writing ritual and process? What did you learn about observing? What did you learn from your choice of audience and genre?

STUDENT WRITING
JENNIFER MACKE

Permanent Tracings

Jennifer Macke, a student in Professor Rachel Henne-Wu's class at Owens Community College in Findlay, Ohio, decided to write her observing essay about a tattoo parlor. She visited the Living Color Tattoo Parlor and took notes on the office, the clientele, the conversations, the artwork of the tattoos, and the owner of the establishment. Ms. Macke wrote that her preconceptions about tattoo parlors were that they were "smoke-filled, dimly lit places" where "undesirables gathered." Gradually, her impressions changed as she saw firsthand the high quality and the remarkable artistry of the tattoos. Reprinted below are some of her original notes, questions and answers, an outline, and the final version of her essay.

NOTES ON A VISIT

- A couple with a young school-aged daughter looks at the artwork on the walls for about 15 minutes before saying anything to the owner. They are looking for a design for the wife for her birthday. They appear to be a typical young couple with a limited amount of money. They ask how much a particular design will be and say they will have to save for it. "How much for this ankle bracelet?" he says. "It'll run you between $45 and $60, depending on how thick you want the rose vine," Gasket says.

- Two Latino men enter the waiting room. One peeks his head into the office and says, "I'm here early for my appointment because I'm not sure exactly what I want. Do you have any books or more pictures I can look through?" Gasket gives him six photo albums full of ideas (designs).

- Five young adult black men enter. They begin browsing through the photos on the wall. There are designs with prices below them so you know what it costs without asking. They too look through the photo albums the Latinos left on the floor. One of the black guys announces, "I'll go first 'cause I want to get it over with." One says, "I'm not going to do this. I can't stand the sound of that needle!" Gasket looks at me and says, "It's amazing how many people just think all you have to do is walk through the door like a walk-in barber shop. They don't know I'm booked for at least a week. During the summer, it's three weeks."

- The phone rings and since his daughter, who normally works there, is gone to visit her mother, he tells me to pick it up. The guy on the other end says, "My uncle wants to know if Jeff's cousin works here?" I relay the message to the owner and he replies, "Yes, that's me." Back on the phone, "He says he's the best in the business. Does he have any time today?" Gasket says, "Here we go again." I tell the guy it will be a week. He says, "OK, I'll call back then." I tell Gasket what he said and he comments, "He'll call back next week, and I'll have to tell him it'll be another week. You would not believe the intelligence level of some people."

- The next girl is going to have lips tattooed on her right hip. She is a petite nurse whom you would never guess would even consider such a thing. Her husband put lipstick on and kissed a napkin which she brought to use for the pattern. Gasket took a photocopy of this and made a transfer from it to use as the template. She dropped her shorts to expose where the art would be placed. She lay down on the table which Gasket explained he had gotten in trade for a tattoo. He also said the stirrups were still in the drawer. The girl smiled and talked the whole time he worked. At one point, he asked her, "Does it hurt?" She said, "No." He said, "I can go deeper!" She said, "Are you supposed to?" He said, laughing, "It's just a joke. If I see someone who's comfortable, I'll ask them this." It only took about 30 minutes to complete this one. You would swear someone just kissed her with bright red lipstick. It's amazing how realistic his work looks.

QUESTIONS AND ANSWERS

1. "Why do people get tattoos?"
   "A tattoo is a very personal thing. It's an expression of one's self."

2. "Does it hurt to get a tattoo?"
   "It all depends on the placement and the person. Guys tend to be bigger wimps. I'd rather do women any day. The most painful areas are the ankle and higher up on the belly. I've had the pain described as something annoying but not necessarily painful to such a point that they cannot stand it. I've never had anyone pass out, though."

3. "What kind of person gets a tattoo?"
   "There's not one particular type of person who gets a tattoo. I once had a call from some lawyers from Findlay. They wanted to know if they had five or so people who wanted a tattoo, would I come over? I said, yes, and I tattooed six lawyers at a party."

4. "What is the process of getting a tattoo?"
   "Depending if it will be freehand or something the people bring in, it starts with drawing the art. It is drawn either on the person or on carbon paper backwards. The carbon design is transferred to the skin with Speed Stick deodorant. The outline is applied first. As the single needle picks up and sews into the skin, excess ink covers the work area."

...*continued* Permanent Tracings, **Jennifer Macke**

As Gasket works, it's hard to see the actual area he's working on because of the excess ink. When asked how he can work with the excess ink obstructing the guidelines, he says he just knows where the line goes. (I wouldn't.) Once the outline is complete he changes to use a 3 or 4 needle set, depending on the coverage necessary. He colorizes the art, which brings it to life. After it's complete, he puts a thick coat of Bacitracin on and covers it with a gauze bandage. The gauze must remain on for one and a half to two hours.

5. "What is the most common place for a tattoo?"
"Placement runs in cycles, sometimes the upper arm, sometimes the ankle." While we were talking, a man came in with one on the back of his neck.

6. "How expensive are tattoos?"
The minimum is $30. Depending on how detailed and how big. Gasket has bartered for the tattoos, too.

7. "Do most people get more than one tattoo?"
"I've seen people go through life with only one or maybe two, but it's said when you get your third, you're hooked. You'll be back for more."

8. "Are there health department requirements?"
"At the beginning, the requirements (laws) weren't very strict. I knew I wanted to be supersterile, so I put my needles and equipment through a much stricter procedure. Since then, the health department has taken on my policy and requires everyone to process their stuff like me. They drop in to make sure the laws are being followed."

9. "How many times do you use your needles?"
"They are single-application needles, but they still need to be sterilized. People ask me if they can watch their needles being sterilized so they can make sure. I say fine, but it will be two and a half hours until I can work on you."

OUTLINE

Working Thesis: "Gasket's creative artistic ability and perfectionist work ethic make his designs worth sewing into your body for a lifetime."

I. Describe the Tattoo Parlor

    A. Outer area (waiting room)

    B. Inner office

II. Describe the owner

    A. The way he looks

    B. The way he feels about his work

III. Describe the people

    A. People getting a tattoo

    B. People not getting a tattoo

FINAL VERSION

Permanent Tracings

At first glance, the Living Color Tattoo Parlor appears to be just another 1
typical tattoo establishment. You enter through a glass door only to find
a waiting room with the decor reminiscent of the 1970s. The dark pan-
eled walls display numerous types of artwork that range from pencil
sketching to color Polaroid snapshots of newly completed tattoos. The
gold and green davenport looks as if it came from a Saturday morning
garage sale. The inner office is celery green with a dental chair and an
obstetrics table that the owner bartered for a tattoo (the stirrups are still
in the drawer). A filing cabinet, desk, and copy machine make you feel as
if you're in a professional office. The sterilizer is in plain sight and is in
operation. Bottle after bottle of brightly colored inks are neatly arranged
on a tiered wooden stand. The sound of the oscillating fan that cools the
client interrupts the buzz of the needle sewing the paint into the client's
skin. A freeze-dried turtle is displayed on a table in the office.

    I still wondered, though. Could tattoos actually be a form of art? 2

    As soon as I could, I asked the owner, a man called Gasket, about his 3
occupation. "I was a suit for fifteen years and now I can work as much as
I want. There's always somebody wanting a tattoo or something pierced,"
Gasket said. He's often asked if he'll scratch out the name of a previous
girlfriend, and he always replies that he would never even consider it.
"That would be defacement," he said. "When I'm done, the design should
look better than when I started." Gasket is not his given name but one he
acquired because of his expert repair work on Harley Davidson motor-
cycles. Gasket is the owner of this establishment, and to look at him, you
would never guess he is a college-educated engineer. His long curly, gray-
ing hair flows from under his Harley hat, and examples of his handiwork
are visible under the rolled up sleeves of his black Harley T-shirt. The
harshness of his heavily bearded face is softened by his slate-blue eyes,
which mirror his gentle demeanor. If you look past his casual exterior,
you will find a code of steel. "At the beginning, the laws weren't very
strict. I knew I wanted to be supersterile, so I put my single-use needles
and equipment through a much stricter procedure. Since then, the health

department has taken on my policy and requires everyone to process their stuff like me," he said.

The appearance of the Living Color Tattoo Parlor may be typical, but 4 two things are distinctly different: the quality and the creativity of the tattoo designs. A young college couple from Toledo was asked why they would drive to Fremont for an appointment. They answered, "Gasket's the best! We wouldn't trust something that's going to be on our body for the rest of our lives to someone other than him."

"I already have two tattoos from you, and I love your work," a mid- 5 dle-aged woman said. Displaying two greeting cards, she asked, "Is it possible to get a combination of these two designs?"

"I can create anything you want," Gasket said.   6

"I'll have to wait a couple of weeks because I'm not working much 7 and my other bills come first," she said.

"Yes, you have to get your priorities straight. When you're ready, I'm 8 here," he said.

Gasket is performing his tattoo magic on a young college female. He's 9 creating a rose with a heart stem wrapping around her belly button, which is pierced. The girl is nervously seated in the green dental chair, which is tilted back to flatten the skin surface. First, Gasket draws the sketch on her belly. He covers his hands with a thin layer of latex once the exact position and specific details are decided upon. A small device resembling a fountain pen with a brightly colored motor and a single needle moving at 1,000 rpm is used to apply the black outline first. As the needle moves up and down, it picks up a small amount of ink and deposits it just under the surface of the skin. When asked how he can work with the excess ink obstructing the guidelines, he simply said he just knows where the line goes. This is a difficult task because unlike a paint-by-number design, the image not only has to be in his mind but he also has to have the artistic ability to convert the image to the skin. The girl asks a pain-filled question, "How much longer?"

"I can stop and let you take a break at any time," Gasket says. His soft 10 tone and slow-paced voice help soothe the girl. "The higher up on the belly, the more painful," he says. The process of colorizing the tattoo begins once the outline is complete. This is accomplished with a three- or four-needle set, depending on the amount of coverage desired. It takes about forty-five minutes to complete the multicolored masterpiece, which is literally sewn into her skin. Some of Gasket's designs can be compared to Picasso's brilliantly colored, dreamlike images. Upon completion, the girl is directed to a full-length mirror to inspect her permanently altered abs.

"It looks fantastic!" she exclaims. "I was a little vague on how I pictured 11 it would look, but it looks even better than I had imagined. I'm thrilled."

Once thought of as green-toned disfigurements that only drunken 12 sailors and lowlife people would don, tattoos are now high fashion. Now

it is possible to see skin art on TV stars, sports superstars, and a multitude of individuals you might not suspect. The future of this trendy fashion has its roots firmly planted in today's society. Young people seem to
be one of its biggest supporters.

"I'll go first 'cause I want to get it over with," one young black man   *13*
states to his four companions.

"I'm not going to do this. I can't stand the sound of that needle!"   *14*
another man proclaims.

"It's amazing how many people think all you have to do is just walk   *15*
through the door like a walk-in barber shop. They don't know I'm
booked for at least a week. During the summer, it's three weeks," Gasket
claims. He explains this to the young men, who make appointments.
They leave, disappointed.

Gasket's tattoo designs can be compared to the famous fashion de-   *16*
signs by Bob Mackie. Like Mackie's one-of-a-kind designs, they are not
mass-produced, but are hand-sewn for a specific individual. As I left, my
first impression of the Living Color Tattoo Parlor was changed by the in-
credibly beautiful skin art and the comments of the satisfied clients. For
many, Gasket's artistic ability and perfectionism make his designs worth
sewing into your body for a lifetime.

QUESTIONS FOR WRITING AND DISCUSSION

1 Review the techniques for writing observing papers at the beginning of the
chapter. Which paragraph(s) in Macke's essay have the best sensory detail,
images, comparisons, and other effective bits of description? Which
paragraphs might use more descriptive detail?

2 Macke describes the office, the owner, the customers, the process of
tattooing, and the prices of a tattoo. Should she also describe several of the
tattoos? Should she describe the colors in a typical tattoo? If she did these
descriptions, where might she put them in her essay?

3 Reread Macke's notes of her visit, including her questions and answers.
What interesting ideas and descriptions in her notes might be included in
her final draft? Why might Macke have left these details out? Assume that
you are a peer reader for Macke's essay. Fill out the peer response questions
printed earlier in this chapter so you can help her with a revision of her
essay.

4 List the three things that you like best about Macke's essay. Which of her
strategies might work for a revision of your own essay? Make a revision
plan for your own essay, based on what you learned from reading
"Permanent Tracings."

STUDENT WRITING

STEPHEN WHITE

Empty Windows

In this essay written for Professor John Boni at Colorado State University, Stephen White describes both what his senses tell him and what he can only imagine about the Anasazi, the ancient Native Americans who more than a thousand years ago built the cliff dwellings at Mesa Verde in southwestern Colorado. Writing about those empty dwellings with their darkened windows, White says, "Perhaps there lurks, behind every blackened window, a certain unexplainable something we can never understand."

It is difficult for me to say exactly what it was that drew me to this solitary *1* place and held me here, virtually entranced, the entire day. It's the silence, maybe, or the empty houses perched precariously on the canyon wall below me. Or could it be the knowledge that something seemingly nonexistent does indeed exist?

I awoke this morning with a sense of unexplainable anticipation *2* gnawing away at the back of my mind, that this chilly, leaden day at Mesa Verde would bring something new and totally foreign to any of my past experiences. It was a sensation that began to permeate my entire being as I sat crouched before my inadequate campfire, chills running up my spine. Chills which, I am certain, were due not entirely to the dreary gray of a winter "sunrise."

It had been my plan to travel the so-called Ruins Road early today *3* and then complete my visit here, but as I stopped along the road and stood scanning the opposite wall of the canyon for ruins, I felt as if some force had seized control of my will. I was compelled to make my way along the rim.

Starting out upon the rock, I weaved in and out repeatedly as the *4* gaping emptiness of the canyon and the weathered standstone of the rim battled one another for territory. At last arriving here, where a narrow peninsula of canyon juts far into the stone, I was able to peer back into the darkness of a cave carved midway in the vertical wall opposite, within whose smoke-blackened walls huddle, nearly unnoticeable, the rooms of a small, crumbled ruin.

They are a haunting sight, these broken houses, clustered together *5* down in the gloom of the canyon. It presents a complete contrast to the tidy, excavated ruins I explored yesterday, lost within a cluster of tourists and guided by a park ranger who expounded constantly upon his wealth of knowledge of excavation techniques and archaeological dating methods. The excavated ruins seemed, in comparison, a noisy, almost modern city, punctuated with the clicking of camera shutters and the bickering of children. Here it is quiet. The silence is broken only by the rush of the wind in the trees and the trickling of a tiny stream of melting snow springing from ledge to ledge as it makes its way down over the rock to the bottom of the canyon. And this small, abandoned village of tiny houses seems almost as the Indians left it, reduced by the passage of nearly a thousand years to piles of rubble through which protrude broken red adobe walls surrounding ghostly jet-black openings, undisturbed by modern man.

Those windows seem to stare back at me as my eyes are drawn to 6 them. They're so horribly empty, yet my gaze is fixed, searching for some sign of the vitality they must surely have known. I yearn for sounds amidst the silence, for images of life as it once was in the bustling and prosperous community of cliff dwellers who lived here so long ago. It must have been a sunny home when the peaceful, agrarian Anasazi, or ancient ones, as the Navajo call them, lived and dreamed their lives here, wanting little more than to continue in their ways and be left alone, only to be driven away in the end by warring people with whom they could not contend.

I long to hear, to see, and to understand, and though I strain all my 7 senses to their limits, my wishes are in vain. I remain alone, confronted only by the void below and the cold stare of those utterly desolate windows. I know only an uneasy sensation that I am not entirely alone, and

Cliff Palace at Mesa Verde National Park.

a quick, chill gust gives birth once again to that restless shiver tracing its path along the length of my spine.

As a gray afternoon fades into a gray evening, I can find neither a true feeling of fear nor one of the quiet serenity one would expect to experience here. It is comforting for me to believe that it was the explorer in me which brought me here, to feel that I was lured to stand above this lonely house by that same drive to find and explore the unknown which motivated the countless others who have come here since seeking knowledge and understanding of the ancient people of the "Green Table." Yet as I begin the journey back to my car and the security of an evening fire, I remain uncomfortably unconvinced.

Perhaps the dreariness of a cloudy day united with my solitude to pave a mental pathway for illusion and mystery. Or perhaps all homes are never truly empty, having known the multitude of experience which is human life. Perhaps there lurks, behind every blackened window, a certain unexplainable something we can never understand. I know only that the Indian has long respected these places and given them wide berth, leaving their sanctity inviolate.

? QUESTIONS FOR WRITING AND DISCUSSION

1 Describe a similar experience you have had with an empty room or a vacant house. White says that "perhaps all homes are never truly empty, having known the multitude of experience which is human life." Based on your experience, do you agree with him?

2 Through his description, what did White help you "see" about the Anasazi and their cliff dwellings? What did you learn?

3 Consider once again the basic techniques for observing—using sensory detail, comparisons, and images; describing what is not there; noting changes; and writing from a clear point of view. Which ones does White use most effectively? Cite an example of each technique from his essay.

4 In which paragraphs does White use each of the following shaping strategies: spatial order, chronological order, comparisons or contrasts, and simile, metaphor, or analogy? Which strategies did you find most effective in organizing the experience for you as a reader?

5 White's essay illustrates how the *occasion* for writing can figure prominently in a writer's rhetorical situation. What sentences and paragraphs best describe the occasion that motivated him to write? Why is occasion so important to the success of his essay? Explain.

6 Consider the relationship between the photograph of Cliff Palace at Mesa Verde Park and White's essay. Does this image add to the overall effect of the essay? Does it detract from the essay by giving the reader an actual picture rather than an imagined one? Should the image be retained, replaced with another image, or removed altogether? Explain your response.

PEARSON
mycomplab

For additional writing, reading, and research resources, go to http://www.mycomplab.com

César Chavez portrait used by special permission of the artist, Bavi Garcia

Described by Robert F. Kennedy as "one of the heroic figures of our time," César Chávez (1927–1993) spent his lifetime improving the conditions of agricultural workers in America. In 1994, President Clinton posthumously awarded Chávez the Presidential Medal of Freedom, the nation's highest and most prestigious civilian award. In his essay in this chapter, "César Chávez Saved My Life," Daniel Alejandrez remembers Chávez's influence on his own life.

Remembering

4

You and several coworkers have formed a committee to draft a report for your company's vice president in charge of personnel. You have grievances about workload, pay scale, daily procedures, and the attitudes of supervisors. Your report needs to recommend changes in current policies. The committee decides that each person will contribute part of the report by describing actual incidents that have had negative effects on efficiency and human relations. You decide to describe a day last June when your immediate supervisor expected you to learn a new word-processing system and at the same time meet a 3:00 P.M. deadline for a thirty-seven-page budget analysis.

This morning you accidentally ran into a certain person whom you knew several years ago, and for several hours you've been in a bad mood. You called your best friend, but no one answered the phone. You went to class and then for your usual jog, but you pooped out after only half a mile. You even watched a game show on television in the middle of the afternoon and ate half a bag of potato chips, but you still felt lousy. You yell at the television: "Why do I always react this way when I see that person?" But the television has no reply. So you grab some paper and begin scrawling out every memory you have of your experiences with the person you ran into this morning, hoping to understand your feelings.

THE HUMAN BRAIN IS A PACK RAT: NOTHING IS TOO SMALL, OBSCURE, OR MUNDANE FOR THE BRAIN'S COLLECTION. OFTEN THE BRAIN COLLECTS AND DISCARDS INFORMATION WITHOUT REGARD TO OUR WISHES. OUT OF THE COLLECTION MAY ARISE, WITH NO WARNING, the image of windblown whitecaps on a lake you visited more than five yeas ago, the recipe for Uncle Joe's incomparable chili, or even the right answer to an exam question that you've been staring at for the past fifteen minutes.

Remembering is sometimes easy, sometimes difficult. Often careful concentration yields nothing, while the most trivial occurrence—an old song on a car radio, the acrid smell of diesel exhaust, the face of a stranger—will trigger a flood of recollections. Someone tells a story and you immediately recall incidents, funny or traumatic, from your own life. Some memories, however, are nagging and troublesome, keeping you awake at night, daring you to deal with them. You pick at these memories. Why are they so important? You write about them, usually to probe that mystery of yesterday and today. Sights, sounds, or feelings from the present may draw you to the past, but the past leads, just as surely, back to the present.

Direct observations are important to learning and writing, but so are your memories, experiences, and stories. You may write an autobiographical account of part of your life, or you may recall a brief event, a person, or a place just as an example to illustrate a point. Whatever form your writing from memory takes, however, your initial purpose is to remember experiences so that you can understand yourself and your world. The point is not to write fiction, but to practice drawing on your memories and to write vividly enough about them so that you and others can discover and learn.

The value of remembering lies exactly here: Written memories have the power to teach you and, through the *empathy* of your readers, to inform or convince them as well. At first, you may be self-conscious about sharing your personal memories. But as you reveal these experiences, you realize that your story is worth telling—not because you're such an egotist, but because sharing experiences helps everyone learn.

Techniques for Writing About Memories

Writing vividly about memories includes all the skills of careful observing, but it adds several additional narrative strategies. Listed below are six techniques that writers use to compose effective remembering essays. As you read the essays that follow in this chapter, notice how each writer uses these techniques.

Then, when you write your own remembering essay, use these techniques in your own essay. Remember: Not all writing about memories uses all of these techniques, but one or two of them may transform a lifeless account into an effective narrative.

66 Time passes and the past becomes the present. . . . These presences of the past are there in the center of your life today. You thought . . . they had died, but they have just been waiting their chance. 99
—CARLOS FUENTES, MEXICAN ESSAYIST AND NOVELIST, AUTHOR OF *THE CRYSTAL FRONTIER*

Techniques for Writing About Memories

Technique	Tips on How to Do It
Using *detailed observation* of people, places, and events	Writing vividly about memories requires many of the skills of careful observation. Use *sensory descriptions*, *comparisons*, and *images*. Include *actual dialogue* where appropriate.
Focusing on *occasion and cultural context*	Think about the personal occasion that motivated you to write about your experience. You may want to set your experiences in a larger cultural context.
Creating *specific scenes* set in time and space	Show your reader the actual events—don't just tell about them. Narrate or recreate specific incidents as they actually happened. Avoid summarizing events or presenting just the conclusions (for instance, "Those experiences really changed my life").
Noting *changes*, *contrasts*, or *conflicts*	Describe changes in people or places. Show contrasts between two different memories or between memories of expectations and realities. Narrate conflicts between people or ideas. Resolving (or sometimes not resolving) these changes, contrasts, or conflicts can often be the point of your memoir.
Making *connections* between *past* events, people, or places and the *present*	The main idea or focus of your narrative may grow out of the connections you make between the past and the present: what you felt then and how you feel now; what you thought you knew and what you know now.
Discovering and focusing on a *main idea*	Your narrative should not be a random account of your favorite memories. It should have a clear main point—something you learned or discovered or realized—without actually stating a "moral" to your story.

All of these techniques are important, but you should also keep several other points in mind. Normally, you should write in the *first person,* using *I* or *we* throughout the narrative. Although you will usually write in *past tense,* sometimes you may wish to lend immediacy to the events by retelling them in the *present tense,* as if they are happening now. Finally, you may choose straightforward *chronological order,* or you may begin near the end and use a *flashback* to tell the beginning of the story.

The key to effective remembering, however, is to get beyond *generalities and conclusions* about your experiences ("I had a lot of fun—those days really changed my life"). Your goal is to *recall specific incidents set in time and place* that *show* how and why those days changed your life. The specific incidents should show your *main point* or *dominant idea.*

The following passage by Andrea Lee began as a journal entry during a year she spent in Moscow and Leningrad following her graduation from college. She then combined these firsthand observations with her memories and published them in a collection called *Russian Journal.* She uses first person and, frequently, present tense as she describes her reactions to the sights of Moscow. In these paragraphs, she weaves observations and memories together to show her main idea: The contrast between American and Soviet Union-style advertising helped her understand both the virtues and the faults of American commercialism. (The annotations in the margin illustrate how Lee uses all five remembering techniques.)

Specific scene

In Mayakovsky Square, not far from the Tchaikovsky Concert Hall, a big computerized electric sign sends various messages flashing out into the night. An outline of a taxi in green dots is accompanied by the words: "Take Taxis—All Streets Are Near." This is replaced by multicolored human figures and a sentence urging Soviet citizens to save in State banks. The bright patterns and messages come and go, making this one of the most sophisticated examples of advertising in Moscow. Even on chilly nights when I pass through the square, there is often a little group of Russians standing in front of the sign, watching in fascination for five and ten minutes as the colored dots go through their magical changes. The first few times I saw this, I chuckled and recalled an old joke about an American town so boring that people went out on weekends to watch the Esso sign.

Detailed observation

Connections past and present

Contrast

Advertising, of course, is the glamorous offspring of capitalism and art: Why advertise in a country where there is only one brand, the State brand, of anything, and often not enough even of that? There is nothing here comparable to the glittering overlay of commercialism that Americans, at least, take for granted as part of our cities; nothing like the myriad small seductions of the marketplace, which have led us to expect to be enticed. The Soviet political propaganda posters that fill up a small part of the Moscow landscape with their uniformly cold red color schemes and monumental robot-faced figures are so unappealing that they are dismissable.

Detailed observation

I realize now, looking back, that for at least my first month in Moscow, I was filled with an unconscious and devastating disappointment. Hardly realizing it, as I walked around the city, I was looking for the constant sensory distractions I was accustomed to in America. **Like many others my age, I grew up reading billboards and singing advertising jingles; my idea of beauty was shaped—perniciously, I think—by the models with the painted eyes and pounds of shining hair whose beauty was accessible on every television set and street corner.**

REMEMBERING PEOPLE

In the following passage from the introduction to *The Way to Rainy Mountain*, N. Scott Momaday remembers his grandmother. While details of place and event are also recreated, the primary focus is on the character of his grandmother as revealed in several *specific,* recurring actions. Momaday does not give us generalities about his feelings (for instance, "I miss my grandmother a lot, especially now that she's gone."). Instead, he begins with specific memories of scenes that *show* how he felt.

Now that I can have her only in memory, I see my grandmother in the several postures that were peculiar to her: standing at the wood stove on a winter morning and turning meat in a great iron skillet; sitting at the south window, bent above her beadwork, and afterwards, when her vision failed, looking down for a long time into the fold of her hands; going out upon a cane, very slowly as she did when the weight of age came upon her; praying. I remember her most often at prayer. She made long, rambling prayers out of suffering and hope, having seen many things. I was never sure that I had the right to hear, so exclusive were they of all mere custom and company. The last time I saw her she prayed standing by the side of her bed at night, naked to the waist, the light of a kerosene lamp moving upon her dark skin. Her long, black hair, always drawn and braided in the day, lay upon her shoulders and against her breasts like a shawl. I do not speak Kiowa, and I never understood her prayers, but there was something inherently sad in the sound, some merest hesitation upon the syllables of sorrow. She began in a high and descending pitch, exhausting her breath to silence; then again and again—and always the same intensity of effort, of something that is, and is not, like urgency in the human voice. Transported so in the dancing light among the shadows of her room, she seemed beyond the reach of time. But that was illusion; I think I knew then that I should not see her again.

Connections past and present

Contrast and change

Main idea

❝A writer is a reader moved to emulation. ❞

—SAUL BELLOW, AUTHOR OF *HENDERSON THE RAIN KING*

❝There are two ways to live. One is as though nothing is a miracle, the other is as though everything is. ❞

—ALBERT EINSTEIN, AUTHOR OF *WHAT I BELIEVE*

❝Some very small incident that takes place today may be the most important event that happens to you this year, but you don't know that when it happens. You don't know it until much later. ❞

—TONI MORRISON, NOBEL PRIZE-WINNING AUTHOR OF *BELOVED* AND *SONG OF SOLOMON*

REMEMBERING PLACES

In the following passage from *Farewell to Manzanar,* Jeanne Wakatsuke Houston remembers the place in California where, as Japanese-Americans, her family was imprisoned during World War II. As you read, look for specific details and bits of description that convey her main idea.

In Spanish, Manzanar means "apple orchard." Great stretches of Owens Valley were once green with orchards and alfalfa fields. It has been a desert ever since its water started flowing south into Los Angeles, sometime during the twenties. But a few rows of untended pear and apple trees were still growing there when the camp opened, where a shallow water table had kept them alive. In the spring of 1943 we moved to block 28, right up next to one of the old pear orchards. That's where we stayed until the end of the war, and those trees stand in my memory for the turning of our life in camp, from the outrageous to the tolerable.

Papa pruned and cared for the nearest trees. Late that summer we picked the fruit green and stored it in a root cellar he had dug under our new barracks. At night the wind through the leaves would sound like the surf had sounded in Ocean Park, and while drifting off to sleep, I could almost imagine we were still living by the beach.

REMEMBERING EVENTS

In the following essay, called "The Boy's Desire," Richard Rodriguez recalls a particular event from his childhood that comes to mind when he remembers Christmas. In his memory, he sorts through the rooms in his house on 39th Street in Sacramento, recalling old toys: a secondhand bike, games with dice and spinning dials, a jigsaw puzzle, and a bride doll. In this passage, Rodriguez describes both the effort to remember and the memory itself—the one memory that still "holds color and size and shape." Was it all right, he wonders, that a boy should have wanted a doll for Christmas?

The fog comes to mind. It never rained on Christmas. It was never sharp blue and windy. When I remember Christmas in Sacramento, it is in gray: The valley fog would lift by late morning, the sun boiled haze for a few hours, then the tule fog would rise again when it was time to go into the house.

The haze through which memory must wander is thickened by that fog. The rooms of the house on 39th Street are still and dark in late afternoon, and I open the closet to search for old toys. One year there was a secondhand bike. I do not remember a color. Perhaps it had no color even then. Another year there were boxes of games that rattled their parts—dice and pegs and spinning dials. Or perhaps the rattle is of a jigsaw puzzle that compressed into an image . . . of what? of Paris? a litter of kittens? I cannot remember. Only one memory holds color and size and shape: brown hair, blue eyes, the sweet smell of styrene.

That Christmas I announced I wanted a bride doll. I must have been seven or eight—wise enough to know not to tell anyone at school, but young enough to whine out my petition from early November.

My father's reaction was unhampered by psychology. A shrug— "Una muñeca?"—a doll, why not? Because I knew it was my mother who would choose all the presents, it was she I badgered. I wanted a bride doll! "Is there something else you want?" she wondered. No! I'd make clear with my voice that nothing else would appease me. "We'll see," she'd say, and she never wrote it down on her list.

By early December, wrapped boxes started piling up in my parents' bedroom closet, above my father's important papers and the family album. When no one else was home, I'd drag a chair over and climb up to see . . . Looking for the one. About a week before Christmas, it was there. I was so certain it was mine that I punched my thumb through the wrapping paper and the cellophane window on the box and felt inside—lace, two tiny, thin legs. I got other presents that year, but it was the doll I kept by me. I remember my mother saying I'd have "to share her" with my younger sister—but Helen was four years old, oblivious. The doll was mine. My arms would hold her. She would sleep on my pillow.

And the sky did not fall. The order of the universe did not tremble. In fact, it was right for a change. My family accommodated itself to my request. My brother and sisters played round me with their own toys. I paraded my doll by the hands across the floor.

The other day, when I asked my brother and sisters about the doll, no one remembered. My mother remembers. "Yes," she smiled. "One year there was a doll."

The closet door closes. (The house on 39th Street has been razed for a hospital parking lot.) The fog rises. Distance tempts me to mock the boy and his desire. The fact remains: One Christmas in Sacramento I wanted a bride doll, and I got one.

WARMING UP   Journal Exercises

The following topics will help you practice writing about your memories. Read all of the following exercises, and then write on three that interest you the most. If another idea occurs to you, write a free entry about it.

1. Go through old family photographs and find one of yourself, taken at least five years ago. Describe the person in the photograph—what he or she did, thought, said, or hoped. How is that person like or unlike the person you are now?

2. Remember the first job you had. How did you get it, and what did you do? What mistakes did you make? What did you learn? Were there any humorous or serious misunderstandings between you and others?

3. What are your earliest memories? Choose one particular event. How old were you? What was the place? Who were the people around you? What happened? After you write down your earliest memories, call members of your family, if possible, and interview them for their memories of this incident. How does what you actually remember differ from what your family tells you? Revise your first memory to incorporate additional details provided by your family.

4. At some point in the past, you may have faced a conflict between what was expected of you—by parents, friends, family, coach, or employer—and your own personality or abilities. Describe one occasion when these expectations seemed unrealistic or unfair. Was the experience entirely negative or was it, in the long run, positive?

5. At least at one point in our lives, we have felt like an outsider. In a selection earlier in this chapter, for instance, Richard Rodriguez recalls feelings of being different, rejected, or outcast. Write about an incident when you felt alienated from your family, peers, or social group. Focus on a key scene or scenes that show what happened, why it was important, and how it affects you now.

PROFESSIONAL WRITING

Beauty: When the Other Dancer Is the Self

Alice Walker

The author of the Pulitzer Prize-winning novel The Color Purple *(1983), Alice Walker has written works of fiction and poetry, including* Love and Trouble: Stories of Black Women *(1973),* Meridian *(1976), and* By the Light of My Father's Smile: A Novel *(1998). "Beauty: When the Other Dancer Is the Self" originally appeared in* Ms. *magazine and was revised and published in Walker's collection of essays,* In Search of Our Mother's Gardens *(1983). Walker, a former editor of* Ms., *refers in this essay to Gloria Steinem and an interview published in* Ms. *titled* "Do You Know This Woman? She Knows You—A Profile of Alice Walker." *As you read the essay reprinted here, consider Walker's purpose: Why is she telling us—total strangers—about a highly personal and traumatic event that shaped her life?*

It is a bright summer day in 1947. My father, a fat, funny man with *1* beautiful eyes and a subversive wit, is trying to decide which of his eight children he will take with him to the county fair. My mother, of course, will not go. She is knocked out from getting us ready: I hold my neck stiff against the pressure of her knuckles as she hastily completes the braiding and then beribboning of my hair.

My father is the driver for the rich old white lady up the road. Her *2* name is Miss Mey. She owns all the land for miles around, as well as the house in which we live. All I remember about her is that she once offered to pay my mother thirty-five cents for cleaning her house, raking up piles of her magnolia leaves, and washing her family's clothes, and that my mother—she of no money, eight children, and a chronic earache— refused it. But I do not think of this in 1947. I am two-and-a-half years old. I want to go everywhere my daddy goes. I am excited at the prospect of riding in a car. Someone has told me fairs are fun. That there is room in the car for only three of us doesn't faze me at all. Whirling happily in my starchy frock, showing off my biscuit polished patent leather shoes and lavender socks, tossing my head in a way that makes my ribbons bounce, I stand, hands on hips, before my father. "Take me, Daddy," I say with assurance, "I'm the prettiest!"

Later, it does not surprise me to find myself in Miss Mey's shiny black *3* car, sharing the backseat with the other lucky ones. Does not surprise me that I thoroughly enjoy the fair. At home that night I tell all the unlucky ones about the merry-go-round, the man who eats live chickens, and the abundance of Teddy bears, until they say: that's enough, baby Alice. Shut up now, and go to sleep.

It is Easter Sunday, 1950. I am dressed in a green, flocked scalloped- *4* hem dress (handmade by my adoring sister Ruth) that has its own smooth satin petticoat and tiny hot-pink roses tucked into each scallop. My shoes, new T-strap patent leather, again highly biscuit polished. I am six years old and have learned one of the longest Easter speeches to be heard in church that day, totally unlike the speech I said when I was two: "Easter lilies/pure and white/blossom in/the morning light." When I rise to give my speech I do so on a great wave of love and pride and expectation. People in the church stop rustling their new crinolines. They seem to hold their breath. I can tell they admire my dress, but it is my spirit, bordering on sassiness (womanishness), they secretly applaud.

"That girl's a little *mess,*" they whisper to each other, pleased.   *5*

...*continued* Beauty: When the Other Dancer Is the Self, **Alice Walker**

Naturally I say my speech without stammer or pause, unlike those 6
who stutter, stammer, or, worst of all, forget. This is before the word
"beautiful" exists in people's vocabulary, but "Oh, isn't she the *cutest*
thing!" frequently floats my way. "And got so much sense!" they gratefully
add . . . for which thoughtful addition I thank them to this day.

It was great fun being cute. But then, one day, it ended.   7

I am eight years old and a tomboy. I have a cowboy hat, cowboy boots, 8
checkered shirt and pants, all red. My playmates are my brothers, two and
four years older than I. Their colors are black and green, the only difference
in the way we are dressed. On Saturday nights we all go to the picture show,
even my mother: Westerns are her favorite kind of movie. Back home, "on
the ranch," we pretend we are Tom Mix, Hopalong Cassidy, Lash LaRue
(we've even named one of our dogs Lash LaRue); we chase each other for
hours rustling cattle, being outlaws, delivering damsels from distress. Then
my parents decide to buy my brothers guns. These are not "real" guns. They
shoot "BBs," copper pellets my brothers say will kill birds. Because I am a
girl, I do not get a gun. Instantly I am relegated to the position of Indian.
Now there appears a great distance between us. They shoot and shoot at
everything with their new guns. I try to keep up with my bow and arrows.

One day while I am standing on top of our makeshift "garage"— 9
pieces of tin nailed across some poles—holding my bow and arrow and
looking out toward the fields, I feel an incredible blow in my right eye.
I look down just in time to see my brother lower his gun.

Both brothers rush to my side. My eye stings, and I cover it with my 10
hand. "If you tell," they say, "we will get a whipping. You don't want that
to happen, do you?" I do not. "Here is a piece of wire," says the older
brother, picking it up from the roof; "say you stepped on one end of it
and the other flew up and hit you." The pain is beginning to start. "Yes,"
I say. "Yes, I will say that is what happened." If I do not say this is what
happened, I know my brothers will find ways to make me wish I had. But
now I will say anything that gets me to my mother.

Confronted by our parents we stick to the lie agreed upon. They place 11
me on a bench on the porch and I close my left eye while they examine the
right. There is a tree growing from underneath the porch, that climbs past
the railing to the roof. It is the last thing my right eye sees. I watch as its
trunk, its branches, and then its leaves are blotted out by the rising blood.

I am in shock. First there is intense fever, which my father tries to 12
break using lily leaves bound around my head. Then there are chills: my
mother tries to get me to eat soup. Eventually, I do not know how, my
parents learn what has happened. A week after the "accident" they take
me to see a doctor. "Why did you wait so long to come?" he asks, looking
into my eye and shaking his head. "Eyes are sympathetic," he says. "If one
is blind, the other will likely become blind too."

This comment of the doctor's terrifies me. But it is really how I look 13 that bothers me most. Where the BB pellet struck there is a glob of whitish scar tissue, a hideous cataract, on my eye. Now when I stare at people—a favorite pastime, up to now—they will stare back. Not at the "cute" little girl, but at her scar. For six years I do not stare at anyone because I do not raise my head.

Years later, in the throes of a mid-life crisis, I ask my mother and sis- 14 ter whether I changed after the "accident." "No," they say, puzzled. "What do you mean?"

What do I mean? 15

I am eight, and for the first time, doing poorly in school, where I have 16 been something of a whiz since I was four. We have just moved to the place where the "accident" occurred. We do not know any of the people around us because this is a different county. The only time I see the friends I knew is when we go back to our old church. The new school is the former state penitentiary. It is a large stone building, cold and drafty, crammed to overflowing with boisterous, ill-disciplined children. On the third floor there is a huge circular imprint of some partition that has been torn out.

"What used to be here?" I ask a sullen girl next to me on our way past 17 it to lunch.

"The electric chair," says she. 18

At night I have nightmares about the electric chair, and about all the 19 people reputedly "fried" in it. I am afraid of the school, where all the students seem to be budding criminals.

"What's the matter with your eye?" they ask, critically. 20

When I don't answer (I cannot decide whether it was an "accident" 21 or not), they shove me, insist on a fight.

My brother, the one who created the story about the wire, comes to my 22 rescue. But then brags so much about "protecting" me, I become sick.

After months of torture at the school, my parents decide to send 23 me back to our old community to my old school. I live with my grandparents and the teacher they board. But there is no room for Phoebe, my cat. By the time my grandparents decide there is room, and I ask for my cat, she cannot be found. Miss Yarborough, the boarding teacher, takes me under her wing, and begins to teach me to play the piano. But soon she marries an African—a "prince," she says—and is whisked away to his continent.

At my old school there is at least one teacher who loves me. She is the 24 teacher who "knew me before I was born" and bought my first baby clothes. It is she who makes my life bearable. It is her presence that finally helps me turn on the one child at the school who continually calls me "one-eyed bitch." One day I simply grab him by his coat and beat him until I am satisfied. It is my teacher who tells me my mother is ill.

My mother is lying in bed in the middle of the day, something I have 25 never seen. She is in too much pain to speak. She has an abscess in her ear. I stand looking down on her, knowing that if she dies, I cannot live. She is being treated with warm oils and hot bricks held against her cheek. Finally a doctor comes. But I must go back to my grandparents' house. The weeks pass, but I am hardly aware of it. All I know is that my mother might die, my father is not so jolly, my brothers still have their guns, and I am the one sent away from home.

"You did not change," they say.   26

Did I imagine the anguish of never looking up?   27

I am twelve. When relatives come to visit I hide in my room. My   28
cousin Brenda, just my age, whose father works in the post office and whose mother is a nurse, comes to find me. "Hello," she says. And then she asks, looking at my recent school picture which I did not want taken, and on which the "glob" as I think of it is clearly visible, "You still can't see out of that eye?"

"No," I say, and flop back on the bed over my book.   29

That night, as I do almost every night, I abuse my eye. I rant and rave   30
at it, in front of the mirror. I plead with it to clear up before morning. I tell it I hate and despise it. I do not pray for sight. I pray for beauty.

"You did not change," they say.   31

I am fourteen and baby-sitting for my brother Bill who lives in   32
Boston. He is my favorite brother and there is a strong bond between us. Understanding my feelings of shame and ugliness, he and his wife take me to a local hospital where the "glob" is removed by a doctor named O. Henry. There is still a small bluish crater where the scar tissue was, but the ugly white stuff is gone. Almost immediately I become a different person from the girl who does not raise her head. Or so I think. Now that I've raised my head, I win the boyfriend of my dreams. Now that I've raised my head, I have plenty of friends. Now that I've raised my head, classwork comes from my lips as faultlessly as Easter speeches did, and I leave high school as valedictorian, most popular student and *queen,* hardly believing my luck. Ironically, the girl who was voted most beautiful in our class (and was) was later shot twice through the chest by a male companion, using a "real" gun, while she was pregnant. But that's another story in itself. Or, is it?

"You did not change," they say.   33

It is now thirty years since the "accident." A beautiful journalist   34
comes to visit and to interview me. She is going to write a cover story for her magazine that focuses on my last book. "Decide how you want to look on the cover," she says. "Glamorous, or whatever."

Never mind "glamorous," it is the "whatever" that I hear. Suddenly   35
all I can think of is whether I will get enough sleep the night before the photography session: if I don't, my eye will be tired and wander, as blind eyes will.

At night in bed with my lover I think up reasons why I should not 36
appear on the cover of a magazine. "My meanest critics will say I've sold
out," I say. "My family will now realize I write scandalous books."

"But what's the real reason you don't want to do this?" he asks.   37

"Because in all probability," I say in a rush, "my eye won't be straight." 38

"It will be straight enough," he says. Then, "Besides, I thought you'd 39
made your peace with that."

And I suddenly remember that I have.   40

I remember: 41

I am talking to my brother Jimmy, asking if he remembers anything 42
unusual about the day I was shot. He does not know I consider that day
the last time my father, with his sweet home remedy of cool lily leaves,
"chose" me, and that I suffered and raged inside because of this. "Well,"
he says, "all I remember is standing by the side of the highway with
Daddy, trying to flag down a car. A white man stopped, but when Daddy
said he needed somebody to take his little girl to the doctor, he drove off."

I remember: 43

I am in the desert for the first time. I fall totally in love with it. I am 44
so overwhelmed by its beauty, I confront for the first time, consciously,
the meaning of the doctor's words years ago: "Eyes are sympathetic. If
one is blind, the other will likely become blind too." I realize I have
dashed about the world madly, looking at this, looking at that, storing up
images against the fading of the light. But I might have missed seeing the
desert! The shock of that possibility—and gratitude for over twenty-five
years of sight—sends me literally to my knees. Poem after poem comes—
which is perhaps how poets pray.

On Sight

I am so thankful I have seen
The Desert
And the creatures in the desert
And the desert Itself.
The desert has its own moon
Which I have seen
With my own eye
There is no flag on it.
Trees of the desert have arms
All of which are always up
That is because the moon is up
The sun is up
Also the sky
The stars
Clouds
None with flags.
If there were flags, I doubt

...continued Beauty: When the Other Dancer Is the Self, **Alice Walker**

the trees would point.
Would you?

But mostly, I remember this: 45

I am twenty-seven, and my baby daughter is almost three. Since   46
her birth I have worried over her discovery that her mother's eyes are
different from other people's. Will she be embarrassed? I wonder.
What will she say? Every day she watches a television program called
"Big Blue Marble." It begins with a picture of the earth as it appears
from the moon. It is bluish, a little battered-looking, but full of light,
with whitish clouds swirling around it. Every time I see it I weep with
love, as if it is a picture of Grandma's house. One day when I am putting Rebecca down for her nap, she suddenly focuses on my eye. Something inside me cringes, gets ready to try to protect myself. All children
are cruel about physical differences, I know from experience, and that
they don't always mean to be is another matter. I assume Rebecca will
be the same.

But no-o-o-o. She studies my face intently as we stand, her inside   47
and me outside her crib. She even holds my face maternally between her
dimpled little hands. Then, looking every bit as serious and lawyerlike as
her father, she says, as if it may just possibly have slipped my attention:
"Mommy, there's a *world* in your eye." (As in, "Don't be alarmed, or do
anything crazy.") And then, gently, but with great interest: "Mommy,
where did you *get* that world in your eye?"

For the most part, the pain left then. (So what if my brothers grew   48
up to buy even more powerful pellet guns for their sons and to carry real
guns themselves. So what if a young "Morehouse man" once nearly fell
off the steps of Trevor Arnett Library because he thought my eyes were
blue.) Crying and laughing I ran to the bathroom, while Rebecca mum-
bled and sang herself off to sleep. Yes indeed, I realized, looking into the
mirror. There *was* a world in my eye. And I saw that it was possible to
love it; that in fact, for all it had taught me, of shame and anger and inner vision, I *did* love it. Even to see it drifting out of orbit in boredom,
or rolling up out of fatigue, not to mention floating back at attention in
excitement (bearing witness, a friend has called it), deeply suitable to my
personality, and even characteristic of me.

That night I dream I am dancing to Stevie Wonder's song "Always" (the   49
name of the song is really "As," but I hear it as "Always"). As I dance, whirling
and joyous, happier than I've ever been in my life, another bright-faced
dancer joins me. We dance and kiss each other and hold each other through
the night. The other dancer has obviously come through all right, as I have
done. She is beautiful, whole and free. And she is also me.

vo·cab·u·lar·y

In your journal, write the meanings of the italicized words in the following phrases.

- a *subversive* wit (**1**)
- rustling their new *crinolines* (**4**)
- Eyes are *sympathetic* (**12**)

- a hideous *cataract* (**13**)
- *boisterous*, ill-disciplined children (**16**)
- bearing *witness* (**45**)

? QUESTIONS FOR WRITING AND DISCUSSION

1 Why does Alice Walker share this story with us? What memories from your own life did her story trigger? Write them down.

2 What does Walker discover or learn about herself? As a reader, what did you learn about your own experiences by reading this essay?

3 Reread the essay, looking for examples of the following techniques for writing about memories: (1) using detailed observations; (2) creating specific scenes; (3) noting changes, contrasts, or conflicts; and (4) seeing relationships between past and present. In your opinion, which of these techniques does she use most effectively?

4 What is Walker's main idea in this autobiographical account? State it in your own words. Where in the essay does she state it most explicitly?

5 How many scenes or episodes does Walker recount? List them according to her age at the time. Explain how each episode relates to her main idea.

6 Walker also uses images of sight and blindness to organize her essay. The story begins with a description of a father who has "beautiful eyes" and ends with her dancing in her dream to a song by Stevie Wonder. Catalog the images of sight and blindness from each scene or episode. Explain how, taken together, these images reinforce Walker's main idea.

7 Walker writes her essay in the present tense, and she uses italics not only to emphasize ideas but to indicate the difference between past thoughts and events and the present. List the places where she uses italics. Explain how the italicized passages reinforce her main point.

8 What is the *occasion* in Walker's life that motivates her to write this narrative? Is it told in the story or does it happen in her life after the story concludes? Explain. Where does Walker include details about the social, historical, or cultural *context* for her story? Locate at least three paragraphs that provide details about context. Explain how these details are important for you as a reader in understanding her narrative.

9 Walker writes a multigenre essay, weaving poetry into her narrative essay. What other multigenre elements—such as photographs, drawings, excerpts from journals, or material from scrapbooks—might also be appropriate in your remembering essay? Might you want to do a "multimedia essay" in which you include not only photographs, images, and childhood artifacts, but also weblog excerpts, streaming video, audio, and Web links?

PROFESSIONAL WRITING

César Chávez Saved My Life

Daniel "Nene" Alejandrez

Labor leader and civil rights worker César Chávez (1927–1993) founded the National Farm Workers Association and used the nonviolent principles of Mahatma Gandhi and Dr. Martin Luther King, Jr. to gain dignity, fair wages, and humane working conditions for farm workers. In addition to his post humously awarded Presidential Medal of Freedom and his induction into the California Hall of Fame, César Chávez has had his birthday, March 31st, recognized in eight states as an official holiday.

The author of the article, Daniel "Nene" Alejandrez, is the founder of Barrios Unidos and has spent his life fighting poverty, drugs, and gangs in Latino communities. In this essay, written in 2005 for Sojourners maga-zine, Alejandrez remembers how the principles and the voice of César Chávez changed his life and inspired him to help others escape the cycle of drugs, violence, and incarceration.

I'm the son of migrant farm workers, born out in a cotton field in *1* Merigold, Mississippi. My family's from Texas. A migrant child goes to five or six different schools in one year, and you try to assimilate to whatever's going on at that time. I grew up not having shoes or only having one pair of pants to wear to school all week. I always remembered my experience in Texas, where Mexicans and blacks couldn't go to certain restaurants. That leaves something in you.

I saw how my father would react when Immigration would come up *2* to the fields or the boss man talked to him. I would see my father bow his head. I didn't know why my father wasn't standing up to this man. As a child working in the rows behind him, I said to myself, "I'll never do that." A deep anger was developing in me.

But it was also developing in my father; the way that he dealt with 3 it was alcohol. He would become violent when he drank on the weekends. I realized later that the reason he would bow his head to the boss is that he had seven kids to feed. He took that humiliation in order to feed me.

I stabbed the first kid when I was 13 years old. I shot another guy 4 when I was 15. I almost killed a guy when I was 17. On and on and on. Then, in the late 1960s, I found myself as a young man in the Vietnam War. I saw more violence, inflicted more violence, and then tried to deal with the violence.

I came back from the war addicted to heroin, as many, many 5 young men did. I came back to the street war, in the drug culture. Suddenly there were farm workers—who lost jobs because of the bringing of machines into the fields—who turned into drug dealers; it's easier money.

But when I was still working in the fields, something happened. I was 6 17 years old, out in the fields of central California, and suddenly I hear this voice coming out of the radio, talking about how we must better our conditions and better our lives in the migrant camps. It was like this voice was talking just to me.

The voice was César Chávez. He said, "You must organize. You must 7 seek justice. You must ask for better wages."

It's 1967. I'm busting my ass off pitching melons with six guys. Be- 8 cause we're the youngest, they put us on the hardest job, but we're getting paid $1.65 an hour. The guys working the harvesting machines are making $8 an hour. We said to ourselves, "Something's not right."

Having the words of César Chávez, I organized the young men and 9 called a strike. After lunch we just stopped working. We didn't go back on the fields. This was sort of a hard thing because my father was a foreman to this contractor, so I was going against him. He was concerned that we were rocking the boat—but I think he was proud of me. We shut down three of the melon machines, which forced the contractor to come, and then the landowner came. "What's going on?" he said. We said, "We're on strike, because we aren't getting our money." After about two hours, they said, "Okay, we're going to raise it to $1.95."

But it wasn't the $1.95—it was the fact that six young men were be- 10 ing abused, and that this little short Indian guy, César Chávez, had an influence. I kept his words.

When I wound up in Vietnam, I heard about Martin Luther King 11 and his stand against the war. Somebody also told me about Mahatma Gandhi. I didn't know who he was, only that he was a bald-headed dude that had done this kind of stuff.

...continued César Chávez Saved My Life, **Daniel "Nene" Alejandrez**

In Vietnam I realized that there were people that I had never met 12 before, that had never done nothing to me, never called me a dirty Mexican or a greaser or nothing, and all of sudden I had to be an enemy to them.

I started looking at the words of César Chávez in terms of nonvio- 13 lence. I looked at the violence in the community, in the fields, yet Chávez was still calling for peace.

It has been an incredible journey since those days. For us this is a 14 spiritual movement. In Barrios Unidos, that's the primary thing—our spirit comes first. How do we take care of ourselves? Whatever people believe in, no matter what faith or religion, how do we communicate to the youngsters who are spiritually bankrupt? Many of us were addicted to drugs or alcohol, and we have to find a spiritual connection. Working with gang members, there's a lot of pain, so you have to find ways for healing. As peacemakers, we are wounded peacemakers.

This work has taken us into the prisons. Throughout the years, we've 15 been talking about the high rate of incarceration among our people, and the drug laws. Many people are doing huge amounts of time for non-violent drug convictions; they did not need to be incarcerated—they need treatment. Currently in this country we deal with treatment by incarcerating people, which leads them to more violence and more negative ways of living.

As community-based organizations, we have had to prove to the 16 correctional institutions that we're not in there to create any revolution. We're there to try to help. I'm asking how I can change the men that have been violent. How do I help change their attitude toward society and toward their own relatives? We see them as our relatives—these are our relatives that are incarcerated. How can we support them?

We go into the prison as a cultural and spiritual group helping 17 men in prison to understand their own culture and those of different cultures. They come from great warrior societies. But the warrior tradition doesn't just mean going to war, but also fighting for peace. The prisoners who help organize the Cinco de Mayo, Juneteenth, and Native powwow ceremonies within the prison system are a true testament of courage to change the madness of violence that has unnecessarily claimed many lives. By providing those ceremonies, we allow them to see who they really are. They weren't born gang members, or drug addicts, or thieves.

My best example of hope in the prisons is when we take the Aztec 18 dancers into the institutions. They do a whole indigenous ceremony. At the end, they invite people to what's called a friendship dance. It's a big figure-eight dance.

The first time that we were in prison in Tracy, California, out on the yard, there were 2,000 men out there. The ceremony was led by Laura Castro, founder of the Xochut Aztec dance group, a very petite woman, very keen to her culture. She says to me, "What do you think, Nane? Do you think that these guys will come out and dance?" I'm looking at those guys—tattoos all over them and swastikas and black dudes that are really big. It's incredible to be in the prison yard. I say to her, "I don't know." *19*

But what ties all those guys together is the drumbeat. Every culture has some ceremonial drum you play. When the drumbeat started in the yard, the men just started coming. They divide themselves by race and then by gang. You got Norteños, Sureños, Hispanos, blacks, whites, Indians, and then "others" (mostly the Asian guys). *20*

When the men were invited into the dance, those guys emptied out the bleachers. They came. They held hands. This tiny woman, Laura, led them through the ceremony of the friendship dance. They went round and round. There were black, white, and brown holding hands, which doesn't happen in prison. And they were laughing. For a few seconds, maybe a minute, there was hope. We saw the smiles of men being children, remembering something about their culture. The COs [correctional officers] came out of the tower wondering what the hell was going on with these men dancing in prison, holding hands. It was an incredible sight. That day, the Creator was present. I knew that God's presence was there. Everyone was given a feeling that something had happened that wasn't our doing. *21*

vo·cab·u·lar·y

In your journal, write the meanings of the italicized words in the following phrases.

- try to *assimilate* (1)
- took that *humiliation* (3)
- the high rate of *incarceration* (15)
- a whole *indigenous* ceremony (18)

QUESTIONS FOR WRITING AND DISCUSSION

1. The motto for César Chávez and his organization, The National Farm Workers Association, was "Si Se Puede," or "It Can Be Done." Although Alejandrez does not specifically refer to this motto, explain where this theme is most apparent in his essay.

2. One key strategy for writing successful narratives is setting and describing specific scenes. Alejandrez does an excellent job of setting two key scenes—one from his childhood and one from later in life. For each of these scenes, explain how Alejandrez (a) sets up the scene, (b) describes what happens

using detailed observations, (c) uses dialogue to make the scene more vivid and dramatic, and (d) makes connections between the past and the present.

❸ One key theme or motif in Alejandrez's essay is the idea of a "spiritual connection." Drawing on your description from question 2, explain how the idea of a spiritual connection is important in both of these key scenes. How does this theme connect to the nonviolent movements of Mahatma Gandhi and Martin Luther King, Jr.? How is this theme evoked in the final sentences of Alejandrez's essay? Explain.

❹ Using Alejandrez's essay as a guide, write a remembering essay about a person in your life who became a role model or was influential at a key point in your life. Be sure to include key scenes showing how, when, and why this person was influential and then what you were able to accomplish because of that influence.

❺ Go to the official Web sites for César Chávez and Barrios Unidos. What parallels are there between the lives of César Chávez and Daniel Alejandrez? How did both organizations use the nonviolent principles of Gandhi and Martin Luther King, Jr.? How are or were the goals of both organizations different? Explain.

Remembering: The Writing Process

"Memory is more indelible than ink."

—ANITA LOOS, AUTHOR OF *KISS HOLLYWOOD GOODBYE*

ASSIGNMENT FOR REMEMBERING

Write an essay about an important person, place, and/or event in your life. Your purpose is to recall and then use specific examples and scenes that *recreate* this memory and *show why* it is important to you. If you don't have a specific audience and genre assigned, use the chart below to help you think about your possible audience and genre. You may be considering a personal audience of family and friends, but you may also want to think about a more public audience. Browsing through specialty magazines or Web sites (sports, nature, outdoors, genealogy, cooking, style) may give you an idea of how writers adapt an autobiographical narrative for a particular audience. Also, personal memoirs often have a place in academic writing in the humanities and social sciences.

Audience	Possible Genres for Writing About Memories
Personal Audience	Autobiographical essay, memoir, journal entry, social networking site entry, blog, photo essay, scrapbook, multigenre document.
Academic Audience	Essay for humanities or social science class, journal entry, forum entry on class site, multigenre document.
Public Audience	Column, memoir or essay in a magazine, newspaper, or newsletter; memoir or essay in a online site or blog; online memoir in a multigenre document.

CHOOSING A SUBJECT

If one of the journal entry exercises suggested a possible subject, try the collecting and shaping strategies below. If none of those exercises led to an interesting subject, consider the following ideas.

- Interview (in person or over the phone) a parent, a brother or sister, or a close friend. What events or experiences does your interviewee remember that were important to you?
- Look at a map of your town, city, state, or country and spend a few minutes doing an inventory of places you have been. Make a list of trips you have taken, with dates and years. Which of those places is the most memorable for you?
- Dig out a school yearbook or look through the pictures and comments on your friends Facebook profiles. Whom do you remember most clearly? What events do you recall most vividly?
- Go to the library and look through news magazines or newspapers from five to ten years ago. What were the most important events of those years? What do you remember about them? Where were you and what were you doing when these events occurred? Which events had the largest impact on your life?
- Choose an important moment in your life, but write from the *point of view* of another person—a friend, family member, or stranger who was present. Let this person narrate the events that happened to you.

Note: Avoid choosing overly emotional topics such as the recent death of a close friend or family member. If you are too close to your subject, responding to your reader's revision suggestions may be difficult. Ask yourself if you can emotionally distance yourself from that subject. If you received a C for that essay, would you feel devastated?

COLLECTING

Once you have chosen a subject for your essay, try the following collecting strategies.

● **BRAINSTORMING**   Brainstorming is merely jotting down anything and everything that comes to mind that is remotely connected to your subject: words, phrases, images, or complete thoughts. You can brainstorm by yourself or in groups, with everyone contributing ideas and one person recording them.

● **LOOPING**   Looping is a method of controlled freewriting that generates ideas and provides focus and direction. Begin by freewriting about your subject for eight to ten minutes. Then pause, reread what you have written, and *underline* the most interesting or important idea in what you've written so far. Then, using that sentence or idea as your starting point, write for eight to ten minutes

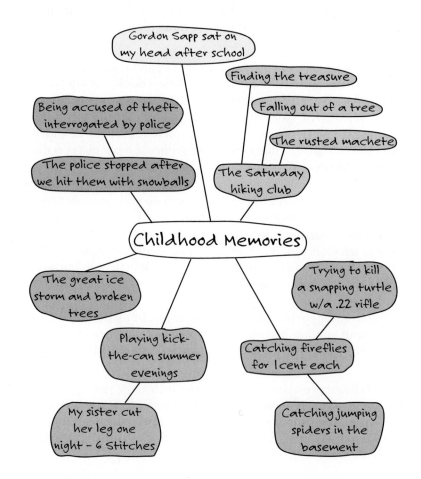

more. Repeat this cycle, or "loop," one more time. Each loop should add ideas and details from some new angle or viewpoint, but overall you will be focusing on the most important ideas that you discover.

● **CLUSTERING**   Clustering is merely a visual scheme for brainstorming and free-associating about your topic. It can be especially effective for remembering because it helps you sketch relationships among your topics and subtopics. As you can see from the sample sketch, the sketch that you make of your ideas should help you see relationships between ideas or get a rough idea about an order or shape you may wish to use.

SHAPING

First, reconsider your purpose; perhaps it has become clearer or more definite since you recorded it in your journal entry. In your journal, jot down tentative answers for the following questions. If you don't have an answer, go on to the next question.

- **Subject:** What is your general subject?
- **Specific topic:** What aspect of your subject interests you?
- **Purpose:** Why is this topic interesting or important to you or your readers?
- **Main idea:** What might your main idea be?
- **Audience:** For whom are you writing? Why might your reader or readers be interested in this topic? (Review possible audiences suggested with the chapter assignment on page 106.)
- **Genre:** What genre might help you communicate your purpose and main idea most effectively to your audience? (Review genre options suggested with the chapter assignment.)

As you think about ways to organize and shape your essay, reread your assignment and think about your purpose and possible audience. Consider several possible *genres* or combinations of genres that might work. Then, for particular parts or sections of your essay, review the strategies described below. *Chronological order* will shape a major part of your narrative, but think also about using *comparison/ contrast* for highlighting past and present or for contrasting two places, two events, or two key people. In addition, *similes*, *metaphors*, and *analogies* will make your writing more vivid, and paying attention to your *voice* and *tone* can help you achieve your purpose.

Most important, be sure to *narrow* and *focus* your subject. If you're going to write a three-page essay, don't try to cover everything in your life. Focus on one person, one episode, one turning point, one discovery, or one day, and do that in depth and detail.

● **GENRE**   As you collect ideas, draft sample passages, and discuss your assignment with your peers, think about appropriate genre possibilities. Start by reviewing the genre alternatives in the chapter assignment. You may choose to write in a traditional narrative format. However, you may want to use a multigenre or multimedia format with photographs, graphics, drawings, scrapbook materials, video, podcasts, and Web links. Check with your instructor to see if a multigenre approach meets the assignment.

● **CHRONOLOGICAL ORDER**   If you are writing about remembered events, you will probably use some form of chronological order. Try making a *chronological list of the major scenes or events.* Then go through the list, deciding what you will emphasize by telling about each item in detail and what you will pass over quickly. Normally, you will be using a straightforward chronological order, but you may wish to use a flashback, starting in the middle or near the end and then returning to tell the beginning. In his paragraph about a personal relationship, for example, student writer Gregory Hoffman begins the story at the most dramatic point, returns to tell how the relationship began, and then concludes the story.

> Her words hung in the air like iron ghosts. "I'm pregnant," she said as they walked through the park, the snow crackling beneath their feet. Carol was looking down at the ground when she told him, somewhat ashamed, embarrassed, and defiant all at once. Their relationship had only started in September, but both had felt the uneasiness surrounding them for the past months. She could remember the beginning so well and in such favor, now that the future seemed so uncertain. The all-night conversations by the bay window, the rehearsals at the university theater—where he would make her laugh during her only soliloquy, and most of all the Christmas they had spent together in Vermont. No one else had existed for her during those months. Yet now, she felt duped by her affections—as if she had become an absurd representation of a tragic television character. As they approached the lake, he put his arm around her, "Just do what you think is best, babe. I mean, I think you know how I feel." At that moment, she knew it was over. It was no longer "their" decision. His hand touched her cheek in a benedictorial fashion. The rest would only be form now. Exchanging records and clothes with an aside of brief conversation. She would see him again, in the market or at a movie, and they would remember. But like his affection in September, her memory of him would fade until he was too distant to see.

● **COMPARISON/CONTRAST**   Although you may be comparing or contrasting people, places, or events from the past, you will probably also be comparing or contrasting the past to the present. You may do that at the beginning, noting how something in the present reminds you of a past person, place, or event. You may do it at the end, as Andrea Lee does in *Russian Journal.* You may do it both at the beginning and at the end, as Richard Rodriguez does in "The Boy's Desire." You may even contrast past and present throughout, as Alice Walker does in "Beauty: When the Other Dancer Is the Self."

Comparing or contrasting the past with the present will often clarify your dominant idea.

● **IMAGE**   Sometimes a single mental picture or recurring image will shape a paragraph or two in an essay. Consider how novelist George Orwell, in his essay "Shooting an Elephant," uses the image of a puppet or dummy to describe his feeling at a moment when he realized that, against his better judgment, he was going to have to shoot a marauding elephant in order to satisfy a crowd of two thousand Burmese who had gathered to watch him. The italicized words emphasize the recurring image.

> Suddenly I realized that I should have to shoot the elephant after all. The people expected it of me and I had got to do it; I could feel their *two thousand wills pressing me forward,* irresistibly. And it was at this moment, as I stood there with the rifle in my hands, that I first grasped the hollowness, the futility of the white man's dominion in the East. Here was I, the white man with his gun, standing in front of the unarmed native crowd—*seemingly the leading actor* of the piece; but in reality I was only an absurd *puppet pushed to and fro* by the will of those yellow faces behind. I perceived in this moment that when the white man turns tyrant it is his own freedom that he destroys. He becomes a sort of *hollow, posing dummy,* the *conventionalized figure* of a sahib. For it is the condition of his rule that he shall spend his life in trying to impress the "natives" and so in every crisis he has got to do what the "natives" expect of him. He *wears a mask,* and his face grows to fit it. I had got to shoot the elephant. I had committed myself to doing it when I sent for the rifle. *A sahib has got to act like a sahib;* he has got to appear resolute, to know his own mind and do definite things.

● **VOICE AND TONE**   When you have a personal conversation with someone, the way you look and sound—your body type, your voice, your facial expressions and gestures—communicates a sense of personality and attitude, which in turn affects how the other person reacts to what you say. In written language, although you don't have those gestures, expressions, or the actual sound of your voice, you can still create the sense that you are talking directly to your listener.

The term *voice* refers to a writer's personality as revealed through language. Writers may use emotional, colloquial, or conversational language to communicate a sense of personality. Or they may use abstract, impersonal language either to conceal their personalities or to create an air of scientific objectivity.

Tone is a writer's attitude toward the subject. The attitude may be positive or negative. It may be serious, humorous, honest, or ironic; it may be skeptical or accepting; it may be happy, frustrated, or angry. Often voice and tone overlap, and together they help us hear a writer talking to us. In the following passage, we hear student writer Kurt Weekly talking to us directly; we hear a clear, honest voice telling the story. His tone is not defensive or guilty: He openly admits he has a "problem."

> Oh no, not another trash day. Every time I see all those trash containers, plastic garbage bags and junk lined up on the sidewalks, it drives me crazy. It all started when I was sixteen. I had just received my driver's license and the most beautiful Ford pickup. It was Wednesday as I remember and trash day. I don't know what happened. All of a sudden I was racing down the street swerving to the right, smashing into a large green Hefty trash bag filled with grass clippings. The bag exploded, and grass clippings and trash flew everywhere. It was beautiful and I was hooked. There was no stopping me.
>
> At first I would smash one or two cans on the way to school. Then I just couldn't get enough. I would start going out the night before trash day. I would go down the full length of the street and wipe out every garbage container in sight. I was the terror of the neighborhood. This was not a bad habit to be taken lightly. It was an obsession. I was in trouble. There was no way I could kick this on my own. I needed help.
>
> I received that help. One night after an evening of nonstop can smashing, the Arapahoe County Sheriff Department caught up with me. Not just one or a few but the whole department. They were willing to set me on the right path, and if that didn't work, they were going to send me to jail. It was a long, tough road to rehabilitation, but I did it. Not alone. I had the support of my family and the community.

● **PERSONA**   Related to voice and tone is the *persona*—the "mask" that a writer can put on. Sometimes in telling a story about yourself, you may want to speak in your own "natural" voice. At other times, however, you may change or exaggerate certain characteristics in order to project a character different from your "real" self. Writers, for example, may project themselves as braver and more intelligent than they really are. Or to create a humorous effect, they may create personas who are more foolish or clumsy than they really are. This persona can shape a whole passage. In the following excerpt, James Thurber, a master of autobiographical humor, uses a persona—along with chronological narrative—to shape his account of a frustrating botany class.

> I passed all the other courses that I took at my university, but I could never pass botany. This was because all botany students had to spend several hours a week in a laboratory looking through a microscope at plant cells, and I could never see through a microscope. I never once saw a cell through a microscope. This used to enrage my instructor. He would wander around the laboratory pleased with the progress all the students were making in drawing the involved and, so I am told, interesting structure of flower cells, until he came to me. I would just be standing there. "I can't see anything," I would say. He would begin patiently enough, explaining how anybody can see through a microscope, but he would always end up in a

fury claiming that I could too see through a microscope but just pretended that I couldn't. "It takes away from the beauty of flowers anyway," I used to tell him. "We are not concerned with beauty in this course," he would say. "We are concerned solely with the mechanics of flowers." "Well," I'd say, "I can't see anything." "Try it just once again," he'd say, and I would put my eye to the microscope and see nothing at all, except now and again a neb- ulous milky substance—a phenomenon of maladjustment. You were sup- posed to see a vivid, restless clockwork of sharply defined plant cells. "I see what looks like a lot of milk," I would tell him. This, he claimed, was the result of my not having adjusted the microscope properly, so he would readjust it for me, or rather, for himself. And I would look again and see milk. I finally took a deferred pass, as they called it, and waited a year and tried again. (You had to pass one of the biological sciences or you could- n't graduate.) The professor had come back from vacation brown as a berry, bright-eyed, and eager to explain cell-structure again to his classes. "Well," he said to me, cheerily, when we met in the first laboratory hour of the semester, "we're going to see cells this time, aren't we?" "Yes, sir," I said. Students to the right of me and to the left of me and in front of me were seeing cells; what's more, they were quietly drawing pictures of them in their notebooks. Of course, I didn't see anything.

"We'll try it," the professor said to me, grimly, "with every adjustment of the microscope known to man. As God is my witness, I'll arrange this glass so that you see cells through it or I'll give up teaching. In twenty-two years of botany, I—" He cut off abruptly for he was beginning to quiver all over, like Lionel Barrymore, and he genuinely wished to hold onto his temper; his scenes with me had taken a great deal out of him.

So we tried it with every adjustment of the microscope known to man. With only one of them did I see anything but blackness or the fa- miliar lacteal opacity, and that time I saw, to my pleasure and amazement, a variegated constellation of flecks, specks, and dots. These I hastily drew. The instructor, noting my activity, came back from an adjoining desk, a smile on his lips and his eyebrows high in hope. He looked at my cell drawing. "What's that?" he demanded, with a hint of a squeal in his voice. "That's what I saw," I said. "You didn't, you didn't, you didn't!" he screamed, losing control of his temper instantly, and he bent over and squinted into the microscope. His head snapped up. "That's your eye!" he shouted. "You've fixed the lens so that it reflects! You've drawn your eye!"

● **DIALOGUE**   Dialogue, which helps to *recreate* people and events rather than just tell about them, can become a dominant form and thereby shape your writing. Recreating an actual conversation, you could possibly write a whole scene using nothing but dialogue. More often, however, writers use dialogue occasionally for dramatic effect. In the account of his battle with the micro- scope, for instance, Thurber uses dialogue in the last two paragraphs to dram- atize his conclusion:

"We'll try it," the professor said to me, grimly, "with every adjustment of the microscope known to man. As God is my witness, I'll arrange this glass so that you see cells through it or I'll give up teaching. In twenty-two years of teaching botany, I—" . . . "What's that?" he demanded. . . . "That's what I saw," I said. "You didn't, you didn't, you didn't!" he screamed. . . . "You've fixed the lens so that it reflects! You've drawn your eye!"

❝I start at the beginning, go on to the end, then stop. ❞

—GABRIEL GARCÍA MÁRQUEZ,
AUTHOR OF *ONE HUNDRED YEARS OF SOLITUDE*

● **TITLE, INTRODUCTION, AND CONCLUSION**   In your journal, sketch out several possible titles you might use. You may want a title that is merely an accurate label, such as *Russian Journal* or "The Boy's Desire," but you may prefer something less direct that gets your reader's attention. For example, for his essay about his hat that appears at the end of this chapter, student writer Todd Petry uses the title "The Wind Catcher." As a reader, what do you think about Alice Walker's title, "Beauty: When the Other Dancer Is the Self"?

Introductions or beginning paragraphs take several shapes. Some writers plunge the reader immediately into the action—as Gregory Hoffman does—and then later fill in the scene and context. Others are more like Kurt Weekly, announcing the subject—trash cans—and then taking the reader from the present to the past and the beginning of the story: "It all started when I was sixteen. . . ." At some point, however, readers do need to know the context—the *who, what, when,* and *where* of your account.

❝I always know the ending; that's where I start. ❞

—TONI MORRISON,
NOBEL PRIZE-WINNING NOVELIST

Conclusions are also of several types. In some, writers will return to the present and discuss what they have learned, as Andrea Lee does in *Russian Journal.* Some, like Alice Walker, end with an image or even a dream. Some writers conclude with dramatic moments, or an emotional scene, as student writer Juli Bovard does in the essay "The Red Chevy" that appears at the end of this chapter. But many writers will try to tie the conclusion back to the beginning, as Richard Rodriguez does at the end of "The Boy's Desire": "The closet door closes . . . the fog rises." In your journal, experiment with several possibilities until you find one that works for your subject.

DRAFTING

When you have experimented with the above shaping strategies, reconsider your purpose, audience, and main idea. Have they changed? In your journal, reexamine the notes you made before trying the shaping activities. If necessary, revise your statements about purpose, audience, or main idea based on what you have actually written.

Working from your journal material and from your collecting and shaping activities, draft your essay. It is important *not* to splice different parts together or just recopy and connect segments, for they may not fit or flow together. Instead, reread what you have written, and then start afresh. Concentrate on what you want to say and write as quickly as possible.

To avoid interruptions, choose a quiet place to work. Follow your own writing rituals. Try to write nonstop. If you cannot think of the right word, put a line or a dash, but keep on writing. When necessary, go back and reread what you have previously written.

REVISING

Revising begins, of course, when you get your first idea and start collecting and shaping. It continues as you redraft certain sections of your essay and rework your organization. In many classes, you will give and receive advice from the other writers in your class. Use the guidelines below to give constructive advice about a remembering essay draft.

> 66 The difference between the right word and the nearly right word is the same as that between lightning and the lightning bug. 99
> —MARK TWAIN, AUTHOR OF *THE ADVENTURES OF HUCKLEBERRY FINN*

GUIDELINES FOR REVISION

* **Reexamine your purpose and audience.** Are you doing what you intended?
* **Reconsider the genre you selected.** Is it working for your purpose and audience? Can you add multigenre elements to make your narrative more effective?
* **Revise to make the main idea of your account clearer.** You don't need a "moral" to the story or a bald statement saying, "This is why this person was important." Your reader, however, should know clearly why you wanted to write about the memory that you chose.
* **Revise to clarify the important relationships in your story.** Consider relationships between past and present, between you and the people in your story, between one place and another place, between one event and another event.
* **Close and detailed observation is crucial.** *Show,* don't just tell. Can you use any of the collecting and shaping strategies for observing discussed in Chapter 3?
* **Revise to show crucial changes, contrasts, or conflicts more clearly.** Walker's essay, for instance, illustrates how *conflict and change* are central to an effective remembering essay. See if this strategy will work in your essay.
* **Have you used a straight chronological order?** If it works, keep it. If not, would another order be better? Should you begin in the middle and do a flashback? Do you want to move back and forth from present to past or stay in the past until the end?

  If you are using a chronological order, cue your reader by occasionally using transitional words to signal changes: *then, when, first, next, last, before, after, while, as, sooner, later, initially, finally, yesterday, today.*

PEER RESPONSE

The instructions below will help you give and receive constructive advice about the rough draft of your remembering essay. You may use these guidelines for an in-class workshop, a take-home review, or a computer e-mail response.

Writer: Before you exchange drafts with another reader, write out the following information about your own rough draft.

1. State the main idea that you hope your essay conveys.
2. Describe the best *one* or *two* key scenes that your narrative creates.
3. Explain one or two problems that you are having with this draft that you want your reader to focus on.

Reader: Without making any comments, read the *entire* draft from start to finish. As you *reread* the draft, answer the following questions.

1. Locate one or two of the *key scenes* in the narrative. Are they clearly set at an identified time and place? Does the writer use vivid description of the place or the people? Does the writer use dialogue? Does the writer include his or her reflections? Which of these areas need the most attention during the writer's revision? Explain.
2. Write out a *time line* for the key events in the narrative. What happened first, second, third, and so forth? Are there places in the narrative where the time line could be clearer? Explain.
3. When you finished reading the draft, *what characters or incidents were you still curious about?* Where did you want more information? What characters or incidents did you want to know more about?
4. What *overall idea* does the narrative convey to you? How does your notion of the main idea compare to the writer's answer to question 1? Explain how the writer might revise the essay to make the main idea clearer.
5. Answer the *writer's questions* in question 3.

After you have some feedback from other readers, you need to distance yourself and objectively reread what you have written. Review the advice you received from your peer readers. Remember, you will get both good and bad advice, so *you* must decide what you think is important or not important. If you are uncertain about advice you received from one of your peers, ask for a third or fourth opinion. In addition, most writing centers will have tutors available who can help you sort through the advice you have received on your draft and figure out a revision plan. Especially for this remembering essay, make sure your memories are recreated on paper. Don't be satisfied with suggesting incidents that merely trigger your own memories: You must *show* people and events vividly for your reader.

- **Be clear about point of view.** Are you looking back on the past from a viewpoint in the present? Are you using the point of view of yourself as a child or at some earlier point in your life? Are you using the point of view of another person or object in your story?
- **What are the key images in your account?** Should you add or delete an image to show the experience more vividly?
- **What voice are you using?** Does it support your purpose? If you are using a persona, is it appropriate for your audience and purpose?
- **Revise sentences to improve clarity, conciseness, emphasis, and variety.**
- **Check your dialogue for proper punctuation and indentation.** See the essay by Alice Walker in this chapter for a model.
- **When you are relatively satisfied with your draft, edit for correct spelling, appropriate word choice, punctuation, and grammar.**

POSTSCRIPT ON THE WRITING PROCESS

After you finish writing, revising, and editing your essay, you will want to breathe a sigh of relief and turn it in. But before you do, think about the problems that you solved as you wrote this essay. *Remember:* Your major goal for this course is to learn to write and revise more effectively. To do that, you need to discover and adapt your writing processes so you can anticipate and solve the problems you face as a writer. Take a few minutes to answer the following questions. Be sure to hand in this postscript with your essay.

1. Review your writing process. Which collecting, shaping, and revising strategies helped you remember and describe incidents most quickly and clearly? What problems were you unable to solve?

2. Reread your essay. With a small asterisk [*], identify in the margin of your essay sentences where you used sensory details, dialogue, or images to show or recreate the experience for your reader.

3. If you received feedback from your peers, identify one piece of advice that you followed and one bit of advice that you ignored. Explain your decisions.

4. Rereading your essay, what do you like best about it? What parts of your essay need work? What would you change if you had another day to work on this assignment?

STUDENT WRITING
TODD PETRY

The Wind Catcher

Todd Petry decided to write about his cowboy hat, observing it in the present and thinking about some of the memories that it brought back. His notes, his first short draft paragraphs, and his revised version demonstrate how observing and remembering work together naturally: The details stimulate memories, and memories lead to more specific details.

NOTES AND DETAILS

DETAILS	MORE SPECIFIC DETAILS
Gray	Dirty, dust coated, rain stained cowdung color
Resistol	The name is stained and blurred
Size 7 3/8	
Diamond shape	Used to be diamond shape, now battered, looks abandoned
4" brim	Front tipped down, curled up in back
1" sweat band	blackish
5 yrs. old	still remember the day I bought it
4x beaver	
What it is not:	it is unlike a hat fresh out of the box
What it compares to:	point of crown like the north star like a pancake with wilted edges battered like General Custer's hat
What I remember:	the day I bought the hat a day at Pray Mesa

FIRST DRAFT

The Wind Catcher

The other day while I was relaxing in my favorite chair and listening to Ian *1* Tyson, I happened to notice my work cowboy hat hanging on the wall. Now I look at that old hat no less than a dozen times a day without too much thought, but on that particular day, my eyes remained fixed on it and my mind went to remembering.

I still remember I had $100 cash in my pocket the day I went hat *2* shopping. The local tack, feed, and western wear CO-OP was my first and only stop. Finding a hat to meet my general specifications was no big deal. I wanted a gray Resistol, size 7 3/8, with a 4-inch brim and diamond-shaped crown. From there on, though, my wants became very particular. I took 30 minutes to find the one that had the right fit, and five times that long to come to terms with the hat shaper. Boy, but I was one proud young fellow the next day when I went to school sporting my new piece of head gear. I've had that wind catcher five years through rough times, but in a way, it really looks better now, without any shape, dirty, and covered with dust and cowdung.

REVISED VERSION

The Wind Catcher

The other day, while I was relaxing in my favorite chair and listening to *1* Ian Tyson, I happened to notice my work cowboy hat hanging on the wall. Now, I look at that old hat no less than a dozen times a day without too much thought, but on that particular day, my eyes remained fixed on it and my mind went to remembering.

I was fifteen years old and had $100 cash in my pocket the day I went *2* hat shopping five years ago. The local tack, feed, and western wear CO-OP was my first and only stop. Finding a hat to meet my general specifications was no big deal. I wanted a gray 4X Resistol, size 7 3/8, with a four-inch brim and diamond-shaped crown. I wanted no flashy feathers or gaudy hatbands, which in my mind were only for pilgrims. From there on, though, my wants became very particular. I took thirty minutes to find the one that had the right fit, and five times that long to come to terms with the hat shaper. Boy, but I was one proud young fellow the next day when I went to school sporting my new piece of head gear.

About that time, Ian Tyson startled me out of my state of reminis- *3* cence by singing "Rose in the Rockies," with that voice of his sounding like ten cow elk cooing to their young in the springtime. As I sat there listening to the music and looking at that old hat, I had to chuckle to myself because that wind catcher had sure seen better days. I mean it looked rode hard and put up wet. The gray, which was once as sharp

...continued The Wind Catcher **Todd Petry**

and crisp as a mountain lake, was now faded and dull where the sun had beat down. Where the crown and brim met, the paleness was suddenly transformed into a gritty black which ran the entire circumference of the hat. This black was unlike any paint or color commercially available, being made up of head sweat, dirt, alfalfa dust, and powdered cow manure. Water blemishes from too much rain and snow mottled the brim, adding to the colors' turbidity. Inside the crown and wherever the slope was less than ninety degrees, dust had collected to hide the natural color even more.

After a while, my attention lost interest in the various colors and began   4
to work its way over the hat's shape, which I was once so critical of. General Custer's hat itself could not have looked worse. All signs of uniformity and definite shape had disappeared. The diamond-shaped crown, which was once round and smooth, now bowed out on the sides and had edges as blunt as an orange crate. The point, which once looked like the North Star indicating the direction, now was twisted off balance from excessive right hand use. Remembering last spring, how I threw that hat in the face of an irate mother cow during calving, I had to chuckle again. Throwing that hat kept my horse and me out of trouble but made the "off-balance look" rather permanent. As I looked at the brim, I was reminded of a three-day-old pancake with all its edges wilted. The back of that brim curled upward like a snake ready to strike, and the front had become so narrow and dipped, it looked like something a dentist would use on your teeth.

For probably half an hour, I sat looking at the wear and tear on that   5
ancient hat. Awhile back, I remember, I decided to try to make my old hat socially presentable by having it cleaned and blocked, removing those curls and dips and other signs of use. However, when a hat shop refused to even attempt the task, I figured I'd just leave well enough alone. As I scanned my eyes over the hat, I noticed several other alterations from its original form, such as the absent hat band, which was torn off in the brush on Pray Mesa, and the black thread that drew together the edges of a hole in the crown. However, try as I might, I could not for the life of me see where any character had been lost in the brush, or any flair had been covered with cowdung.

 QUESTIONS FOR WRITING AND DISCUSSION

1 Close observation often leads to specific memories. In the opening paragraph of his revised version, Todd Petry says that "on that particular

day, my eyes remained fixed on it and my mind went to remembering." He then recalls the time when he was fifteen years old and bought his hat. Identify two other places where observation leads Petry to remember specific scenes from the past.

2 Petry chose "The Wind Catcher" as the title for his essay. Reread the essay and then brainstorm a list of five other titles that might be appropriate for this short essay. Which title do you like best?

3 Where does Petry most clearly express the main idea of his essay? Write out the main idea in your own words.

STUDENT WRITING

JULI BOVARD

The Red Chevy

In the following essay, Juli Bovard recalls several of the most traumatic days of her life. She remembers not just the day she was raped by an unknown assailant, but the days she had to spend in the police station, the day she confronted her attacker in the courtroom, and the days she spent regaining control of her life. In the end, Bovard helps us understand how she overcame being a rape victim and reclaimed her life.

From the moment the man in the Chevy stopped to offer me a ride *1* on that blistering September afternoon, I knew I was in trouble. Before I could say, "No, but thanks anyway," the man in the passenger side of the car jumped at me, twisted my arm and held a shiny piece of steel to my side. I was pushed into the car and driven 30 miles over the county line. During the ride, I did everything every article or specialist on abduction had advised against: I cried, I babbled, and I lost control. In the end it was all futile. Two hours later—after they dumped me off near my home—I was another statistic. I had been raped, and was now a victim of the brutal, demeaning, sad violent crime of sexual assault. I was officially one of the 1,871 rapes that occur each day in the United States ("Sexual Assault Statistics").

Rape not only has physical repercussions, but has an enormous *2* psychological and emotional impact as well. During my "event" as I like to call it, I remembered an initial feeling of shock and numbness, and soon found myself babbling incoherently. I begged my attackers to let me go. I tried to talk my way out of the car. I even tried to beg or bargain my way out. However, the driver was very much in control of the situation, and my weak efforts failed. Eventually my babbling gave way to cold reason, and I became convinced that not only would I be raped, but that I would also die. My life did not pass before me—as is said to happen to dying people. In fact, I did not think of the past at all, but only the future and all the things I had not yet done. I had never ridden a horse other than the ponies at the fair. I had not learned to play golf—though I had intended to—or learned to snow ski down a mountain with my son. There were too many people I had not told how I really felt, too many people to whom I wanted to say good-bye. I seriously doubted I would ever be given another chance.

I did not die. In fact, other than a few bruises and scratches from 3 the field grass (where I was forced to lie during my rape), and several cuts on my neck and cheek—left by the brass knuckle style knife, I was remarkably, physically unhurt. The greatest trauma was to my mind. The psychological and emotional wounds in the ensuing months were far worse than the actual sexual assault.

Within a week of my report, the man who raped me was arrested and 4 held without bail (he had previously been convicted of attempted rape), his accomplice was not accused since he agreed to turn state's evidence—which means he made a deal to cover himself and agreed to testify against my assailant. What followed these events, I remember, was a long investigation that involved many tedious hours in the police station, and numbing revisits to the scene of the crime. Through it all I was alone, and I halfheartedly tried to comfort myself for enduring the stress so well. By late October, the month of the preliminary hearing, I had gone back to work, and was back in control of my life—or so I thought. The actual hearing proved me wrong.

Though I do not remember much about the actual courtroom or its 5 proceedings, I will always remember the warmth of the day and the overwhelming odor of my perpetrator's cologne (to this day I become nauseous if I smell the cologne Obsession). Seeing my assailant again had an effect on me that I was not prepared for. I felt the same fear that I had experienced the day of my rape, and for the second time in my life I felt terror so deep it paralyzed me. The pressure from the entire incident finally overwhelmed me, and when I returned home that afternoon I climbed into bed and did not leave it for three days. I spent seventy-two hours staring at the ceiling and vomiting. When I finally emerged from my emotional coma, I could not eat or sleep. Everything seemed unreal and unclear to me. It was weeks before I could focus on everyday tasks, even something as simple as showering.

By the middle of November, I had lost close to fifteen pounds. I 6 had constant diarrhea, my menstrual cycle had stopped, and I was constantly bombarded by anxiety attacks. I could no longer get up each day and go to work and act like nothing had happened. Leaving the house left me with cold sweats, and sleeping through the night became impossible. I became paranoid and despondent. I knew I would have to seek professional help.

Fortunately, through counseling I learned that my reactions were *7* very common, and are shared by most rape victims. Through research, I found that all the feelings I was having were very normal. My fear that the rapist would return was natural, and my inability to face unfamiliar situations or people was a classic symptom. I also learned that the guilt that plagued me, which made me think that somehow I had provoked the rape or "wore" the wrong clothes to entice the rapist, was simply untrue. I was feeling a great amount of shame and embarrassment—a stigma I learned society often places on rape victims. My anger, which was the most natural response, was also the most helpful. When you are angry, you tend to want to fight back. My way of fighting back was to get on with living. Still I asked, "Why me?" I had followed all the rules set by society. I did not walk the streets at night, hang out in bars, or talk to strangers. I was an actively employed member of society. So why me? I found it wasn't just me or something I did. It could have been any woman walking the streets that day, and it went far beyond what I wore or how I walked, something noted author Susan Brownmiller eloquently affirms in her statement that, "any female may become a victim of rape. Factors such as youth, advanced age, physical homeliness and virginal lifestyle do not provide a fool-proof deterrent to render a women impervious to sexual assault" (Brownmiller 348).

Through my experience and in talking with other victims I have *8* learned that rape has no typical "face." Certainly the man who raped me looked normal (He was not obscene, ugly, or disfigured). He could have been my neighbor, my grocer, or even my boyfriend. Rape victims and its perpetrators are colorless and ageless. There is no stereotypical rapist *or* victim. We can be doctors, lawyers, mothers, or fathers. We are tall, short, fat, and skinny. And, as in most victims' cases, simply in the wrong place at the wrong time.

After the question of "why me?" I asked, "WHY, at all?" Why *does* a *9* man rape a woman? Initially I thought it was obvious—for sex. But I was wrong. The motivations of rape include anger, aggression, dominance, hostility, and power, but generally are not usually associated with just the actual act of sex. Quite simply it is violence. Men who rape do so because they are violent and psychotic. There is no other reason, and no valid excuse.

In the end, before I was to testify, the man who attacked me changed *10* his plea to guilty. I walked out of the district attorney's office and never asked how many years the rapist would serve in prison. It did not matter.

He would be behind bars, but more importantly, I would be free to begin living again. Now, instead of dreading the month of September, I celebrate it. I celebrate the month, in which, instead of just existing, I started living. I was a victim of rape, but through years of counseling and support I am not a victim any longer.

Works Cited

Brownmiller, Susan. Against Our Will. New York: Simon and Schuster, 1975. Print.

"Sexual Assault Statistics." Abuse Counseling and Treatment. n.d. Web. 22 Oct. 2000.

vo·cab·u·lar·y

In your journal, write down the meanings of the italicized words in the following phrases.

- babbling *incoherently* (2)
- the greatest *trauma* (3)
- a *stigma* (7)

- render a woman *impervious* (7)
- they are violent and *psychotic* (9)

QUESTIONS FOR WRITING AND DISCUSSION

1. Psychological research has shown that people remember traumatic events more vividly and with more detail than other events. Has that been true in your experience? Recall two experiences—one happy, one traumatic—and consider whether your experiences support or do not support the research.

2. Remembering essays should have a purpose—that is, they should focus on having a specific effect on their audience. Why is Juli Bovard writing about this experience? What effect does she want to have on her readers? Is she just giving information or does she want to convince us about something? Explain.

3. Review the techniques for writing a remembering essay listed at the beginning of this chapter. Which of these techniques does Bovard use? Where does she use them? Which are, in your opinion, most effective? Why?

4. In addition to remembering specific scenes, Bovard uses some research and explains the causes and effects of the event. Should she have research and cite sources in a narrative essay? Do her explanations and her research help achieve her purpose or do they detract from the story? Support your response by citing specific sentences from her essay.

5 Bovard chose the title "The Red Chevy" for her essay. Brainstorm five other titles she might use for her essay. Compare your ideas with those of your classmates. Did you come up with titles that might be more effective for the purpose of her essay? Explain.

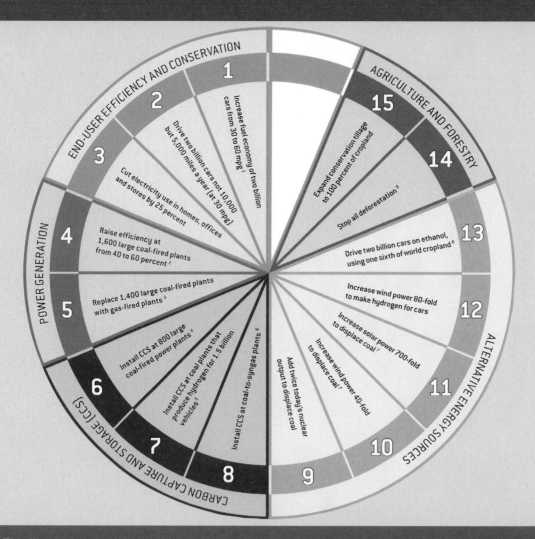

15 Ways to Make a Wedge
Illustrated by Janet Chao

END-USER EFFICIENCY AND CONSERVATION

1 — Increase fuel economy of two billion cars from 30 to 60 mpg [1]

2 — Drive two billion cars not 10,000 but 5,000 miles a year (at 30 mpg) [1]

3 — Cut electricity use in homes, offices and stores by 25 percent

POWER GENERATION

4 — Raise efficiency at 1,600 large coal-fired plants from 40 to 60 percent [2]

5 — Replace 1,400 large coal-fired plants with gas-fired plants [3]

CARBON CAPTURE AND STORAGE (CCS)

6 — Install CCS at 800 large coal-fired power plants [4]

7 — Install CCS at coal plants that produce hydrogen for 1.5 billion vehicles [5]

8 — Install CCS at coal-to-syngas plants [6]

ALTERNATIVE ENERGY SOURCES

9 — Add twice today's nuclear output to displace coal

10 — Increase wind power 40-fold to displace coal [7]

11 — Increase solar power 700-fold to displace coal [7]

12 — Increase wind power 80-fold to make hydrogen for cars

AGRICULTURE AND FORESTRY

13 — Drive two billion cars on ethanol, using one sixth of world cropland [8]

14 — Stop all deforestation [9]

15 — Expand conservation tillage to 100 percent of cropland

This illustration, "15 Ways to Make a Wedge," by Janet Chao, first appeared in "A Plan to Keep Carbon on Track," by Robert H. Socolow and Stephen W. Pacala, in the September 2006 issue of *Scientific American*. According to the caption, "An overall carbon strategy for the next half a century produces seven wedges' worth of emissions reductions. Here are 15 technologies from which those seven can be chosen [taking care to avoid double-counting]. Each of these measures, when phased in over 50 years, prevents the release of 25 billion tons of carbon. Leaving one wedge blank symbolizes that this list is by no means exhaustive." After reading the articles on climate change in this chapter, see Discussion Question 4 on page 158.

Reading

5

After discussing in class how to write letters to the editor, you decide to respond to Margaret Atwood's "Letter to America." Atwood, the award-winning Canadian author of *Surfacing* and *The Handmaid's Tale*, addresses America personally, arguing that what was great about America in previous centuries—its great writers like Twain and Dickinson, its great films, and its history and Constitution—is now being lost through its deteriorating economy and foreign policy. In your response, you acknowledge areas where you agree with Atwood, but then argue that not everything in America's past was as rosy as Atwood portrays. Moreover, even current events show flaws but also continued signs of greatness. America, you conclude, "is still that city upon a hill."

As an assignment in class, you are reading and critiquing an article by Deborah Tannen on how men and women respond differently during class conversations. As you read the article, you have trouble locating the main focus of the article, and then you are disturbed by some unsupported assertions that she makes about typical behavior of men and women. Do men really like to argue and dominate class discussions? Do women always benefit from smaller, more intimate group discussions? You reread the article and make notes in the margin. After discussing your reactions with other readers, you decide to argue that readers should expect clearer organization and fewer unsupported assertions about the gender-based differences between men and women.

> If we think of it, all that a University, or final highest School can do for us, is still but what the first School began doing—teach us to read.
>
> —THOMAS CARLYLE, AUTHOR OF *ON HEROES AND HERO WORSHIP*

> Reading is not a passive process by which we soak up words and information from the page, but an active process by which we predict, sample, and confirm or correct our hypotheses about the written text.
>
> —CONSTANCE WEAVER, AUTHOR OF *READING PROCESS AND PRACTICE*

A T FIRST GLANCE, A CHAPTER ON READING IN A TEXTBOOK ON WRITING MAY CATCH YOU BY SURPRISE. THIS CHAPTER, HOWEVER, IS NOT ABOUT LEARNING YOUR ABC'S OR ABOUT READING *THE CAT IN THE HAT*. IT IS ABOUT LEARNING TO READ TEXTS ACTIVELY AND critically. It is about learning how to summarize and respond to what you read. It is about using reading—along with observing and remembering—as a source for your writing.

At the beginning of this chapter, we need to define two key terms: *texts* and *reading*. Normally, when you think about a text, you may think of a textbook. A text, however, can be any graphic matter—a textbook, an essay, a poem, a newspaper editorial, a photograph, or an advertisement. Some people expand the definition of texts to include any thing or phenomenon in the world. In this widest sense, the layout of a restaurant, the behavior of children on a playground, or clouds in the sky could be "texts" that can be read.

Similarly, the term *reading* has both narrow and broad senses. In a narrow sense, reading is simply understanding words on a page. But reading has a variety of wider meanings as well. Reading can mean analyzing, as when an architect "reads" blueprints and knows how to construct a roof. Reading can also mean interpreting, as when a sailor "reads" the sky and knows that the day will bring winds and rough weather. Reading can also mean examining texts or cultural artifacts and perceiving messages of racism, gender bias, or cultural exploitation. All of these "readings" require close, critical reading of the text and an ability to engage, analyze, probe, respond to, and interpret the text.

In this chapter, you will practice active, critical reading and responding to academic and cultural texts. (In Chapter 6, you will focus specifically on analyzing and responding to images, photographs, advertisements, and other visual texts.) Implied in active, critical reading are both writing about the texts and discussing the texts with other readers. Writing requires reading with your pen in your hand to annotate the texts you read with comments, questions, and observations. You can also write double-entry logs that will help you become an active, critical reader. You may consider reading a solitary activity, but texts appear in social contexts and should be read in social contexts. Active reading, therefore, also involves sharing ideas in small groups, engaging in a class conversation, posting e-mail responses, or writing for an online discussion forum.

This chapter provides guidelines for critical reading, tips for summarizing ideas accurately, and techniques for responding to academic essays, editorials, and other texts you will encounter in college, on the job, and in your community.

Techniques for Analyzing and Responding to Texts

Analysis of texts requires several different techniques to ensure both comprehension and intelligent response. Although the strategies below are listed in a typical order for any reading assignment, remember that the analytical reading process is just like the writing process. You may need to circle back and reread, summarize a second time, research key terms or topics, or double check on the context or author's background as you work.

Techniques for Analyzing and Responding to Texts

Technique	Tips on How to Do It
Using active and responsive reading, writing, and discussing strategies	Preview the author's background and the writing context. Prewrite about your own experiences with the subject. Read initially for information but then reread, make annotations, ask questions, research on the internet, or do a double-entry log. Discuss the text with other readers in class or online.
Summarizing the main ideas or features of the text	A summary should accurately and objectively represent the key ideas. Cite the author and title, accurately represent the main ideas, directly quote key phrases or sentences, and describe the main ideas or features of the text.
Responding to or critiquing the ideas in the text	Responses may *agree or disagree* with the argument in the text; they may *analyze* the argument, organization, or quality of evidence in the text; and/or they may *reflect* on assumptions or implications.
Supporting the response with evidence	Evidence should cite examples of strengths or weaknesses in the argument, cite evidence from other texts or outside reading, and/or use examples from personal experience.
Combining summary and response into a coherent essay	Usually the summary appears first, followed by the reader's response, but be sure to integrate the two parts. Your response should focus quickly on your main idea. Use a transition between the summary and response or integrate the summary and response throughout.

> 66 Reading involves a fair measure of push and shove. You make your mark on a book and it makes its mark on you. Reading is not simply a matter of hanging back and waiting for a piece, or its author, to tell you what the writing has to say. 99
> —DAVID BARTHOLOMAE AND ANTHONY PETROSKY, AUTHORS OF *WAYS OF READING*

As you work on these techniques, don't simply read the text, listen to a class discussion, and write out your critique. Instead, annotate the text by circling key ideas and writing your questions and responses in the margin. Continue reading and discussing your ideas after you have written out a draft. Use the interactive powers of reading, writing, and discussing to help you throughout your writing process.

CRITICAL READING STRATEGIES

Critical reading does not mean that you always criticize something or find fault. *Critical reading simply means questioning what you read.* You may end up liking or praising certain features of a text, but you begin by asking questions, by resisting the text, and by demanding that the text be clear, logical, reliable, thoughtful, and honest.

You begin your critical reading by asking questions about every element in the rhetorical situation. Who is the *author,* and what is his or her background or potential bias? What was the *occasion,* and who was the intended *audience?* Is the writer's *purpose* achieved for that occasion and audience? Did the writer understand and fairly represent other writers' positions on this topic? Did the writer understand the *genre* and use it to achieve the purpose? How did the *cultural context* affect the author and the text? How did the context affect you as a reader?

You continue your critical reading by asking about the writer's claim or argument, the representation of the background information, the organization, the logical use of evidence, and the effectiveness of the style, tone, and word choice. You may find these elements effective or ineffective, but you start your critical reading by reading and then rereading, by probing key passages, by looking for gaps or ideas not included, by discussing the text with other readers, by assessing your position as a reader, and by continually making notes and asking questions.

● **DOUBLE-ENTRY LOG** One of the most effective strategies to promote critical reading is a double-entry log. Draw a line down the middle of a page in your notebook. On the left-hand side, keep a running summary of the main ideas and features that you notice in the text. On the right-hand side, write your questions and reactions.

Author and Title:_____

Summary	Response
Main ideas, key features	Your reactions, comments, and questions

● **CRITICAL REREADING GUIDE** If your double-entry log did not yield some good ideas, try the ideas and suggestions in this rereading guide. First, read the essay in its entirety. Then, let the following set of questions guide your

Summary and Analysis of Text	Critical Response
I. Purpose • Describe the author's overall *purpose* (to inform, explain, explore, evaluate, argue, negotiate, or other purpose). • How does the author/text want to affect or change the reader?	• Is the overall purpose clear or muddled? • Was the actual purpose different from the stated purpose? • How did the text actually affect you?
II. Audience/Reader • Who is the *intended* audience? • What *assumptions* does the author make about the reader's knowledge or beliefs? • From what *point of view* or *context* is the author writing?	• Are you part of the intended audience? • Does the author misjudge the reader's knowledge or beliefs? • Examine your own personal or cultural bias or point of view. How does that hinder you from being a critical reader of this text?
III. Occasion, Genre, Context • What was the *occasion* for this text? • What *genre* is this text? • What is the *cultural* or *historical context* for this text?	• What conversation was taking place on this topic? • Does the author's chosen genre help achieve the purpose for the audience? • What passages show the cultural forces at work on the author and the text?
IV. Thesis and Main Ideas • What key *question* or *problem* does the author/ text address? • What is the author's *thesis*? • What *main ideas* support the thesis? • What are the key passages or key moments in the text?	• Where is the thesis stated? • Are the main ideas related to the thesis? • Where do you agree or disagree? • Does the essay have contradictions or errors in logic? • What ideas or arguments does the essay omit or ignore? • What experience or prior knowledge do you have about the topic? • What are the implications or consequences of the essay's ideas?

Continued

Summary and Analysis of Text	Critical Response
V. Organization and Evidence • Where does the author *preview* the essay's organization? • How does the author *signal* new sections of the essay? • What kinds of *evidence* does the author use (personal experience, descriptions, statistics, interviews, other authorities, analytical reasoning, or other)?	• At what point could you accurately predict the organization of the essay? • At what points were you confused about the organization? • What evidence was most or least effective? • Where did the author rely on assertions rather than on evidence? • Which of your own personal experiences did you recall as you read the essay?
VI. Language and Style • What is the author's *tone* (casual, humorous, ironic, angry, preachy, academic, or other)? • Are *sentences* and *vocabulary* easy, average, or difficult? • What key *words* or *images* recur throughout the text?	• Did the tone support or distract from the author's purpose or meaning? • Did the sentences and vocabulary support or distract from the purpose or meaning? • Did recurring words or images relate to or support the purpose or meaning?

rereading. The questions on the left-hand side will help you summarize and analyze the text; the questions on the right-hand side will start your critical reading and help focus your response.

Remember that not all these questions will be relevant to any given essay or text, but one or two of these questions may suggest a direction or give a *focus* to your overall response. When one of these questions suggests a focus for your response to the essay, *go back to the text, to other texts, and to your experience* to gather *evidence* and *examples* to support your response.

GUIDELINES FOR CLASS DISCUSSION

Class discussions are an important part of the reading, writing, and discussing process. Often, however, class discussions are not productive because not everyone knows the purpose of the discussion or how to discuss openly and fairly. Following is a suggested list of goals for class discussion. Read them carefully. Make notes about any suggestions, revisions, or additions for your class. Your class can then review these goals and agree to adopt, modify, or revise them for your own class discussions for the remainder of the semester.

Discussion Goals

1. To understand and accurately represent the views of the author(s) of an essay. The first discussion goal should be to summarize the author's views fairly.

2. To understand how the views and arguments of individual authors relate to each other. Comparing and contrasting different authors' views help clarify each author's argument.

3. To encourage all members of the class to articulate their understanding of each essay and their response to the ideas in each essay. Class discussions should promote multiple responses rather than focus on a single "right" interpretation or response.

4. To hear class members' responses in an open forum. All points of view must be recognized. *Discussions in class should focus on ideas and arguments, not on individual class members.* Class members may attack ideas but not people.

5. To relate class discussions to the assigned reading/writing task. What effective writing strategies are illustrated in the essay the class is discussing? How can class members use any of these strategies in writing their own essays?

Summarizing and Responding to an Essay

Following is an essay by Barbara Ehrenreich, "Teach Diversity—with a Smile." First, write for five minutes on the suggested Prereading Journal Entry that precedes the essay. The purpose of the journal entry is to allow you to collect your thoughts about the subject *before* you read Ehrenreich's essay. You will be a much more responsive reader if you reflect on your experiences and articulate your opinions *before* you are influenced by the author and her text. If possible, discuss your experiences and opinions with your classmates after you write your entry but before you read the essay. Next, read the introductory note about Barbara Ehrenreich to understand her background and the context for the essay. Finally, practice active reading techniques as you read. Read first for information and enjoyment. Then, reread with a pen in your hand. Either write your comments and questions directly in the text or do a double-entry log, summarizing the main ideas on one side of a piece of paper and writing your questions and reactions on the other.

PREREADING JOURNAL ENTRY

Describe the ethnic groups of people who live in your neighborhood or who attended your previous school. List all the groups you can recall. Then choose one of the following terms and briefly explain what it means: *diversity, multiculturalism,* or *political correctness.* Finally, describe one personal experience that taught you something about diversity or political correctness. What was the experience and how did you react?

PROFESSIONAL WRITING

Teach Diversity—with a Smile

Barbara Ehrenreich

Barbara Ehrenreich was born in Butte, Montana, in 1941 and received a B.A. degree from Reed College and a Ph.D. from Rockefeller University. She has been a health policy adviser and a professor of health sciences, but since 1974, she has spent most of her time writing books and articles about socialist and feminist issues. She has received a Ford Foundation Award and a Guggenheim Fellowship for her writings, which include The Worst Years of Our Lives: Irreverent Notes from a Decade of Greed *(1990),* The Snarling Citizen: Essays *(1995),* Nickel and Dimed: On (Not) Getting by in America *(2001), and* This Land Is Their Land: Reports from a Divided Nation *(2008). Her articles and essays have appeared in* Esquire, Mother Jones, Ms., New Republic, The New York Times Magazine, *and* Time. *The following essay on cultural diversity appeared in* Time *magazine.*

Something had to replace the threat of communism, and at last a workable substitute is at hand. "Multiculturalism," as the new menace is known, has been denounced in the media recently as the new McCarthyism, the 1 new fundamentalism, even the new totalitarianism—take your choice. According to its critics, who include a flock of tenured conservative scholars, multiculturalism aims to toss out what it sees as the Eurocentric bias in education and replace Plato with Ntozake Shange and traditional math with the Yoruba number system. And that's just the beginning. The Jacobins of the multiculturalist movement, who are described derisively as P.C., or politically correct, are said to have launched a campus reign of terror against those who slip and innocently say "freshman" instead of "freshperson," "Indian" instead of "Native American" or, may the Goddess forgive them, "disabled" instead of "differently abled."

So you can see what is at stake here: freedom of speech, freedom of 2 thought, Western civilization and a great many professorial egos. But before we get carried away by the mounting backlash against multiculturalism, we ought to reflect for a moment on the system that the P.C. people aim to replace. I know all about it; in fact it's just about all I do know, since I—along with so many educated white people of my generation—was a victim of monoculturalism.

American history, as it was taught to us, began with Columbus's "dis- 3 covery" of an apparently unnamed, unpeopled America, and moved on to the Pilgrims serving pumpkin pie to a handful of grateful red-skinned folks. College expanded our horizons with courses called Humanities or sometimes Civ, which introduced us to a line of thought that started with Homer, worked its way through Rabelais and reached a poignant climax in the pensées of Matthew Arnold. Graduate students wrote dissertations on what long-dead men had thought of Chaucer's verse or Shakespeare's dramas; foreign languages meant French or German. If there had been high technology in ancient China, kingdoms in black Africa or women anywhere, at any time, doing anything worth noticing, we did not know it, nor did anyone think to tell us.

Our families and neighborhoods reinforced the dogma of mono- 4 culturalism. In our heads, most of us '50s teenagers carried around a social map that was about as useful as the chart that guided Columbus to the "Indies." There were "Negroes," "whites" and "Orientals," the latter meaning Chinese and "Japs." Of religions, only three were known—Protestant, Catholic and Jewish—and not much was known about the last two types. The only remaining human categories were husbands and wives, and that was all the diversity the monocultural world could handle. Gays, lesbians, Buddhists, Muslims, Malaysians, Mormons, etc. were simply off the map.

So I applaud—with one hand, anyway—the multiculturalist goal of 5 preparing us all for a wider world. The other hand is tapping its fingers impatiently, because the critics are right about one thing: when advocates of multiculturalism adopt the haughty stance of political correctness,

...*continued* Teach Diversity—with a Smile, **Barbara Ehrenreich**

they quickly descend to silliness or worse. It's obnoxious, for example, to rely on university administrations to enforce P.C. standards of verbal in-offensiveness. Racist, sexist and homophobic thoughts cannot, alas, be abolished by fiat but only by the time-honored methods of persuasion, education and exposure to the other guy's—or, excuse me, woman's—point of view.

And it's silly to mistake verbal purification for genuine social re- 6 form. Even after all women are "Ms." and all people are "he or she," women will still earn only 65¢ for every dollar earned by men. Minori-ties by any other name, such as "people of color," will still bear a hugely disproportionate burden of poverty and discrimination. Disabilities are not just "different abilities" when there are not enough ramps for wheel-chairs, signers for the deaf or special classes for the "specially" endowed. With all due respect for the new politesse, actions still speak louder than fashionable phrases.

But the worst thing about the P.C. people is that they are such 7 poor advocates for the multicultural cause. No one was ever won over to a broader, more inclusive view of life by being bullied or relentlessly "corrected." Tell a 19-year-old white male that he can't say "girl" when he means "teen-age woman," and he will most likely snicker. This may be the reason why, despite the conservative alarms, P.C.-ness remains a relatively tiny trend. Most campuses have more serious and ancient problems: faculties still top-heavy with white males of the monocul-tural persuasion; fraternities that harass minorities and women; date rape; alcohol abuse; and tuition that excludes all but the upper fringe of the middle class.

So both sides would be well advised to lighten up. The conservatives 8 ought to realize that criticisms of the great books approach to learning do not amount to totalitarianism. And the advocates of multicultural-ism need to regain the sense of humor that enabled their predecessors in the struggle to coin the term P.C. years ago—not in arrogance but in self-mockery.

Beyond that, both sides should realize that the beneficiaries of mul- 9 ticulturalism are not only the "oppressed peoples" on the standard P.C. list (minorities, gays, etc.). The "unenlightened"—the victims of mono-culturalism—are oppressed too, or at least deprived. Our educations, whether at Yale or at State U, were narrow and parochial and left us ill-equipped to navigate a society that truly is multicultural and is becom-ing more so every day. The culture that we studied was, in fact, *one* culture and, from a world perspective, all too limited and ingrown. Di-versity is challenging, but those of us who have seen the alternative know it is also richer, livelier and ultimately more fun.

SUMMARIZING

The purpose of a summary is to give a reader a condensed and objective account of the main ideas and features of a text. Usually, a summary has between one and three paragraphs or one hundred to three hundred words, depending on the length and complexity of the original essay and the intended audience and purpose. Typically, a summary will do the following:

- **Cite the author and title of the text.** In some cases, the place of publication or the context for the essay may also be included.
- **Indicate the main ideas of the text.** Accurately representing the main ideas (while omitting the less important details) is the major goal of a summary.
- **Use direct quotation of key words, phrases, or sentences.** *Quote* the text directly for a few key ideas; *paraphrase* the other important ideas (that is, express the ideas in your own words).
- **Include author tags.** ("According to Ehrenreich" or "as Ehrenreich explains") to remind the reader that you are summarizing the author and the text, not giving your own ideas. ***Note:*** Instead of repeating "Ehrenreich says," choose verbs that more accurately represent the purpose or tone of the original passage: "Ehrenreich argues," "Ehrenreich explains," "Ehrenreich warns," "Ehrenreich asks," "Ehrenreich advises."
- **Avoid summarizing specific examples or data** unless they help illustrate the thesis or main idea of the text.
- **Report the main ideas as objectively as possible.** Represent the author and text as accurately and faithfully as possible. Do not include your reactions; save them for your response.

> 66 Inferences about the writer's intentions appear to be an essential building block—one that readers actively use to construct a meaningful text. 99
>
> —LINDA FLOWER,
> AUTHOR OF "THE CONSTRUCTION OF PURPOSE"

SUMMARY OF "TEACH DIVERSITY— WITH A SMILE"

Following is a summary of Ehrenreich's essay. Do *not* read this summary, however, until you have tried to write your own. After you have made notes and written a draft for your own summary, you will more clearly understand the key features of a summary. ***Note:*** There are many ways to write a good summary. If your summary conveys the main ideas and has the features described previously, it may be just as good as the following example. (Key features of a summary are annotated in the margin.)

In "Teach Diversity—with a Smile," journalist Barbara Ehrenreich explains the current conflict between people who would like to replace our Eurocentric bias in education with a multicultural approach and those critics and conservative scholars who are leading the backlash

Title and author

Main idea paraphrase

Context for essay

against multiculturalism and "political correctness." Writing for [readers of *Time* magazine] Ehrenreich uses her own experience growing up in the 1950s to explain that her narrow education left her a "victim of monoculturalism," ill-equipped to cope with America's growing cultural diversity.

Author tag

Ehrenreich applauds multiculturalism's goal of preparing people for a culturally diverse world, but she is impatient at the "haughty stance" of

Direct quotations

the P.C. people because they mistake "verbal purification for genuine social reform" and they arrogantly bully people and "correct" their

Main idea paraphrase

language. Since actions speak louder than words, Ehrenreich argues, the multiculturalists should focus more on genuine social reform—paying equal salaries to men and women, creating access for people with disabilities, and reducing date rape and alcohol abuse. The solution to the

Author tag
Main idea paraphrase

problem, according to Ehrenreich, is for both sides to "lighten up." The conservatives should recognize that criticizing the great books of Western civilization is not totalitarian, and the multiculturalists should be less arrogant and regain their sense of humor.

> 66 Reading the world always precedes reading the word, and reading the word implies continually reading the world. 99
>
> —PAULO FREIRE
> AUTHOR OF *LITERACY: READING THE WORD AND THE WORLD*

RESPONDING

A response requires your reaction and interpretation. Your own perspective—your experiences, beliefs, and attitudes—will guide your particular response. Your response may be totally different from another reader's response, but that does not necessarily make yours better or worse. Good responses say what you think, but then they *show why* you think so. They show the relationships between your opinions and the text, between the text and your experience, and between this text and other texts.

Depending on its purpose and intended audience, a response to a text can take several directions. Responses may focus on one or more of the following strategies. Consider your purpose and audience or check your assignment to see which type(s) you should emphasize.

TYPES OF RESPONSES

- **Analyzing the effectiveness of the text.** In this case, the response analyzes key features such as the clarity of the main idea, the rhetorical situation, the organization of the argument, the logical reasoning of an argument, the quality of the supporting evidence, and/or the effectiveness of the author's style, tone, and voice.
- **Agreeing and/or disagreeing with the ideas in the text.** Often responders react to the ideas or the argument of the essay. In this case, the responders show why they agree and/or disagree with what the author/text says.
- **Interpreting and reflecting on the text.** The responder explains key passages or examines the underlying assumptions or the implications

of the ideas. Often, the responder reflects on how his or her own experiences, attitudes, and observations relate to the text.

Analyzing, agreeing/disagreeing, and interpreting are all slightly different directions that a response may take. But regardless of the direction, responses must be supported by evidence, examples, facts, and details. A responder cannot simply offer an opinion or agree or disagree. Good responses draw on several kinds of supporting evidence.

KINDS OF EVIDENCE

- **Personal experience.** Responders may use *examples* from their personal experiences to show why they interpreted the text as they did, why they agreed or disagreed, or why they reacted to the ideas as they did.
- **Evidence from the text.** Responders should cite *specific phrases or sentences* from the text to support their explanation of a section, their analysis of the effectiveness of a passage, or their agreement or disagreement with a key point.
- **Evidence from other texts.** If appropriate, responders may bring in ideas and information from other relevant essays, articles, books, or graphic material.

Not all responses use all three kinds of supporting evidence, but all responses *must* have sufficient examples to support the responder's ideas, reactions, and opinions. Responders should not merely state their opinions. They must give evidence to *show* how and why they read the text as they did.

One final—and crucial—point about responses: A response should make a coherent, overall main point. It should not be just a laundry list of reactions, likes, and dislikes. Sometimes the main point is that the text is not convincing because it lacks evidence. Sometimes the overall point is that the text makes an original statement even though it is difficult to read. Perhaps the basic point is that the author/text stimulates the reader to reflect on his or her experience. Every response should focus on a coherent main idea.

RESPONSE TO "TEACH DIVERSITY — WITH A SMILE"

Following is one possible response to Ehrenreich's essay. Before you read this response, however, write out your own reactions. You need to decide what you think before other responses influence your reading. There are, of course, many different but legitimate responses to any given essay. As you read this response, note the marginal annotations indicating the different types of responses and the different kinds of evidence this writer uses.

<table>
<tr><td>

Analyzing effectiveness of text
Responder's main point

</td><td>

What I like best about Barbara Ehrenreich's article is her effective use of personal experience to clarify the issues on both sides of the multiculturalism debate. However, her conclusion, that we should "lighten up" and accept diversity because it's "more fun," weakens her argument by ignoring the social inequalities at the heart of the debate. The issue in this debate, I believe, is not just enjoying diversity, which is easy to do, but changing cultural conditions, which is much more difficult.

</td></tr>
<tr><td>

Evidence from text

Evidence from text

</td><td>

Ehrenreich effectively uses her own experiences—and her common sense—to let us see both the virtues and the excesses of multiculturalism. When she explains that her monocultural education gave her a social map that was "about as useful as the chart that guided Columbus to the 'Indies,'" she helps us understand how vital multicultural studies are in a society that is more like a glass mosaic than a melting pot. Interestingly, even her vocabulary reveals—perhaps unconsciously—her Western bias: *Jacobins, pensées, fiat,* and *politesse* are all words that reveal her Eurocentric education. When Ehrenreich shifts to discussing the P.C. movement, her commonsense approach to the silliness of excessive social correctness ("the other guy's—or, excuse me, woman's—point of view") makes us as readers more willing to accept her compromise position.

</td></tr>
<tr><td>

Reflecting on the text

Personal experience

Evidence from other

</td><td>

My own experience with multiculturalism certainly parallels Ehrenreich's impatience with the "haughty stance" of the P.C. people. Of course, we should avoid racist and sexist terms and use our increased sensitivity to language to reduce discrimination. But my own backlash began several years ago when a friend said I shouldn't use the word *girl.* I said, "You mean, not ever? Not even for a ten-year-old female child?" She replied that the word had been so abused by people referring to a "woman" as a "girl" that the word *girl* now carried too many sexist connotations. Although I understood my friend's point, it seems that *girl* should still be a perfectly good word for a female child under the age of twelve. Which reminds me of a book I saw recently, *The Official Politically Correct Dictionary.* It is loaded with examples of political correctness out of control: Don't say *bald,* say *hair disadvantaged.* Don't use the word *pet,* say *nonhuman companion.* Don't call someone *old,* say that they are *chronologically gifted.*

</td></tr>
<tr><td>

Analyzing effectiveness of text

Responder's main point

</td><td>

Ehrenreich does recommend keeping a sense of humor about the P.C. movement, but the conclusion to her essay weakens her argument. Instead of focusing on her earlier point that "it's silly to mistake verbal purification for genuine social reform," she advises both sides to lighten up and have fun with the diversity around us. Instead, I wanted her to conclude by reinforcing her point that "actions still speak louder than fashionable phrases." Changing the realities of illiteracy, poverty, alcohol abuse, and sexual harassment should be the focus of the multiculturalists. Of course, changing language is crucial to changing the world, but the language revolution has already happened—or at least begun. Ehrenreich's article would be more effective, I believe, if she

</td></tr>
</table>

concluded her essay with a call for both sides to help change cultural conditions rather than with a reference to the silly debate about what to call a teenage woman.

WARMING UP   Journal Exercises

The following topics will help you practice your reading and responding.

1 **Community Service Learning Project.** Go to your agency or organization and collect texts, images, and brochures that advertise the organization or explain its mission. Choose one or two documents and write a summary and response addressed both to your classmates and to the organization itself. Consider the rhetorical context of these documents (author, purpose, audience, occasion, genre, and cultural context) as you explain why they are or are not effective or appropriate and/or how you interpret the assumptions and implications contained in these texts or images. Your goal is to provide constructive suggestions about ways to revise or improve these texts.

2 Study the print by Maurits Escher reproduced here. How many different ways of perceiving this picture can you see? Describe each perspective. How is "reading" this picture similar to reading a printed text? How is it different?

3 **Writing across the Curriculum.** Because previewing material is an important part of active reading, most recent psychology and social science textbooks use previewing or prereading strategies at the beginning

Day and Night by M. C. Escher. © 1997 Cordon Art-Baarn-Holland.
All rights reserved.

of each new chapter. Find one chapter in a textbook that uses these previewing techniques. How does the author preview the material? Does the preview help you understand the material in the chapter?

4 Reading the following paragraph illustrates how our prior experience can combine with our predictions to make meaning. The following passage describes a common procedure in our lives. Read the passage. Can you identify the procedure?

> The procedure is actually quite simple. First, you arrange things into different groups. Of course, one pile may be sufficient depending on how much there is to do. If you have to go somewhere else because of lack of facilities, that is the next step; otherwise you are pretty well set. It is important not to overdo things. That is, it is better to do too few things at once than too many. In the short run this may not seem important, but complications can easily arise. A mistake can be expensive as well. At first, the whole procedure will seem complicated. Soon, however, it will become just another facet of life. It is difficult to foresee any end to the necessity for this task in the immediate future, but then one can never tell. After the procedure is completed, one arranges the materials into different groups again. Then they can be put into their appropriate places. Eventually, they will be used once more, and the whole cycle will then have to be repeated. However, that is part of life.

As you read, record your guesses. What words helped to orient you? Where did you make wrong guesses? Discuss your reactions in class.

5 Reprinted below is a letter written by Margaret Atwood, which appeared in *The Nation*. The editors of *The Nation* had asked several foreign writers and political commentators to "share their reflections" about the debate concerning America's foreign policy. An award-winning Canadian novelist, Margaret Atwood has written many volumes of poetry and short fiction as well as over a dozen novels, including *Surfacing* (1973), *The Handmaid's Tale* (1986), and *Oryx and Crake* (2003). Read her "Letter to America," and then write your own summary and response to her ideas.

LETTER TO AMERICA
Margaret Atwood

Dear America

This is a difficult letter to write, because I'm no longer sure who you are. Some of you may be having the same trouble.

I thought I knew you: We'd become well acquainted over the past fifty-five years. You were the Mickey Mouse and Donald Duck comic books I read in the late 1940s. You were the radio shows—*Jack Benny, Our Miss Brooks.* You were the music I sang and danced to: the Andrews Sisters, Ella Fitzgerald, the Platters, Elvis. You were a ton of fun.

You wrote some of my favorite books. You created Huckleberry Finn, and Hawkeye, and Beth and Jo in *Little Women,* courageous in their different ways. Later, you were my beloved Thoreau, father of environmentalism, witness to individual conscience; and Walt Whitman, singer of the great Republic; and Emily Dickinson, keeper of the private soul. You were Hammett and Chandler, heroic walkers of mean streets; even later, you were the amazing trio, Hemingway, Fitzgerald and Faulkner, who traced the dark labyrinths of your hidden heart. You were Sinclair Lewis and Arthur Miller, who, with their own American idealism, went after the sham in you, because they thought you could do better.

You were Marlon Brando in *On the Waterfront,* you were Humphrey Bogart in *Key Largo,* you were Lillian Gish in *Night of the Hunter.* You stood up for freedom, honesty and justice; you protected the innocent. I believed most of that. I think you did, too. It seemed true at the time.

You put God on the money, though, even then. You had a way of thinking that the things of Caesar were the same as the things of God: That gave you self-confidence. You have always wanted to be a city upon a hill, a light to all nations, and for a while you were. Give me your tired, your poor, you sang, and for a while you meant it.

We've always been close, you and us. History, that old entangler, has twisted us together since the early seventeenth century. Some of us used to be you; some of us want to be you; some of you used to be us. You are not only our neighbors: In many cases—mine, for instance—you are also our blood relations, our colleagues and our personal friends. But although we've had a ringside seat, we've never understood you completely, up here north of the 49th parallel. We're like Romanized Gauls—look like Romans, dress like Romans, but aren't Romans—peering over the wall at the real Romans. What are they doing? Why? What are they doing now? Why is the haruspex eyeballing the sheep's liver? Why is the soothsayer wholesaling the Bewares?

Perhaps that's been my difficulty in writing you this letter. I'm not sure I know what's really going on. Anyway, you have a huge posse of experienced entrail-sifters who do nothing but analyze your every vein and lobe. What can I tell you about yourself that you don't already know?

This might be the reason for my hesitation: embarrassment, brought on by a becoming modesty. But it is more likely to be embarrassment of another sort. When my grandmother—from a New England background—was confronted with an unsavory topic, she would change the subject and gaze out the window. And that is my own inclination: Keep your mouth shut, mind your own business.

But I'll take the plunge, because your business is no longer merely your business. To paraphrase Marley's Ghost, who figured it out too late, mankind is your business. And vice versa: When the Jolly Green Giant goes on the rampage, many lesser plants and animals get trampled underfoot. As for us, you're our biggest trading partner: We know perfectly well that if you go down the plug-hole, we're going with you. We have every reason to wish you well.

I won't go into the reasons why I think your recent Iraqi adventures have been—taking the long view—an ill-advised tactical error. By the time you read this, Baghdad may or may not be a pancake, and many more sheep entrails will have been examined. Let's talk, then, not about what you're doing to other people but about what you're doing to yourselves.

You're gutting the Constitution. Already your home can be entered without your knowledge or permission, you can be snatched away and incarcerated without cause, your mail can be spied on, your private records searched. Why isn't this a recipe for widespread business theft, political intimidation and fraud? I know you've been told that all this is for your own safety and protection, but think about it for a minute. Anyway, when did you get so scared? You didn't used to be easily frightened.

You're running up a record level of debt. Keep spending at this rate and pretty soon you won't be able to afford any big military adventures. Either that or you'll go the way of the USSR: lots of tanks, but no air conditioning. That will make folks very cross. They'll be even crosser when they can't take a shower because your shortsighted bulldozing of environmental protections has dirtied most of the water and dried up the rest. Then things will get hot and dirty indeed.

You're torching the American economy. How soon before the answer to that will be not to produce anything yourselves but to grab stuff other people produce, at gunboat-diplomacy prices? Is the world going to consist of a few mega-rich King Midases, with the rest being serfs, both inside and outside your country? Will the biggest business sector in the United States be the prison system? Let's hope not.

If you proceed much further down the slippery slope, people around the world will stop admiring the good things about you. They'll decide that your city upon the hill is a slum and your democracy is a sham, and therefore you have no business trying to impose your sullied vision on them. They'll think you've abandoned the rule of law. They'll think you've fouled your own nest.

The British used to have a myth about King Arthur. He wasn't dead, but sleeping in a cave, it was said: and in the country's hour of greatest peril, he would return. You too have great spirits of the past you may call upon: men and women of courage, of conscience, of prescience. Summon them now, to stand with you, to inspire you, to defend the best in you. You need them.

Casebook on Responses to Climate Change

The importance of critical reading, interpretation, and response is dramatically illustrated today in our public discussion about climate change. The central scientific document is still the report of the 2007 Intergovernmental Panel on Climate Change. The next IPCC report is due in 2014, but in the meantime, scientific articles on the increase of greenhouse gases, the melting of glaciers, and the changes to animal habitat continue to support earlier IPCC findings. With the Obama administration, the focus has shifted to mitigating the effects of greenhouse gases through alternative energies, cap-and-trade policies, and more efficient houses, factories, and automobiles.

The articles in this casebook begin with a summary of and response to the 2007 IPCC report written by the editor of Environmental Science & Technology magazine. Following that are two articles from Scientific American, "A Climate Repair Manual," by Gary Stix, and "The Rise of Renewable Energy," by Daniel M. Kammen, which briefly explain the effects of climate change and discuss how best to reduce greenhouse gases. The final document, "Take the Campus Carbon Challenge: 50 Things You Can Do" from an Oregon State Web site at http://oregonstate.edu/~johnsonc/50%20 Things .html, typifies the efforts made by schools, colleges, local communities, and state governments to involve citizens in a cooperative effort to use alternative energies, reduce our carbon footprint, and be more efficient in our use of traditional carbon-based energies.

Critical reading and response requires asking questions of any document we read or graphic that we see. For example, does the graphic at the beginning of this chapter, "15 Ways to Make a Wedge," help us think more constructively about the problem? As you read the following articles, consider these questions: Is there still a "debate" about whether climate change is happening or whether it is significantly caused by the activities of human beings? How can we reduce greenhouse gases without further harming the economy? What changes in our personal lives will bring about the best results?

But critical readers must also ask questions about themselves as readers. Are we climate change skeptics or believers? What arguments or evidence are we most likely to believe? Who seems to be an authority—and why? Finally, what media—scientific journals, popular magazines, Web sites, blogs, or videos—seem most convincing for us?

As you read the following articles and documents, write your questions in the margin. What bits of evidence are most or least persuasive? What topics, questions, or arguments are not addressed? Your purpose in reading these articles is not just to confirm your current belief, but to consider how your position is changing—and why.

PROFESSIONAL WRITING

The IPCC Fourth Assessment

Jerald L. Schnoor, Editor
Environmental Science & Technology

Will history show that February 2, 2007, marked the beginning of the end 1 of the fossil-fuel age? That's when the scientific basis of the Intergovernmental Panel on Climate Change's (IPCC's) Fourth Assessment Report (AR4) was unveiled in Paris. It also may be the day when we first took seriously the threat of human-induced global warming, the gravest environmental problem of our time.

Climate Change 2007: The Physical Science Basis AR4 from Working 2 Group 1 is a consensus report written by 150 authors from 100 countries and vetted by 600 reviewers. It states, with 90% certainty, that human activities, especially the burning of fossil fuels, have *caused* global warming during the past 50 years. Predicting a warming for the 21st century of 2.0–4.5 °C, it narrows the range of 1.4–5.8 °C from the Third Assessment Report. The tone of the assessment has become more strident (and certain) with each report:

". . . the observed increase could be largely due to this natural vari- 3 ability; alternatively this variability and other human factors could have offset a still larger human-induced green-house warming."—IPCC First Assessment Report, 1990

"The balance of evidence suggests a discernible human influence on 4 global climate."—IPCC Second Assessment Report, 1995

"There is new and stronger evidence that most of the warming over 5 the last 50 years is attributable to human activities."—IPCC Third Assessment Report, 2001

Despite the fact that these reports are *consensus* documents, the real- 6 ity is still lost on many Americans. The Bush Administration has done an amazingly effective job of creating confusion where little existed. And the press has contributed to the fiasco by "fair and balanced" reporting, that is, by always finding an opposing quotation despite the lack of support for its research content or the questionable credentials of the interviewee.

AR4 tracks 20 climate models from groups all over the world. Unanimous agreement exists among model results that the 21st century will be significantly warmer. Modelers disagree only on exactly how much warmer it will be. Understanding climate sensitivity to increasing CO_2 is still crucial, and the uncertainties are narrowing.

Like a vigilant lawyer, the report lays out multiple lines of evidence 7 as to how we know that humans are causing global warming: satellite corroboration of land surface warming, parallel ocean warming and commensurate sea-level rise, stratospheric cooling, increasing nighttime minimum temperatures, and melting ice shelves and glaciers.

Why is AR4 so important? For the first time, it seeks to define "dan- 8 gerous climate interference". Earth's vulnerabilities include the potential disintegration of Greenland and Antarctic ice sheets, increased storm severity, rapidly rising sea levels, and shutdown of the thermohaline circulation in the North Atlantic. Most researchers estimate that those effects initiate at 2 °C of total warming. Because we have already experienced 0.6 °C of warming and we likely have already loaded an additional ~1.0 °Cof warming into the sluggish climate system, we don't have much leeway before anthropogenic interference becomes dangerous. That is why nations must begin to reduce emissions within the next decade or so.

Drastic measures are needed—an–80% cut in emissions to stabi- 9 lize the atmospheric concentration of CO_2 at 550 ppmv by 2100 (a doubling from preindustrial times). The Kyoto Protocol was designed to achieve a reduction of a few percent, and it will fall short of that target. Eighty percent is a formidable goal, a much greater challenge than sending a man to the moon or rebuilding Europe and Japan after World War II. It is *the* environmental challenge defining our century and future generations.

Actually, I'm optimistic that (finally) we are beginning to accept and 10 respond to the challenge. Bob Dylan sang that you don't need a weatherman to know which way the wind blows and, for the first time, you can feel the winds shifting. Companies in the EU, North America, Japan, and even China are announcing their own emission reduction programs; states are passing legislation to serve as incubators for greenhouse-gas mitigation; and people understand that emitting CO_2 has consequences and that there's a price to pay. The much-debated Stern report from the U.K., *The Economics of Climate Change*, states that price: 5–20% of gross world product (GWP) if we fail to act, compared with 1% of GWP if we respond now. I believe even the laggard U.S. will enact a cap-and-trade program within the next year.

In case you missed the nuance, the release of the IPCC report coincided 11 with Groundhog Day in the U.S., the day when that awkward furry animal wakes from hibernation to predict what the weather will be in the future. Let's hope the U.S. can make the right choice.

A Climate Repair Manual

Gary Stix

Explorers attempted and mostly failed over the centuries to establish *1* a pathway from the Atlantic to the Pacific through the icebound North, a quest often punctuated by starvation and scurvy. Yet within just 40 years, and maybe many fewer, an ascending thermometer will likely mean that the maritime dream of Sir Francis Drake and Captain James Cook will turn into an actual route of commerce that competes with the Panama Canal.

The term "glacial change" has taken on a meaning opposite to its com- *2* mon usage. Yet in reality, Arctic shipping lanes would count as one of the more benign effects of accelerated climate change. The repercussions of melting glaciers, disruptions in the Gulf Stream and record heat waves edge toward the apocalyptic: floods, pestilence, hurricanes, droughts—even itchier cases of poison ivy. Month after month, reports mount of the deleterious effects of rising carbon levels. One recent study chronicled threats to coral and other marine organisms, another a big upswing in major wildfires in the western U.S. that have resulted because of warming.

The debate on global warming is over. Present levels of carbon diox- *3* ide—nearing 400 parts per million (ppm) in the earth's atmosphere—are higher than they have been at any time in the past 650,000 years and could easily surpass 500 ppm by the year 2050 without radical intervention.

The earth requires greenhouse gases, including water vapor, carbon *4* dioxide and methane, to prevent some of the heat from the received solar radiation from escaping back into space, thus keeping the planet hospitable for protozoa, Shetland ponies and Lindsay Lohan. But too much of a good thing—in particular, carbon dioxide from SUVs and local coal-fired utilities—is causing a steady uptick in the thermometer. Almost all of the 20 hottest years on record have occurred since the 1980s.

No one knows exactly what will happen if things are left *5* unchecked—the exact date when a polar ice sheet will complete a phase change from solid to liquid cannot be foreseen with precision. . . . But no climatologist wants to test what will arise if carbon dioxide levels drift much higher than 500 ppm.

A LEAGUE OF RATIONS

Preventing the transformation of the earth's atmosphere from green- *6* house to unconstrained hothouse represents arguably the most imposing scientific and technical challenge that humanity has ever faced. Sustained marshaling of cross-border engineering and political resources over the course of a century or more to check the rise of carbon emissions makes a moon mission or a Manhattan Project appear comparatively straightforward.

Climate change compels a massive restructuring of the world's energy economy. Worries over fossil-fuel supplies reach crisis proportions only when safeguarding the climate is taken into account. Even if oil production peaks soon—a debatable contention given Canada's oil sands, Venezuela's heavy oil and other reserves—coal and its derivatives could tide the earth over for more than a century. But fossil fuels, which account for 80 percent of the world's energy usage, become a liability if a global carbon budget has to be set.   7

Translation of scientific consensus on climate change into a consensus on what should be done about it carries the debate into the type of political minefield that has often undercut attempts at international governance since the League of Nations.[1] The U.S. holds less than 5 percent of the world's population but produces nearly 25 percent of carbon emissions and has played the role of saboteur by failing to ratify the Kyoto Protocol[2] and commit to reducing greenhouse gas emissions to 7 percent below 1990 levels. . . .   8

Kyoto may have been a necessary first step, if only because it lit up the pitted road that lies ahead. But stabilization of carbon emissions will require a more tangible blueprint for nurturing further economic growth while building a decarbonized energy infrastructure. An oil company's "Beyond Petroleum" slogans will not suffice. . . .   9

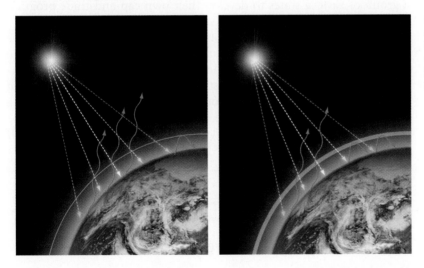

GREENHOUSE EFFECT
A prerequisite for life on earth, the greenhouse effect occurs when infrared radiation (heat) is retained within the atmosphere.

[1] The League of Nations was established after World War 1, but failed in its mission to prevent further conflicts. The U.S. did not join the League, despite the role of President Woodrow Wilson in establishing it.

[2] The Kyoto Protocol was a 1997 international agreement to limit greenhouse gas emissions. The U.S. Senate rejected the agreement by a 95–0 vote.

Perhaps a solar cell breakthrough will usher in the photovoltaic age, al- *10* lowing both a steel plant and a cell phone user to derive all needed watts from a single source. But if that does not happen—and it probably won't—many technologies (biofuels, solar, hydrogen and nuclear) will be required to achieve a low-carbon energy supply. All these approaches are profiled by leading experts in this special issue, as are more radical ideas, such as solar power plants in outer space and fusion generators, which may come into play should today's seers prove myopic 50 years hence.

NO MORE BUSINESS AS USUAL

Planning in 50-or 100-year increments is perhaps an impossible dream. *11* The slim hope for keeping atmospheric carbon below 500 ppm hinges on aggressive programs of energy efficiency instituted by national governments. To go beyond what climate specialists call the "business as usual" scenario, the U.S. must follow Europe and even some of its own state governments in instituting new policies that affix a price on carbon— whether in the form of a tax on emissions or in a cap-and-trade system (emission allowances that are capped in aggregate at a certain level and then traded in open markets). These steps can furnish the breathing space to establish the defense-scale research programs needed to cultivate fossil fuel alternatives. The current federal policy vacuum has prompted a group of eastern states to develop their own cap-and-trade program under the banner of the Regional Greenhouse Gas Initiative.

A steady chorus of skeptics continues to cast doubt on the massive *12* peer-15 reviewed scientific literature that forms the cornerstone for a consensus on global warming. "They call it pollution; we call it life," intones a Competitive Enterprise Institute advertisement on the merits of carbon dioxide. Uncertainties about the extent and pace of warming will undoubtedly persist. But the consequences of inaction could be worse than the feared economic damage that has bred overcaution. If we wait for an ice cap to vanish, it will simply be too late.

PROFESSIONAL WRITING

The Rise of Renewable Energy

Daniel M. Kammen

No plan to substantially reduce greenhouse gas emissions can succeed *1* through increases in energy efficiency alone. Because economic growth continues to boost the demand for energy—more coal for powering new factories, more oil for fueling new cars, more natural gas for heating new homes—carbon emissions will keep climbing despite the introduction of more energy-efficient vehicles, buildings and appliances. To counter the alarming trend of global warming, the U.S. and other countries must make a major commitment to developing renewable energy sources that generate little or no carbon.

Renewable energy technologies were suddenly and briefly fashion- 2 able three decades ago in response to the oil embargoes of the 1970s, but the interest and support were not sustained. In recent years, however, dramatic improvements in the performance and affordability of solar cells, wind turbines and biofuels—ethanol and other fuels derived from plants—have paved the way for mass commercialization. In addition to their environmental benefits, renewable sources promise to enhance America's energy security by reducing the country's reliance on fossil fuels from other nations. What is more, high and wildly fluctuating prices for oil and natural gas have made renewable alternatives more appealing.

We are now in an era where the opportunities for renewable energy 3 are unprecedented, making this the ideal time to advance clean power for decades to come. But the endeavor will require a long-term investment of scientific, economic and political resources. Policymakers and ordinary citizens must demand action and challenge one another to hasten the transition.

LET THE SUN SHINE

Solar cells, also known as photovoltaics, use semiconductor materials to 4 convert sunlight into electric current. They now provide just a tiny slice of the world's electricity: their global generating capacity of 5,000 megawatts (MW) is only 0.15 percent of the total generating capacity from all sources. Yet sunlight could potentially supply 5,000 times as much energy as the world currently consumes. And thanks to technology improvements, cost declines and favorable policies in many states and nations, the annual production of photovoltaics has increased by more than 25 percent a year for the past decade and by a remarkable 45 percent in 2005. The cells manufactured last year added 1,727 MW to worldwide generating capacity, with 833 MW made in Japan, 353 MW in Germany and 153 MW in the U.S.

Solar photovoltaics are particularly easy to use because they can be 5 installed in so many places—on the roofs or walls of homes and office buildings, in vast arrays in the desert, even sewn into clothing to power portable electronic devices. The state of California has joined Japan and Germany in leading a global push for solar installations; the "Million Solar Roof" commitment is intended to create 3,000 MW of new generating capacity in the state by 2018. Studies done by my research group, the Renewable and Appropriate Energy Laboratory at the University of California, Berkeley, show that annual production of solar photovoltaics in the U.S. alone could grow to 10,000 MW in just 20 years if current trends continue.

The biggest challenge will be lowering the price of the photovoltaics, 6 which are now relatively expensive to manufacture. Electricity produced by crystalline cells has a total cost of 20 to 25 cents per kilowatt-hour, compared with four to six cents for coal-fired electricity, five to seven cents for power produced by burning natural gas, and six to nine cents for biomass power plants. (The cost of nuclear power is harder to pin down because experts disagree on which expenses to include in the analysis; the estimated range is two to 12 cents per kilowatt-hour.) Fortunately, the prices of solar cells have fallen consistently over the past decade, largely because of improvements in manufacturing processes. In Japan, where 290 MW of solar generating capacity were added in 2005 and an even larger amount was exported, the cost of photovoltaics has declined 8 percent a year; in California, where 50 MW of solar power were installed in 2005, costs have dropped 5 percent annually.

BLOWING IN THE WIND

Wind power has been growing at a pace rivaling that of the solar indus- 7 try. The worldwide generating capacity of wind turbines has increased more than 25 percent a year, on average, for the past decade, reaching nearly 60,000 MW in 2005. The growth has been nothing short of explosive in Europe—between 1994 and 2005, the installed wind power capacity in European Union nations jumped from 1,700 to 40,000 MW. Germany alone has more than 18,000 MW of capacity thanks to an aggressive construction program. The northern German state of Schleswig-Holstein currently meets one quarter of its annual electricity demand with more than 2,400 wind turbines, and in certain months wind power provides more than half the state's electricity. In addition, Spain has 10,000 MW of wind capacity, Denmark has 3,000 MW, and Great Britain, the Netherlands, Italy and Portugal each have more than 1,000 MW.

In the U.S. the wind power industry has accelerated dramatically in 8 the past five years, with total generating capacity leaping 36 percent to 9,100 MW in 2005. Although wind turbines now produce only 0.5 percent of the nation's electricity, the potential for expansion is enormous, especially in the windy Great Plains states. (North Dakota, for example, has greater wind energy resources than Germany, but only 98 MW of generating capacity is installed there.) If the U.S. constructed enough wind farms to fully tap these resources, the turbines could generate as much as 11 trillion kilowatt-hours of electricity, or nearly three times the total amount produced from all energy sources in the nation last year. The wind industry has developed increasingly large and efficient turbines, each capable of yielding 4 to 6 MW. And in many locations, wind power is the cheapest form of new electricity, with costs ranging from four to seven cents per kilowatt-hour.

The growth of new wind farms in the U.S. has been spurred by a pro- 9 duction tax credit that provides a modest subsidy equivalent to 1.9 cents per kilowatt-hour, enabling wind turbines to compete with coal-fired plants. Unfortunately, Congress has repeatedly threatened to eliminate the tax credit. Instead of instituting a long-term subsidy for wind power, the lawmakers have extended the tax credit on a year-to-year basis, and the continual uncertainty has slowed investment in wind farms. Congress is also threatening to derail a proposed 130-turbine farm off the coast of Massachusetts that would provide 468 MW of generating capacity, enough to power most to Cape Cod, Martha's Vineyard and Nantucket.

The reservations about wind power come partly from utility compa- 10 nies that are reluctant to embrace the new technology and partly from so-called NIMBY-ism. ("NIMBY" is an acronym for Not in My Back-yard.) Although local concerns over how wind turbines will affect land-scape views may have some merit, they must be balanced against the social costs of the alternatives. Because society's energy needs are grow-ing relentlessly, rejecting wind farms often means requiring the construc-tion or expansion of fossil fuel-burning power plants that will have far more devastating environmental effects.

GREEN FUELS

Researchers are also pressing ahead with the development of biofuels that 11 could replace at least a portion of the oil currently consumed by motor ve-hicles. The most common biofuel by far in the U.S. is ethanol, which is typ-ically made from corn and blended with gasoline. The manufacturers of ethanol benefit from a substantial tax credit: with the help of the $2-billion annual subsidy, they sold more than 16 billion liters of ethanol in 2005 (al-most 3 percent of all automobile fuel by volume), and production is ex-pected to rise 50 percent by 2007. Some policymakers have questioned the wisdom of the subsidy, pointing to studies showing that it takes more en-ergy to harvest the corn and refine the ethanol than the fuel can deliver to combustion engines. In a recent analysis, though, my colleagues and I dis-covered that some of these studies did not properly account for the energy content of the by-products manufactured along with the ethanol. When all the inputs and outputs were correctly factored in, we found that ethanol has a positive net energy of almost five megajoules per liter.

We also found, however, that ethanol's impact on greenhouse gas 12 emissions is more ambiguous. Our best estimates indicate that substitut-ing corn-based ethanol for gasoline reduces greenhouse gas emissions by 18 percent, but the analysis is hampered by large uncertainties regarding certain agricultural practices, particularly the environmental costs of fer-tilizers. If we use different assumptions about these practices, the results of switching to ethanol range from a 36 percent drop in emissions to a 29

...continued The Rise of Renewable Energy, **Daniel M. Kammen**

percent increase. Although corn-based ethanol may help the U.S. reduce its reliance on foreign oil, it will probably not do much to slow global warming unless the production of the biofuel becomes cleaner.

But the calculations change substantially when the ethanol is made 13 from cellulosic sources: woody plants such as switch-grass or poplar. Whereas most makers of corn-based ethanol burn fossil fuels to provide the heat for fermentation, the producers of cellulosic ethanol burn lignin—an unfermentable part of the organic material—to heat the plant sugars. Burning lignin does not add any greenhouse gases to the atmosphere, because the emissions are offset by the carbon dioxide absorbed during the growth of the plants used to make the ethanol. As a result, substituting cellulosic ethanol for gasoline can slash greenhouse gas emissions by 90 percent or more.

Another promising biofuel is so-called green diesel. Researchers have 14 produced this fuel by first gasifying biomass—heating organic materials enough that they release hydrogen and carbon monoxide—and then converting these compounds into long-chain hydrocarbons using the Fischer-Tropsch process. (During World War II, German engineers employed these chemical reactions to make synthetic motor fuels out to coal.) The result would be an economically competitive liquid fuel for motor vehicles that would add virtually no greenhouse gases to the atmosphere. Oil giant Royal Dutch/Shell is currently investigating the technology.

THE NEED FOR R&D

Each of these renewable sources is now at or near a tipping point, the cru- 15 cial stage when investment and innovation, as well as market access, could enable these attractive but generally marginal providers to become major contributors to regional and global energy supplies. At the same time, aggressive policies designed to open markets for renewables are taking hold at city, state and federal levels around the world. Governments have adopted these policies for a wide variety of reasons: to promote market diversity or energy security, to bolster industries and jobs, and to protect the environment on both the local and global scales. In the U.S. more than 20 states have adopted standards setting a minimum for the fraction of electricity that must be supplied with renewable sources. Germany plans to generate 20 percent of its electricity from renewables by 2020, and Sweden intends to give up fossil fuels entirely.

But perhaps the most important step toward creating a sustainable 16 energy economy is to institute market-bases schemes to make the prices of carbon fuels reflect their social cost. The use of coal, oil and natural gas imposes a huge collective toll on society, in the form of health care expenditures for ailments caused by air pollution, military spending to secure oil supplies, environmental damage from mining operations, and the potentially devastating economic impacts of global warming. A fee on carbon emissions would provide a simple, logical and transparent method to reward renewable, clean energy sources over those that harm the economy and the environment. The tax revenues could pay for some of the social costs of carbon emissions, and a portion could be designated to compensate low-income families who spend a larger share of their income on energy. Furthermore, the carbon fee could be combined with a cap-and-trade program that would set limits on carbon emissions but also allow the cleanest energy suppliers to sell permits to their dirtier competitors. The federal government has used such programs with great success to curb other pollutants, and several northeastern states are already experimenting with greenhouse gas emissions trading.

Best of all, these steps would give energy companies an enormous financial incentive to advance the development and commercialization of renewable energy sources. In essence, the U.S. has the opportunity to foster an entirely new industry. The threat of climate change can be a rallying cry for a clean-technology revolution that would strengthen the country's manufacturing base, create thousands of jobs and alleviate our international trade deficits—instead of importing foreign oil, we can export high-efficiency vehicles, appliances, wind turbines and photovoltaics. This transformation can turn the nations' energy sector into something that was once deemed impossible: a vibrant, environmentally sustainable engine of growth. *17*

PROFESSIONAL WRITING

50 Things You Can Do[1]

Take the Campus Carbon Challenge. Pledge to try 5 carbon-reducing actions in February. Choose from our list of 50 or make up one of your own. *1*

[1]This excerpt from the Oregon State University web page shows only the first nine suggestions.

...*continued* The Rise of Renewable Energy, **Daniel M. Kammen**

On the Go

1. Carpool instead of going it alone (at least 1 day a week)

   Burning just one gallon of gasoline produces about 20 pounds of carbon emissions. Find out more about carbon emissions from Terrapass, then check out local Ride Shares to find out if someone is going your way.

2. Take the bus instead of driving (at least 1 day a week)

   According to Public Transportation, the typical public transit rider uses half the gas consumed by car commuters. On average, public transportation saves 4 million gallons of gas in the United States every day. That is the equivalent of 300,000 fill-ups! Check out the Corvallis bus schedule, then sit back, relax, and enjoy the ride for free with a valid Oregon State University ID.

3. Bike instead of driving (at least 1 day a week)

   Biking is 50 times more energy efficient than driving. If you are new to cycling, Commuting by Bike has a Biking 101 class to get you started, and Corvallis has extensive bike paths to get you where you need to go. If you don't have a bike yet, there are usually cycles for sale at OSU's Wednesday Salvage Sale or on Craigslist.

4. Work or study from home instead of commuting (at least 1 day a week)

   According to a recent study, 3.9 million people in the U.S. work from home at least one day a week. By avoiding the average 22-mile commute to the office, and taking into account the increased use of home power, telecommuting saves about 840 million gallons of gas, which is equivalent to taking two million cars off the road for a year.

5 Consolidate errands instead of making multiple car trips (at least twice this month)

   Fewer trips means fewer emissions. Visit Sustainable Choices to find out more. Then call a friend to see if he or she needs to run similar errands, toss your reusable bags in the car, and hit the road.

6. Inflate your tires (check your air pressure of your tires to make sure they are properly inflated)

   According to Click and Clack, "The softer your tires are, the greater the friction between the road and the rubber, and the harder your engine will have to work to move the car." Inflating your tires to recommended pressure levels can increase gas mileage by about 1–4%. Good for your wallet and the environment.

7. Lighten your load (every 100 lbs. in your car increases gas consumption by 1–2%)

Every extra 100 pounds in your car increases gas consumption by 1–2%. So clean out your trunk, then find out more about getting better fuel economy from Click and Clack.

8. Slow down (go the speed limit and get better gas millage)

According to Click and Clack, for every ten miles per hour you floor it, you lose as much as 15% in fuel economy.

At Home

9. Light up with compact fluorescents (change at least half the light bulbs in your house)

Compact fluorescents (CFLs) use one quarter of the electricity and last years longer than incandescent bulbs. According to Energy Star, if every American home replaced just one light bulb with a CFL bulb, "we would save enough energy to light more than 3 million homes for a year, more than $600 million in annual energy costs, and prevent greenhouse gases equivalent to the emissions of more than 800,000 cars." When your CFLs finally do burn out, remember to recycle them because they contain mercury.

vo·cab·u·lar·y

In your journal, write the meanings of the italicized words in the following phrases.

"The IPCC Fourth Assessment"

- *vetted* by 600 reviewers (**2**)
- Has become more *strident* (**2**)
- Due to this natural *variability* (**2**)
- Contributed to the *fiasco* (**3**)
- Satellite *corroboration* of land and surface warming (**5**)
- Shutdown of the *thermocline* circulation (**6**)
- *anthropogenic* interference (**6**)
- Greenhouse gas *mitigation* (**8**)

"A Climate Repair Manual"

- *benign* effects (**2**)
- *deleterious* effects (**2**)
- become a *liability* (**7**)
- role of *saboteur* (**8**)
- decarbonized energy *infrastructure* (**9**)
- should today's seers prove *myopic* (**10**)
- are capped in *aggregate* (**11**)

"The Rise of Renewable Energy"

- the oil *embargoes* (**2**)
- wisdom of the *subsidy* (**11**)
- is more *ambiguous* (**12**)
- heat for *fermentation* (**13**)
- *sustainable* energy economy (**16**)

"Take the Campus Carbon Challenge"

- that is the *equivalent* (**2**)
- *telecommuting* saves (**4**)
- longer than *incandescent* bulbs (**9**)

QUESTIONS FOR WRITING AND DISCUSSION

1 Analyze Jerald Schnoor's article about the IPCC Fourth Assessment Report for its summary and response techniques. Where does he cite the original IPCC study? Where does he give the main ideas of the IPCC report? Where does he use paraphrase and direct quotation from the IPCC report? Where does he give his response to the report? What is the thesis or main point of his response?

2 In "A Climate Repair Manual," Gary Stix states that "the debate on global warming is over." Explain why you agree or disagree with this statement. What facts, issues, or arguments might you use to support your response?

3 Of the alternative energies that Daniel Kammen cites in "The Rise of Renewable Energy," which do you have some personal knowledge about? Are solar cells, wind turbines, or green fuels used in your community or state? Which are developing and growing the fastest?

4 Analyze the full-page visual, "15 Ways to Make a Wedge" that appears at the beginning of this chapter. Read the caption under the graphic. Which of these wedges or reductions of carbon emissions does Kammen discuss? How would the cap-and-trade proposals or the "market-based schemes" that Kammen discusses in paragraph 16 help promote the carbon savings depicted in these wedges? What makes this graphic effective (or ineffective) at showing workable solutions for reducing carbon emissions?

5 Use your library's databases or reliable Web sites, such as the Environmental Protection Agency (http://www.epa.gov) or RealClimate (http://www.realclimate.org/), to research the latest information about climate change, its recent effects, or new ways to reduce carbon emissions. How has the conversation or the focus of the conversation changed since the last IPCC report? Write your own summary and response to one of the articles that you discover in your research.

Reading and Writing Processes

ASSIGNMENT FOR READING/WRITING

Write an essay that summarizes and then responds to one or more essays, articles, or advertisements. As you review your particular assignment, make sure you understand what text or texts you should respond to, how long your summary and response should be, and what type(s) of responses you should focus on.

Your purpose for this assignment is to represent the text(s) accurately and faithfully in your summary and to explain and support your response. Taken together, your summary and response should be a coherent essay, with a main idea and connections between summary and response. Assume that your audience is other members of the class, including the instructor, with whom you are sharing your reading.

Your instructor's assignment should indicate which of the possible audiences and genres suggested below you should use.

Audience	Possible Genres for Reading/Writing Assignments
Personal Audience	Class or laboratory notes, journal entry, blog, scrapbook, multigenre document
Academic Audience	Academic summary, summary and response, synopsis, critique, review, journal entry, forum entry on class site, multigenre document
Public Audience	Column, editorial, letter to the editor, article in a magazine, newspaper, online site, newsletter, or multigenre document

---

CHOOSING A SUBJECT

Suggested processes, activities, and strategies for reading and writing will be illustrated in response to the following essay by Dudley Erskine Devlin.

PROFESSIONAL WRITING

Teaching Tolerance in America

Dudley Erskine Devlin

Dudley Erskine Devlin was born in Syracuse, New York, and attended the University of Kansas. Originally trained as a scientist, he currently teaches English at Colorado State University and writes columns and editorials on contemporary problems. The targets for his editorials are often the large and complicated issues of the day, such as education, violence, health care, and the media. "My first goal as a writer," Devlin said in a recent interview, "is to provoke response. If just one reader is angry enough to write me a letter of response, then my time is not wasted." As you read Devlin's essay, note places where you agree or disagree with his ideas. How would you respond to Devlin's argument?

In the past few years, American high schools have struggled with a variety of forces that have threatened to tear them apart: reduced funding, increased class sizes, fewer music and art classes, violence in schools, and racial and class divisions among students. Although educational reform in America tends to focus on curriculum issues, class sizes, and security issues, one lesson seems increasingly hard to teach—helping students appreciate and welcome differences in culture, racial heritage, and personal identity. Despite the emphasis on increasing respect and tolerance in schools, teenagers still bring the social and racial divisions found in society at large back into the halls of high schools across America. Social cliques based on race, gender, athletic prowess, income, social class, dress, and even body piercings still define the culture at most schools. 1

America, we fervently believe, is still the land of opportunity, the land where we can be judged on our merits and achievements, not on stereotypes or preconceptions or prejudices. Yet the social clique is based on the notion that one group imagines it is superior to another and thus can ridicule, taunt, or even bully another group. And nowhere does the social clique have more devastating and long-lasting effects than in our high schools. 2

High school cliques, which reproduce the class divisions found in society, originate from three distinct sources: racial differences, gender differences, and social differences. Racial problems in high schools need no explanation. Every high school in America has racial problems that have led to continuing conflicts. A reporter visiting one typical suburban high school found that each ethnic group—Hispanics, whites, blacks, Asians—had a place where they gathered between classes and after school. Although individual members in an ethnic group gain security from being in the group, they make outsiders—people who do not belong to their racial group—feel insecure and often threatened. As one student put it, "The problem is that some people think they are better than others. So they make disparaging remarks about one another, creating tension and conflict in the school." 3

The ongoing gender problems in America's high schools are mentioned—if at all—on the back pages of newspapers, as if the sexist treatment of girls is a normal and inconsequential behavior. Nan Stein, author of *Classrooms and Courtrooms: Facing Sexual Harassment in K-12 Schools,* 4 recounts numerous incidents where school administrations overlook student-on-student sexual harassment. In a recent interview with *Harvard Educational Letter,* Stein recalled a case in which "15 boys harassed this one girl verbally, mooing like cows whenever they saw her and talking about the size of her breasts. They did this outside of school, in school, on the way to school. Other kids heard it and saw it. Teachers and custodians told the administrator, who kept saying, 'It's not a big deal.'" When the case involves males of status, the chances are even more likely that school administrators will look the other way. Ignoring the flagrant behavior of the popular students happens at every school in America—despite a recent Supreme Court ruling that now holds schools liable in such cases of sexual harassment.

Finally, the differences in social classes among the various cliques— 5 most notably between the jocks and the geeks, between the powerful and the weak—is a continuing source of conflict. As one student put it, "If you're not a jock in this school . . . you're not part of it." The outsiders, geeks, and gays are ridiculed by everyone and harassed, bullied, and picked on by the jocks and by other members of the elite social class. Bullying is sometimes connected to cliques and gangs, and it affects both boys and girls. Allan Beane, author of *The Bully-Free Classroom,* writes that he has "heard from so many adults who are still very angry and hurt from when they were mistreated in school." Frequently school bullies are boys—and the ridicule and intimidation they inflict has played a role, Beane says, in "almost all of the school shootings that have outraged the nation in the past two years." Hara Marano, an editor for *Psychology Today,* points out that girls, too, engage in physical aggression even though they are "more apt to be masters of indirect bullying, spreading lies and rumors and destroying reputations." The result is that about one in seven schoolchildren is either a bully or a victim of bullying.

How do we solve these problems? First we need to eliminate those 6 liberal solutions that simply aren't working—thus releasing funds for more effective deterrents. Many schools, for example, have introduced diversity issues into English and social studies classes, and some schools even have sensitivity training classes that seek to "instill respect for others and training students how to speak up when they hear insulting or intimidating comments." However, most students react negatively to such classes. In a recent report, one student said that he really didn't like having notions of tolerance and acceptance drilled into him: "It's like shoving something down our throats." . . .

There are, however, some real and sensible solutions that could solve 7 the intolerance problem in our high schools. For years, parents and educators have recommended that schools adopt uniforms, so that every student wears the same clothing to school. Already, many schools ban specific colors or types of hats, shirts, or jewelry. We need uniforms not just to eliminate gangs, but to reduce the visual cues that enable one group to maintain social power. And we need to enforce those dress rules

---

...continued Teaching Tolerance in America, **Dudley Erskine Devlin**

---

with a zero tolerance policy. Second, schools need to make single-sex classes a standard practice. Not only do boys and girls learn better in single-sex environments, but the segregated classes will reduce the differences and thus reduce conflicts. Finally, schools need to improve security—both to protect students from the outside and to protect students from each other. Schools need more video cameras, drug sniffing dogs, and spot checks of cars and lockers. Governor Jesse Ventura had an excellent idea when he suggested that every school needs to have teachers with paramilitary and anti-riot training. Last but not least, students need to wear picture ID tags hung on ribbons around their necks—so videotapes can easily identify any troublemakers.

The class system that is created and perpetuated by student cliques 8 is the most important problem in our high schools today. In any high school on any day, we see the strong picking on the weak, the bullies intimidating the outcasts, and the jocks and the social elite dominating everyone else. Only when we apply our zero tolerance policy to the dress code, the gender makeup of our classes, and the security of our schools will students learn how to treat all people and social classes with acceptance and tolerance.

COLLECTING

Once a text has been selected or assigned for your summary and response, try the following reading, writing, and discussing activities.

PREREADING JOURNAL ENTRY

In your journal, write what you already know about the subject of the essay. The following questions will help you to recall your prior experiences and think about your own opinions before you read the essay. The purpose of this entry is to think about your own experiences and opinions *before* you are influenced by the arguments of the essay.

- What classes or programs at your high school were designed to improve tolerance of social differences among students? Did they increase or decrease tolerance for social, sexual, or racial difference among students at your school?
- Were cliques a big problem at your school? Did your high school have bullies who picked on other students? Were the jocks or the upper-class students given preferential treatment?

> • What measures to increase security, reduce potential violence, and increase tolerance has your high school taken in the last few years? Were these changes necessary? Did they improve the quality of your education? Did they make you feel more secure at school?

● **TEXT ANNOTATION**   Most experts on reading and writing agree that you will learn more and remember more if you actually write out your comments, questions, and reactions in the margins of the text you are reading. Writing your responses helps you begin a conversation with the text. Reproduced below are one reader's marginal responses to paragraph 7 of Devlin's essay.

Second, schools need to make single-sex classes a standard practice. Not only do

boys and girls learn better in single-sex environments, but the segregated classes

will reduce the differences and thus reduce conflicts. Finally, schools need to

improve security—both to protect students from the outside and to protect

students from each other. Schools need more video cameras, drug sniffing dogs,

and spot checks of cars and lockers. Governor Jesse Ventura had an excellent idea

when he suggested that every school needs to have teachers with paramilitary and

anti-riot training. Last but not least, students need to wear picture ID tags hung

on ribbons around their necks—so videotapes can easily identify any trouble-

makers.

Why not have them optional for some subjects?

In the real world men and women work together, so why not start now?

A few cameras will provide security, but spot checks invade our privacy.

What? Schools are not wrestling arenas and we don't have riots.

Students should not be treated like jail inmates!

● **READING LOG**   A reading log, like text annotation, encourages you to interact with the author/text and write your comments and questions as you read. While text annotation helps you identify specific places in the text for commentary, a reading log encourages you to write out longer, more thoughtful responses. In a reading log, you can keep a record of your thoughts *while you read and reread* the text. Often, reading-log entries help you focus on a key idea to develop later in your response.

Below is one reader's response to Devlin's ideas about single-sex classes and bullying.

I attended a private elementary school and junior high where a school uniform was required and some of the classes were single-sex. Personally, I can say that the uniform did not make a bit of difference where bullying was an issue. Kids still made fun of other kids no matter what they were wearing. The real reason that kids make fun of others is because of social differences and because they themselves do not want to be picked on, so they deflect the attention onto others.

It is true that bullying is carried on with people throughout life, which is why there should be no tolerance at all for teasing. For example, I was talking with a very good friend of mine who told me that he is still haunted by memories of when children would call him a "fag" on the playground. This has affected him for a long time, and he is still fearful of admitting his homosexuality because he feels as if he is letting the bullies win and proving that they were right.

SHAPING

Summaries and responses have several possible shapes, depending on the writer's purpose and intended audience. Keep in mind, however, that in a summary/response essay or critique, *the summary and the response should be unified by the writer's overall response.* The summary and the response may be organized or drafted separately, but they are still parts of one essay, focused on the writer's most important or overall response.

SUMMARY SHAPING

Summaries should convey the main ideas, the essential argument, or the key features of a text. The purpose should be to represent the author's/text's ideas as accurately and as faithfully as possible. Summaries rely on description, paraphrase, and direct quotation. Below are definitions and examples for each of these terms.

● **DESCRIPTION**   The summary should *describe* the main features of an essay, including the author and title, the context or place of publication of the essay (if appropriate), the essay's thesis or main argument, and any key text features, such as sections, chapters, or important graphic material.

In the article "Teaching Tolerance in America," Dudley Erskine Devlin reports some disturbing issues concerning America's high schools. Devlin states that intimidation, through dress, social cliques, gender, and race, is causing tension and danger in high schools today. According to Devlin, sexual harassment is allowed and condoned, and in some cases jocks bully geeks and racial and social groups intimidate one another. As a solution, Devlin suggests that schools enforce strict, zero-tolerance dress codes, segregate the sexes in classes, increase security through surveillance cameras and drug-sniffing dogs, and require students to wear photo IDs.

● **PARAPHRASE**   A paraphrase restates a passage or text in different words. The purpose of a paraphrase is to recast the author's/text's words in your own language. A good paraphrase retains the original meaning without plagiarizing from the original text.

ORIGINAL: High school cliques, which reproduce the class divisions found in society, originate from three distinct sources: racial differences, gender differences, and social differences.

PARAPHRASE: Peer groups in high school mirror society's class distinctions, which stem from differences in race, gender, and social status.

PLAGIARISM: Peer groups in high school *reproduce the class divisions found in society* and come *from three distinct sources: race, gender, and social differences.* [This is plagiarism because the writer uses exact phrases (see italics) from the original without using quotation marks.]

● **DIRECT QUOTATION**   Often, summaries directly quote a few key phrases or sentences from the source. *Remember: Any words or phrases within the quotation marks must be accurate, word-for-word transcriptions of the original.* Guidelines for direct quotation and examples are as follows. Use direct quotations sparingly to convey the key points in the essay:

> Devlin focuses on what he believes is the school system's largest problem today, the issue of "helping students appreciate and welcome differences in culture, racial heritage, and personal identity."

Use direct quotations when the author's phrasing is more memorable, more concise, or more accurate than your paraphrase might be:

> Devlin claims that teenagers "still bring the social and racial divisions found in society at large back into the halls of high schools across America."

Use direct quotations for key words or phrases that indicate the author's attitude, tone, or stance:

> According to Devlin, we should "eliminate those liberal solutions that simply aren't working" in order to fund his solutions.

Don't quote long sentences. Condense the original sentence to the most important phrases. Use just a short phrase from a sentence or use an ellipsis (three spaced points . . .) to indicate words that you have omitted.

ORIGINAL: Although educational reform in America tends to focus on curriculum issues, class sizes, and security issues, one lesson seems increasingly hard to teach—helping students appreciate and welcome differences in culture, racial heritage, and personal identity.

CONDENSED QUOTATION: Educational reform, according to Devlin, should focus less on curriculum issues and class sizes and more on helping students "appreciate . . . differences in culture, racial heritage, and personal identity."

● **AVOIDING PLAGIARISM**   As you work with your sources, paraphrasing key ideas and quoting key phrases or sentences, keep in mind that in order to avoid plagiarizing, you need to document any ideas, facts, statistics, or actual language you use in your text and in a Works Cited or References page. *Plagiarism* is knowingly and deliberately using the language, ideas, or visual materials of another person or source without acknowledging that person or source. Use the following guidelines to avoid plagiarism.

- Do not use language, ideas, or graphics from any essay, text, or visual image that you find online, in the library, or from commercial sources without acknowledging the source.
- Do not use language, ideas, or visual images from any other student's essay without acknowledging the source.

Students who deliberately plagiarize typically fail the course and face disciplinary action by the university.

Sometimes, however, students plagiarize out of carelessness or inadequately citing words, specific languages, ideas, or visual images. You can avoid this inadvertent plagiarism by learning how to quote accurately from your sources, how to paraphrase using your own words, and how to cite your sources accurately. In this chapter, you will learn how to quote accurately, to paraphrase without plagiarizing, and to use author tags to indicate your sources. In addition, Chapter 7, "Investigating," and Chapter 13, "Writing a Research Paper," have examples illustrating how to do in-text citation and how to do a Works Cited page.

The best way to avoid inadvertent plagiarism is to ask your instructor how to document a source you are using. Your instructor will help you with conventions of direct quotation, paraphrasing, and in-text reference or citation.

SAMPLE SUMMARIES

Following are summaries of Devlin's essay written by two different readers. Notice that while both convey the main ideas of the essay by using description, paraphrase, and direct quotation, they are not identical. Check each summary to see how well it meets these guidelines:

- Cite the author and title of the text.
- Indicate the main ideas of the text.
- Use direct quotation of key words, phrases, or sentences.

- Include author tags.
- Do not summarize most examples or data.
- Be as accurate, fair, and objective as possible.

Summary 1

Dudley Erskine Devlin's essay "Teaching Tolerance in America" addresses several hot topics concerning the American public school system. Devlin focuses on what he believes is the school system's largest problem today, the issue of "helping students appreciate and welcome differences in culture, racial heritage, and personal identity." According to Devlin, the root of the problem lies within the social clique, particularly the social cliques found inside the halls of your local high school. According to Devlin, these cliques originate from three different sources: social, racial, and gender differences. Devlin suggests that we solve the problems these cliques create by eliminating "those liberal solutions that simply aren't working—thus releasing funds for more effective deterrents." Devlin's solutions to eradicate the intolerance are to impose dress codes or uniforms, to create single-sex classrooms, and to markedly increase security at every high school.

Summary 2

The idea of social reform in education has been a pressing issue given the increase in youth violence in high schools across America. In Dudley Erskine Devlin's article "Teaching Tolerance in America," he outlines some of the problems in schools caused by members of cliques and bullies who feed on the "racial differences, gender differences, and social differences" found in society at large. Devlin's argument then moves on to attack the "liberal solutions" (such as introducing diversity issues in classes) and proposes to replace them with "more effective deterrents" such as instituting single-sex classes, school uniforms, picture IDs, and heightened security measures. This zero-tolerance policy, Devlin believes, will teach students how to accept diversity and "appreciate and welcome differences in culture, racial heritage, and personal identity."

RESPONSE SHAPING

Strategies for organizing a response depend on the purpose of the response. Typically, responses include one or more of the following three purposes:

- Analyzing the effectiveness of the text.
- Agreeing and/or disagreeing with the ideas in the text.
- Interpreting and reflecting on the text.

As the following explanations illustrate, each of these types of responses requires supporting evidence from the text, from other texts, and/or from the writer's own experience.

● **ANALYZING**   Analysis requires dividing a whole into its parts in order to better understand the whole. In order to analyze a text for its effectiveness, start by examining key parts or features of the text, such as the purpose, the intended audience, the thesis and main ideas, the organization and evidence, and the language and style. Notice how the following paragraph analyzes Devlin's illogical argument.

> Devlin's essay has some clear problems with the logic of his argument. The title of his essay is "Teaching Tolerance in America," but his solutions contradict his stated purpose. Devlin's proposal to tighten security in our high schools is not going to teach tolerance in high schools across America. As a teenager in a post-Columbine era, I can tell you that ID card checks, patrolling security officers, and hall monitors do not create an atmosphere conducive to teaching tolerance. Students who are treated like prisoners in a maximum security ward do not feel increased warm wishes to faculty and administrators nor are they more likely to tolerate differences in their classmates. Being watched like a hawk by a hall monitor does nothing to make a person more socially outgoing or more tolerant of difference. These security measures will increase fear during the school hours and not encourage tolerance once students leave the school grounds. In short, Devlin's solutions do not, in fact, solve the problems with tolerance created by racial, gender, or social differences.

● **AGREEING/DISAGREEING**   Often, a response to a text focuses on agreeing and/or disagreeing with its major ideas. Responses may agree completely, disagree completely, or agree with some points but disagree with others. Responses that agree with some ideas but disagree with others are often more effective because they show that the responder sees both strengths and weaknesses in an argument. In the following paragraphs, notice how the responder agrees and disagrees and then supports each judgment with evidence.

> About Devlin's recommendation that schools can "reduce conflicts" and teach tolerance by creating single-sex classrooms, I have mixed feelings. From my own personal experience, I agree that single-sex classes can have benefits. Perhaps I am biased, but attending an all-girls high school was very beneficial for me and many of my classmates. Although I have always been a very outgoing individual, I watched many of my friends grow from timid, shy freshmen to independent, strong women. Furthermore, I was never sexually harassed by a classmate, nor did I hear of any of the kinds of harassment Devlin mentions. On the other hand, however, I must disagree with Devlin that single-sex

classes are a long-term solution. In the real world, women and men constantly interact, so they need to learn how to positively interact as girls and boys in school. Students need to be comfortable and learn to work with the opposite sex in preparation for college and the workplace. Although my high school gave me academic confidence, it did not really prepare me for the diverse world I met once I went to college. Single-sex classrooms may just postpone learning about tolerance and difference rather than actually teaching it.

● **INTERPRETING AND REFLECTING**   Many responses contain interpretations of passages that might be read from different points of view or reflections on the assumptions or implications of an idea. An interpretation says, "Here is what the text says, but let me explain what it means, what assumptions the argument carries, or what the implications might be." Here is a paragraph from an interpretive response to Devlin's essay.

If we stop a moment and reflect on the purpose of schools, we realize that schools should be a place where learning and growth can take place. All of Devlin's solutions, however, are designed to increase security and control rather than actually teach tolerance. Perhaps Devlin has modeled his "final solution" on prisons, where students as inmates would have no rights, no privacy, no room to express either tolerance or hatred. Rather than place students in a maximum security prison, we should return to the more liberal approach of teaching tolerance and understanding—the very solution that Devlin initially rejects. While the simple method of teaching about cultural, social, and ethnic differences does not guarantee a conflict-free school environment, it does ensure that students have the opportunity to embrace rather than just accept differences. The forced tolerance that Devlin recommends through dress codes and maximum security measures ultimately discourages students from using their schools to actively examine and freely embrace the differences among their peers.

OUTLINES FOR SUMMARY/ RESPONSE ESSAYS

Three common outlines for summary/response essays follow. Select or modify one of these outlines to fit your audience, purpose, and kind of response. Typically, a summary/response takes the following form

I. Introduction to text(s)

II. Summary of text(s)

   III. Response(s)
      A. Point 1
      B. Point 2
      C. Point 3, etc.
  IV. Conclusion

A second kind of outline focuses initially on key ideas or issues and then examines the text or texts for their contribution to these key ideas. This outline begins with the issues, then summarizes the text(s), and then moves to the reader's responses

    I. Introduction to key issues
   II. Summary of relevant text(s)
  III. Response(s)
      A. Point 1
      B. Point 2
      C. Point 3, etc.
  IV. Conclusion

A third outline integrates the summary and the response. It begins by introducing the issue and/or the text, gives a brief overall idea of the text, but then summarizes and responds point by point.

    I. Introduction to issues and/or text(s)
   II. Summary of text's Point 1/response to Point 1
  III. Summary of text's Point 2/response to Point 2
  IV. Summary of text's Point 3/response to Point 3, etc.
   V. Conclusion

DRAFTING

If you have been reading actively, you have been writing throughout the reading/ writing/discussing process. At some point, however, you will gather your best ideas, have a rough direction or outline in mind, and begin writing a draft. Some writers like to have their examples and evidence ready when they begin drafting. Many writers have outlines in their heads or on paper. Perhaps you like to put your rough outline on the computer and then just expand each section as you write. Finally, most writers like to skim the text and *reread their notes* immediately before they start their drafts, just to make sure everything is fresh in their minds.

Once you start drafting, keep interruptions to a minimum. Because focus and concentration are important to good writing, try to keep writing as long as possible. If you come to a spot where you need an example that you don't have at your fingertips, just put in parentheses—(put the example about cosmetics and animal abuse here)—and keep on writing. Concentrate on making all your separate responses add up to a focused, overall response.

REVISING

Revision means, literally, *reseeing*. Revising requires rereading the text and rewriting your summary and response. While revision begins as you read and reread the text, it continues until—and sometimes after—you turn in a paper or send it to its intended audience.

A major step in your revision is receiving responses from peer readers and deciding on a revision plan, based on the feedback. Use the following guidelines as you read your peers' papers and respond to their advice.

GUIDELINES FOR REVISION

- **Review the purpose and audience for your assignment.** Is your draft addressed to the appropriate audience? Does it fulfill its intended purpose?
- **Reconsider the genre you selected.** Is the genre you selected (essay, letter, letter to the editor) still working for your audience and purpose? Are there multigenre elements you could add to make your summary and response more effective?
- **Continue to use your active reading/writing/discussing activities as you revise your draft.** If you are uncertain about parts of your summary or response, reread the text, check your notes, or discuss your draft with a classmate.
- **Reread your summary for key features.** Make sure your summary indicates author and title, cites main ideas, uses an occasional direct quotation, and includes author tags. Check your summary for accuracy and objectivity.
- **Check paraphrases and direct quotations.** If you are paraphrasing (without quotation marks), you should put the author's ideas into your own language. If you are quoting directly, make sure the words within the quotation marks are accurate, word-for-word transcriptions.
- **Review the purpose of your response.** Are you analyzing, agreeing/ disagreeing, interpreting, or some combination of all three? Do your types of responses fit the assignment or address your intended audience and satisfy your purpose?
- **Amplify your supporting evidence.** Summary/response drafts often need additional, relevant evidence. Be sure you use sufficient personal experience, evidence from the text, or examples from other texts to support your response.

PEER RESPONSE

The instructions below will help you give and receive constructive advice about the rough draft of your summary/response essay. You may use these guidelines for an in-class workshop, a take-home review, or a computer e-mail response.

Writer: Before you exchange drafts with another reader, write out the following information about your own rough draft.

1. On your draft, *label* the parts that are summary and the parts that are your own response.
2. *Underline* the sentence(s) that signal to the reader that you are shifting from objective summary to personal response.
3. Indicate your purpose, intended audience, and any special genre features such as graphs or images.
4. Explain *one or two problems* that you are having with this draft that you want your reader to comment on.

Reader: Without making any comments, read the *entire* draft from start to finish. As you *reread* the draft, answer the following questions.

1. Review the guidelines for writing summaries. Has the writer remained *objective* in his or her summary? Does the summary *omit* any key ideas? Does the writer use *author tags* frequently and accurately? Can you clearly understand the main ideas of the article? Is the summary written in language appropriate for the intended audience? Do any added images or graphic material support the writer's purpose?
2. Review the guidelines for writing responses. What type(s) of response is the writer using? In the margin, label the types. What kinds of evidence does the writer use in support of his or her response? In the margin, label the kinds of supporting evidence. Is this response addressed appropriately to the audience?
3. In your own words, state the main idea or the focus that organizes the writer's response.
4. Write out your own reactions to the writer's response. Where do you disagree with the writer's analysis or interpretation? Explain.
5. Answer the writer's questions in number 4, above.

- **Focus on a clear, overall response.** Your responses should all add up to a focused, overall reaction. Delete or revise any passages that do not maintain your focus.
- **Revise sentences to improve clarity, conciseness, emphasis, and variety.** (See Handbook.)
- **Edit your final version.** Use the spell check on your computer. Have a friend help proofread. Check the Handbook for suspected problems in usage, grammar, and punctuation.

POSTSCRIPT ON THE WRITING PROCESS

1. As you finish your essay, what questions do you still have about how to summarize? What questions do you have about writing a good response?
2. Which paragraphs in your response contain your most effective supporting evidence? What kinds of evidence (analysis of the text, evidence from other texts, or personal experience) did you use?
3. What sentences in your response contain your overall reaction to the text?
4. If you had one more day to work on your essay, what would you change? Why?
5. Review the guidelines for critical reading at the beginning of this chapter. Which of those strategies was most successful for you? What did you learn about active, critical reading that you applied to the writing of your response? Cite one passage that illustrates what you learned about critical reading.

STUDENT WRITING
DEAN C. SWIFT

Letter to Margaret Atwood

After reading Margaret Atwood's "Letter to America," which is reprinted earlier in this chapter, Dean Swift decided to write a letter of response to Ms. Atwood. In his letter, he focuses particularly on Ms. Atwood's rosy picture of America's past and her claim that America is no longer a "city on a hill," but instead a country where a war with Iraq, problems with erosion of constitutional rights, and looming economic problems have threatened America's standing in the world. In his letter of response, Swift

---

...*continued* Letter to Margaret Atwood, **Dean C. Swift**

---

argues that the America in the past faced significant problems with civil rights, with assassinations of our great leaders, and with a severe economic depression. Before you read Swift's response, however, be sure to read Atwood's letter and form your own opinion.

1763 Fox Wood Ct.
Rockford, IL 61106
March 11, 2004

Ms. Margaret Atwood
C/o Editors, *The Nation*
33 Irving Place
New York, New York 10003

Dear Ms. Atwood

I am writing in response to your "Letter to America." Although I do not agree *1* totally with everything you say in the letter, I do agree that you can get a much better sense of your country through the eyes of another. There are many things we do not see or realize as Americans until we look at America from the outside. We get tunnel vision. Yet when reading your letter and hearing your description of the America you "once knew," I believe you also have tunnel vision. Throughout the letter you seem to compare the negative things about America today to all the positive things of the past. You fail to mention any negative aspects of America during those days. Maybe you should take a look at someone else's view on America today versus America in the past.

You started your letter by relating the America you once knew to its popular *2* culture. For one thing, I don't really think that is an appropriate subject on which to judge a country. There are more important aspects to our history than what the hit movies and songs were. But on that subject, of course it has changed—that was fifty years ago! You can't expect all the music and books to be the same; we are a completely different generation. Now we have our Dave Mathews Band and our Jennifer Lopez—we go to the movies to see *Lord of the Rings*. What is wrong with that? You've drawn us a picture that the America you once knew was flawless. Why don't you try to tell that to the African Americans living in this country back at that time? Would they really believe that America was so much better back then? I'll guarantee that if you were to ask Rosa Parks today whether America has changed for the better or worse, she would go on for hours on how great this country has become. African Americans have been used as slaves, abused, discriminated against, and even tortured to death for hundreds of years until the later 1950s and '60s. Violent race riots and disturbing demonstrations took place during the Civil Rights Movement. Didn't it bother you that women didn't have equal rights until 1964? How was that such a perfect country when people were being discriminated against and in some cases beaten, simply because of their race or gender?

Our economy now and the debt we have gotten ourselves into is frustrating 3 to everyone, but what about the economy in the past? Were there no problems with it in the 1930s during the Great Depression? I understand that you feel there are many corrupt things in our country today, but it is no more corrupt than it was in the past. Our country has been going to war as far back as our history dates. What about all the assassinations that took place back then? Your generation lost some great people. Throughout America's history, these tragedies have taken place: the assassination of President Lincoln and President Kennedy, Martin Luther King, Jr., Senator Robert Kennedy—yet these disturbing events don't seem to have left an impression on you.

On the subject of gutting the constitution, it's hard to draw a clear line as to 4 where I stand on that issue. On the one hand, according to our amendments, it is wrong for the government to be able to do such things as tap phone lines, enter a home without a warrant, and incarcerate suspects without cause. These are our rights as Americans. But is this invasion of our privacy really wrong? Why should this bother us unless we are on the guilty side or under suspicion of a crime? I know I don't have anything to hide myself. Although everyone in the U.S. should be entitled to certain privacy rights, isn't it in our best interest—for safety purposes—to sacrifice some rights in order to gain better knowledge and leads on subjects such as terrorism, gang violence, drug deals, and other serious matters? From my point of view, I believe that the Patriot Act is good for our country, and for our own safety. If you have nothing to hide, then why worry—if you are guilty or have information on something serious, then it should be in our best interest to apprehend the suspects or information by any means possible.

You say that our "city upon a hill" is slipping to the slums, but I say you are 5 far from the truth. Though we have fallen in some ways, we have also risen in many. Look at all the technological and medical advances we have made. Our efforts to improve equal rights among all people have clearly improved since your time. We are still a great country. To be sure, there are flaws along the way, but that doesn't change for any country, at any time in history. I felt you were a little narrow minded in your judgment about how America has changed since the time period you grew up in. From generation to genera-

...*continued* Letter to Margaret Atwood, **Dean C. Swift**

tion, people will always have different views on other time periods. I think you should try to open your mind and see that there were many flaws in your time also, and that although there are still many today, we have changed many things for the better. America is still that city upon a hill.

Sincerely,

Dean C. Swift

QUESTIONS FOR WRITING AND DISCUSSION

1 Reread Margaret Atwood's "Letter to America" reprinted earlier in this chapter. Write your own summary of her main ideas. Then reread Dean Swift's essay. Which of her points or arguments does he mention and respond to? Which ones does he ignore? Would he have a more effective letter if he responded to all of her points? Why or why not?

2 Dean Swift chose to use the genre of a letter to respond to Atwood's own letter. How are the stylistic conventions of a letter different from the conventions of an academic essay? How would Swift's response be different if he were writing a letter to the editor of *The Nation?* Does Swift use the more informal conventions of a letter to make his point in a more effective or personal way? Explain.

3 Responses typically analyze the logic and presentation of the argument, agree or disagree with the main ideas, and/or offer an interpretation or an examination of assumptions and implications behind an argument. Which of these does Swift do most effectively? Where could he add more supporting analysis, evidence, or interpretation? Should he use more of his own personal experience? Explain, referring to specific paragraphs in his essay.

STUDENT WRITING
JENNIFER KOESTER AND SONJA H. BROWE

Two Responses to Deborah Tannen

The two essays reprinted here were written in response to an essay by Deborah Tannen, "How Male and Female Students Use Language Differently," which appears in Chapter 8. Jennifer Koester and Sonja H. Browe have opposite responses to Tannen's essay. Jennifer Koester, a political science major at Colorado State University, argues that Tannen's essay is effective because she uses sufficient evidence and organizes her essay clearly.

On the other hand, Sonja Browe, an English education major at the University of Wyoming, writes an essay that is critical of Deborah Tannen's focus and supporting evidence. Be sure to read Tannen's essay and decide for yourself before you read the following essays.

A Response to Deborah Tannen's Essay

JENNIFER KOESTER

Deborah Tannen's "How Male and Female Students Use Language Differently" addresses how male and female conversational styles influence classroom discussions. Tannen asserts that women speak less than men in class because often the structure of discussion is more "congenial" to men's style of conversing. *1*

Tannen looks at three differences between the sexes that shape classroom interaction: classroom setting, debate format, and contrasting attitudes toward classroom discussion. First, Tannen says that during childhood, men "are expected to seize center stage: by exhibiting their skill, displaying their knowledge, and challenging and resisting challenge." Thus, as adults, men are more comfortable than women when speaking in front of a large group of strangers. On the other hand, women are more comfortable in small groups. *2*

Second, men are more comfortable with the debate format. Tannen asserts that many classrooms use the format of putting forth ideas followed by "argument and challenge." This too coincides with men's conversational experiences. However, Tannen asserts that women tend to "resist discussion they perceive as hostile." *3*

Third, men feel it is their duty to think of things to say and to voice them. On the other hand, women often regulate their participation and hold back to avoid dominating discussion. *4*

Tannen concludes that educators can no longer use just one format to facilitate classroom discussion. Tannen sees small groups as necessary for any "non-seminar" class along with discussion of differing styles of participation as solutions to the participation gap between the sexes. *5*

Three things work together to make Deborah Tannen's essay "How Male and Female Students Use Language Differently" effective: the qualifications of her argument, the evidence used, and the parallel format of comparison/ contrast. *6*

First, Tannen's efforts to qualify her argument prevent her from committing logical errors. In the first paragraphs of her essay, she states, "This is not to say that all men talk in class, nor that no women do. It is simply that a greater percentage of discussion time is taken by men's voices." By acknowledging exceptions to her claim, Tannen avoids the mistake of oversimplification. She also strengthens her argument because this qualification tells the reader that she is aware of the complexity of this issue. *7*

Later, Tannen uses another qualification. She says, "No one's conver- 8 sational style is absolute; everyone's style changes in response to the context and others' styles." Not only does this qualification avoid a logical fallacy, but it also strengthens Tannen's argument that classroom discussion must have several formats. By acknowledging that patterns of participation can change with the setting, Tannen avoids oversimplifying the issue and adds to her argument for classroom variety.

Second, Tannen's evidence places a convincing argument before her 9 reader. In the beginning of her essay, Tannen states that a greater percentage of discussion time in class is taken by men and that those women who attend single-sex schools tend to do better later in life. These two pieces of evidence present the reader with Tannen's jumping-off point. These statistics are what Tannen wants to change.

In addition, Tannen effectively uses anecdotal evidence. She presents 10 the reader with stories from her colleagues and her own research. These stories are taken from the classroom, a place which her audience, as educators, are familiar with. Her anecdotal evidence is persuasive because it appeals to the common sense and personal experiences of the audience. While some might question the lack of hard statistics throughout the essay, the anecdotal evidence serves Tannen best because it reminds her audience of educators of their own experiences. When she reminds the audience of their experiences, she is able to make them see her logic.

Third, the parallel format of comparison/contrast between the genders 11 highlights for the reader Tannen's main points. Each time Tannen mentions the reactions of one gender, she follows with the reaction of the other gender. For example, Tannen states, "So one reason men speak in class more than women is that many of them find the 'public' classroom setting more conducive to speaking, whereas most women are more comfortable speaking in private to a small group of people they know well." Here, Tannen places the tendencies of men and of women together, thus preventing the reader from having to constantly refer back to another section of the essay.

In an earlier example, Tannen discusses men's comfort with the de- 12 bate format in class discussion. The majority of that paragraph relates why men feel comfortable with that format. After explaining this idea, Tannen then tells the reader how women feel about the debate structure. Because how men and women feel about the debate format is placed within a paragraph, the readers easily see the difference between the genders. Tannen's use of the parallel format in the above examples and the rest of the essay provides a clear explanation of the differences in men's and women's interactions in the classroom.

Tannen writes her essay effectively. She makes the essay convincing by 13 qualifying her claims about gender participation. This strengthens her argument that just as the classroom is diverse, so should the format be diverse.

Her supporting evidence is convincing because it comes from Tannen's own experience, reminds the audience of its own experiences, and appeals to the audience's common sense. Finally, her parallel format for discussing the differences between men and women enhances the reader's understanding. Overall, Tannen's essay is effective because she qualifies her argument, uses convincing evidence, and makes clear how men and women use language differently through a parallel comparison/contrast format.

Is Deborah Tannen Convincing?

SONJA H. BROWE

In her article entitled "How Male and Female Students Use Language 1 Differently," Deborah Tannen explores the issue of gender as it affects the way we use language to communicate. Specifically, she discusses how differences in the way males and females are socialized to use language affect their classroom interactions. She explains that as females are growing up, they learn to use language to talk to friends, and to tell secrets. She states that for females, it is the "telling of secrets, the fact and the way they talk to each other, that makes them best friends." Boys, on the other hand, are "expected to use language to seize center stage: by exhibiting their skill, displaying their knowledge, and challenging and resisting challenge."

According to Tannen, these differences make classroom language use 2 more conducive to the way males were taught to use language. Tannen suggests that speaking in front of groups and the debatelike formats used in many classrooms are more easily handled by male students.

Finally, Tannen describes an experiment she conducted in her own 3 classroom which allowed students to evaluate their own conversation transcripts. From this experience, she deduced that small-group interaction is essential in the classroom because it gives students who don't participate in whole-class settings the opportunity for conversation and interaction.

Though Tannen's research is a worthwhile consideration and pro- 4 vides information which could be of great interest to educators, this particular article lacks credibility and is unfocused. The points she is trying to make get lost in a world of unsupported assertions, and she strays from her main focus, leaving the reader hanging and confused.

Tannen does take some time at the beginning of her article to estab- 5 lish her authority on linguistic analysis, but we may still hold her accountable for supporting her assertions with evidence. However, Tannen makes sweeping declarations throughout the essay, expecting the reader to simply accept them as fact. For example, when discussing the practice of the teacher playing devil's advocate and debating with the students, she states that "many, if not most women would shrink from such a challenge, experiencing it as public humiliation." Following such an assertion, we expect to see some evidence. Whom did Tannen talk to? What did they say? What percentage of women felt this way? This sort of evidence is completely lacking, so that what Tannen states as fact appears more like conjecture.

Tannen makes another such unsupported pronouncement when she 6 discusses the debatelike formats used in many classrooms. She explains that this type of classroom interaction is in opposition to the way that females, in contrast to males, approach learning. She states that "it is not that females don't fight, but that they don't fight for fun. They don't ritualize opposition." Again, where is Tannen's evidence to support such a claim?

When Tannen does bother to support her assertions, her evidence is 7 trite and unconvincing. For example, she reviews Walter Ong's work on the pursuit of knowledge, in which he suggested that "ritual opposition . . . is fundamental to the way males approach almost any activity." Tannen supports this claim of Ong's in parentheses, saying, "Consider, for example, the little boy who shows he likes a little girl by pulling her braids and shoving her." This statement may serve as an example but is not enough to convince the reader that ritual opposition is fundamental to the way males approach "almost any activity."

Other evidence which Tannen uses to support her declarations 8 comes in the form of conversations she has had with colleagues on these issues. Again, though these may provide examples, they do not represent a broad enough database to support her claims.

Finally, Tannen takes three pages of her article to describe in detail an 9 experiment she conducted in her classroom. Though the information she collected from this experiment was interesting, it strayed from the main point of the essay. Originally, Tannen's article was directed specifically at gender differences in communication. In this classroom activity, she looked at language-use differences in general, including cultural differences. She states that some people may be more comfortable in classes where you are expected to raise your hand to speak, while others prefer to be able to talk freely. She makes no mention of gender in regard to this issue.

Finally, at the close of her essay, where we can expect to get the thrust 10 of her argument or at least some sort of summary statement which ties into her main thesis, Tannen states that her experience in her classroom convinced her that "small-group interaction should be a part of any classroom" and that "having students become observers of their own interaction is a crucial part of their education." Again, these are interesting points, but they stray quite a bit from the original intention of the article.

In this article, Tannen discusses important issues of which those of 11 us who will be interacting with students in the classroom should be aware. However, her article loses a great deal of its impact because she does not stay focused on her original thesis and fails to support her ideas with convincing evidence.

QUESTIONS FOR WRITING AND DISCUSSION

1 Do your own double-entry log for Tannen's essay (see Chapter 8). On the left-hand side of a piece of paper, record Tannen's main points. On the right-hand side, write your own questions and reactions. Compare your notes to Koester's and Browe's responses. Whose response most closely matches your own? Where or how does your response differ from each?

2 Review the critical reading strategies at the beginning of this chapter (see pages 130–132). Identify specific places in both Koester's and Browe's essays where they analyze elements of the rhetorical situation—such as purpose, audience, or context. Where do they analyze the effectiveness of the organization, use of evidence, or the style? Based on your analyses of both essays, which writer does a better job of critically reading Tannen's essay? Explain your choice.

3 Responses to texts may analyze the effectiveness of the text, agree or disagree with the ideas in the text, and/or interpret or reflect on the text. What kinds of responses do Koester and Browe give? Would a different kind of response work better for either writer? Why or why not?

4 Koester focuses on three writing strategies that Tannen uses to make her essay more effective. What are they? What weaknesses of Tannen's essay does Koester ignore or downplay?

5 Browe's response focuses on two criticisms of Tannen's essay. What are they? In which paragraphs does Browe develop each criticism? What strengths of Tannen's essay does Browe ignore or downplay?

6 Neither Browe nor Koester uses personal experience as supporting evidence. Think of one experience that you have had in a specific class illustrating the conversational preferences of men and women. Write out that specific example. Could either Browe or Koester use such a specific example? Where might each writer use it in her response?

7 Reread the essays by Tannen, Koester, and Browe. Review your reactions with your classmates. Then write your own summary and response. In your response, mention both the strengths and the weaknesses of Tannen's article. Then indicate whether or not you found Tannen's essay, in general, thought-provoking or convincing.

PEARSON
mycomplab

For additional writing, reading, and research resources,
go to http://www.mycomplab.com

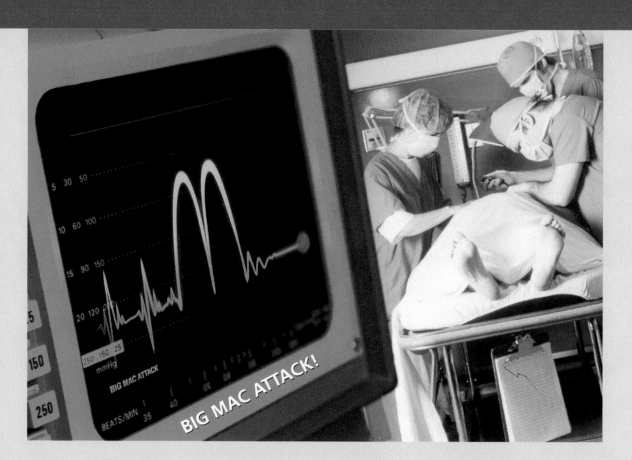

The above spoof ad appears on the Adbusters Web site. After analyzing the composition, images, and contexts for this advertisement, read and respond to Journal Exercise 2 on page 201.

Analyzing and Designing Visuals

6

For one of your composition class projects, you work with the managers of a local adult fitness center in writing a brochure that they can use to promote their fitness, healthy diet, and weight loss programs. First you research information about healthy approaches to weight loss programs. Then you prepare a draft with information organized into key topics from your research and, working with the adult center, decide how to best select, organize, and present this information for their adult clients. As you revise, you focus on giving good, concise advice for adults, presented in an easy-to-read, visually appealing document. Your final product is a four-color brochure with your information, advice, photographs, and graphs that the center will print and distribute.

The editor of your college newspaper asks you to write an article calling attention to upcoming events celebrating César Chávez Day on March 31. You interview organizers of the day's activities to gather basic information. After researching César Chávez's life, however, you decide to write your article primarily to let readers know about his life and accomplishments. You plan to have a calendar of the day's events accompany your biographical information. Your final article features your profile, two pictures of Cesar Chavez, and a sidebar of the campus and community activities.

> 66 Graphic design creates visual logic and seeks an optimal balance between visual sensation and graphic information. Without the visual impact of shape, color, and contrast, pages are graphically boring and will not motivate the viewer. 99
> —PATRICK LYNCH AND SARAH HORTON, *WEB STYLE GUIDE*

> 66 Now we make our networks, and our networks make us. 99
> —WILLIAM MITCHELL, *CITY OF BITS*

COMMUNICATION IN THE 21ST CENTURY IS, INCREASINGLY, MULTIMEDIA COMMUNICATION. WRITTEN TEXTS ARE INTERWOVEN WITH PICTURES, NEWS PHOTOGRAPHS, GRAPHIC DESIGNS, WORKS OF ART, CHARTS, AND DIAGRAMS. IN ADDITION, WEB SITES AND ELECTRONIC COMMUNICATION contain sound and video, with music, podcasts, and video clips often only a mouse click away. High-tech cell phones now offer true multimedia communication, with e-mail, text messaging, photographs, news updates, video and text files, and music.

Even though our digital-age technology is new, our means for analyzing and designing visuals remains very traditional. In every case, we analyze and design by asking basic rhetorical questions. What is the purpose of this image or bit of media? Who is the intended audience? In what social, political, or cultural context does this visual appear? Who is the author or group of authors? What appeals to logic, emotion, or character do these hybrid or multimedia texts make?

This chapter begins by providing the rhetorical questions you need to analyze visuals and hybrid texts. After you understand how to analyze visuals, you can practice composing and designing hybrid texts of your own. This chapter focuses primarily on visuals as one key element of a multimedia text, but the rhetorical principles will help you analyze other kinds of media as well. The diagram below will help you analyze visuals, their contexts, and their meanings.

The chapter begins with you as the reader, viewer, or member of the audience. You will examine the visual and its relationship to any accompanying text. Then you will consider how the visual and the text interact with the cultural, political, or social context in which the image appears. The context is both immediate (the magazine, newspaper, essay, Web site, or blog in which the image appears) and more general (the cultural context of the image, the

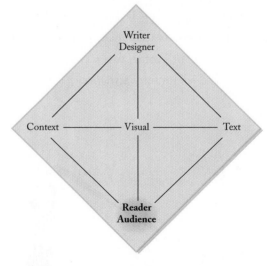

written or spoken conversation that is occurring about this image). Finally, throughout the process of analyzing, you will estimate the rhetorical effect: What is the purpose and audience for this image and its text? What appeals to logic and reason, to emotion and feelings, to reliability and character is the writer making? How effective are those appeals?

After you practice analyzing the rhetorical effect of visuals, you will be better prepared to switch roles from reader or audience to writer or designer of visuals for your own documents. In the second half of this chapter, you will practice several possible visual or design choices. You will analyze which visuals help support your purpose for your specific audience, and how effectively the visuals add to your audience appeals.

Techniques for Analyzing Visuals

As you analyze images and visuals—as well as any accompanying text or surrounding context—always consider the rhetorical situation, the purpose of the visual, and the intended audience for the visual or hybrid text. The techniques explained here help you **analyze**—that is, look at each part of the visual separately—but the ultimate goal is to **synthesize**, to put the pieces together in an explanation that shows how the parts work together (or do not work together) to achieve a rhetorical purpose for an intended audience. Your conclusion about the visual's significance or meaning becomes your **claim**. These techniques shouldn't necessarily be followed in lock-step order. If you begin by analyzing the genre of a visual, for example, you may more quickly see how the text and the visual work together. Similarly, returning to analyze the visual *after* you know more about the context can be very important.

Techniques for Analyzing Visuals

Technique	Tips on How to Do It
Analyzing the composition of the visual itself	Describe the *layout, balance, color, key figures, symbols,* and *cultural references.* What message or messages is/are being conveyed? Based on your analysis, what is the purpose and who is the audience? What claim can you make about the significance or meaning of the visual?

Continued

Technique	Tips on How to Do It
Analyzing the visual in combination with any accompanying text	Does the *accompanying text or caption* work to complement the meaning of the visual? How does the text add to or distract from the visual? What do the words help you notice in the visual? (What do the words distract you from noticing?) Do the words and the visual work together to achieve the same purpose for the intended audience?
Analyzing the visual and the text in context	In what magazine, essay, newspaper, or Web site does the visual appear? What does this *context* tell you about its purpose and audience? In what larger cultural, political, or social context does the visual appear? How does analyzing the visual, the accompanying text, and the larger context help you arrive at a thesis or claim?
Analyzing the genre of the visual	Visual genres include advertisements, photographs, art, graphics, posters, brochures, and charts. Compare the visual you are analyzing with other similar ones. What features do they share? How is your example different? How do those similarities/differences affect the overall meaning and purpose of the visual or its effect on the audience?
Analyzing the rhetorical appeals of a visual	What appeals to reason and logic, to emotion, or to character and credibility does the visual make? Does the writer or designer use multiple appeals (to reason and to emotion, for example)? How effective are these appeals in achieving the writer's purpose for the intended audience? How does your analysis of these appeals lead to your thesis or claim?

ANALYZING VISUALS

When we analyze stand-alone visuals and images, we need to pay particular attention to the details of composition, focus, narrative, and genre. We rely primarily on this analysis to reach conclusions about the purpose, intended audience, and effectiveness of the visual. These conclusions will become your claim or thesis for your analysis. Use the following sets of questions to guide your analysis. Depending on the particular image, of course, some questions will be more important than others.

● COMPOSITION

- Who or what is pictured in the main figure?
- How are key images arranged or organized on the page?
- What is the relationship between the main figure and the background?
- What is excluded from the main figure or background?
- When and where was the image or photograph made?
- What use of color, contrasts of light and shade, or repeated figures are present?
- How do these composition details come together to create a purpose or message for the intended audience/viewer?

● FOCAL POINT

- What point or image first draws your attention?
- Is this focal point centered or offset?
- Do background figures or diagonal lines draw your attention to or away from the focal point?
- How does the focus (or lack of focus) contribute to the purpose or message of the image?

● NARRATIVE

- What story or narrative does the image or visual suggest?
- Do certain objects or figures act as symbols or metaphors?
- How do these story elements support (or not support) the purpose or message for the intended audience?

● THEMES

- Who has the power in this visual? Who does not? Who is included or excluded?
- What sexist, racist, or body image stereotypes exist? Are these stereotypes promoted and reproduced or are they resisted or challenged? Explain.
- What is this image trying to sell? Does the image make a commodity out of social or cultural values, including holidays (Christmas or Independence Day), ideals (patriotism, charity, or religion), or personal values (integrity or status)?

Now practice applying these questions to two photographs taken by Dorothea Lange. One of America's most famous documentary photographers of migrant workers and sharecroppers, Lange took the following images during the Great Depression of the 1930s, near Berkeley, California.

In the first picture, the composition focuses on several main figures—the two women and the three children. The makeshift tarp helps to frame these figures,

and the diagonal lines from the chair and the woman on the left bring the viewer's focus to the children standing in the center and then to the mother holding her child on the right. The half-opened suitcase of clothes appears in the foreground. The background helps establish the rural, agricultural setting.

In contrast, the second picture has much a much stronger **composition**. The main figure is the woman, with her two children, looking away from the camera. The background—the tent—does not distract from this central, pyramid-like image. The children's faces are also turned away from the camera, leaving the **focal point** on the mother. The picture is in black and white, which helps focus the viewer's attention on the figures of the mother and the children. Even the angle of the mother's arm, and her chin in her hand, lead the eye to the woman's face. Her expression is determined, but without much hope. All of these compositional features support the purpose and message of the photograph: A migrant mother is caring for her family, as best as she can, in the most primitive of environments.

As viewers, we can construct our own **narrative** based on the information in the picture. This woman is caring for her children in a migrant worker environment. She has no apparent support. This shelter appears to be where she is living, both during the day and at night. She may have other family members working in the area, but we can only guess at their whereabouts.

Our own conjectural narrative is, in fact, not very different from the description that Dorothea Lange herself gives of the day when she took these photographs:

"I saw and approached the hungry and desperate mother, as if drawn by a magnet. I do not remember how I explained my presence or my camera to her, but I do remember she asked me no questions. I made five exposures, working closer and closer from the same direction. I did not ask her name or her history. She told me her age, that she was thirty-two. She said that they had been living on frozen vegetables from the surrounding fields, and birds that the children killed. She had just sold the tires from her car to buy food. There she sat in that lean-to tent with her children huddled around her, and seemed to know that my pictures might help her, and so she helped me. There was a sort of equality about it." (*Popular Photography,* Feb., 1960)

We can put all these analytical pieces together to better understand the purpose and meaning of this photograph. For its **theme**, the photograph brings something hidden (the human story of poverty and exploitation) out into the open and gives it dignity. Lange's purpose was to call attention to the predicament of migrant workers in order to gather support for governmental reform. Her purpose was thus persuasive: she hoped to change public awareness as a first step to improving governmental assistance programs.

ANALYZING VISUALS WITH TEXT

Analyzing visuals with accompanying words or text requires considering how the composition of the image and the written text function together. Text serves to call attention to and support the message of the visual. Often, words serve as a focusing device, calling our attention to key features, guiding us to "read" the visual in a certain way. (Of course, a text that encourages us to see one meaning in the visual may keep us from seeing other possible meanings or messages in that visual.) Ideally, image and text should not just duplicate each other; they should each contribute something unique so that the combined effect is more powerful, appealing, or persuasive than either the text or the image taken separately.

In the following recruiting poster for the American Red Cross, the text is spare, simple, and direct: "Join." Notice how the composition of the picture supports this appeal. The foreground figure contrasts clearly with the less distinct background, a representation of a flood-ravaged town. And the figures in the background—a rundown house and a Red Cross nurse who is caring for children—seem to hover in the middle distance, perhaps connected, perhaps not, to the flooded town. The nurse in the foreground extends her hand to the viewer, inviting her or him to join. Thematically, women rather than men are featured in the foreground and background in this stereotypical service role. The patriotic red, white, and blue colors of the nurse's blouse and cape are repeated as a

66 There can be no words without images. 99
—ARISTOTLE, AUTHOR OF *RHETORIC*

66 My eyes make pictures when they are shut. 99
—SAMUEL TAYLOR COLERIDGE, AUTHOR OF "*THE RIME OF THE ANCIENT MARINER*"

motif in the red of the cross, the blue of the word *join*, and the white of the immediate foreground. The focus on the foreground figure, the color, the center focal point, and the balance of the background figures on the right and left function with the text and the implied narrative (Join the Red Cross and serve your country!) to achieve this visual's persuasive purpose.

In the next image with accompanying text, photographer Jim Goldberg effectively illustrates how visual and text should combine to create a more powerful message than either word or image alone. The photograph, taken in San Francisco in 1982, shows the lady of the house, Mrs. Stone, standing in her modern kitchen with her servant, Vickie Figueroa, standing in the background. The diagonal lines of the white counter and window to the right send us first to the figure of Mrs. Stone, and then to Ms. Figueroa in the background. This foreground/background juxtaposition sets up a power relationship, confirmed by Mrs. Stone's hands grasping (and owning) the counter while Ms. Figueroa's hands are tucked behind her. The contrast between the pointed and poignant writing and the rather conventional kitchen scene gives the visual a special, combined power. The language in Ms. Figueroa's note supports the power relationship of the image: "I am used to standing behind Mrs. Stone." Finally, Goldberg's choice to present the text in what is apparently Ms. Figueroa's own handwriting, complete with crossed out letters, uneven lines, and signature,

My dream was to became a shool teacher.
Mrs Stone is rich.
I have talents but not opportunity.
I ~~tom~~ am used to standing behind
Mrs Stone.
I have been a servant for 40 years.
Vickie Figueroa.

Jim Goldberg, USA, San Francisco, 1982

gives her lost dream of becoming a school teacher remarkable power. If Goldberg had simply put her note in typeface, much of the authenticity and power of the visual would be lost.

ANALYZING VISUALS IN CONTEXT

Often, the key to analyzing a visual lies in understanding and explaining the context of the image. The context is the publication or medium in which the image appeared, but taken more widely, the context is the surrounding political, social, and cultural context of the times. The following image of Michael J. Fox does not, in itself, appear to be unusual. But this still photograph actually represents a frame in a video in which Fox is speaking in support of a political candidate who supports stem cell research. On the video, Fox shows visible tremors, a symptom of his battle with Parkinson's disease. As a result of the controversy created by Rush Limbaugh's criticism of the video—followed by Limbaugh's apology—this image became a focal point in a larger cultural and political battle over governmental support for stem cell research.

In the following short commentary in *Newsweek*, one of hundreds of articles and editorials appearing in the media at the time, Jonathan Alter explains how the video image impacted the political debate on stem cell research.

Progress or Not
Jonathan Alter

Oct. 25, 2006—"The ad was in extremely poor taste," said a spokesman for Michael Steele, Republican candidate for the Senate in Maryland, referring to a TV spot made for his opponent, Rep. Ben Cardin.

That will be the line of Republicans under assault from what could become one of the most powerful political advertisements ever made. The new ad features an ailing Michael J. Fox talking about politicians who oppose embryonic stem-cell research. This is not just another celebrity ad, like those cut by the late Christopher Reeve. It's a celebrity shot to the solar plexus of the GOP. Whatever happens in the campaign, the ad is already a classic and will be mentioned in the same breath as LBJ's famous 1964 "Daisy" ad and other unforgettable political moments on television.

Rush Limbaugh helped cement the ad's place in history with his astonishingly insensitive remark that Fox "was either off his medication or was acting." Limbaugh quickly

apologized but the damage to his own reputation was already done.

Fox, star of megahit TV shows and movies like "Family Ties" and *Back to the Future,* was for years one of the most popular actors in the United States. He still works, but is clearly debilitated by Parkinson's. Throughout the ad, he sways back and forth, showing signs of advanced disease.

In the version cut for Democrat Claire McCaskill, who is running against Sen. Jim Talent in Missouri, the actor, wearing a blue blazer and open-collared shirt, says, "Senator Talent even wanted to criminalize the science that gives us a chance for hope." This is in apparent reference to Talent's early support for Sen. Sam Brownback's view that embryonic stem-cell research should be illegal. Then comes the clincher: "They say all politics is local, but it's not always the case. What you do in Missouri matters to millions of Americans—Americans like me."

Sometimes, the accompanying text for a visual carries a message that in the larger social context creates controversy and anger. Consider the following two photographs showing people wading through the floodwaters in New Orleans following hurricane Katrina in 2005. The first, taken by Associated Press photographer Dave Martin, has a caption stating that the young man, an African American, was "looting a grocery store." The second, taken by photographer

Chris Graythen for Getty Images, has a caption stating that two white residents are wading through the floodwaters after "finding bread and soda from a local grocery store." Several Internet sites and bloggers picked up these photographs and highlighted the key words with a red box in order to illustrate racial bias in media coverage of Hurricane Katrina.

The controversy created by these images was reported one week later by Tania Ralli in a *New York Times* article titled "Who's a Looter?" Read her account of the circumstances surrounding this media event. When you finish reading her article, you may want to Google the photographers, Dave Martin and Chris Graythen, to read more about their accounts of the events and the story surrounding their photographs. This controversy shows the dramatic power of images, but it also emphasizes the power of our reading or interpretation of these images. A picture may be worth a thousand words, but sometimes a single word is more powerful than a dramatic picture.

> " In any hypertext, the text originates in an interaction that neither the author nor the reader can completely predict or control. "
> —JAY DAVID BOULTER, "LITERATURE IN THE ELECTRONIC WRITING SPACE"

A young man walks through chest deep flood water after looting a grocery store in New Orleans on Tuesday, Aug. 30, 2005. Flood waters continue to rise in New Orleans after Hurricane Katrina did extensive damage. Associated Press

Two residents wade through chest-deep water after finding bread and soda from a local grocery store after Hurricane Katrina came through the area in New Orleans, Louisiana. (AFP/Getty Images/Chris Graythen) AFP/Getty Images Tue Aug 30, 3:47 AM ET

Who's a Looter?
Tania Ralli

Two news photographs ricocheted through the Internet last week and set off a debate about race and the news media in the aftermath of Hurricane Katrina.

The first photo, taken by Dave Martin, an Associated Press photographer in New Orleans, shows a young black man wading through water that has risen to his chest. He is clutching a case of soda and pulling a floating bag. The caption provided by The A.P. says he has just been "looting a grocery store."

The second photo, also from New Orleans, was taken by Chris Graythen for Getty Images and distributed by Agence France-Presse. It shows a white couple up to their chests in the same murky water. The woman is holding some bags of food. This caption says they are shown "after finding bread and soda from a local grocery store."

Both photos turned up Tuesday on Yahoo News, which posts automatic feeds of articles and photos from wire services. Soon after, a user of the photo-sharing site Flickr juxtaposed the images and captions on a single page, which attracted links from many blogs. The left-leaning blog Daily Kos linked to the page with the comment, "It's not looting if you're white."

The contrast of the two photo captions, which to many indicated a double standard at work, generated widespread anger toward the news media that quickly spread beyond the Web.

On Friday night, the rapper Kanye West ignored the teleprompter during NBC's live broadcast of "A Concert for Hurricane Relief," using the opportunity to lambast President Bush and criticize the press. "I hate the way they portray us in the media," he said. "You see a black family, it says they're looting. You see a white family, it says they're looking for food."

Many bloggers were quick to point out that the photos came from two different agencies, and so could not reflect the prejudice of a single media outlet. A writer on the blog BoingBoing wrote: "Perhaps there's more factual substantiation behind each copywriter's choice of words than we know. But to some, the difference in tone suggests racial bias, implicit or otherwise."

According to the agencies, each photographer captioned his own photograph. Jack Stokes, a spokesman for The A.P., said that photographers are told to describe what they have seen when they write a caption.

Mr. Stokes said The A.P. had guidelines in place before Hurricane Katrina struck to distinguish between "looting" and "carrying." If a photographer sees a person enter a business and emerge with goods, it is described as looting. Otherwise The A.P. calls it carrying.

Mr. Stokes said that Mr. Martin had seen the man in his photograph wade into a grocery store and come out with the sodas and bag, so by A.P.'s definition, the man had looted.

The photographer for Getty Images, Mr. Graythen, said in an e-mail message that he had also stuck to what he had seen to write his caption, and had actually given the wording a great deal of thought. Mr. Graythen described seeing the couple near a corner store from an elevated expressway. The door to the shop was open, and things had floated out to the street. He was not able to talk to the couple, "so I had to draw my own conclusions," he said.

In the extreme conditions of New Orleans, Mr. Graythen said, taking necessities like food and water to survive could not be considered stealing. He said that had he seen people coming out of stores with computers and DVD players, he would have considered that looting.

"If you're taking something that runs solely from a wall outlet that requires power from the electric company—when we are not going to have power for weeks, even months—that's inexcusable," he said.

Since the photo was published last Tuesday Mr. Graythen has received more than 500 e-mail messages, most of them supportive, he said.

Within three hours of the photo's publication online, editors at Agence France-Presse rewrote Mr. Graythen's caption. But the original caption remained online as part of a Yahoo News slide show. Under pressure to keep up with the news, and lacking the time for a discussion about word choice, Olivier Calas, the agency's director of multimedia, asked Yahoo! to remove the photo last Thursday.

Now, in its place, when readers seek the picture of the couple, a statement from Neil Budde, the general manager of Yahoo! News, appears in its place. The statement emphasizes that Yahoo! News did not write the photo captions and that it did not edit the captions, so that the photos can be made available as quickly as possible.

Mr. Calas said Agence France-Presse was bombarded with e-mail messages complaining about the caption. He said the caption was unclear and should have been reworded earlier. "This was a consequence of a series of negligences, not ill intent," he said.

For Mr. Graythen, whose parents and grandparents lost their homes in the disaster, the fate of the survivors was the most important thing. In his e-mail message he wrote: "Now is no time to pass judgment on those trying to stay alive. Now is no time to argue semantics about finding versus looting. Now is no time to argue if this is a white versus black issue."

ANALYZING THE GENRE OF THE VISUAL

Visuals, like other texts, are of certain kinds or types that we call *genres*. Common visual genres are advertisements, works of art, photographs, charts, and other kinds of graphics. We can learn more about the purpose, audience, and context by understanding how a visual that we are analyzing is similar to (and different from) other visuals belonging to its genre. The World War II posters on the next page, for example, illustrate a visual genre from the 1940s. The purpose of these

Rosie the Riveter

"She's a WOW"

Patriotism Means Silence

posters was to recruit men and women to the war effort. The posters featured here were intended to appeal to women to help with war-related tasks or even to join the Women's Army Corps.

The first poster is possibly the most famous example of this genre: Rosie the Riveter. The focus is on Rosie's strong right arm, with her sleeves rolled up, ready for work. The strong diagonal of her arm points back to Rosie's face and to the text at the top of the poster. The purpose of this poster was to encourage women to participate in the war effort, both by direct exhortation ("We Can Do It!") and by offering an image of an attractive, capable, and courageous woman. The Rosie the Riveter poster helped revolutionize gender images during the war.

The second poster, "She's a WOW," presents a similarly strong image designed to recruit women for ordnance work. Like Rosie, she is capable, attractive, and ready for work, with her hair wrapped in a red and white bandana. Although she is in the foreground against the background image of the soldier, the text keeps her in a supportive role: "The Girl He Left Behind Is Still Behind Him." She is not looking out at the viewer, as Rosie is, but back at the soldier. Still, her color image, accented in red and white, is larger than the soldier's background picture.

The war poster genre continues in contemporary satiric posters questioning our Homeland Security laws. The poster on the left suggests that patriotism requires being silent and refraining from speaking out against these laws or against other government policies. It uses a popular and patriotic image to imply that the Homeland Security Office is trying to silence freedom of speech. We understand this message partly from the words and partly from the genre of the patriotic wartime poster.

RHETORICAL APPEALS TO THE AUDIENCE

All of the features of visuals analyzed earlier—the composition of the visual, the accompanying text, the context, and the genre—contribute to the overall rhetorical purpose and the effect on its audience or viewer. Visuals, like written texts, also make specific rhetorical appeals to reason and logic (logos), to emotion (pathos), and to character and credibility (ethos).

● **APPEAL TO REASON**   Usually charts, graphs, and diagrams contain appeals to reason, logic, facts, and other kinds of data. The following visual diagram, which accompanied a newspaper story about alternative sources of energy, illustrates the appeal to reason (*logos*). Using a sequence of logical steps, it explains in text and in image how wind could be used to generate hydrogen to power electric grids as well as automobiles. Its purpose is apparently to inform or explain, but because the information for the graphic is provided by an energy company, its more subtle purpose is to improve public relations by persuading customers that Xcel Energy is doing its part in the search for alternative energies.

Storing the power of the wind

Xcel Energy and the National Renewable Energy Laboratory are teaming up to explore the potential of using wind power to generate electricity at any time — even after the wind has stopped blowing. How the process will work:

1 **Turbine** is turned by wind, generating electricity.

2 **Electrolyzer,** powered by electricity from turbine, separates water into oxygen and hydrogen gases.

3 **Storage tanks,** hold the hydrogen after it has been compressed.

4 **Engine,** or a fuel cell, powered by hydrogen creates electricity.

5 **Electricity** is sent to the utility grid during times of greater demand.

6 **In the future** hydrogen gas could be piped to fueling stations and used to power vehicles.

Sources: Xcel Energy; National Renewable Energy Laboratory

Jonathan Moreno and Thomas McKay | The Denver Post

● **APPEAL TO EMOTION**   Typically, advertisements use strong appeals to emotion (*pathos*), simply because emotions are so effective in persuading viewers to buy a product. Emotional appeals include positive feelings (beauty, sex, status, image, and sometimes even humor) as well as negative emotions (fear, anxiety, insecurity, and pity). These appeals come from the composition of the image, the text, the context, and even the genre of the visual. Magazines are a good source for advertisements relying primarily on emotional appeals.

● **APPEAL TO CHARACTER AND CREDIBILITY**   Often visuals use a strong appeal to character and credibility (*ethos*) to convince, move, or persuade viewers. This appeal is not to the character of any person pictured in the visual, but to the character and credibility of the designer or creator of the image. If viewers sense that the visual conveys a sense of integrity and authenticity, that the maker of the image is sincere and is not relying on cheap emotional appeals, or that the visual communicates a sense of humanity and goodwill, the appeal to character is successful. Look again at Dorothea Lange's images of a migrant mother on page 188. These pictures have an emotional appeal, to be sure, but they are composed with an integrity and credibility that give them a strong character appeal, too. Lange's pictures give the mother and her children dignity at the same time that they call attention to their plight.

● **COMBINED APPEALS IN AN AD**   Often visuals and their texts will combine appeals to logic, emotion, and character. Consider the following spoof-ad posted on Adbusters of the popular ads for Absolut, a brand of vodka. Emotional appeals emerge from the blood-colored reds and dramatic blacks, the long shadows and spilt liquids, the white chalk outline of the body (the bottle), the police officer taking notes, and the red taillights of the car. The bold caption, "Absolute End," (notice how the spelling has been changed from *Absolut* to *Absolute*) and the statistics cited

below the picture appeal to logic, connecting the 100,000 alcohol ads teenagers see with the fact that 50% of automobile fatalities are linked to alcohol. This visual also generates an ethos or character appeal because the creator of the ad is apparently someone we can trust, someone of good character whose goal is to prevent the needless and tragic fatalities associated with drinking and driving.

As you practice analysis of a variety of visuals, remember three important points. First, not all types of analysis will be important for a particular visual or hybrid text. Focus on the kinds of analysis that work best for your project. Second, techniques for analysis should be repeated or combined until you discover the key features of the visual. Start with the visual, work through accompanying text, consider the context and the genre, and analyze the rhetorical appeals, but come back to the visual after you know more about the context and have thought about appeals. Third, remember that the ultimate goal of your analysis will be **synthesis**. You examine the parts and pieces of a multimedia text in order to support your synthesis of these parts into a meaningful whole. Your explanation of the meaning and

Adbusters

significance of the visual or the rhetorical purpose and effectiveness of the visual in its context becomes your thesis or **claim**.

Techniques for Designing Visuals

When you practiced analyzing visuals, you were the reader or audience in the diagram shown here, judging the visual with its accompanying text, in its context, and considering how the creator of the image worked to achieve a particular purpose for the intended audience.

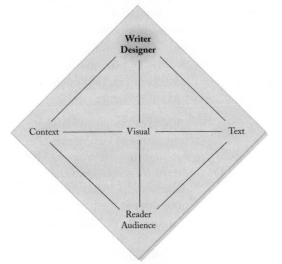

Now you need to switch roles. After you have practiced analyzing a variety of visuals for their overall rhetorical effect, you are better prepared to add or design visuals for your own essay, article, pamphlet, or Web site. As the primary designer or creator, you will likely be using visuals and diagrams, but you should also consider the layout of your text as a visual element: typeface, size of font, margins, color, and use of white space all have visual appeal for your readers.

Visuals, illustrations, graphics, photographs, and document design are all elements of your writing that have a rhetorical effect. Use the following techniques as you consider visuals and text layout possibilities for your essay, article, brochure, or other document.

> 66 Effective visual presentation . . . [requires] minimizing the possibility of competition between picture and text and ensuring that the pictures used are relevant to the material presented. 99
> —JENNIFER WILEY, "COGNITIVE AND EDUCATIONAL IMPLICATIONS OF VISUAL RICH MEDIA"

Techniques for Designing Visuals

Technique	Tips on How to Do It
Designing for your audience and purpose	Your *purpose* and *audience* should guide your selection of an appropriate genre, the most effective visual(s), and a clear document design. *Example:* The image taken by Jim Goldberg on page 191 places Vickie Figueroa in the background in order to support his purpose, that Vickie's dreams are subordinate to Mrs. Stone's power.
Choosing and understanding your genre	Collect and study several *examples of your genre,* whether it is an article, brochure, poster, or Web site. Does your genre use many visuals and only a few words? Does it use mostly text with a few visuals or diagrams? Take notes on the layout typically used, and then choose the best features and creatively modify them for your own purposes. *Examples:* Examine more posters like "Rosie the Riveter" by searching Google images for World War II posters. Take notes on the common features of the genre.
Selecting or designing visuals for your document	Choose or design visual elements with *strong compositional features:* key figures, strong diagonals, appropriate color, and balance. Make your diagrams, graphs, and charts clear and easy to understand. Choose the most striking illustrations but use them sparingly. Avoid clutter. *Examples:* In the World War II posters on page 196, notice the strong central figures, bright colors (red, white, blue, yellow), strong diagonals, and large, bold font. Look again at the "Absolute End" visual on page 198 or the American Red Cross image on page 190 for examples of strong compositional features.
Designing your written text to support your purpose	Choose *typeface, font, white space,* and *margins* with an eye to your purpose and audience. Balance chunks of text with visuals on the page. Use bold type and white space to create emphasis. Make your visuals or illustrations compatible with your text. *Examples:* The World War II posters and the American Red Cross poster are excellent examples of bold type and effective use of white space.

WARMING UP   Journal Exercises

The following exercises will help you practice analyzing and designing visuals. Respond to these exercises individually, in groups, or on your class Web site.

1. Go to the Web site of a newspaper or news organization. Choose a section that you like to read, such as world news, business, sports, fashion, dining, home and garden, books, movies, or music. Find an interesting article and see what visuals or graphics accompany the article. Copy the article into a Word file. Then design an additional graph or select an additional or alternative image that would be appropriate for that article. Practice designing a simple bar graph or pie graph if the article has statistics. For alternative visuals, search Google Images for appropriate art or photos. After you have designed your graph or selected your image, explain why your choice or design fits the subject, purpose, and audience of the original article.

2. In a visual that contains text or a caption, the image and the words should complement each other, working toward a single meaning. *The New Yorker* regularly sponsors a cartoon caption contest. Drawings are initially published without captions, and readers are invited to contribute their best lines during the next two weeks. Study the cartoon below. By yourself

"Well, then, it's unanimous." Anne Whiteside, San Francisco, Calif. (The winning caption.)

"So that settles it. This year, instead of cooking the books, we'll bake them in a light, flaky pastry." Michael Hirson, Washington, D.C.

"Who else found Gary's report a little too angry, white, and male?" Grant Ruple, Morristown, N.J.

World War II Kiss

Gordon Parks, *American Gothic*

or in a group, suggest possible captions. Once you have a caption or two, explain why your entry complements the drawing. (Below the cartoon are the three finalist suggestions, printed upside down. Don't read them until you've made your own suggestions.)

3 Analyze the spoof-ad that appears on the opening page of this chapter. First, examine the visual for composition, focus, narrative, theme, and rhetorical appeals. After you have written your analysis, search the Internet and your library databases for a short, full-text news article, report, editorial, or op-ed column that discusses the dietary or health problems associated with fast foods. Download a full-text version of this article into a Word file, and then download and insert this image in an appropriate place in that article. Write a paragraph explaining why this McDonald's spoof-ad is (or perhaps is not) appropriate to the purpose and audience of that article.

4 Study the two famous photographs presented on this page. Choose one and write your own analysis of that image. First, analyze the image. Then write a narrative of what you imagine happened before, during, and after the moment recorded in this image. Finally, *research* these two photographs and their photographers on the internet and add a final paragraph explaining how the information you discovered confirms or revises your analysis and your narrative.

5. Find three advertisements that advertise the same product (or same kind of product, such as cars, jeans, or perfume) in different magazines directed at different audiences. For example, you might find similar ads in *Time, Wired,* and *Seventeen.* Analyze each ad for its compositional features, and then describe how the ad changes in its composition, focus, narrative, theme, or appeals based on different target audiences. Which of these ads is most effective for its target audience? Why?

6. Choose an essay that you have already written for this course or for a previous writing course. Revise and format it on your computer for a more public audience, choosing the genre of a short newspaper article, brochure, flyer, or poster. Practice using the layout features (sidebars, inserted visuals, double columns, pulled quotations, drop caps, tables, and color) appropriate for that genre. As a postscript for your revision, explain why you made the choices you did during your revision.

7. Analyze the following cartoon, which appeared in *The New Yorker*. What are the main compositional features? Is this cartoon humorous, serious, or both? If you were looking for a visual to use in an article about possible cell phone legislation, would this image be effective? Research your library's databases for recent newspaper articles or editorials about cell phone use and abuse. Find a short article or editorial, copy it into your computer Word file, and insert this image at an appropriate place. Then write a paragraph explaining why this

"I was distracted for a moment. Go on."

THERE'S ANOTHER LANGUAGE INSIDE YOU. GIVE IT A VOICE.

Do you want to communicate a new voice to the world, to express another side of you? With Rosetta Stone® you can. In any language.

- We teach language naturally, pairing words spoken by native speakers with vivid, real-life imagery in context, activating your mind's inherent ability to learn a language.
- Speech recognition coaches you to the right pronunciation, so you'll be speaking quickly and correctly. In no time at all, you'll find that the new language you tried on is a perfect fit.

Rosetta Stone. The fastest way to learn a language. Guaranteed.

Over 30 languages available.

SAVE 10%

Level 1	$233
Level 1&2	$377
Level 1,2&3	$494

100% six-month money-back guarantee.

PICK UP A NEW LANGUAGE TODAY!
(866) 833-8301   RosettaStone.com/sas029a
Use promo code sas029a when ordering. Offer expires June 30, 2009.

RosettaStone

The woman in this advertisement appears to be a successful and affluent professional based upon her attire. Many of the members of the audience for this publication are likely to be part of this elite class, since 82% of readers have a college degree. There is also an intellectual appeal in the picture: this woman is seeking to broaden her horizons even though she is already successful. Since 51% of readers for *Scientific American Mind* are women, a large number of audience members may be able to identify with her or aspire to her status and success.

The Rosetta Stone program is relatively expensive and must therefore seek to target an affluent audience. *Scientific American Mind* is a good publication to appeal to this audience because the average household income is $119,000, and average household net worth is $827,000.

The bright yellow of the Rosetta Stone logo also frames the picture and serves as a backdrop for the saying "There's another language inside you. Give it a voice." This effectively unifies the elements of the advertisement. The bright yellow is an active appeal to initiative, which is likely to draw the attention of this magazine's audience. *Scientific American Mind's* web site says in its mission statement that it is "aimed at inquisitive adults who are passionate about knowing more about how the mind works". These same individuals who want to know more about the mind are likely to be interested in learning about other cultures and languages.

Analysis of Rosetta Stone ad by Sarah Kay Hurst

image complements the message of the article. On Google Images, find another image about cell phone use that would be effective for your article or editorial. Which of the two images (the cartoon shown here or the visual you found) would be more effective? Explain.

8 Choose an advertisement in a magazine and analyze it for how it works in the context of that particular magazine. First, research the magazine to profile its readers (typical income, class, occupations, or interests). Then examine several advertisements from this magazine to see which ads make the most effective appeals to this group of readers. Choose one particular ad and annotate it for appeals to audience as well as use of key images, color, graphics, balance, layout, diagonals, and accompanying text. Use the analysis of a Rosetta Stone advertisement in *Scientific American* by student writer Sarah Kay Hurst as an example (see page 204).

PROFESSIONAL WRITING

Miss Clairol's "Does She . . . Or Doesn't She?": How to Advertise a Dangerous Product

James B. Twitchell

A longtime professor of English at the University of Florida, James B. Twitchell has written a dozen books on a variety of academic and cultural topics. His recent books on advertising and popular culture include Carnival Culture: The Trashing of Taste in America *(1992),* Adcult USA: The Triumph of Advertising in American Culture *(1996), and* Living It Up: Our Love Affair with Luxury *(2002). In "Miss Clairol's Does She . . . Or Doesn't She?" taken from* Twenty Ads That Shook the World *(2000), Twitchell examines the Miss Clairol advertising campaign, which was designed by Shirley Polykoff. Twitchell explains how Polykoff's ads, which ran for nearly twenty years, revolutionized the hair-coloring industry. Part of the success of the ad was in the catchy title, Twitchell notes, but equally important were the children in the ads and the follow-up phrase, "Hair color so natural, only her hairdresser knows for sure." (Before you read Twitchell's essay, however, look at several of Polykoff's Clairol ads by searching for Shirley Polykoff on Google.)*

Two types of product are difficult to advertise: the very common and *1* the very radical. Common products, called "parity products," need contrived distinctions to set them apart. You announce them as "New and Improved, Bigger and Better." But singular products need the illusion of acceptability. They have to appear as if they were *not* new and big, but old and small.

So, in the 1950s, new objects like television sets were designed to look *2* like furniture so that they would look "at home" in your living room. Meanwhile, accepted objects like automobiles were growing massive tail fins to make them seem bigger and better, new and improved.

...continued Miss Clairol's "Does She . . . Or Doesn't She?," **James B. Twitchell**

Although hair coloring is now very common (about half of all [3] American women between the ages of thirteen and seventy color their hair, and about one in eight American males between thirteen and seventy does the same), such was certainly not the case generations ago. The only women who regularly dyed their hair were actresses like Jean Harlow, and "fast women," most especially prostitutes. The only man who dyed his hair was Gorgeous George, the professional wrestler. He was also the only man to use perfume.

In the twentieth century, prostitutes have had a central role in de- [4] veloping cosmetics. For them, sexiness is an occupational necessity, and hence anything that makes them look young, flushed, and fertile is quickly assimilated. Creating a full-lipped, big-eyed, and rosy-cheeked image is the basis of the lipstick, eye shadow, mascara, and rouge industries. While fashion may come *down* from the couturiers, face paint comes *up* from the street. Yesterday's painted woman is today's fashion plate.

In the 1950s, just as Betty Friedan was sitting down to write *The Feminine Mystique,* there were three things a lady should not do. She should not smoke in public, she should not wear long pants (unless under an overcoat), and she should not color her hair. Better she should pull out each gray strand by its root than risk association with those who bleached or, worse, dyed their hair.

This was the cultural context into which Lawrence M. Gelb, a chem- [6] ical broker and enthusiastic entrepreneur, presented his product to Foote, Cone & Belding. Gelb had purchased the rights to a French hair-coloring process called Clairol. The process was unique in that unlike other available hair-coloring products, which coated the hair, Clairol actually penetrated the hair shaft, producing softer, more natural tones. Moreover, it contained a foamy shampoo base and mild oils that cleaned and conditioned the hair.

When the product was first introduced during World War II, the ap- [7] plication process took five different steps and lasted a few hours. The users were urban and wealthy. In 1950, after seven years of research and development, Gelb once again took the beauty industry by storm. He introduced the new Miss Clairol Hair Color Bath, a single-step hair-coloring process.

This product, unlike any haircolor previously available, lightened, [8] darkened, or changed a woman's natural haircolor by coloring and shampooing hair in one simple step that took only twenty minutes. Color results were more natural than anything you could find at the corner beauty parlor. It was hard to believe. Miss Clairol was so technologically advanced that demonstrations had to be done onstage at the International Beauty Show, using buckets of water, to prove to the industry that it was not a hoax. This breakthrough was almost too revolutionary to sell.

In fact, within six months of Miss Clairol's introduction, the number of women who visited the salon for permanent hair-coloring services increased by more than 500 percent! The women still didn't think they could do it themselves. And *Good Housekeeping* magazine rejected hair-color advertising because they too didn't believe the product would work. The magazine waited for three years before finally reversing its decision, accepting the ads, and awarding Miss Clairol's new product the "Good Housekeeping Seal of Approval." 9

FC&B passed the "Yes you *can* do it at home" assignment to Shirley Polykoff, a zesty and genial first-generation American in her late twenties. She was, as she herself was the first to admit, a little unsophisticated, but her colleagues thought she understood how women would respond to abrupt change. Polykoff understood emotion, all right, and she also knew that you could be outrageous if you did it in the right context. You can be very naughty if you are first perceived as being nice! Or, in her words, "Think it out square, say it with flair." And it is just this reconciliation of opposites that informs her most famous ad. 10

She knew this almost from the start. On July 9, 1955, Polykoff wrote to the head art director that she had three campaigns for Miss Clairol Hair Color Bath. The first shows the same model in each ad, but with slightly different hair color. The second exhorts "Tear up those baby pictures! You're a redhead now," and plays on the American desire to refashion the self by rewriting history. These two ideas were, as she says, "knock-downs" en route to what she really wanted. In her autobiography, appropriately titled *Does She . . . Or Doesn't She?: And How She Did It*, Polykoff explains the third execution, the one that will work: 11

> #3. Now here's the one I really want. If I can get it sold to the client. Listen to this: "*Does she . . . or doesn't she?*" (No, I'm not kidding. Didn't you ever hear of the arresting question?) Followed by: "*Only her mother knows for sure!*" or "*So natural, only her mother knows for sure!*"
>
> I may not do the mother part, though as far as I'm concerned mother is the ultimate authority. However, if Clairol goes retail, they may have a problem of offending beauty salons, where they are presently doing all of their business. So I may change the word "mother" to "hairdresser." This could be awfully good business—turning the hairdresser into a color expert. Besides, it reinforces the claim of naturalness, and not so incidentally, glamorizes the salon.
>
> The psychology is obvious. I know from myself. If anyone admires my hair, I'd rather die than admit I dye. And since I feel so strongly that the average woman is me, this great stress on naturalness is important [Polykoff 1975, 28–29].

While her headline is naughty, the picture is nice and natural. Exactly 12
what "Does She . . . or Doesn't She" do? To men the answer was clearly sexual, but to women it certainly was not. The male editors of *Life* magazine balked about running this headline until they did a survey and found out women were not filling in the ellipsis the way they were.

Women, as Polykoff knew, were finding different meaning because 13
they were actually looking at the model and her child. For them the picture was not presexual but postsexual, not inviting male attention but expressing satisfaction with the result. Miss Clairol is a mother, not a love interest.

If that is so, then the product must be misnamed: it should be *Mrs.* 14
Clairol. Remember, this was the mid-1950s, when illegitimacy was a powerful taboo. Out-of-wedlock children were still called bastards, not love children. This ad was far more dangerous than anything Benetton or Calvin Klein has ever imagined.

The naughty/nice conundrum was further intensified *and* diffused 15
by some of the ads featuring a wedding ring on the model's left hand. Although FC&B experimented with models purporting to be secretaries, schoolteachers, and the like, the motif of mother and child was always constant.

So what was the answer to what she does or doesn't do? To women, 16
what she did had to do with visiting the hairdresser. Of course, men couldn't understand. This was the world before unisex hair care. Men still went to barber shops. This was the same pre-feminist generation in which the solitary headline "Modess . . . because" worked magic selling female sanitary products. The ellipsis masked a knowing implication that excluded men. That was part of its attraction. Women know, men don't. This you-just-don't-get-it motif was to become a central marketing strategy as the women's movement was aided *and* exploited by Madison Avenue nichemeisters.

Polykoff had to be ambiguous for another reason. As she notes in her 17
memoir, Clairol did not want to be obvious about what they were doing to their primary customer—the beauty shop. Remember that the initial product entailed five different steps performed by the hairdresser, and lasted hours. Many women were still using hairdressers for something they could now do by themselves. It did not take a detective to see that the company was trying to run around the beauty shop and sell to the end-user. So the ad again has it both ways. The hairdresser is invoked as the expert—only he knows *for sure*—but the process of coloring your hair can be done without his expensive assistance.

The copy block on the left of the finished ad reasserts this intimacy, 18
only now it is not the hairdresser speaking, but another woman who has used the product. The emphasis is always on *returning* to young and ra-

diant hair, hair you used to have, hair, in fact, that glistens exactly like your current companion's—your child's hair.

The copy block on the right is all business and was never changed dur- 19 ing the campaign. The process of coloring is always referred to as "automatic color tinting." *Automatic* was to the fifties what *plastic* became to the sixties, and what *networking* is today. Just as your food was kept automatically fresh in the refrigerator, your car had an automatic transmission, your house had an automatic thermostat, your dishes and clothes were automatically cleaned and dried, so, too, your hair had automatic tinting.

However, what is really automatic about hair coloring is that once 20 you start, you won't stop. Hair grows, roots show, buy more product . . . automatically. The genius of Gillette was not just that they sold the "safety razor" (they could give the razor away), but that they also sold the concept of being *clean-shaven*. Clean-shaven means that you use their blade every day, so, of course, you always need more blades. Clairol made "roots showing" into what Gillette had made "five o'clock shadow."

As was to become typical in hair-coloring ads, the age of the model 21 was a good ten years younger than the typical product user. The model is in her early thirties (witness the age of the child), too young to have gray hair.

This aspirational motif was picked up later for other Clairol prod- 22 ucts: "If I've only one life . . . let me live it as a blonde!" "Every woman should be a redhead . . . at least once in her life!" "What would your husband say if suddenly you looked 10 years younger?" "Is it true blondes have more fun?" "What does he look at second?" And, of course, "The closer he gets the better you look!"

But these slogans for different brand extensions only work because Miss 23 Clairol had done her job. She made hair coloring possible, she made hair coloring acceptable, she made at-home hair coloring—dare I say it—empowering. She made the unique into the commonplace. By the 1980s, the hairdresser problem had been long forgotten and the follow-up lines read, "Hair color so natural, they'll never know for sure."

The Clairol theme propelled sales 413 percent higher in six years and 24 influenced nearly 50 percent of all adult women to tint their tresses. Ironically, Miss Clairol, bought out by Bristol-Myers in 1959, also politely opened the door to her competitors, L'Oreal and Revlon.

Thanks to Clairol, hair coloring has become a very attractive business 25 indeed. The key ingredients are just a few pennies' worth of peroxide, ammonia, and pigment. In a pretty package at the drugstore it sells for four to ten dollars per application. To put it mildly, the cost-revenue spread is what is really enticing. Gross profits of 70 percent are standard. As is common in the beauty industry, advertising and promotion cost far more than the product.

If you want to see how well this Clairol campaign did, just look at 26 how L'Oreal sells its version of hair dye. In L'Oreal's pitch, a rapturous beauty proudly proclaims that her coloring costs more, but that "I'm

...continued Miss Clairol's "Does She . . . Or Doesn't She?," **James B. Twitchell**

worth it." In a generation, hair coloring has gone from a surreptitious whisper (Does she . . . ?) to a heroic trumpet (You better believe I do!). The user may be dangerous, the product certainly isn't. L'Oreal now dominates the worldwide market.

But by taking control of how the new woman presented herself, Miss 27 Clairol did indeed make it possible to come a long way, baby. In a current ad for Miss Clairol's descendant Nice 'n' Easy, the pixieish Julia Louis Dreyfus, from *Seinfeld*, shows us how the unique and dangerous has become common and tame. In her Elaine persona, she interrupts a wedding, telling the bride, "Even if your marriage doesn't last, your haircolor will." The guests are not shocked; they nod understandingly.

vo•cab•u•lar•y

In your journal, write down the meanings of the following words.

- is quickly *assimilated* (**4**)
- from the *couturiers* (**4**)
- enthusiastic *entrepreneur* (**6**)
- *reconciliation* of opposites (**10**)
- filling in the *ellipsis* (**12**)
- models *purporting* to be secretaries (**15**)
- the *motif* of mother and child (**15**)
- had to be *ambiguous* (**17**)

QUESTIONS FOR WRITING AND DISCUSSION

❶ Recall the first time you colored your hair—or cut or styled it in a particular way. What was your attitude toward making a change? Did you change because of influences from peers, family, friends, advertisements, or other social pressure? What was the effect of the change on your attitude, personality, or relationships with others?

❷ A key part of any successful advertising campaign is understanding the rhetorical situation: the product, the purpose and audience, the occasion, the selected text and images, and the cultural context. First consider the cultural context. Twitchell subtitles his essay, "How to Advertise a Dangerous Product." According to Twitchell, what was culturally "dangerous" about a hair-coloring product at that time? What specifically were the dangers? How did Shirley Polykoff's Miss Clairol ads diffuse each of those dangers?

❸ Understanding and successfully appealing to the audience is a second key to any successful text or advertisement. Who was the audience or audiences for the Clairol advertisements? Cite particular paragraphs where Twitchell explains how the Clairol advertisements anticipated and successfully managed the problem of audience.

④ Key word choices (diction) played an important role in the success of the Clairol advertisements. Find three examples from the essay that show how Polykoff used—or didn't use—a key word in order to make the advertisement more successful.

⑤ In paragraph 15, Twitchell briefly mentions the "motif of mother and child" that appears in every Miss Clairol advertisement. Using the Internet or your library's databases, research cultural images of mother and child. Start by examining traditional Christian imagery. Consider Dorothea Lange's famous photograph of a migrant mother. How does the mother-child imagery work in these pictures to make them more effective? Then, working in a small group in your class, develop Twitchell's idea about the motif of mother and child. Why is this image culturally so important? Why was it rhetorically so important in the Miss Clairol advertisements?

Processes for Analyzing and Designing Visuals

ASSIGNMENT FOR ANALYZING VISUALS

Choose an audience and genre and analyze the effectiveness of a visual by itself or a visual with accompanying text and/or social context. For example, you might analyze an advertising campaign, political document with photographs, prize-winning or historical photograph, fine art, Internet visual, or other scientific, cultural, or social text that uses images and visuals.

Your purpose for this assignment is to analyze the visual for its composition, focus, narrative, themes, and/or rhetorical appeals in order to show how—and how effectively—it works with any accompanying text in its social context for the intended purpose and audience.

Audience	Possible Genres for Analyzing Visuals
Personal Audience	Class notes, journal entry, blog, scrapbook, social networking page.
Academic Audience	Academic analysis, media critique, review, journal entry, forum entry on class site, multi-genre document.
Public Audience	Column, editorial, article, or critique in a magazine, newspaper, online site, newsletter, or multi-genre document.

ASSIGNMENT FOR DESIGNING VISUALS

Choose a piece of writing that you are currently working on or have already written for this class or another class you are taking. Your assignment is to add visual elements (pictures, art, charts, graphic material) to your writing that will help illustrate the subject for your particular audience. Start by explaining the audience, purpose, genre, and context for this particular piece of writing. Then look for opportunities to provide visual elements that will help achieve your purpose for your audience. Select or design the visuals you will be using and insert them into your document. When you finish this assignment, write a postscript explaining the process you went through of selecting, designing, and integrating the material into your piece of writing. Illustrate your choices by referring to graphs or visuals that you decided **not** to use because they were not effective or appropriate for your audience or purpose.

Audience	Possible Visual Genres
Personal Audience	Photographs, art, digitized scrapbook images, collage, video, comics.
Academic Audience	Graphs, charts, diagrams, flow charts, organizational diagrams, photographs, digital images, art, video.
Public Audience	Graphs, charts, diagrams, flow charts, organizational diagrams, photographs, digital images, art, comics, graphic novel, video.

CHOOSING A SUBJECT

Unless you have a particular assignment, choose a contemporary image that you find incorporated in your reading for your other classes, reading and research that you do for your job, news items, Internet sites, billboards, or any other place where visuals appear in a clear rhetorical context. (If you choose to analyze a Web site, read the essay "Evaluating a Web Site," reprinted on pages 351–354.) Video clips from the Internet can work if they are short and if you are submitting your document online or in a digital environment. You may wish to choose a visual and compare it to other examples from that genre. You may wish to consider several similar images used for different gender, racial, or cultural contexts. Your assignment may even be to analyze a variety of possible visuals you could choose for an essay you are writing and to show why the ones you select are best suited to your purpose, audience, and genre. *Remember that when you download images from the Internet, you must give credit to the photographer, artist, or designer of the visual.*

COLLECTING

Many images are available on the Internet through Google or Yahoo! searches, or on popular image sites such as Corbis. Once you locate several appropriate visuals, begin by analyzing and taking notes on them, looking for key parts of the composition, focus, narrative, themes, and rhetorical appeals. However, you should also collect and analyze any accompanying texts or evidence that illustrates the social or historical context. Collecting visuals belonging to the same genre (historical photographs, advertising campaigns, political photographs, or Internet images) will also provide evidence helpful for your analysis. Researching the background, context, origin, or maker/designer of the image can be important, as is finding other commentaries and analyses of your particular type or genre of visuals. Use your *critical reading skills* to understand key points in these commentaries. Be sure to use your *observing* skills to help your analysis. Try closing your eyes and drawing the visual for yourself—what details did you remember and reproduce and what details did you forget? If you have any particular *memories* of this image or of the first time you saw this visual, you may want to add those to your account.

SHAPING

How you organize your analysis depends on the assignment, purpose, audience, and genre for your analysis. Three effective strategies for organizing are explained and illustrated here.

● **ANALYSIS FOCUSED ON THE VISUAL**   Often the specific details of the visual are the primary focus of the analysis. This is often the case with detailed or complex images whose meaning or significance may not be immediately obvious. The analysis focuses on composition, arrangement, focus, foreground and background images, images in the center and on the margin, symbols, cultural references, and key features of the genre. Only after analyzing these details will the commentary explain how these details are related to the cultural or historical context and thus contribute to the overall meaning.

The following analysis, by Charles Rosen and Henri Zerner, appeared in the *New York Review of Books*, and is of a painting by Norman Rockwell that appeared on the cover of *The Saturday Evening Post* in 1960. The authors devote over half of their essay to an analysis of the picture before they interpret the significance of Rockwell's self-portrait. Before you read Rosen's and Zerner's analysis, however, study the painting presented on page 213. What are the important details in the picture? What is the overall meaning or significance, based on your analysis?

Triple Self-Portrait
Charles Rosen and Henri Zerner

Claim: The portrait is a clever and witty comment on his own art.

Layout and composition of portrait

Description of details

More description of details

Triple Self-Portrait of 1960 is clever and witty. It is not simply a portrait of the artist by himself but represents the process of painting a self-portrait, and in the bargain Rockwell takes the opportunity to comment on his brand of "realism" and his relation to the history of art. A sheet of preparatory drawings in different poses is tacked onto the left of the canvas. The artist represents himself from the back; the canvas he works on already has a fully worked-out black-and-white drawing of his face with the pipe in his mouth, based on the central drawing of the sketch sheet. The artist gazes at his own reflection in a mirror propped up on a chair. The reflection we see in the mirror is similar to, but not identical with, the portrait sketched on the canvas. The artist wears glasses, and the glare of the lenses completely obliterates his gaze, while the portrait he works on is without glasses and a little younger-looking, certainly less tense than the reflection. Rockwell seems to confess that the reality of his depicted world, compelling as it may be, is in fact a make-believe.

Tacked on the upper right corner of the canvas is a series of reproductions of historical self-portraits: Dürer, Rembrandt, Van Gogh, and Picasso—grand company to measure oneself against, although the humorous tone of the image preserves it from megalomania. But there is a problem: "If Rockwell nodded humbly in Picasso's direction," as Robert Rosenblum suggests, how humbly was it? It is "most surprising," Rosenblum observes, that Rockwell chose "a particularly difficult Picasso that mixes in idealized self-portrait in profile with an id-like female monster attacking from within" rather than something easily recognizable. This was a cover for *The Saturday Evening Post*. The strength of Rockwell is that he knew his public, and knew that such subtleties would be entirely lost on its readers, that most of them would not recognize the Picasso as a self-portrait at all but would consider it as pretentious humbug compared to Rockwell's honest picture and those of the illustrious predecessors he claims. Nor does he seem to have been particularly anxious to change their minds, whatever he himself may have thought.

Interpreting the meaning and significance of the painting

● **ANALYSIS FOCUSED ON THE SOCIAL CONTEXT**   Often the visual or image is not detailed or complex, but the social, political, or historical context is complex, involved, or highly controversial. The following analysis, "Out of the Picture on the Abortion Ban," by Ellen Goodman, appeared in the *Boston Globe*. In this case, the photograph is not particularly complex or difficult, but it reveals much about the political and social context. The photograph is described at the beginning and then referred to at the end, providing a framework for Goodman's comment about the abortion debate.

Out of the Picture on the Abortion Ban
Ellen Goodman

Maybe this picture isn't worth a thousand words. That honor probably belongs to the flight deck portrait of the president under the sign, "Mission Accomplished." Maybe the presidential photo op now flying around the Internet and soon to be available on your local T-shirt is only worth 750 words.

Early reference to another frequently appearing photograph

The picture shows the president surrounded by an all-male chorus line of legislators as he signs the first ban on an abortion procedure. It's a single-sex class photo of men making laws governing something they will never have: a womb.

Short description and analysis of the photograph

This was not just a strategic misstep, a rare Karl Rove lapse. It perfectly reflected the truth of the so-called partial-birth abortion law. What's wrong with this picture? The legislators had indeed erased women. They used the law as if it were Photoshop software, to crop out real women with real problems.

Indeed, just days after the shutter snapped, three separate courts ordered a temporary halt to the ban on these very grounds: It doesn't have any exemption for the health of a woman.

*Analysis: What is missing from the photograph
Analysis: How the photograph connects to abortion*

This is what brings me back, kicking and screaming, to the subject of abortion. I don't want to write about this. Like most Americans, I want the abortion debate to end. I want abortion to be safe and rare. That's safe and rare. And early.

Over the years, I've rejoiced at sonograms and picked names for what we call a baby when it's wanted and a fetus when it isn't. I'm aware that medicine has put the moment of viability on a collision course with the moment of legal abortion. And I am also aware that not every pregnancy goes well, that sometimes families face terrible, traumatic choices.

Sixty-eight percent of Americans have been convinced by a public relations coup that this new law bans only a fringe and outrageous procedure. But the refusal to include an exception for the health of a pregnant woman takes this from the fringe to the heart of the debate. It's a deliberate, willful first strike at some of the most vulnerable women, those who need medical help the most.

Social and political contexts

The moment the anti-abortion leaders invented the term "partial-birth abortion," they made women invisible. The cartoon figures shown at congressional debates were, literally, drawings of a headless womb holding a perfect Gerber baby of some six or more months.

Social and political contexts

As Priscilla Smith, legal director of the Center for Reproductive Rights, said, "they turned the argument from the right of a woman to have an abortion to the reasons women have abortions." And then they declared those reasons to be frivolous.

The headless womb belonged to a generic woman who, as one opponent said, would get an abortion to fit into a prom dress. She would carry a pregnancy for months and then casually flip a coin between birth and an abortion "inches from life."

Time and again, abortion-rights supporters said they too would vote for the ban if opponents recognized that some pregnancies go terribly awry for the fetus or the woman and that some doctors found this procedure safest. But anti-abortion forces simply declared—against the evidence of the AMA or the American College of Obstetrics and Gynecology—that it was never medically necessary.

Reference to the abortion ban being signed in the photograph

Some years ago, when President Clinton vetoed a similar bill, he was surrounded by women. These women had been through pregnancies that came with words like hydrocephalus and polyhydramnia, and came with risks like hysterectomies. But the men around Bush see a health exception as a giant loophole. They believe a woman would leap through this loophole to get to the prom.

Reminder that another president had not signed a similar bill

Behind this is simply a mistrust of women as moral decision-makers. A mistrust so profound that their health is now in the hands of the courts. Not long ago, the Supreme Court ruled by exactly one vote that a law similar to this one violated the Constitution.

This should be a wake-up call to young women, because it's their health at risk, their role as moral decision-makers disparaged.

The most reliable supporters of abortion rights today are women over 50. It is, ironically, post-menopausal women who still lead the struggle to keep abortion legal for younger women. Everyone will tell you that the younger generation simply doesn't remember a time when abortion was illegal. They can't believe that it will ever be illegal again. How many believe they could be among those who need it?

Days before signing this ban, the president tried to reassure voters that it wasn't the time to "totally ban abortions." But young women should put this picture up on their desktops. The folks in that photo op don't trust you. They don't even see you.

Final reference to the omission of women in the photograph and in the making of laws directly affecting women

● **ANALYSIS FOCUSED ON THE STORY** In this organizational pattern, the visual or photograph receives some analysis and commentary, but most of the analysis is of the history of the photograph and the life story of the key figures in the photograph. A narrative or story can often be very effective as a means of understanding the significance or true meaning behind a picture. The following example, "Coming Home," by Carolyn Kleiner Butler, was published in *Smithsonian* in 2003. Her article appeared at a time when many families in the United States had loved ones serving in Iraq or Afghanistan. Butler chooses to analyze a famous Vietnam era photograph by Sal Veder, which he titled *Burst of Joy* and which won a Pulitzer Prize in 1974. Usually an analysis of an image focuses on what the image reveals and what it represents. In this case, however, Butler emphasizes how the reality behind the photograph contrasts sharply with the reality in the photograph. In other words, Butler contrasts the happy story of what the image reveals with the reality that it conceals.

Coming Home

Carolyn Kleiner Butler

To a war-weary nation, a U.S. POW's return from captivity in Vietnam in 1973 looked like the happiest of reunions.

The story just before the photograph was taken

SITTING IN THE BACK SEAT of a station wagon on the tarmac at Travis Air Force Base, in California, clad in her favorite fuchsia miniskirt, 15-year-old Lorrie Stirm felt that she was in a dream. It was March 17, 1973, and it had been six long years since she had last seen her father, Lt. Col. Robert L. Stirm, an Air Force fighter pilot who was shot down over Hanoi in 1967 and had been missing or imprisoned ever since. She simply couldn't believe they were about to be reunited. The teenager waited while her father stood in front of a jubilant crowd and made a brief speech on behalf of himself and other POW's who had arrived from Vietnam as part of "Operation Homecoming."

Lorrie's memories of her feelings when her dad returned

The minutes crept by like hours, she recalls, and then, all at once, the car door opened. "I just wanted to get to Dad as fast as I could," Lorrie says. She tore down the runway toward him with open arms, her spirits—and feet—flying. Her mother, Loretta, and three younger siblings—Robert Jr., Roger and Cindy—were only steps behind. "We

A hero's welcome: Lorrie, Robert Jr., Cindy, Loretta and Roger Stirm greet Lt. Col. Robert Stirm after his six years as a prisoner of war.

didn't know if he would ever come home," Lorrie says. "That moment was all our prayers answered, all our wishes come true."

Associated Press photographer Slava "Sal" Veder, who'd been standing in a crowded bullpen with dozens of other journalists, noticed the sprinting family and started taking pictures. "You could feel the energy and the raw emotion in the air," says Veder, then 46, who had spent much of the Vietnam era covering antiwar demonstrations in San Francisco and Berkeley. The day was overcast, meaning no shadows and near-perfect light. He rushed to a makeshift darkroom in a ladies' bathroom on the base (United Press International had commandeered the men's). In less than half an hour, Veder and his AP colleague Walt Zeboski had developed six remarkable images of that singular moment. Veder's pick, which he instantly titled *Burst of Joy*, was sent out over the news-service wires, published in newspapers around the nation and went on to win a Pulitzer Prize in 1974.

Shift to the photographer's story

The photographer's recollection of the emotions of that day

It remains the quintessential homecoming photograph of the time. Stirm, 39, who had endured gunshot wounds, torture, illness, starvation and despair in North Vietnamese prison camps, including the infamous Hanoi Hilton, is pictured in a crisp new uniform. Because his back is to the camera, as Veder points out, the officer seems anonymous, an everyman who represented not only the hundreds of POW's released that spring but all the troops in Vietnam who would return home to the mothers, fathers, wives, daughters and sons they'd left behind. "It's a hero's welcome for guys who weren't always seen or treated as heroes," says Donald Goldstein, a retired Air Force lieutenant colonel and a coauthor of *The Vietnam War: The Stories and The Photographs*, of the Stirm family reunion picture. "After years of fighting a war we couldn't win, a war that tore us apart, it was finally over, and the country could start healing."

The story from the soldier's or father's point of view

But there was more to the story than was captured on film. Three days before Stirm landed at Travis, a chaplain had handed him a Dear John letter from his wife. "I can't help but feel ambivalent about it," Stirm says today of the photograph. "I was very pleased to see my children—I loved them all and still do, and I know they had a difficult time—but there was a lot to deal with." Lorrie says, "So much had happened—there was so much that my dad missed out on—and it took a while to let him back into our lives and accept his authority." Her parents were divorced within a year of his return. Her mother remarried in 1974 and lives in Texas with her husband. Robert retired from the Air Force as a colonel in 1977 and worked as a corporate pilot and businessman. He married and was divorced again. Now 72 and retired, he lives in Foster City, California.

Events behind the moment of this photograph

As for the rest of the family, Robert Jr. is a dentist in Walnut Creek, California; he and his wife have four children, the oldest of whom is a marine. Roger, a major in the Air Force, lives outside Seattle. Cindy Pierson, a waitress, resides in Walnut Creek with her husband and has

How the lives of all the family members have changed

a daughter in college. And Lorrie Stirm Kitching, now 47, is an executive administrator and mother of two sons. She lives in Mountain View, California, with her husband. All four of Robert Stirm Sr.'s children have a copy of *Burst of Joy* hanging in a place of honor on their walls. But he says he can't bring himself to display the picture.

Three decades after the Stirm reunion, the scene, having appeared in countless books, anthologies and exhibitions, remains part of the nation's collective consciousness, often serving as an uplifting postscript to Vietnam. That the moment was considerably more fraught than we first assumed makes it all the more poignant and reminds us that not all war casualties occur on the battlefield.

"We have this very nice picture of a very happy moment," Lorrie says, "but every time I look at it, I remember the families that weren't reunited, and the ones that aren't being reunited today—many, many families—and I think, I'm one of the lucky ones."

Concluding comments leading up to Butler's thesis: Pictures do not always tell the complete story, and not all casualties occur on the battlefield.

DRAFTING

Before you begin drafting, collect all your notes, your visuals, and your research. Based on your materials, determine what you want the *focus* of your analysis to be—the visual itself, its relationship to any accompanying text or context, its relation to other images in its genre, or the rhetorical appeals that the visual makes. Depending on the assignment, your visuals, and your own purpose, narrow the strategies to the few that are most helpful in understanding the rhetoric of the visual.

If you are designing your own document, write out your accompanying text in a draft, and then experiment with the overall placement of text, images, and graphs. Cut out and arrange/rearrange the chunks of your text and visuals on a blank page until you find a combination of text, image, and use of white space that has the best effect for your purpose and audience.

Finally, obtain feedback or peer response to help you as you move from drafting to revising.

REVISING

As you revise your visual analysis or visual design project, consider your peer-response feedback. Some of it will be helpful, but some may not help you achieve your purpose. You must decide which changes to make.

GUIDELINES FOR REVISION

- **Review the purpose and audience for your assignment.** Does your draft analyze the key parts of the visual? If you are designing a document, give a draft to someone who is your intended audience or who might understand the needs of your intended audience. What suggestions does that person have?

- **Reexamine the visual.** What else do you notice about its composition, focus, narrative, or themes?
- **Reconsider relationships between the image and its text and context.** Much of the meaning and impact of the visual depends on the

PEER RESPONSE

The instructions that follow will help you give and receive constructive advice about the rough draft of your visual analysis or design document. Use these guidelines for an in-class workshop, a take-home review, or an electronic class forum response.

Writer: Before you exchange drafts, write out your responses to the following questions.

1. **Purpose** Briefly describe the purpose and intended audience of your essay or document. What is the main point you are trying to communicate?
2. **Revision Plans** Point out one part of your essay that is successful at achieving your purpose. Describe the parts of your essay that do not seem to be working or are not yet completed.
3. **Questions** Write out one or two specific questions that you still have about your visual analysis or your design. Where exactly would you like help on this project?

Reader: First, read the entire draft or document from start to finish without making any comments. Then as you reread the draft, answer the following questions.

1. **Techniques for analyzing visuals** Where in the draft do you see the writer using the techniques for analyzing visuals discussed in this chapter? Which techniques should be more developed to help achieve the writer's purpose? Explain.
2. **Context** Where do you see the writer analyzing or using the social, political, or cultural context of the visuals? What other aspects of context might the writer consider?
3. **Responses to visuals** Write out your response to these visuals. What key elements of these visuals do you see that the writer does not comment on? Where would you disagree with the writer's analysis? Explain.

Continued

4. **Response to design** Analyze the writer's document design. Is it too busy, cluttered, or crowded? Does the document need more text and fewer visuals? Does it need to cut text and increase white space? What might the audience for this document say about its attractiveness, simplicity of message, or overall effectiveness?

5. **Response to the assignment** The visual analysis or document design needs to respond to the assignment. Where does this draft respond to the assignment? Where doesn't it respond to the assignment? Explain.

6. **Answer the writer's questions** Briefly respond to the writer's questions listed above.

accompanying text and on the social, political, and cultural context. Look again at these possible relationships.

- **Reconsider the genre of your visual or your document.** If you are analyzing a visual, have you collected other examples of visuals in that genre? How are these examples similar to or different from your visual? If you are designing a document, have you checked other documents belonging to this genre? How does yours compare to them? How could you use their ideas to improve your document?

- **Check your visual or your document for its rhetorical appeals.** Make sure your draft comments on or makes use of appropriate rhetorical appeals to logic, to character, and to emotion. Are these appeals effective for the purpose and audience of the visual or the document?

- **Organize your analysis.** Check your draft to make sure the parts of your analysis add up to or contribute to your overall thesis or claim.

- **Revise and edit sentences to improve clarity, conciseness, and emphasis.** Check your handbook for suspected problems with usage, grammar, and punctuation. Be sure to spell check your final version.

POSTSCRIPT ON THE WRITING PROCESS

1. Describe the process you used to analyze your visual in its context or to design your own document. What did you do first? How did your research help? What advice did you get from your peers? What major change(s) did you make for your final version?

2. Write out the sentence or sentences that contain your thesis or main claim of your visual analysis. If you are designing a document, explain where you put the focus and how you related both your text and your images to that focus or main idea.

3. Explain the two or three most important things you learned about visual analysis or document design as you wrote your analysis or worked through your project.

4. What parts of your analysis or document still need revision? If you had one more day to work on the project, what changes would you make? Explain.

KARYN M. LEWIS

Some Don't Like Their Blues at All

Karyn Lewis decided to write an analysis of an advertisement for Fila jeans that she found in a magazine. She chose this particular advertisement because it created an image for the product that was based on stereotyped portrayals of gender roles. Instead of using its power to break down gender stereotypes, Fila deliberately used common stereotypes (men are strong and hard; women are weak and soft) to help sell their clothing. Lewis's analysis explains how Fila's images perpetuate the myth that men are "creatures of iron," while women are soft and "silly bits of fluff," leaving viewers of the advertisement without positive gender role models.

He strides toward us in navy and white, his body muscled and heavy-set, one *1* arm holding his casually flung jeans jacket over his shoulder. A man in his prime, with just the right combination of macho and sartorial flair.

He is also black. *2*

She is curled and giggling upon a chair, her hair loose and flowing *3* around her shoulders, leaning forward innocently—the very picture of a blossoming, navy flower.

She is white. *4*

They are each pictured on a magazine page of their own, situated op- *5* posite each other in a complementary two-page spread. They are stationed in front of a muted photograph which serves as a background for each one. They both merit their own captions: bold indigo letters presiding over them in the outer corners of each page.

His says: SOME LIKE THEIR BLUES HARD. *6*

Hers says: SOME LIKE THEIR BLUES SOFT. *7*

His background depicts a thrusting struggle between a quarterback *8* and a leaping defender, a scene of arrested violence and high tension.

Her background is a lounging, bikini-clad goddess, who looks at the 9
camera with intriguing, calm passion. She raises her hand to rest behind
her head in a languid gesture as she tries to incite passion within the viewer.

At the bottom of the page blazes the proud emblem of the company 10
that came up with this ad: FILA JEANS.

This advertisement blatantly uses stereotypes of men and women to 11
sell its product. It caters to our need to fit into the roles that society has
deemed right for the individual sexes ever since patriarchal rule rose up
and replaced the primitive worship of a mother goddess and the rever-
ence for women. These stereotypes handed down to us throughout the
centuries spell out to us that men are violence and power incarnate, and
that the manly attitude has no room for weakness or softness of nature.
And we find our role model of women in the compliant and eager female
who obeys her man in all things, who must not say no to a male, and who
is not very bright—someone who flutters her eyelashes, giggles a lot, and
uses tears to get her way.

This ad tells us, by offering the image of a hard, masculine male, who 12
is deified in violence, that he is the role model men should aspire to, and
that for women, their ideal is weak but sexual, innocent and at the same
time old enough to have sex. In viewing this ad, we see our aspirations
clothed in Fila jeans, and to be like them, we must buy the clothes pictured here. This ad also suggests that a man can become hard and powerful (or at least look it) dressed in these jeans; a woman can become
sexually intense and desirable dressed in Fila's clothing.

The words of the captions tantalize with their sexual innuendo. The 13
phrase "Some like their blues hard" hints at male sexual prowess. Most
men and women in this country are obsessed with males' need to prove
their virility, and Fila plays on this obsession. Females too have their own
stereotype of what constitutes their sexuality. "Some like their blues soft"
exemplifies this ideal: A woman should be soft and yielding. Her soft,
sensuous body parts, which so excite her partners, have been transformed into her personal qualities. By using the term *soft,* Fila immediately links the girl with her sexuality and sexual organs.

We are shown by the models' postures that men and women are 14
(according to Fila) fundamentally different and total antonyms of one
another. He is standing and walking with purpose; she sits, laughing
trivially at the camera. Even the background hints at separation of the
sexes.

The football players on the man's page are arranged in a diagonal 15
line which starts at the upper left-hand corner and runs to the opposite
corner, which is the center of the ad. On her page, the enchanting
nymph in the bathing suit runs on a diagonal; beginning where his ends,
and traveling up to the upper right-hand corner of her page. These two

photos in effect create a *V*, which both links the two models and suggests movement away from one another. Another good example of their autonomy from one another is their skin color. He is a black man, she's white. Black is the opposite color of white on an artist's color wheel and palette and symbolizes dynamically opposed forces: good and evil, night and day, man and woman. This ad hits us with the idea that men and women are not parallel in nature to one another but are fundamentally different in all things. It alienates the sexes from each other. Opposites may attract, but there is no room for understanding a nature completely alien to your own.

So in viewing this ad, and reading its captions, the consumer is left 16 with the view that a woman must be "soft" and sensual, a male's sexual dream, and must somehow still retain her innocence after having sex. She must be weak, the opposite of the violence which contrasts with her on the opposite page. The men looking at this ad read the message that they are supposed to be well-dressed and powerful and possess a strength that borders on violence. As we are told by the caption, men should be "hard." Furthermore, men and women are opposite creatures, as different as two sides of a coin.

This ad is supposed to cause us to want to meet these requirements, 17 but it fills me with a deep-rooted disgust that we perpetuate the myth that men are unyielding creatures of iron and women are silly bits of fluff. The ad generates no good role models to aspire to, where men and women are equal beings, and both can show compassion and still be strong. Fila may like their blues hard and soft, but I don't like their blues at all.

 ## QUESTIONS FOR WRITING AND DISCUSSION

1. Fila did not grant permission to reproduce their advertisement for this text. However, Lewis does an excellent job of describing the layout, balance, color, key figures, diagonals, and background. In the margin of this essay, indicate those sentences where Lewis describes the advertisement, enabling us to clearly visualize it.

2. Parts of Lewis's essay describe and analyze the text that accompanies the advertisement, but she spends most of her time discussing the social, cultural, and gendered contexts of the advertisement. In the margin of the essay, indicate places where she analyzes the accompanying *text* and where she analyzes the *context* of the advertisement. Where in her analysis do you see her showing how text and context relate to each other? Explain.

3 Examine how Lewis *organizes* her analysis of the Fila advertisement. How does her organization reflect her thesis that the two figures, hers and his, are opposites? In other words, where and how does she use sentences and paragraphs to show that these two figures are "fundamentally different and total antonyms of each other"?

4 The genre of the Fila promotion is the clothing or fashion advertisement. Find at least three other advertisements for clothing or fashion. Use Lewis's strategy and analyze how the images, text, and context function together. How are the overall messages in these advertisements similar to or different from the messages that Lewis finds? Explain.

STUDENT WRITING

LAWRENCE FLETCHER

Weight Loss 101 for the Adult Fitness Program

For his class assignment, Lawrence Fletcher was asked to work with a community organization to produce a brochure, flyer, or pamphlet. Fletcher's site partner was the Adult Fitness Center, which needed a four-page informative pamphlet to help increase its members' understanding of weight-loss strategies that use good nutrition and dieting practices. After researching effective dieting strategies, Fletcher wrote a sixteen-page document for the adult members, which he then revised and cut down to the length required by the center. To make his pamphlet more attractive, Fletcher used bulleted lists, photographs, and charts to illustrate key strategies and highlight important information.

Are you working hard in the gym and still not shedding the pounds? Is 1 your face dripping in sweat and you're out of breath from the cardio, but you still have unwanted weight? Are your muscles sore from weightlifting, but your arms are just not as toned as you think they should be? If you have answered YES to even one of these questions, you can do one more thing to fight the fat and enjoy that fit and youthful body you have always wanted. The key to obtaining your weight loss goal is through choosing a healthy diet!

Two main ways adults become overweight are through eating too 2 much food and not being active enough (kind of a no brainer, right?). We all know the reasons why we get big, but fighting the problem is not so easy.

With good nutritional habits combined with the right fitness levels, 3 you should have no trouble in dropping extra pounds to feel healthy and good about yourselves. Take the challenge of fighting the fat and become the new you! It will be fun and easy!

FAD DIETS—KICK 'EM OUT!

In our fast paced world, we are very concerned with the quick and easy 4 solution to weight loss. People discuss the low-fat, low-carb, and miracle diets that swarm our everyday lives. These diets are not the key to long-term weight loss.

The low-carbohydrate diet popularized through the Atkins and 5 South Beach programs poses many health risks to a person. Low intake of fruits and vegetables from the diet limits the vitamins, minerals, phytochemicals, and especially fiber you can get through the course of a day leaving yourself nutrient deficient. Meals rich in saturated fats from the diet produce long-term negative health effects such as heart disease according to Dr. Chris Melby, a professor of Advanced Nutrition at CSU. The low-carb diet is not an eating regimen you could possibly meet the rest of your life. Forget the low-carb craze!

Low-fat diets are not the best solution to shed pounds. Low-fat foods 6 associated with diets can be extremely high in sugar content and will actually make a person overeat and gain weight. Low-fat cookies and ice cream are not your friends. Forget the fads! Let's focus on a safe and easy approach to weight loss that will last a lifetime.

CALORIE BALANCE = A HEALTHY WEIGHT

The American Dietetic Association claims calorie balance is the one easy 7 and correct way to your weight loss solution. Dieters must simply manage their calories to ensure weight loss success. Making sure you eat fewer calories than what you use in a day will guarantee that you finally lose that extra baggage you carry around today.

One pound of body fat is equal to 3,500 calories. So to lose 1 pound 8 of fat in a week, a person must cut out 3,500 calories from their diet in that week. Dropping 1 pound may sound like a lot of work, but it's not if you follow a few simple rules.

TO CUT OUT THE CALORIES, YOU MUST:

- Know your nutritional requirements
- Eat the right foods
- Understand food labels
- Control the portions you eat
- Diet while dining out

...continued Weight Loss 101 for the Adult Fitness Program **Lawrence Fletcher**

FABULOUS FOODS

The key to a good diet is the food you are "allowed to eat." But let's not think of it as the food we're allowed to eat but rather the food we choose to eat to get that flat stomach.   9

Here are a few tips in choosing the right foods for you: *10*

- Eat more fruits and vegetables. Your mother has always told you this, and she was right. Eating fruits and vegetables replaces those "bad" foods high in sugar and fat which plague your body into obesity.
- Eat a variety of fruits! Eatright.org, supervised by the American Dietetic Association, suggests eating 2 cups of fruit each day whether frozen, fresh, canned, or dried.
- Eat your fruit, don't just drink them. Eat whole fruits rather than drinking fruit juices. Juices contain many sugar calories. Whole fruits will maintain your feeling of fullness longer.
- Vary your vegetables! Choose a wide variety of veggies including orange and dark green varieties like carrots, sweet potatoes, broccoli, and dark leafy greens to fill your appetite.
- Eat the lean meat! Meats such as fish and poultry are the champions.
- Stay away from the red meat! Red meat is loaded with saturated fat which is hard for the body to shed. If you prefer red meat, the US de-

Your Metabolism Will
Burn More Calories!

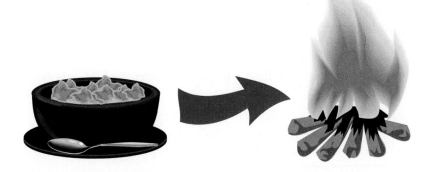

partment of Agriculture claims the leanest beef cuts include round
steaks and roasts as well as top loin and top sirloin.

- Choose turkey, ham, or roast beef for your sandwiches. These are the
lean deli meats. Salami, bologna, and bacon should be eaten minimally
because they contain much more fat and calories than other luncheon
meats.

- Eat whole grains in your diet, while tossing the refined carbohydrates
(sugars and white floured grains) into the garbage.

- Drink fewer alcoholic beverages. Alcohol is a temptation which leads
to big bellies and thighs. Many adults get home from work and want
to enjoy a glass of beer or wine to relax. Another way to relax is to
enjoy a nice cup of green tea full of anti-oxidants which fight cancer
as well as being low in calories.

- Drink six to eight glasses of water each day. Drinking water helps one
feel a sense of fullness which limits your need or urge to eat. Good hy-
dration will also lead to increased energy. Energy is motivation to
burn more calories in the gym!

- Choose dairy products which are low in fat or fat free. Many cheeses,
creams, and milk products are loaded with fat. Fat-free cottage cheese
or yogurt are smart choices for any dieter's dairy needs.

- Eat foods with more monounsaturated fats than polyunsaturated fat
and saturated fat. Olive oil, avocados, natural peanut butter, and cold
water fish contain good fats that are highly monounsaturated.

- Choose foods prepared by baking, grilling, and broiling more often
than frying. Fried foods are high in fat and calories that contribute to

...continued Weight Loss 101 for the Adult Fitness Program, **Lawrence Fletcher**

becoming overweight. Forget the hot wings; try something else! Grilled chicken also pleases the taste buds.

- Eat Breakfast! Breakfast jumpstarts your metabolism and helps you curb hunger throughout your day so you will be less prone to overeating.

By following some of these simple guidelines, weight loss will be within your reach!

READING THE LABELS AND COUNTING THE CALORIES

Keep your calories in check. Counting the calories you consume is not a hard *11* task and will aid in your weight loss. The key to your success in limiting calories will be to understand the food label placed on every food package in your cabinet and refrigerator.

Understanding the Label   *12*

- Check the food's fat and calorie content listed on the label. Choose foods that are lower in fats, especially saturated and trans fats, and low in calories. Foods with a smaller fat content will help you cut calories from your normal diet and lose some pounds with ease.

- Servings per container can be deceiving. One container may be more than 1 serving. Don't eat the whole box! Eat the appropriate serving size for your weight loss goal.

- Let the percent daily values (DVs) guide you to your weight loss goals. Use DVs to assist you in deciding how a particular food should fit into your diet.

- The FDA claims that DVs on labels today for the energy-producing nutrients such as protein, fat, and carbohydrates are based on the number of calories a person eats per day. The reference amount is 2000 calories, so do not be fooled. If you require more than 2000 calories per day, your DVs will be larger than what the label reads. If you require less than 2000 calories a day to maintain your weight, your DVs will be less than what the label says.

PORTION CONTROL: BE THE LEADER!

Portion control is a major part to winning your battle in weight loss. *13* Overeating is a common problem among Americans because of increased portion sizes. Super-sized foods and bigger bags of chips are leading to bigger waistlines in this fast-food nation.

You can still enjoy your favorite foods by keeping them in modera- *14* tion. Read the labels to determine if 3 cookies are really OK for your snack. ONE cookie may be more reasonable.

To lose weight, the Department of Health and   *15*
Human Services lists many suggestions to control
portion sizes.

- Serve food on individual plates! Placing food on individual plates helps reduce the opportunity to overeat by keeping excess food out of reach.

- Keep the serving dishes off the table and out of sight so you will not be tempted to dig in a second or third time.

- Take control when eating out! Split large entrees with a friend so you do not overeat and keep some money in your pocket and fat off your stomach.

- Ask your server for a "to-go" box as your food comes out so that you can split the meal in half and limit your intake at one meal. Now you will have food for tomorrow's lunch as well.

- Ask about child size portions that may be available to you.

- Order an appetizer as your entrée.

- Control portions by creating a diet-friendly environment! One suggestion is to replace a candy or cookie jar with a fruit basket, so you'll steal a piece of nutritious food between meals.

...continued Weight Loss 101 for the Adult Fitness Program, **Lawrence Fletcher**

For a quick reference of your portion sizes, here are some easy reminders 16 provided by the American Dietetic Association:

Food	Serving Size	About the size of...
Meat, Poultry, Fish	2 to 3 ounces	Deck of cards or palm of your hand
Pasta, Rice	1/2 cup	Small computer mouse or the size of your fist
Cooked Vegetables	1/2 cup	Small computer mouse
Fruit	1/2 cup	Small computer mouse or a medium apple, pear, or orange
Cheese	1 1/2 ounces hard cheese	C battery or your thumb

American Dietetic Association—eatright.org

CALCULATE THE CALORIES—JOT THEM DOWN

To keep yourself in check while cutting calories, try making a diary of 17 the food you eat and the beverages you consume throughout the course of a week. Record the calories at each meal and your total calories for a day. Jotting down all of your calories will assist in exposing hidden calories you did not realize you were taking in.

EATING OUT, DON'T LET IT RUIN YOUR GOAL!

Eating out on a regular basis can ruin your plan for weight loss as well 18 as diminish your healthy lifestyle. The Heart and Stroke Foundation has filled out the Fast Food Report Card and has reported failing grades for your fast-food choices!

Fast foods tend to be high in fat, calories, and sodium content. 19 Eating excess fat, especially saturated and trans fats, at your favorite fast-food establishment can increase your blood cholesterol levels, which puts you at a higher risk for heart disease, stroke, diabetes, and cancer. These excess calories from that burger and fries will also lead to weight gain, which is your enemy today!

If you are like many Americans who find it hard to make time to 20 cook nutritious meals at home or rely on the inexpensive option of fast-food meals, here's some advice to think about before you swallow that juicy burger:

- Stay away from the fried foods. French fries, fried fish, and fried chicken, like the world famous McNuggets, are villains to a healthy lifestyle. Instead of fried foods, choose grilled varieties of foods from your favorite fast-food stop.
- Grilled options such as chicken and fish are cooked without added fat, therefore will lack the fat and calorie content their fried counterparts have.
- Get rid of the fattening condiments. Condiments such as mayonnaise, ranch, and bleu cheese dressings are loaded with fat calories. Stay away from these unhealthy condiments and choose items such as ketchup, barbeque sauce, salsa, and hot sauce in moderation to add to your sandwich.
- Stay clear of the big sodas! Soda is composed mostly of high fructose corn syrup, also known as sugar, which can destroy your diet. A large 32-ounce soda may contain as much as 310 calories. Drink diet beverages instead.
- Drink tea without added sugar or water at a fast food joint. Tea and water are low in calories.

BEYOND FAST FOOD

As adults, it is fun to go out with friends, family, and coworkers for the *21* occasional meal full of hearty foods and good drinks. Your diet should not restrict the good times to be had! When you are out for a night on the town, make good decisions about what you eat so that you can stay true to your diet and weight loss goals.

The Heart and Stroke Foundation offers great suggestions for *22* healthy choices.

- *At the coffee shop* eat healthier options, such as a low-fat whole-grain muffin or bagel with a small amount of light cream cheese, coffee or tea.
- *At the deli or sandwich counter* good options include: whole-grain bread or bun; lean meats like ham, chicken, turkey, and roast beef; green salad, fruit salad, or bean salad; unsweetened juices or low-fat milk.
- *At the pizza place* choose smart options like: vegetarian or Hawaiian pizza, whole-wheat or grain crust, and lower-fat toppings such as ham, chicken, mushrooms, peppers, tomatoes, zucchini, artichokes, and low-fat cheese. Red-pepper is fine to give your pizza a little spice, but put the parmesan cheese back on the table. Your pizza already has plenty of cheese. Extra cheese equals extra fat and calories.
- *At the Asian café* healthy options include: steamed dumplings and buns; grilled/steamed/or stir-fried veggies; spring rolls, sushi, and cucumber salad; steamed rice (not fried!), noodles in soup, and light soy sauce with no MSG (monosodium glutamate).

...*continued* Weight Loss 101 for the Adult Fitness Program, **Lawrence Fletcher**

- *At your best burger stand* cut some calories with these choices: plain or child-size burgers (stay away from the double and triple patties if you want to lose extra pounds), light menu items, chili, and veggie burgers. Choose buffalo burgers over beef because buffalo is naturally a leaner meat.

- *At your Italian bistro* excellent choices include broiled, baked, grilled, or poached fish, grilled chicken, or veal. Pasta with vegetables in a red sauce will include the least amount of fat and calories. Stay clear of the lasagna and pastas drenched in creamy sauces. White sauce = excessive fat + calories!

    Enjoy your favorite restaurants by choosing healthy options on your quick and easy path to weight loss success. Many restaurants will include a 23 "healthy options" section on their menu.

DEVELOP ENERGY FOR LIFE WITH GOOD NUTRITION! GET OFF THE COUCH AND GET ACTIVE!

GET ON YOUR PATH TO SUCCESSFUL WEIGHT LOSS

It's now time to apply the knowledge 24 in this brochure to successfully shed those unwanted pounds! Get back into your favorite pair of jeans, tone those arms, and feel better about yourself today. Nutritional discipline combined with an effective workout routine (supplied to you by the wonderful people at the Adult Fitness Program) will lead you to your goal of a shaped and toned body and higher energy levels to take on the day.

Good luck meeting your weight loss 25 goals!

Further Information for Dieters:

In addition to this brochure, additional information to assist in your weight loss success can be found at many government supported Web sites which include:

www.mypyramid.gov
www.eatright.org
www.nutrition.gov
www.smallstep.gov

QUESTIONS FOR WRITING AND DISCUSSION

1 The first principle of designing documents with accompanying visuals is to consider purpose and audience. What is the purpose of Fletcher's brochure? Where do you find him stating or restating that purpose? Where do you find him adapting his text and his visuals to his adult audience? Find examples of both specific sentences and visuals that address his audience. Are there places where he could revise his language or his visuals to appeal more effectively to his audience? Explain.

2 To be effective, visuals must be relevant to the accompanying text. Ideally, however, they should not only be relevant, but they should also add attractiveness and impact that the text does not have by itself. Choose three of Fletcher's visuals and analyze their relevance, attractiveness, and impact. Which are his strongest and which are his weakest visuals? What substitutions might you suggest?

3 Assume that you are one of the managers of the Adult Fitness Center, and that you are going to revise and then actually print this brochure. What typeface and fonts would you use? Where would you want more white space? What colors might you use? Would you want to use Fletcher's text in a full-page brochure, or in a folding brochure? Would you add a sidebar indicating diet or exercise classes at your center? Write out your complete design plan for the finished brochure.

4 At your place of work, talk to your managers about a poster, flyer, instructional leaflet, or brochure that they could use. The project might be addressed to current customers, future customers, or even to employees. The resulting document should use both text and visuals, should be attractively designed, and should be addressed to and clearly appeal to its audience. Write your first draft of that document.

PEARSON
mycomplab

For additional writing, reading, and research resources, go to http://www.mycomplab.com

Investigating can be a fruitful technique for writers, even though writers may not get results as dramatic as the police officers do on *CSI: Crime Scene Investigation*. After examining this photo from the television program, do Journal exercise 7 on page 249.

Investigating

7

While watching joggers running in the park one day, you notice their straining muscles, their labored breathing, and the grimaces etched on their faces. Why, you wonder, do people go through the pain of running? Does it have a physical or a psychological benefit? Or can it even become an addiction for those people who *have* to run every day? You decide to investigate this question in runners' magazines and professional journals and then interview a few serious runners to determine their motives and the effects that running has on them, both physically and psychologically. The results of your report, you hope, will prove interesting to those who run as well as to those who merely watch others run.

For your campus magazine, you decide to write a profile of the professor who is leading the climate change initiatives at your college. First you e-mail her to see if she is willing to be interviewed and then shadowed during a typical day of activities and meetings. You prepare for the interview by researching her academic background, the classes she teaches, and her leadership of the climate change program. With this background, you conduct an hour-long interview during a mid-morning coffee break. At the interview, she suggests a day when you can go with her to a couple of meetings and attend one of her classes. With the information from your research, your interview, and your personal observations, you write a profile that appears in the campus magazine.

> " When you stop learning, stop listening, stop looking and asking questions, always new questions, then it is time to die. "
> —LILLIAN SMITH, CIVIL RIGHTS ACTIVIST, JOURNALIST, AUTHOR OF *KILLERS OF THE DREAM*

> " As the free press develops, the paramount point is whether the journalist, like the scientist or scholar, puts truth in the first place or in the second. "
> —WALTER LIPPMANN, JOURNALIST AND AUTHOR

NVESTIGATING BEGINS WITH QUESTIONS. WHAT CAUSES THE GREENHOUSE EFFECT? WHEN WILL THE WORLD BEGIN TO RUN OUT OF OIL? HOW DOES ILLITERACY AFFECT A PERSON'S LIFE? HOW WAS THE WORLD WIDE WEB CREATED? IS TALKING ON A CELL PHONE WHILE DRIVING AS DANGEROUS AS driving drunk? How do colleges recruit applicants? What can you find out about a famous person's personality, background, and achievements? What is Bono really like?

Investigating also carries an assumption that probing for answers to such questions—by observing and remembering, researching sources, interviewing key people, or conducting surveys—will uncover truths not generally known or accepted. As you dig for information, you learn *who, what, where,* and *when.* You may even learn *how* and *why.*

The purpose of investigating is to uncover or discover facts, opinions, information, and reactions and then to report that information to other people who want to know. Although no writing is ever free from cultural or personal bias, investigative writing strives to be as neutral and objective as possible. It may summarize other people's judgments, but it does not consciously editorialize. It may represent opposing viewpoints or arguments, but it does not argue for one side or the other. Investigative writing attempts to be a window on the world, allowing readers to see the information for themselves.

Techniques for Investigative Writing

> Curiosity is my natural state and has led me headlong into every worthwhile experience . . . I have ever had.
> —ALICE WALKER, AUTHOR OF *THE COLOR PURPLE*

Investigative writing begins with asking questions and finding informed sources: published material, knowledgeable people, or both. In most cases, collecting information in an investigation requires the ability to use a library and online resources and then to summarize, paraphrase, and quote key ideas accurately from other people's writing. In addition, personal interviews are often helpful or necessary. For an investigation, you might talk to an expert or an authority, an eyewitness or participant in an event, or the subject of a personality profile. Finally, you may wish to survey the general public to determine opinions, trends, or reactions. Once you have collected your information, you must then present your findings in a written form suitable for your audience, with clear references in the text to your sources of information.

The following texts illustrate a few of the many types of investigative writing: a summary of a research study, a brief report with graphics, a profile of a person, and a published interview. Though some investigative writing is brief, intended to be only short news items, other efforts are full-length features.

Techniques for Investigative Writing

Technique	Tips on How to Do It
Beginning with an interesting title and a catchy lead-in	Titles should announce the topic in a *concise but original* way. Lead-in sentences should arouse your *readers' interest* and focus their attention on the subject.
Giving background information by answering relevant who, what, when, where, how, and why questions	Answering the reporter's "Wh" questions *early in your report or article* ensures that readers have sufficient information to understand your report.
Stating the main idea, question, or focus of the investigation	The purpose of a report is to convey information as *clearly as possible*. Readers shouldn't have to guess the main idea.
Summarizing or quoting information from written or oral sources	Reports quote *accurately* any statistics, data, or sentences from the sources; they cite authors and titles in the text of the report.
Following appropriate genre conventions	A news report, a profile, an interview, and an investigative report follow different style and format conventions. Learn the key features of the particular *genre* with which you are working.
Writing in a readable and interesting style for the intended audience	*Clear, direct, and readable language* is essential in a report. Be as *accurate* and *factual* as possible. Use visuals, photos, graphs, and charts as appropriate.

The intended audience for each report is often determined by the publication in which the report appears: *Psychology Today* assumes that its readers are interested in personality and behavior; *Discover* magazine is for readers interested in popular science; readers of *Ms.* magazine expect coverage of contemporary issues concerning women.

REPORT ON A RESEARCH STUDY

The following report, prepared by the University of Utah News Center, describes a research study on the effects of driving while using cell phones. The article presents the results of the study conducted by psychology Professor David Strayer and his colleagues Frank Drews and Dennis Crouch. Notice that the report cites the authors, gives the research methodology, and summarizes the detailed findings of the study.

PROFESSIONAL WRITING

Attention-getting title

Background information on study

Drivers on Cell Phones Are as Bad as Drunks

June 29, 2006—Three years after the preliminary results first were pre- 1 sented at a scientific meeting and drew wide attention, University of Utah psychologists have published a study showing that motorists who talk on handheld or hands-free cellular phones are as impaired as drunken drivers.

Most important findings of study

"We found that people are as impaired when they drive and talk on a 2 cell phone as they are when they drive intoxicated at the legal blood-alcohol limit" of 0.08 percent, which is the minimum level that defines illegal drunken driving in most U.S. states, says study co-author Frank Drews, an assistant professor of psychology. "If legislators really want to address driver distraction, then they should consider outlawing cell phone use while driving."

"Who" information: the authors of the study

Psychology Professor David Strayer, the study's lead author, adds: 3 "Just like you put yourself and other people at risk when you drive drunk, you put yourself and others at risk when you use a cell phone and drive. The level of impairment is very similar."

"When" and "Where" information: When and Where the study was published.

"Clearly the safest course of action is to not use a cell phone while 4 driving," concludes the study by Strayer, Drews and Dennis Crouch, a research associate professor of pharmacology and toxicology. The study was set for publication June 29 in the summer 2006 issue of *Human Factors: The Journal of the Human Factors and Ergonomics Society.*

The study reinforced earlier research by Strayer and Drews showing 5 that hands-free cell phones are just as distracting as handheld cell phones because the conversation itself—not just manipulation of a handheld phone—distracts drivers from road conditions.

Human Factors Editor Nancy J. Cooke praised the study: "Although 6 we all have our suspicions about the dangers of cell phone use while driving, human factors research on driver safety helps us move beyond mere suspicions to scientific observations of driver behavior."

Key Findings: Different Driving Styles, Similar Impairment

"How" information: The methodology of the study

Each of the study's 40 participants "drove" a PatrolSim driving simula- 7 tor four times: once each while undistracted, using a handheld cell phone, using a hands-free cell phone and while intoxicated to the 0.08 percent blood-alcohol level after drinking vodka and orange juice. Participants followed a simulated pace car that braked intermittently.

Both handheld and hands-free cell phones impaired driving, with no *8* significant difference in the degree of impairment. That "calls into question driving regulations that prohibited handheld cell phones and permit hands-free cell phones," the researchers write.

The study found that compared with undistracted drivers:

- Motorists who talked on either handheld or hands-free cell phones drove slightly slower, were 9 percent slower to hit the brakes, displayed 24 percent more variation in following distance as their attention switched between driving and conversing, were 19 percent slower to resume normal speed after braking and were more likely to crash. Three study participants rear-ended the pace car. All were talking on cell phones. None were drunk.

  Results of the study

- Drivers drunk at the 0.08 percent blood-alcohol level drove a bit more slowly than both undistracted drivers and drivers using cell phones, yet more aggressively. They followed the pace car more closely, were twice as likely to brake only four seconds before a collision would have occurred, and hit their brakes with 23 percent more force. "Neither accident rates, nor reaction times to vehicles braking in front of the participant, nor recovery of lost speed following braking differed significantly" from undistracted drivers, the researchers write.

  Results of the study

"Impairments associated with using a cell phone while driving can be as *9* profound as those associated with driving while drunk," they conclude.

Are Drunken Drivers Really Less Accident-Prone than Cell Phone Users?

Drews says the lack of accidents among the study's drunken drivers *10* was surprising. He and Strayer speculate that because simulated drives were conducted during mornings, participants who got drunk were well-rested and in the "up" phase of intoxication. In reality, 80 percent of all fatal alcohol-related accidents occur between 6 P.M. and 6 A.M. when drunken drivers tend to be fatigued. Average blood-alcohol levels in those accidents are twice 0.08 percent. Forty percent of the roughly 42,000 annual U.S. traffic fatalities involve alcohol.

Analysis and discussion of results

While none of the study's intoxicated drivers crashed, their hard, late *11* braking is "predictive of increased accident rates over the long run," the researchers wrote.

One statistical analysis of the new and previous Utah studies showed *12* cell phone users were 5.36 times more likely to get in an accident than undistracted drivers. Other studies have shown the risk is about the same as for drivers with a 0.08 blood-alcohol level.

Analysis and discussion of results

Strayer says he expects criticism "suggesting that we are trivializing *13* drunken-driving impairment, but it is anything but the case. We don't

...continued Drivers on Cell Phones Are as Bad as Drunks

think people should drive while drunk, nor should they talk on their cell phone while driving."

Drews says he and Strayer compared the impairment of motorists 14 using cell phones to drivers with a 0.08 percent blood-alcohol level because they wanted to determine if the risk of driving while phoning was comparable to the drunken driving risk considered unacceptable.

"This study does not mean people should start driving drunk," says 15 Drews. "It means that driving while talking on a cell phone is as bad as or maybe worse than driving drunk, which is completely unacceptable and cannot be tolerated by society."

BRIEF REPORT WITH GRAPHICS

The following passage illustrates the genre of the brief report with graphics that was popularized by *USA Today*. Abigail Sullivan Moore's report, which appeared in the Education Life section of the *New York Times*, illustrates how a simple graphic can enhance the impact of a report.

PROFESSIONAL WRITING

Gimme an A (I Insist!)

Abigail Sullivan Moore

Grade inflation seems to be reaching record levels at the nation's high 1 schools, according to a new survey of incoming freshmen at more than 400 colleges and universities. Almost half reported an A average in high school, up from 18 percent in 1968. "Something is amiss," says Linda J. Sax, who directed the survey of 276,000 students for the Higher Education Research Institute at the University of California at Los Angeles. At the same time, she says, "students are studying, but not as often as they were."

Based on conversations with educators, Dr. Sax believes that parents 2 and pupils are pushing teachers for higher grades amid the intense competition for desirable colleges. Also, she says: "What I'm hearing is that teachers feel a pressure to not shatter students' self-esteem. Teachers are caught up in this web of pressure."

A study by the College Board released in January confirms the find- 3 ings: high school seniors' grades have climbed but SAT scores remain nearly unchanged. Wayne J. Camara, the board's vice president for research and development, says the trend started to accelerate in the early 90's, when "more and more middle-income families had much more awareness of college, and at the same time there was more discretionary income" to pay for the expensive, hard-to-get-into institutions. He predicts a correction is due. "Everyone can't get A's," he says.

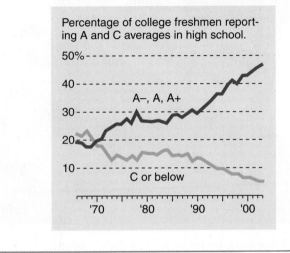

Percentage of college freshmen reporting A and C averages in high school.

PROFILE OF A PERSON

The following article is a profile of a person—a biographical sketch intended to give a sense of the person's appearance, character, and accomplishments. The following article, "Face to Face," by David Kushner, appeared in *Rolling Stone* and profiles Mark Zuckerberg, creator of Facebook.

PROFESSIONAL WRITING

Face to Face

David Kushner

It's an unseasonably warm afternoon in Palo Alto, California, as Silicon *1*
Valley's hottest whiz kid hurries down the street. Mark Zuckerberg, slight and bushy-haired, strides quickly past the tree-lined shops and cafes. He's late for a meeting with the venture capitalist who just gave him $12.7 million. And after another all-nighter plotting world domination, fending off investors and wooing execs from dot-com rivals, this Harvard dropout is feeling the heat. "Being a CEO at twenty-one is not normal," he says wearily.

Zuckerberg is the face of Facebook, the most popular and contro- *2*
versial site to hit college campuses since Napster. What makes the site—

with its candid photos, booty shots and cheeky profiles—unique from networks like Friendster and MySpace is that it's exclusively for academia. Which is precisely how students like it, thanks. And with a whopping 7 million members from more than 2,100 universities and 22,000 high schools, Facebook is now the seventh-most-trafficked site on the Net, valued at over $1 billion. While other online communities are rife with poseurs, Facebook members use their ".edu" e-mail addresses; as a result, there's inherent social pressure to be real.

Ostensibly, this gives the site academic potential, and plenty of 3 people are using it for stuff like Chaucer study groups and car pools to ichthyology lab. But these are the children of the *Real World* nation, and Facebook is their chance to let it all hang out: cell-phone numbers, spring-break plans, topless photos. Surfing the site can feel like wandering through a giant dorm where every door is open and every kid is swilling Jack Daniel's.

As Zuckerberg and his legions are discovering, though, openness 4 has a price. With students posting their skin shots and class schedules, Facebook has been called a stalkers' handbook. Employers are using the site to weed out applicants based on their profiles. Blogs have been buzzing about celebs and their spawn supposedly shown in flagrante: the son of NBC's Tim Russert and a bevy of scantily clad beauties in a hot tub; Tony Danza's daughter ripping bong hits; Lindsay Lohan acting naughty with her girlfriends. Twenty years from now, presidential candidates will have to answer to Facebook.

Zuckerberg grew up in tony Dobbs Ferry, New York, a gifted 5 prodigy with a knack for computers. After creating a custom MP3 player for a school project, he was courted by Musicmatch and

Microsoft but brashly turned down a $950,000 offer in order to go to Harvard. Once there, frustrated by the school's delay in getting a campus-wide student directory online, he hacked together his own solution and launched Facebook.com in February 2004. Within weeks, the site exploded—but not without a few setbacks. A trio of Harvard classmates soon claimed he stole the idea and are suing Zuckerberg. Though he maintains his innocence and is countersuing for defamation of character, Zuckerberg figures if Harvard's other beleaguered dropout Bill Gates is any indication, it's par for the course. "This won't be the last time I get sued," he says coldly.

It's 10 P.M., midday at Facebook HQ, the dormlike office that 6 houses the company's nearly 100 employees. Tonight the team is getting ready to launch the Pulse, which enables students to get weird stats on their school, such as the fact that sixty percent of Berkeley students prefer *The Simpsons* to *Arrested Development*. It's the stuff of a direct-marketer's dream, and another reason why this hub for the eighteen-to-twenty-four-year-old demographic has been valued by industry insiders at more than $1 billion. Zuckerberg insists, however, "We're not doing this to cash in. We're doing this to build something cool."

Cool, as he's learning, is often controversial. Even though students 7 can restrict access to their pages, some neglect to do so and are paying a price. North Carolina State and Northern Kentucky University have disciplined underage students shown drinking on their Facebook pages. In January, Michael Guinn, a student at John Brown University in Siloam Spring, Arkansas, was expelled when authorities at his Christian college discovered through his page that he is gay. And sometimes where there's smoke, there's fire: In January, Matthew Cloyd, a student at Alabama-Birmingham, posted, "It is time to reconvene the season of evil!" on his friend's page. He was arrested in March, along with two other students, for setting fire to nine Alabama churches.

But it's not just *bad* behavior that's raising red flags. Cameron 8 Walker, the twenty-year-old student-body president of Fisher College in Boston, and another student were expelled after starting a Facebook group to rally against an unpopular campus cop. First Amendment or not, John McLaughlin, Fisher College spokesman, says Walker's conspiratorial language violated the campus code of conduct. "As a private institution, we have the ability to decide what discipline is appropriate," he says. Sarah Wunsch, an attorney with the ACLU, is concerned that the reactionary uproar over Facebook is just that. "Colleges are supposed to be places where students can engage in heated debate," she says.

Zuckerberg is doing his best to endure the growing pains. "I was 9 just a shy kid and computer dork," he says. "Being a CEO is as far from being a student as you can get." But he's learning: There are two

...continued Face to Face, **David Kushner**

versions of business cards in Zuckerberg's wallet. One has the title CEO, the other I'M CEO . . . BITCH. He's phasing out the latter. "Now I can look someone in the eye and say, 'I want you to give me a half-million dollars,'" he says. "I can feel myself changing."

INTERVIEW

Typically, interviews are conducted by one person, the interviewer, who asks questions in person, over the phone, or in writing. The person or persons being interviewed answer the questions and then the interviewer often edits the interview in order to focus on the most relevant questions and answers. Sometimes, however, newsmakers, writers, or celebrities agree to write responses to questions submitted by the public. In that case, the newspaper, magazine, or online site conducting the interview selects questions submitted by the public and then edits them for that particular publication. As an example of this second type of interview, *Time* magazine published the following interview, "Henry Louis Gates Jr. Will Now Take Your Questions," shortly after the inauguration of President Barack Obama. Henry Louis Gates Jr. is an historian at Harvard University and is the Director of the W. E. B. Du Bois Institute for African and African American Research.

PROFESSIONAL WRITING

Henry Louis Gates Jr. Will Now Take Your Questions

You recently wrote about the complex feelings Abraham Lincoln held toward black people. Could you expand on that?
Bill Bre, Bremen, Germany

A fundamental part of Lincoln's moral compass was his opposition to slavery. But it took him a long time to embrace black people. We were raised with a fairy-tale representation that because he hated slavery, he loved the slaves. He didn't. He was a recovering racist. He used to use the *N* word. He told darky jokes. He resisted abolition as long as he could. But in the end, he was on an upward arc, one that was quite noble.

Can you define the word *race*?
Treva Gholston, Stone Mountain, Ga.

People use the words *ethnicity* and *race* interchangeably. But race is not a biological concept. It's socially constructed. We are [influenced by] the environment in which we live, but our physical features are inherited from our biology. If we all traced our family trees 50,000 years back, we're all in Ethiopia. There's no question about that.

What were you doing the night Barack Obama was elected?

Rick Klein, La Crosse, Wis.

I was at my friend's house in Cambridge, Mass. Everyone kept saying, "He's winning, he's winning," but I wouldn't let myself celebrate until Wolf Blitzer said he was President. Then I cheered, and we all cried and drank about another gallon of champagne.

After devoting your life to African-American studies, what are you most proud of?

Vern Nicholson, Dover, N.H.

My most cherished accomplishment is helping to edit the *Encyclopaedia Africana*. Every people in the world had an encyclopedia but black people. There's an *Encyclopaedia Judaica, Encyclopaedia Britannica* and finally, at the turn of the 21st century, we have one as well.

Is African-American history taught enough in our schools?

David Veigel, Virginia Beach

No. African-American history is generally taught only in Black History Month, which is February, the coldest, darkest, shortest month. It's like the month that was left over, they gave to black people. I'm a big advocate of teaching history in our public schools on a multicultural level.

Will there ever be a time when race ceases to matter?

Loren Anthony, Pretoria, South Africa

I would hope one day. But I can't imagine such a reality when I think about South Africa, when I think of the U.S. and when I think about France, where race is not even an official category but black people and North Africans are suffering under great implicit discrimination. Race will remain a primary signifier for a long, long time.

Is it right for African Americans to use the *N* word?

Pitufo Geiger, Baguio City, Philippines

I was raised hearing black people using the *N* word and I don't find it offensive at all. I do find it offensive when a nonblack person uses it.

Have you learned anything new while exploring your ancestry?

Jackie Lantry, Rehoboth, Mass.

Yes. We can now trace my family back to the 18th century. An Irishman fathered the children of Jane Gates, my great-great-grandmother, who was born a slave in 1819. It's a miracle of DNA technology.

How expensive is it to trace one's genetic roots?

Sheron Mitchell, Brundidge, Ala.

It's cheaper than a pair of sneakers. You're not confined to the foibles of your ancestors, but it helps to understand your place in the world if you can look at your family tree.

People refer to President Obama as black, even though he is of mixed race. What language should we use?

Johh Malick, London

We can't reinvent language each day or even each generation. Obama is an African American—literally. His father was African, his mother was American. It took us all these years to get a black man into the White House. We're not giving that brother up anytime soon.

WARMING UP   Journal Exercises

The following exercises will help you practice investigative writing. Read all of the following exercises and then, in your journal, write about the three that interest you most. One of these exercises may suggest an idea for your investigative essay.

❶ Write an "authority" list of topics about which you have some information or experience. Consider your hobbies, academic interests, job skills, community experiences, or other experience with art, music, sports, travel, films, and so forth. Jot down a few sentences about three or four possible topics. Then go to the Internet and use your favorite search engine to continue investigating these topics. When you are finished browsing, write out the key questions you could answer about each of these topics.

❷ **Writing Across the Curriculum.** Look through the assignments and texts from another course you are taking or have taken recently. Find an article or research report from that class that was recommended or assigned reading. Following the model of the report on cell phone research earlier in this chapter, write a summary of the research that answers the "Who," "What," "When," "Where" questions about the study and then summarizes the findings of the study. Write this summary so that other members of your writing class can understand the research findings.

❸ Next semester, you will be taking a course in your major field, but you aren't sure which professor you should pick. To investigate the differences among the teachers, interview several students who have taken this course from different professors. Prepare questions that encourage factual responses: How many papers or tests does the teacher require? What is the grade distribution? What text-book is required? What is the reading or homework load? What are typical lecture topics? Is the teacher available outside class?

❹ As a member of the student governing board, your job is to solicit student opinions about some aspect of campus life that needs improving. Choose a subject such as dorms, classes, the library, parking, student clubs, the film or fine art series, or recreational opportunities.

Then choose a question to focus your investigation and write a one-page questionnaire that you might distribute to students. (See the section on writing questionnaires in this chapter.)

5 Watch an investigative news show such as *60 Minutes* or *Nightline,* taking notes on the interviewer's techniques. Is there a sequence to the questions—say, from gentle and polite to critical or controversial? What information does the interviewer have *before* the interview? Can you tell which questions are planned or scripted and which are spontaneous? After taking notes on a show, explain what you think are the three most important tips for successful interviewing.

6 Interview a classmate for a 200- to 250-word "personality profile." Your object is to profile this person and one of his or her major interests. First, in your daybook, prepare questions you need to ask for biographical information. Then, in an eight- to ten-minute interview, ask questions about the person and about several topics from that person's "authority" list. After the interview, take two or three minutes to review your notes. At home, write up the results of your interview, which will appear in your local or campus newspaper.

7 If you have watched the television program, *CSI: Crime Scene Investigation,* explain the kinds of investigations that the CSI team uses during a typical case. How does the team use crime scene observations, interviews, online or file research, or other investigative strategies in order to solve their crimes? Support your explanation with specific references to a program you have seen recently or that you watch specifically for this assignment.

8 Read the following article by Elizabeth Larson, "Surfin' the Louvre." Use her model to write your own investigative essay comparing online learning to a traditional textbook-based course. Choose a course you are taking or have recently taken, and then find and report on key Web sites that enable you to learn about your subject without going to a single class, reading a textbook, or taking an exam.

(PROFESSIONAL WRITING)

Surfin' the Louvre

Elizabeth Larsen

I first studied art history the old-fashioned way: scribbling notes in a dark [1] auditorium as a parade of yellowing slides whizzed past in an overwhelming progression from ancient Greece to Andy Warhol. Four years and tens of thousands of dollars later, I had traveled from the ruins of Tikal in Guatemala to a tiny Giotto-decorated chapel in Padua to Rodin's Paris atelier without ever leaving my college's urban campus.

Today it's possible to get a similar education—minus the sometimes inspired (and sometimes not-so-inspired) comments of a professor—on the Internet. In the past few years, virtually every museum of note has established a presence on the World Wide Web. While some sites still stick to the basics (cost of admission, hours, information about the permanent collection and current exhibits), more and more institutions are following the lead of the Fine Arts Museums of San Francisco (www.thinker.org/index.shtml) which is using the Web to promote its new commitment to "behave more like a resource and less like a repository." Currently the site houses over 65,000 images—from Mary Cassatt's *Woman Bathing* to more than 3,000 examples of Japanese ukiyo-e printmaking—with plans to double that number as the museum digitizes its entire collection.

That's a heck of a lot more reproductions than you'll find in that chiro- 2 practically unfriendly art history text, H. W. Janson's *History of Art*. Inspired by the sheer volume of images available on FAMSF's "Imagebase," I decided to try my hand at digitally designing my own art education.

My self-directed syllabus started in Spain at the new Guggenheim 3 Museum in Bilbao (www.bm30.es/guggenheim), the recently opened critic's darling designed by maverick California architect Frank Gehry. As befits a museum where the architecture is as much a piece of art history as the works it houses, much of the site is devoted to Gehry's oddly gorgeous design, which looks like a cross between a medieval fortress and a bouquet of flowers sculpted in titanium. But there's a lot of other great stuff as well, including reproductions of the museum's most famous acquisitions—like Richard Serra's *Snake*, an appropriately jarring-yet-graceful panel of curving steel set smack dab in the middle of a gallery.

Eager to see more, I moved on to the Museums page of the World Wide 4 Web Virtual Library (www.comlab.ox.ac.uk/archive/other/museums.html). A clearinghouse of links to museums, the site is most helpful for those who want to search according to the countries the museums are in. I started in Italy, which I soon discovered doesn't include that country-within-a-country, the Vatican (www.christusrex.org/www1citta/O-Citta.html). At the Uffizi Gallery in Florence (www.italink.com/eng/egui/hogui.html), I checked out a number of Renaissance heavy hitters, including Botticelli's The Birth of Venus and Paolo Ucello's Battle of San Romano. To get more of a feeling for Florentine art as it exists on the streets and in the churches of Florence, I used the Florence Art Guide to take me all over the city, from the Ponte Vecchio to the Piazzale Michelangelo.

My next stop was Paris, where my first visit was to—where else?— 5 the Louvre (www.mistral.culture.fr/Louvre/Louvrea.html), where I lingered over a Watteau and a Poussin before getting absorbed in the history of the building. From there it was an easy trek to the countryside and the Giverny home page (www.giverny.org/index.html) to check out the gardens that inspired Monet.

From Giverny I hopped over to Greece and the Hellenic Ministry 6
of Culture's Guide to Athens (www.culture.gr/maps/sterea/attiki/
athens.html) where I gazed out over the Acropolis. Then I spent the
rest of the afternoon in Japan at the Kyoto National Museum (www
.kyohaku.go.jp/), where I studied up on the intricacies of Chinese and
Japanese lacquerware.

I know I'm starting to sound pretty starry-eyed about my cyber- 7
education, so I'll temper my enthusiasm with a few caveats. From the
vantage point of my office chair, I obviously wasn't able to glean insights
from the people standing next to me as I contemplated de Kooning's
Woman I. But I don't require that every symphony I listen to be live, and
I'm equally comfortable with the trade-offs inherent in a digital visual
experience. Especially since I won't need to worry about those threatening
form letters from the bursar's office.

PROFESSIONAL WRITING

The Homeless and Their Children

Jonathan Kozol

In his most famous book, Illiterate America (1985), *Jonathan Kozol says
that because more than one-third of America's adults are at least partially
illiterate, we should organize a massive government and volunteer army to
liberate people imprisoned by illiteracy. More recently, Kozol has written
about children in underclass America in* Amazing Grace: The Lives of
Children and the Conscience of a Nation (1996) *and* Ordinary Resurrec-
tions (2000). *In* "The Homeless and Their Children," *taken from* Rachel
and Her Children (1988), *Kozol investigates individual cases of poverty in
a New York City welfare hotel. Although welfare laws have changed and the
Martinique Hotel has since been renovated, Kozol's investigative report
accurately chronicles the effects of illiteracy on the lives of the poor. Kozol
uses his own observations and interview transcripts to demonstrate vividly
the connection between illiteracy and poverty. However, instead of arguing
indignantly for literacy programs to save the lives of the poor and illiterate,
Kozol simply reports the case of a single illiterate woman trying to raise her
four children. The woman he calls Laura cannot decipher labels on products
at the grocery store, cannot read notices from the welfare office, and cannot
understand letters from the hospital warning of her children's lead poisoning.*

The Martinique Hotel, at Sixth Avenue and Thirty-second Street, 1
is one of the largest hotels for homeless people in New York City.

...continued The Homeless and Their Children, **Jonathan Kozol**

When I visited it, in December of 1985, nearly four hundred homeless families, including some twelve hundred children, were lodged in the hotel, by arrangement with the city's Human Resources Administration. One of the residents I spoke to at some length was an energetic, intelligent woman I'll call Kim. During one of our conversations, she mentioned a woman on the seventh floor who had seemingly begun to find her situation intolerable. Kim described this woman as "a broken stick," and offered to arrange for us to meet.

The woman—I will call her Laura, but her name, certain other 2 names, and certain details have been changed—is so fragile that I find it hard to start a conversation when we are introduced, a few nights later. Before I begin, she asks if I will read her a letter from the hospital. The oldest of her four children, a seven-year-old boy named Matthew, has been sick for several weeks. He was tested for lead poisoning in November, and the letter she hands me, from Roosevelt Hospital, says that the child has a dangerous lead level. She is told to bring him back for treatment. She received the letter some weeks ago. It has been buried in a pile of other documents that she cannot read.

Although Laura cannot read, she knows enough about the dangers 3 of lead to grasp the darker implications of this information. The crumbling plaster in the Martinique Hotel is covered with sweet-tasting paint, and children eat or chew chips of the paint as it flakes off the walls. Some of the paint contains lead. Children with lead poisoning may suffer loss of coordination or undergo convulsions. The consequences of lead poisoning may be temporary or long lasting. They may appear at once or not for several years. This final point is what instills so much uneasiness; even months of observation cannot calm a parent's fear.

Lead poisoning, then, is Laura's first concern, but she has other prob- 4 lems. The bathroom plumbing has overflowed and left a pool of sewage on the floor. A radiator valve is broken, and every now and then releases a spray of scalding steam at the eye level of a child. A crib provided by the hotel appears to be unstable. A screw that holds two of its sides together is missing. When I test the crib with my hand, it starts to sway. There are four beds in the room, and they are dangerous, too. They have metal frames with unprotected corners, and the mattresses do not fit the frames; at one corner or another, metal is exposed. If a child has the energy or the playfulness to jump or turn a somersault or wrestle with a friend, and if he falls and strikes his head against the metal corner, the consequences can be serious. The week before, a child on the fourteenth floor fell in just this way, cut his forehead, and required stitches. Most of these matters have been brought to the attention of the hotel management; in Laura's case, complaints have brought no visible results.

All of this would be enough to make life difficult for an illiterate 5 young woman in New York, but Laura has one other urgent matter on her hands. It appears that she has failed to answer a request for information from her welfare office, and, for reasons that she doesn't understand, she did not receive her benefits this week. The timing is bad; it's a weekend. The city operates a crisis center in the Martinique, where residents can go for food and other help, but today the crisis center is not open, so there's nobody around to tide her over with emergency supplies. Laura's children have been eating cheese and bread and peanut butter for two days. "Those on welfare," the Community Service Society of New York said in a report published in 1984, may be suddenly removed from welfare rolls "for reasons unrelated to their actual need," or even to eligibility standards. Welfare workers in New York City call this practice "churning." Laura and her children are being churned.

The room is lighted by fluorescent tubes in a ceiling fixture. They 6 cast a stark light on four walls of greenish paint smeared over with sludge draining from someone's plumbing on the floor above. In the room are two boys with dark and hollowed eyes and an infant girl. A third boy is outside and joins us later. The children have the washed-out look of the children Walker Evans photographed for "Let Us Now Praise Famous Men." Besides the four beds and the crib, the room contains two chairs, a refrigerator, and a television set, which doesn't work. A metal hanger serves as an antenna, but there is no picture on the screen. Instead, there is a storm of falling flakes and unclear lines. I wonder why Laura keeps it on. There are no table lamps to soften the fluorescent glare, no books, no decorations. Laura tells me that her father is of Panamanian birth but that she went to school in New York City. Spanish is her first language. I don't speak Spanish well. We talk in English.

"I cannot read," Laura says. "I buy the New York *Post* to read the pictures. 7 In the grocery, I know what to buy because I see the pictures."

What of no-name products—generic brands, whose labels have no 8 pictures but which could save her a great deal of money?

"If there are no pictures, I don't buy it," she says. "I want to buy pan- 9 cakes, I ask the lady, 'Where's the pancakes?' So they tell me."

She points to the boys and says, "He's two. He's five. Matthew's seven. 10 My daughter is four months. She has this rash." She shows me ugly skin eruptions on the baby's neck and jaw. "The carpets, they was filthy from the stuff, the leaks that come down on the wall. All my kids have rashes, but the worst she has it. There was pus all over. Somewhere here I have a letter from the nurse." She shuffles around but cannot find the letter. "She got something underneath the skin. Something that bites. The only way you can get rid of it is with a cream."

She finds the letter. The little girl has scabies. 11

Laura continues, "I have been living here two years. Before I came 12 here, I was in a house we had to leave. There was rats. Big ones, they crawl on us. The rats, they come at night. They come into our house, run over my son's legs. The windows were broken. It was winter. Snow, it used to come inside. My mother lived with us before. Now she's staying at my grandma's house. My grandma's dying in the bed. She's sixty-five. My mother comes here once a week to do the groceries. Tomorrow she comes. Then she goes back to help my grandma."

"I know my name, and I can write my name, my children's names. 13 To read, I cannot do it. Medicines, I don't know the instructions. I was living here when I was pregnant with Corinne. No, I didn't see no doctor. I was hungry. What I ate was rice and beans, potato chips and soda. Up to now this week we don't have food. People ask me, 'Can you help? Do you got this? Do you got that?' I don't like to tell them no. If I have something, I give it. This week, I don't got. I can read baby books—like that, a little bit. If I could read, I would read newspapers. I would like to know what's going on. Matthew, he tells me I am stupid. 'You can't read.' You know, because he wants to read. He don't understand what something is. I tell him, 'I don't know it. I don't understand.' People laugh. You feel embarrassed. On the street. Or in the store." She weeps. "There's nothing here."

Laura sweeps one hand in a wide arc, but I can't tell whether she 14 means the gesture to take in the room or something more. Then she makes her meaning clear: "Everything I had, they put it on the sidewalk when I was evicted. I don't know if that's the law. Things like that—what is the law, what isn't? I can't read it, so I didn't understand. I lost everything I had. I sign papers. Somebody could come and take my children. They could come. 'Sign this. Sign that.' I don't know what it says. Adoption papers—I don't know. This here paper that I got I couldn't understand."

She hands me another letter. This one is from the management of the 15 hotel: "This notice is to inform you that your rent is due today. I would appreciate your cooperation in seeing to it that you go to your center today." Another form that she hands me asks her to fill out the names and the ages of her children.

"Papers, documents—people give it to me. I don't know it: I don't un- 16 derstand." She pauses, and then says, "I'm a Catholic. Yes—I go two weeks ago to church. This lady say they have these little books that learn me how to spell. You see the letters. Put them together. I would like to read. I go to St. Francis' Church. Go inside and kneel—I pray. I don't talk to the priest. I done so many things—you know, bad things. I buy a bottle of wine. A bottle of beer. That costs a dollar. I don't want to say to God. I get a hundred and seventy-three dollars restaurant allowance. With that money I buy clothes. Food stamps, I get two hundred dollars. That's for groceries. Subway tokens I take out ten dollars. Washing machine, I do downstairs. Twenty-five dollars to dry and wash. Five dollars to buy soap. Thirty dollars twice a month."

Another woman at the Martinique calculates her laundry costs at my 17 request, and they come out to nearly the same figure. These may be the standard rates for a midtown site. The difficulty of getting out and traveling to find lower prices, whether for laundromats or for groceries, cannot be overstated. Families at the Martinique are trapped in a commercial district.

I ask Laura who stays with the children when she does her chores. 18

"My mother keeps the children when I do the wash," she replies. "If 19 she can't, I ask somebody on the floor. 'Give me three dollars. I watch your kids.' For free? Nothing. Everything for money. Everybody's poor."

Extending a hand, she says, "This is the radiator. Something's 20 wrong." She shows me where the steam sprays out. I test it with my hand. "Sometimes it stops. The children get too close. Then it starts— like that! Leak is coming from upstairs down." I see the dark muck on the wall. "The window is broke. Lights broke." She points to the fluorescent tubes. They flicker on and off. "I ask them, 'Please, why don't you give me ordinary lights?' They don't do nothing. So it been two weeks. I go downstairs. They say they coming up. They never come. So I complain again. Mr. Tuccelli—Salvatore Tuccelli, the manager of the Martinique—said to come here to his office. Desks and decorations and a lot of pictures. It's above the lobby. So the manager was there. Mr. Tuccelli sat back in his chair. He had a gun. He had it here under his waist. You know, under his belt. I said, 'Don't show it to me if you isn't going to use it.' I can't tell what kind of gun it was. He had it in his waist. 'You are showing me the gun so I will be afraid.' If he was only going to show it, I would not be scared. If he's going to use it, I get scared."

"So he says, 'You people bring us trouble.' I said, 'Why you give my 21 son lead poison and you didn't care? My child is lead-poisoned.' He said, 'I don't want to hear of this again.' What I answer him is this: 'Listen. People like you live in nice apartments. You got a home. You got TV. You got a family. You got children in a school that learn them. They don't got lead poison.'"

"I don't know the reason for the guards. They let the junkies into 22 the hotel. When my mother comes, I have to sign. If it's a family living good, they make it hard. If it's the drug dealers, they come in. Why they let the junkies in but keep away your mother? The guards, you see them taking women in the corner. You go down twelve-thirty in the night, they're in the corner with the girls. This is true. I seen it."

She continues, "How I know about the lead is this: Matthew sits 23 there and he reaches his fingers in the plaster and he put it in his mouth. So I ask him, 'Was you eating it?' He says, 'Don't hit me. Yes, I was.' So then I took him to the clinic and they took the blood. I don't know if something happen to him later on. I don't know if it affects him. When he's older . . ."

I ask Laura why she goes to church. 24

"I figure: Go to church. Pray God. Ask Him to help. I go on my 25 knees. I ask Him from my heart. 'Jesus Christ, come help me, please. Why do you leave me here?' When I'm lying down at night, I ask, 'Why people got to live like this?' On the street, the people stare at you when you go out of the hotel. People look. They think, I wonder how they live in there. Sometimes I walk out this door. Garbage all over in the stairs. When it's hot, a lot of bugs around the trash. Sometimes there are fires in the trash. I got no fire escape. You have to get out through the hall. I got no sprinkler. Smoke detector doesn't work. When I cook and food is burning, it don't ring. If I smoke, it starts to ring. I look up. I say, 'Why you don't work? When I need you, you don't work. I'm gonna knock you down.' I did!" She laughs.

There is a sprinkler system in the corridor. In 1987, the hotel man- 26 agement informed residents that the fire-alarm system was "inoperable."

I ask Laura if the older children are enrolled in school. Nodding at 27 Michael, her middle son, she says, "This one doesn't go to school. He's five. I need to call tomorrow. Get a quarter. Then you get some papers. Then you got to sign those papers. Then he can start school."

"For this room I pay fifteen hundred dollars for two weeks. I don't 28 pay. The welfare pays. I got to go and get it." The room, although it is undivided, was originally a two-room suite and is being rented at the two-room rate. "They send me this. I'm suppose to sign. I don't know what it is. Lots of things you suppose to sign. I sign it but I don't know what it is."

While we are talking, Matthew comes in and sits beside his 29 mother. He lowers his eyes when I shake his hand.

Laura goes on, "Looking for a house, I got to do it." She explains 30 that she's required to give evidence that she is searching for a place to live. "I can't read, so I can't use the paper. I get dressed. I put my makeup on. If I go like this, they look afraid. They say, 'They going to destroy the house!' You got to dress the children and look nice. Owners don't want homeless. Don't want welfare. Don't want kids. What I think? If they pay one thousand and five hundred dollars every two weeks, why not pay five hundred dollars for a good apartment?"

She hands me another paper. "Can you tell me what is this?" 31

It's a second letter from the hospital, telling her to bring her son 32 for treatment.

She says, "Every day, my son this week, last week was vomiting. Every 33 time he eat his food, he throw it right back out. I got to take him to the clinic."

"Christmas, they don't got. For my daughter I ask a Cabbage 34 Patch. For my boys I ask for toys. I got them stockings." She shows me four cotton stockings tacked to the wall with nothing in them. "They say, 'Mommy, there's no toys.' I say not to worry. 'You are going to get something.' But they don't. They don't get nothing. I could not afford. No, this isn't my TV. Somebody lended it to me. Christmas tree I can't afford. Christmas I don't spend it happy. I am thinking of the kids. What we do on Christmas is we spend it laying on the bed. If I go outside, I feel a little better. When I'm here, I see those walls, the bed, and I feel sad. If I had my own apartment, maybe there would be another room. Somewhere to walk. Walk back and forth."

I ask her, "How do you relax?"   35

"If I want to rest, relax, I turn out the light and lie down on the bed," 36 she says. "When I met his father, I was seventeen." She says she knew him before she was homeless, when she lived in Brooklyn with her mother. He was working at a pizza parlor near her mother's home. "One night, he bought me liquor. I had never tasted. So he took me to this hallway. Then my mother say that what I did is wrong. So I say that I already did it. So you have to live with what you did. I had the baby. No. I did not want to have abortion. The baby's father I still see. When he has a job, he brings me food. In the summer, he worked in a flower store. He would bring me flowers. Now he don't have any job. So he don't bring me flowers."

She sweeps her hand in a broad arc and says again, "Nothing here. 37 I feel embarrassed for the room. Flowers, things like that, you don't got. Pretty things you don't got. Nothing like that. No."

In the window is a spindly geranium plant. It has no flowers, but 38 some of the leaves are green. Before I go, we stand beside the window. Blowing snow hits the panes and blurs the dirt.

"Some of the rooms high up, they got a view," Laura says. "You see 39 the Empire State."

I've noticed this—seen the building from a window. It towers high 40 above the Martinique.

"I talk to this plant. I tell him, 'Grow! Give me one flower!' He 41 don't do it." Then, in an afterthought, "No pets. No. You don't got. Animals. They don't allow."

It occurs to me that this is one of the few places I have been except 42 a hospital or a reform school where there are hundreds of children and virtually no pets. A few people keep cats illegally.

"I wish I had a dog," Laura says. "Brown dog. Something to hug." 43

vo·cab·u·lar·y

In your journal, write the meanings of the italicized words in the following phrases.

- the darker *implications* (**3**)
- call this practice "*churning*" (**5**)
- ugly skin *eruptions* (**10**)
- girl has *scabies* (**11**)

QUESTIONS FOR WRITING AND DISCUSSION

1 Describe your intellectual and emotional reaction to Kozol's article. What information about the lives of the poor and illiterate did you already know? What information surprised you? How did Kozol's essay make you feel about this problem?

2 The purpose of an investigative report is to give information without editorializing or arguing for or against a solution. In which paragraphs does Kozol remain most objective and unemotional? Which passages reveal Kozol's sympathy for Laura's situation? Does he avoid editorializing?

3 Reread the essay, marking those places where Laura's illiteracy causes her problems. Based on your notes, explain how her illiteracy (rather than her poverty) causes or magnifies her problems.

4 Describe the investigative techniques that Kozol probably used to write his essay. In addition to his interviews with Laura, what were his other probable sources of information?

5 According to the information provided by Kozol, what support does the welfare system provide Laura and her children? How does the welfare system encourage Laura to improve her life? List three changes that you believe the welfare system should make to solve Laura's problems and make her more self-sufficient.

6 On your next trip to the grocery store, see which products would appeal to an illiterate person. List the items (and their prices) that you might buy based on the pictures on the labels. Write a paragraph describing your findings. Is Kozol correct in assuming that Laura pays too much for her groceries?

Investigating: The Writing Process

ASSIGNMENT FOR INVESTIGATING

Choose a subject to investigate: one aspect of a current social or political policy, a scientific discovery or principle, a historical event, a profile of a controversial public figure, or perhaps just an ordinary event, person, process, or place that you find interesting. Your initial purpose should be to discover or learn about your subject. Then, with a specific audience in mind, report your findings. A report presents the information that you find; it should not argue for or against any idea or plan. With the final copy of your investigative report, turn in photocopies of any sources you have summarized or cited, notes from your interview(s), and/or copies of questionnaires that you used.

Selecting your audience and genre is especially important for your investigative report. If an audience is not specified in your assignment, check out newspapers, magazines, and Web sites for appropriate audiences and genres. Use the chart below to brainstorm about possible audiences and genres. Where possible, think globally but focus locally—what global or national topic has local implications that you can investigate, and what local publication might be interested in your report?

Audience	Possible Genres for Investigating Assignments
Personal Audience	Personal or family interview or profile, journal entry, social networking site profile, photo essay, multigenre document.
Academic Audience	Reports for academic classes, summary of article or research study, forum entry on class site, multigenre document.
Public Audience	Survey, interview, profile, investigation, or report of research for a newspaper, magazine, blog, newsletter, community service organization, online site, or multigenre document.

CHOOSING A SUBJECT

If one of your journal topics does not suggest a subject for your investigation, consider the following ideas. If you have a subject, go on to the collecting and shaping strategies.

- Choose some idea, principle, process, or theory discussed in a class that you are currently taking. In biology, you might focus on the Krebs cycle; in art, investigate the Dutch school of painters; or in education, investigate community literacy programs. In physics, research low-temperature conductivity or hydrogen fuels, or in astronomy, investigate competing theories about the formation of the universe. Begin by interviewing a professor, graduate students, or classmates about how to research the history, development, or personalities behind this idea. With information from the interview, continue your investigation in the library and online. As you read, focus your question to one narrow or specific area.

- Investigate and report on a campus or community service organization. Choose any academic, minority, cultural, or community organization. Visit the office. Interview an official. Read the organization's literature. Talk to students or community members who have used the service. Check the library for background information. Find people who are dissatisfied with or critical of the organization. Select an audience who might use this service or who might be interested in volunteering for the organization, and report the relevant *who, what, when, where, why,* and/or *how* information.

- At your workplace, investigate how something does or does not work, research how the business (or your part of the business) is organized, do a profile of a coworker, or survey your customers to find out what they like best or least about your store or company.

- For practice, investigate one of the following questions on the Internet and/or in the library (be prepared to explain your answers to your class members): How can you minimize jet lag? Can aspirin prevent heart attacks? How expensive is television advertising? What is a wind tunnel used for? Why is the Antarctic ice shelf melting? How do endorphins work? What is a melanoma? What causes seasonal affective disorder? How does a "Zamboni" work? What effects does Megan's law have? Do Americans spend more money on cosmetics than on education? What are the newest ways to repair torn ACLs (anterior cruciate ligaments) in your knee? What is computer morphing, and how does it work?

- Investigate an academic major, a career, or a job in which you are interested. List some of the *who, what, when, where,* and *why* questions you want to answer. Who is interested in this major? What background or courses are required? What is the pay scale or opportunities for advancement? What appeals to you about this major or job? What are the disadvantages of this major or career? Research your major or career on the Internet and in the library. Plan to interview an adviser, a friend who majors in the field, or a person who works at that job. Be prepared to report your findings to your classmates.

COMMUNITY SERVICE LEARNING

If you have a service-learning project connected with your writing course, below is some background information that will help you understand your project.

Definition Community service learning is simply a mutually beneficial partnership with a community agency.

Goals Teachers, students, and the partnering agency work together to set mutual goals promoting both civic action and academic learning. The agency receives your assistance with projects involving planning, writing, and communicating. You receive valuable experience related to your writing class goals: working and writing collaboratively, assessing and addressing agency needs, and getting practice with real-world writing situations, tasks, and genres.

Requirements Most service-learning projects require both a certain number of hours of service and a portfolio of pieces of writing *about* the agency, *for* the agency, and *with* the agency. A major requirement of service-learning projects is a reflective account about your participation, about the agency and its mission, and about what you have learned.

Writing Situations and Genres Depending on the goals and mission of the agency, you may write any combination of the following genres or kinds of writing: journal writing, online discussion forums, observation of the agency, profile of the agency, research, needs assessment, audience analysis, interviews, pamphlets, Web site design, public service announcements, feature articles, and impact assessment.

Benefits The agency benefits from your help with its ongoing projects (but remember that it also gives its time to help you learn). You benefit from getting to write in real-world situations—not just for your teacher and classmates. You also gain civic and crosscultural awareness, experience in working and writing collaboratively, increased problem-solving skills, contacts for possible job or career choices, and personal satisfaction for helping with a worthy civic cause.

COLLECTING

The collecting strategies discussed in Chapters 3, 4, and 5 (brainstorming, clustering, looping, mapping, sketching, reading, summarizing, taking double-entry notes) may be useful as you collect ideas. Other strategies particularly useful for investigating are suggested here. Try each of the following collecting strategies for your subject.

● **ASKING QUESTIONS**   Asking the *right questions* is crucial to investigative writing. Sets of questions (often called *heuristics*) will help you narrow and focus your subject and tailor your approach to the expectations or needs of your audience. You don't know what information you need to collect until you know what questions your investigation needs to answer.

1. The "reporter's" or the familiar "Wh" questions are one basic heuristic: Who? What? When? Where? Why? Asking these questions of a topic ensures that you're not leaving out any crucial information. If, for example, you are investigating recreational opportunities in your city or on campus, you might ask the following questions to focus your investigation (remember to ask the negative version of each question, too).

> 66 Had I known the answer to any of these questions, I would never have needed to write. 99
>
> —JOAN DIDION, ESSAYIST AND NOVELIST

- *Whom* is the recreation for?
- *Who* runs the programs?
- *Who* is excluded from the programs?
- *Who* pays for the programs?
- *What* is the program?
- *What* sports are included in the program?
- *What* sports are not included?
- *What* is the budget for these programs?
- *When* are these opportunities available or not available?
- *Where* do the activities take place?
- *Where* are they restricted?
- *Why* are these programs offered?
- *Why* are certain activities not offered?
- *Why* have activities been changed?

These questions might lead you to focus your investigation on the scheduling, on why soccer has been excluded, or on why participants are charged a fee for one class or program but not for another.

2. The classical "topics" provide a second set of questions for an investigation.

Definition:	What is it?
Comparison:	What is it like or unlike?
Relationship:	What caused it? What are its consequences?
Testimony:	What has been said or written about it?

These questions can be used in conjunction with the reporter's questions to focus an investigation. Applied to the topic on recreational opportunities, the questions might be as follows.

Definition:	What activities exist?
	How can the activities be described, classified, or analyzed?
Comparison:	What are similarities to or differences from other programs?
Relationship:	What caused these programs to be offered?
	What causes people to use or avoid these activities?
	What are the consequences of these programs?
Testimony:	What do students think about these activities?
	What do administrators think?
	What have other schools done?
	What does research show?
	What proverbs or common sayings apply here?

Research Tips  GO

As you work on your investigating essay, use the following research strategies. For additional information, see Chapter 13.

Library Orientation Every library is different, so be sure to take your library's tour and find out how the online catalog searches and databases work. Knowing which databases to use and how to effectively use their search strategies makes your research quicker and more effective.

Internet Searches Use Internet search engines such as Google primarily for introductory or background information. Remember that the sites you find online may not be as reliable as information you find through your library's academic databases.

Evaluate Your Sources For all your Internet and library database sources, be sure to carefully evaluate the reliability, accuracy, and bias of your sources. Is the author of the text or Web site an authority on the subject? What is the author's connection to the subject, point of view, or bias? Has the text been published by a reputable magazine, or is it a self-published Web site?

Talk to Your Reference Librarian An informal interview with a reference librarian may be the most important ten minutes you spend doing research. Start by telling the librarian about your assignment—the topic and issue you're investigating—and then ask which databases, sources, or reference guides might be most helpful. Remember, there are no stupid questions in a library.

Include Field Research Field research, including personal observations, interviews, and questionnaires, can be effective in almost every research project. An interview with a campus or community expert on your topic may be a great place to start. A questionnaire for other students or potential readers may give you a better sense of what your audience knows or does not know about your topic and what points of view they have on the issue.

These two sets of questions will *expand* your information, helping you collect facts, data, examples, and ideas—probably more than you can use in a short essay. Once you have all of this information, you can then *narrow* your topic.

● **SUMMARIZING**   As explained in Chapter 5, a *summary* is a concise explanation of the main and supporting ideas in a passage, report, essay, book, or speech. It is usually written in the present tense. It identifies the author and title of the source; it may refer to the context or the actual place where the study took place; it contains the passage's main ideas; and it may quote directly a few force-ful or concise sentences or phrases. It will not usually cite the author's examples. A *paraphrase* usually expresses all the information in the passage—including examples—in your own words. Summary, paraphrase, and direct quotation often occur together as you use sources. (See Chapter 5 for more details.)

● **CITING SOURCES IN YOUR TEXT**   Typically, journalistic reports refer to their sources directly in the text, without using footnotes or a works-cited page. In the University of Utah report, which appears earlier in this chapter, quotations are attributed, the authors are identified, and the journal is cited directly in the text:

> "Clearly the safest course of action is not to use a cell phone while driv-ing," concludes the study by Strayer, Drews and Dennis Crouch, a re-search associate professor of pharmacology and toxicology. The study was set for publication June 29 in the summer 2006 issue of *Human Factors: The Journal of the Human Factors and Ergonomics Society*.

In the profile of Mark Zuckerberg, however, *Rolling Stone* writer David Kushner refers to a date and a place where an incident occurs but does not actually cite the source for his information:

> And sometimes where there's smoke, there's fire: In January, Matthew Cloyd, a student at Alabama-Birmingham, posted, "It is time to reconvene the season of evil!" on his friend's page. He was arrested in March, along with two other students, for setting fire to nine Alabama churches.

The policy of not citing sources is common in magazines and newspapers where articles and news reports typically go through a fact-checking process to ensure accuracy. If you are writing an academic report, however, your professor may require you to use in-text citation, footnotes, or a works-cited page. Be sure to check with your teacher to see how to refer to or document your sources for your investigating report. For information on citing sources using the Modern Language Association (MLA) style or American Psychological Association (APA) style, see Chapter 13, Researching.

DOING FIELD RESEARCH

Field research is essential for many kinds of investigative reports. Typically, field research—as opposed to library research—involves first-hand observations, in-terviews, and questionnaires. For observing strategies, see Chapter 3, "Observ-ing." Using interviews and writing questionnaires are discussed below.

● **INTERVIEWING**   After you have done some initial research, interviews are a logical next step. Remember that the more you know about the subject (and the person you're interviewing), the more productive the interview will be. In planning an interview, keep the following steps in mind.

1. Make an *appointment* with the person you wish to interview. Although you may feel hesitant or shy about calling or e-mailing someone for an interview, remember that most people are flattered that someone else is interested in them and wants to hear their opinions or learn about their areas of expertise.

2. Make a *list of questions,* in an appropriate *sequence,* that you can ask during the interview. The interview itself will generate additional topics, but your list will jog your memory if the interview gets off track. Begin with relatively objective or factual questions and work your way, gradually, to more subjective questions or controversial issues. Try to phrase your questions so that they require more than a yes or no answer.

3. Begin the interview by *introducing yourself* and describing your investigation. Keep your biases or opinions out of the questions. Be sure to *listen* carefully and ask follow-up questions: "What information do you have on that? What do the statistical studies suggest? In your opinion, do these data show any trends? What memorable experiences have you had relating to this topic?" Like a dog with a good bone, a reporter doesn't drop a topic until the meat's all gone.

4. During the interview, *take notes* and, if appropriate, use a tape recorder to ensure accuracy. Don't hesitate to ask your interviewee to repeat or clarify a statement. Remember: People want you to get the facts right and quote them accurately. Especially if you're doing a personality profile, describe notable features of your interviewee: hair color, facial features, stature, dress, gestures, and nervous habits, as well as details about the room or surroundings. Finally, don't forget to ask your interviewee for additional leads or sources. At the conclusion of the interview, *express your thanks* and ask if you can check with him or her later, perhaps by e-mail, for additional details or facts.

5. Immediately after the interview, *go over your notes.* If you recorded the interview, listen to the tape and transcribe important responses. List other questions you may still have.

● **WRITING QUESTIONNAIRES** Questionnaires are useful when you need to know the attitudes, preferences, or opinions of a large group of people. If you are surveying customers in your business, you may discover that 39 percent of those surveyed would prefer that your business stay open an additional hour, from 5 P.M. to 6 P.M. If you are surveying students to determine their knowledge of geography, you might discover that only 8 percent can correctly locate Beirut on a map of the Middle East. The accuracy and usefulness of a survey depend on the kinds of questions you ask, on the number of people you survey, and on the sample of people you select to respond to your questionnaire.

Open questions are easy to ask, but the answers can be difficult to interpret. For example, if you want to survey customers at a department store where you work, you might ask questions requiring a short written response:

- What is your opinion of the service provided by clerks at Macy's?
- What would make your shopping experience at Macy's more enjoyable?

While these questions may give you interesting—and often reliable—responses, the results may be difficult to tabulate. Open questions are often valuable in initial surveys because they can help you to determine specific areas or topics for further investigation.

Closed questions are more typical than open questions in surveys. They limit responses so that you can focus on a particular topic and accurately tabulate the responses. Following are several types of closed questions.

- *Yes/no questions:* Have you shopped at Macy's in the last three months?

  _____ Yes

  _____ No

- *Multiple choice:* How far did you travel to come to Macy's?

  _____ 0–5 miles

  _____ 5–10 miles

  _____ 10–15 miles

  _____ Over 15 miles

- How would you characterize the salespeople at Macy's?

  _____ Exceptionally helpful

  _____ Helpful

  _____ Indifferent

  _____ Occasionally rude

  _____ Usually rude

- *Checklists:* Which departments at Macy's do you usually visit?

  _____ Women's Wear

  _____ Sporting Goods

  _____ Children's Wear

  _____ Lingerie

  _____ Men's Wear

  _____ Household Goods

- *Ranking lists:* Rank the times you prefer to shop (1 indicates most convenient time, 2 indicates slightly less convenient, and so on).

  _____ 9 A.M.–11 A.M.

  _____ 11 A.M.–1 P.M.

  _____ 1 P.M.–4 P.M.

  _____ 4 P.M.–8 P.M.

As you design, administer, and use your questionnaire, keep the following tips in mind.

- Limit and focus your questions so that respondents can fill out the questionnaire quickly.
- Avoid loaded or biased questions. For example, don't ask, "How do you like the high-quality merchandise in Macy's sports department?"
- At the top of your questionnaire, write one or two sentences describing your study and thanking participants.
- Pretest your questionnaire by giving it to a few people. Based on their oral and written responses, focus and clarify your questions.
- Use a large sample group. Thirty responses will give you more accurate information about consumer attitudes than will three responses.
- Make your sample as *random* or as evenly representative as possible. Don't survey customers on only one floor, in only one department, or at only one time of day.
- Be sure to include a copy of your questionnaire with your article or essay.

Note: If you intend to do a formal study using questionnaires, check your library for additional sources to help you design and administer statistically reliable surveys.

SHAPING

As you begin shaping your material, reconsider your purpose and audience. Limit your subject to create a *narrowed* and *focused* topic. Don't try to cover everything; focus on *the most interesting questions and information*. Take the time to write out a statement of your topic, key questions, purpose, and audience. Then try the following strategies.

● INVERTED PYRAMID A common form for reports, especially in journalism, is the *inverted pyramid*. The writer begins with a succinct but arresting title, opens the story with a sentence or short paragraph that

> 66 But for whom have I tried so steadfastly to communicate? Who have I worried over in this writing? Who is my audience? 99
>
> —CHERRIE MORAGA, SOCIAL CRITIC AND POET

"Wh" question lead: Who, What, When, Where, Why
Most important information and details

Important information and details

Least important information and details

answers the reporter's "Wh" questions, and then fills in the background information and details in order of importance, from the *most important* to the *least important.*

Writers use the inverted pyramid when concrete information and the convenience of the reader are most important. The advantage of the inverted pyramid is that a hurried reader can quickly gather the most important information and determine whether the rest of the story is worth reading. The disadvantage is that some details or information may be scattered or presented out of clear sequence. In investigative writing, therefore, writers often supplement the inverted pyramid with other forms of development: chronological order, definition, classification, or comparison/contrast.

● **CHRONOLOGICAL ORDER**   Often, writers present their information in the order in which they discovered it, enabling the reader to follow the research as if it were a narrative or a story. In this format, the writer presents the steps of the investigation, from the earliest incidents, to the discoveries along the way, to the final pieces of information.

Elizabeth Larsen, for example, uses chronological order to make a story out of her report on Web sites in art history. The following sentences—most of them appearing at the beginning of paragraphs—illustrate how she uses time signals ("first," "today," "started," "my next stop," and "then") to create an interesting story about surfing the Web.

> I first studied art history the old-fashioned way: scribbling notes in a dark auditorium . . .
>
> Inspired by the sheer volume of images available . . . I decided to try my hand at digitally designing my own art education.
>
> My self-directed syllabus started in Spain . . .
>
> Eager to see more, I moved on to the Museums page of the World Wide Web Virtual Library.
>
> I started in Italy, which I soon discovered doesn't include . . . the Vatican.
>
> My next stop was Paris, where my first visit was to . . . the Louvre.
>
> From Giverny I hopped over to Greece . . .

As these sentences illustrate, chronological order can transform a potentially boring list of Web sites into an interesting narrative journey through the information.

● **COMPARISON AND CONTRAST**   Comparison and contrast are as essential to investigating and reporting as they are to observing and remembering. In "Surfin' the Louvre," Elizabeth Larsen organizes her essay around a comparison between her traditional campus art course and her online education. Jonathan Kozol, in "The Homeless and Their Children," concludes his investigative report about Laura and her children with a comparison to other places where children have no pets: "It occurs to me that this is one of the few places I have been except a hospital or a reform school where there are hundreds of children and virtually no pets."

● **ADDITIONAL SHAPING STRATEGIES**   Other shaping strategies, discussed in previous chapters, may be useful for your investigation, too. *Classifying people, places,* or *things* may help organize your investigation. *Simile, metaphor,* or *analogy* may develop and shape parts of your article. Even in investigative reporting, writers may create an identifiable *persona* or adopt a humorous tone. In the example report given earlier in this chapter, David Kushner assumes a reporter's objective persona and uses a serious, straightforward tone. In contrast, Elizabeth Larsen, in "Surfin' the Louvre," establishes a friendly and humorous tone: "That's a heck of a lot more reproductions than you'll find in that chiropractically unfriendly art history text, H. W. Janson's *History of Art.*" Larsen demonstrates that even journalistic writing can have a sense of fun.

● **TITLE, INTRODUCTION, AND CONCLUSION**   Especially in an investigative report, a catchy title is important to help get your readers' interest and attention. Jot down several ideas for titles now and add to that list *after* you've drafted your essay.

In your introductory paragraph(s), answering the "Wh" questions will help focus your investigation. Or you may wish to use a short *narrative,* as Larsen does in "Surfin' the Louvre." Other types of lead-ins, such as a short *description,* a *question,* a *statement of a problem,* a *startling fact* or *statistic,* or an arresting *quotation,* may get the reader's interest and focus on the main idea you wish to investigate. (See Chapter 8 for additional examples of lead-ins.)

The conclusion should resolve the question or questions posed in the investigation, summarize the most important information (useful primarily for long or complicated reports), and give the reader a sense of completion, often by picking up an idea, fact, quotation, narrative, or bit of description used in the introduction.

Some writers like to have a title and know how they're going to start a piece of writing before they begin drafting. However, if you can't think of the perfect title or introduction, begin drafting and continue working on the title, the introduction, and the conclusion after the first draft.

DRAFTING

Before you begin a first draft, reconsider your purpose in writing and further focus your questions, sense of audience, and shaping strategies.

The actual drafting of an investigative essay requires that you have all your facts, statistics, quotations, summaries, notes from interviews, or results of surveys ready to use. Organize your notes, decide on an overall shaping strategy, or write a sketch outline. In investigative writing, a primary danger is postponing writing too long in the mistaken belief that if you read just one

> 66 All good writing is swimming under water and holding your breath. 99
> —F. SCOTT FITZGERALD, AUTHOR OF *THE GREAT GATSBY*

more article or interview just one more person, you'll get the information you need. At some point, usually *before* you feel ready, you must begin writing. (Professional writers rarely feel they know enough about their subject, but deadlines require them to begin.) Your main problem, you'll quickly discover, will be having too much to say rather than not enough. If you have too much, go back to your focusing questions and see whether you can narrow your topic further.

REVISING

After you have drafted your essay, you may wish to get some feedback from your peers about your work in progress. The peer response guidelines below will help you to review your goals for this investigative assignment and to construct a revision plan. When you read other students' drafts or ideas, be as constructively critical as possible. Think carefully about the assignment. Be honest about your own reactions as a reader. What would make the draft better?

GUIDELINES FOR REVISION

As you add, delete, substitute, or rearrange materials, keep the following tips in mind.

- **Reexamine your purpose and audience.** Are you doing what you intended? You should be *reporting* your findings; you should *not* be arguing for or against any idea.
- **Is the genre of your report responsive to audience needs and expectations?** Use samples of other writing for your audience (from newspapers, magazines, or journals) as models. Would visuals be appropriate or effective in your essay?
- **Can you add any of your own observations or experiences to the investigation?** Remember that your own perceptions and experiences as a reporter are also relevant data.
- **Review the reporter's "Wh" questions.** Are you providing your readers with relevant information *early* in the report and also catching their interest with a key statistic, fact, quotation, example, question, description, or short narrative?
- **Recheck your summaries, paraphrases, or direct quotations.** Are they accurate, and have you cited these sources in your text?
- **Use signals, cues, and transitions to indicate your shaping strategies.** *Chronological order:* before, then, afterward, next, soon, later, finally, at last *Comparison/contrast:* likewise, similarly, however, yet, even so, in contrast *Analysis:* first, next, third, fourth, finally

PEER RESPONSE

The instructions that follow will help you give and receive constructive advice about the rough draft of your investigating essay. You may use these guidelines for an in-class workshop, a take-home review, or a computer e-mail response.

Writer: Before you exchange drafts with another reader, write out the following on your essay draft or in an e-mail message.

1. **Purpose** Briefly describe your purpose and intended audience. For your audience, write out the title of a newspaper or magazine that might print your investigative report.
2. **Revision plans** Obviously, your draft is just a draft. What still needs work as you continue revising? Explain. (You don't want your reader to critique problems you are already intending to fix.)
3. **Questions** Write out one or two questions that you still have about your draft. What questions would you like your reader to answer?

Reader: First, read the entire draft from start to finish. As you reread the draft, answer the following questions.

1. **Purpose** Remember that the purpose of this essay is to accurately and objectively report information, not argue or editorialize. Does this writer go beyond reporting to editorializing or arguing? If so, point out specific sentences that need revision.
2. **Evidence** List the kinds of evidence the writer uses. What additional kinds of sources might the writer use: An additional interview? A source on the Web? Personal observation? Other print sources? A survey? Make a specific suggestion about additional, appropriate sources.
3. **Key investigative question** When you read the essay, the key question should become apparent. Write it out. If there are places in the essay that don't relate to that key question, should they be omitted? Explain. Are there other aspects of the key question that the writer should address? Explain.
4. **Reader's response** An investigative essay should satisfy your curiosity about the topic. What did you want to learn about the topic that the essay did not answer? Write out any questions that you would like the writer to answer as he or she revises the essay.
5. **Answer the writer's questions in number 3.**

- **Revise sentences for directness, clarity, and conciseness.** Avoid unnecessary passive voice.
- **Edit your report for appropriate word choice, usage, and grammar.** Check your writing for problems in spelling and punctuation.

> ❝ We are all apprentices at a craft where no one ever becomes a master. ❞
>
> —ERNEST HEMINGWAY, NOVELIST

STUDENT WRITING

LAUREN STRAIN

The Hollywood Indian

As the granddaughter of a Cherokee Indian, Lauren Strain decided to investigate how Native Americans have been portrayed in Hollywood films. How accurately have films such as Dances with Wolves, The Last of the Mohicans, *and Disney's* Pocahontas *portrayed American Indians? What stereotypes are presented in these films? Which Native American actors have helped change these stereotypes? In order to answer these questions, Strain watched old films, interviewed her grandfather, and researched several popular films about American Indians.*

INVESTIGATING PAPER PROPOSAL

Being a quarter Indian, I have grown up with only a few Indian images in my life. Those images come from my grandfather, a Cherokee, and from the Indians in movies and on television. I have always been curious about Hollywood's portrayal of Indians. My grandfather, being adopted, did not grow up with any traditional Indian beliefs or values, so I heard of none. So I wonder if my perceptions about Indian culture and value systems are correct. I would like to look into that more for my paper.

Using sources from movies, TV, photos and articles, I would like to go into the Native American resource center and speak to a full-blood Indian who has experienced some of the traditional ways and values. Using my grandfather as a resource will also be an option. I would like to ask him how he felt seeing the images of Indians on television, and if he thought that they truly reflected how he saw himself as an Indian.

I would start out my paper with the perception of Tonto in *The Lone Ranger*. Using Sherman Alexie's story, *The Lone Ranger and Tonto Fistfight in Heaven* as one view of Tonto, I would continue with written accounts of the actor who played Tonto in the TV show. Next, I would look at Hollywood's perceptions of Indians on reservations. I could use *Smoke Signals* and other movies for those images. I will also look for movie reviews in journals in the library's database for any articles on Indians in Hollywood. I will finish my paper with the perception of the traditional "soak" Indian in Hollywood—I mean when Indians had just been taken over by the white man. For this I will use old westerns and the written and visual accounts of the movies *Dances with Wolves* and *The Last of the Mohicans*.

I am looking forward to this assignment, although it will be challenging to collect all of the information. It will, however, give me the chance to talk with other Indians and perhaps I will be able to grow as a person as well as a Cherokee Indian. I will also have a reason to ask my grandfather all of the questions that I have had for him ever since I was a child. I would like to direct this paper to all white and red people to help them see that although many of us believe almost everything we see on television and in movies, some of that information might be false. It will be a journey to find out what is true and what is false about some of the first people to inhabit America.

OUTLINE: THE HOLLYWOOD INDIAN

I. Introduce Topic
   A. How are Indians portrayed in Hollywood?
   B. Grandfather Cherokee and how I grew up with the TV and movie Indians as my models.
   C. Introduce movies like *Dances with Wolves* and *The Last of the Mohicans.*

II. Movie portrayal of Native Americans
   A. The accurate portrayal and inaccurate portrayal of *Dances with Wolves.*
   B. *The Last of the Mohicans*—are they really gone?
   C. *Pocahontas*—an inaccurate portrayal of true women?

...continued The Hollywood Indian, **Lauren Strain**

> **D.** Jack Strain's account of Indians on the reservation in the movie theaters.
>
> **E.** Tonto.

III. Indian actors and their movies
  A. *Outlaw Josey Wales* (Chief Dan George)
  B. *Maverick* (Graham Green)
  C. *Last of the Mohicans* (Russell Means)

IV. Movies and ideals of Native Americans throughout history
  A. The early movie portrayal of Native Americans
  B. President Ulysses S. Grant's quote and ideal
  C. John Ford's *Stagecoach* interprets Indians as enemies

V. Conclusions
  A. My own beliefs of how Native Americans are portrayed in Hollywood
  B. Interview with a Native American student at CSU and what his or her views are about Native Americans in movies

THE HOLLYWOOD INDIAN

I am the granddaughter of an adopted Cherokee who grew up knowing only *1* the ways of the white man. Not knowing much about the traditional American Indian, my only perceptions of them were through movies and Hollywood. Now that I am older, I stop and ask myself: What is the perception of Indians in Hollywood movies? Some of the most popular movies portraying Indians came out in my younger years (late 1980's early 1990's). I remember sneaking in to watch *Dances with Wolves* with my parents in the movie theater, which is a source of my perceptions of Indians. I even watched *Last of the Mohicans* in my freshman history class. Not only do I wonder how accurate movies like these are, I am very curious about the actors who play the Indians. During this research I want to answer certain questions. Are recent movies historically correct and do they eliminate stereotypes that people have given to Native Americans? What Native American actors have helped to portray their people accurately? And lastly, how has history helped to portray Native Americans better?

Three films that, despite historical inaccuracies, helped to popular- *2* ize the life and culture of Native Americans were *Dances with Wolves, Last of the Mohicans,* and *Pocahontas. Dances with Wolves* has been the most critically acclaimed movie that portrays the "correct" Indian. When asking my grandfather about whether or not he thought this movie was a correct portrayal, he said, "Yes, except for one thing." He told me that at the end of the movie, you see a winter camp deep in the mountains. The Indians would never keep their camp that deep in the mountains during the winter; they would move on to a warmer place. This was a detail that I had never known about. In Armando J. Prats' essay about the comparison between the two cinematic versions of *Dances with Wolves,* he states that there was a normal film version shown in the theaters and the one released in a TV miniseries that added scenes. He brings up a very valid point: even though, in this movie, the Indians are portrayed in a valid way, the story's main character is a white man. This title is even the white man's given Indian name (6). Watching the movie myself, I noticed that the portrayal of the Sioux Indians was very human and realistic to tradition. The film showed strong bonds between family and tribesmen. I too—as well as many others I know—also have strong bonds with family and friends. The Indian characters even had a sense of humor, which also helped me connect to them easier.

The movie *Last of the Mohicans* is also a very realistic film but it has 3
some historical misrepresentations. It takes place during the French and Indian War in 1757. This movie was shown to me in my freshman history class to illustrate brutalities of the war itself. Those details of the movie were portrayed very clearly. In one scene, an Indian from the Mohawk tribe eats the heart of a British general. I am not quite sure whether or not this type of brutality actually happened but I do know that scalpings were regular occurrences during the French and Indian War. Just like humans today, people kill people in savage ways. And although there are many accurate historical details about the war itself, like the Mohegan tribe helping out the settlers in Canada, there are misrepresentations about the details concerning the Mohegan tribe.

One plot point that is incorrect is that the Mohegan tribe is extinct, 4
as the movie suggests. Melissa Sayet, in her essay "The Lasting of the Mohegans," tells us "[I am] a Mohegan Indian, alive and well in 1993" (55). The Mohegan tribe still exists, although it is very small, in Uncasville, Connecticut. The small tribe has a church, museum and an all-Indian run institution that has existed for sixty-two years to help show their history. Sayet tells us that the media is responsible for putting the thought into people's heads that the tribe has been dead for a long time. The myth was actually created by Lydia Howard Sigourney. Sayet writes, "It seems that it was far easier for Lydia to romanticize dead Mohegans than to deal with the realities of alcoholism and poverty among living ones" (56). A well-known poet that knew of the Mohegan tribe, Sigourney wrote of their extinction anyway.

An additional inaccuracy in *The Last of the Mohicans,* although it 5
may be small, is that the spelling of the tribe's name is different in the movie compared to the spelling that the tribe uses (Mohican vs. Mohegan). According to Sayet, this was because of the miscommunication between the tribe and Europeans during first contact. The Mohegan tribe did not have an alphabet to help convey the correct spelling (56). Another reason for the misspelling is the fact that there are two tribes with

the same name spelled differently. One tribe comes from Connecticut and the other from the Hudson Valley in New York. The author of *The Last of the Mohicans* just accidentally switched the names unknowingly, according to the First Nations Web Site (First Nations).

When I watched the movie, I saw the romantic reasons for saying 6 that the tribe was extinct at the end. The Mohegan men were very stoic, smart, athletic and heroic. I have never met a Mohegan Indian, so I am not sure how they carry themselves. I do know that not all the Indians were known heroes. It was hard not to fall in love with these characters, though. The movie was designed to pull at your heart. In the end, when the character Changachook, the father of Uncas and the second-to-last Mohegan, tells us he is the only remaining Mohegan, it is very convincing and sad. This is how Hollywood wants us to feel. If movies did not leave people with any type of feeling, whether humor, sadness or happiness, then there would be no reason to watch.

In contrast to the more accurate portrayals of Native Americans in 7 *Dances with Wolves* and *Last of the Mohicans,* a third popular Native American film, *Pocahontas,* is very inaccurate historically speaking. Disney's version of *Pocahontas* focuses on a very historic American Indian. This movie is very factually inaccurate, however. The Indians were portrayed as very peaceful and loving in this film. Pocahontas is an Indian princess who falls in love with the handsome John Smith, an English soldier looking for land in the New World. She ends up saving his life, and he asks her to come with him back to England to be his wife. She declines his offer, saying she could never leave her family and her land.

The true story of Pocahontas is different in many ways. The age of 8 the character in the Disney movie seems to be in her early twenties. The real Pocahontas was sixteen years old. She did save the life of John Smith, but she fell in love with his friend, John Rolfe. She also ended up leaving America and going to England to marry him. Shortly upon her arrival, she died of smallpox. Although the film is historically inaccurate, telling children the real story of Pocahontas would not have been a wise decision on the part of Disney. They like to show a happy story that promotes values. A sixteen-year-old girl marrying an older man is not a common thing these days. Plus, the main character never dies in Disney movies. I can see why Disney changed the story. They did, however, keep the happy and peaceful image of the Indians, thus promoting them; but they didn't tell the story in a historically correct manner.

The second question that I had was who were/are the Native American 9 actors who have helped Hollywood portray a historically unstereotypical Indian? Three of the most recognized Indian actors in Hollywood who have portrayed historically accurate Indian characters are Graham Green, Russell Means, and Chief Dan George.

Graham Green is best known for his portrayal of Kicking Bird in 10
Dances with Wolves. He received an Academy Award Nomination for best supporting actor for that role. Green is also a well-known draftsman, steel worker, civil technologist, and sound engineer. He graduated from a Native American theater school, where his comedy skills shined (Green).

We see Green's comic acting shine through in the movie *Maverick*. 11
In this movie, his character, Joseph, is earning money for his tribe by running around in war paint and having his tribe beat their drums for a European who wants to experience the "real west." When we see him encounter the European, he begins to speak the man's native language. When the European tells Joseph to speak as they do in the movies, Joseph says "How, white man," a stereotypical greeting. Joseph tells his friend Maverick how stupid he feels acting as if he is foolish and savage when in fact we see he is a very intellectual person (*Maverick*). I believe that Graham Green chose this role because he was able to show people how inaccurate and stupid the stereotypical Indian can be, when in reality Indians can be intellectual, caring people.

Russell Means is known more for his work outside Hollywood, but 12
he is still praised for the roles he has taken in movies. He has been involved in civil rights for Native Americans since the 1960s. He has also done work with the United Nations for over twelve years. His most recent spot in the public eye was not in a movie, but rather in the demonstration against Columbus Day celebrations. Means got involved in acting in 1991. His most recognizable role was in *Last of the Mohicans*, where he plays the eldest Mohegan, a wise and brave man. His character was the leader of the family of Mohegans in this movie and he never strayed and helped to keep the spirit of the tribe alive when it was "lost" with the passing of his son.

Chief Dan George (1899–1981) also helped to show film viewers 13
that American Indians were intelligent and civilized and not the typical savages. George was the chief of the Salish Band in the Burrard Inlet, in British Columbia, Canada. He was a very gifted actor and the author of many books, such as *My Heart Soars* and *My Spirit Soars*. George was also nominated for an Academy Award for his role in *Little Big Man*. He was also in the TV miniseries "Centennial" (*Chief Dan George*).

In the movie *The Outlaw Josey Wales*, Chief Dan George's character, 14
Lone Watie, explains to Josey Wales how he was part of the tribe the white man called "the civilized tribe," or the Cherokee. His character is wearing a top hat and a suit when we first see him in the film. He tells Wales that he dressed up as Abe Lincoln to impress Lincoln when he met him. Later we see Watie burning his clothes, wearing less casual traveling garments. He tells Wales how he forgot things and lost his way when he became "civilized" (*The Outlaw Josie Wales*). The clothes Chief Dan George wore in that movie were very symbolic in the story that he told. Although these

were the words of a fictional character, I believe that they helped reflect the struggle of a Native American to be accepted as "civilized." Because of Hollywood, these struggles and lifestyles were able to get out to movie watchers.

The final question I was curious about was when and if historical 15 events helped to change the portrayal of Native Americans in Hollywood. The change from the savage enemy Indian came with World War II because the Nazis became the enemy rather than Native Americans. Angela Aleiss writes, "Previous images of menacing warriors who blocked Westward expansion gradually began to fade into one in which Indians stood as allies—rather than enemies—alongside America's frontier heroes" (25). Most movies changed stereotypes, but there were still some that had inaccurate portrayals like *Geronimo* (1939) and *They Died With Their Boots On* (1941).

In addition to the change brought on by World War II, Aleiss tells us 16 that there were three other contributions. The first one was to keep the relations between America, the United Kingdom, and Canada on good terms. Puritanical leaders wanted a good portrayal of Americans with other races. The second contribution, Alesiss says, is "the pro-interventionist politics of Hollywood studios [that] helped to create a mindset that would reshape the Indians image at least two years before America's entry into the war" (26). Hollywood executives were trying to rid the movie industry of fascist ideals. The final element was that the image of the ally Indian was not a fad, but rather a gateway for other Western movie themes.

My grandfather grew up next to a reservation before World War II, so 17 I asked him in my interview how Native Americans reacted to the westerns depicting them as the enemy. He told me that most of them went to the movies for the cartoons before the movie itself. "They did not show any emotional reaction to it," he said. I found it interesting that they would even go to the movies at all. When telling my grandfather this, he told me that, "It was a way for the Indians to break into the western culture." That helped me to understand their reasons for going.

When conducting my survey of students in my class, three out of ten 18 thought that movies still portray Indians in a stereotypically savage manner. Two of them thought that Hollywood was doing a good job in the portrayal of the "correct" Native American. One person wrote, "Hollywood is more worried about offending anybody who is not white. Because people today are very sensitive, everyone, including Hollywood, watches what they say and do."

Throughout my research, I have found that Native Americans are 19 portrayed in a very positive light. The negative stereotypical Indian has slowly faded with images of "the true west." Although there are still few exceptions, one aspect that I see in movies with Native Americans is historical details being left out. For example, the Mohegan tribe still existing and the movie *Last of the Mohicans* portraying their extinction. Also, the Indians in the last scene of *Dances with Wolves,* who use an incorrect stopping ground during the winter. I believe that Hollywood is concerned about offending Native Americans, but historical context comes into play in what they write and put in movies. Hollywood has a duty to add accurate historical context to the films; movies are taken very seriously in today's culture. Children learn from what they see in movies and on TV. But should Hollywood risk a good story just for entertainment value? I believe that the film industry can mix fact and fiction while still pulling off a good story. They should learn the correct history of America and all its people.

Works Cited

Aleiss, Angela. "Prelude to World War II: Racial Unity and the Hollywood Indian." *Journal of American Culture* 18. 2 (1995): 25–34. Print.

"Chief Dan George." *Indigenous Peoples' Literature.* American Indian Heritage Foundation, 14 Dec. 1998. Web. 7 May 2001.

First Nations. Ed. Jordan S. Dill. 2000. Web. 23 Apr. 2001.

Green, Graham. Home page. 16 Jan. 2000. Web. 6 May 2001. <http://www.geocities/Hollywood/guild/9621/grahamgreen.html>

The Last of the Mohicans. Dir. Michael Mann. Perf. Russell Means and Daniel Day-Lewis. Twentieth Century Fox, 1992. DVD.

Maverick. Dir. Richard Donner. Perf. Graham Green and Mel Gibson. Warner Brothers, 1994. Videocassette.

The Outlaw Josey Wales. Dir. Clint Eastwood. Perf. Clint Eastwood and Chief Dan George. Warner Brothers, 1976. DVD.

Prats, Armando J. "The Image of the Other and the Other 'Dances with Wolves': The Refigured Indian and the Textual Supplement." *Journal of Film and Video* 50.1 (1998): 3–19. Print.

Sayet, Melissa F. "The Lasting of the Mohegan." *Essence* 23.11 (March 1993): 55–57. Print.

Strain, Jack. Phone interview. 11 April 2001.

Strain, Lauren. Personal survey. 3 May 2001.

vo·cab·u·lar·y

In your journal, write down the meanings of the italicized words in the following sentences.

- some historical *misrepresentations* (3)
- the *romantic* reasons (6)
- *pro-interventionist* politics of Hollywood studios (16)
- rid the movie industry of *fascist* ideals (16)

? QUESTIONS FOR WRITING AND DISCUSSION

1 Make a list of films you have seen that have Native American characters. Choose two of those films—one older, one more recent. Which characters in both films seemed most realistic and which most stereotypical? Describe the changes you notice between these two films' representations of Native American culture, language, politics, or heritage.

2 At the end of her essay, Strain says that Hollywood can "mix fact and fiction" while still creating a good story. Would you agree with that statement, or do you think historical accuracy should come first and entertainment values second? Choose a film about Native Americans— or any ethnic group—and explain what that film loses or gains by placing entertainment values over historical and cultural accuracy (or, conversely, by giving historical/cultural accuracy much more importance than entertainment values).

3 Strain conducts both a short survey and an interview which she reports on at the end of her paper. Assume you are in a peer-response group, giving her feedback on her essay. Would you advise her to integrate the information in paragraphs 17 and 18 earlier in her essay rather than tacking them on at the end? Where might that information fit? (How do you plan to integrate any interview or survey information in your own essay?)

4 Read the essay by Margaret Lazarus in Chapter 9, titled "All's Not Well in Land of 'The Lion King.'" Rent *Pocahontas* from a video store and watch it. Are there racist or sexist scenes or images in Disney's version of *Pocahontas?* Does the film ultimately promote Native American cultural values or mainstream white American values? Explain.

STUDENT WRITING
BRIDGID STONE

My Friend Michelle, an Alcoholic

Bridgid Stone, a student at Southeast Missouri State University, decided to write her investigative essay on alcoholism. In the library, she was able to find quite a lot of information and statistics about alcohol. In her friend, Michelle, she had a living example of the consequences of alcohol abuse. The question, however, was how to combine the two. As you read her essay, notice how she interweaves description and dialogue with facts and statistics.

Five million teenagers are problem drinkers, according to *Group* maga- 1 zine's article "Sex, Drugs, and Alcohol." One of these five million teenagers is my friend, Michelle.

"I can't wait to go out tonight and get drunk," Michelle announces *2* as she walks into my dorm room. I just sigh and shake my head. Michelle has been drunk every night since Wednesday. In the last three days, she has been to more fraternity parties than classes.

We leave a few hours later for a Sig Tau party. Even though I have *3* been attending these parties for weeks now, the amount of alcohol present still amazes me. Almost everyone is walking around with a twelve-pack of beer. Others are carrying fifths of vodka or Jack Daniels whiskey. As cited in *Fraternities and Sororities on Contemporary College Campuses,* 73 percent of fraternity advisers believe that alcohol is a problem in fraternities. I wish the other 27 percent could be here now. Fraternities are synonymous with drinking.

Michelle and I both have innocent-looking squeeze bottles, but inside *4* are very stiff screwdrivers. They probably have more vodka than orange juice. Michelle finishes her drink before I am halfway through mine. So she finishes off mine, too, before disappearing into the throng of people at the party. The next time I see her, she is holding a beer in each hand. Her speech is slurred, and she can barely stand up on her own.

We head back to the dorm when Michelle starts vomiting. Once we *5* are in her room, I help her undress and put her to bed.

"Bridgid, I am so sorry," Michelle cries, "I promise never to drink *6* again."

"Okay, just get some sleep," I tell her as I leave. *7*

It's Thursday night and Michelle is ready to party again. *8*

"I haven't been to my Friday 8:00 class in a month. Do you think I *9* should just stay up all night after the party and go to class drunk? Or should I just not go to class and sleep in?" Michelle asks.

"Don't go out and get drunk. Stay home tonight and get up and go *10* to your classes tomorrow," I advise.

"I am just going to sleep in," Michelle informs me as she leaves for *11* the party.

Like Michelle, an estimated 4.6 million adolescents experience nega- *12* tive consequences of alcohol abuse, such as poor school performance. This was reported in a survey conducted by NIAAA for a United States Congressional report.

Early Friday morning, I get a phone call from the on-duty resident *13* adviser. Michelle has passed out in the lobby of the Towers Complex. She couldn't remember her phone number or even what floor she lived on, but I had written my phone number on Michelle's hand, so she could call me if she got into any trouble. The R.A. had seen my number and decided to call, since Michelle was too drunk to dial the four digits.

"Could you please escort your friend up to your room?" the R.A. *14* asks. She doesn't sound very happy.

"Sure, I will be down in a few minutes," I promise. It takes me and *15* another girl from our floor to get Michelle onto the elevator. She keeps lying down or passing out. Thirty minutes later, we get Michelle into bed.

She is mumbling incoherently, and she reeks of alcohol. Needless to say, Michelle doesn't make it to her 8:00 A.M. class, again.

Saturday afternoon, I confront Michelle about the Thursday night 16 incident. This is rather hard to do, since she doesn't remember any of it.

"I just drink to loosen up. I'm much more fun if I've been drink- 17 ing," Michelle tells me.

"You are not much fun when you are puking or passing out," I re- 18 ply. A desire to loosen up is one of the main reasons that teenagers drink, reports *Group* magazine. Other reasons include a need to escape and to rebel.

"I have to release steam every once in a while," she argues. "School 19 is really stressing me out."

"Michelle, you don't even go to class," I tell her.   20

"Everyone else drinks!" she says. "Why are you picking on me?" 21 She stomps out of my room.

Michelle was partially correct, though, when she stated, "Everyone 22 else drinks." As reported in *Alcohol and Youth,* more than 80 percent of all college students surveyed had been drinking in the previous month. But this doesn't mean that what Michelle is doing is any less serious. In all probability, Michelle is an alcoholic.

A test that is often used to determine if someone has a drinking 23 problem can be found in *Getting Them Sober,* by Toby Rice Andrews. There are twenty questions on the test. A "yes" answer to two of the questions indicates a possible drinking problem. Questions include: "Do you miss time from school or work due to drinking?" "Do you drink to escape from worries or troubles?" "Do you drink because you are shy?" "Have you ever had a memory loss due to drinking?" Michelle would probably have answered "yes" to all of the above questions.

I moved out of the dorm at the beginning of the second semester, 24 so I haven't seen much of Michelle. The last time I saw her was about three weeks ago. She had gotten arrested while in New Orleans for spring break. Apparently, Michelle had been out drinking and eventually had been arrested for public drunkenness.

"It wasn't that bad," she told me. "I don't even remember being in 25 the jail cell. I was pretty trashed."

Works Cited

Andrews, Toby Rice. *Getting Them Sober.* South Plainfield, N.J.: Bridge, 1980. Print.

Barnes, Grace. *Alcohol and Youth.* Westport, Conn.: Greenwood, 1982. Print.

Pruett, Harold, and Vivian Brown. *Crisis Intervention and Prevention.* San Francisco: Jossey-Bass, 1987. Print.

"Sex, Drugs, and Alcohol." *Group.* February 1992: 17–20. Print.

Van Pelt, Rich. *Intensive Care*. Grand Rapids: Zondervan, 1988. Print.

Winston, Roger, William Nettles III, and John Opper, Jr. *Fraternities and Sororities on Contemporary College Campuses*. San Francisco: Jossey-Bass, 1987. Print.

 QUESTIONS FOR WRITING AND DISCUSSION

1 Investigative reports should provide information without editorializing or arguing for or against one perspective or another. Even though Stone is writing about her friend, Michelle, does she sympathize with Michelle or make excuses for her? Does she censure Michelle for her behavior? How effectively does Stone maintain a reporter's distance as she describes Michelle's behavior and presents statistics and other background information? Explain, referring to specific passages in the essay.

2 Who is Stone's audience for her essay? Where would you recommend that Stone send her essay for possible publication? List two possible publication sources (magazines or newspapers), and explain your choices.

3 If Stone were revising her essay, what advice would you give her about balancing statistics and personal experience? Should she have more statistics? Should she have more narrative? Refer to specific paragraphs and examples in your response.

4 Stone's use of the present tense adds dramatic impact to her essay. Reread her essay, noticing where she uses the present tense and where she shifts to the past tense. Where was the use of the present tense most effective? Did her tense shifting confuse you at any point? Where?

5 Compare Stone's essay with Kozol's essay earlier in this chapter. What reporting strategies does Stone adapt from Kozol? How are their reporting strategies different? Explain your response by referring to specific passages from each author.

PEARSON
mycomplab

For additional writing, reading, and research resources, go to http://www.mycomplab.com

Examine the image above, captured from Google Street Views. Although many Google street views show people unaware that the Google camera car is passing, these people knew the camera car was coming and prepared to have their picture taken. After studying this image, answer Journal question 6 on page 295.

Explaining

8

You have decided to quit your present job, so you write a note to your boss giving thirty days' notice. During your last few weeks at work, your boss asks you to write a three-page job description to help orient the person who will replace you. The job description should include a list of your current duties as well as advice to your replacement on how to execute them most efficiently. To write the description, you record your daily activities, look back through your calendar, comb through your records, and brainstorm a list of everything you do. As you write up the description, you include specific examples and illustrations of your typical responsibilities.

As a gymnast and dancer, you gradually become obsessed with losing weight. You start skipping meals, purging the little food you do eat, and lying about your eating habits to your parents. Before long, you weigh less than seventy pounds, and your physician diagnoses your condition: anorexia nervosa. With advice from your physician and counseling from a psychologist, you gradually begin to control your disorder. To explain to others what anorexia is, how it is caused, and what its effects are, you write an essay in which you explain your ordeal, alerting other readers to the potential dangers of uncontrolled dieting.

> Become aware of the two-sided nature of your mental make-up: one thinks in terms of the connectedness of things, the other thinks in terms of parts and sequences.
> —GABRIELE LUSSER RICO, AUTHOR OF *WRITING THE NATURAL WAY*

> What [a writer] knows is almost always a matter of the relationships he establishes, between example and generalization, between one part of a narrative and the next, between the idea and the counter idea that the writer sees is also relevant.
> —ROGER SALE, AUTHOR OF *ON WRITING*

E XPLAINING AND DEMONSTRATING RELATIONSHIPS IS A FREQUENT PURPOSE FOR WRITING. EXPLAINING GOES BEYOND INVESTIGATING THE FACTS AND REPORTING INFORMATION; IT ANALYZES THE COMPONENT PARTS OF A SUBJECT AND THEN SHOWS HOW THE PARTS FIT in relation to one another. Its goal is to clarify for a particular group of readers *what* something is, *how* it happened or should happen, and/or *why* it happens.

Explaining begins with assessing the rhetorical situation: the writer, the occasion, the intended purpose and audience, the genre, and the cultural context. As you begin thinking about a subject, topic, or issue to explain, keep in mind your own interests, the expectations of your audience, the possible genre you might choose to help achieve your purpose (essay, article, pamphlet, multigenre essay, Web site), and finally the cultural or social context in which you are writing or in which your writing might be read.

Explaining any idea, concept, process, or effect requires analysis. Analysis starts with dividing a thing or phenomenon into its various parts. Then, once you explain the various parts, you put them back together (synthesis) to explain their relationship or how they work together.

Explaining how to learn to play the piano, for example, begins with an analysis of the parts of the learning process: playing scales, learning chords, getting instruction from a teacher, sight reading, and performing in recitals. Explaining why two automobiles collided at an intersection begins with an analysis of the contributing factors: the nature of the intersection, the number of cars involved, the condition of the drivers, and the condition of each vehicle. Then you bring the parts together and show their *relationships:* you show how practicing scales on the piano fits into the process of learning to play the piano; you demonstrate why one small factor—such as a faulty turn signal—combined with other factors to cause an automobile accident.

The emphasis you give to the *analysis* of the object or phenomenon and the time you spend explaining *relationships* of the parts depends on your purpose, subject, and audience. If you want to explain how a flower reproduces, for example, you may begin by identifying the important parts, such as the pistil and stamen, that most readers need to know about before they can understand the reproductive process. However, if you are explaining the process to a botany major who already knows the parts of a flower, you might spend more time discussing the key operations in pollination or the reasons why some flowers cross-pollinate and others do not. In any effective explanation, analyzing parts and showing relationships must work together for that particular group of readers.

Because its purpose is to teach the reader, *expository writing,* or writing to explain, should be as clear as possible. Explanations, however, are more than organized pieces of information. Expository writing contains information that is focused by your point of view, by your experience, and by your reasoning powers. Thus, your explanation of a thing or phenomenon makes a point or has a thesis: This is the *right* way to define *happiness.* This is how one *should* bake lasagne or do a calculus problem. These are the *most important* reasons why the senator from New York was elected. To make your explanation clear, you show what you mean by using specific support: facts, data, examples, illustrations, statistics, comparisons, analogies, and images. Your thesis is a *general* assertion about the relationships of the *specific* parts. The support helps your reader identify the parts and see the relationships. Expository writing teaches the reader by alternating between generalizations and specific examples.

Techniques for Explaining

Explaining requires first that you assess your rhetorical situation. Your purpose must work for a particular audience, genre, and context. You may revise some of these aspects of the rhetorical situation as you draw on your own observations and memories about your topic. As you research your topic, conduct an interview, or do a survey, keep thinking about issues of audience, genre, and context. Below are techniques for writing clear explanations.

66 The main thing I try to do is write as clearly as I can. 99

—E. B. WHITE,
JOURNALIST AND COAUTHOR OF
ELEMENTS OF STYLE

Techniques for Explaining

Technique	Tips on How to Do It
Considering (and reconsidering) your purpose, audience, genre, and social context	As you change your *audience* or your *genre,* you must change how you explain something as well as how much and what kind of evidence you use.
Getting the reader's attention and stating the thesis	Devise an accurate but interesting *title.* Use an attention-getting *lead-in.* State the *thesis* clearly.
Defining key terms and describing *what* something is	Analyze and define by *describing, comparing, classifying* and/or *giving examples.*
Identifying the steps in a process and showing *how* each step relates to the overall process	Describe *how* something should be done or *how* something typically happens. *Continued*

Technique	Tips on How to Do It
Describing causes and effects and showing *why* certain causes lead to specific effects	Analyze how several causes lead to a *single effect,* or show how a single cause leads to *multiple effects.*
Supporting explanations with specific evidence	Use descriptions, examples, comparisons, analogies, images, facts, data, or statistics to *show* what, how, or why.

In *Spirit of the Valley: Androgyny and Chinese Thought,* psychologist Sukie Colgrave illustrates many of these techniques as she explains an important concept from psychology: the phenomenon of *projection.* Colgrave explains how we "project" attributes missing in our own personality onto another person—especially someone we love:

Explaining what: Definition example

Explaining why: Effects of projection

Explaining how: The process of freeing ourselves from dependency

> A one-sided development of either the masculine or feminine principles has [an] unfortunate consequence for our psychological and intellectual health: it encourages the phenomenon termed "projection." This is the process by which we project onto other people, things, or ideologies, those aspects of ourselves which we have not, for whatever reason, acknowledged or developed. The most familiar example of this is the obsession which usually accompanies being "in love." A person whose feminine side is unrealised will often "fall in love" with the feminine which she or he "sees" in another person, and similarly with the masculine. The experience of being "in love" is one of powerful dependency. As long as the projection appears to fit its object nothing awakens the person to the reality of the projection. But sooner or later the lover usually becomes aware of certain discrepancies between her or his desires and the person chosen to satisfy them. Resentment, disappointment, anger and rejection rapidly follow, and often the relationship disintegrates. . . . But if we can explore our own psyches we may discover what it is we were demanding from our lover and start to develop it in ourselves. The moment this happens we begin to see other people a little more clearly. We are freed from some of our needs to make others what we want them to be, and can begin to love them more for what they are.

EXPLAINING *WHAT:* DEFINITION

Explaining *what* something is or means requires showing the relationship between it and the *class* of beings, objects, or concepts to which it belongs. *Formal definition,* which is often essential in explaining, has three parts: the thing or term to be defined, the class, and the distinguishing characteristics of the thing or term. The thing being defined can be concrete, such as a turkey, or abstract, such as democracy.

Thing or Term	Class	Distinguishing Characteristics
A turkey is a	bird	that has brownish plumage and a bare, wattled head and neck; it is widely domesticated for food.
Democracy is	government	by the people, exercised directly or through elected representatives.

Frequently, writers use *extended definitions* when they need to give more than a mere formal definition. An extended definition may explain the word's etymology or historical roots, describe sensory characteristics of something (how it looks, feels, sounds, tastes, smells), identify its parts, indicate how something is used, explain what it is not, provide an example of it, and/or note similarities or differences between this term and other words or things.

The following extended definition of democracy, written for an audience of college students to appear in a textbook, begins with the etymology of the word and then explains—using analysis, comparison, example, and description—what democracy is and what it is not:

Since democracy is government of the people, by the people, and for the people, a democratic form of government is not fixed or static. Democracy is dynamic; it adapts to the wishes and needs of the people. The term *democracy* derives from the Greek word *demos,* meaning "the common people," and -*kratia,* meaning "strength or power" used to govern or rule. Democracy is based on the notion that a majority of people creates laws and then everyone agrees to abide by those laws in the interest of the common good. In a democracy, people are not ruled by a king, a dictator, or a small group of powerful individuals. Instead, people elect officials who use the power temporarily granted to them to govern the society. For example, the people may agree that their government should raise money for defense, so the officials levy taxes to support an army. If enough people decide, however, that taxes for defense are too high, then they request that their elected officials change the laws or they elect new officials. The essence of democracy lies in its responsiveness: Democracy is a form of government in which laws and lawmakers change as the will of the majority changes.

Formal definition
Description: What democracy is
Etymology: Analysis of the word's roots

Comparison: What democracy is not

Example

Formal definition

Figurative expressions—vivid word pictures using similes, metaphors, or analogies—can also explain what something is. During World War II, for example, the Writer's War Board asked E. B. White (author of *Charlotte's Web* and many *New Yorker* magazine essays, as well as other works) to provide an explanation of democracy. Instead of giving a formal definition or etymology, White responded with a series of imaginative comparisons showing the *relationship* between various parts of American culture and the concept of democracy.

> Surely the Board knows what democracy is. It is the line that forms on the right. It is the don't in Don't Shove. It is the hole in the stuffed shirt through which the sawdust slowly trickles; it is the dent in the high hat. Democracy is the recurrent suspicion that more than half of the people are right more than half of the time. It is the feeling of privacy in the voting booths, the feeling of communion in the libraries, the feeling of vitality everywhere. Democracy is the score at the beginning of the ninth. It is an idea which hasn't been disproved yet, a song the words of which have not gone bad. It's the mustard on the hot dog and the cream in the rationed coffee. Democracy is a request from a War Board, in the middle of a morning in the middle of a war, wanting to know what democracy is.

EXPLAINING *HOW:* PROCESS ANALYSIS

Explaining *how* something should be done or how something happens is usually called *process analysis.* One kind of process analysis is the "how-to" explanation: how to cook a turkey, how to tune an engine, how to get a job. Such recipes or directions are *prescriptive:* You typically explain how something *should* be done. In a second kind of process analysis, you explain how something happens or is typically done—without being directive or prescriptive. In a *descriptive* process analysis, you explain how some natural or social process typically happens: how cells split during mitosis, how hailstones form in a cloud, how students react to the pressure of examinations, or how political candidates create their public images. In both prescriptive and descriptive explanations, however, you are analyzing a *process*—dividing the sequence into its parts or steps—and then showing how the parts contribute to the whole process.

Cookbooks, automobile-repair manuals, instructions for assembling toys or appliances, and self-improvement books are all examples of *prescriptive* process analysis. Writers of recipes, for example, begin with analyses of the ingredients and the steps in preparing the food. Then they carefully explain how the steps are related, how to avoid problems, and how to serve mouth-watering concoctions. Farley Mowat, naturalist and author of *Never Cry Wolf,* gives his readers the following detailed—and humorous—recipe for creamed mouse. Mowat became interested in this recipe when he decided to test the nutritional content of the wolf's diet. "In the event that any of my readers may be interested in personally exploiting this hitherto overlooked source of excellent animal protein," Mowat writes, "I give the recipe in full."

Souris à la Crème

Ingredients:

One dozen fat mice	Salt and pepper	One cup white flour
Cloves	One piece sowbelly	Ethyl alcohol

Skin and gut the mice, but do not remove the heads; wash, then place in a pot with enough alcohol to cover the carcasses. Allow to marinate for about two hours. Cut sowbelly into small cubes and fry slowly until most of the fat has been rendered. Now remove the carcasses from the alcohol and roll them in a mixture of salt, pepper and flour; then place in frying pan and sauté for about five minutes (being careful not to allow the pan to get too hot, or the delicate meat will dry out and become tough and stringy). Now add a cup of alcohol and six or eight cloves. Cover the pan and allow to simmer slowly for fifteen minutes. The cream sauce can be made according to any standard recipe. When the sauce is ready, drench the carcasses with it, cover and allow to rest in a warm place for ten minutes before serving.

Explaining *how* something happens or is typically done involves a *descriptive* process analysis. It requires showing the chronological relationship between one idea, event, or phenomenon and the next—and it depends on close observation. In *The Lives of a Cell,* biologist and physician Lewis Thomas explains that ants are like humans: while they are individuals, they can also act together to create a social organism. Although exactly how ants communicate remains a mystery, Thomas explains how they combine to form a thinking, working organism.

[Ants] seem to live two kinds of lives: they are individuals, going about the day's business without much evidence of thought for tomorrow, and they are at the same time component parts, cellular elements, in the huge, writhing, ruminating organism of the Hill, the nest, the hive. . . .

A solitary ant, afield, cannot be considered to have much of anything on his mind; indeed, with only a few neurons strung together by fibers, he can't be imagined to have a mind at all, much less a thought. He is more like a ganglion on legs. Four ants together, or ten, encircling a dead moth on a path, begin to look more like an idea. They fumble and shove, gradually moving the food toward the Hill, but as though by blind chance. It is only when you watch the dense mass of thousands of ants, crowded together around the Hill, blackening the ground, that you begin to see the whole beast, and now you observe it thinking, planning, calculating. It is an intelligence, a kind of live computer, with crawling bits for its wits.

At a stage in the construction, twigs of a certain size are needed, and all the members forage obsessively for twigs of just this size. Later, when outer walls are to be finished, thatched, the size must change, and as though given new orders by telephone, all the workers shift the search to the new twigs. If you disturb the arrangement of a part of the Hill, hundreds of ants will set it vibrating, shifting, until it is put right again. Distant sources of food are somehow sensed, and long lines, like tentacles, reach out over the ground, up over walls, behind boulders, to fetch it in.

EXPLAINING *WHY:* CAUSAL ANALYSIS

"Why?" may be the question most commonly asked by human beings. We are fascinated by the reasons for everything that we experience in life. We ask questions about natural phenomena: Why is the sky blue? Why does a teakettle whistle? Why do some materials act as superconductors? We also find human attitudes and behavior intriguing: Why is chocolate so popular? Why do some people hit small leather balls with big sticks and then run around a field stomping on little white pillows? Why are America's family farms economically depressed? Why did the United States go to war in Iraq? Why is the Internet so popular?

Explaining *why* something occurs can be the most fascinating—and difficult—kind of expository writing. Answering the question "why" usually requires analyzing *cause-and-effect relationships.* The causes, however, may be too complex or intangible to identify precisely. We are on comparatively secure ground when we ask *why* about physical phenomena that can be weighed, measured, and replicated under laboratory conditions. Under those conditions, we can determine cause and effect with precision.

Fire, for example, has three *necessary* and *sufficient* causes: combustible material, oxygen, and ignition temperature. Without each of these causes, fire will not occur (each cause is "necessary"); taken together, these three causes are enough to cause fire (all three together are "sufficient"). In this case, the cause-and-effect relationship can be illustrated by an equation:

Cause 1	+	Cause 2	+	Cause 3	=	Effect
(combustible material)		(oxygen)		(ignition temperature)		(fire)

Analyzing both necessary and sufficient causes is essential to explaining an effect. You may say, for example, that wind shear (an abrupt downdraft in a storm) "caused" an airplane crash. In fact, wind shear may have *contributed* (been necessary) to the crash but was not by itself the total (sufficient) cause of the crash: an airplane with enough power may be able to overcome wind shear forces in certain circumstances. An explanation of the crash is not complete until you analyze the full range of necessary *and* sufficient causes, which may include wind shear, lack of power, mechanical failure, and even pilot error.

Sometimes, explanations for physical phenomena are beyond our analytical powers. Astrophysicists, for example, have good theoretical reasons for believing that black holes cause gigantic gravitational whirlpools in outer space, but they have difficulty explaining why black holes exist—or whether they exist at all.

In the realm of human cause and effect, determining causes and effects can be as tricky as explaining why black holes exist. Why, for example, do some children learn math easily while others fail? What effect does failing at math have on a child? What are necessary and sufficient causes for divorce? What are the effects of divorce on parents and children? Although you may not be able to explain all the causes or effects of something, you should not be satisfied until you have considered a wide range of possible causes and effects. Even then, you need to qualify or modify your statements, using such words as *might, usually, often, seldom, many,* or *most,* and then giving as much support and evidence as you can.

In the following paragraphs, Jonathan Kozol, a critic of America's educational system and author of *Illiterate America,* explains the multiple effects of a single cause: illiteracy. Kozol supports his explanation by citing specific ways that illiteracy affects the lives of people:

Illiterates cannot read the menu in a restaurant.

They cannot read the cost of items on the menu in the window of the restaurant before they enter.

Illiterates cannot read the letters that their children bring home from their teachers. They cannot study school department circulars that tell them of the courses that their children must be taking if they hope to pass the SAT exams. They cannot help with homework. They cannot write a letter to the teacher. They are afraid to visit in the classroom. They do not want to humiliate their child or themselves. . . .

Many illiterates cannot read the admonition on a pack of cigarettes. Neither the Surgeon General's warning nor its reproduction on the package can alert them to the risks. Although most people learn by word of mouth that smoking is related to a number of grave physical disorders, they do not get the chance to read the detailed stories which can document this danger with the vividness that turns concern into determination to resist. They can see the handsome cowboy or the slim Virginia lady lighting up a filter cigarette; they cannot heed the words that tell them that this product is (not "may be") dangerous to their health. Sixty million men and women are condemned to be the unalerted, high-risk candidates for cancer. . . .

Illiterates cannot travel freely. When they attempt to do so, they encounter risks that few of us can dream of. They cannot read traffic signs and, while they often learn to recognize and to decipher symbols, they cannot manage street names which they haven't seen before. The same is true for bus and subway stops. While ingenuity can sometimes help a man or woman to discern directions from familiar landmarks, buildings, cemeteries, churches, and the like, most illiterates are virtually immobilized. They seldom wander past the streets and neighborhoods they know. Geographical paralysis becomes a bitter metaphor for their entire existence. They are immobilized in almost every sense we can imagine. They can't move up. They can't move out. They cannot see beyond.

WARMING UP   Journal Exercises

The following exercises will help you practice writing explanations. Read all of the following exercises and then write on the three that interest you most. If another idea occurs to you, write about it.

1. **Writing Across the Curriculum.** Write a one-paragraph explanation of an idea, term, or concept that you have discussed in a class that you are currently taking. From biology, for example, you might define *photosynthesis* or *gene splicing*. From psychology, you might define *psychosis* or *projection*. From computer studies, you might define *cyberspace* or *morphing*. First, identify someone who might need to know about this subject. Then give a definition and an illustration. Finally, describe how the term was discovered or invented, what its effects or applications are, and/or how it works.

2. Imitating E. B. White's short "definition" of democracy, use imaginative comparisons to write a short definition—serious or humorous—of one of the following words: *freedom, adolescence, mathematics, politicians, parents, misery, higher education, luck,* or a word of your own choice.

3. Novelist Ernest Hemingway once defined courage as "grace under pressure." Using this definition, explain how you or someone you know showed this kind of courage in a difficult situation.

4. When asked what jazz is, Louis Armstrong replied, "Man, if you gotta ask you'll never know." If you know quite a bit about jazz, explain what Armstrong meant. Or choose a familiar subject to which the same remark might apply. What can be "explained" about that subject, and what cannot?

5. Choose a skill that you've acquired (for example, playing a musical instrument, operating a machine, playing a sport, drawing, counseling others, driving in rush-hour traffic, dieting) and explain to a novice how he or she can acquire that skill. Reread what you've written. Then write another version addressed to an expert. What parts can you leave out? What must you add?

6 Examine the illustration of Google Street Views shown on the opening page of this chapter. Do some research online about what Google Street Views are, how these images are captured, and how to access them online. Then consider the possible effects. Although Google says that they blur the faces of people so that they are not identifiable, is this always true? Are there examples of images that are clear invasions of privacy? Google has already captured images of apparent crimes—does that mean that these images could protect public safety or help send alleged criminals to jail? For a private, public, or academic audience, write your own blog or essay explaining the real or possible good or bad effects of Google Street Views.

7 Sometimes writers use standard definitions to explain a key term, but sometimes they need to resist conventional definition in order to make a point. LaMer Steptoe, an eleventh-grader in West Philadelphia, was faced with a form requiring her to check her racial identity. Like many Americans of multicultural heritage, she decided not to check one box. In the following paragraphs, reprinted from National Public Radio's *All Things Considered,* Ms. Steptoe explains how she decided to (re)define herself. As you read her response, consider how you might need to resist a conventional definition in your own explaining essay.

Multiracialness

Caucasian, African-American, Latin American, Asian-American. Check one. I look black, so I'll pick that one. But, no, wait, if I pick that, I'll be denying the other sides of my family. So I'll pick white. But I'm not white or black, I'm both, and part Native American, too. It's confusing when you have to pick which race to identify with, especially when you have family who, on one side, ask, "Why do you talk like a white girl?" when, in the eyes of the other side of your family, your behind is black.

I never met my dad's mom, my grandmother, Maybelle Dawson Boyd Steptoe, and my father never knew his father. But my aunts or uncles or cousins all think of me as black or white. I mean, I'm not the lightest-skinned person, but my cousins down South swear I'm white. It bothers them, and that bothers me, how people could care so much about your skin color.

My mother's mother, Sylvia Gabriel, lives in Connecticut, near where my aunt, uncle and cousins on that side of the family live. Now, they're white, and where my grandma lives, there are very few black people or people of color. And when we visit, people look at us a lot, staring like, "What is that woman doing with those people?" It shocks the heck out of them when my brother and I call her Grandma.

My mother's side is Italian. I really didn't get any Italian culture except for the food. My father was raised much differently from my mother. My father is superstitious; he believes that a child should know his or her place and not speak unless spoken to. My father is very much into both his African-American and Native American heritage.

Multiracialness is a very tricky subject for my father. He'll tell people that I'm Native, African-American and Caucasian American, but at the same time he'll say things like, "Listen to jazz, listen to your cultural music." He says, "LaMer, look in the mirror. You're black. Ask any white person: they'll say you're black." He doesn't get it. I really would rather be colorless than to pick a race. I like other music, not just black music.

The term African-American bugs me. I'm not African. I'm American as a hot dog. We should have friends who are yellow, red, blue, black, purple, gay, religious, bisexual, trilingual, whatever, so you don't have a stereotypical view. I've met mean people and nice people of all different backgrounds. At my school, I grew up with all these kids, and I didn't look at them as white or Jewish or heterosexual; I looked at them as, "Oh, she's funny, he's sweet."

I know what box I'm going to choose. I pick D for none of the above, because my race is human.

PROFESSIONAL WRITING

How to Take Control of Your Credit Cards
Suze Orman

The author of several best selling books, including The Nine Steps to Financial Freedom *(1997),* The Money Book for the Young, Fabulous & Broke *(2005), and* Women and Money: Owning the Power to Control Your Destiny *(2007), Suze Orman was born in 1951 in Chicago, earned a degree in social work from the University of Illinois, and started her career not as a financial expert but as a waitress in Berkeley, California. After working at a restaurant for seven years, she talked her way into a job as a financial advisor with Merrill Lynch. She then started her own business and published her first book* You've Earned It, Don't Lose It. *Six of her most recent books have been* New York Times *bestsellers. Now that she is young(ish), fabulous, and very wealthy, Suze Orman has her own CNBC TV show, and she appears on* Oprah, *the* Today Show, The View, *and* Larry King. *She is also the winner of 2 Emmy Awards for her PBS specials and has been the recipient of the most GRACIE Awards in the history of the AWRT (American Women in Radio and Television). "How to Take Control of Your Credit Cards" appeared originally as one of her regular columns for* Money Matters *on Yahoo! Finance.*

I'm all for taking credit where credit is due, but when it comes to credit cards, way too many of you are overdoing it. For Americans who don't pay their entire credit card bill each month, the average balance is close to $4,000. And when we zoom in on higher-income folks—those with annual incomes between $75,000 and $100,000—the average balance clocks in at nearly $8,000. If you're paying, say, 18 percent interest on an $8,000 balance, and you make only the 2 percent minimum payment due each month, you are going to end up paying more than $22,000 in interest over the course of the 54 years it will take to get the balance down to zero. *1*

That's absolute insanity. *2*

And absolutely unnecessary. *3*

If you have the desire to take control of your credit card mess, you can. It's just a matter of choice. I am not saying it will be easy, but there are plenty of strategies that can put you on a path out of credit card hell. And as I explain later, even those of you who can't seem to turn the corner and become credit responsible on your own, can get plenty of help from qualified credit counseling services. *4*

How to Be a Credit Card Shark

If you overspend just because you like to buy buy buy on credit, then you are what I call Broke by Choice. You are willfully making your own mess. I am not going to lecture you about how damaging this is; I'm hoping the fact that you're reading this article means you are ready to make a change. *5*

But I also realize that some of you are Broke by Circumstance. I actually tell young adults in the dues-paying stage of their careers to lean on their credit cards if they don't yet make enough to always keep up with their bills. But the key is that if you rely on your credit cards to make ends meet, you must limit the plastic spending to true necessities, not indulgences. Buying groceries is a necessity. Buying dinner for you and your pals at a swank restaurant is an indulgence you can't afford if it will become part of your unpaid credit card balance. *6*

But whether you are broke by choice or by circumstance, the strategy for getting out of credit card debt is the same: to outmaneuver the card companies with a strategy that assures you pay the lowest possible *7*

...continued How to Take Control of Your Credit Cards, **Suze Orman**

interest rate, for the shortest possible time, while avoiding all of the many snares and traps the card companies lay out for you.

Here's how to be a Credit Card Shark.   *8*

Take an Interest in Your Rate

The average interest rate charged on credit cards is 15 percent, with *9* plenty of folks paying 18 percent, 20 percent, or even more. If you carry a balance on any credit cards, your primary focus should be to get that rate down as low as possible.

Now then. If you have a FICO score of at least 720, and you make at *10* least the minimum payment due each month, on time, you should be able to negotiate with your current credit card issuer to lower your rate. Call 'em up and let them know you plan to transfer your entire balance to another card with a lower rate—more on this in a sec—if they don't get your rate down.

If your card issuer doesn't step up to the plate and give you a better *11* deal, then do indeed start shopping around for a new card with a sweet intro offer. For those of you with strong FICO scores, a zero-rate deal ought to be possible. You can search for top card deals at the Yahoo! Finance Credit Card Center.

Don't forget, though, that the key with balance transfer offers is to *12* find out what your rate will be when the intro period expires in six months to a year. If your zero rate will skyrocket to 20 percent, that's a crappy deal, unless you are absolutely 100 percent sure you will get the balance paid off before the rate changes. (And if you got yourself into card hell in the first place, I wouldn't be betting on you having the ability to wipe out your problem in just six months. . . .)

Once you are approved for the new low- or zero-rate card, move as *13* much of your high-rate balances onto this new card. But don't—I repeat, do NOT—use the new card for new purchases. Hidden in the fine print on these deals are provisions stating, first, that any new purchases you make on the card will come with a high interest rate, and second, that you'll be paying that high interest on the entirety of your new purchase charges until you pay off every last cent of the balance transfer amount. This, to put it mildly, could really screw up your zero-rate deal. So please, use the new card only to park your old high-rate debt, and not to shop with.

Another careless mistake you can make is to cancel your old cards. *14* Don't do that either. Those cards hold some valuable "history" that's used to compute your FICO credit score. If you cancel the cards, you cancel your history, and your FICO score can take a hit. If you are woried about the temptation of using the cards, just get out your scissors and give them a good trim. That way you can't use 'em, but your history stays on your record.

Coddle Your New Card

When you do a balance transfer, you need to protect your low rate as *15*
if it were an endangered species—because if the credit card issuer has
anything to say about it, it will be. Look, you don't really think the card
company is excited about charging you no interest, do you? How the heck
do they make money off of that? They only offer up the great deal to lure
you over to their card. Then they start working overtime trying to get you
to screw up so they have an excuse to change your zero interest rate, often to as much as 20 percent or more.

And the big screw-up they are hoping you don't know about is *16*
buried down in the fine print of your card agreement: make one late payment and you can kiss your zero deal good-bye. Even worse is that card
companies are now scouring all your credit cards—remember, they can
check your credit reports—to see if you have been late on any card, not
just their card. So even if you always pay the zero-rate card on time, if you
are late on any other card, your zero deal can be in jeopardy.

That's why I want you to make sure every credit card bill is paid ahead *17*
of schedule. Don't mail it in on the day it is due; that's late. Mail it in at least
five days early. Better yet, convert your card to online bill pay so you can zap
your payments over in time every month. And remember, it's only the minimum monthly payment that needs to be paid. That's not asking a lot.

Dealing with High-Rate Debt

Okay, I realize not everyone is going to qualify for these low-rate bal- *18*
ance transfer deals, so let's run through how to take control of your cards
if you are stuck with higher rates.

I want you to line up all your cards in descending order of their in- *19*
terest rates. Notice I said the card with the highest interest rate comes
first. Not the one with the biggest balance.

Your strategy is to make the minimum monthly payment on every *20*
card, on time, every month. But your card with the highest interest rate
gets some special treatment. I want you to pay more than the minimum
amount due on this card. The more you can pay, the better; but everyone
should put in, at the minimum, an extra $20 each month. Push yourself
hard to make that extra payment as large as possible. It can save you
thousands of dollars in interest charges over time.

Keep this up every month until your card with the highest rate is paid *21*
off. Then turn your attention to the card with the next highest rate. In addition to the usual monthly minimum payment due on that second card, I
want you to add in the entire amount you were previously paying on the
first card (the one that's now paid off). So let's say you were paying a total of
$200 a month on your original highest-rate card, and making a $75 monthly
minimum on the second card. Well, now you are going to fork over $275
a month to the second card. And, of course, you'll continue to make the

...continued How to Take Control of Your Credit Cards, **Suze Orman**

minimum monthly payment due on any other cards. Once your second card is paid off, move on to the third. If your monthly payment on that second card was $275, then that's what you should add to the minimum payment due on your third card. Get the idea? Rinse and repeat as often as needed, until you have all your debt paid off. For some of you this may take a year, for others it may take many years. That's okay. Just get yourself moving in the right direction and you'll be amazed how gratifying it is to find yourself taking control of your money rather than letting it control you.

And be sure to keep an eye on your FICO credit score. As you pay 22
down your card balances—and build a record of paying on time—your score is indeed going to rise. Eventually your score may be high enough to finally qualify for a low-rate balance transfer offer.

Is Credit Counseling Right for You?

There is plenty of help available if you can't seem to get a solid grip 23
on dealing with your credit card debt. But not all the help is good. Given that so many Americans are drowning in card debt, it's really no surprise that some enterprising—and underhanded—folks have figured out a way to make money off of this epidemic by charging high fees for counseling and advice.

So you need to make sure you choose an honest and fair credit coun- 24
seling service. Start by getting references from the National Foundation for Credit Counseling.

Next, make an appointment to talk with a counselor face-to-face. A 25
good counselor will question you thoroughly and in detail about your financial situation before proposing anything. If you are simply told right off the bat that you need a Debt Management Plan, you should run out the door PDQ. That firm is not interested in truly helping you. They just want to hit you up with a bunch of fees.

A good counselor is also going to require that you attend education 26
classes. This is not punishment! On the contrary, it's the best help you can get. Quite often, you can make the changes necessary to take control of your credit card spending just by learning a few good habits.

vo·cab·u·lar·y

In your journal, write the meaning of the italicized words in the following phrases.

- true necessities, not *indulgences* (**6**)
- to *outmaneuver* the card companies (**7**)
- you have a *FICO* score (**10**)
- deal can be in *jeopardy* (**16**)
- make money off this *epidemic* (**23**)

? QUESTIONS FOR WRITING AND DISCUSSION

❶ Writers of effective explaining essays focus their thesis for a specific audience. Describe the audience Orman addresses in her essay. Which sentences help you identify this audience? Which sentences in Orman's essay most clearly express her thesis?

❷ Explaining essays typically use definition of terms, explanation of processes, and analyses of causes and effects. Identify at least one example of each of the following strategies in Orman's essay: definition, process analysis, and causal analysis. In each case, decide if the information Orman gives is clear to you. Where do you need additional information or clarification?

❸ Two strategies that Orman uses to connect with her readers is addressing them in the second person, "you," and using informal language such as "you and your pals," "call 'em up," "more on this in a sec," and "sweet intro offer." Find other examples of informal language in her essay. Does this language work for her audience? Does it make the essay more lively and readable for you? Is this language appropriate in an essay about finances? Explain.

❹ Appeals to the audience often involve more than simply using informal language. Effective appeals connect to the readers' sense of identity and their personal and social values. Read the following introduction to Chapter I in Orman's book, *Women and Money: Owning the Power to Control Your Destiny*. Cite specific sentences from the following paragraph to explain how Orman identifies with her readers while at the same time suggesting that they need to make changes in their lives.

> I never thought I'd write a book about money just for women. I never thought it was necessary. So then why am I doing just that in my eighth book? And why now? Let me explain. All my previous books were written with the belief that gender is not a factor on any level in mastering the nuts and bolts of smart financial management. Women can invest, save, and handle debt just as well and skillfully as any man. I still believe that—why would anyone think differently? So imagine my surprise when I learned that some of the people closest to me in my life were in the dark about their own finances. Clueless. Or, in some cases, willfully resisting doing what they knew needed to be done.

❺ Find one of the offers for credit cards that you, a friend, or a family member has recently received. Study the fine print. Then, in your own words, explain what the fine print means in language that another member of your class can understand. Is Orman right about the "many snares and traps" that the card companies set for their customers?

❻ Write a profile of Suze Orman that recounts key events in her life and explains why she has been so successful as a writer, motivator, and financial advisor. Check your online library databases as well as online reviews and Web sites. Write your profile so that it could appear in a local newspaper, on a Web site, or as a promotion for one of Suze Orman's latest books.

PROFESSIONAL WRITING

How Male and Female Students Use Language Differently

Deborah Tannen

Everyone knows that men and women communicate differently, but Deborah Tannen, a linguist at Georgetown University, has spent her career studying how and why their conversational styles are different. Tannen's books include Conversational Style: Analyzing Talk Among Friends *(1984), her best-selling* You Just Don't Understand: Women and Men in Conversation *(1990), and* I Only Say This Because I Love You *(2001). In the following article from* The Chronicle of Higher Education, *Tannen applies her knowledge of conversational styles to the classroom. How do men and women communicate differently in the classroom? What teaching styles best promote open communication and learning for both sexes? As you read her essay, think about your own classes. Do the men in your classes talk more than the women? Do men like to argue in large groups, while women prefer conversations in small groups? How clearly—and convincingly—does Tannen explain discussion preferences and their effects in the classroom?*

When I researched and wrote my latest book, *You Just Don't Under- 1 stand: Women and Men in Conversation,* the furthest thing from my mind was reevaluating my teaching strategies. But that has been one of the direct benefits of having written the book.

The primary focus of my linguistic research always has been the 2 language of everyday conversation. One facet of this is conversational style: how different regional, ethnic, and class backgrounds, as well as age and gender, result in different ways of using language to communicate. *You Just Don't Understand* is about the conversational styles of women and men. As I gained more insight into typically male and female ways of using language, I began to suspect some of the causes of the troubling facts that women who go to single-sex schools do better in later life, and that when young women sit next to young men in classrooms, the males talk more. This is not to say that all men talk in class, nor that no women do. It is simply that a greater percentage of discussion time is taken by men's voices.

The research of sociologists and anthropologists such as Janet Lever, 3 Marjorie Harness Goodwin, and Donna Eder has shown that girls and boys learn to use language differently in their sex-separate peer groups. Typically, a girl has a best friend with whom she sits and talks, frequently telling secrets. It's the telling of secrets, the fact and the way that they talk to each other, that makes them best friends. For boys, activities are central: their best friends are the ones they do things with. Boys also tend to play in larger groups that are hierarchical. High-status boys give orders and push low-status boys around. So boys are expected to use language to seize center stage: by exhibiting their skill, displaying their knowledge, and challenging and resisting challenges.

These patterns have stunning implications for classroom interaction. *4* Most faculty members assume that participating in class discussion is a necessary part of successful performance. Yet speaking in a classroom is more congenial to boys' language experience than to girls', since it entails putting oneself forward in front of a large group of people, many of whom are strangers and at least one of whom is sure to judge speakers' knowledge and intelligence by their verbal display.

Another aspect of many classrooms that makes them more hospitable *5* to most men than to most women is the use of debate-like formats as a learning tool. Our educational system, as Walter Ong argues persuasively in his book *Fighting for Life* (Cornell University Press, 1981), is fundamentally male in that the pursuit of knowledge is believed to be achieved by ritual opposition: public display followed by argument and challenge. Father Ong demonstrates that ritual opposition—what he calls "adversativeness" or "agonism"—is fundamental to the way most males approach almost any activity. (Consider, for example, the little boy who shows he likes a little girl by pulling her braids and shoving her.) But ritual opposition is antithetical to the way most females learn and like to interact. It is not that females don't fight, but that they don't fight for fun. They don't *ritualize* opposition.

Anthropologists working in widely disparate parts of the world have *6* found contrasting verbal rituals for women and men. Women in completely unrelated cultures (for example, Greece and Bali) engage in ritual laments: spontaneously produced rhyming couplets that express their pain, for example, over the loss of loved ones. Men do not take part in laments. They have their own, very different verbal ritual: a contest, a war of words in which they vie with each other to devise clever insults.

When discussing these phenomena with a colleague, I commented *7* that I see these two styles in American conversation: many women bond by talking about troubles, and many men bond by exchanging playful insults and put-downs, and other sorts of verbal sparring. He exclaimed: "I never thought of this, but that's the way I teach: I have students read an article, and then I invite them to tear it apart. After we've torn it to shreds, we talk about how to build a better model."

This contrasts sharply with the way I teach: I open the discussion of *8* readings by asking, "What did you find useful in this? What can we use in our own theory building and our own methods?" I note what I see as weaknesses in the author's approach, but I also point out that the writer's discipline and purposes might be different from ours. Finally, I offer personal anecdotes illustrating the phenomena under discussion and praise students' anecdotes as well as their critical acumen.

These different teaching styles must make our classrooms wildly different places and hospitable to different students. Male students are more likely to be comfortable attacking the readings and might find the inclusion of personal anecdotes irrelevant and "soft." Women are more likely to resist discussion they perceive as hostile, and, indeed, it is women in my classes who are most likely to offer personal anecdotes. 9

A colleague who read my book commented that he had always taken for granted that the best way to deal with students' comments is to challenge them; this, he felt it was self-evident, sharpens their minds and helps them develop debating skills. But he had noticed that women were relatively silent in his classes, so he decided to try beginning discussion with relatively open-ended questions and letting comments go unchallenged. He found, to his amazement and satisfaction, that more women began to speak up. 10

Though some of the women in his class clearly liked this better, perhaps some of the men liked it less. One young man in my class wrote in a questionnaire about a history professor who gave students questions to think about and called on people to answer them: "He would then play devil's advocate . . . *i.e.,* he debated us. . . . That class *really* sharpened me intellectually. . . . We as students do need to know how to defend ourselves." This young man valued the experience of being attacked and challenged publicly. Many, if not most, women would shrink from such "challenge," experiencing it as public humiliation. 11

A professor at Hamilton College told me of a young man who was upset because he felt his class presentation had been a failure. The professor was puzzled because he had observed that class members had listened attentively and agreed with the student's observations. It turned out that it was this very agreement that the student interpreted as failure: since no one had engaged his ideas by arguing with him, he felt they had found them unworthy of attention. 12

So one reason men speak in class more than women is that many of them find the "public" classroom setting more conducive to speaking, whereas most women are more comfortable speaking in private to a small group of people they know well. A second reason is that men are more likely to be comfortable with the debate-like form that discussion may take. Yet another reason is the different attitudes toward speaking in class that typify women and men. 13

Students who speak frequently in class, many of whom are men, assume that it is their job to think of contributions and try to get the 14 floor to express them. But many women monitor their participation not only to get the floor but to avoid getting it. Women students in my class tell me that if they have spoken up once or twice, they hold back for the rest of the class because they don't want to dominate. If they have spoken a lot one week, they will remain silent the next. These different ethics of participation are, of course, unstated, so those who speak freely assume that those who remain silent have nothing to say, and those who are reining themselves in assume that the big talkers are selfish and hoggish.

When I looked around my classes, I could see these differing ethics *15* and habits at work. For example, my graduate class in analyzing conversation had twenty students, eleven women and nine men. Of the men, four were foreign students: two Japanese, one Chinese, and one Syrian. With the exception of the three Asian men, all the men spoke in class at least occasionally. The biggest talker in the class was a woman, but there were also five women who never spoke at all, only one of whom was Japanese. I decided to try something different.

I broke the class into small groups to discuss the issues raised in *16* the readings and to analyze their own conversational transcripts. I devised three ways of dividing the students into groups: one by the degree program they were in, one by gender, and one by conversational style, as closely as I could guess it. This meant that when the class was grouped according to conversational style, I put Asian students together, fast talkers together, and quiet students together. The class split into groups six times during the semester, so they met in each grouping twice. I told students to regard the groups as examples of interactional data and to note the different ways they participated in the different groups. Toward the end of the term, I gave them a questionnaire asking about their class and group participation.

I could see plainly from my observation of the groups at work that *17* women who never opened their mouths in class were talking away in the small groups. In fact, the Japanese woman commented that she found it particularly hard to contribute to the all-woman group she was in because "I was overwhelmed by how talkative the female students were in the female-only group." This is particularly revealing because it highlights that the same person who can be "oppressed" into silence in one context can become the talkative "oppressor" in another. No one's conversational style is absolute; everyone's style changes in response to the context and others' styles.

Some of the students (seven) said they preferred the same-gender *18* groups; others preferred the same-style groups. In answer to the question "Would you have liked to speak in class more than you did?" six of the seven who said yes were women; the one man was Japanese. Most startlingly, this response did not come only from quiet women; it came from women who had indicated they had spoken in class never, rarely, sometimes, and often. Of the eleven students who said the amount they had spoken was fine, seven were men. Of the four women who checked "fine," two added qualifications indicating it wasn't completely fine: One wrote in "maybe more," and one wrote, "I have an urge to participate but often feel I should have something more interesting/relevant/wonderful/intelligent to say!!"

I counted my experiment a success. Everyone in the class found the   19 small groups interesting, and no one indicated he or she would have preferred that the class not break into groups. Perhaps most instructive, however, was the fact that the experience of breaking into groups, and of talking about participation in class, raised everyone's awareness about classroom participation. After we had talked about it, some of the quietest women in the class made a few voluntary contributions, though sometimes I had to ensure their participation by interrupting the students who were exuberantly speaking out.

Americans are often proud that they discount the significance of   20 cultural differences: "We are all individuals," many people boast. Ignoring such issues as gender and ethnicity becomes a source of pride: "I treat everyone the same." But treating people the same is not equal treatment if they are not the same.

The classroom is a different environment for those who feel comfortable putting themselves forward in a group than it is for those who   21 find the prospect of doing so chastening, or even terrifying. When a professor asks, "Are there any questions?" students who can formulate statements the fastest have the greatest opportunity to respond. Those who need significant time to do so have not really been given a chance at all, since by the time they are ready to speak, someone else has the floor.

In a class where some students speak out without raising hands, those   22 who feel they must raise their hands and wait to be recognized do not have equal opportunity to speak. Telling them to feel free to jump in will not make them feel free; one's sense of timing, of one's rights and obligations in a classroom, are automatic, learned over years of interaction. They may be changed over time, with motivation and effort, but they cannot be changed on the spot. And everyone assumes his or her own way is best. When I asked my students how the class could be changed to make it easier for them to speak more, the most talkative woman said she would prefer it if no one had to raise hands, and a foreign student said he wished people would raise their hands and wait to be recognized.

My experience in this class has convinced me that small-group inter-   23 action should be part of any class that is not a small seminar. I also am convinced that having the students become observers of their own interaction is a crucial part of their education. Talking about ways of talking in class makes students aware that their ways of talking affect other students, that the motivations they impute to others may not truly reflect others' motives, and that the behaviors they assume to be self-evidently right are not universal norms.

The goal of complete equal opportunity in class may not be attainable, but realizing that one monolithic classroom-participation structure is not equal opportunity is itself a powerful motivation to find more-diverse methods to serve diverse students—and every classroom is diverse. 24

vo·cab·u·lar·y

In your journal, write the meanings of the italicized words in the following phrases.

- ritual opposition is *antithetical* (**5**)
- personal *anecdotes* (**8**)
- *conducive* to speaking (**13**)

- *ethics* of participation (**14**)
- *monolithic* classroom-participation structure (**24**)

? QUESTIONS FOR WRITING AND DISCUSSION

1 Reread Tannen's essay, noting places where your experiences as a student match or do not match her observations. In what contexts were your experiences similar to or different from Tannen's? Explain what might account for the different observations.

2 In her essay, Tannen states and then continues to restate her thesis. Reread her essay, underlining all the sentences that seem to state or rephrase her main idea. Do her restatements of the main idea make her essay clearer? Explain.

3 Explaining essays may explain *what* (describe and define), explain *how* (process analysis), and/or explain *why* (causal analysis). Find one example of each of these strategies in Tannen's essay. Which of these three is the dominant shaping strategy? Support your answer with references to specific sentences or paragraphs.

4 Effective explaining essays must have supporting evidence—specific examples, facts, quotations, testimony from experts, statistics, and so on. Choose four consecutive paragraphs from Tannen's essay and list the kinds of supporting evidence she uses. Based on your inventory, rate her supporting evidence as weak, average, or strong. Explain your choice.

5 Does the style of Tannen's essay support her thesis that men and women have different ways of communicating? Does Tannen, in fact, use a "woman's style" of writing that is similar to women's conversational style? Examine Tannen's tone (her attitude toward her subject and audience), her voice (the projection of her personality in her language), and her supporting evidence (her use of facts and statistics or anecdotal, contextual evidence). Cite specific passages to support your analysis.

6 In another class where students discuss frequently, sit in the back row where you can observe the participation of men and women. First, record the number of men and the number of women in the class. Then, during one class period, record the following: (a) when the teacher calls on a student, record whether the student is male or female; (b) when a student talks without raising his or her hand, record whether the student is male or female; and (c) when students speak in class, record how long they talk and whether they are male or female. Once you have collected and analyzed your data, explain whether they seem to support or refute Tannen's claims.

7 On the Internet, visit Deborah Tannen's home page at http://www .georgetown.edu/faculty/tannend. Click on the link "Interviews with Deborah Tannen." How do her responses during these interviews shed light on the conversational styles of men and women? What points does she make that might apply to how men and women communicate and learn differently in the classroom?

Explaining: The Writing Process

ASSIGNMENT FOR EXPLAINING

After assessing your rhetorical situation, *explain* what something means or is, *how* it should be done or *how* it occurs, and/or *why* something occurs. Your purpose is to explain something as clearly as possible for your audience by analyzing, showing relationships, and demonstrating with examples, facts, illustrations, data, or other information.

With a topic in mind, use the grid below to think about a possible audience and genre that would meet your assignment. Once you've chosen an audience, think about how much they already know about the subject. Are they experts, novices, or somewhere in between? What can you assume that they already know? What points or information are they least likely to know?

Audience	Possible Genres for Explaining
Personal Audience	Class notes, annotations in a textbook, journal entry, blog, scrapbook, social networking page
Academic Audience	Expository essay, academic analysis and synthesis, journal entry, forum entry on class site, multigenre document
Public Audience	Column, editorial, letter, or article, or in a magazine, newspaper, online site, newsletter, or multigenre document

CHOOSING A SUBJECT

If one of your journal entries suggested a possible subject, go on to the collecting and shaping strategies. If you still need an interesting subject, consider the following suggestions.

- Reread your authority list or the most interesting journal entries from previous chapters. Do they contain ideas that you might define or explain, processes suitable for how-to explanations, or causes or effects that you could analyze and explain for a certain audience?

- **Writing Across the Curriculum**. Reread your notes from another class in which you have an upcoming examination. Select some topic, idea, principle, process, famous person, or event from the text or your notes. Investigate other texts, popular magazines, or journals for information on that topic. If appropriate, interview someone or conduct a survey. Explain this principle or process to a member of your writing class.

- **Community Service Learning**. If you are doing a community-service-learning project, consider a writing project explaining the agency's mission to the public or to a potential donor. You might also write an article for a local or campus newspaper explaining some aspect of their service or a recent contribution the agency has made to the community.

- Consider writing an artistic, cultural, historical, or social explanation of a particular visual image or a set of visual images. One excellent Web site for famous photographs is the Pulitzer site at http://www.gallerym.com/pulitzerphotos.htm. Decide on a particular audience, genre, and context appropriate for the photograph.

> 66 You can write about anything, and if you write well enough, even the reader with no intrinsic interest in the subject will become involved. 99
> —TRACY KIDDER, NOVELIST

- Choose a current controversy to explain. Instead of arguing for one side or the other, however, explain the different points of view in this controversy. Who are the leading figures or groups representing each of several different positions? Choose a particular audience, genre, and context, and explain what each of these people or groups have to gain or lose and how their personal investments in the topic determine their position.

COLLECTING

● **QUESTIONS**   Once you have a tentative subject and audience in mind, consider which of the following will be your primary focus (all three may be relevant).

- *What* something means or is
- *How* something occurs or is done (or should be done)
- *Why* something occurs or what its effects are

Focus on Definition.   To explain *what* something is, jot down answers to each of the following questions. The more you can write on each question, the more details you'll have for your topic.

- What are its class and distinguishing characteristics?
- What is its etymology?
- How can you describe it?
- What examples can you give?
- What are its parts or its functions?
- What is it similar to? What is it *not?*
- What figurative comparisons apply?
- How can it be classified?
- Which of the above is most useful to your audience?

Focus on Process Analysis.   To explain *how* something occurs or is done, answer the following questions.

- What are the component parts or steps in the whole process?
- What is the exact sequence of steps or events?
- Are several of the steps or events related?
- If steps or events were omitted, would the outcome change?
- Which steps or events are most crucial?
- Which steps or events does your audience most need to know?

Focus on Causal Analysis. To explain *why* something occurs or what its effects are, consider the following issues.

- Which are the necessary or sufficient causes?
- Which causes are remote in time, and which are immediate?
- What is the order or sequence of the causes? Do the causes occur simultaneously?
- What are the effects? Do they occur in a sequence or simultaneously?
- Do the causes and effects occur in a "chain reaction"?
- Is there an action or situation that would have prevented the effect?
- Are there comparable things or events that have similar causes or effects?
- Which causes or effects need special clarification for your audience?

● **BRANCHING**   Often, *branching* can help you visually analyze your subject. Start with your topic and then subdivide each idea into its component parts. The resulting analysis will not only help generate ideas but may also suggest ways to shape an essay.

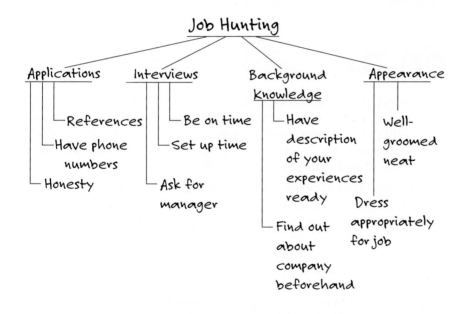

● **OBSERVING**   If you can observe your subject, try drawing it, describing it, or taking careful notes. Which senses can you use to describe it—sight, sound, touch, smell, taste? If it is a scientific experiment that you can reproduce or a social situation you can reconstruct, go through it again and observe carefully. As you observe it, put yourself in your readers' shoes: What do you need to explain it to them?

• **REMEMBERING**   Your own experience and memory are essential for explaining. *Freewriting, looping,* and *clustering* may all generate detailed information, good examples, and interesting perspectives that will make your explanation clearer and move vivid. (See Chapter 4 for an explanation of looping and clustering.)

• **READING**   When you find written texts about your subject, be sure to use your active reading strategies. You may need only a few sources if you reread them carefully. Write out a short summary for each source. Respond to each source by analyzing its effectiveness, agreeing or disagreeing with its ideas, or interpreting the text. The quality of your understanding is more important than the sheer number of sources you cite.

• **INVESTIGATING**   Use sources available in the library, textbooks containing relevant information, or interviews with teachers, participants, or experts. Interview your classmates about their own subjects for this assignment: Someone else's subject may trigger an idea that you can write about or may suggest a fresh approach to the subject that you have already chosen.

> ❝ Readers may be strangers who have no immediate reason to care about your writing. They want order, clarity, and stimulation. ❞
>
> —ELIZABETH COWAN NEELD,
> TEACHER AND AUTHOR

SHAPING

As you collect information and generate ideas from your collecting activities, be sure to *narrow* and *focus* your subject into a topic suitable for a short essay. You will not be able to cover everything you've read, thought, or experienced about your subject. Choose the most interesting ideas—for you and for your audience—and shape, order, and clarify those ideas.

• **AUDIENCE AND GENRE**   As you consider ways to organize and shape your explaining essay, think about a possible audience and genre. An essay directed at a general audience composed of peers like your classmates is just one possibility. A letter to the editor, a pamphlet for a community agency, a job analysis for your employer, an article for a local or school newspaper, a posting or response to a listserve, or an essay for students in your major are other possibilities. Once you have a tentative audience and genre, you'll have a better idea about how to organize your explanation. Reread your assignment for specific suggestions and guidelines about audience and genre.

• **DEFINITION AND CLASSIFICATION**   An essay explaining *what* something means or is can be shaped by using a variety of definition strategies or by classifying the subject.

Definition itself is not a single organizing strategy; it supports a variety of strategies that may be useful in shaping your essay: description, analysis of

Research Tips

Review your audience, purpose, and possible focus. Which of the following four research strategies would help you gather information on your topic?

1. Direct *observation* (see Chapter 3)
2. Use of *memories* and personal experience (see Chapter 4)
3. *Field research* including interviews and surveys (see Chapter 7)
4. *Library/internet research* (see Chapter 13)

As you do your research, keep the following tips in mind:

- Save all your *links* or *Word files* or make *photocopies* or *printouts* of all the sources that you plan to cite in your essay.
- Be sure to *write all relevant bibliographic information,* such as author, date, publisher, place of publication, journal title, and volume and issue numbers. in your Word files or on the photocopies or printouts. Note the Web site sponsor and your access date for Web sources.
- When you cite sources in the text, be sure to *introduce* your sources. Make sure your direct quotations are *accurate* word-for-word transcriptions.

For more details on these suggestions, see Chapter 13.

parts or function, comparison/contrast, development by examples, or figures of speech such as simile, metaphor, and analogy.

Classification, on the other hand, is a single strategy that can organize a paragraph or even a whole essay quickly. Observers of human behavior, for example, love to use classification. Grocery shoppers might be classified by types: racers (the ones who seem to have just won forty-five seconds of free shopping and run down the aisles filling their carts as fast as possible), talkers (the ones whose phone must be out of order because they stand in the aisles gossiping forever), penny-pinchers (who always have their calculators out and read the unit price labels for everything), party shoppers (who camp out in the junk food aisles, filling their carts with potato chips, dip, candy, peanuts, and drink mixers), and dawdlers (who leave their carts crosswise in the aisles while they read twenty-nine different soup can labels). You can write a sentence or two about each type or devote a whole paragraph to explaining a single type.

● **EXAMPLE** Development by example can effectively illustrate what something is or means, but it can also help explain how or why something happens. Usually, an example describes a specific incident, located at a certain place and occurring at a particular time, that *shows* or *demonstrates* the main idea. In the following paragraph from *Mediaspeak,* Donna Woolfolk Cross explains what effects soap operas can have on addicted viewers. This paragraph is developed by several examples—some described in detail, others referred to briefly.

> Dedicated watchers of soap operas often confuse fact with fiction. . . . Stars of soap operas tell hair-raising stories of their encounters with fans suffering from this affliction. Susan Lucci, who plays the promiscuous Erica Kane on "All My Children," tells of a time she was riding in a parade: "We were in a crowd of about 250,000 traveling in an antique open car moving ver-r-ry slowly. At that time in the series I was involved with a character named Nick. Some man broke through, came right up to the car and said to me, 'Why don't you give me a little bit of what you've been giving Nick?'" The man hung onto the car, menacingly, until she was rescued by the police. Another time, when she was in church, the reverent silence was broken by a woman's astonished remark, "Oh, my god, Erica prays!" Margaret Mason, who plays the villainous Lisa Anderson in "Days of Our Lives," was accosted by a woman who poured a carton of milk all over her in the supermarket. And once a woman actually tried to force her car off the Ventura Freeway.

● **VOICE AND TONE**   Writers also use voice and tone to shape and control whole passages, often in combination with other shaping strategies. In the following paragraph, Toni Bambara, author of *The Salt Eaters* and numerous short stories, explains *what* being a writer is all about. This paragraph is shaped both by a single extended example and by Bambara's voice talking directly to the reader.

> When I replay the tapes on file in my head, tapes of speeches I've given at writing conferences over the years, I invariably hear myself saying—"A writer, like any other cultural worker, like any other member of the community, ought to try to put her/his skills in the service of the community." Some years ago when I returned south, my picture in the paper prompted several neighbors to come visit. "You a writer? What all you write?" Before I could begin the catalogue, one old gent interrupted with—"Ya know Miz Mary down the block? She need a writer to help her send off a letter to her grandson overseas." So I began a career as the neighborhood scribe—letters to relatives, snarling letters to the traffic chief about the promised stop sign, nasty letters to the utilities, angry letters to the principal about that confederate flag hanging in front of the school, contracts to transfer a truck from seller to buyer, etc. While my efforts have been

graciously appreciated in the form of sweet potato dumplings, herb teas, hair braiding, and the like, there is still much room for improvement—"For a writer, honey, you've got a mighty bad hand. Didn't they teach penmanship at that college?" Another example, I guess, of words setting things in motion. What goes around, comes around, as the elders say.

● **CHRONOLOGICAL ORDER AND PROCESS ANALYSIS** Writers use chronological order in expository writing to help explain how to do something or how something is typically done. In her essay "Anorexia Nervosa," student writer Nancie Brosseau uses transitional words to signal the various stages of anorexia. In the following sentences, taken from the third paragraph of her essay, the *italicized* words mark the chronological stages of her anorexia.

> Several serious health problems bombarded me, and it's a wonder I'm still alive. . . . *As my weight plummeted,* my circulation grew *increasingly worse.* . . . My hair *started* to fall out, and my whole body took on a very skeletal appearance. . . . I would force myself to vomit *as soon as possible* if I was forced to eat. The enamel on my teeth *started to be eaten away* by the acid in the vomit, and my lips cracked and bled regularly. I *stopped* menstruating completely because I was not producing enough estrogen. . . . *One time,* while executing a chain of back handsprings, I broke all five fingers on one hand and three on the other because my bones had become so brittle. . . . I chose to see a psychologist, and she helped me sort out the emotional aspects of anorexia, *which in turn* solved the physical problems.

● **CAUSAL ANALYSIS** In order to explain *why* something happens or what the effects of something are, writers often use one of the following three patterns of cause and effect to shape their material:

Cause 1 + Cause 2 + Cause 3 . . . + Cause $n \rightarrow$ Effect

In the case of fire, for example, we know that three causes lead to a single effect. These causes do not occur in any special sequence; they must all be present at the same time. For historical events, however, we usually list causes in chronological order.

Sometimes one cause has several effects. In that case, we reverse the pattern:

Cause $\rightarrow$ Effect 1 + Effect 2 + Effect 3 . . . + Effect n

For example, an explanation of the collapse of the economy following the stock market crash of 1929 might follow this pattern. The crash (itself a symptom of other causes) led to a depreciated economy, widespread unemployment, bankruptcy for thousands of businesses, foreclosures on farms,

TIPS FOR INTEGRATING IMAGES

For your explaining essay, you may wish to integrate images (photographs, images, graphics, or charts), and you may wish to work with your document design. To integrate images with your text, first consider your rhetorical situation.

- **What is your purpose?** Does the visual contribute to your thesis or main idea, or is it just a distraction?
- **Who is your audience?** Is the image appropriate for your target audience? Would it make your document more appealing or attractive? Would it offend them? Would it amuse them? Would it make your point in a way that words could not?
- **What is your intended genre?** Look at other examples of your genre. Find several examples of the kind of essay, pamphlet, Web page, article, advertisement, brochure, laboratory report, letter, or flyer. How do they use images or graphics?
- **What is the social/cultural context of your text?** Consider whether the subject, topic, or issue you are discussing could or should be illustrated with an image or a certain document design.

Use search engines and library sources to find a variety of images relevant to your topic. Start with an image search on Google or Yahoo!, but don't forget that your library has a wealth of online image databases. If you're looking for paintings or fine art, check Web sites for museums around the world. Having several potential images enables you to choose the one most effective for your rhetorical situation.

Finally, don't forget about your document design. Start with your purpose, audience, and genre. Consider how the genre you have selected uses the following document features.

- **Columns** Would a text with two columns work for your purpose?
- **Margins and white space** Avoid overcrowding words, images, and graphics on a page. Use margins and white space to emphasize key parts of your text.
- **Fonts** Use a font appropriate to your purpose, genre, and audience. Times New Roman and Palatino Linotype are widely accepted, but do you need **Franklin Gothic Demi** for particular parts of your text? For special situations, perhaps consider a script face such as Felt Tip or a bolder face such as TRADE GOTHIC. If appropriate for your purpose, genre, and audience, play around with the available fonts on your computer.
- **Sidebars** If appropriate for your text, use a sidebar for text emphasis or to add related information.

> **Is the image appropriate for your target audience? Does the image contribute to your thesis?**

and so forth. An essay on the effects of the crash might devote one or two paragraphs to each effect.

In the third pattern, causes and effects form a pattern of chain reactions. One cause leads to an effect that then becomes the cause of another effect, and so on:

Cause 1 → Effect 1 (Cause 2) → Effect 2 (Cause 3) → Effect 3

We could analyze events in the Middle East during and after the Iraq War as a series of actions and reactions in which each effect becomes the cause of the next effect in the chain of car bombings, air raids, terrorist hijackings, and kidnappings. An essay on the chain reaction of events in the Middle East might have a paragraph or two on each of the links in this chain.

● **INTRODUCTION AND LEAD-IN** Often, the first sentences of the introductory paragraph of an essay are the hardest to write. You want to get your reader's attention and focus on the main idea of your essay, but you don't want to begin, boringly, with your thesis statement. Below are several kinds of opening sentences designed to grab your reader's interest. Consider your topic—see if one of these strategies will work for you.

A Personal Example

I knew my dieting had gotten out of hand, but when I could actually see the movement of my heart beating beneath my clothes, I knew I was in trouble.

—"Anorexia Nervosa," Nancie Brosseau

A Description of a Person or Place

He strides toward us in navy and white, his body muscled and heavy-set, one arm holding his casually flung jeans jacket over his shoulder. A man in his prime, with just the right combination of macho and sartorial flair.

—"Some Don't Like Their Blues at All," Karyn M. Lewis

It's still there, the Chinese school on Yale Street where my brother and I used to go. Despite the new coat of paint and the high wire fence, the school I knew ten years ago remains remarkably, stoically the same.

—"The Struggle to Be an All-American Girl," Elizabeth Wong

An Example from a Case Study

Susan Smith has everything going for her. A self-described workaholic, she runs a Cambridge, Massachusetts, real estate consulting company with her husband Charles and still finds time to cuddle and nurture their two young kids, David, 7, and Stacey, 6. What few people know is that Susan, 44, needs a little chemical help to be a supermom: She has been taking the antidepressant Prozac for five years.

—"The Personality Pill," Anastasia Toufexis

A Startling Statement, Fact, or Statistic

Embalming is indeed a most extraordinary procedure, and one must wonder at the docility of Americans who each year pay hundreds of millions of dollars for its perpetuation, blissfully ignorant of what it is all about, what is done, how it is done.

—"To Dispel Fears of Live Burial," Jessica Mitford

A Statement from a Book

The American novelist John Barth, in his early novel *The Floating Opera,* remarks that ordinary, day-to-day life often presents us with embarrassingly obvious, totally unsubtle patterns of symbolism and meaning—life in the midst of death, innocence vindicated, youth versus age, etc.

—"I'm O.K., but You're Not," Robert Zoellner

A Striking Question or Questions

Do non-human animals have rights? Should we humans feel morally bound to exercise consideration for the lives and well-being of individual members of other animal species? If so, how much consideration, and by what logic?

—"Animal Rights and Beyond," David Quammen

A Common Error or Mistaken Judgment

There was a time when, in my search for essences, I concluded that the canyonland country has no heart. I was wrong. The canyonlands did have a heart, a living heart, and that heart was Glen Canyon and the golden, flowing Colorado River.

—"The Damnation of a Canyon," Edward Abbey

Combined Strategies

Last December a man named Robert Lee Willie, who had been convicted of raping and murdering an 18-year-old woman, was executed in the Louisiana state prison. In a statement issued several minutes before his death, Mr. Willie said: "Killing people is wrong. . . . It makes no difference whether it's citizens, countries, or governments. Killing is wrong."

—"Death and Justice," Edward Koch

● **LEAD-IN, THESIS, AND ESSAY MAP**   The introduction to an explaining essay—whether one paragraph or several—usually contains the following features.

- **Lead-in:** Some example, description, startling statement, statistic, short narrative, allusion, or quotation to get the reader's interest *and* focus on the topic the writer will explain.
- **Thesis:** Statement of the main idea; a "promise" to the reader that the essay fulfills.
- **Essay map:** A sentence, or part of a sentence, that *lists* (in the order in which the essay discusses them) the main subtopics for the essay.

In her essay on anorexia nervosa at the end of this chapter, Nancie Brosseau's introductory paragraph has all three features.

I knew my dieting had gotten out of hand, but when I could actually see the movement of my heart beating beneath my clothes, I knew I was in trouble. At first, the family doctor reassured my parents that my rapid weight loss was a "temporary phase among teenage girls." However, when I, at fourteen years old and five feet tall, weighed in at sixty-three pounds, my doctor changed his diagnosis from "temporary phase" to "anorexia nervosa." Anorexia nervosa is the process of self-starvation that affects over 100,000 young girls each year. Almost 6,000 of these girls die every year. Anorexia nervosa is a self-mutilating disease that affects its victim both physically and emotionally.	*Lead-in: Startling statement* *Description* *Statistics* *Thesis and essay map*

The essay map is contained in the phrase "both physically and emotionally": The first half of the essay discusses the physical effects of anorexia nervosa; the second half explains the emotional effects. Like a road map, the essay map helps the reader anticipate what topics the writer will explain.

● **PARAGRAPH TRANSITIONS AND HOOKS**   Transition words and paragraph hooks are audience cues that help the reader shift from one paragraph to the next. These connections between paragraphs help the reader see the relationships of the various parts. Transition words—*first, second, next, another, last, finally,* and so forth—signal your reader that a new idea or a new part of the idea is coming up. In addition to transition words, writers often tie paragraphs together by using a key word or idea from a previous paragraph in the first sentence of the following paragraph to "hook" the paragraphs together. The following paragraphs from James Twitchell's "Miss

Clairol's 'Does She . . . Or Doesn't She?'" illustrate how transition words and paragraph hooks work together to create smooth connections between paragraphs. (The complete essay appears in Chapter 6.)

As was to become typical in hair-coloring ads, the age of the model was a good ten years younger than the typical product user. The model is in her early thirties (witness the age of the child), too young to have gray hair.

Hook: "aspirational motif"

This inspirational motif was picked up later for other Clairol products: "If I've only one life . . . let me live it as a blonde!" "Every woman should be a redhead . . . at least once in her life!" "What would your husband say if suddenly you looked 10 years younger?" "Is it true blondes have more fun?" "What does he look at second?" And, of course, "The closer he gets, the better you look!"

Transition: "But"

But these slogans for different brand extensions only work because Miss Clairol had done her job. She made hair coloring possible, she made hair coloring acceptable, she made at-home hair coloring—dare I say it—empowering. She made the unique into the commonplace. By the 1980s, the hairdresser problem had been long forgotten and the follow-up lines read, "Hair color so natural, they'll never know for sure."

Hook: "these slogans"

● **BODY PARAGRAPHS**   Body paragraphs in expository writing are the main paragraphs in an essay, excluding any introductory, concluding, or transition paragraphs. They often contain the following features.

- **Topic sentence:** To promote clarity and precision, writers often use topic sentences to announce the main ideas of paragraphs. The main idea should be clearly related to the writer's thesis. A topic sentence usually occurs early in the paragraph (first or second sentence) or at the end of the paragraph.

- **Unity:** To avoid confusing readers, writers focus on a single idea for each paragraph. Writing unified paragraphs helps writers—and their readers—concentrate on one point at a time.

- **Coherence:** To make their writing flow smoothly from one sentence to the next, writers supplement their shaping strategies with coherence devices: repeated key words, pronouns referring to key nouns, and transition words.

The following body paragraphs from James Twitchell's "Miss Clairol's 'Does She . . . Or Doesn't She?'" illustrates these features. The second sentence in the first paragraph is the *topic sentence* for the first paragraph—and the second paragraph as well. That topic sentence focuses our attention on the process of "automatic color tinting." These two paragraphs have *unity* because they keep the focus on the "automatic" process of hair tinting. The two paragraphs also achieve *coherence* through the use of transitions and repeated key words and ideas.

> The copy block on the right is all business and was never changed during the campaign. *The process of coloring is always referred to as "automatic color tinting."* Automatic was to the fifties what *plastic* became to the sixties, and what *networking* is today. Just as your food was kept automatically fresh in the refrigerator, your car had an automatic transmission, your house had an automatic thermostat, your dishes and clothes were automatically cleaned and dried, so, too, your hair had automatic tinting.
>
> *However,* what is really automatic about hair coloring is that once you start, you won't stop. Hair grows, roots show, buy more product . . automatically. The genius of Gillette was not just that they sold the "safety razor" (they could give the razor away), *but that they also sold* the concept of being *clean-shaven.* Clean-shaven means that you use their blade every day, so, of course, you always need more blades. Clairol made "roots showing" into what Gillette had made "five o'clock shadow."

Topic sentence

Coherence & repeated key words

Transitions

DRAFTING

Before you begin drafting, reconsider your purpose and audience. What you explain depends on what your audience needs to know or what would demonstrate or show your point most effectively.

As you work from an outline or from an organizing strategy, remember that all three questions—*what, how,* and *why*—are interrelated. If you are writing about causes, for example, an explanation of *what* the topic is and *how* the causes function may also be necessary to explain your subject clearly. As you write, balance your sense of plan and organization with a willingness to pursue ideas that you discover as you write. While you need to have a plan, you should be ready to change course if you discover a more interesting idea or angle.

REVISING

As you revise your explaining essay, concentrate on making yourself perfectly clear, on illustrating with examples where your reader might be confused, and on signaling the relationship of the parts of your essay to your reader.

PEER RESPONSE

The instructions that follow will help you give and receive constructive advice about the rough draft of your explaining essay. You may use these guidelines for an in-class workshop, a take-home review, or a computer e-mail response.

Writer: Before you exchange drafts with another reader, write out the following on your essay draft.

1. **Purpose** Briefly describe your purpose, genre, and intended audience.
2. **Revision plans** What do you still intend to work on as you revise your draft?
3. **Questions** Write out one or two questions that you still have about your draft. What questions would you like your reader to answer?

Reader: First, read the entire draft from start to finish. As you reread the draft, answer the following questions.

1. **Clarity** What passages were clearest? Where were you most confused? Refer to specific sentences or passages to support your response. How and where could the writer make the draft clearer?
2. **Evidence** Where does the writer have good supporting evidence (specific examples, facts, visuals, statistics, interview results, or citations from sources)? Where does the writer need additional evidence? Refer to specific sentences or passages to support your response.
3. **Organization** Summarize or briefly outline the main ideas of the essay. Where was the organization most clear? Where were you confused? Refer to specific passages as you suggest ways to improve the draft.
4. **Purpose** Underline sentences that express the purpose or contain the thesis of the essay. Does your understanding of the essay's purpose match the writer's statement about purpose? Explain. How might the writer clarify the thesis for the intended audience?
5. **Reader's response** Overall, describe what you liked best about the draft. Then identify one major area that the writer should focus on during the revision. Does your suggestion match the writer's revision plans? Explain. Answer the writer's own question or questions about the draft.

GUIDELINES FOR REVISION

- **Review your purpose, audience, and genre.** Is your purpose clear to your target audience? Should you modify your chosen genre to appeal to your audience?

- **Review possibilities for visuals or graphics.** What additions or changes to images might be appropriate for your purpose, genre, or audience?

- **Compare your thesis sentence with what you say in your conclusion.** You may have a clearer statement of your thesis near the end of your paper. Revise your original thesis sentence to make it clearer, more focused, or more in line with what your essay actually says.

- **Explaining means *showing* and *demonstrating* relationships.** Be sure to follow general statements with *specific examples, details, facts, statistics, memories, dialogues,* or other *illustrations.*

- **In a formal definition, be sure to include the class of objects or concepts to which the term belongs.** Avoid ungrammatical writing, such as "Photosynthesis is *when* plants absorb oxygen" or "The lymphatic system is *where* the body removes bacteria and transports fatty cells."

- **Avoid introducing definitions with "Webster says . . . ."** Instead, read definitions from several dictionaries and give the best or most appropriate definition.

- **Remember that you can modify the dictionary definition of a term or concept to fit your particular context.** For example, to you, *heroism* may mean having the courage to *say* what you believe, not just to endanger your life through selfless actions.

- **Don't mix categories when you are classifying objects or ideas.** If you are classifying houses *by floor design* (ranch, bilevel, split-level, two-story), don't bring in other categories, such as passive-solar, which could be incorporated into any of those designs.

- **In explaining *how* something occurs or should be done, be sure to indicate to your audience which steps are *most important*.**

- **In cause-and-effect explanations, avoid post hoc fallacies.** This term comes from the Latin phrase *post hoc, ergo propter hoc:* "After this, therefore because of this." For example, just because Event B occurred after Event A, it does not follow, necessarily, that A caused B. If, for example, statistics show that traffic fatalities in your state actually

> 66 I wish he would explain his explanation. 99
>
> —LORD BYRON, POET

declined after the speed limit on interstate highways was increased, you should not conclude that higher speeds actually caused the reduction in fatalities. Other causes—increased radar patrols, stiffer drunk-driving penalties, or more rigorous vehicle-maintenance laws—may have been responsible for the reduction.

- **As you revise to sharpen your meaning or make your organization clearer, use appropriate transitional words and phrases to signal the *relationships among the various parts of your subject.***
  - —*To signal relation in time:* before, meanwhile, later, soon, at last, earlier, thereafter, afterward, by that time, from then on, first, next, now, presently, shortly, immediately, finally
  - —*To signal similarity:* likewise, similarly, once again, once more
  - —*To signal difference:* but, yet, however, although, whereas, though, even so, nonetheless, still, on the other hand, on the contrary
  - —*To signal consequences:* as a result, consequently, therefore, hence, for this reason

---

POSTSCRIPT ON THE WRITING PROCESS

Before you hand in your essay, reflect on your writing and learning process. In your journal, spend a few minutes answering the following questions.

1. Describe the purpose and intended audience for your essay.

2. What was the best workshop advice that you received? What did you revise in your draft because of that advice? What piece of advice did you ignore? Why?

3. What caused you the most difficulty with this essay? How did you solve the problem—or attempt to solve it? With what parts are you still least satisfied?

4. What are the best parts of your paper? Refer to specific paragraphs—what do you like most about them?

5. If you added visual images or special document-design features to your essay, explain how they supported your purpose or rhetorical goals.

6. What was the most important thing you learned about writing or your writing process as you wrote this paper?

CHRIS BLAKELY

White Lies: White-Collar Crime in America

Chris Blakely decided to write his essay on white-collar crime after the recent collapse of financial institutions such as AIG and the wave of collapsed pyramid schemes such as the one perpetrated by Bernie Madoff that cost investors $65 billion. After gathering information about the nature of white-collar crime and its devastating effects on workers and investors, Blakely decided to focus on two examples: the Enron collapse and the Adelphia Communications scandal. His purpose was to explain what white-collar crime is and how its effects can, in fact, be more devastating than those of street crime. As his essay overview explains, he also wrote a graphic novel to help make his point more visually and memorably for his audience. Some sample pages from his graphic novel appear on the next page.

ESSAY OVERVIEW

In this paper, I planned to analyze the state of white collar crime *1* and how it is perceived by the general public and the justice system. I found in my early research that white-collar criminals are perceived as less of a threat than street criminals (Holtfreter). This helped me to realize that public perception needs to change—and helping to change that perception was the main goal of my paper. I first needed to define white-collar crime, which I limited to cases where an employee of a public company engaged in illegal activity that seems to benefit that person and the company, but in the end harms the company, its employees, and its stockholders. I found examples of crime on a large scale, such as the Enron, Tyco, and WorldCom scandals, to show how damaging white-collar crime can be at its highest levels.

Understanding this type of crime first became important to me *2* when I found that, "according to the Federal Bureau of Investigation, white-collar crime is estimated to cost the United States more than $300 billion annually" (Cornell Law Index). Despite a recent rise in white-collar crime awareness, I was outraged that the justice system had not shifted its efforts to reduce white-collar crime. How are white-collar criminals getting away with $300 billion dollars every year? What happens to the employees when companies go bankrupt as a result of this crime? It is necessary to understand all types of crime so that society can treat all criminals in a fair and just manner.

...*continued* White Lies: White-Collar Crime in America, **Chris Blakely**

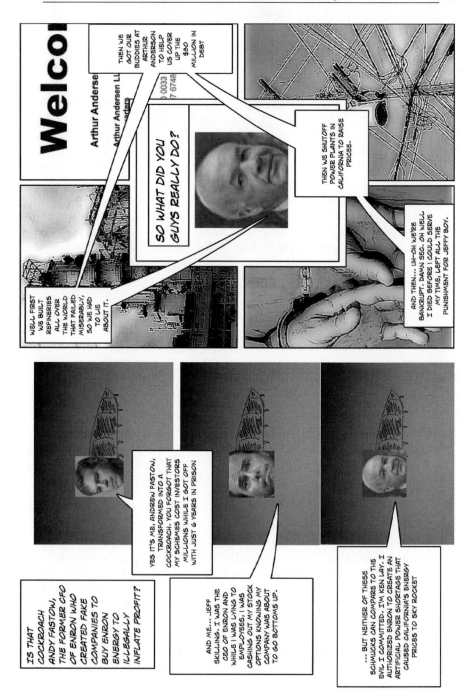

I also wanted to understand why people didn't take white-collar 3 crime seriously, so the second part of my paper used studies, mainly one by Florida State University, which look at public perception of white-collar crime. I wanted to show how white-collar crime can be just as damaging to the general public as street crime. This part helped to validate my thesis and show that this paper is exigent.

One major audience for this paper is business students. It will be 4 their decisions that shape the business world, and the ethical decisions they make could reduce white-collar crime. It will be their bosses, coworkers, and corporations committing white-collar crime—and maybe asking them to participate. If they have a better understanding of the term, as well as a sense of how damaging it can be, businesses may act more ethically.

Considering the audience of students, I then created a short 5 graphic novel about a CEO who is tempted to commit white-collar crime, but is dissuaded after meeting characters like Jeff Skilling, Dennis Kozlowski, and Karl Marx. My graphic novel, "Hope for America," looks at the illegal activity orchestrated by the CEOs of Enron. I wanted readers to be intrigued but not overwhelmed by the magnitude of the crimes. This genre is more likely to interest students by presenting the facts about white-collar crime in an accessible and humorous manner. I imagine that clips of the novel could be published in magazines that accept reader submitted cartoons. I felt that the graphic novel, which I created by learning and using the program "Comic Life," would be a great medium for presenting the information because it can be informal and is driven by visuals. It is also a much faster way for the audience to understand my point than reading a research paper—and maybe can interest them in later reading more details.

FINAL DRAFT OF ESSAY

In the prosperous days before the current economic crisis, stories 1 about misdoings among corporate executives got little more than a nod and a wink; businesspeople, it seemed, were expected to cut corners and bend the rules in seeking the profits expected of their shareholders. After all, were these "real" crimes?

But times have changed. In the face of growing unemployment, 2 numerous bankruptcies, and shrinking retirement funds, suddenly the public (and the justice system) has turned their attention—and sometimes their rage—toward the white-collar criminal. Joe Nacchio, CEO of Qwest Communication has been sentenced to six years in federal prison; Bernie Madoff, who pled guilty to defrauding clients out of some sixty-five billion dollars, has faced not only criminal penalties but also death threats; and bonuses paid to executives at the American International Group (AIG) has caused public outrage by citizens and legislators. But while these and countless other abuses have finally caught the public and governmental eye, white-collar crime is no new phenomenon. We are, in short, now paying the price for not paying attention to the long history of this phenomenon. And if we do not come to understand the problem, the outrage will not solve it. A look back at the all-but forgotten Aldephia Communications scandal and the Enron debacle before that demonstrates how, despite the spectacular headlines, we have largely ignored this building storm until it was too late.

On March 27, 2002, John Rigas and his executive board at Adel- 3 phia prepared for a routine financial check by the Securities and Exchange Commission. The investigation disclosed that the Rigas family had illegally co-borrowed $2.3 billion from the company. To cover the loans, it was estimated that Adelphia would have to borrow $1 billion. In response, investors pushed Adelphia's stock down 30% the very next day. Adelphia's shares were temporarily taken off the market and by summer the company filed for bankruptcy. On July 24, 2002 Rigas and his sons were arrested in New York City. Rigas's son, Tim, was sentenced to twenty years, while his father was given fifteen year for securities fraud (Cauley). After his trial, John Rigas maintained that, "It was a case of being in the wrong place at the wrong time. If this happened a year before, there would have been no headlines" (Cauley). In other words, Rigas felt that few would have noticed his actions if he had been caught before the Enron and the other corporate scandals of 2001 were exposed. And perhaps he was right.

The manner in which Rigas broke the law, and to the extent which 4 he abused his power, was and is astounding. At one point Rigas was embezzling one million dollars every month (Meier). Rigas built a private golf course in his backyard, bought the Buffalo Sabres hockey team, and maintained his three private jets (Huffington 1). But the spectacular nature of this greed hides the damage that those crimes have caused to the people surrounding Adelphia. At its peak Adelphia was the largest cable company in America (Cauley). After Rigas's actions were exposed, share values dropped from eighty-seven dollars to twelve cents, costing investors and employees millions of dollars (Huffington 41). While some employees were re-hired when Adelphia was bought-up by several companies, most employees lost their jobs and all the securities that they had invested in company stock. Despite all the financial damage that the Rigas family caused, they were able to avoid jail for five years. It wasn't until 2004 that the Rigases were convicted of fraud, and because they hired a team of elite lawyers, they did not have to report to prison until the summer of 2007 (Cauley).

The Adelphia story would be a tragedy in its own right, but when 5 it is looked at in conjunction with companies like Enron, WorldCom, Tyco, Global Crossing, Qwest, Xerox, and several other Fortune 500 companies that went bankrupt after white-collar crime was exposed, a pattern of corruption that has existed for many years emerges. In the film *Enron: The Smartest Guys in the Room,* Bethany Mclean, a co-author of the book of the same title, shows a significant problem with how white-collar crime is perceived: "The Enron story is so fascinating because people perceive it as a story that's about numbers, that it's some how about all these complicated transactions. In reality it's a story about people, and it's really a human tragedy" (Gibney). Mclean here demonstrates that the complicated transactions that surround the case distract people from the heart of the matter: the human tragedy.

By explaining the human costs behind these white collar crimes, I 6 hope to show why the public must pay attention to this public scourge. First, I want to show how the sentencing of these criminals, as compared to the sentencing of street criminals, sends the wrong message about the serious nature of white-collar crime. Second, I hope to demonstrate that public perception of white-collar crime is flawed and out of sync with the personal tragedies that crime causes.

The term white-collar crime was originally coined by Edward 7 Sutherland in 1939. Sutherland defined white-collar crime as "crime committed by a person of high social status and respectability, in the course of their occupation." Recently, sociologists and criminologists have debated what crimes are actually considered white-collar. Often, the term refers to a crime committed in the course of a person's occupation—no matter the social class. But, as Sutherland suggests, true white-collar crime is that which has a great impact upon society.

White-collar crime is often very difficult to detect. The crimes 8 take place in private offices where there are rarely eye-witnesses. The government has to base their prosecution on complex paper trails instead of concrete evidence (Strader 1-4). Also, white-collar criminals of high social status are able to hire better-trained, more experienced lawyers. This makes convicting white-collar criminals much more difficult than street criminals.

Because white-collar crimes are often not given due attention, it is 9 difficult for the majority of Americans to understand their financial complexity. Understanding the methods used to commit the crimes, however, is not nearly as important as recognizing the damage that is done to countless employees who lose everything that they worked years to accomplish. Americans need to realize that their ignorance of the effects of white collar crime has allowed the American justice system to be unfairly lax in the way it treats white-collar criminals.

If we compare white collar crime to a typical armed robbery, we 10 can see the inequality of the current justice system. For example, just compare the sentencing of John Rigas to that of three Kentuckians who robbed a small grocery store. In November, 2007, Morgan Wallace, 30, entered the grocery store with a handgun and demanded money. Geneva S. Goodin and Megan Johnston assisted in the escape before the three were apprehended on a highway near the scene of the crime. All three were held in a detention center after the robbery. On April 11, 2008, Wallace and Goodin were sentenced to ten years in prison while Johnston was sentenced to five years (McCreary County Voice). Unlike Rigas, Wallace, Goodin, and Johnston were not able to obtain bail money so that they could go to their homes before their trial. The three robbers were arrested, tried, and convicted within five to six months. That period is a stark contrast to the five years of freedom that Rigas was allowed, before a judge requested he begin his jail time (Cauley). There is also a clear disparity in the punishment that was handed out in relation to the damage of the crimes to society. The amount that the Kentuckians made off with was not disclosed, but it is certainly a miniscule amount compared with the $2.3 billion that Rigas gained, followed by the millions of dollars that were lost to shareholders. However, Wallace's term is only five years shorter than that of John Rigas, and there was no stipulation that the sentence could be as short as two years (as with Rigas' case), if Wallace's health declined.

Wallace and his accomplices are clearly criminals. That is not 11 the point. What *is* important here is the clear bias between the ways that these two cases were tried. If the two cases are looked at separately, there is little ground to claim injustice in either case. If the two cases are compared, however, the injustice is clear. Wallace's armed robbery did not kill anyone and it robbed a store owner of a very small amount of money compared to the 2.3 billion that Rigas took from his employees.

The Rigas case is important in its own right, but it is impossible to 12 explain the devastation caused by white-collar crime without also examining the Enron scandal. In January 2001, Enron was the seventh largest corporation in America. Enron had built oil-extracting stations all over the world, but most of them were performing terribly. However, instead of accurately releasing the correct financial statistics, Enron's executives included prospective profits in its bottom-line. Enron, and its accounting firm, Arthur Anderson, were able to hide the fact that they were $30 million in debt. Enron's CFO Andy Fastow created fake partnerships that would buy energy from Enron, in order to increase Enron's value. However, Fastow was merely working under Kenneth Lay, the founder of the company, and Jeffrey Skilling, the CEO. When investors started to question Enron's finances, Enron was not able to provide legitimate documentation for their profits. The final straw was when Enron began shutting down power plants in California in order to create artificial power shortages to increase the price of energy. The SEC began to inquire into Enron. In response, Enron began to release massive restatements, and Arthur Anderson began to shred the documents concerning Enron. Six weeks after the investigations began, Enron filed for bankruptcy (Gibney). Ken Lay passed away before he could be sentenced. Jeff Skilling was sentenced to twenty-four years and $60 million in fines; however, he was allowed to keep his $5 million mansion and $50 million in stocks and bonds. Andy Fastow was sentenced to just six years in prison. The term was reduced because of his cooperation with the government (MSNBC).

The difference between Enron and other corporate scandals is that 13 no other company has ever been so high and fallen with such damaging consequences. While Adelphia was partially bought up by Time Warner (Cauley), Enron completely collapsed. The stock value went from $90.75 at its peak to just $.08 after the company filed for bankruptcy. Five thousand employees lost their jobs, along with $800 million in pension funds. The total market loss for the company was $68 million (Huffington 12). These numbers do not include the money that was lost by California residents during the artificial power outages or the prospective earnings that thousands of Enron employees lost when they were fired. Despite efforts to re-coop money lost by employees, most of the damage was irreversible. It is also important to remember that not all of the damage was financial. Enron employees and investors were personally affected. After losing their jobs, they were forced to deal with the stress that surrounds finding a new job, and making ends meet while providing for a family. The employees went from having a secure future in a successful company to being unemployed with most of their stock and their retirement funds erased. Enron was white-collar crime at its worst.

These personal tragedies are often lost in the extravagant numbers 14 and complex business practices. As a result of the fraud committed by a small group of men, thousands of people lost their livelihood. This problem cannot be considered an isolated incident. Doing that would ignore the damage that white-collar crime has already done, as well as be ignorant of future corporate fraud. As Ben Lerach, the chief attorney for Enron employees stated, "It's the same old adage; if it looks to good to be true, then it is. Enron was making millions of dollars out of nowhere, and no one inside the company was there to stand up and question where this money was coming from" (Gibney). But is the public aware?

Following these high profile white-collar crimes, researchers took 15 specific interest in how white-collar crime is perceived by the general public. Researchers at the College of Criminology at Florida State University published a study in February 2008 that addressed this topic. In preliminary research it was found that white-collar crime costs the United States about $250 billion per year, whereas personal, or "street crimes," and household crimes account for only $17.6 billion lost. Despite this large disparity, the focus of criminal justice authorities and criminologists has been on explaining and preventing personal crime. Previous research found that authorities focus on street crime because the public perceives it as more of a threat. In a study of 402 participants nation-wide, researchers found that in a case where a white-collar criminal stole $1,000 and a street criminal stole $1,000 about two thirds of the participants believed that the street criminal was more likely to be caught. Two-thirds also believed that the street criminal should be given a harsher punishment than the white-collar criminal. In contrast, two-thirds of participants believed that the government should devote more resources to catching white-collar criminals (Holtfreter). This research shows that while Americans see white-collar crime as a problem, they are still more threatened by street crime and believe it should be dealt with more harshly. If Americans feel more threatened by street crime, authorities will respond by devoting their efforts to stopping it.

A study by researchers at Cal State and the University of Florida 16 published in February 2007 provides more data on the topic. Researchers used data from a national phone poll of 1,106 participants and found that three-quarters of the sample believed that street criminals were more likely to be caught and more likely to receive a harsher punishment. The sample was split in who *should* receive a harsher punishment. This study suggests that while the public may believe all criminals should receive the same punishment, it is clear that Americans believe white-collar criminals will receive less of a punishment (Schoepfer).

Interesting conclusions can be drawn from both of these studies. 17 From the Florida State study, participants believed that in a case where a white-collar and a street criminal commit crimes of equal financial damage, the street criminal should receive a harsher punishment. This may be because street crime is usually a crime where the victim is personally involved in a confrontation, whereas white-collar crime is a more indirect form of victimization. However, it is obvious, due to the large gap in total damages, that white-collar criminals are acting more frequently and doing more financial damage than street criminals. The second study shows that the public acknowledges a disparity in the sentencing of white-collar and street criminals, yet no major reforms have attempted to change this pattern. These studies show that public perception is inaccurate as based on the threat that each type of crime poses financially.

The American business model is an institution that has shown sustainability and reliability for the past two hundred years. However, it is through this institution that Americans are stealing nearly fifteen times more money than through conventional street crimes. The devastating effects of white collar crime need to be discussed by all Americans and addressed in a systematic way. The current outrage is not sufficient for a long-term fix. People lock their doors when they leave their house, but they see no problem in putting ninety percent of their 401k stock options into one company. White-collar crime has produced real damage and without change in public opinion, there are no signs that it will decline. Understanding white-collar crime now can prevent or reduce the damage that white-collar crime inflicts on America. *18*

Works Cited

Cauley, Leslie. "John Rigas Tells His Side of the Adelphia Story." *USA Today*. Gannett, 10 Apr. 2008. Web. 12 Apr. 2009.

Enron: The Smartest Guys in the Room. Dir. Alex Gibney. Perf. Peter Coyote. Jigsaw, 2005. Film.

"Former Enron CEO Skilling Gets 24 Years." *Associated Press*. Associated Press, 23 Oct. 2006. Web. 11 Apr. 2009.

Holtfreter, Kristy., et al. "Public Perception of White-Collar Crime." *Journal of Criminal Justice* 36:1 (2008): 50–60. Print.

Meier, Barry. "Founder of Adelphia Is Found Guilty of Conspiracy." *New York Times*. New York Times, 8 July 2004. Web.13 Apr. 2009.

Schoepfer, Andrea., et al. "Do Perceptions of Punishment Vary Between White Collar and Street Crimes?" *Journal of Criminal Justice* 35:2 (2007): 151–163. Print.

Strader, Kelly. "Understanding White Collar Crime." *Understanding White Collar Crime*. New York: Mathew Bender, 2002. 1–13. Print.

"Three Plead Guilty in Store Robbery." *McCreary County Voice*. McCreary County Voice, 11 Apr. 2008. Web. 13 Apr. 2009.

QUESTIONS FOR WRITING AND DISCUSSION

1 In his essay overview, Blakely says his purpose is to change public perception about the effects of white-collar crime. Cite at least two specific sentences from his essay where Blakely states this purpose.

❷ Explaining essays typically use definition, process analysis, and cause and effect reasoning to demonstrate the main points. Reread Blakely's essay. Then cite examples of all of the above strategies from his paper. Which of these strategies is most closely related to his purpose or thesis? Explain.

❸ As he explains the effects of white-collar crime on society, Blakely makes a comparison between a "street crime" and white-collar crime. What two crimes is he comparing? How does Blakely say they are similar and different? Are there other differences that Blakely doesn't explain that may account for the public's fear of street crime but their complacency about white-collar crime?

❹ In an explaining essay, transitions from paragraph to paragraph help to clarify the subject for the audience. Review the section on "Paragraph Transitions and Hooks" in this chapter (page 319). Then find two places where Blakely makes clear and smooth transitions from one paragraph to the next. Identify the transition words and hooks he uses to connect these paragraphs.

❺ Review the selections from Blakely's graphic novel. How do the scenes he depicts relate to the subject and purpose of his essay? Do the cartoon-like pictures and captions make white-collar crime seem too humorous? How do Blakely's images and captions convey the seriousness of these crimes? Explain, citing specific images and dialogue.

STUDENT WRITING
NANCIE BROSSEAU

Anorexia Nervosa

In her essay on anorexia nervosa, Nancie Brosseau writes from her own experience, explaining what anorexia nervosa is and what its effects are. Her essay succeeds not only because it is organized clearly, but also because it is so vivid and memorable. Relying on specific details, her explanation shows the effects of anorexia on her life.

1   I knew my dieting had gotten out of hand, but when I could actually see the movement of my heart beating beneath my clothes, I knew I was in trouble. At first, the family doctor reassured my parents that my rapid weight loss was a "temporary phase among teenage girls." However, when I, at fourteen years old and five feet tall, weighed in at sixty-three pounds, my doctor changed his diagnosis from "temporary

phase" to "anorexia nervosa." Anorexia nervosa is the process of self-starvation that affects over 100,000 young girls each year. Almost 6,000 of these girls die every year. Anorexia nervosa is a self-mutilating disease that affects its victim both physically and emotionally.

As both a gymnast and a dancer, I was constantly surrounded by 2 lithe, muscular people, all of them extremely conscious about their weight. Although I wasn't overweight to begin with, I thought that if I lost five to ten pounds I would look, feel, dance, and tumble better. I figured the quickest way to accomplish this was by drastically limiting my intake of food. By doing this, I lost ten pounds in one week and gained the approval of my peers. Soon, I could no longer control myself, and ten pounds turned into twenty, twenty into forty, and so on, until I finally ended up weighing fifty-eight pounds.

Several serious health problems bombarded me, and it's a wonder 3 I'm still alive. Because my body was receiving no nourishment at all, my muscles and essential organs, including my heart, liver, kidneys, and intestines, started to compensate by slowly disintegrating. My body was feeding on itself! As my weight plummeted, my circulation grew increasingly worse. My hands, feet, lips, and ears took on a bluish-purple tint, and I was constantly freezing cold. My hair started to fall out and my whole body took on a very skeletal appearance. My eyes appeared to have sunken into my face, and my forehead, cheekbones, and chin protruded sharply. My wrists were the largest part of my entire arm, as were my knees the widest part of my legs. My pants rubbed my hips raw because I had to wear my belts at their tightest notch to keep them up. I would force myself to vomit as soon as possible if I was forced to eat. The enamel on my teeth started to be eaten away by the acid in the vomit, and my lips cracked and bled regularly. I stopped menstruating completely because I was not producing enough estrogen. Instead of improving my skills as a dancer and a gymnast, I drastically reduced them because I was so weak. One time, while executing a chain of back handsprings, I broke all five fingers on one hand and three on the other because my bones had become so brittle. My doctor realized the serious danger I was in and told me I either had to see a psychologist or be put in the hospital. I chose to see a psychologist, and she helped me sort out the emotional aspects of anorexia, which in turn solved the physical problems.

The emotional problems associated with anorexia nervosa are 4 equally disastrous to the victim's health. Self-deception, lying, and depression are three examples of the emotions and actions an anorexic often experiences. During my entire bout with anorexia, I deceived myself into thinking I had complete control over my body. Hunger pains became a pleasant feeling, and sore muscles from overexercising just proved to me that I still needed to lose more weight. When my

...continued Anorexia Nervosa, **Nancie Brosseau**

psychologist showed me pictures of girls that were of normal weight for my age group, they honestly looked obese to me. I truly believed that even the smallest amount of food would make me extremely fat.

Another problem, lying, occurred most often when my parents 5 tried to force me to eat. Because I was at the gym until around eight o'clock every night, I told my mother not to save me dinner. I would come home and make a sandwich and feed it to my dog. I lied to my parents every day about eating lunch at school. For example, I would bring a sack lunch and sell it to someone and use the money to buy diet pills. I always told my parents that I ate my own lunch. I lied to my doctor when he asked if I was taking an appetite suppressant. I had to cover one lie with another to keep from being found out, although it was obvious that I was not eating by looking at me.

Still another emotion I felt, as a result of my anorexia, was severe 6 depression. It seemed that, no matter how hard I tried, I kept growing fatter. Of course, I was getting thinner all the time, but I couldn't see that. One time, I licked a postage stamp to put on a letter and immediately remembered that there was 1/4 of a calorie in the glue on the stamp. I punished myself by doing 100 extra situps every night for one week. I pinched my skin until it bruised as I lay awake at night because I was so ashamed of the way I thought I looked. I doomed myself to a life of obesity. I would often slip into a mood my psychologist described as a "blue funk." That is, I would become so depressed, I seriously considered committing suicide. The emotional instabilities associated with anorexia nervosa can be fatal.

Through psychological and physical treatment, I was able to over- 7 come anorexia nervosa. I still have a few complications today due to anorexia, such as dysmenorrhea (severe menstrual cramps) and the tendency to fast. However, these problems are minute compared to the problems I would have had if I hadn't received immediate help. Separately, the physical and emotional problems that anorexia nervosa creates can greatly harm its victim. However, when the two are teamed together, the results are deadly.

 QUESTIONS FOR WRITING AND DISCUSSION

❶ Without looking back at this essay, jot down the specific examples that you found most memorable. How would you describe these examples: tedious and commonplace, eye-opening, shocking, upsetting, persuasive? Explain.

2 Identify the thesis statement and essay map. Referring to paragraph numbers, show how the essay map sets up the organization of the essay.

3 Reread the opening sentences of each body paragraph. Identify one opening sentence that creates a smooth transition from the previous paragraph. Identify one opening sentence in which the transition could be smoother. Revise this sentence to improve the transition with a paragraph hook.

4 In this essay, Brosseau defines anorexia nervosa, explains its physical and emotional effects (and hints at its causes), and analyzes the process of the disorder, from its inception to its cure. Identify passages that illustrate each of these strategies: definition, cause-and-effect analysis, and process analysis.

5 A study by Judith Rabek-Wagener and her colleagues has shown that the "mass marketing of body images through print media and television and advertising" has helped cause nearly 65 percent of young women and 35 percent of young men to "experience significant dissatisfaction with their body size, shape, condition, or appearance." For the complete article, see "The Effect of Media Analysis on . . . Body Image Among College Students" in the *Journal of American College Health,* August 1, 1998. Read the research on the connection between the media and eating disorders and then write your own essay explaining the causes of eating disorders or the effects that the media have on college students' self-images.

PEARSON
mycomplab

For additional writing, reading, and research resources, go to http://www.mycomplab.com

Study the details in "American Gothic" by Grant Wood and then read the review of
"American Gothic" by Paul Richard on page 345 of this chapter.

Evaluating

9

During your fall semester library-orientation tour, you discover a small office tucked away in the corner of the library building: the interlibrary loan office. Because you occasionally need to see articles and books that your library does not have, you decide to investigate the interlibrary loan service and evaluate the helpfulness of the staff as well as the convenience, speed, and cost of obtaining materials. As part of your evaluation, you interview the office coordinator as well as several teachers and students who have used the service. Their responses—combined with your own observations—indicate that although an interlibrary loan can sometimes take a couple of weeks, the loan office gets high marks for its service. The staff is always helpful and patient, the service is easily accessible through electronic mail, and the cost of books and articles is surprisingly low.

In an e-mail to your parents, you explain that you are considering transferring to a different school for the following year. You have some misgivings about your decision to change, but after listing your criteria and ranking them in order from most to least important, you are convinced that you're making the right choice. In the message, you explain your decision, based on your criteria, and ask that your parents continue to support your education.

> " When we evaluate, we have in mind ... an ideal of what a good thing—pianist, painting, or professor—should be and do, and we apply that ideal to the individual instance before us. "
>
> —JEANNE FAHNESTOCK AND MARIE SECOR, AUTHORS OF *A RHETORIC OF ARGUMENT*

> " Purpose and craftsmanship—ends and means—these are the keys to your judgment. "
>
> —MARYA MANNES, JOURNALIST AND SOCIAL COMMENTATOR

H ARDLY A DAY PASSES THAT WE DO NOT EXPRESS OUR LIKES OR DISLIKES. WE CONSTANTLY PASS JUDGMENT ON PEOPLE, PLACES, OBJECTS, EVENTS, IDEAS, AND POLICIES. "SUE IS A WONDERFUL PERSON." "THE FOOD IN THIS CAFETERIA IS HORRIBLE." "THAT movie we saw Saturday night ought to get an Oscar nomination for best picture." "The bailout for America's banks and auto industry was a horrible waste of tax-payers' money." In addition to our own reactions, we are constantly exposed to the opinions of our friends, family members, teachers, and business associates. The media also barrage us with claims about products, famous personalities, and candidates for political office.

A claim or opinion, however, is not an *evaluation*. Your reaction to a person, a sports event, a meal, a movie, or a public policy becomes an evaluation *only* when you support your value judgment with clear standards and specific evidence. Your goal in evaluating something is not only to express your viewpoint, but also to *persuade* others to accept your judgment. You convince your readers by indicating the standards for your judgment and then supporting it with evidence: "The food in this cafeteria is horrible [your claim]. I know that not all cafeteria food tastes great, but it should at least be sanitary [one standard of judgment]. Yesterday, I had to dig a piece of green mold out of the meat loaf, and just as I stuck my fork into the green salad, a large black roach ran out [evidence]."

Most people interested in a subject agree that certain standards are impor-tant, for example, that a cafeteria be clean and pest-free. The standards that you share with your audience are the *criteria* for your evaluation. You convince your readers that something is good or bad, ugly or beautiful, tasty or nauseating by analyzing your subject in terms of your criteria. For each separate criterion, you support your judgment with specific *evidence:* descriptions, statistics, testimony, or examples from your personal experience. If your readers agree that your stan-dards or criteria are appropriate, and if you supply detailed evidence, your read-ers should be convinced. They will take your evaluation seriously—and think twice about eating at that roach-infested cafeteria.

Techniques for Writing Evaluations

The most common genre for evaluations is the review. Most frequently, we read reviews of films, books, restaurants, commercial products, public performances, and works of art. Reviews vary widely depending on the topic, the place of pub-lication, and the social context. Some reviews seem to be little more than thinly disguised promotions, while other reviews are thorough, complex, and highly critical. For any substantive evaluation, the review must set standards of judgment, rely on fair criteria, balance positive and negative evaluations, and provide sufficient evidence to persuade its readers. Use the following techniques as you write your evaluation.

> It is as hard to find a neutral critic as it is a neutral country in a time of war.
>
> —KATHERINE ANNE PORTER,
>
> NOVELIST AND SHORT STORY WRITER

Techniques for Evaluating

Technique	Tips on How to Do It
Assessing the *rhetorical situation*	What is the occasion and context for your review? Find examples of the genre you propose to write— where are these reviews or critiques typically published? Who is the audience, and what do they already believe or know about the topic?
Stating an *overall claim* about your subject	The overall claim is your *thesis* for your evaluation. It sums up both the positive and negative judgments you make for each criterion.
Clarifying the *criteria* for your evaluation	A criterion is a standard of judgment that most people who are knowledgeable about your subject agree is important. A criterion serves as a yardstick against which you measure your specific subject.
Stating a *judgment* for each criterion	The overall claim is based on your *judgment* of each separate criterion. Avoid being too critical or too enthusiastic by including both positive and negative judgments.
Supporting each judgment with *evidence*	Support should include *detailed observations, facts, examples, testimonials, quotations from experts,* or *statistics.*
Balancing your evaluation with both *positive* and *negative* judgments about your subject	Evaluations that are all positive are merely advertisements; evaluations that are entirely negative may seem too harsh or mean-spirited.

In the following evaluation of a Chinese restaurant in Washington, D.C., journalist and critic Phyllis C. Richman illustrates the main features of an evaluation.

Hunan Dynasty

215 Pennsylvania Ave. SE. 546–6161

Open daily 11 A.M. TO 3 P.M. for lunch, 3 P.M. TO 10 P.M. for dinner, until 11 P.M. on Friday and Saturday.

Reservations suggested for large parties.

Information and description

Prices for lunch: appetizers $2 to $4.50, entrees $4.75 to $6.50. For dinner: appetizers $1 to $13.95 (combination platter), entrees $6.75 to $18.

Complete dinner with wine or beer, tax, and tip about $20 a person.

Description

Chinese restaurants in America were once places one went just to eat. Now one goes to dine. There are now waiters in black tie, cloths on the tables and space between those tables, art on the walls and decoratively carved vegetables on the plate—elegance has become routine in Chinese restaurants. What's more, in Chinese restaurants the ingredients are fresh (have you ever found frozen broccoli in a Chinese kitchen?), and the cooking almost never sinks below decent. . . . And it is usually moderately priced. In other words, if you're among unfamiliar restaurants and looking for good value, Chinese restaurants now are routinely better than ever.

Overall claim

The Hunan Dynasty is an example of what makes Chinese restaurants such reliable choices. A great restaurant? It is not. A good value? Definitely. A restaurant to fit nearly any diner's need? Probably.

Criterion #1: Nice setting
Judgment: Attractive
Evidence

First, it is attractive. There are no silk tassels, blaring red lacquer or Formica tables; instead there are white tablecloths and subtle glass etchings. It is a dining room—or dining rooms, for the vastness has been carved into smaller spaces—of gracefulness and lavish space.

Criterion #2: Good service
Judgment: Often expert
Evidence

Second, service is a strong priority. The waiters look and act polished, and serve with flourishes from the carving of a Peking duck to the portioning of dishes among the diners. I have found some glitches—a forgotten appetizer, a recommendation of two dishes that turned out nearly identical—but most often the service has been expert. . . .

Criterion #3: Good main dishes
Judgment: Good but not memorable
Evidence

As for the main dishes, don't take the "hot and spicy" asterisks too seriously, for this kitchen is not out to offer you a test of fire. The peppers are there, but not in great number. And, like the appetizers, the main dishes are generally good but not often memorable. Fried dishes—and an inordinate number of them seem to be fried—are crunchy and not greasy. Vegetables are bright and crisp. Eggplant with hot garlic sauce is properly unctuous; Peking duck is as fat-free and crackly-skinned as you could hope (though pancakes were rubbery). And seafoods—shrimp, scallops, lobster—are tenderly cooked, though they are not the most full-flavored examples of those ingredients.

I have found only one dismal main dish in a fairly broad sampling: lemon chicken had no redeeming feature in its doughy, greasy, overcooked and underseasoned presentation. Otherwise, not much goes wrong. Crispy shrimp with walnuts might be preferable stir-fried rather than batter-fried, but the tomato-red sauce and crunchy walnuts made a good dish. Orange beef could use more seasoning but the coating was nicely crusty and the meat tender. . . .

Criterion #3 cont.
Judgment: Sometimes
bad
Evidence

So with the opening of the Hunan Dynasty, Washington did not add a stellar Chinese restaurant to its repertoire, but that is not necessarily what the city needed anyway. Hunan Dynasty is a top-flight neighborhood restaurant—with good food, caring service and very fair prices—that is attractive enough to set a mood for celebration and easygoing enough for an uncomplicated dinner with the family after work.

Overall claim restated

EVALUATING COMMERCIAL PRODUCTS OR SERVICES

Writers frequently evaluate commercial products or services. Consumer magazines test and rate every imaginable product or service—from cars and dishwashers to peanut butter and brokerage houses. Guidebooks evaluate tourist spots, restaurants, colleges, and hunting lodges. Specialty magazines, such as *Modern Photography, Road and Track, Skiing,* and *Wired,* often rate products and services of interest to their readers. To qualify as evaluation—and not just advertising—the authors and the publishers must maintain an independent status, uninfluenced by the manufacturers of the products or services they are judging.

Consider, first, the following "evaluation" of a wine, found on a bottle of Cabernet Sauvignon:

This Cabernet Sauvignon is a dry, robust, and complex wine whose hearty character is balanced by an unusual softness.

This "evaluative" language is so vague and esoteric that it may mean very little to the average consumer who just wants some wine with dinner. *Dry:* How can a liquid be dry? *Robust:* Does this refer to physique? *Soft:* Wine is not a pillow, though it might put you to sleep. *Complex:* Are they describing a wine or conducting a psychological analysis? While an independent evaluator may legitimately use these terms for knowledgeable wine drinkers, this particular description suggests that the wine is absolutely everything the buyer would like it to be—dry yet robust, hearty but at the same time soft. Apparently, the writer's purpose here is not to evaluate a product but to flatter readers who imagine themselves connoisseurs of wine.

Now consider the following evaluation of two popular cell phones, Apple's iPhone and the Palm Pre. In this comparative evaluation, the editors at *Consumer Reports* judge the two cell phones in terms of their display functions, cameras, Web search capabilities, and voice qualities. After providing evidence to support their judgments for each of these criteria, the editors conclude with their overall assessment.

Cell-phone Face-off

Apple's iPhone 3G S ($200, two-year contract, AT&T) is a slight update on its previous version and now sits atop our smart-phone Ratings. The new Palm Pre ($200, two-year contract, Sprint) ranked close, turning in a fine performance. Here are the details:

Display. The iPhone offers superb multimedia functionality via a 3.5-inch touch screen. That provides access to most controls and allows you to move or enlarge photos and Web pages with your fingertips. The Pre lets you shuffle multiple applications on its 3.1-inch touch screen like a deck of cards without losing your place. Flick the application off the page to close it.

Camera. The Pre's 3.1-megapixel camera has a flash and produces decent 8 x 10 prints. The iPhone's 3.1-megapixel camera, which also made fine 8 x 10 prints, has auto-focus and can shoot videos.

Search. Type a name or word on the Pre's slide-out keyboard and it will check your contacts and applications for that term, listing them for quick access. It also offers a useful Web search option. On the iPhone, typing a name or word on its virtual keyboard will provide an extensive internal search of your contacts, e-mail messages, applications, and music.

Voice. The phones have very good voice quality when talking, fair when listening.

Bottom line. The iPhone 3G S has a slight edge overall and is the best for multimedia. The Pre is better if you do a lot of messaging and prefer a real keyboard.

EVALUATING WORKS OF ART

Evaluations of commercial products and services tend to emphasize usefulness, practicality, convenience, and cost. Evaluations of works of art, on the other hand, focus on form, color, texture, design, balance, image, or theme. Even the phrase "appreciating a work of art" suggests that we are making a value judgment, though usually not one based on money. Through evaluation, writers teach us to appreciate all kinds of art: paintings, sculpture, photographs, buildings, antique cars or furniture, novels, short stories, essays, poems, and tapestries. A Dior fashion, a quilt, a silverware pattern, even an old pair of jeans might be evaluated primarily on aesthetic rather than practical grounds.

In the following selection, Paul Richard, art critic for *The Washington Post,* evaluates the painting, "American Gothic," by Grant Wood. (This painting is reproduced on the opening page of this chapter.) Although the painting was completed in 1930, the occasion for Richard's review was a 2006 Grant Wood exhibition at the Renwick Gallery of the Smithsonian American Art Museum. Richard's overall claim is that "American Gothic" is a famous and even iconic example of American art—as well known as Andy Warhol's Campbell soup can or Norman Rockwell's Thanksgiving turkey. The fact that "American Gothic" has so often been the subject of parody (search Google images, "American Gothic Parodies") is further evidence of the painting's iconic status.

PROFESSIONAL WRITING

"American Gothic," Pitchfork Perfect

Paul Richard

Is "American Gothic" America's best-known painting? Certainly it's one *1* of them. Grant Wood's dual portrait—with its churchy evocations, its stiffness and its pitchfork—pierced us long ago, and got stuck into our minds. Now, finally, it's here.

"American Gothic," which hasn't been in Washington in 40 years, *2* goes on view today at the Renwick Gallery of the Smithsonian American Art Museum. By all means, take it in—although, of course, you have already.

It should have gone all fuzzy—it's been parodied so often, and *3* parsed so many ways—but the 1930 canvas at the Renwick is as sharp as ever. Its details are finer than its travesties suggest, its image more absorbing. It's also smaller than one might have imagined, at only two feet wide. Wood painted it in his home town of Cedar Rapids, Iowa, showed it only once and then sold it, with relief, to the Art Institute of Chicago—for $300.

The picture with a pitchfork is an American unforgettable. Few *4* paintings, very few, have its recognizability. Maybe Whistler's mother. Maybe Warhol's soup can. Maybe Rockwell's Thanksgiving turkey. They're national emblems, all of them, visual manifestations of the American dream.

Whistler's figure, stiff and dark, looks half-enthroned and half- *5* embalmed; what she evokes is Mom. Family and food are the twin themes of the Rockwell. And with his Campbell's can, fluorescent-lit, Warhol nails shopping.

"American Gothic," too, hits the psychic bull's-eye. Wood's sly painting gives us the bedrock Christian values, the sober rural rectitude and the gnawing fear of sex that have made this country great. 6

The dangers of the dirty deed might not be depicted, but they're present nonetheless. The sinful is suggested by the serpent made of hair that slithers up the woman's neck to whisper in her ear, by the lightning rod atop the house and, of course, by the Devil's pitchfork. Wood's painting has a wink in it. No wonder it has been so frequently cartooned. 7

"The couple in front of the house have become preppies, yuppies, hippies," writes critic Robert Hughes, "Weathermen, pot growers, Ku Kluxers, jocks, operagoers, the Johnsons, the Reagans, the Carters, the Fords, the Nixons, the Clintons, and George Wallace with an elderly black lady." 8

But cartoons tend toward the slapdash, and Wood's calculated image is not at all haphazard. Nothing's out of place. The bright tines of the fork have been echoed one, two, three, by, at the left, the distant steeple, the window's pointed arch and the sharp roof at the right. The pitchfork rhymes as well with the seams of the man's overalls. When Wood painted "American Gothic," he fit its symmetries together as if he were making a watch. 9

Often, for self-portraits, the painter posed in overalls. But don't fall for the costume. Grant Wood (1891–1942) was no hick. He'd been four times to Europe. He taught in universities. He'd studied art in Paris, Germany and Italy, and it's clear he'd learned a lot. He was an exceptionally skillful painter, although not for long. Most of his best pictures—a dozen are included in "Grant Wood's Studio: Birthplace of 'American Gothic,'" the Renwick's exhibition—were painted in the five years after 1930. He had other things to do. 10

He was, this show reminds us, a carpenter, a carver, a skilled interior decorator. He could make a metal lampshade, or devise a chandelier, or embellish a posh room with faux rococo decorations. He could design a woman's necklace or a stained-glass window. He hammered teapots out of copper. Examples are on view. 11

They're here for a reason. And two works of art are key to Jane C. Milosch's exhibition. One is Wood's strict picture; the other is the vaguely medieval studio in which he made that painting—a charming, hand-built place acquired by the Cedar Rapids Museum of Art in 2002. They have a lot in common. The painting and the studio demonstrate the principles—the insistence on the local, the display of traditional craftsmanship—of the decorative movement known as American Arts and Crafts. 12

The picture takes its title from an architectural fashion. In its higher 13 manifestations, American Gothic gave us the Washington Cathedral and the colleges at Yale. Far out in the sticks (in, for instance, rural Iowa), the style left its mark on the factory-made windows, porch columns and pattern books that in the 19th century were shipped in by train.

"American Gothic's" farmhouse, with its pointed gable window, is 14 another local artifact. Wood discovered that wooden building in nearby Eldon, Iowa. It's still there. His figures were local, too. The bald man is his dentist, B.H. McKeeby. The woman is Wood's sister, Nan. (She was 30 at the time, McKeeby, 62.) Their eyes are cold, their mouths are prim. They wear period clothes. He stares the viewer down, she averts her gaze. They understand their roles.

Modern art, this isn't. Wood's painting is behind its times, rather 15 than ahead of them. What gives the work its punch is its slippery ambiguities. These haven't aged at all.

Try asking it a question. Is the woman the farmer's wife, or might 16 she be (nudge, nudge) the famous farmer's daughter of countless naughty jokes?

What does this painting mean to do, celebrate or satirize? Do its fig- 17 ures dwell in paradise, where the pioneering Protestant verities still hold, or is their rural neighborhood not so far from Hell? . . .

I don't know whether Wood expected "American Gothic" to become 18 an American icon, but he wouldn't have been surprised. In the early 1930s, mythic American icons were very much on his mind.

Had you asked him to identify America's best-known paintings, you 19 can bet he would have named two pictures of George Washington: Gilbert Stuart's likeness, the so-called Atheneum Portrait of 1796, the one that's on the dollar; and "Washington Crossing the Delaware" (1851), Emanuel Leutze's famous river scene with ice floes. In fact, both of these chestnuts can be found in Wood's own art. . . .

What is remarkable about "American Gothic" is its famousness. 20 What is equally remarkable is that the picture's fame was not achieved by accident. The Renwick's show suggests that's what Grant Wood had in mind.

EVALUATING PERFORMANCES

Evaluating live, recorded, or filmed performances of people in sports, dance, drama, debate, public meetings or lectures, and music may involve practical criteria, such as the prices of tickets to sports events or rock concerts. However, there are also aesthetic criteria that apply to people and their performances. In film evaluations, for example, the usual criteria are good acting and directing, an entertaining or believable story or plot, memorable characters, dramatic special effects, and so forth.

In the following review of *Slumdog Millionaire,* Manohla Dargis, writing for *The New York Times,* evaluates key elements of this Academy Award winning film: the director, the actors, the story, and the cinematography. As is typical of the film review genre, Dargis is writing for readers who have seen the film but also for those still deciding whether to watch it. To appeal to both sets of readers, Dargis weaves her evaluation into a summary of the film that gives a sense of the story and its context without revealing too much about the twists and turns of the plot. Dargis' overall judgment is that the film has a "resolutely upbeat pitch and seductive visual style" even though it feels "blithely glib" and calculated in places.

PROFESSIONAL WRITING

"Slumdog Millionaire"

Manohla Dargis

A gaudy, gorgeous rush of color, sound and motion, "Slumdog Million- 1 aire," the latest from the British shape-shifter Danny Boyle, doesn't travel through the lower depths, it giddily bounces from one horror to the next. A modern fairy tale about a pauper angling to become a prince, this sensory blowout largely takes place amid the squalor of Mumbai, India, where lost children and dogs sift through trash so fetid you swear you can smell the discarded mango as well as its peel, or could if the film weren't already hurtling through another picturesque gutter.

Mr. Boyle, who first stormed the British movie scene in the mid- 2 1990s with flashy entertainments like "Shallow Grave" and "Trainspotting," has a flair for the outré. Few other directors could turn a heroin addict rummaging inside a rank toilet bowl into a surrealistic underwater reverie, as he does in "Trainspotting," and fewer still could do so while holding onto the character's basic humanity. The addict, played by Ewan McGregor, emerges from his repulsive splish-splashing with a near-beatific smile (having successfully retrieved some pills), a terrible if darkly funny image that turns out to have been representative not just of Mr. Boyle's bent humor but also of his worldview: better to swim than to sink.

Swimming comes naturally to Jamal (the British actor Dev Patel in 3 his feature-film debut), who earns a living as a chai-wallah serving fragrant tea to call-center workers in Mumbai and who, after a series of alternating exhilarating and unnerving adventures, has landed in the hot seat on the television game show "Who Wants to Be a Millionaire." Yet while the story opens with Jamal on the verge of grabbing the big prize,

Simon Beaufoy's cleverly kinked screenplay, adapted from a novel by Vikas Swarup, embraces a fluid view of time and space, effortlessly shuttling between the young contestant's past and his present, his childhood spaces and grown-up times. Here, narrative doesn't begin and end: it flows and eddies—just like life.

By all rights the texture of Jamal's life should have been brutally 4 coarsened by tragedy and poverty by the time he makes a grab for the television jackpot. But because "Slumdog Millionaire" is self-consciously (perhaps commercially) framed as a contemporary fairy tale cum love story, or because Mr. Boyle leans toward the sanguine, this proves to be one of the most upbeat stories about living in hell imaginable. It's a life that begins in a vast, vibrant, sun-soaked, jampacked ghetto, a kaleidoscopic city of flimsy shacks and struggling humanity and takes an abrupt, cruel turn when Jamal (Ayush Mahesh Khedekar), then an exuberant 7, and his cagier brother, Salim (Azharuddin Mohammed Ismail), witness the murder of their mother (Sanchita Choudhary) by marauding fanatics armed with anti-Muslim epithets and clubs.

Cast into the larger, uncaring world along with another new or- 5 phan, a shy beauty named Latika (Rubina Ali plays the child, Freida Pinto the teenager), the three children make their way from one refuge to another before falling prey to a villain whose exploitation pushes the story to the edge of the unspeakable. Although there's something undeniably fascinating, or at least watchable, about this ghastly inter- lude— the young actors are very appealing and sympathetic, and the images are invariably pleasing even when they shouldn't be—it's unsettling to watch these young characters and, by extension, the young nonprofessionals playing them enact such a pantomime. It doesn't help even if you remember that Jamal makes it out alive long enough to have his 15 televised minutes.

It's hard to hold onto any reservations in the face of Mr. Boyle's res- 6 olutely upbeat pitch and seductive visual style. Beautifully shot with great sensitivity to color by the cinematographer Anthony Dod Mantle, in both film and digital video, "Slumdog Millionaire" makes for a better viewing experience than it does for a reflective one. It's an undeniably attractive package, a seamless mixture of thrills and tears, armchair tourism (the Taj Mahal makes a guest appearance during a sprightly interlude) and crackerjack professionalism. Both the reliably great Irrfan Khan ("A Mighty Heart"), as a sadistic detective, and the Bollywood star Anil Kapoor, as the preening game-show host, run circles around the young Mr. Patel, an agreeable enough if vague centerpiece to all this co-ordinated, insistently happy chaos.

In the end, what gives me reluctant pause about this bright, cheery, 7 hard-to-resist movie is that its joyfulness feels more like a filmmaker's calculation than an honest cry from the heart about the human spirit (or,

...continued "Slumdog Millionaire", **Manohla Dargis**

better yet, a moral tale). In the past Mr. Boyle has managed to wring giggles out of murder ("Shallow Grave") and addiction ("Trainspotting"), and invest even the apocalypse with a certain joie de vivre (the excellent zombie flick "28 Days Later"). He's a blithely glib entertainer who can dazzle you with technique and, on occasion, blindside you with emotion, as he does in his underrated children's movie, "Millions." He plucked my heartstrings in "Slumdog Millionaire" with well-practiced dexterity, coaxing laughter and sobs out of each sweet, sour and false note.

WARMING UP   Journal Exercises

The following exercises will help you practice writing evaluations. Read all of the following exercises and then write on the three that interest you most. If another idea occurs to you, write about it.

1 **Writing Across the Curriculum.** Choose the best of the courses that you are currently taking. To persuade a friend to take it, evaluate the course, the teacher, or both. What criteria and evidence would you select to persuade your friend?

2 Evaluate an object related to one of your hobbies or special interests—stereo or video equipment, water or snow skis, a cooking appliance or utensil, diving or hiking equipment, photography or art equipment, ranching or farming apparatus, fishing rods or reels, some part of a car, or computers. Write an evaluation of that object following the format used by *Consumer Reports*.

3 Evaluate a TV show that you find particularly irritating, boring, or insipid, but that you find yourself watching occasionally anyway. Watch the show, taking notes about scenes, characters, dialogue, and plot. Write a critique of the show for other students in this class.

4 To gather some information for yourself about a possible job or career, interview a person in your prospective field about his or her job or profession. Focus your questions on the person's opinions and judgments about this career. What criteria does this person use to judge it? What other jobs serve as a good basis for comparison? What details from this person's daily routine support his or her judgments?

5 At your place of work, evaluate one of your products or services. Write down the criteria and evidence that your business might use to determine whether it is a "good" product or service. Then list the criteria and evidence that your customers or patrons probably use. Are these two sets of criteria and evidence identical? Explain.

6 Choose a piece of modern art (painting, drawing, poster, sculpture, ceramics, and so forth). Describe and evaluate it for an audience that is indifferent or possibly even hostile to contemporary art. Explain why your readers should appreciate this particular art object.

7 Read the following short essay, "Evaluating a Web Site," by Robin Williams and John Tollett. Using the guidelines and criteria that they develop in their essay, evaluate a Web site that you choose or a site that you are designing. Which areas are especially effective? Which are least effective? How might the site be improved? Explain how you would evaluate the site overall. (For additional ideas about putting the authors' guidelines into practice, check out their own Web site at www .peachpit.com.)

PROFESSIONAL WRITING

Evaluating a Web Site

Robin Williams and John Tollett

The World Wide Web has become an important and integral communication tool around the world. Standards have been developed and users expect certain features to exist. Every time you land on a Web page you automatically evaluate how well the site works, how the page design impacts you, what makes the site usable, and what sorts of things hinder the communication. Your gut reactions determine whether or not you'll return to that site.

When John and I design a new site or visit a site we haven't been to before (many times a day, of course), we consciously evaluate a large number of features. Whether designing the site or visiting it, our evaluation criteria is pretty much the same. These are the sorts of things we look at:

Style: Does the theme or graphic style fit the goals of the site and appeal to the target audience? This is an extremely important consideration. Imagine if the Gumps.com site looked like the Disney site—would that suit the market for Gumps customers?

Animation and Flash and lots of large images can be perfectly appropriate on a site designed for a tech-savvy target audience, an audience you assume has a fast computer and the latest software. If the target audience is seniors who have inherited older machines from their kids, the site should probably have fewer flashy gizmos that require up-to-the-minute hardware and software.

Organization: Web sites can contain huge amounts of information. Organization is the critical element that makes the information accessible, and this can make or break a site. Organizing information on a large Web site requires serious thought and planning and testing and more thought and planning and testing. The Apple and Adobe Web sites are incredible examples of clear organization—each site has thousands of pages, but you can find what you need in seconds.

Recently I needed to buy a new carafe for my coffee pot. I went to the Web site our local store recommended, and in THREE SECONDS I found exactly the carafe I needed. The site wasn't beautiful, but I didn't need beautiful—I needed a carafe. This site (that sold hundreds of coffee-related products) was so well organized that I could scan and find the first topic I needed in about one second; I clicked the button and saw the second level of information; I clicked the button, and there was exactly the carafe I needed. Amazing.

Presentation: Web pages don't have to be masterpieces of art, but they do need to be pleasant and easy to look at. A very simple, well-organized page is more pleasing than an overdesigned, busy page that is badly organized. When Google.com first appeared, long before we recognized what a superior search engine it used, we loved it because it was simple. All of the other existing search pages were horrendously busy and cluttered and obnoxious; Google was white and clean with almost nothing on the page except the field in which to type my search. It was so comforting that since I found that site, I have never used another search page.

These are some of the features we see on poorly presented sites. These are easily fixable:

Too much bold text, especially when it is in color on a colored background.
Busy, distracting backgrounds.
Long lines of text that stretch out across the page.
Text in lots of all caps or italic.
Underlined text that is not a link.
Meaningless graphics.
Giant link buttons.
Borders turned on in tables.
Anything that blinks.
Anything that makes me scroll sideways (unless it is a specific and conscious design element).
Too many focal points on the page.
Clutter.

Logical and consistent: We don't like sites that are a puzzle we're expected to solve. We don't have time to figure out that if we click on a bubble as it floats up the page, we'll find the photographer's portfolio—I'll spend the time finding another photographer instead. We might find that kind of site interesting—for about twelve seconds.

Every page must be as intuitive and logical as possible and consistent with other pages in the site. You never know where visitors are going to drop into a site; they might find an obscure page through a search tool and pop into the archives. This means that no matter where visitors enter your site, they should know instantly whose site it is, have a rough idea of what the site is about, and know how to get to the home page.

The entire site should feel familiar so the visitor feels comfortable and confident wherever they are in it. Don't invent a variety of ways to navigate from page to page. Don't use underlines on the links on most pages, then eliminate them from other pages. Don't arbitrarily change the color scheme or layout.

Forgiving: Site visitors often make mistakes—they go to the wrong page or click a wrong button. If a site design is forgiving, a mistake is not a big problem. Every page should have familiar navigation to make it easy to return to any section of the site.

We hate orphan pages, which are those that dead end without links to return to previous pages or to the home page. Visitors often bookmark pages and return by choosing that bookmark; if they go to a bookmarked orphan page, they may not be able to find the rest of the site.

No chain-yanks: A chain-yank sets you up with expectations, then abruptly disappoints you. For example, you click a link next to a graphic that says "Click here for a larger image." You click, expecting a larger image and perhaps some additional information, but you get a page with the same image on a bare page, or perhaps the image is a quarter-inch larger. This makes you feel stupid. Or worse, it makes you think the Web site is stupid. If there is a link to another page, it must be worth the trip.

I read an online article about Steve Wozniak, co-creator of the Macintosh computer. The article included a paragraph on how Woz felt about his father, and the word "father" was an underlined link. Now, where would you expect that link to go? Probably to a page about Wozniak's father, right? No—the link was to Fathers.com, a nice site but totally irrelevant to the article. Chain-yank.

Link visibility: The underline below text is a visual clue that indicates a link. I agree that it's an ugly look. Designers sometimes remove the underline and use colored text to indicate the links. The problem with removing the underline is that if the designer uses more than one color on the Web page, it's difficult to tell which text is a link and which is just in color. I'm forced to run the mouse over any text in any color on the page to see whether or not it's a link. The only pages I've seen where this was done well were pages where no other text colors were used (see the Adobe.com site for a great example).

It's better to make text links obvious and easy with an underline than to have a fancier page that's harder to use. Whether or not you choose to use the underline, be consistent so the visitor doesn't get confused.

Communication, not decoration: Visuals should enhance the content or repeat a design theme, making pages seem familiar, friendly, consistent, and useful. When photos or illustrations merely decorate a page, they have little effect other than slowing the download time. Now, we're not discouraging visual elements—it's just that every element should have a purpose. Nothing should be on the page arbitrarily.

Dazzle me sparingly: There are many dazzling techniques, such as Flash animation, that advanced Web designers can add to a site. Flash is great stuff. Love it, love it, love it. It can be entertaining, dramatic, and compelling. It can also be annoying, especially when it's so dazzling you can't figure out how to get to another page. Most of us have grown tired of circles and squares that get bigger, then smaller, then fade out. The sites that use Flash effectively, use it sparingly. Visit the Adobe Flash Web pages and notice that even the creators of Flash use it in small bits. If I have to wait for a Flash animation to load before I can even see the first link, I'm gone.

Pop-up windows: Pop-up windows can be wonderful when used appropriately. They are great for giving visitors extra bits of information without making them go to an entirely different page. (Pop-up ads are hateful and annoying!)

Help: Large sites can be cumbersome even with good design. Any good, large site will have a site map, a site outline with links to all pages, or a search feature that a visitor can use to locate information.

This is just a brief overview of the sorts of things that one can evaluate on any Web site in just a few minutes. It's a good exercise to spend an hour or so with a complex Web site and really see what makes it work or not work. Try to accomplish a task, such as find a particular item, buy a product, search for information, contact someone, print a page, dig down deep in the structure and see if you can get out easily. Is the design consistent so you always know when you are in the site? Can you easily find what you need through the navigation bar? Is the search feature useful or annoying? Can you scan the page and know what the major topics of the site are? Is it so cluttered that it's difficult to find what you need? Once you spend the time to really evaluate a large site, you will feel more confident in appraising and using any Web site.

The following two articles present other alternatives for writing reviews. In the first example, Margaret Lazarus writes a cultural critique of Walt Disney's *The Lion King*. Instead of the typical review that evaluates the plot, acting, and cinematography, Lazarus focuses on the cultural stereotyping contained in a film targeted at children. Read her review and decide if you find her evaluation persuasive. In the second short review, David Sedaris, author of the best-selling *Me Talk Pretty One Day,* uses humor to evaluate one of the "precious little bistros" that have sprung up in New York. Sedaris provides an excellent model of how to use a personal narrative and humor to create a memorable review.

PROFESSIONAL WRITING

All's Not Well in Land of "The Lion King"

Margaret Lazarus

It's official: Walt Disney's *The Lion King* is breaking box-office records. Unfortunately, it's not breaking any stereotypes.

My sons, along with millions of other kids around the world, joyously awaited *The Lion King.* I was intrigued because this time Disney appeared to be skipping the old folk-tales with their traditional and primal undercurrents.

I hoped Disney had grown weary of reinforcing women's subordinate status by screening fables about a beauty who tames an angry male beast or a mermaid who gives up her glorious voice and splits her body to be with a prince.

So off we went to the movies, figuring we would enjoy an original, well-animated story about animals on the African plain. Even before the title sequence, however, I started to shudder.

Picture this (and I apologize for spilling the plot): The golden-maned—that is, good—lion is presenting his first born male child to his subjects. All the animals in the kingdom, known as Pride Lands, are paying tribute to the infant son that will someday be their king. These royal subjects are basically lion food—zebras, monkeys, birds, etc.—and they all live together in supposed harmony in the "circle of life."

Outside the kingdom, in a dark, gloomy, and impoverished elephant graveyard, are the hyenas. They live dismally jammed together among bones and litter. The hyenas are dark—mostly black—and they are nasty, menacing the little lion prince when he wanders into their territory.

One of their voices is done by Whoopie Goldberg, in a clearly inner-city dialect. If this is not the ghetto, I don't know what is.

All is not perfect inside Pride Lands, however. The king's evil brother Scar has no lionesses or cubs. Scar has a black mane, and speaks in an effeminate, limp-pawed, British style done by Jeremy Irons—seemingly a gay caricature.

Scar conspires with the hyenas to kill the king and send the prince into exile. In exchange for their support, Scar allows the hyenas to live in

...continued All's Not Well in Land of "The Lion King", **Margaret Lazarus**

Pride Lands. But property values soon crash: The hyenas overpopulate, kill all the game, and litter the once-green land with bones.

Already Disney has gays and blacks ruining the "natural order," and the stereotypes keep rolling. The lionesses never question whether they should be serving Scar and the hyenas—they just worry a lot. They are mistreated, but instead of fighting back these powerful hunters passively await salvation. (Even my 7-year-old wondered why the young, strong lioness didn't get rid of Scar.)

The circle of life is broken; disaster awaits everyone. But then the first-born male returns to reclaim power. The royal heir kills the gay usurper, and sends the hyenas back to the dark, gloomy, bone-filled ghetto. Order is restored and the message is clear: Only those born to privilege can bring about change.

This is not a story about animals—we know animals don't behave like this. This is a metaphor for society that originated in the minds of Disney's creators. These bigoted images and attitudes will lodge deeply in children's consciousness.

I'm not sure I always understand the law of the Hollywood jungle, but my boys definitely don't. Scared and frightened by *The Lion King*, they were also riveted, and deeply affected. But entranced by the "Disney magic," they and millions of other children were given hidden messages that can only do them—and us—harm.

PROFESSIONAL WRITING

Today's Special

David Sedaris

It is his birthday, and Hugh and I are seated in a New York restaurant, *1* awaiting the arrival of our fifteen-word entrées. He looks very nice, dressed in the suit and sweater that have always belonged to him. As for me, I own only my shoes, pants, shirt, and tie. My jacket belongs to the restaurant and was offered as a loan by the maître d', who apparently thought I would feel more comfortable dressed to lead a high-school marching band.

I'm worrying the thick gold braids decorating my sleeves when the *2* waiter presents us with what he calls "a little something to amuse the palette." Roughly the size and color of a Band-Aid, the amusement floats on a shallow, muddy puddle of sauce and is topped with a sprig of greenery.

"And this would be . . . what, exactly?" Hugh asks.   3

"This," the waiter announces, "is our raw Atlantic sword-fish served in   4
a dark chocolate gravy and garnished with fresh mint."

"Not again," I say. "Can't you guys come up with something a little less   5
conventional?"

"Love your jacket," the waiter whispers.   6

As a rule, I'm no great fan of eating out in New York restaurants. It's   7
hard to love a place that's outlawed smoking but finds it perfectly acceptable to serve raw fish in a bath of chocolate. There are no normal
restaurants left, at least in our neighborhood. The diners have all been
taken over by precious little bistros boasting a menu of indigenous
American cuisine. They call these meals "traditional," yet they're rarely
the American dishes I remember. The patty melt has been pushed aside
in favor of the herb-encrusted medallions of baby artichoke hearts,
which never leave me thinking, Oh, right, those! I wonder if they're as
good as the ones my mom used to make.

Part of the problem is that we live in the wrong part of town. SoHo is   8
not a macaroni salad kind of place. This is where the world's brightest
young talents come to braise carmelized racks of corn-fed songbirds or
offer up their famous knuckle of flash-seared crappie served with a collar of chided ginger and cornered by a tribe of kiln-roasted Chilean
toadstools, teased with a warm spray of clarified musk oil. Even when
they promise something simple, they've got to tart it up—the meatloaf
has been poached in sea water, or there are figs in the tuna salad. If cooking is an art, I think we're in our Dada phase.

I've never thought of myself as a particularly finicky eater, but it's   9
hard to be a good sport when each dish seems to include no fewer than
a dozen ingredients, one of which I'm bound to dislike. I'd order the
skirt steak with a medley of suffocated peaches, but I'm put off by the
aspirin sauce. The sea scallops look good until I'm told they're served
in a broth of malt liquor and mummified litchi nuts. What I really want
is a cigarette, and I'm always searching the menu in the hope that some
courageous young chef has finally recognized tobacco as a vegetable.
Bake it, steam it, grill it, or stuff it into littleneck clams, I just need
something familiar that I can hold on to.

When the waiter brings our entrées, I have no idea which plate   10
might be mine. In yesterday's restaurants it was possible both to visualize and to recognize your meal. There were always subtle differences,
but for the most part, a lamb chop tended to maintain its basic shape.
That is to say that it looked choplike. It had a handle made of bone and
a teardrop of meat hugged by a thin rind of fat. Apparently, though,

that was too predictable. Order the modern lamb chop, and it's likely to look no different than your companion's order of shackled pompano. The current food is always arranged into a senseless, vertical tower. No longer content to recline, it now reaches for the sky, much like the high-rise buildings lining our city streets. It's as if the plates were valuable parcels of land and the chef had purchased one small lot and unlimited air rights. Hugh's saffron linguini resembles a miniature turban, topped with architectural spires of shrimp. It stands there in the center while the rest of the vast, empty plate looks as though it's been leased out as a possible parking lot. I had ordered the steak, which, bowing to the same minimalist fashion, is served without the bone, the thin slices of beef stacked to resemble a funeral pyre. The potatoes I'd been expecting have apparently either been clarified to an essence or were used to stoke the grill.

"Maybe," Hugh says, "they're inside your tower of meat."   *11*

This is what we have been reduced to. Hugh blows the yucca pollen off *12*
his blackened shrimp while I push back the sleeves of my borrowed sport coat and search the meat tower for my promised potatoes.

"There they are, right there." Hugh uses his fork to point out what *13*
could easily be mistaken for five cavity-riddled molars. The dark spots must be my vegetable.

Because I am both a glutton and a masochist, my standard com- *14*
plaint, "That was so bad," is always followed by "And there was so little of it!"

Our plates are cleared, and we are presented with dessert menus. I *15*
learn that spiced ham is no longer considered just a luncheon meat and that even back issues of *Smithsonian* can be turned into sorbets.

"I just couldn't," I say to the waiter when he recommends the white *16*
chocolate and wild loganberry couscous.

"If we're counting calories, I could have the chef serve it without the *17*
crème fraîche."

"No," I say. "Really, I just couldn't."   *18*

We ask for the check, explaining that we have a movie to catch. It's *19*
only a ten-minute walk to the theater, but I'm antsy because I'd like to get something to eat before the show. They'll have loads of food at the concession stand, but I don't believe in mixing meat with my movies. Luckily there's a hot dog cart not too far out of our way.

Friends always say, "How can you eat those? I read in the paper that *20*
they're made from hog's lips."

"And . . . ?"   *21*

"And hearts and eyelids."   *22*

That, to my mind, is only three ingredients and constitutes a refresh- 23
ing change of pace. I order mine with nothing but mustard, and
am thrilled to watch the vendor present my hot dog in a horizontal position. So simple and timeless that I can recognize it, immediately, as
food.

vo·cab·u·lar·y

In your journal, write the meaning of the italicized words in the following phrases.

- *garnished* with fresh mint (**4**)
- we're in the *Dada* phase (**8**)
- *mummified* litchi nuts (**9**)
- same *minimalist* fashion (**10**)

- a *glutton* and a *masochist* (**14**)
- turned into *sorbets* (**15**)
- without the crème *fraiche* (**17**)

 QUESTIONS FOR WRITING AND DISCUSSION

1 In his essay, David Sedaris claims to enjoy simple food like potatoes and hot
dogs, yet he knows and uses the vocabulary of a sophisticated gourmand.
List the words and phrases Sedaris uses to describe the cuisine of this
particular restaurant. Does he use this vocabulary to praise the cooking of
this restaurant or to ridicule it? Explain.

2 As a humorist, Sedaris looks for the amusing and absurd in people, places,
and events. As a restaurant critic, however, Sedaris uses evaluation to make
a serious point. He doesn't explicitly state his overall claim about this
particular restaurant, but his opinion is evident throughout. What exactly
does Sedaris like and dislike? Write your own three-column log for this
essay. List the *criteria* (such as ambiance, food taste, service, presentation,
etc.) that Sedaris uses in this review, the *evidence* he gives, and his *judgment*
for each of the criteria. State in your own words Sedaris' overall judgment
or claim.

3 In his review, Sedaris uses several descriptive and narrative strategies to
convey the scene and describe the action. Review the techniques for
observing and remembering in Chapters 3 and 4. Where in his essay does
Sedaris give vivid and detailed descriptions or use images, similes, and
metaphors? Where does Sedaris use narrative techniques such as scene
setting, dialogue, and characterization? Support your response by citing
specific sentences, phrases, or images.

④ Visit a local restaurant—preferably one you are already familiar with—for the purpose of writing a review. If you wish, bring some of your friends. Take notes during the meal so you won't miss any names of foods or service details. Then write two versions of your review. For the first one, follow the informative model of the Hunan Dynasty review at the beginning of this chapter. Organize your comments clearly by the criteria you choose. For your second version, write in a narrative fashion as Sedaris does, including scene description, key events, characters, and dialogue. When you finish, evaluate your reviews. Which do you like best? What magazine, newspaper, or Web site would be the best choice for each of your versions?

Evaluating: The Writing Process

> ❝ I love criticism so long as it's unqualified praise. ❞
>
> —NOEL COWARD, PLAYWRIGHT, SONGWRITER, NOVELIST, DIRECTOR, AND PERFORMER

ASSIGNMENT FOR EVALUATING

With a specific audience and genre in mind, evaluate a product or service, a work of art, or a performance. Choose a subject that is reobservable—that you can revisit or review as you write your essay. Select criteria appropriate for your subject, genre, and audience. Collect evidence to support your judgment for each criterion. *Remember: In order to remain objective and credible, your review or critique should contain both positive and negative judgments.*

As the grid below indicates, the review is the most common genre for evaluating, but "reviews" cover a wide range of documents. Some film reviews, for example, are academic and critical whereas others merely indicate the major plot line without much critical evaluation. As you choose your topic, be sure to reread your assignment and consider the requirements or expectations of your audience. Are they expecting merely to be informed or entertained, or do they want the thorough and critical evaluation described in this chapter?

Audience	Possible Genres for Evaluating
Personal Audience	Class notes, journal entry, blog, scrapbook, or social networking page
Academic Audience	Academic critique, media critique, review, journal entry, forum entry on class site, multigenre document
Public Audience	Column, editorial, article, or critique in a magazine, newspaper, newsletter, online site, or multigenre document

CHOOSING A SUBJECT

If you have already settled on a possible subject, try the following collecting and shaping strategies. If you have not found a subject, consider these ideas.

- Evaluating requires some expertise about a particular person, performance, place, object, or service. You generate expertise not only through experience but also through writing, reading, and rewriting. Review your authority list from Chapter 7. Which of those subjects could you evaluate? Reread your journal entries on observing and investigating. Did you observe or investigate some person, place, or thing that you could write about again, this time for the purpose of evaluating it?

- Comparing and contrasting lead naturally to evaluation. For example, compare two places you've lived, two friends, or two jobs. Compare two newspapers for their coverage of international news, local features, sports, or business. Compare two famous people from the same profession. Compare your expectations about a person, place, or event with the reality. The purpose of your comparison is to determine, for a specific audience, which is "better," based on the criteria you select and the evidence you find.

- Evaluating a possible career choice can help you choose courses, think about possible summer jobs, and prepare for job interviews. Begin by describing several jobs that fit your particular career goals. Then go to several of the following Web sites and gather information.

  http://www.monster.com   http://www.bestjobsusa.com
  http://www.careers.com   money.cnn.com/services/careerbuilder
  http://careers.yahoo.com   http://www.getthatgig.com

  Choose the career criteria that are most important for you, such as job satisfaction, location, benefits, salary, education requirements, and so forth. Decide which criteria are most important for **you**. Is job satisfaction more important than pay or location? Choose your criteria and rank them in order of importance. Then write an evaluation of one or two jobs that you find described on the Internet or in your local newspaper.

- **Community Service Learning.** Community service-learning projects often require an assessment at the end of the period of service. These reflective evaluations start with the goals of the agency, the goals of your class project, and your goals as a learner as the major criteria. Then you gather evidence to see how well the actual experiences and projects met these overall project goals. Sometimes participants use short evaluation questionnaires to get feedback at the midpoint and then again at the end of the project. If you are participating in a community service-learning project, check with your teacher or coordinator about how to write this assessment.

COLLECTING

Once you have a tentative subject and audience in mind, ask the following questions to focus your collecting activities

- Can you *narrow, restrict,* or *define* your subject to focus your paper?
- What *criteria* will you use to evaluate your subject?
- What *evidence* might you gather? As you collect evidence, focus on three questions:
  What *comparisons* can you make between your subject and similar subjects?
  What are the *uses* or *consequences* of this subject?
  What *experiments* or *authorities* might you cite for support?
- What initial *judgments* are you going to make?

● **OBSERVING** Observation and description of your subject are crucial to a clear evaluation. In most cases, your audience will need to know *what* your subject is before they can understand your evaluation.

- Examine a place or object repeatedly, looking at it from different points of view. Take notes. Describe it. Draw it, if appropriate. Analyze its component parts. List its uses. To which senses does it appeal— sight, sound, touch, smell, taste? If you are comparing your subject to other similar subjects, observe them carefully. Remember: The second or third time you observe your subject, you will see even more key details.
- If you are evaluating a person, collect information about this person's life, interests, abilities, accomplishments, and plans for the future. If you are able to observe the person directly, describe his or her physical features, write down what he or she says, and describe the person's environment.
- If you are evaluating a performance or an event, a tape recording or videotape can be extremely useful. If possible, choose a concert, film, or play on tape so that you can stop and review it if and when necessary. If a tape recording or videotape is not available, attend the performance or event twice.

Making notes in a *three-column log* is an excellent collecting strategy for evaluations. Using the following example from Phyllis Richman's evaluation of the Hunan Dynasty restaurant, list the criteria, evidence, and judgments for your subject.

Subject: Hunan Dynasty Restaurant

Criteria	Evidence	Judgment
Attractive setting	No blaring red-lacquer tables	Graceful
	White tablecloths	
	Subtle glass etchings	
Good service	Waiters serve with flourishes	Often expert
	Some glitches, such as forgotten appetizer	

● **REMEMBERING**   You are already an authority on many subjects, and your personal experiences may help you evaluate your subject. Try *freewriting, looping, branching,* or *clustering* your subject to help you remember relevant events, impressions, and information. In evaluating appliances for consumer magazines, for example, reporters often use products over a period of months, recording data, impressions, and experiences. Those experiences and memories are then used to support criteria and judgments. Evaluating a film often requires remembering similar films that you have liked or disliked. An evaluation of a great athlete may include your memories of previous performances. A vivid narrative of those memories can help convince an audience that a performance is good or bad.

● **READING**   Some of the ideas and evidence for your evaluation may come from reading descriptions of your subject, other evaluations of your subject, or the testimony of experts. Be sure you read these texts critically: Who is the intended audience for the text? What evidence does the text give? What is the author's bias? What are other points of view? Read your potential sources critically.

● **INVESTIGATING**   All evaluations involve some degree of formal or informal investigation as you probe the characteristics of your subject and seek evidence to support your judgments.

Use the Library or the Internet   Check the library and Internet resources for information on your subject, for ideas about how to design and conduct an evaluation of that subject, for possible criteria, for data in evaluations already performed, and for a sense of different possible audiences. In its evaluation of chocolate chip cookies, for example, *Consumer Reports* suggests criteria and outlines procedures. The magazine rated some two dozen popular store-bought brands, as well as four "boutique" or freshly baked varieties, on "strength of chocolate flavor and aroma, cookie and chip texture, and freedom from sensory defects." When the magazine's evaluators faced a problem sampling the fresh cookies in the lab, they decided to move the lab: "We ended up loading a station wagon with scoresheet, pencils, clipboards, water containers, cups, napkins . . . and setting off on a tasting safari to shopping malls."

Gather Field Data You may want to supplement your personal evaluation with a sample of other people's opinions by using *questionnaires* or *interviews*. (See Chapter 7.) If you are rating a film, for example, you might give people leaving the theater a very brief *questionnaire*, asking for their responses on key criteria relating to the movie that they just saw. If you are rating a class, you might want to *interview* several students in the class to support your claim that the class was either effective or ineffective. The interviews might also give you some specific examples: descriptions of experiences that you can then use as evidence to support your own judgments.

SHAPING

While the shaping strategies that you have used in previous essays may be helpful, the strategies that follow are particularly appropriate for shaping evaluations.

● **AUDIENCE AND GENRE** As you consider ways to organize and shape your explaining essay, think about your probable audience and genre. Reviews vary greatly in length, critical depth, complexity, and reader appeal. Think about your own purpose and goal; find several magazines, newspapers, or Web sites that publish the kind of review you would like to write, and use the best ones as genre models—not as blueprints—to guide your own writing.

● **ANALYSIS BY CRITERIA** Often, evaluations are organized by criteria. You decide which criteria are appropriate for the subject and audience, and then you use those criteria to outline the essay. Your first few paragraphs of introduction establish your thesis or overall claim and then give background information: what the subject is, why you are evaluating it, what the competition is, and how you gathered your data. Then you order the criteria according to some plan: chronological order, spatial order, order of importance, or another logical sequence. Phyllis Richman's evaluation of the Hunan Dynasty restaurant follows the criteria pattern:

- **Introductory paragraphs:** *information* about the restaurant (location, hours, prices), general *description* of Chinese restaurants today, and *overall claim:* The Hunan Dynasty is reliable, a good value, and versatile.
- **Criterion #1/judgment:** Good restaurants should have an attractive setting and atmosphere/Hunan Dynasty is attractive.

- **Criterion #2/judgment:** Good restaurants should give strong priority to service/Hunan Dynasty has, despite an occasional glitch, expert service.
- **Criterion #3/judgment:** Restaurants that serve moderately priced food should have quality main dishes/Main dishes at Hunan Dynasty are generally good but not often memorable. (*Note:* The most important criterion—the quality of the main dishes—is saved for last.)
- **Concluding paragraphs:** Hunan Dynasty is a top-flight neighborhood restaurant.

● **COMPARISON AND CONTRAST**   Many evaluations compare two subjects in order to demonstrate why one is preferable to another. Books, films, restaurants, courses, music, writers, scientists, historical events, sports—all can be evaluated by means of comparison and contrast. In evaluating two Asian restaurants, for example, student writer Chris Cameron uses a comparison-and-contrast structure to shape her essay. In the following body paragraph from her essay, Cameron compares two restaurants, the Unicorn and the Yakitori, on the basis of her first criterion—an atmosphere that seems authentically Asian.

> Of the two restaurants, we preferred the authentic atmosphere of the Unicorn to the cultural confusion at the Yakitori. On first impression, the Yakitori looked like a converted truck stop, sparsely decorated with a few bamboo slats and Japanese print fabric hanging in slices as Bruce Springsteen wailed loudly in the ears of the customers. The feeling at the Unicorn was quite the opposite as we entered a room that seemed transported from Chinatown. The whole room had a red tint from the light shining through the flowered curtains, and the place looked truly authentic, from the Chinese patterned rug on the wall to the elaborate dragon on the ceiling. Soft oriental music played as the customers sipped tea from small porcelain cups and ate fortune cookies.

Cameron used the following *alternating* comparison-and-contrast shape for her whole essay.

- Introductory paragraph(s)
- **Thesis:** Although several friends recommended the Yakitori, we preferred the Unicorn for its more authentic atmosphere, courteous service, and well-prepared food.
- **Authentic atmosphere:** Yakitori versus Unicorn
- **Courteous service:** Yakitori versus Unicorn
- **Well-prepared food:** Yakitori versus Unicorn
- Concluding paragraph(s)

On the other hand, Cameron might have used a *block* comparison-and-contrast structure. In this organizational pattern, the outline would be as follows.

- Introductory paragraph(s)
- **Thesis:** Although several friends recommended the Yakitori, we preferred the Unicorn for its more authentic atmosphere, courteous service, and well-prepared food.
- **The Yakitori:** atmosphere, service, and food
- **The Unicorn:** atmosphere, service, and food as compared to the Yakitori's
- Concluding paragraph(s)

● **CHRONOLOGICAL ORDER**   Writers often use chronological order, especially in reviewing a book or a film, to shape parts of their evaluations. Film reviewers rely on chronological order to sketch the main outlines of the plot as they comment on the quality of the acting, directing, or cinematography.

● **CAUSAL ANALYSIS**   Evaluations of works of art, performances, or visuals often measure the *effect* on the audience. Robin Williams and John Tollett, in "Evaluating a Web Site," use several criteria, including using a clear organization and avoiding irritating "chain-yanks." Their evidence illustrates that Web sites should have a positive effect on the user.

- **Criteria:** The organization of a Web site must make information easily accessible for the user.
  EVIDENCE: "Recently I needed to buy a new carafe for my coffee pot. I went to the Web site our local store recommended, and in THREE SECONDS I found exactly the carafe I needed. . . . This site was so well organized that I could scan and find the first topic I needed in about one second. . . . Amazing."
- **Judgment:** The site was very well organized for the user.

- **Criteria:** Web sites should not create false expectations or "chain-yanks" for the user.
  EVIDENCE: "For example, you click next to a graphic that says 'Click here for a larger image.' You click, expecting a larger image and perhaps some additional information, but you get a page with the same image. . . . This makes you feel stupid. Or worse, it makes you think the Web site is stupid."
- **Judgment:** The Web site frustrated the user.

● **TITLE, INTRODUCTION, AND CONCLUSION**   Titles of evaluative writing tend to be short and succinct, stating what product, service, work of art, or performance you are evaluating ("Slumdog Millionaire" or "'American Gothic,'

Pitchfork Perfect") or suggesting a key question or conclusion in the evaluation ("Borrowers Can Be Choosy").

Introductory paragraphs provide background information and description and usually give an overall claim or thesis. In some cases, however, the overall claim comes last, in a concluding "Recommendations" section or in a final summary paragraph. If the overall claim appears in the opening paragraphs, the concluding paragraph may simply review the strengths or weaknesses or may just advise the reader: This *is* or *is not* worth seeing, reading, watching, doing, or buying.

> 66 I have to stop being afraid of being wrong; I can't wait until everything is perfect before the work comes out. I don't have that kind of time. 99
>
> —SHERLEY ANNE WILLIAMS, NOVELIST AND CRITIC

Research Tips   GO

Before you draft your evaluating essay, stop for a moment and *evaluate your sources* of information and opinion. If you are citing ideas or information from library articles—or especially from the Internet—be skeptical. How reliable is your source? What do you know about your source's reliability or editorial slant? Does the author have a particular bias? Be sure to *qualify* any biased or absolute statements you use from your sources. (See Chapter 13 for additional ideas on evaluating written sources.)

If you cite observations or field sources (interviews, surveys), evaluate the information you collected. Does it reflect only one point of view? How is it biased? Are your responses in surveys limited in number or point of view? Remember: You may use sources that reflect a limited perspective, but *be sure to alert your readers to those limitations*. For example, you might say, "Obviously, these reactions represent only four viewers who saw this film, but . . ." or "Of course, the administrator wanted to defend this student program when he said. . . ."

PEER RESPONSE

The instructions that follow will help you give and receive constructive advice about the rough draft of your evaluating essay. You may use these guidelines for an in-class workshop, a take-home review, or an e-mail computer response.

Writer: Before you exchange drafts, write out the following information about your essay draft.

1. **Purpose, audience, and genre.** Briefly, describe your overall purpose, your genre, and your intended audience. Do you plan to incorporate visuals? If so, where?

2. **Revision plans.** What do you know you still need to work on as you revise your draft?

3. **Questions.** Write one or two questions about your draft that you would like your reader to answer.

Reader: Before you answer the following questions, read the entire draft from start to finish. As you *reread* the draft, do the following.

1. Underline the sentence(s) that state the writer's *overall claim* about the subject.

2. In the margin, put large brackets [ ] around paragraphs that *describe* what the writer is evaluating.

3. On a separate piece of paper or at the end of the writer's essay, make a *three-column log* indicating the writer's criteria, evidence, and judgments. (Does the log include both positive and negative judgments?)

4. Identify with an asterisk (*) any passages in which the writer needs more *evidence* to support the judgments.

5. Write out one *criterion* that is missing or that is not appropriate for the given subject.

6. Assess how well the writer explains the purpose and addresses the intended audience. Do you agree with the writer about his or her revision plans? Finally, answer the writer's questions.

Writer: As you read your peer reviewer's notes and comments, do the following.

1. Consider your peer reviewer's comments and notes. Has your reviewer correctly identified your overall claim? Do you need to add more description of your subject? Does the reviewer's three-column log look like yours? Do you need to revise your criteria or add additional evidence? Do you balance positive and negative judgments?

2. Based on your review, draw up a *revision plan*. Write out the three most important things you need to do as you revise your essay.

66 I have rewritten—often several times—every word I have ever published. My pencils outlast their erasers. 99
—VLADIMIR NABOKOV, NOVELIST

DRAFTING

With your criteria in front of you, your data or evidence at hand, and a general plan or sketch outline in mind, begin writing your draft. As you write, focus on your audience. If your evaluation needs to be short, you may have to use only those criteria that will appeal most effectively to your audience. As you write, check occasionally to be sure that you are including your key criteria. While some parts of the essay may seem forced or awkward as you write, other parts will grow and expand as you get your thoughts on paper. As in other papers, don't stop to check spelling or worry about an occasional awkward sentence. If you stop and can't get going, reread what you have written, look over your notes or sketch outline, and pick up the thread again.

REVISING

Remember that revision is not just changing a word here and there or correcting occasional spelling errors. Make your evaluation more effective for your reader by including more specific evidence, changing the order of your paragraphs to make them clearer, cutting out an unimportant point, or adding a point that one of your readers suggests.

GUIDELINES FOR REVISION

* **Review your purpose, audience, and genre.** Is your purpose clear to your target audience? Should you modify your chosen genre to appeal to your audience?
* **Review possibilities for visuals or graphics.** What additions or changes to images might be appropriate for your purpose, genre, or audience?
* **Criteria are *standards of value.*** They contain categories and judgments, as in "good fuel economy," "good reliability," or "powerful use of light and shade in a painting." Some categories, such as "price," have clearly implied judgments ("low price"), but make sure that your criteria refer implicitly or explicitly to a standard of value.
* **Examine your criteria from your audience's point of view.** Which criteria are most important in evaluating your subject? Will your readers agree that the criteria you select are indeed the most important ones? Will changing the order in which you present your criteria make your evaluation more convincing?
* **Include both positive and negative evaluations of your subject.** If all of your judgments are positive, your evaluation will sound like an advertisement. If all of your judgments are negative, your readers may think you are too critical.
* **Be sure to include supporting evidence for each criterion.** Without any data or support, your evaluation will be just an opinion that will not persuade your reader.
* **Avoid overgeneralizing in your claims.** If you are evaluating only three software programs, you cannot say that Lotus 1-2-3 is the best business program around. You can say only that it is the best among the group or the best in the particular class that you measured.

- **Unless your goal is humor or irony, compare subjects that belong in the same class.** Comparing a Ford Focus to a BMW is absurd because they are not similar cars in terms of cost, design, or purpose.
- **If you need additional evidence to persuade your readers, review the questions at the beginning of the "Collecting" section of this chapter.** Have you addressed all the key questions listed there?
- **If you are citing other people's data or quoting sources, check to make sure your summaries and data are accurate.**
- *Signal* **the major divisions in your evaluation to your reader using clear transitions, key words, and paragraph hooks.** At the beginning of new paragraphs or sections in your essay, let your reader know where you are going.
- **Revise sentences for directness and clarity.**
- **Edit your evaluation for correct spelling, appropriate word choice, punctuation, usage, and grammar.**

POSTSCRIPT ON THE WRITING PROCESS

When you finish writing your essay, answer the following questions.

1. Who is the intended audience for your evaluation? Write out one sentence from your essay in which you appeal to or address this audience.

2. Describe the main problem that you had writing this essay, such as finding a topic, collecting evidence, or writing or revising the draft.

3. What parts or paragraphs of your essay do you like best? Indicate the words, phrases, or sentences that make it effective. What do you like about them?

4. Explain what helped you most with your revision: advice from your peers, conference with the teacher, advice from a writing center tutor, rereading your draft several times, or some other source.

5. Write out one question that you still have about the assignment or about your writing and revising process.

STUDENT WRITING

LINDA MEININGER

Borrowers Can Be Choosy

Linda Meininger wrote her evaluation essay on the Interlibrary Loan Office at her campus library. Her purpose was to advise her readers—other students—about the usefulness of the interlibrary loan service. In order to gather information for her essay, she visited the office, learned how to access an interlibrary loan with her computer, interviewed the coordinator of the office, and surveyed nine people who had used the library service. Overall, she discovered that the interlibrary loan office provided a surprisingly convenient, helpful, and inexpensive service. Included here are the following writing-process materials: a draft of her interview and survey questions, a three-column log, her first rough draft, questions for a conference with her instructor, and her final draft.

DRAFT OF INTERVIEW AND SURVEY QUESTIONS

Interview Questions for Interlibrary Loan Office (ILL) Coordinator

1. Have you surveyed your clients to get their impressions about the service? Results? Favorable—why? Unfavorable—why? Valid or not—why?
2. How do you and your employees rate your service?
3. Do you offer any special services for your clients?
4. Have you received any recognition for your work in the ILL?
5. What institutions lend documents to our library?
6. How convenient do you make it for clients to use your services?

Survey Questions

1. Were you satisfied with the interlibrary loan service you received? Why? Why not?
2. How often do you use the service?
3. How much lead time did you allow for your request?
4. What was your area of research?
5. What type of materials did you request? Periodicals? Books? Documents? Theses?
6. What was the cost of using the service?

DRAFT OF THREE-COLUMN LOG

CLAIM: The Interlibrary Loan Office runs a well-organized and efficient operation.

AUDIENCE: Students.

PURPOSE: To evaluate the service and encourage students to use it.

...continued Borrowers Can Be Choosy, **Linda Meininger**

CRITERIA	EVIDENCE	JUDGMENT
1. Timely delivery of materials	Survey results	Mixed
2. Helpful service	Personal experience	Positive
3. Convenience for users	Survey	Positive
4. Scope of libraries available	Interview and brochure	Positive
5. Reasonable cost	Survey and interview	Positive

FIRST ROUGH DRAFT

Are you someone who has searched endlessly through the library's computer database or the card catalog only to have that elusive title never appear? Go directly to Room 210, Morgan Library, and collect an Interlibrary Loan request card, or if that's too far to walk, place your order via e-mail from your PC.   *1*

How useful can this service be to you? Stay tuned and I'll show you everything you need to know about Morgan Library Interlibrary Loan (ILL). In evaluating this service, available to all who are affiliated with CSU as a student or employee, I will be looking at the following criteria: convenience and ease of use; timely arrival of materials requested; cooperation and assistance from the ILL staff; and reasonable fees for use of loaned materials.   *2*

Jane Smith of the ILL department informed me that request cards can be found in many locations in the library. These color-coded cards are used to request documents, periodicals, theses, or books. The color of the card corresponds to the type of material. Requests may be left at any of the reference desks, or you may drop off your request in person in Room 210 of the library, Monday through Friday.   *3*

Students and employees with a PC and a modem may request materials from their office or home. According to Jane Smith, electronic access was developed in-house by the ILL department. A new service has also been established, called the Library Retrieval and Delivery Service (LRDS). This is available to disabled students on campus. Requests may be made by the computer or manually.   *4*

Jane Smith of the ILL office informed me that normal turnaround for requests is 24 hours. That translates to one day from the time the requests leave the ILL office for another lending institution. Unless . . . it's spring semester. Then, look out! Deadlines for theses and research are closing in and everyone is in need of the materials yesterday. Then the turnaround time is a week. Most likely materials will not arrive until the end of the school year. Requests in spring semester jump to 300–400 per day compared to a norm of approximately 200 daily.   *5*

I would say that being able to fill 300 requests for material is efficient by my standards. Jane was delighted to inform me that Morgan   *6*

Library was chosen most efficient in the state by other ILLs in Colorado. I think that could be comparable to a Good Housekeeping Seal of Approval or a five-star rating by AAA.

When I visited the ILL office I discovered a staff willing to answer my questions and with a sense of humor. They made me feel comfortable and at ease. One of the brochures I picked up was a pamphlet with their job descriptions: Queen of the World, Resident Geek, ILL's Mouthpiece, Double Agent, ILL's Movie Star and answer to Greta Garbo, and Leading (Lending) Lady. The pamphlet shows me that these people like what they do and can laugh at themselves and their idiosyncrasies. I believe this impression is relayed to their patrons. *7*

CONFERENCE QUESTIONS

1. Are the criteria I have sufficient? Should I have chosen more of the criteria from my log? Or other criteria from my list?

2. My development needs improvement. I need more evidence to substantiate my criteria. What if I didn't secure the surveys necessary (ten) to be fairly objective?

3. Should I introduce my criteria in a subtle manner or just come right out and state them?

4. After class today, I felt that I needed to state judgments for each of my criteria, although they could change after the survey results.

5. Does it sound like I'm writing to a student audience?

REVISED VERSION
Borrowers Can Be Choosy

Are you someone who has searched endlessly through the library's computer listing, the card catalog, or even the stacks, only to have that elusive title never appear? Don't give up. Go directly to Room 210, Morgan Library, and collect an Interlibrary Loan request card. If that's too far to walk, just place your order via e-mail with your PC, a modem, and some communications software. *1*

This service can be useful to you during your four-year educational experience at Colorado State University. So stay tuned, and I'll review four characteristics of Morgan Library Interlibrary Loan (ILL). In evaluating this service, which is available to all CSU students, faculty, or staff, I will be looking at the following criteria: convenience and ease of use, timely arrival of materials requested, reasonable fees for materials, and cooperation and assistance from the ILL staff. To gain evidence about the performance of this department, I interviewed the staff, observed their operation, and conducted a survey of CSU students, faculty, and employees (see Appendix for results of survey). Out of nine *2* survey respondents, the level of usage varied from four one-time users to two weekly users.

The convenience and ease of using the interlibrary loan service was definitely a high point. Jane Smith of the ILL department informed me that request cards have been placed in many locations in the library for convenient access. These color-coded cards are used to request documents, periodicals, theses, or books. The color of the card corresponds to the type of material requested. Cards may be left at any of the reference desks, or you may drop off your request in person in Room 210 of the library, just off to your left at the top of the stairs, Monday through Friday, 8:00 A.M.–5:00 P.M. 3

The addition of computer access to interlibrary loans also adds to the ease of requesting materials. At the present time, students, faculty, and employees with a PC and a modem may request materials from their office or home. According to Ms. Smith, electronic access was developed in-house by the ILL department, making their service available 24 hours per day. Julie Wessling, coordinator of the Interlibrary Loan department, said, "About one third of our users request their specific information via our electronic service." 4

The ILL has also established another convenient new service, called Library Retrieval and Delivery Service (LRDS). This is available to disabled students on campus and other off-campus users. Requests may be made by computer or by using the request cards. Delivery or notice of nonavailability of materials will be made within 48 hours to three sites on campus: Braiden Hall, the RDS Office in 116 Student Services Building, and the ILL office. There is also dial-up access to the library's computer listings. This service is especially valuable to off-campus users or students with mobility problems. The ILL staff retrieves requests, most of which—according to Ms. Wessling—are in the CSU stacks, and then delivers them to one of the collection sites for pickup by the patron. 5

Overall, I found the request forms and located the ILL office without any problem, and according to nine out of the nine people surveyed, the ILL service was "easy to use and locate." Judy Lira, a Rocky Mountain High School media specialist, faxes her requests and feels that the technology is a service to the staff and students at her school. Bonnie Mueller, a Morgan Library cataloguing employee, uses LAN to order materials, and she states, "It's wonderful!" While I was in the ILL office, a student was filling out request cards. I tried to enlist her aid for my survey, but she declined, saying that this was her first time using the Interlibrary Loan service. However, she did have one comment for me: "They [the ILL office] need to make us [students] more aware of this." It appears that the convenient access to the ILL system makes it an asset to CSU students and to the local schools. 6

I wished to experiment personally with the ILL to evaluate the timely 7 arrival of requests, but Ms. Smith explained to me that it would be impossible to receive anything within the time frame I was allotted to finish this essay. Therefore, I will be relying on the experiences and testimony of others.

The normal processing turnaround time for requests, Ms. Smith in- 8 formed me, is 24 hours. That means that it takes one day from the time the request is made by the borrower to the time it leaves the ILL office for another lending institution. Unless . . . it's spring semester. Then look out! Deadlines for theses and research papers are closing in, and students and faculty need their materials yesterday. Ms. Smith related the story of a student who recently came in on a Wednesday and wanted the item by Monday. She had to tell him, "Sorry, it's not possible, especially now." She said at this time of the year—spring semester—the processing time is approximately one week, and that's just until the request leaves the CSU ILL office. Most likely, materials will not arrive until April or the end of the school year. Normal arrival time seems to vary between ten days and two weeks, according to survey results. Requests at spring semester jump to 300–400 per day, and these requests include not only the CSU customers, but the borrowers from other institutions who are requesting materials from Morgan Library, reported Ms. Wessling.

The normal processing time can be speeded up, however, in some 9 cases. Ms. Wessling explained that "the use of e-mail allows us to locate and help process customers' requests faster. This allows the student or professor to receive the information more quickly. The only thing holding the process back is the time it takes to get the specific request in the mail." Also, articles from periodicals or a document can be sent electronically or by fax. When materials are needed in a hurry, a RUSH may be affixed to the card and a last usable date recorded. This will bring the request to the attention of the office, and they will give it priority to try to locate a copy at a nearby library for pickup by the client. Of the nine people I surveyed, six reported that their materials arrived within 24 hours to two weeks, but one person reported that it took eight weeks and didn't arrive in time to be of use. He allowed two weeks of lead time, but he ordered the material in April. Another person stated that she had to wait over six weeks for materials to arrive. Her materials were "very difficult to locate." My accounting professor, Dr. Middlemist, usually allows a two-week lead time when ordering and said that the "time taken to arrive depended on where the materials were coming from." Dr. Middlemist stated that she uses the service 10–12 times per year, maybe more, depending on what her needs are.

By my standards, being able to fill 300 requests for materials is ef- 10 ficient. In addition, Ms. Smith was delighted to inform me that Morgan Library was chosen most efficient by other ILLs in Colorado and will be "looked over" by a team from the state so that their efficient and innovative ideas may be used in other libraries. I think that could be comparable to a Good Housekeeping Seal of Approval or a four-star rating by AAA.

While the timely arrival of materials was a problem, especially in the 11 spring semester, the cost of materials received was very reasonable. For most requests, there is no charge for the service. I found that only on the journal request card was there a line item for maximum cost. This is in the event that there could be photocopying charges. Eight of my nine respondents said they received their materials (books, theses, and journals) free of charge, and the other paid a reasonable fee for Xeroxing one time. It is through the lending and borrowing reciprocal agreement between libraries that the ILL service can be offered at no cost or low cost to the user.

Perhaps the strongest feature of the ILL service was the willingness 12 of the staff to help patrons, answer questions, and keep their sense of humor. They made me feel comfortable and at ease. One of the brochures I picked up was a pamphlet with their job descriptions: Queen of the World, Resident Geek, ILL's Mouthpiece, Double Agent, ILL's Movie Star and Answer to Greta Garbo, and Leading (Lending) Lady. This pamphlet shows that these people like what they do and can laugh at themselves and their idiosyncrasies. Something else Ms. Smith said really sticks in my mind. She said, "I think we're the only department in the whole library where everyone really likes what they do." I believe this impression is relayed to the patrons. My survey results concurred with this, as seven respondents felt that the staff was friendly and helpful. One dissenting student felt that the office could have presented the information she needed over the phone, saving her a trip to the library. The other person felt there wasn't any follow-up on a trace request to see if a book had been lost. Morgan Library has lost this patron to another library. Some of the positive comments received were as follows: "The ILL personnel went out of their way to help me." "What I needed was extremely obscure, and they got most of it." "They found a German book in Berlin, and they Xeroxed it and sent the whole thing FREE!"

As a result of my investigation and evaluation of the ILL office, I 13 hope I have occasion to use their service in the future. I know from my conversations with the staff and other users of ILL that the service and staff are reliable and willing to assist at any time (during office hours, of course). The cost is well within the reach of all patrons, and we have two methods of booking our requests: manually on cards and electronically by computer. So the next time you need an item that the CSU library doesn't own, remember that you do have another resource available at your fingertips: Morgan Library's Interlibrary Loan.

APPENDIX

MORGAN LIBRARY INTERLIBRARY LOAN SURVEY

The following survey was completed by nine students and faculty members. Responses follow each question.

1. What was the subject area of the materials requested?

Accounting—1	Ben Jonson—17th C writer & critic—1
Agriculture—1	Cognitive development—1
Ancient Roman Art—1	Popular fiction—1
Anthropology—1	Travelogues—1800s—1
Archaeology—1	Various subjects—1

2. What type of material did you request?

Book—7	Journal—6
Thesis—1	Documents—0

3. How much lead time did you allow the Interlibrary Loan office to secure your materials?

   No deadline—5
   24 hours—1
   1 week—1
   2 weeks—2

4. At what time of the year did you request materials?

Fall semester	Specify month 3 in Oct, Nov, and Dec
Spring semester	Specify month 1—Jan, 4—Feb & Mar,
	2—April, 1—May

5. Did your materials arrive in a timely manner? How much time did it take?

24 hours—1	Very quickly—1
1 week—1	Not more than $1\frac{1}{2}$–2 months—1
8 weeks—1	Over 3 weeks—1
Typically timely—1	10 days—1

6. Were you satisfied with the service you received? Why? Why not?

   No, not friendly, no follow-up if lost—1
   Yes, friendly and helpful—1
   Yes—2
   Yes, very satisfied—1
   Very, needed extremely obscure stuff & got most of it—1

Extremely satisfied, wonderful to have access to otherwise unreachable materials—1
No problem with service or individuals, satisfied—1
Friendly—1

7. How often do you use the service?
   1 time—3   Weekly—1
   2 times/year—1   One semester a lot of times—1
   10–12 times/year—1
   Goes to Boulder-CU library—1
   2–3 times/week avg., usually turns in requests in batches—1

8. Was there a charge for your requested materials? If so, did you feel the charge was reasonable or not? How much was it?
   No charge—8
   Xeroxing charge, reasonable—1

9. Was the staff of the Interlibrary Loan office helpful? Friendly? Did it give out-of-the-ordinary service?
   Not friendly, not helpful, no out-of-ordinary service—1
   Could have presented info over phone, save trip to library—1
   Staff went out of their way to help—1
   Worked hard on obscure stuff—1
   Always do their best—1
   Very friendly—3   Friendly & helpful—3
   Regular service—1   Fax requests—1

10. Did you feel that the service was convenient to use (e.g., easy to order materials and pick them up, forms to be filled out, the open hours of the office)?
    Easy to use—2   Very—2   Yes—2
    Used LAN—1
    Yes, feels guilty about amt. of paper involved in all of the requests—1
    Fax technology availability real service to students & staff—1

11. From which institution did you receive your materials?
    Northwestern—1
    Dartmouth—1
    Berlin—1
    Denver Public Library—1
    Oklahoma State University—1
    CU-Boulder—1
    Don't know—2

? QUESTIONS FOR WRITING AND DISCUSSION

1 Evaluate Meininger's final draft, using the peer response guidelines in this chapter. What are the strengths and weaknesses of her essay? Now read Meininger's first rough draft. Which areas did she improve most in her revision?

2 Based on her final draft, make a revised version of Meininger's three-column log. Write out each criterion, the main supporting evidence for that criterion, and the judgment. Indicate the paragraphs (by number) that Meininger devotes to each of her criteria.

3 In her postscript, Meininger wrote, "I revised my criteria and rearranged them in a different order after we talked in class. I didn't want to have my weakest criteria last." Compare her criteria (see her three-column log) with her revised draft. Explain how her additions, deletions, and reordering improved her criteria—and her essay.

4 Reread the questionnaire in Meininger's Appendix. How might she improve that questionnaire? What questions might she add or delete? How might she rephrase the questions?

5 Brainstorm a list of other campus services or organizations that you could evaluate. Choose one of those services or organizations and write a three-column log, indicating the subject, the audience, the criteria, and the possible kinds of evidence that you might collect for your essay.

STUDENT WRITING
COURTNEY KLOCKEMAN

Vulgar Propriety

For her evaluative essay, Courtney Klockeman wrote a critical review of the 2001 Oscar Award-winning musical, Moulin Rouge. *The original story is of a young English writer who comes to the Paris of Toulouse-Lautrec in 1899 and falls in love with the nightclub's leading performer and courtesan, Satine. The director's challenge, as Klockeman explains, is to convey the exciting and sensual scene of Montmartre in 1899 for a twenty-first century audience. As you read her essay, see if Klockeman evaluates the film based on clear criteria and evidence that support her thesis that the film "is over the top, but intentionally and meticulously so."*

Baz Luhrmann's rock opera *Moulin Rouge* has been called everything   *1* from vulgar and over the top to innovative and spectacular. Love it or hate it, Luhrmann knows how to draw attention. Edward Guthmann calls Luhrmann's vision "two hours of cranked up movie trailers: the volume is punishing, the pacing relentlessly fast and the gestures broad and obvious. Everything is punched up, overstressed" (C1). Indeed, Luhrmann seems to have emulated the things that entertain us: music videos, rock concerts, and "high octane thrill ride" movies. He managed to create a musical romance with the thrills and explosive appeal of all of the above, successfully captivating the A.D.D. MTV generation. The pure opulence of the film, especially the club, might over-stimulate some, but it accurately conveys the exciting lure that the Moulin Rouge has represented since its opening. The film *is* over the top, but intentionally and meticulously so. Each artistic decision reflects careful consideration for historical context and authenticity of costumes and sets while still keeping modern audiences enthralled.

Luhrmann faced a tremendous challenge in trying to shock a desensitized generation. He had to convey to a 21st century audience the temptations of the Moulin Rouge to its 19th century audience while still being fairly faithful to the period. In today's world girls walk around in low cut crop tops and high cut shorts on a regular basis, and shows on HBO would have been deemed pornography 30 years ago. The only way to shock us anymore is with excess—vibrant color, ornate detail and flamboyant movement so that we are repulsed yet strangely attracted to the frenzied energy of it all. It is a delicate and complex balance, for which Luhrmann turned to his wife and artistic director Catherine Martin. He had a vision and she made it a reality.

With an ambition for authenticity Martin and her co-costume designer Angus Strathie thoroughly researched 19th century France and the Moulin Rouge before beginning production. Their research spanned over several years and included much time in Montmartre and Paris Libraries (Litson 22). The trouble was to reconcile their vision of the film's impact with their research. To remain historically accurate while still connecting to their modern audience, they agreed to follow one main rule: if it existed in the 19th century, even if it wasn't used in every day life, they could use it. For instance, there is a bohemian musician wearing sunglasses when Christian first arrives in Montmartre. Martin explains that "sunglasses did exist in the 19th century, but they were a specific purpose item. Like if you were climbing Mount Everest and there was a glare from the snow" (Kaye 58). The sunglasses are a tiny stretch, but they make the musician easier for us to relate to, like one we might see on Pearl Street in Boulder.

Through their research, Martin and Strathie also learned that part of the appeal at the actual Moulin Rouge was that the dancers wore knickers that were split down the middle. If some of us were wondering what was so naughty about the cancan . . . mystery solved. Leaving that dirty little detail out was not an option if they were going to stay true to the times. At the same time an uncensored split knicker cancan would have earned them an R or possibly NC-17 rating, effectively eliminating a large portion of the movie-going public. Martin solved the problem by "conceal[ing] the areas that can be seen [so the girls had] a pink, smooth, Barbie-like area!" (Litson 22). Corsets, of course, were also essential to the costuming. Women used to cinch themselves up so tightly that they would fracture ribs and sometimes damage their internal organs. Naturally, clothing so tight restricts movement and makes dancing extremely difficult. Martin designed smaller corsets to mitigate the issue while keeping the extreme hourglass figures, but Nicole Kidman still cracked a rib during a scene (Litson 22).

Compared to the costumes, the set was fairly straightforward. The 5 original Moulin Rouge was excessive enough that Martin and Strathie needed only to create a replica of it. Even Satine's Hindi elephant was a part of the original (Litson 22). The inside of the dance hall was and still is very much like a circus, as it is portrayed in the film (Mac Devitt). There were some minor changes to the design for the sake of convenience or emphasis. The garden was placed in front instead of to the side of the dance hall to allow for smooth filming in and out of the club. Martin also added the gothic "brothel room." There were such rooms near the notorious dance hall and the dancers were, in fact, prostitutes, but there wasn't one in the hall itself (Litson 22). Martin's addition makes these particulars more assertive by visually and spatially combining the dance hall with its shady brothel aspect.

For some sets Martin sacrificed authenticity for effect. The city of 6 Paris from afar looks more like a picture book than a movie set. Some question the choice to use such post-card like scenery, but the dreamy image with the Eiffel Tower surrounded by quaint little buildings is just a flimsy romanticized façade for the gritty truth. Why not portray it for what it is? Montmartre was, and nightly still is, a seedy district. It is home to pimps and prostitutes, where beatnik artists earn wages on the streets. In the film, Christian seeks the romantic, iconic version and discovers instead the disturbing truth. The styles of the sets represent their distance from or closeness to the truth. During "Your Song" the set becomes surreal with a miniature Eiffel Tower and a singing moon while Satine and Christian dance on the clouds. In that scene, Satine is under the false impression that Christian is the Duke and Christian seems to be naïve of Satine's work as a prostitute. Essentially, they fall in love under false pretenses and the scenery reflects that falseness. Alternately, in the scene where they declare their love with full awareness of each others' identities ("Elephant Love Medley"), realism returns because there is no deception or misunderstanding. The scenes with Christian, Satine, and the Duke once again enter the realm of surreal due to his blissful ignorance of their love affair.

...*continued* Vulgar Propriety, **Courtney Klockeman**

To keep us spellbound, Strathie and Martin replaced a line of girls in 7 matching outfits with a fascinating diversity in color and style to "make [it as] extraordinary for now" as it was in 1899 (Litson 22). They turned an already challenging task into a Herculean feat by designing each individual dancer's costume with a theme in mind. There is a Hindi girl, a baby doll, a Greek goddess, a very heavily tattooed dominatrix, and more than 50 others. They started with sexual fetishes and moved on to nationalities when they ran out (Litson 22). Even in the "Tango de Roxanne," each dancer sports a unique undergarment. By the end of filming, the creative duo had meticulously clothed 15 primary actors, 60 dancers, and more than 600 extras in various scenes. Nicole Kidman alone wears more than 20 costumes throughout (Kaye 58).

The Moulin Rouge seems all the more opulent because of its stark 8 contrast from the outside world. The costumes and sets are more overwhelming in and around the Moulin Rouge than anywhere else. The color scheme is all red, black and gold and everything is heavily ornamented. Away from its influence, Christian's "humble abode" is comparatively minimalistic. It is dominated by whites and light neutrals and has only the bare essentials in furniture. Satine's costumes tend to match the surroundings. In and around the Moulin Rouge she is always corseted and fully accessorized. Like all of the dancers, she is trapped where "the show must go on." At Christian's flat, she is usually wearing only a white sheet or robe, free to be herself—not the temptress of the stage. The view from Christian's flat is the Moulin Rouge, seemingly innocent by day but lit up and dangerously alluring by night. The story's conflict arises in trying to reconcile these apparently incompatible worlds or else leave one behind.

Moulin Rouge may be an "audacious, rapid-fire assault on the 9 senses," but even Guthmann concedes that "it works" (C1). The gaudy display is not without a purpose, exposing us to the lurid temptations of the "tantric cancan" in a way we understand while revealing their destructive consequences. David Ansen and Dan Ephron eloquently conclude that "by reveling in all things artificial, [Moulin Rouge] arrives, giddily, at the genuine" (61). Luhrmann and Martin set out to shock us, thrill us, entertain us, and give us a musical like never before. Even their most "over-stimulated" and conservative critics can't deny that they achieved just that.

Works Consulted

Ansen, David and Dan Ephron. "Yes, 'Rouge' Can Can Can." *Newsweek* 137.22 (2001): 61. *LexisNexis Academic.* Web. 5 Mar. 2009.

Guthmann, Edward. "Red Hot." *San Francisco Chronicle* 1 June 2001 final ed: C1. *LexisNexis Academic.* Web. 5 Mar. 2009.

Kaye, Lori. "Clothes that Cancan." *Advocate* 839 (2001): 58. *Academic Search Premiere.* Web. 5 Mar. 2009.

Litson, Jo. "Rouging It." *Entertainment Design* 35.5 (2001): 22. *LexisNexis Academic.* Web. 5 Mar. 2009.

Mac Devitt, Aedin. "Le Moulin Rouge Cabaret." *About.com.* New York Times, 2008. Web. 5 Mar. 2009.

Moulin Rouge. Dir. Baz Luhrmann. Perf. Nicole Kidman, Ewan McGregor. 2001. 20th Century Fox, 2003. DVD.

QUESTIONS FOR WRITING AND DISCUSSION

1 In her review, Klockeman explains that the director's main task was to maintain historical accuracy while updating the context, costumes, and sets for a modern audience. If you have seen the film, would you agree that these adjustments do in fact make the film historically real and yet contemporary and exciting for a twenty-first century audience? Explain your response by commenting on scenes that you remember from the film.

2 Reread Klockeman's essay and then write out a three-column log (criteria, evidence, judgments) that she might have used to organize her evaluation. List the pieces of evidence that she uses for each of her criteria. Does she have sufficient evidence from the film to support her judgment of each criterion? Explain.

3 In her title, Klockeman tries to capture the edginess of the film by using the phrase, "vulgar propriety." Is this title effective for the essay? Would other oxymorons or phrases such as "tasteful pornography" also work for her title? Explain your choices.

4 Go online and read other reviews of *Moulin Rouge.* After reading those reviews, do you agree with Klockeman's evaluation? Do these reviews consider other criteria such as acting ability, plot, or character dialogue that you believe are important for evaluating the film? What criteria would you choose for your evaluation of this film?

5 Klockeman wrote her essay primarily for her writing class, but if she wanted to publish her essay, what newspaper, magazine, or online site would be most appropriate? Find two possible publications sites for her essay and explain why Klockeman's style and content would (or would not) be appropriate for that particular audience.

mycomplab

For additional writing, reading, and research resources, go to http://www.mycomplab.com

The MyPyramid campaign, "Steps to a Healthier You," by the United States Department of Agriculture, is designed to bring healthy diet advice to the American public. After analyzing the graphic and reading the advice in the text, answer discussion question 5 on page 403.

Problem Solving

10

After reading the headlines about the bankruptcies and closings of newspapers across America, you wonder what the future of journalism will be. Citizen journalism has become widespread, so you decide to investigate whether it can solve the problems created by the deterioration of professional print journalism. To replace professional journalists, citizen journalists would need to be able to inform the public and expose corruption and injustice in government and business. You decide to write your research questions and then create a questionnaire to gather information from students at your college about the effectiveness of online citizen journalism. After compiling your survey results and doing research on the current state of citizen journalism, you decide to argue that citizen journalism clearly has the potential to pick up the pieces left by traditional print journalism.

Trying to take notes in your Psych I lecture class—along with 250 other students— you realize that you are completely lost and confused. So you raise your hand to ask a question, but the professor keeps on talking, throwing out more new terms and examples. After class, when you think about how hard you've worked to pay your tuition, you realize that you deserve better classes for your money. The problem, you decide, is in the large lecture format—there are just too many students for the teacher to answer questions and explain difficult concepts. So you decide to write a letter to the head of the psychology department (with a copy to the dean of arts and sciences) outlining your problems with this class and proposing that Psychology I be taught in classes no larger than fifty.

> ❝ This country has more problems than it should tolerate and more solutions than it uses. ❞
> —RALPH NADER,
> CONSUMER RIGHTS ADVOCATE AND PRESIDENTIAL CANDIDATE

> ❝ Whenever life doesn't seem to give an answer, we create one. ❞
> —LORRAINE HANSBERRY
> AUTHOR OF *A RAISIN IN THE SUN*

W E DON'T HAVE TO LOOK DILIGENTLY TO LOCATE PROBLEMS IN OUR LIVES. THEY HAVE A HABIT OF SEEKING US OUT. IT SEEMS THAT IF SOMETHING CAN GO WRONG, IT WILL. COUNTRIES ARE FIGHTING EACH OTHER, GREENHOUSE GASES ARE CAUSING climate changes, prejudice is still rampant, television shows are too violent, sports are corrupted by drugs and money, education is too impersonal, and people drive so recklessly that you take your life in your hands every time you go across town. Everywhere we look, someone else creates problems for us—from minor bureaucratic hassles to serious or life-threatening situations. (On rare occasions, of course, we're part of the problem ourselves.)

Once we identify a potential problem, we must critically question and investigate the issue. Just because we think something is a problem does not mean that other people in other social, political, or cultural contexts will agree that it is a problem. For example, let's critically analyze what appears to be a straightforward issue: grade inflation. First, notice the language used to describe the issue. In this case, the word *inflation* suggests a negative bias; we are predisposed to think that any "inflation" is a bad thing. Next, we need to know who is involved in this issue and who has the most to gain or lose by its existence. What different positions are students, teachers, parents, school administrators, admissions officers at colleges, and companies who hire applicants likely to take on this issue? Some of these groups may see grade inflation as a serious problem, while others may not agree that it is a problem or that it even exists. Finally, we must gather the "facts" about grade inflation and the various definitions commonly used to describe it. There are statistics both proving and disproving that grade inflation exists and a variety of definitions for grade inflation.

Once you can identify something that is actually a problem for a specific group of people, the difficult part is to propose a solution and then persuade others that your solution will in fact solve the problem—without creating new problems and without costing too much. Because your proposal may ask readers to take some action, vote in a certain way, or actually work to implement your proposal, you must make sure that your readers vividly perceive the problem and agree that your plan outlines the most logical and feasible solution.

Techniques for Problem Solving

Problem solving requires all your skills as a writer. You need to observe carefully to see if a problem exists. You may need to remember experiences that illustrate the seriousness of the problem. You need to read and investigate which solutions have worked or have not worked. You often have to explain what the problem is and why or how your proposal would remedy the situation. You may need to evaluate both the problem and alternative solutions. To help you identify the problem and convince your readers of the soundness of your proposal, keep the following techniques in mind.

Techniques for Problem Solving

Technique	Tips on How to Do It
Analyzing the political, social, and cultural *contexts* of the problem	*When, where,* and *why* do some people perceive this issue as a problem? *What* groups of people are affected, and what do they have to gain or lose? *Who* would be most affected by a particular solution?
Identifying and understanding your *audience*	If you want something changed, fixed, improved, subsidized, banned, reorganized, or made legal or illegal, be sure to write to an audience that has the *power to help make this change.*
Demonstrating that a *problem exists*	Some problems are so obvious that your readers will readily acknowledge them: conflicts in the Middle East, air pollution and greenhouse gases in industrialized nations, high childhood obesity rates, high unemployment, and outsized CEO bonuses. Often, however, you must first convince your audience that a problem exists: Are genetically engineered crops a problem or would eliminating them cause even more problems?
Proposing a *solution* that will solve the problem	After convincing your readers that a serious problem exists, you must then propose a *remedy, plan,* or *course of action* that will reduce or eliminate the problem.
Persuading your readers that your proposal *will work*	You need to show that your solution is *feasible* and that it is better than *alternative solutions.* You convince your readers by supporting your proposal with *reasons* and *evidence.*

❝You see things; and you say, "Why?" But I dream things that never were; and I say, "Why not?" ❞
—GEORGE BERNARD SHAW, DRAMATIST

As you start your problem-solving paper, concentrate on ways to *narrow and focus* your topic. When you think about possible topics, follow the advice of environmentalists: "Think Globally, Act Locally." Rather than talk about education or drugs or crime or pollution on a national scale, find out how your community or campus is dealing with a problem. A local focus will help narrow your topic—and provide possibilities for using firsthand observations, personal experience, and interviews.

DEMONSTRATING THAT A PROBLEM EXISTS

A proposal begins with a description of a problem. Demonstrating that the problem exists (and is serious) will make your readers more receptive to your plan for a solution. The following selection from Frank Trippett's *Time* magazine essay "A Red Light for Scofflaws" identifies a problem and provides sufficient examples to demonstrate that scofflawry is pervasive and serious enough to warrant attention. Even if we haven't been personally attacked while driving the Houston or Miami or Los Angeles freeways, Trippett convinces us that *scofflawry*—deliberately disobeying ("scoffing at") laws—is serious. His vivid description makes us aware of the problem.

Demonstrating that a problem exists

Law and order is the longest-running and probably the best-loved political issue in U.S. history. Yet it is painfully apparent that millions of Americans who would never think of themselves as lawbreakers, let alone criminals, are taking increasing liberties with the legal codes that are designed to protect and nourish their society. Indeed, there are moments today—amid outlaw litter, tax cheating, illicit noise, and motorized anarchy—when it seems as though the scofflaw represents the wave of the future. Harvard sociologist David Riesman suspects that a majority of Americans have blithely taken to committing supposedly minor derelictions as a matter of course. Already, Riesman says, the ethic of U.S. society is in danger of becoming this: "You're a fool if you obey the rules."

Evidence: Authority

Evidence: Examples

The dangers of scofflawry vary wildly. The person who illegally spits on the sidewalk remains disgusting, but clearly poses less risk to others than the company that illegally buries hazardous chemical waste in an unauthorized location. The fare beater on the subway presents less threat to life than the landlord who ignores fire safety statutes. The most immediately and measurably dangerous scofflawry, however, also happens to be the most visible. The culprit is the American driver, whose lawless activities today add up to a colossal public nuisance. The hazards range from routine double parking that jams city streets to the drunk driving that kills some 25,000 people and injures at least 650,000 others yearly.

Evidence: Statistics

The most flagrant scofflaw of them all is the red-light runner. The flouting of stop signals has got so bad in Boston that residents tell an anecdote about a cabby who insists that red lights are "just for decoration." The power of the stoplight to control traffic seems to be waning everywhere. In Los Angeles, red-light running has become perhaps the city's most common traffic violation. In New York City, going through an intersection is like Russian roulette. Admits Police Commissioner Robert J. McGuire: "Today it's a 50–50 toss-up as to whether people will stop for a red light." Meanwhile, his own police largely ignore the lawbreaking.

Evidence: Authority

The prospect of the collapse of public manners is not merely a matter of etiquette. Society's first concern will remain major crime, but a foretaste of the seriousness of incivility is suggested by what has been happening in Houston. Drivers on Houston freeways have been showing an increasing tendency to replace the rules of the road with violent outbreaks. Items from the Houston police department's new statistical category—freeway traffic violence: (1) Driver flashes high-beam lights at car that cut in front of him, whose occupants then hurl a beer can at his windshield, kick out his tail lights, slug him eight stitches worth. (2) Dump-truck driver annoyed by delay batters trunk of stalled car ahead and its driver with steel bolt. (3) Hurrying driver of 18-wheel truck deliberately rear-ends car whose driver was trying to stay within 55 m.p.h. limit.

Evidence: Examples

PROPOSING A SOLUTION AND CONVINCING YOUR READERS

Once you have vividly described the problem, you are ready to propose a solution and persuade your readers. In the following selection from his book *Fist Stick Knife Gun,* Geoffrey Canada proposes ways to create a safer world for our children. Geoffrey Canada is president and CEO of Harlem's Rheedlen Center for Children and Families, an organization that serves at-risk inner-city children. He was recognized in 2009 for his work, with a nomination for *Time* magazine's most influential people. As you read Canada's proposal, notice how he narrows the problem to saving the lives of inner-city children. When he makes a recommendation, he talks about the advantages of his solution, but he talks about *feasibility problems* and real drawbacks. At several points, he gives *reasons* why we must change and supports his reasons with *evidence* from statistics and from his own personal experience.

If I could get the mayors, the governors, and the president to look into the eyes of the 5-year-olds of this nation, dressed in old raggedy clothes, whose jacket zippers are broken but whose dreams are still alive, they would know what I know—that children need people to fight for them. To stand with them on the most dangerous streets, in the dirtiest hallways, in their darkest hours. We as a country have been too willing to take from our weakest when times get hard. People who allow this to happen must be educated, must be challenged, must be turned around.

Personal experience

If we are to save our children we must become people they will look up to. We must stand up and be visible heroes. I want people to

Proposal

understand the crisis and I want people to act: Either we address the murder and mayhem in our country or we simply won't be able to continue to have the kind of democratic society that we as Americans cherish. Violence is not just a problem of the inner cities or of the minorities in this country. This is a national crisis and the nation must mobilize differently if we are to solve it.

Part of what we must do is change the way we think about violence. Trying to catch and punish people after they have committed a violent act won't deter violence in the least. In life on the street, it's better to go to jail than be killed, better to act quickly and decisively even if you risk being caught.

There are, however, things that governments could and should do right away to begin to end the violence on our streets. They include the following:

Specific recommendations

Specific details

Create a peace officer corps. Peace officers would not be police; they would not carry guns and would not be charged with making arrests. Instead they would be local men and women hired to work with children in their own neighborhoods. They would try to settle "beefs" and mediate disputes. They would not be the eyes and ears of the regular police force. Their job would be to try to get these young people jobs, to get them back into school, and, most importantly, to be at the emergency rooms and funerals where young people come together to grieve and plot revenge, in order to keep them from killing one another.

Recommendation

Reduce the demand for drugs. Any real effort at diverting the next generation of kids from selling drugs must include plans to find employment for these children when they become teenagers. While that will require a significant expenditure of public funds, the savings from reduced hospitalization and reduced incarceration will more than offset the costs of employment. . . .

Recommendation

Reduce the amount of violence on television and in the movies. Violence in the media is ever more graphic, and the justification for acting violently is deeply implanted in young people's minds. The movie industry promotes the message that power is determined not merely by carrying a gun, but by carrying a big gun that is an automatic and has a big clip containing many bullets.

Reason + evidence

What about rap music, and especially "gangsta rap"? It is my opinion that people have concentrated too much attention on this one source of media violence. Many rap songs are positive, and some are neither positive nor negative—just kids telling their stories. But there are some rap singers who have decided that their niche in the music industry will be the most violent and vile. I would love to see the record industry show some restraint in limiting these rappers' access to fame and fortune.

Reduce and regulate the possession of handguns. I believe all handgun sales should be banned in this country. Recognizing, however, that other Americans may not be ready to accept a ban on handguns, I believe there are still some things we must do.

Recommendation

Licensing. Every person who wants to buy a handgun should have to pass both a written test and a field test. The cost for these new procedures should be paid by those who make, sell, and buy handguns. . . .

Recommendation

Gun buy-backs. The federal government, which recently passed a $32 billion crime bill, needs to invest billions of dollars over the next ten years buying guns back from citizens. We now have more than 200 million guns in circulation in our country. A properly cared-for gun can last for decades. There is no way we can deal with handgun violence until we reduce the number of guns currently in circulation. We know that young people won't give up their guns readily, but we have to keep in mind that this is a long-term problem. We have to begin to plan now to get the guns currently in the hands of children out of circulation permanently.

Recommendation

Statistics

The truth of the matter is that reducing the escalating violence will be complicated and costly. If we were fighting an outside enemy that was killing our children at a rate of more than 5,000 a year, we would spare no expense. What happens when the enemy is us? What happens when those Americans' children are mostly black and brown? Do we still have the will to invest the time and resources in saving their lives? The answer must be yes, because the impact and fear of violence has over-run the boundaries of our ghettos and has both its hands firmly around the neck of our whole country. And while you may not yet have been visited by the spectre of death and fear of this new national cancer, just give it time. Sooner or later, unless we act, you will. We all will.

Response to feasibility problems

Evidence

Call to action

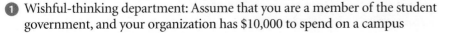

WARMING UP **Journal Exercises**

The following exercises will help you practice problem solving. Read all of the following exercises and then write on one or two that interest you most. If another idea occurs to you, write about it.

1 Wishful-thinking department: Assume that you are a member of the student government, and your organization has $10,000 to spend on a campus

improvement project. Think of some campus problem that needs solving. Describe why it is a problem. Then outline your plan for a solution, indicating how you would spend the money to help solve the problem.

2 Reread Frank Trippett's analysis of the scofflaw problem. Write a letter to the city council recommending a solution to one of the problems that Trippett identifies—a solution that the city council has the power to implement.

3 Eldridge Cleaver once said, "You're either part of the solution or part of the problem." Examine one of your activities or pastimes—sports, shopping, cruising, eating, drinking, or even studying. How does what you do possibly create a problem from someone else's point of view? Explain.

4 The following visual, with an accompanying paragraph, appears on the United Nations Children's Fund (UNICEF) Web site at http://www .unicef.org. Analyze the effectiveness of the image and text in demonstrating the problem of child labor. What details in the picture support the argument that child labor is a problem we must solve?

> **66** A good solution solves more than one problem, and it does not make new problems. I am talking about health as opposed to almost any cure, coherence of pattern as opposed to almost any solution produced piecemeal or in isolation. **99**
>
> —WENDELL BERRY,
> AUTHOR OF *THE GIFT OF THE GOOD LAND*

A small boy sleeps at the table where he was making softballs in the village of Cholomo, Honduras.

Some people say that boycotts—that is, refusing to buy goods made by children—will help put an end to child labour. But boycotts can also hurt working children and their families, as the children lose their jobs, and then their families have even less money to live on. If employers provided parents with jobs at a living wage, fewer children would be forced to go to work. (UNICEF/89-0052/Vauclair)

5. "Let the buyer beware" is a time-honored maxim for all consumers. Unless you are vigilant, you can easily be ripped off. Write a letter to the Better Business Bureau explaining some consumer problem or rip-off that you've recently experienced and suggest a solution that will prevent others from being exploited.

6. Changing the rules of some sports might make them more enjoyable, less violent, or fairer: moving the three-point line farther out, introducing the 30-second clock in NCAA basketball, using TV instant replays in professional and college football and basketball, imposing stiffer fines for brawls in hockey games, requiring boxers to wear padded helmets, giving equal pay and media coverage to women's sports. Choose a sport you enjoy as a participant or observer, identify and explain the problem you want to solve, and justify your solution in a letter to the editors of *Sports Illustrated*.

7. The increasing use of sites such as Turnitin.com to check student papers for plagiarism has led to disagreement about how best to respond to possible cases of plagiarism. In the following passage, John Barrie, President of Turnitin.com, says that plagiarism is a "digital problem [that] demands a digital solution." Representing the point of view of many writing teachers, Rebecca Moore Howard claims that the best solution is to prevent plagiarism by teaching students how to access, use, and document sources. Read these two responses and decide which writer proposes the better overall solution.

> 66 God, give us grace to accept with serenity the things that cannot be changed, courage to change the things which should be changed, and the wisdom to distinguish the one from the other. 99
>
> —REINHOLD NIEBUHR, AUTHOR AND THEOLOGIAN

PROFESSIONAL WRITING

Should Educators Use Commercial Services to Combat Plagiarism?

Pro

The following is a summary of John Barrie's argument, which appeared in the CQ Researcher *in 2003. (Mr. Barrie declined to give permission to reproduce his remarks as they appear there.) The entire article can be read on the* CQ Researcher *Web site (http://library.cqpress.com/cqresearcher).*

Mr. Barrie believes that because we all "draw from the past to create the present," our writing and learning in schools and colleges should take advantage of the power of collaboration. Students should, Barrie believes, be able to "share ideas and criticism" as they work to prepare a high school report about a Shakespeare play or a college level paper about Nietzsche's philosophy. "The problem begins," Barrie acknowledges, "when faculty cannot determine whether a student wrote a term paper or plagiarized it from other sources." Barrie cites a recent study by Rutgers University Professor Donald McCabe that concludes that "nearly 40% of college undergraduates admitted to plagiarizing term papers" by lifting information directly from Internet sources. Solving this growing problem of plagiarism, Barrie argues, requires a solution that goes beyond the "status quo" of campus honor codes, detective work by faculty, and punishments for plagiarism. "Digital plagiarism," Barrie says, "is a digital problem [that] demands a digital solution." According to Barrie, TurnItIn is an important part of that solution. It receives thousands of essays to check each day and finds that "30 percent of those papers are less than original." Barrie concludes by arguing that educators and administrators should not "shirk their responsibility" as educators and should "demand original work" from all students by using plagiarism detection programs such as TurnItIn.

Con

Rebecca Moore Howard

Associate Professor of Writing and Rhetoric, Syracuse University

Teaching, not software, is the key to preventing plagiarism. Today's students can access an array of electronic texts and images unimaginable just 20 years ago, and students' relationship to the practice of information-sharing has changed along with the technology.

But today's students lack extensive training and experience in working carefully from print sources, and they may not understand that they need to learn this skill. They may also find it difficult to differentiate between kinds of sources on the Internet. With information arriving as a cacophony of electronic voices, even well-intentioned students have difficulty keeping track of—much less citing—who said what.

Moreover, the sheer volume of available information frequently leaves student writers feeling that they have nothing new to say about an issue. Hence too many students—one in three, according to a recent survey conducted by Rutgers University Professor Donald McCabe—may fulfill assignments by submitting work they have not written.

Were we in the throes of widespread moral decay, capture-and-punishment might provide an appropriate deterrent. We are, however, in the midst of a revolution in literacy, and teachers' responses must be more complex. They must address the underlying issues: students' ability to conduct research, comprehend extended written arguments, evaluate sources and produce their own persuasive written texts, in explicit dialogue with their sources.

Classrooms must engage students in text and in learning—communicating a value to these activities that extends beyond grades earned and credentials accrued. McCabe, who is a founder of the renowned Center for Academic Integrity at Duke University, recommends pedagogy and policies that speak to the causes of plagiarism, rather than buying software for detection and punishment. In a 2003 position statement, the Council of Writing Program Administrators urges, "Students should understand research assignments as opportunities for genuine and rigorous inquiry and learning." The statement offers extensive classroom suggestions for teachers and cautions that using plagiarism-catching software may "justify the avoidance of responsible teaching methods."

Buying software instead of revitalizing one's teaching means that teachers, like students, have allowed the electronic environment to encourage a reductive, automated vision of the educational experience. As one of my colleagues recently remarked, "The 'world's leading plagiarism-prevention system' is not TurnItIn.com—it's careful pedagogy."

PROFESSIONAL WRITING

One Thing to Do About Food

Eric Schlosser, Marion Nestle, Michael Pollan, Troy Duster and Elizabeth Ransom, Peter Singer, and Jim Hightower

It is well known that the United States faces an epidemic of problems related to food: childhood obesity, type II diabetes in adults, junk food advertising to children, unhealthy eating by adults, exploitative farm legislation, unsafe working conditions for agricultural laborers, factory farm cruelty to animals, and overall ignorance on the part of the American public about how food is produced. In a forum edited by Alice Waters for The Nation *magazine, the following seven authors were among a group of twelve writers contributing short responses about reforming food production, regulation, and consumption in the United States. Following each short response, Alice Waters provides a brief biographical sketch of the author. As you read each selection, consider how each author's proposal relates to his or her professional expertise and how all these potential solutions relate to each other and to an overall solution to the problem.*

Eric Schlosser

Every year the fast-food chains, soda companies and processed-food *1* manufacturers spend billions marketing their products. You see their ads all the time. They tend to feature a lot of attractive, happy, skinny people having fun. But you rarely see what's most important about the food: where it comes from, how it's made and what it contains. Tyson ads don't show chickens crammed together at the company's factory farms, and Oscar Mayer ads don't reveal what really goes into those wieners. There's a good reason for this. Once you learn how our modern industrial food system has transformed what most Americans eat, you become highly motivated to eat something else.

The National Uniformity for Food Act of 2005, passed by the House *2* and now before the Senate, is a fine example of how food companies and their allies work hard to keep consumers in the dark. Backed by the American Beverage Association, the American Frozen Food Association, the Coca-Cola Company, ConAgra Foods, the National Restaurant Association, the International Food Additives Council, Kraft Foods, the National Cattlemen's Beef Association and the US Chamber of Commerce, among many others, the new law would prevent states from having food safety or labeling requirements stricter than those of the federal government. In the name of "uniformity," it would impose rules that are uniformly bad. State laws that keep lead out of children's candy and warn pregnant women about dangerous ingredients would be wiped off the books.

What single thing could change the US food system, practically *3* overnight? Widespread public awareness—of how this system operates and whom it benefits, how it harms consumers, how it mistreats animals and pollutes the land, how it corrupts public officials and intimidates the press, and most of all, how its power ultimately depends on a series of cheerful and ingenious lies. The modern environmental movement began forty-four years ago when *Silent Spring* exposed the deceptions behind the idea of "better living through chemistry." A similar movement is now gaining momentum on behalf of sustainable agriculture and real food. We must not allow the fast-food industry, agribusiness and Congress to deceive us. "We urgently need an end to these false assurances, to the sugar-coating of unpalatable facts," Rachel Carson famously argued. "In the words of Jean Rostand, 'The obligation to endure gives us the right to know.'"

Eric Schlosser is the author of Fast Food Nation: The Dark Side of the All-American Meal *and, with Charles Wilson,* Chew on This: Everything You Don't Want to Know About Fast Food *(both Houghton Mifflin).*

Marion Nestle

From a public health perspective, obesity is the most serious nutri- *1* tion problem among children as well as adults in the United States. The roots of this problem can be traced to farm policies and Wall Street. Farm subsidies, tariffs and trade agreements support a food supply that provides 3,900 calories per day per capita, roughly twice the average need, and 700 calories a day higher than in 1980, at the dawn of the obesity epidemic. In this overabundant food economy, companies must compete fiercely for sales, not least because of Wall Street's expectations for quarterly growth. These pressures induce companies to make highly profitable "junk" foods, market them directly to children and advertise such foods as appropriate for consumption at all times, in large amounts, by children of all ages. In this business environment, childhood obesity is just collateral damage.

Adults may be fair game for marketers, but children are not. Chil- 2 dren cannot distinguish sales pitches from information unless taught to do so. Food companies spend at least $10 billion annually enticing children to desire food brands and to pester parents to buy them. The result: American children consume more than one-third of their daily calories from soft drinks, sweets, salty snacks and fast food. Worse, food marketing subverts parental authority by making children believe they are supposed to be eating such foods and they—not their parents—know what is best for them to eat.

Today's marketing methods extend beyond television to include 3 Internet games, product placements, character licensing and word-of-mouth campaigns—stealth methods likely to be invisible to parents. When restrictions have been called for, the food industry has resisted, invoking parental responsibility and First Amendment rights, and proposing self-regulation instead. But because companies cannot be expected to act against corporate self-interest, government regulations are essential. Industry pressures killed attempts to regulate television advertising to children in the late 1970s, but obesity is a more serious problem now.

It is time to try again, this time to stop all forms of marketing foods 4 to kids—both visible and stealth. Countries in Europe and elsewhere are taking such actions, and we could too. Controls on marketing may not be sufficient to prevent childhood obesity, but they would make it easier for parents to help children to eat more healthfully.

Marion Nestle, Paulette Goddard Professor of Nutrition, Food Studies and Public Health at New York University, is the author of Food Politics (*California*) *and* What to Eat (*North Point*).

Michael Pollan

Every five years or so the President of the United States signs an ob- 1 scure piece of legislation that determines what happens on a couple of hundred million acres of private land in America, what sort of food Americans eat (and how much it costs) and, as a result, the health of our population. In a nation consecrated to the idea of private property and

...continued One Thing to Do About Food, **Michael Pollan**

free enterprise, you would not think any piece of legislation could have such far-reaching effects, especially one about which so few of us—even the most politically aware—know anything. But in fact the American food system is a game played according to a precise set of rules that are written by the federal government with virtually no input from anyone beyond a handful of farm-state legislators. Nothing could do more to reform America's food system—and by doing so improve the condition of America's environment and public health—than if the rest of us were suddenly to weigh in.

The farm bill determines what our kids eat for lunch in school 2 every day. Right now, the school lunch program is designed not around the goal of children's health but to help dispose of surplus agricultural commodities, especially cheap feedlot beef and dairy products, both high in fat.

The farm bill writes the regulatory rules governing the production of 3 meat in this country, determining whether the meat we eat comes from sprawling, brutal, polluting factory farms and the big four meatpackers (which control 80 percent of the market) or from local farms.

Most important, the farm bill determines what crops the govern- 4 ment will support—and in turn what kinds of foods will be plentiful and cheap. Today that means, by and large, corn and soybeans. These two crops are the building blocks of the fast-food nation: A McDonald's meal (and most of the processed food in your supermarket) consists of clever arrangements of corn and soybeans—the corn providing the added sugars, the soy providing the added fat, and both providing the feed for the animals. These crop subsidies (which are designed to encourage overproduction rather than to help farmers by supporting prices) are the reason that the cheapest calories in an American supermarket are precisely the unhealthiest. An American shopping for food on a budget soon discovers that a dollar buys hundreds more calories in the snack food or soda aisle than it does in the produce section. Why? Because the farm bill supports the growing of corn but not the growing of fresh carrots. In the midst of a national epidemic of diabetes and obesity our government is, in effect, subsidizing the production of high-fructose corn syrup.

This absurdity would not persist if more voters realized that the 5 farm bill is not a parochial piece of legislation concerning only the interests of farmers. Today, because so few of us realize we have a dog in this fight, our legislators feel free to leave deliberations over the farm bill to the farm states, very often trading away their votes on agricultural policy for votes on issues that matter more to their constituents. But what could matter more than the health of our children and the health of our land?

Perhaps the problem begins with the fact that this legislation is 6 commonly called "the farm bill"—how many people these days even know a farmer or care about agriculture? Yet we all eat. So perhaps that's where we should start, now that the debate over the 2007 farm bill is about to be joined. This time around let's call it "the food bill" and put our legislators on notice that this is about us and we're paying attention.

Michael Pollan, Knight Professor of Journalism at the University of California, Berkeley, is the author of The Omnivore's Dilemma: A Natural History of Four Meals *(Penguin).*

Troy Duster and Elizabeth Ransom

Strong preferences for the kinds of food we eat are deeply rooted 1 in the unexamined practices of the families, communities and cultural groups in which we grow up. From more than a half-century of social science research, we know that changing people's habitual behavior— from smoking to alcohol consumption, from drugs to junk food—is a mighty task. Individuals rarely listen to health messages and then change their ways.

If we as a nation are to alter our eating habits so that we make a no- 2 table dent in the coming health crisis around the pandemic of childhood obesity and Type II diabetes, it will be the result of long-term planning that will include going into the schools to change the way we learn about food. With less than 2 percent of the US population engaged with agriculture, a whole generation of people has lost valuable knowledge that comes from growing, preserving and preparing one's own food. A recent initiative by the City of Berkeley, California, represents a promising national model to fill this void. The city's Unified School District has approved a school lunch program that is far more than just a project to change what students eat at the noon hour. It is a daring attempt to change the institutional environment in which children learn about food at an early age, a comprehensive approach that has them planting and growing the food in a garden, learning biology through an engaged process, with some then cooking the food that they grow. If all goes well, they will learn about the complex relationship between nutrition and physiology so that it is an integrated experience—not a decontextualized, abstract, rote process.

But this is a major undertaking, and it will need close monitoring 3 and fine-tuning. Rather than assuming that one size fits all in the school, we will need to find out what menu resonates with schools that are embedded within local cultures and climatic conditions—for example, teaching a health-mindful approach to Mexican, Chinese, Italian, Puerto Rican, Caribbean and Midwestern cuisine. Finally, we need to regulate the kinds of food sold in and around the school site—much as we now do with smoking, alcohol and drugs. The transition from agrarian to modern society has created unforeseen health challenges. Adopting an

...continued One Thing to Do About Food, **Troy Duster and Elizabeth Ransom**

engaged learning approach through agricultural production and consumption will help future generations learn what it means to eat healthy food and live healthy lives.

Troy Duster, director of the Institute for the History of Production of Knowledge at New York University, holds an appointment as Chancellor's Professor at the University of California, Berkeley. Elizabeth Ransom is a sociologist at the University of Richmond whose work focuses on globalization, food and the changing structure of agriculture.

Peter Singer

There is one very simple thing that everyone can do to fix the food *1* system. Don't buy factory-farm products.

Once, the animals we raised went out and gathered things we could *2* not or would not eat. Cows ate grass, chickens pecked at worms or seeds. Now the animals are brought together and we grow food for them. We use synthetic fertilizers and oil-powered tractors to grow corn or soybeans. Then we truck it to the animals so they can eat it.

When we feed grains and soybeans to animals, we lose most of their *3* nutritional value. The animals use it to keep their bodies warm and to develop bones and other body parts that we cannot eat. Pig farms use six pounds of grain for every pound of boneless meat we get from them. For cattle in feedlots, the ratio is 13:1. Even for chickens, the least inefficient factory-farmed meat, the ratio is 3:1.

Most Americans think the best thing they could do to cut their personal contributions to global warming is to swap their family car for a fuel-efficient hybrid like the Toyota Prius. Gidon Eshel and Pamela Martin of the University of Chicago have calculated that typical meat-eating Americans would reduce their emissions even more if they switched to a vegan diet. Factory farming is not sustainable. It is also the biggest system of cruelty to animals ever devised. In the United States alone, every year nearly 10 billion animals live out their entire lives confined indoors. Hens are jammed into wire cages, five or six of them in a space that would be too small for even one hen to be able to spread her wings. Twenty thousand chickens are raised in a single shed, completely covering its floor. Pregnant sows are kept in crates too narrow for them to turn around, and too small for them to walk a few steps. Veal calves are similarly confined, and deliberately kept anemic.

This is not an ethically defensible system of food production. But in *5* the United States—unlike in Europe—the political process seems powerless to constrain it. The best way to fight back is to stop buying its products. Going vegetarian is a good option, and going vegan, better still. But if you continue to eat animal products, at least boycott factory farms.

Peter Singer is a professor of bioethics at Princeton University. His most recent book, co-written with Jim Mason, is The Way We Eat: Why Our Food Choices Matter *(Rodale).*

Jim Hightower

In the very short span of about fifty years, we've allowed our politi- 1
cians to do something remarkably stupid: turn America's food-policy decisions over to corporate lobbyists, lawyers and economists. These are
people who could not run a watermelon stand if we gave them the melons and had the Highway Patrol flag down the customers for them—yet,
they have taken charge of the decisions that direct everything from how
and where food is grown to what our children eat in school.

As a result, America's food system (and much of the world's) has 2
been industrialized, conglomeratized and globalized. This is food we're
talking about, not widgets! Food, by its very nature, is meant to be agrarian, small-scale and local.

But the Powers That Be have turned the production of our edibles away 3
from the high art of cooperating with nature into a high-cost system of always trying to overwhelm nature. They actually torture food—applying
massive doses of pesticides, sex hormones, antibiotics, genetically manipu-
lated organisms, artificial flavorings and color, chemical preservatives,
ripening gas, irradiation . . . and so awfully much more. The attitude of
agribusiness is that if brute force isn't working, you're probably just not using enough of it.

More fundamentally, these short-cut con artists have perverted the 4
very concept of food. Rather than being both a process and product that
nurtures us (in body and spirit) and nurtures our communities, food is
approached by agribusiness as just another commodity that has no
higher purpose than to fatten corporate profits.

There's our challenge. It's not a particular policy or agency that must 5
be changed but the most basic attitude of policy-makers. And the only way
we're going to get that done is for you and me to become the policy-makers, taking charge of every aspect of our food system—from farm to fork.

The good news is that this "good food" movement is already well un- 6
der way and gaining strength every day. It receives little media coverage, but
consumers in practically every city, town and neighborhood across America are reconnecting with local farmers and artisans to de-industrialize, de-
conglomeratize, de-globalize—de-Wal-Martize—their food systems.

Of course, the Powers That Be sneer at these efforts, saying they can't 7
succeed. But, as a friend of mine who is one of the successful pioneers in
this burgeoning movement puts it: "Those who say it can't be done
should not interrupt those who are doing it."

Look around wherever you are and you'll find local farmers, con- 8
sumers, chefs, marketers, gardeners, environmentalists, workers, churches,
co-ops, community organizers and just plain folks who are doing it. These
are the Powers That Ought to Be—and I think they will be. Join them!

Jim Hightower (www.jimhightower.com) *is a syndicated newspaper columnist, a radio commen-
tator and the author of six books including* Thieves in High Places (*Plume*).

vo·cab·u·lar·y

In your journal, write the meaning of the italicized words in the following phrases.

Eric Schlosser
- series of cheerful and *ingenious* lies **(3)**
- *sustainable* agriculture **(3)**
- sugar-coating of *unpalatable* facts **(3)**

Marion Nestle
- food marketing *subverts* parental authority **(2)**
- *product placements* **(3)**
- *stealth* methods **(3)**

Michael Pollan
- a nation *consecrated* to the idea of private property **(1)**
- *subsidizing* the production **(4)**
- not a *parochial* piece of legislation **(5)**

Troy Duster and Elizabeth Ransom
- the *pandemic* of childhood obesity **(2)**
- not a *decontextualized*, abstract, *rote* process **(2)**

- what menu *resonates* with schools **(3)**
- transition from *agrarian* to modern society **(3)**

Peter Singer
- use *synthetic* fertilizers **(2)**
- switched to a *vegan* diet **(4)**
- factory farming is not *sustainable* **(4)**
- deliberately kept *anemic* **(4)**
- not an *ethically* defensible system **(5)**

Jim Hightower
- has been industrialized, *conglomeratized* and globalized **(2)**
- attitude of *agribusiness* **(3)**
- pioneers in this *burgeoning* movement **(7)**

 QUESTIONS FOR WRITING AND DISCUSSION

1 Choose one of the short essays and annotate it for the analysis of the problem and then for the proposed solution. For this author, how much discussion is about the problem and how much about the solution? Which part—the discussion of the problem or the explanation of the solution—is more specific, detailed, and supported? What parts could be explained further to make the author's recommendations more effective or more persuasive? Be prepared to present your findings in class.

2 Find and underline each author's claim statement. What "one thing" does each author recommend should be done to address the problem? What reasons and evidence does each author offer in support of his or her claim? Explain.

3 Do your own library or Web research on issues related to the topics in these responses. Check out an award-winning cartoon critiquing factory farms at www.themeatrix.com. A popular Web site for issues related to animal rights and vegetarianism is People for the Ethical Treatment of Animals (PETA) at http://www.peta.org. For an overview of effective farming practices, visit Polyface Farms at http://polyface.com. Finally, Michael Pollan's book *The Omnivore's Dilemma* addresses many of the issues raised in these authors' responses. Write up your research notes in a short investigative report to the members of your class.

4 Assume that Alice Waters has asked you to contribute a short essay to this forum. Write an essay that explains your position about food production and eating habits, and offer your best suggestion for resolving the problems presented in these essays.

5 Analyze the MyPyramid graphic that appears on the opening page of this chapter. Find at least one passage in each of the above essays that relates to the MyPyramid guidelines. Which of these articles mention solutions that most closely parallel the dietary solutions suggested in the MyPyramid campaign? Explain your choice.

PROFESSIONAL WRITING

The Argument Culture

Deborah Tannen

A professor of linguistics at Georgetown University, Deborah Tannen is also a best-selling author of many books on discourse and gender, including You Just Don't Understand: Women and Men in Conversation *(1990),* Talking from 9 to 5 *(1994),* The Argument Culture: Moving from Debate to Dialogue *(1998), and* I Only Say This Because I Love You *(2001). Throughout her career, Tannen has focused on how men and women have different conversational habits and assumptions, whether they talk on the job or at home. In the following essay, taken from* The Argument Culture, *Tannen tries to convince her readers that adversarial debates—which typically represent only two sides of an issue and thus promote antagonism—create problems in communication. As a culture, Tannen believes, we would be much more successful if we didn't always think of argument as a war or a fight but as a dialogue among a variety of different positions. As you read her essay, does Tannen persuade you that our "argument culture" really is a problem and that her solutions will help solve that problem?*

Balance. Debate. Listening to both sides. Who could question these *1* noble American traditions? Yet today, these principles have been distorted. Without thinking, we have plunged headfirst into what I call the "argument culture."

...*continued* The Argument Culture, **Deborah Tannen**

"What about here? This looks like a good spot for an argument."

The argument culture urges us to approach the world, and the people in it, in an adversarial frame of mind. It rests on the assumption that opposition is the best way to get anything done: The best way to discuss an idea is to set up a debate; the best way to cover news is to find spokespeople who express the most extreme, polarized views and present them as "both sides"; the best way to settle disputes is litigation that pits one party against the other; the best way to begin an essay is to attack someone; and the best way to show you're really thinking is to criticize.

More and more, our public interactions have become like arguing with a spouse. Conflict can't be avoided in our public lives any more than we can avoid conflict with people we love. One of the great strengths of our society is that we can express these conflicts openly. But just as spouses have to learn ways of settling their differences without inflicting real damage, so we, as a society, have to find constructive ways of resolving disputes and differences.

The war on drugs, the war on cancer, the battle of the sexes, politicians' turf battles—in the argument culture, war metaphors pervade our talk and shape our thinking. The cover headlines of both *Time* and *Newsweek* one recent week are a case in point: "The Secret Sex Wars," proclaims *Newsweek*. "Starr at War," declares *Time*. Nearly everything is framed as a battle or game in which winning or losing is the main concern.

The argument culture pervades every aspect of our lives today. Is- 5 sues from global warming to abortion are depicted as two-sided arguments, when in fact most Americans' views lie somewhere in the middle. Partisanship makes gridlock in Washington the norm. Even in our personal relationships, a "let it all hang out" philosophy emphasizes people expressing their anger without giving them constructive ways of settling differences.

Sometimes You Have to Fight

There are times when it is necessary and right to fight—to defend 6 your country or yourself, to argue for your rights or against offensive or dangerous ideas or actions. What's wrong with the argument culture is the ubiquity, the knee-jerk nature of approaching any issue, problem or public person in an adversarial way.

Our determination to pursue truth by setting up a fight between 7 two sides leads us to assume that every issue has two sides—no more, no less. But if you always assume there must be an "other side," you may end up scouring the margins of science or the fringes of lunacy to find it.

This accounts, in part, for the bizarre phenomenon of Holocaust 8 denial. Deniers, as Emory University professor Deborah Lipstadt shows, have been successful in gaining TV air time and campus newspaper coverage by masquerading as "the other side" in a "debate." Continual reference to "the other side" results in a conviction that everything has another side—and people begin to doubt the existence of any facts at all.

The power of words to shape perception has been proved by re- 9 searchers in controlled experiments. Psychologists Elizabeth Loftus and John Palmer, for example, found that the terms in which people are asked to recall something affect what they recall. The researchers showed subjects a film of two cars colliding, then asked how fast the cars were going; one week later they asked whether there had been any broken glass. Some subjects were asked, "How fast were the cars going when they bumped into each other?" Others were asked, "How fast were the cars going when they smashed into each other?"

Those who read the question with "smashed" tended to "remem- 10 ber" that the cars were going faster. They were also more likely to "remember" having seen broken glass. (There wasn't any.) This is how language works. It invisibly molds our way of thinking about people, actions and the world around us.

In the argument culture, "critical" thinking is synonymous with crit- 11 icizing. In many classrooms, students are encouraged to read someone's life work, then rip it to shreds.

...continued The Argument Culture, **Deborah Tannen**

When debates and fighting predominate, those who enjoy verbal *12* sparring are likely to take part—by calling in to talk shows or writing letters to the editor. Those who aren't comfortable with oppositional discourse are likely to opt out.

How High-Tech Communication Pulls Us Apart

One of the most effective ways to defuse antagonism between two *13* groups is to provide a forum for individuals from those groups to get to know each other personally. What is happening in our lives, however, is just the opposite. More and more of our communication is not face to face, and not with people we know. The proliferation and increasing portability of technology isolates people in a bubble.

Along with the voices of family members and friends, phone lines *14* bring into our homes the annoying voices of solicitors who want to sell something—generally at dinnertime. (My father-in-law startles phone solicitors by saying, "We're eating dinner, but I'll call you back. What's your home phone number?" To the nonplused caller, he explains, "Well, you're calling me at home; I thought I'd call you at home, too.")

It is common for families to have more than one TV, so the adults can *15* watch what they like in one room and the kids can watch their choice in another—or maybe each child has a private TV.

E-mail, and now the Internet, are creating networks of human con- *16* nection unthinkable even a few years ago. Though e-mail has enhanced communication with family and friends, it also ratchets up the anonymity of both sender and receiver, resulting in stranger-to-stranger "flaming."

"Road rage" shows how dangerous the argument culture—and espe- *17* cially today's technologically enhanced aggression—can be. Two men who engage in a shouting match may not come to blows, but if they express their anger while driving down a public highway, the risk to themselves and others soars.

The Argument Culture Shapes Who We Are

The argument culture has a defining impact on our lives and on our *18* culture.

- **It makes us distort facts,** as in the Nancy Kerrigan-Tonya Harding story. After the original attack on Kerrigan's knee, news stories focused on the rivalry between the two skaters instead of portraying Kerrigan as the victim of an attack. Just last month, *Time* magazine called the event a "contretemps" between Kerrigan and Harding. And a recent joint TV interview of the two skaters reinforced that skewed image by putting the two on equal footing, rather than as victim and accused.

- **It makes us waste valuable time,** as in the case of scientist Robert Gallo, who co-discovered the AIDS virus. Gallo was the object of a groundless four-year investigation into allegations he had stolen the virus from another scientist. He was ultimately exonerated, but the toll was enormous. Never mind that, in his words, "These were the most painful and horrible years of my life." Gallo spent four years fighting accusations instead of fighting AIDS.

- **It limits our thinking.** Headlines are intentionally devised to attract attention, but the language of extremes actually shapes, and mis-shapes, the way we think about things. Military metaphors train us to think about, and see, everything in terms of fighting, conflict and war. Adversarial rhetoric is a kind of verbal inflation—a rhetorical boy-who-cried-wolf.

- **It encourages us to lie.** If you fight to win, the temptation is great to deny facts that support your opponent's views and say only what supports your side. It encourages people to misrepresent and, in the extreme, to lie.

End the Argument Culture by Looking at All Sides

How can we overcome our classically American habit of seeing issues 19 in absolutes? We must expand our notion of "debate" to include more dialogue. To do this, we can make special efforts not to think in twos. Mary Catherine Bateson, an anthropologist at Virginia's George Mason University, makes a point of having her class compare three cultures, not two. Then, students are more likely to think about each on its own terms, rather than as opposites.

In the public arena, television and radio producers can try to avoid, 20 whenever possible, structuring public discussions as debates. This means avoiding the format of having two guests discuss an issue. Invite three guests—or one. Perhaps it is time to re-examine the assumption that audiences always prefer a fight.

Instead of asking, "What's the other side?" we might ask, "What are 21 the other sides?" Instead of insisting on hearing "both sides," let's insist on hearing "all sides."

We need to find metaphors other than sports and war. Smashing 22 heads does not open minds. We need to use our imaginations and ingenuity to find different ways to seek truth and gain knowledge through intellectual interchange, and add them to our arsenal—or, should I say, to the ingredients for our stew. It will take creativity for each of us to find ways to change the argument culture to a dialogue culture. It's an effort we have to make, because our public and private lives are at stake.

vo·cab·u·lar·y

In your journal, write the meanings of the italicized words in the following phrases.

- in an *adversarial* frame of mind (2)
- the *ubiquity* (6)
- *synonymous* with criticizing (11)
- with *oppositional* discourse (12)
- the *proliferation* (13)

- a *contretemps* between Kerrigan and Harding (18)
- he was ultimately *exonerated* (18)
- imaginations and *ingenuity* (22)

? QUESTIONS FOR WRITING AND DISCUSSION

1. List three controversial topics currently in the news. Then choose one of those topics and explain the two "sides" of this argument. Now, imagine a third point of view. How is it different from the first two positions? Does coming up with a third position help you think creatively about how to resolve this dispute? Explain.

2. As she writes her essay, Tannen initially outlines the nature of the problem with the "argument culture" before she gives her solution. Which paragraphs most clearly demonstrate the problem? Which paragraphs explain her solution? Does she ignore any aspects of the problem? Would her solution really solve the problem she describes? Why or why not?

3. Critically analyzing the social, political, or cultural context is an important strategy for solving a problem. Where does Tannen explain the context(s) for the problem? Where does she argue that her solution will help resolve social, political, or cultural problems? Are there contexts where her solution might not work? Explain.

4. Read Tannen's advice in the final four paragraphs of her essay. Does she follow her own advice in writing this essay? Which pieces of advice does she follow and which does she ignore? Cite examples from the essay to support your analysis. Would her essay be more effective if she followed her own advice? Explain.

5. As a professor of linguistics, Tannen can write in a formal, academic style, but she can also write in an informal style for general audiences. In this essay, is Tannen writing for academics or for anyone interested in culture and communication? Find examples of Tannen's "academic" style as well as her informal style. Does she successfully integrate the two or is she too informal or too academic? Explain.

6. According to Tannen, the language we choose and the metaphors we use affect our perceptions of the world. Where does Tannen discuss how words

or metaphors shape our perceptions? What examples does she give? In her own argument, does Tannen herself avoid language or metaphors referring to war, violence, or conflict?

7 The *New Yorker* cartoon by BEK, "This looks like a good spot for an argument," did not originally appear with Tannen's essay. Evaluate the appropriateness of this visual image for Tannen's essay. Does the cartoon support Tannen's thesis? Does it contribute to the essay's appeal, or does it distract from Tannen's argument? Citing details from the cartoon and passages from Tannen's essay, explain your response.

8 On the Internet, log on to the Web site of a national news magazine such as *Newsweek* or *Utne* magazine and read their e-mail letters in response to an essay on a controversial topic such as stem cell research, climate change, public transportation, educational testing, and so forth. Read several letters or responses. Can you find at least *three* positions on that issue—rather than just the standard "pro" and "con"? Explain the controversial topic and then write out at least three different positions or points of view which you discover in the responses.

Problem Solving: The Writing Process

ASSIGNMENT FOR PROBLEM SOLVING

Select a problem that you believe needs a solution. Narrow and focus the problem and choose an appropriate audience. Describe the problem and, if necessary, demonstrate for your audience that it needs a solution. State your solution, and justify it with reasons and evidence. Where appropriate, weigh alternative solutions, examine the feasibility of your own solution, and answer objections to your solution.

The problem-solving assignment leads naturally to the genre of a proposal. Some proposals are long, formal documents addressed to knowledgeable readers, while others are short and informal, intended for general audiences. Review your assignment, and then use the following grid to brainstorm possible genres that would meet your purpose for your selected audience.

Continued

Audience	Possible Genres for Problem Solving
Personal Audience	Class notes, journal entry, blog, social networking page
Academic Audience	Academic proposal, analysis, editorial, review, journal entry, forum entry on class site, multigenre document
Public Audience	Column, editorial, article, blog, or critique in a magazine, newspaper, online site, newsletter, or multigenre document

CHOOSING A SUBJECT

If one of your journal entries suggests a possible subject, try the collecting and shaping strategies below. If none of these leads to a workable subject, consider the following suggestions:

- Evaluating leads naturally into problem solving. Reread your journal entries and topic ideas for "evaluating." If your evaluation of your

"I can't think of anything I have no problem with."

subject was negative, consider what would make your evaluation more positive. Based on your evaluation, write a proposal, addressed to the proper audience, explaining the problem and offering your solution.

- Organized groups are already trying to solve a number of national and international problems: homelessness, illegal immigrants, the slaughter of whales, acid rain, abuse of animals in scientific experiments, drug and alcohol abuse, toxic-waste disposal, and so forth. Read several current articles on one of these topics. Then narrow the problem to one aspect that students or residents of your town could help to resolve. Write an essay outlining the problem and proposing some *specific and limited* actions that citizens could take.

- **Community Service Learning.** An important part of any community-service-learning project is collaborating with the agency to assess problems and propose possible solutions. If you have a community-service-learning project in one of your classes, work collaboratively with the agency to assess the community's and/or the agency's needs as well as the knowledge and skills you might bring to the agency to contribute to a possible solution. Working with the agency, decide on a purpose, audience, and genre for your proposal.

- Every day, the news media features images that seem to suggest a problem that needs a solution. Choose one image that you have found in the media and investigate the issue. What problem does the image suggest? What does your research and investigation reveal about the rhetorical situation and cultural context surrounding this image and this issue? Choose a possible audience, genre, and context, and write your own problem-solving essay based on the issue raised by this image.

COLLECTING

With a possible subject and audience in mind, write out answers for each of the following topics. Remember that not all of these approaches will apply to your subject; some topics will suggest very little, while others may prompt you to generate ideas or specific examples appropriate to your problem and solution. A hypothetical problem—large classes that hinder learning—illustrates how these topics may help you focus on your subject and collect relevant ideas and information.

● **IDENTIFY AND FOCUS ON THE SPECIFIC PROBLEM**   Answer the first four "Wh" questions:

WHO: A Psychology I professor; the Psychology Department
WHAT: Psychology I class

WHEN: Spring semester (the structure of this class may be slightly different from previous semesters)

WHERE: University of Illinois (large lecture classes at one school may be different from those at another)

You may want to generalize about large lecture classes everywhere, but begin by identifying the specific problem at hand.

● **DEMONSTRATE THAT THE PROBLEM NEEDS A SOLUTION** Map out the *effects* of a problem. (See the diagram.)

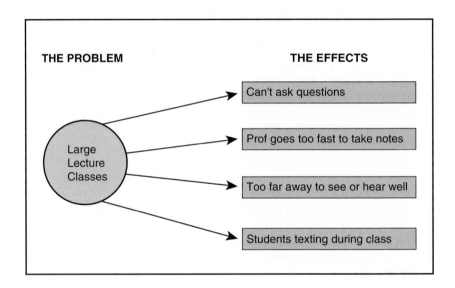

You may want to map out both *short-term effects* and *long-term effects*. Over the short term, large lecture classes prevent you from asking questions; over the long term, you may do poorly on examinations, get a lower grade in the class, lose interest in the subject, be unable to cope with your own and others' psychological problems, or end up in a different career or job.

● **DISCOVER POSSIBLE SOLUTIONS** One strategy is to map out the history or the causes of the problem. If you can discover what caused the problem in the first place, you may have a possible solution. (See the following diagram.)

A second strategy takes the imaginative approach. Brainstorm hypothetical cases by asking, "What if. . . ."

"What if students petitioned the president of the university to abolish all lecture classes with enrollments over 100 students?" Would that work?

"What if students invited the professor to answer questions at a weekly study session?" Would the professor attend? Would students attend?

"What if students taught each other in a psychology class?" How would that work?

"What if all lecture classes were in smart-media classrooms with computer projection, i-clickers, twitter, and in-class videos?"

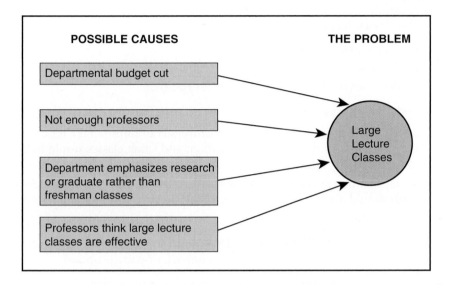

● **EVALUATE POSSIBLE SOLUTIONS**   Apply the "If . . . then . . ." test on each possible solution: Consider whether each proposal would:

    A. actually solve the problem;

    B. meet certain criteria, such as cost-effectiveness, practicality, ethicality, legality;

    C. not create new problems.

"*If* classes were smaller, *then* students would learn more":

If classes were smaller, students might learn more, but a small class size does not necessarily guarantee greater learning.

Although students might learn more, do smaller classes meet other criteria? While they are legal and ethical, are they practical and cost-effective?

Would smaller classes create new problems? Smaller classes might mean fewer upper-level course offerings. Is that a serious new problem?

● **CONVINCE YOUR READERS**   Support your proposed solutions by stating *reasons* and finding supporting *evidence*.

    Reason: Smaller classes are worth the additional expense because students actually engage the material rather than just memorizing for exams.

Evidence: Data from studies comparing large and small classes; personal testimony by students, interviews, or questionnaires; testimony or evidence from authorities on teaching.

● **ANSWER POSSIBLE OBJECTIONS TO YOUR PROPOSAL** Every solution has a down side or possible drawbacks. You need to respond to the most important objections.

List Drawbacks

Small classes cost more.
Small classes might reduce course offerings.
Small classes might mean less money for research.

List Your Responses

Good education does cost more. The University of Illinois has a reputation as an excellent undergraduate institution, and small classes would help it maintain quality education.

Perhaps some classes with low demand could be cut, but the necessary funds should not be taken out of upper-division classes for psychology majors or research projects.

● **LIST POSSIBLE STEPS FOR IMPLEMENTATION** If appropriate, indicate the key steps or chronological sequence of your proposal.

1. Poll students and teachers in large lecture classes to confirm that the problem warrants attention.
2. Gather evidence from other colleges or universities to show how they reduced class sizes.
3. Present results of polls and other evidence to the state legislature to request more funds.

● **OBSERVING** As you gather evidence and examples, use your observation skills. If the problem is large lecture classes, attend classes and *observe* the behavior of students and professors. Are students distracted by noise? Can they ask questions? Does the professor talk too softly to be heard in the back row? Remember that *repeated* observation is essential. If necessary, observe your subject over a period of several days or weeks.

● **REMEMBERING** Use *freewriting, looping,* or *clustering* to help you remember examples from your experience of the problem or of possible solutions. Brainstorm or freewrite about previous class sessions in Psychology I. Do looping or mapping on other small-enrollment classes: What made these classes effective or ineffective? What teaching strategies, projects, or small-group activities were possible in these classes that would not be possible in a class of 250 students?

> ❝The best time for planning . . . is when you're doing the dishes. ❞
>
> —AGATHA CHRISTIE, MYSTERY WRITER

Research Tips ⬛ GO

As you begin researching your problem, don't spend all your time on the Internet or on the library's databases. Remember to interview people who may know about your problem. Use your investigating skills to locate local authorities and interview them in person, via e-mail, or on the telephone (see Chapter 7). Find out what other people think about this problem. How do they explain or define the problem? What are they already doing to solve the problem? Why are current solutions not working or not working effectively enough? Interview a teacher who knows about the problem, a student who has firsthand experience with the problem, an owner of a local business, or the coordinator of a community service or agency. Combining your online and library research with interviews makes your research more interesting, more local and current, and more effective.

● **READING AND INVESTIGATING**   *Use the library* to find books or articles about the particular problem. Other writers have no doubt offered solutions to your problem that you could consider. Articles may even suggest objections to your proposed solution that you need to answer.

Interview participants or authorities on the problem. The professor who is teaching your Psychology I class may have some ideas about a solution. Administration—department chairs, deans, even the president—may agree to answer your questions and react to your possible solutions.

Design a questionnaire that addresses aspects of your problem. Responses to questionnaires provide evidence that a problem is serious, immediate, and in need of a solution. If the results of a questionnaire show that 175 of the 200 people in Psychology I who returned it favor smaller sections, you can include those data in your letter to the head of the department and the dean of the college.

SHAPING

● **GENRES FOR PROBLEM SOLVING**   Initially, you must consider possible genres appropriate for your issue and your particular rhetorical situation. Typical genres used for proposals include articles in magazines, letters to the editor, academic essays, self-help essays, political essays, and business proposals. Depending on the genre and audience you choose, proposals often do the following.

- Identify, analyze, and demonstrate the problem
- Describe and evaluate alternative solutions
- Make proposals
- Give reasons and evidence to support the proposal
- Answer objections; discuss feasibility problems
- Indicate implementation and call for action

Of course, not all problem-solving essays have all six elements. Some do not discuss feasibility in detail or do not describe and evaluate alternative solutions. Adam Richman's essay at the end of this chapter, for example, does not consider alternative solutions to the gradual demise of professional print journalism because his focus is on demonstrating that citizen journalism is a workable solution. Reconsidering your rhetorical situation and genre helps you decide how to shape your proposal.

● **OUTLINES FOR PROBLEM SOLVING**   The following patterns indicate four possible ways to organize a problem-solving essay. One of these patterns may help you organize your proposal.

Problem-Solving Pattern
   I. Introduction
  II. The problem: Identify and demonstrate
 III. The solution(s)
 IV. Answering possible objections, costs, drawbacks
  V. Conclusion: Implementation plan; call to action

Point-by-Point Pattern
   I. Introduction
  II. The overall problem: Identify and demonstrate
 III. One part of the problem, solution, evidence, answers to possible objections, feasibility
 IV. Second part of the problem, solution, evidence, answers to possible objections, feasibility
  V. Third part of the problem, solution, evidence, and so on
 VI. Conclusion: Implementation; call to action

Alternative Pattern
   I. Introduction
  II. The problem: Identify and demonstrate
 III. Alternative Solution 1; why it's not satisfactory
 IV. Alternative Solution 2; why it's not satisfactory

   V. Alternative Solution 3; why it works best: Evidence, objections, feasibility
   VI. Conclusion: Implementation; call to action

Step-by-Step Pattern

   I. Introduction
   II. The problem: Identify and demonstrate
   III. Plan for implementing the solution or how solution has worked in the past:
      A. Step 1: Reasons and evidence showing why this step is necessary and feasible
      B. Step 2: Reasons and evidence showing why this step is necessary and feasible
      C. Step 3: Reasons and evidence showing why this step is necessary and feasible

   IV. Conclusion

● **CAUSAL ANALYSIS**   Causal analysis can be used to organize some paragraphs of a proposal. In arguing the benefits or advantages of a proposed solution, you are actually explaining the *effects* of your solution.

- The effects or advantages of smaller class sections in Psychology I would be greater student participation, fewer distractions, more discussion during lectures, and more individual or small-group learning.
- Shortening the work week to thirty-two hours would increase the number of jobs, reduce tensions for working parents, and give employees time to learn new skills.

   In each of these cases, each effect or advantage can become a separate point and, sometimes, a separate body paragraph.

● **CRITERIA ANALYSIS**   In some cases, the *criteria* for a good solution are quite clear. For example, cost-effectiveness, feasibility, and worker morale might be important criteria for a business-related proposal. If you work in a fast-food restaurant and are concerned about the increasing number of crimes, for example, you might propose that your manager add a video surveillance system. In order to overcome the manager's resistance to spending the needed funds, you could defend your proposal (and answer possible objections) by discussing relevant criteria.

   Proposal: To reduce theft and protect the employees of the restaurant by installing a video surveillance system.

- **Cost-effectiveness.** Citing evidence from other stores that have video cameras, you could prove that the equipment would pay for itself in less than a year. In addition, you could argue that if the life of just one employee—or possibly one manager—were saved, the cost would be worth it.

66 Vigorous writing is concise. 99

—WILLIAM STRUNK, JR., AUTHOR AND TEACHER

- **Feasibility.** Installing a security system would not require any extensive remodeling or any significant training time for employees to learn how to operate the system.
- **Employee morale.** The benefits to employee morale would be significant: Workers would feel more secure, they would feel that the management cares about them, and they would work more productively.

● **CHRONOLOGICAL ORDER** If your proposal stresses the means of implementing your solution to a problem, you may organize several paragraphs or even an entire essay using a chronological order or step-by-step pattern.

A proposal to improve the reading skills of children might be justified by a series of coordinated steps, beginning by organizing seminars for teachers and PTA meetings to discuss possible solutions; establishing minimal reading requirements in grades K–6 that teachers and parents agree on; offering reading prizes; and organizing media coverage of students who participate in reading programs.

DRAFTING

Using your examples, recorded observations, reading, interviews, results from questionnaires, or your own experience, make a sketch outline and begin writing. As you write, let your own proposal and your intended audience guide you. In your first draft, get as much as possible on paper. Don't worry about spelling or awkward sentences. If you hit a snag, stop and read what you have written so far or reread your collecting and shaping notes.

PEER RESPONSE

Writer: Provide the following information about your essay before you exchange drafts with a peer reader.

1. a. Audience and genre
   b. Statement of problem and context of problem
   c. Possible or alternative solutions
   d. Your recommended solution(s)
2. Write out one or two questions about your draft that you want your reader to answer.

Reader: Read the writer's entire draft. As you *reread* the draft, do the following.

1. Without looking at the writer's responses, describe (a) the essay's intended audience, (b) the main problem that the essay identifies, (c) the possible or alternative solutions, and (d) the writer's recommended solution. What feasibility problems or additional solutions should the writer consider? Why?

2. Indicate one paragraph in which the writer's evidence is strong. Then find one paragraph in which the writer needs more evidence. What additional *kinds* of evidence (personal experience, testimony from authorities, statistics, specific examples, etc.) might the writer use in this paragraph? Explain.

3. Number the paragraphs in the writer's essay and then describe, briefly, the purpose or main idea of each paragraph: paragraph 1 introduces the problem, paragraph 2 gives the writer's personal experience with the problem, and so on. When you finish, explain how the writer might improve the organization of the essay.

4. List the three most important things that the writer should focus on during revision.

5. Respond to the writer's questions in number 2.

Writer: When your essay is returned, read the comments by your peer reader(s) and do the following.

1. Compare your description of the audience, the problem, and the solutions with your reader's description. Where there are differences, try to clarify your essay.

2. Reconsider and revise your recommended solution(s).

3. What additional kinds of evidence will make your recommendations stronger?

4. Make a revision plan. List, in order, the three most important things that you need to do as you revise your essay.

REVISING

When you have a completed draft and are ready to start revising your essay, get another member of your class to read and respond to your essay. Use the peer response guidelines that follow to get—and give—constructive advice on your draft.

Use the following revising guidelines to identify areas for improving your draft. Even at this point, don't hesitate to collect additional information, if necessary, or reorganize your material. If a reader makes suggestions, reread your draft to see if those changes will improve your essay.

GUIDELINES FOR REVISION

- **Review your rhetorical situation.** How can you revise your selected genre to make it more effectively communicate your purpose to your intended audience?
- **Review to make sure you critically analyze the problem.** Don't just assume that everyone will agree with your definition or representation of the problem. Investigate and describe the groups of people who are affected by the problem.
- **Have a classmate or someone who might understand your audience read your draft and play devil's advocate.** Have your reader pretend to be hostile to your solution and ask questions about alternative solutions or weaknesses in your own solution. Revise your proposal so that it answers any important objections.
- **Review your proposal for key elements.** If you are missing one of the following, would adding it make your proposal more effective for your audience? *Remember:* Proposals do not necessarily have to have all of these elements.

  Develop the items that are most applicable to your proposal.

  Show that a problem exists and needs attention.

  Evaluate alternative solutions.

  Propose your solution.

  Show that your solution meets certain criteria: feasibility, cost-effectiveness, legality.

  Answer possible objections.

  Suggest implementation or call for action.
- **Be sure that you *show* what you mean, using specific examples, facts, details, statistics, quotations from interviews or articles.** Don't rely on general assertions.
- **Signal the major parts of your proposal with key words and transitions.**
- **Avoid the following errors in logic and generalization.**

  Don't commit an "either-or" fallacy. For example, don't say that "*either* we reduce class sizes *or* students will drop out of the university." There are more than two possible alternatives.

Don't commit an "ad hominem" fallacy by arguing "to the man" or "to the woman" rather than to the issue. Don't say, for example, that Deborah Tannen is wrong about argument because she is just another pushy woman who should stick to teaching linguistics.

Test your proposal for "If . . . then . . ." statements. Does it really follow that "if we reduce class size, teaching will be more effective"?

Avoid overgeneralizing your solution. If all your research applies to solving problems in large lecture classes in psychology, don't assume that your solution will apply to, say, classes in physics or physical education.

- **If you are citing data or quoting sources, make sure that your material is accurately cited.**

- **Read your proposal aloud for flabby, wordy, or awkward sentences.** Revise your sentences for clarity, precision, and forcefulness.

- **Edit your proposal for spelling, appropriate word choice, punctuation, usage, mechanics, and grammar.** Remember that, in part, your form and audience help determine what are appropriate usage and mechanics.

POSTSCRIPT ON THE WRITING PROCESS

Before you turn in your essay, answer the following questions in your journal.

1. As you worked on your essay, what elements of the rhetorical situation did you revise? How did you change the purpose, audience, or genre elements as you drafted your essay? Cite specific sentences or paragraphs from your essay as examples.

2. List the skills you used in writing this paper: observing people, places, or events; remembering personal experience; using questionnaires and interviews; reading written material; explaining ideas; evaluating solutions. Which of these skills was most useful to you in writing this essay?

3. What was your most difficult problem to solve while writing this paper? Were you able to solve it yourself, or did your readers suggest a solution?

4. In one sentence, describe the most important thing you learned about writing while working on this essay.

5. What were the most successful parts of your essay?

Can Citizen Journalism Pick Up the Pieces?

In a writing class focusing on the future of literacies, Adam Richman decided to write his essay on citizen journalism. He began by assembling research questions that he wanted to answer. Because many traditional newspapers were going bankrupt and ceasing publication, Richman wondered whether citizen journalism might potentially fill the gap left by these disappearing traditional news sources. If citizen journalism could be a solution to the problem, he needed to know whether it was capable of meeting the responsibilities of professional journalism. Citizen journalism must be able to inform the public and serve as a public watchdog for injustice and corruption in government and business. After brainstorming his list of questions, he decided to design a questionnaire that would assess whether citizen journalism—as opposed to professional journalism—kept students informed and whether students thought citizen journalism was as reliable as professional journalism. After tabulating the results of his survey and completing his research, he decided that the evidence showed that citizen journalism definitely had the potential to replace professional journalism. Printed below are some of Richman's research questions, his survey questions, and his essay.

RESEARCH QUESTIONS

Overall Question: Is citizen journalism good for journalism as a whole?

- What percentage of journalism consumers read/watch/listen to a) primarily professional journalism, b) primarily citizen journalism, or c) about an even mix?
- Which of the three groups is best informed on current events?
- Which of the three groups spends the most time consuming news?
- Which of the three groups is the best informed on current events?
- What percentage of journalism consumers says professional journalism has a) more credibility than citizen journalism b) less credibility than citizen journalism, or c) about the same credibility as citizen journalism?
- Which of these three groups is the best informed on current events?
- What percentage of journalism consumers fact-checks the news they consume?

- Which type of journalism gets fact-checked more: professional or citizen?
- What percentage of people considers citizen journalism to be journalism?
- Who is more informed on current events: those who say *yes* above or those who say *no* above?

QUESTIONNAIRE

This questionnaire is part of a research project conducted by Adam Richman. The topics to be covered include encyclopedias, media consumption and current events. Any information you provide will be kept entirely confidential, and your identity will not be requested.

1. **Which of the following do you use more often?**
   A. User-edited encyclopedias (Wikipedia, etc.)
   B. Staff-written encyclopedias (Encyclopedia Britannica, etc.)

2. **Which of the following statements best applies to you?**
   A. To get the news, I primarily use professional journalism (newspapers, TV news programs, news magazines, etc.).
   B. To get the news, I primarily use citizen journalism (weblogs, video logs, etc.).
   C. To get the news, I use an even mix of professional and citizen journalism.

3. **Which of the following has more credibility?**
   A. Professional journalism does.
   B. Citizen journalism does.
   C. They are about the same.

4. **Do you consider citizen journalism (weblogs, video logs, etc.) to be true journalism?**
   A. Yes
   B. No

5. **When reading, watching, or listening to the news, which of the following do you prefer?**
   A. An attempt at objectivity
   B. A transparent bias
   If you answered B, move on to question 6. If you answered A, skip to question 7.

6. **Which of the following statements best applies to you?**
   A. I primarily seek bias I agree with.
   B. I primarily seek bias I disagree with.
   C. I seek an even mix of bias I agree with and bias I disagree with.

7. **When reading, watching, or listening to the news, how often do you check facts?**

   1 (Never)   2 (Rarely)   3 (Sometimes)   4 (Often)   5 (Always)

8. **Who is the Vice President of the United States?**
9. **Which political party has the majority in both houses of Congress?**
10. **Which radio host has recently been pegged by opposition as the de facto leader of the Republican Party?**
11. **What kind of pet was recently shot and killed by police after the pet mauled its owner's friend?**
    A. Pit bull
    B. Chimpanzee
    C. Bobcat
    D. Horse
12. **Which former First Lady recently underwent open heart surgery?**
13. **Which CNN host recently cancelled his own show?**
14. **Which New York Yankees star has recently come under fire for steroid use?**
15. **Which radio legend recently died?**

ESSAY

Print journalism has recently seen historic cuts. In February, the *Rocky Mountain News* closed just weeks shy of its 150th anniversary. Also that month, Philadelphia Newspapers L.L.C., which owns the city's *Inquirer* and *Daily News,* filed for bankruptcy (Lieberman). Four years shy of its 150th anniversary, the *Seattle Post-Intelligencer* transferred 100 percent of its operations to the Internet (Richman and James). Most recently, Harrisburg's *Patriot-News* announced March 24 that all full-time employees must take 10 days off over the next five months ("Local Newspaper Announces Mandatory Furloughs"). This alarming string of newspaper closings appears to be just the beginning of a fundamental change in journalism. We may well wonder how or if journalism—and our democratic way of life that depends on journalism—can survive these upheavals. [1]

The problem is nothing less than the gradual demise of print journalism. But is there a solution? One possible solution could be the rise of citizen journalists, or "people without professional journalism training using the tools of modern technology and the global distribution of the Internet to create, augment or fact-check media on their own or in collaboration with others" (Glaser). User "djussila" of the citizen journalistic *NowPublic.com* defines journalism as one-third of the democratic [2] equation: Politicians + Public + Publication = Democracy. The publication element is necessary, djussila argues, because direct democracy is obsolete. "People do not really have a say in modern democracy, aside from their vote, unless they are a politician themselves," djussila said. "Journalism serves as a window."

Like a chemical reaction equation, each entity of a functioning 3 democracy needs to remain balanced. But with the gradual reduction of print journalism, the equation becomes unstable. In a piece for the *Washington Post*, Marc Fisher quotes Warren Fiske of the *Virginia Pilot* lamenting the job cuts facing the newspaper industry: "When we had the larger bureaus, you could do the good investigative piece. Most sessions, somebody would find someone doing something wrong," Fiske said. "Now, we can only really cover the flow of legislation."

The number of citizen journalism sites that might replace print jour- 4 nalism has been growing dramatically in recent years. The most popular of these Web sites include the following:

- *NowPublic.com*, one of *Time's* 50 Coolest Web sites of 2007. The magazine said, "Nowhere are the merits of citizen journalism more apparent than at NowPublic.com" ("NowPublic Blog").

- CyberJournalist.net, one of Cnet's Top 100 Blogs. *USA Today* and the *Columbia Journalism Review* have both recommended the site ("About *CyberJournalist.net*").

- *Wanabehuman.blogspot.com*, a UK blog "founded on the principles of participatory or citizen journalism." Their site proudly declares, "We believe every citizen can be a journalist (*Wanabehuman*: About Wanabehuman).

The growth of these news sources and many others like them 5 raises a key question. Can citizen journalism pick up the pieces being left by professional journalism? To answer this, we first must answer other questions: 1) Can citizen journalism be considered real journalism? and 2) Does citizen journalism have the necessary characteristics to bridge the gap?

According to Mark Pearson's and Jane Johnston's *Breaking into* 6 *Journalism*, news media serves "to inform . . . and to act as a public watchdog over government." If citizen journalism can accomplish these tasks to a degree that meets or exceeds the standards currently set by professional journalism, it can be considered real journalism. A survey I conducted of 100 York College students seems to suggest that citizen journalism may already be meeting the current standards. This survey included an eight-question current events quiz. Those who primarily used professional journalism to get the news answered an average of 3.98 questions correctly. Those who primarily used citizen journalism to get the news answered an average of 4.29 questions correctly. Although it is difficult to generalize this data across the nation, it does suggest that citizen journalism at least has the potential to inform the public to a degree that meets or exceeds the standards set by professional journalism.

In addition to providing the public with civic information, citizen 7 journalism has also demonstrated the potential to act as a public watchdog. In a PBS online article, Mark Glaser showed occasions when blogs have acted as a public watchdog, outlining four events:

- "Trent Lott resigns as majority leader of the U.S. Senate in December 2002 after blogs keep up pressure over a racist remark he made."

- "Conservative bloggers helped discredit documents related to President Bush's National Guard service used in an episode of '60 Minutes II' in 2004. This became known as Rathergate."

- "Various people worked together online to help identify the star of the Lonelygirl15 videos on YouTube as a New Zealand actress."

- "A former Lockheed Martin engineer takes his story about security flaws with Coast Guard ships straight to YouTube after the mainstream media ignored his entreaties. Later, the *Washington Post* wrote about it."

As these cases demonstrate, citizen journalism can indeed serve as a public watchdog.

Because citizen journalism has shown the potential to inform and 8 serve as a watchdog to a degree that meets or exceeds the standards set by professional journalism, it can be considered real journalism. The next question is, "Can citizen journalism solve the problem by bridging the gap left by the fading of professional journalism?"

Professional journalism has three key functions: 1) to offer credible 9 reporting of the news, 2) to report on the deliberations and decisions of state and local government, and 3) to do investigative work on public issues. Currently, there are already weaknesses in all of these areas. The *Columbia Journalism Review's* Web site laments the deterioration of credibility obvious in the media when CNN, Fox News, ABC News, and CNBC all focused heavily on a story revolving around a commercial being shot by Kevin Federline—better known as K-Fed or "Britney's ex," (Colby). Also, a *Washington Post* story explains, "as long as people buy property, look for jobs, send kids to school and pay taxes, they will need credible information about state government." Finally, Fiske says that professional journalism institutions no longer have the resources to commit to investigative reporting (Fisher).

Although there are current weaknesses in professional journalism, 10 both media critics and the public disagree about whether citizen journalism can serve these functions credibly. My survey of York College students suggested a lack of respect for citizen journalism. Seventy-nine percent of respondents said professional journalism is more credible, and fifty three percent said that citizen journalism isn't even real journalism. Supporting that position, a Virginian politics blogger and maintainer of *RichmondSunlight.com*, Waldo Jaquith, admits an inability to cover local news as objectively as institutional journalists. "What I can't offer on my blogs is the relationships, the institutional memory, the why, the history that reporters who know the capital can bring to their stories," Jaquith said. "Newspapers can describe the candidates for governor in a more balanced, deeper way because you don't have a dog in the race. Webloggers do" (Fisher).

On the other hand, many professionals do support the job that citizen journalists are doing. Dave Berlind, a blogger with *zdnet.com*, denies that blogs lack credibility. "Bloggers and so called 'citizen journalists' have to earn their credibility, and the community at large does a good job of regulating the environment—quality will usually rise to the top." Providers of citizen journalism have earned praise from organizations like *Time, USA Today*, and the *Columbia Journalism Review*. In addition, the citizen journalistic *Chi-Town Daily News* covers Chicago's local happenings in depth, especially compared to the only eight local stories you may find in an average edition of the *Chicago Tribune* ("Investigative Journalism Done Better, Faster and Cheaper Without Newspapers"): "We publish articles written by our team of seasoned beat reporters covering citywide topics like education, the environment, public housing and health," the site's About Us section reads. "Their work is supported by trained volunteer neighborhood reporters." Another Web site, the *Voice of San Diego*, operates similarly. Undeniably, citizen journalism has the ability to cover local news.

One citizen journalism Web site, which was born during the Florida recounts of 2000, has earned praise from *techdirt.com*. "*Talking Points Memo* has been quite successful with its investigative reporting, which does a lot to leverage its community to help out in the process," *techdirt.com*'s 'let's-get-real' department said, "while still employing full time journalists who are doing tremendous investigative reporting—which should only improve as better tools are created to enable more to be done." With this site and others like it—others like those who broke open the four stories bulleted above—it is clear that citizen journalism has the ability to conduct investigative reporting.

Because citizen journalism has shown the ability to adequately accomplish these tasks, the potential exists for new media outlets to fill the vacuum being left by the downturn in professional journalism. Citizen journalism is able to pick up the pieces left by a fragmented and faltering print-based press. The fix will be neither immediate nor perfect, but a solid journalistic foundation supports the very capable field of citizen journalism. Potentially life-altering stories may go unnoticed, but for every one of those, another important story will see daylight that professional journalism alone could have never have shown. With every keystroke, with every click of the mouse on a button reading "post," citizen journalism is proving itself to the public. As accessibility to the Internet grows and as professional journalism continues to circle the drain, citizen journalism continues to grow stronger. Thanks to the brand-less brand of journalism that fosters independence, personal responsibility, and healthy skepticism, professional journalism's faltering need not throw the democratic equation off balance—if citizen journalism can meet its potential.

Works Cited

"About *CyberJournalist.net*." *CyberJournalist.net.* Jonathan Dube, 28 Mar 2009. Web. 28 Mar. 2009.

Berlind, David. "Can Technology Close Journalism's Credibility Gap?" *ZDNet.* CBS Interactive, 19 Jan. 2005. Web. 28 Mar. 2009.

Chi-Town Daily News. Chi-Town Daily News, 28 Mar. 2009. Web. 28 Mar. 2009.

Colby, Edward B. "A Penny 'Saved' Is Media Credibility Burned." *Columbia Journalism Review.* Columbia Journalism Review, 23 June 2006. Web. 28 Mar 2009.

djussila, "The Role of Journalism in a Democracy." *NowPublic.* NowPublic Technologies, 09 Mar. 2009. Web. 28 Mar. 2009.

Fisher, Marc. "Bloggers Can't Fill the Gap Left by a Shrinking Press Corps." *The Washington Post.* Washington Post, 1 Mar. 2009. Web. 28 Mar. 2009.

Glaser, Mark. "MediaShift: Your Guide to Citizen Journalism." *PBS.* PBS, 27 Sep. 2006. Web. 25 Mar. 2009.

"Investigative Journalism Done Better, Faster and Cheaper Without Newspapers." *techdirt.* Floor64, 18 Mar. 2009. Web. 28 Mar. 2009.

Lieberman, David. "Newspaper Closings Raise Fears about Industry." *USA Today.* Gannett, 19 Mar. 2009. Web. 28 Mar. 2009.

"Local Newspaper Announces Mandatory Furloughs." *WGAL News.* WGAL, Lancaster, 24 Mar. 2009. Television.

"NowPublic Blog." *NowPublic.com.* NowPublic News Coverages, 28 Mar. 2009. Web. 28 Mar. 2009.

Pearson, Mark, and Jane Johnston. *Breaking into Journalism.* Crow's Nest, Australia: Allen & Unwin, 1998. Print.

Richman, Dan, and Andrea James. "Seattle P-I to Publish Last Edition Tuesday." *Seattle Post-Intelligencer.* Seattle Post-Intelligencer, 16 Mar. 2009. Web. 28 Mar. 2009.

"Wanabehuman: About Wanabehuman." *Wanabehuman.* Wanabehuman, 28 Mar. 2009. Web. 28 Mar. 2009.

QUESTIONS FOR WRITING AND DISCUSSION

1. Problem-solving essays need to clearly demonstrate an existing problem. According to Adam Richman, what is the problem facing journalism in America today? In what paragraphs does Adam Richman state this problem? Do you agree with his statement of the problem, or could other forces be creating the problem? Explain.

2. What solution to this problem does Richman propose? In what paragraphs does he state his solution most directly? What evidence does he present to convince you that his solution will work? Which pieces of evidence did you find most persuasive?

3. Richman presents one possible solution to this problem, but there are other alternative solutions to the problem of declining print journalism. Some people say that newspapers can be saved by selling articles online. Others say that newspapers and other print journalism ought to have nonprofit status in order to pay professional journalists to protect our democratic way of life. In addition, critics of citizen journalism say that ordinary citizens are not trained to investigate and deliver news accurately and objectively. Should Richman consider these alternative ideas in order to convince you that citizen journalism has the potential to replace traditional print journalism?

4. Richman is writing for an audience composed of his fellow students at his college. Are the results of this study likely to convince students? Why or why not? If he were writing for an audience of Americans over the age of 50, would this study convince these readers? Why or why not?

STUDENT WRITING

JESSICA COOK

New Regulations and You

For her problem-solving essay, Jessica Cook decided to write about current solutions for solving a recent outbreak of mad cow disease. Her purpose was "to persuade cattle ranchers that the new regulations and changes in policy that arose in the wake of the discovery of mad cow disease (BSE) in the U.S. are necessary and can even be beneficial." Her audience was beef producers and ranchers, and she chose Beef *magazine as a target publication. After reviewing current issues of* Beef *magazine, she modeled her essay on the genre features of their articles: a personal voice combined with current research, short paragraphs with headings and bullets, a two-column format, and graphics to illustrate her point. Cook also wrote a Works Cited page, but did not use in-text citation because that was not the format used by* Beef *magazine. As you read her essay, decide how successful she is at arguing for the recommended policies, addressing her target audience, and meeting the genre requirements.*

NEW REGULATIONS AND YOU

1 When I was growing up, my mother always told me that I was just one small pebble on a very large beach, meaning that I was just an insignificant part of the world, and as a single person, I couldn't bring about any huge changes.

2 It may sound demeaning, but the truth is, most people will never change the world.

3 However, after seeing how much of an impact one dairy cow in Washington can have on American agriculture and world trade, I am beginning to think my mother might have been wrong.

4 In case you hadn't already guessed, the infamous cow I am referring to is the Holstein that tested positive for mad cow disease, or bovine spongiform encephalopathy (BSE), on December 23, 2003.

5 According to a special report in *Cattle-Fax*, this discovery caused nearly all of our trading partners to ban the import of U.S. beef, a plunge in beef prices, and a recall of 10,400 pounds of beef associated with the cow. Consumer confidence in beef and bovine-derived products also plummeted. In addition, this cow spawned several new government-issued regulations and changes to procedures.

THE NEW RULES

6 In two articles in the *New York Times*, Denise Grady and Donald G. McNeil, Jr., the two writers following mad cow disease, discuss the new regulations, including bans on the following:

- Feeding cattle blood to calves as a milk replacer
- Allowing chicken litter—feathers, spilled feed, bedding, and feces—in cattle feed
- Using the same equipment that makes feed containing bone meal for making cattle feed
- Allowing dead or downer cattle to be used for human food or products, including dietary supplements, cosmetics or soups

- Feeding "plate waste" or table scraps to cattle
- Air-injection stunning

Also, carcasses that are tested for BSE must be held until the re- *7* sults are known.

Even more changes are being considered for the future, including *8* testing more cattle, mandatory identification and tracking systems, and banning all animal protein from cattle feed.

WHAT THIS MEANS TO YOU

By now, beef producers have realized how these new rules will aff- *9* ect them, and most have already implemented the government-mandated changes.

Although many producers share the opinion that these new regu- *10* lations just increase the time, effort and money it takes to produce beef, I disagree.

I believe that the new regulations and changes in policy that arose *11* in the wake of the discovery of BSE in the U.S. are necessary and can even be beneficial to the cattle industry.

Although I realize that these changes will be expensive and tedious *12* to implement, I believe that the advantages will outweigh the disadvantages. These regulations will increase food safety, open opportunities in niche markets, facilitate exportation, and boost consumer confidence and demand.

Because I was raised in a small town by the name of Burns, *13* Wyoming, and grew up in an agricultural community, I know what it takes to produce our nation's food supply. I am familiar with the "blood, sweat and tears" that go hand-in-hand with raising cattle, or any other species of livestock.

THE DOWNSIDE

Anyone who has been around agriculture and cattle knows that *14* the new regulations will be expensive and time consuming to implement, and I acknowledge this.

Many ranchers feel that changing the way things have always been *15* done is pointless; the current methods were passed down from our successful elders, and "if it isn't broke, why fix it?" Another argument against the new rules is that changing the way a ranch operates takes an exorbitant effort.

A group of government officials, many of whom have no idea *16* what goes into raising cattle, have made several new rules that ranchers must follow. As Wes Ishmael phrased it in the February 1, 2004, issue of *Beef* magazine, "How many laws would a lawmaker make if a lawmaker could make laws without pause or cause?"

...*continued* New Regulations and You, **Jessica Cook**

Despite all of those negative side effects, there are some redeem- 17 ing features to the new regulations.

INCREASED FOOD SAFETY

Although the beef industry is quick to claim that the beef supply 18 is safe (after all, there has only been one case of mad cow disease out of the nearly 36 million cattle slaughtered per year in the U.S.), there is evidence to the contrary.

Dave Louthan (as recorded by McNeil of the *New York Times*), the 19 man who killed the infected cow at the slaughterhouse in Moses Lake, WA, warns of the danger.

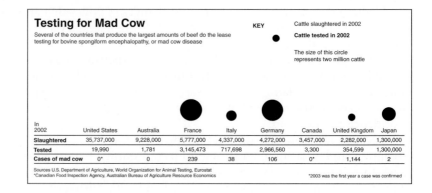

Testing for Mad Cow

Several of the countries that produce the largest amounts of beef do the lease testing for bovine spongiform encephalopathy, or mad cow disease

KEY

● Cattle slaughtered in 2002
● **Cattle tested in 2002**

The size of this circle represents two million cattle

In 2002	United States	Australia	France	Italy	Germany	Canada	United Kingdom	Japan
Slaughtered	35,737,000	9,228,000	5,777,000	4,337,000	4,272,000	3,457,000	2,282,000	1,300,000
Tested	19,990	1,781	3,145,473	717,698	2,966,560	3,300	354,599	1,300,000
Cases of mad cow	0*	0	239	38	106	0*	1,144	2

Sources U.S. Department of Agriculture, World Organization for Animal Testing, Eurostat
*Canadian Food Inspection Agency, Australian Bureau of Agriculture Resource Economics

*2003 was the first year a case was confirmed

Louthan claims that the infected cow was not a downer when it 20 was killed, which contradicts the official reports from the federal De-partment of Agriculture, and would thus make the discovery of it just a fluke. Because the guidelines only mandate testing for downer cattle, this could mean BSE-infected cattle are slipping through the testing procedures and into the food chain.

According to another of McNeil's articles, last year only about 21 20,000 cattle were tested for BSE, which is only 0.06% of those slaugh-tered. New testing protocol calls for doubling the number tested, which is an improvement whose worth is easily demonstrated.

Even if only one cow slips by the testing, which is statistically in- 22 significant, I sure don't want to be the person innocently consuming that meat and risking a fatal disease. Do you want to be the rancher re-sponsible for creating another disaster because you didn't implement the changes to move your enterprise into the future?

Louthan also claims that the carcass splitting process is unsafe as 23 well. When the carcass is split the blade cleaves the spinal column while jets of water blast away the fat and bone dust.

The "slurry" containing spinal column matter, a portion of the 24 carcass that can transmit BSE, "runs all over the beef." Obviously, this poses a risk, and if a way to change this process is feasible, it should be implemented.

NICHE MARKET OPPORTUNITIES

Another potential benefit of the new regulations is the opportu- 25 nity to move into niche markets. Currently, raising beef is a commodity market, where one rancher's beef is basically the same as the next rancher's.

There have been some recent changes to help ranchers differenti- 26 ate their products, like the Certified Angus Beef campaign.

In theory, the kind of packaging and label on a product shouldn't 27 play a part in consumer's decisions, yet in reality, it does. In the text book *Scientific Farm Animal Production,* Drs. Taylor and Field, professors at Colorado State University, state that the five main factors used to determine value of meat products are palatability, fat composition, presentation, price, and convenience.

As the producers who can place the sticker that says "Certified An- 28 gus Beef" on their packages in the supermarket have found out, making your product just a little different so that it stands out from the crowd can be an effective marketing technique.

Although labeling of products, mandatory identification, and 29 traceability are not yet required, I believe that the implementation of these procedures now—before they are deemed necessary—could benefit a producer in the same way.

According to Dr. Field during a lecture in Introduction to Animal 30 Science, some Japanese producers can already testify to its effectiveness.

One ranch decided to raise all of its beef cattle from birth to 31 slaughter on their family-owned ranch, and advertise their beef in that way. They stated that all of their beef was raised solely on that farm. Consumers liked knowing that they only had to trust one ranch instead of several places and businesses.

Another ranch put a picture of their family on the beef packaging, 32 making it more personal. When the consumers saw the nice, honest-looking family on the package of steak, it made them choose it over the standard package beside it.

When marketing beef, producers must consider opportunities like 33 these in order to move into niche markets and leave the commodity market in the past. Implementing things like identification and traceability before they are required can give producers a jump on the market and a chance to become more profitable.

EXPORTATION

As American agriculturalists, we know the importance of expor- 34 tation. When BSE was discovered, our export markets were drastically affected.

According to an article from Mexico City on AOLNews, "U.S. beef 35 exports came to a virtual halt after the Dec. 23 announcement that mad cow had been found." This is a major concern; last year alone, the U.S. exported $3.8 billion worth of beef products.

Many of the new regulations were essential in convincing our major 36 trading partners, namely Mexico, Japan and South Korea, into reopening borders.

In a market where we are such a big player, we cannot afford to allow 37 the borders to remain closed for long. Some of the regulations that might seem like they go beyond what is actually necessary for food safety are vital in meeting the requirements of other countries.

CONSUMER CONFIDENCE

Boosting consumer confidence is the most important advantage of 38 the new rules and regulations. In a consumer-driven market, the importance of consumer confidence in the product cannot be overstated.

If confidence sinks, so will demand and prices. However, if we come 39 up with a way to buoy their belief in the product, we can save the market from disaster during the mad cow crisis.

Many of the new regulations serve this purpose. While some of the 40 rules may seem like they are more restricting than absolutely necessary for food safety, if they put the consumer's mind at ease, then they are indispensable.

For example, consider the rule that bans feeding cow blood to calves 41 as a milk replacer. So far, there has been no conclusive evidence that BSE can be transmitted through blood, but once the topic had been brought up and consumers heard about this common practice, measures had to be taken.

Grady writes in the *New York Times,* consumers "imagine bucolic 42 scenes of nursing calves and cows munching on grass."

Realistically, this isn't productive, but we must cater to the more del- 43 icate nature of consumers wherever possible to insure that they will buy the product.

According to one of Dr. Field's lectures in my animal science class, 44 when you are producing a product for consumers, you have to produce it in a way that consumers want to buy it, not just in a way that you want to produce it.

An example of this is producing a product in a way that is inexpen- 45 sive and easy, but yields a poor quality product that won't sell or bring a good price, so you are better off not producing anything at all.

If you produce *for* the consumers, giving them what they want, it will 46 be worth the extra effort and money required.

That is why the new regulations are crucial. They force producers 47 to yield to consumer desires on specific things, increasing the consumer's confidence in the product and therefore the demand for the product.

WHY THE GOVERNMENT?

Finally, I would like to discuss why it actually makes sense that the gov- 48 ernment is making these rules, when they really don't know much about cows. From their city dwellings, government officials might not know the exact nutrients that a lactating cow requires, but they have a much more comprehensive understanding of the economics of production.

They have the knowledge of other countries requirements and what 49 is necessary to facilitate exportation. They understand the effects that the rules will have on consumer confidence and demand. Government officials also have scientific information that isn't available to the general public to help them make their decisions.

And the last critical piece to the puzzle is the fact that they don't have a 50 vested interest. They can attempt to satisfy all groups without favoring any.

THE DECISION

It's incredible to think that all of these issues stemmed from one cow, 51 one incidence of a disease. However, now that it has occurred, we must accept and flow with the changes if we hope to be productive in the future.

The government's regulations have already been passed and ranch- 52 ers are forced to comply. Although the changes will be expensive and a pain-in-the-round to implement they do have benefits.

It is up to each rancher to decide if they will plant their feet in re- 53 sistance, hoping to hold on to the ways of the past, or embrace the changes and the increased food safety, niche market opportunities, export markets, and boosted consumer confidence that they will bring. If ranchers choose the latter, they will have the opportunity to profit and grow with the future of beef and make their product stand out from the rest of the herd.

...continued New Regulations and You, **Jessica Cook**

Before you make your decision about how to react to these new reg- 54
ulations, consider all of the benefits. I'm sure they will tip the scale in favor of being proactive and optimistic.

Works Cited

Field, Thomas G., and Robert E. Taylor. *Scientific Farm Animal Production.* Ed.
Debbie Yarnell. 8th ed. Upper Saddle River, NJ: Pearson, 2003. Print.

Grady, Denise. "Mad Cow Quandary: Making Animal Feed." *New York Times*
6 Feb. 2004: A20. Print.

Grady, Denise, and Donald G. McNeil, Jr. "Rules Issued on Animal Feed and Use
of Disabled Cattle." *New York Times* 27 Jan. 2004: A12. Print.

Ismael, Wes. "Raining Regulations." *Beef* Feb. 2004. Web. 3 Mar. 2004.

McNeil, Donald G., Jr. "Doubling Tests for Mad Cow Doesn't Quiet Program
Critics." *New York Times* 9 Feb. 2004: A8. Print.

McNeil, Donald G., Jr. "Man Who Killed the Mad Cow Has Questions of His
Own." *New York Times* 3 Feb. 2004: D2. Print.

"Mexico to Ban U.S. Beef Until Mad Cow Controlled." *Reuters.* 10 Feb. 2004. Web.
10 Feb 2004.

"Time for Perspective." *Cattle-Fax* 36 (2004): 1. Print.

QUESTIONS FOR WRITING AND DISCUSSION

1 In her essay, Cook takes a slightly different approach to her problem-
solving essay. Instead of trying to prove that a problem exists, she
assumes that her readers are aware of the problem and argues for
accepting a solution already in place. List the reasons she gives in
arguing that the advantages of this policy outweigh the disadvantages.
What evidence or support does she provide for each reason? Will the
readers of *Beef* magazine find her reasons and evidence persuasive? Why
or why not?

2 In addressing her target audience, Cook uses a personal voice and an
appeal to character (*ethos*). Voice is the personality of the writer as
revealed through her language and personal experience. The appeal to
character or *ethos* (see Chapter 11, p. 448) is based on the writer's
character as honest, fair-minded, ethical, and knowledgeable about the
key issues. Find examples in which Cook uses a personal voice and
makes appeals based on her character. For each example, evaluate the
effectiveness of her appeal. Overall, does her personal approach make

her argument more effective or less effective for her target audience? Explain.

3 In the library, find a copy of *Beef* magazine and read one or two sample articles. What are the key genre features of articles that appear in this magazine? Pay attention to audience, reference to sources, voice, style, article length, use of pictures and graphics, organization and use of headings, and paragraph length. Then find examples where Cook successfully models these genre features. Are there genre features that Cook does not imitate? Explain why you believe that Cook has or has not effectively modeled the genre features of her target publication.

4 For your own problem-solving essay, choose a target magazine or newspaper where you might publish your essay. Analyze the genre features of articles that appear in that publication. Write out your own plan for revising your essay to meet the requirements of that publication. Specifically, list and explain the genre features that you would include in your essay.

PEARSON
mycomplab

For additional writing, reading, and research resources, go to http://www.mycomplab.com

Jerome Lawrence and
Robert E. Lee
Inherit the Wind (1960)
Stanley Kramer, Director

STANLEY KRAMER presents SPENCER TRACY | FREDRIC MARCH | GENE KELLY in

"INHERIT THE WIND"

...IT'S ALL ABOUT THE 'MONKEY TRIAL' THAT ROCKED AMERICA...

co-starring DICK YORK · DONNA ANDERSON · with HARRY MORGAN · CLAUDE AKINS · and FLORENCE ELDRIDGE · Screenplay by NATHAN E. DOUGLAS and HAROLD JACOB SMITH
Based upon the play by JEROME LAWRENCE and ROBERT E. LEE · Produced and Directed by STANLEY KRAMER · Released thru UNITED ARTISTS

For twelve swelteringly hot days in July 1925, the famous Scopes "Monkey Trial" in Dayton, Tennessee, tested a state law banning the teaching of evolution. The original debate between Clarence Darrow and William Jennings Bryan is recreated in this film version of the play *Inherit the Wind*. Written arguments sometimes recreate the pro–con debate style of a trial, but frequently, they represent multiple points of view, just as parents, teachers, administrators, and students might gather to recommend policy changes at a school or citizens get together to solve problems in the community. This chapter encourages you to imagine multiple situations for written argument as you adapt to different audiences, genres, and social contexts.

Arguing

11

As a recent high school graduate, you decide to write about the increasing number of standardized tests currently required of primary and secondary school students. The question you want to investigate is whether schools are teaching students important skills and making them better members of society or whether schools are just teaching them how to do well on tests. After reading current articles on tests mandated by No Child Left Behind and interviewing your classmates, you decide to write to politicians who are in favor of standardized tests and argue that, while the tests should not be thrown out, they should be changed in order to solve several serious problems they have created for students, teachers, and parents.

After being cited for not wearing a seat belt while operating a motor vehicle, you decide that your rights have been violated. In order to write a convincing argument to your representative that seat belt laws are unfair, you research current articles about the law and interview a law professor on the issue. You decide to claim that seat belt laws should be repealed because they are a fundamental violation of individual liberty. You believe that the opposing argument—that seat belts save lives and reduce insurance rates for everyone—is not relevant to the issue of individual liberty. Because your representative has supported seat belt laws, you present both sides of the issue but stress the arguments supporting your viewpoint.

> Give me liberty to know, to utter, and to argue freely according to conscience, above all liberties.
> —JOHN MILTON, POET

> Freedom of speech is established to achieve its essential purpose only when different opinions are expounded in the same hall to the same audience. . . . The opposition is indispensable.
> —WALTER LIPPMANN, JOURNALIST

WHEN PEOPLE ARGUE WITH EACH OTHER, THEY OFTEN BECOME HIGHLY EMOTIONAL OR CONFRONTATIONAL. REMEMBER THE LAST HEATED ARGUMENT YOU HAD WITH A FRIEND OR FAMILY MEMBER: AT THE END OFTHE ARGUMENT, ONE PERSON STOMPED out of the room, slammed the door, and didn't speak to the other for days. In the aftermath of such a scene, you felt angry at the other person and angry at yourself. Nothing was accomplished. Neither of you came close to achieving what you wanted when you began the argument. Rather than understanding each other's point of view and working out your differences, you effectively closed the lines of communication.

When writers construct arguments, however, they try to avoid the emotional outbursts that often turn arguments into displays of temper. Strong feelings may energize an argument—few of us make the effort to argue without emotional investment in the subject—but written argument stresses a fair presentation of opposing or alternative arguments. Because written arguments are public, they take on a civilized manner. They implicitly say, "Let's be reasonable about this. Let's look at the evidence on all sides. Before we argue for our position, let's put all the reasons and evidence on the table so everyone involved can see what's at stake."

As writers construct written arguments, they carefully consider the rhetorical situation:

- What is the social or cultural context for this issue?
- Where might this written argument appear or be published?
- Who is the audience, and what do they already know or believe?
- Do readers hold an opposing or alternative viewpoint, or are they more neutral and likely to listen to both sides before deciding what to believe?

> 66 All writing . . . is propaganda for something. 99
> —ELIZABETH DREW, WRITER AND CRITIC

A written argument creates an atmosphere of reason, which encourages readers to examine their own views clearly and dispassionately. When successful, such argument convinces rather than alienates an audience. It changes people's minds or persuades them to adopt a recommended course of action.

Techniques for Writing Arguments

A written argument is similar to a public debate—between attorneys in a court of law or between members of Congress who represent different political parties. It begins with a debatable issue: Is this a good bill? Should we vote for it? In such debates, one person argues for a position or proposal, while the other argues against it. The onlookers (the judge, the members of Congress, the jury, or the public) then decide what to believe or what to do. The chapter opening art, which shows a scene from *Inherit the Wind,* pictures the debate about evolution between Clarence Darrow and William Jennings Bryan during the 1925 Scopes trial. The judge in the picture makes sure the trial follows certain rules, and the audience (not in the picture) decides what or whom to believe.

Written argument, however, is not identical to a debate. *In a written argument, the writer must play all the different roles.* The writer is first of all the person arguing for the claim. But the writer must also represent what the opposition might say. In addition, the writer must think like the judge and make sure the argument follows appropriate rules. Perhaps certain arguments and evidence are inadmissible or inappropriate in this case. Finally, the writer often anticipates the responses of the audience and responds to them as well.

Written argument, then, represents several different points of view, responds to them reasonably and fairly, and gives reasons and evidence that support the writer's claim. An effective written argument uses the following techniques.

Techniques for Arguing

Technique	Tips on How to Do It
Analyzing the *rhetorical situation*	Reviewing your purpose, audience, genre, occasion, and context helps you understand how to write your essay. Pay particular attention to your *audience.* Knowing what your audience already knows and believes helps you convince or persuade them.
Focusing on a *debatable* claim	This claim becomes the *thesis.*
Representing and evaluating the *opposing points of view* on the issue fairly and accurately	The key to a successful arguing paper is *anticipating and responding* to the most important alternate or opposing positions.
Arguing reasonably *against opposing arguments* and *for your claim*	Respond to or refute alternate or opposing arguments. Present the best arguments supporting your claim. Argue reasonably and fairly.
Supporting your claims with sufficient *evidence*	Use firsthand observations; examples from personal experience; results of surveys and interviews; graphs, charts, and visuals; and statistics, facts, and quotations from your reading.

In an article titled "Active and Passive Euthanasia," James Rachels claims that active euthanasia may be defensible for patients with incurable and painful diseases. The following paragraphs from that article illustrate the key features of argument.

Opposing position

The distinction between active and passive euthanasia is thought to be crucial for medical ethics. The idea is that it is permissible, at least in some cases, to withhold treatment and allow a patient to die, but it is never permissible to take any direct action designed to kill the patient. This doctrine seems to be accepted by most doctors. . . .

Claim

However, a strong case can be made against this doctrine. In what follows I will set out some of the relevant arguments, and urge doctors

Audience

to reconsider their views on this matter.

Argument for claim

To begin with a familiar type of situation, a patient who is dying of incurable cancer of the throat is in terrible pain, which can no longer be satisfactorily alleviated. He is certain to die within a few days, even if

Example

present treatment is continued, but he does not want to go on living for those days, since the pain is unbearable. So he asks the doctor for an end to it, and his family joins in the request.

Example

Suppose the doctor agrees to withhold treatment, as the conventional doctrine says he may. The justification for his doing so is that the patient is in terrible agony, and since he is going to die anyway, it would be wrong to prolong his suffering needlessly. But now notice this. If one simply withholds treatment, it may take the patient longer to die, and so he may suffer more than he would if more direct action were taken and a lethal injection given. This fact provides strong reason for

Argument against opposition

thinking that, once the initial decision not to prolong his agony has been made, active euthanasia is actually preferable to passive euthanasia, rather than the reverse. To say otherwise is to endorse the option that leads to more suffering rather than less, and is contrary to the humanitarian impulse that prompts the decision not to prolong his life in the first place.

CLAIMS FOR WRITTEN ARGUMENT

The thesis of your argument is a *debatable claim.* Opinions on both sides of the issue must have some merit. Claims for a written argument usually fall into one of four categories: claims of fact, claims about cause and effect, claims about value, and claims about solutions and policies. A claim may occasionally fall into several categories or may even overlap categories.

● **CLAIMS OF FACT OR DEFINITION**   These claims are about facts that are not easily determined or about definitions that are debatable. If I claim that a Lhasa apso was an ancient Chinese ruler, you can check a dictionary and find out that I am wrong. A Lhasa apso is, in fact, a small Tibetan dog. There is no argument. But people do disagree about some supposed "facts": Are polygraph tests accurate? Do grades measure achievement? People also disagree about definitions: Gender discrimination exists in the marketplace, but is it "serious"? What is discrimination, anyway? And what constitutes "serious" discrimination? Does the fact that women currently earn only seventy-three cents for every dollar that men earn qualify as serious discrimination?

In "*American Gothic,* Pitchfork Perfect," a review of Grant Wood's famous painting, Paul Richard opens with a claim of fact and definition (the complete essay appears in Chapter 9). His claim is that *American Gothic* is an American emblem or icon. Although reviews typically contain claims of value, Richard begins his essay with a claim of fact or definition, arguing that the painting is a visual manifestation of the American dream.

> Is "American Gothic" America's best-known painting? Certainly it's one of them. Grant Wood's dual portrait—with its churchy evocations, its stiffness and its pitchfork—pierced us long ago, and got stuck into our minds. Now, finally, it's here.
>
> "American Gothic," which hasn't been in Washington in 40 years, goes on view today at the Renwick Gallery of the Smithsonian American Art Museum. By all means, take it in—although, of course, you have already.
>
> It should have gone all fuzzy—it's been parodied so often, and parsed so many ways—but the 1930 canvas at the Renwick is as sharp as ever. Its details are finer than its travesties suggest, its image more absorbing. It's also smaller than one might have imagined, at only two feet wide. Wood painted it in his home town of Cedar Rapids, Iowa, showed it only once and then sold it, with relief, to the Art Institute of Chicago—for $300.
>
> The picture with a pitchfork is an American unforgettable. Few paintings, very few, have its recognizability. Maybe Whistler's mother. Maybe Warhol's soup can. Maybe Rockwell's Thanksgiving turkey. They're national emblems, all of them, visual manifestations of the American dream.

● CLAIMS ABOUT CAUSE AND EFFECT

- Testing in the schools improves the quality of education.
- Secondhand smoke causes lung cancer.
- Capital punishment does not deter violent crime.

Unlike the claim that grades affect admission to college—which few people would deny—the above claims about cause and effect are debatable. No Child Left Behind requires tests in order to evaluate individual schools. But do these tests ultimately improve students' education, or do they just make students better test-takers? The claim that secondhand smoke causes cancer is behind the rush to make all public and commercial spaces smoke-free. But what scientific evidence demonstrates a cause-and-effect link? Finally, the deterring effect of capital punishment is still an arguable proposition with reasonable arguments on both sides.

In a selection from her book *The Plug-In Drug: Television, Children, and the Family,* Marie Winn argues that television has a negative effect on family life. In her opening paragraphs, she sets forth both sides of the controversy and then argues that the overall effect is negative.

> Television's contribution to family life has been an equivocal one. For while it has, indeed, kept the members of the family from dispersing, it has not served to bring them *together.* By its domination of the time families spend together, it destroys the special quality that depends to a great extent on what a family does, what special rituals, games, recurrent jokes, familiar songs, and shared activities it accumulates.
>
> "Like the sorcerer of old," writes Urie Bronfenbrenner, "the television set casts its magic spell, freezing speech and action, turning the living into silent statues so long as the enchantment lasts. The primary danger of the television screen lies not so much in the behavior it produces—although there is danger there—as in the behavior it prevents: the talks, the games, the family festivities and arguments through which much of the child's learning takes place and through which his character is formed. Turning on the television set can turn off the process that transforms children into people."
>
> Yet parents have accepted a television-dominated family life so completely that they cannot see how the medium is involved in whatever problems they might be having.

● CLAIMS ABOUT VALUE

- Boxing is a dehumanizing sport.
- Internet pornography degrades children's sense of human dignity.
- Toni Morrison is a great American novelist.

Claims about value typically lead to evaluative essays. All the strategies discussed in Chapter 9 apply here, with the additional requirement that you must anticipate and respond to alternate or opposing arguments. The essay that claims that boxing is dehumanizing must respond to the argument that boxing is merely another form of competition that promotes athletic excellence. The claim that pornography degrades children's sense of dignity must respond to the claim that restricting free speech on the Internet would cause greater harm. Arguing that Morrison is a great American novelist requires setting criteria for great American novels and then responding to critics who argue that Morrison's work does not reach those standards.

In "College Is a Waste of Time and Money," teacher and journalist Caroline Bird argues that many students go to college simply because it is the "thing to do." For those students, Bird claims, college is not a good idea.

Nowadays, says one sociologist, you don't have to have a reason for going to college; it's an institution. His definition of an institution is an arrangement everyone accepts without question; the burden of proof is not on why you go, but why anyone thinks there might be a reason for not going. The implication is that an 18-year-old . . . should listen to those who know best and go to college.

I don't agree. I believe that college has to be judged not on what other people think is good for students, but on how good it feels to the students themselves.

I believe that people have an inside view of what's good for them. If a child doesn't want to go to school some morning, better let him stay at home, at least until you find out why. Maybe he knows something you don't. It's the same with college. If high-school graduates don't want to go, or if they don't want to go right away, they may perceive more clearly than their elders that college is not for them. It is no longer obvious that adolescents are best off studying a core curriculum that was constructed when all educated men could agree on what made them educated, or that professors, advisors, or parents can be of any particular help to young people in choosing a major or a career. High-school graduates see college graduates driving cabs and decide it's not worth going. College students find no intellectual stimulation in their studies and drop out.

● CLAIMS ABOUT SOLUTIONS OR POLICIES

- Pornography on the Internet should be censored.
- The penalty for drunk driving should be a mandatory jail sentence and loss of driver's license.
- To reduce exploitation and sensationalism, the news media should not be allowed to interview victims of crime or disaster.

Claims about solutions or policies sometimes occur *along with* claims of fact or definition, cause and effect, or value. Because grades do not measure achievement (argue that this is a fact), they should be abolished (argue for this policy). Boxing is a dehumanizing sport (argue this claim of value); therefore, boxing should be banned (argue for this solution). Claims about solutions or policies involve all the strategies used for problem solving (see Chapter 10), but with special emphasis on countering opposing arguments: "Although advocates of freedom of speech suggest that we cannot suppress pornography on the Internet, in fact, we already have self-monitoring devices in other media that could help reduce pornography on the Internet."

In *When Society Becomes an Addict,* psychotherapist Anne Wilson Schaef argues that our society has become an "Addictive System" that has many characteristics in common with alcoholism and other addictions. Advertising becomes addictive, causing us to behave dishonestly; the social pressure to be "nice" can become addictive, causing us to lie to ourselves. Schaef argues that the solution for our social addictions begins when we face the reality of our dependency.

> We cannot recover from an addiction unless we first admit that we have it. Naming our reality is essential to recovery. Unless we admit that we are indeed functioning in an addictive process in an Addictive System, we shall never have the option of recovery. Once we name something, we own it. . . . Remember, to name the system as addict is not to condemn it: It is to offer it the possibility of recovery.
>
>   Paradoxically, the only way to reclaim our personal power is by admitting our powerlessness. The first part of Step One of the AA [Alcoholics Anonymous] Twelve-Step Program reads, "We admitted we were powerless over alcohol." It is important to recognize that admitting to powerlessness over an addiction is not the same as admitting powerlessness as a person. In fact, it can be very powerful to recognize the futility of the illusion of control.

APPEALS FOR WRITTEN ARGUMENT

❝ Mere knowledge of the truth will not give you the art of persuasion. **❞**

—PLATO,
PHAEDRUS

To support claims and respond to opposing arguments, writers use *appeals* to the audience. Argument uses three important types of appeals: to *reason* (logic and evidence support the claim), to *character* (the writer's good character itself supports the claim), and to *emotion* (the writer's expression of feelings about the issue may support the claim). Effective arguments emphasize the appeal to reason but may also appeal to character or emotion.

● **APPEAL TO REASON**   An appeal to reason depends most frequently on *inductive logic,* which is sometimes called the *scientific method.* Inductive logic draws a general conclusion from personal observation or experience, specific facts, reports, statistics, testimony of authorities, and other bits of data.

Experience is the best teacher, we always say, and experience teaches inductively. Suppose, using biologist Thomas Huxley's famous example, you pick a green apple from a tree and take a bite. Halfway through the bite you discover that the apple is sour and quickly spit it out. But, you think, perhaps the next green apple will be ripe and will taste better. You pick a second green apple, take a bite, and realize that it is just as sour as the first. However, you know that some apples—like the Granny Smith—look green even when they're ripe, so you take a bite out of a third apple. It is also sour. You're beginning to draw a conclusion. In fact, if you taste a fourth or fifth apple, other people may begin to question your intelligence. How many green apples from this tree must you taste before you get the idea that all of these green apples are sour?

Experience, however, may lead to wrong conclusions. You've tasted enough of these apples to convince *you* that all these apples are sour, but will others think that these apples are sour? Perhaps you have funny taste buds. You may need to ask several friends to taste the apples. Or perhaps you are dealing with a slightly weird tree—in fact, some apple trees are hybrids, with several different kinds of apples grafted onto one tree. Before you draw a conclusion, you may need to consult an expert in order to be certain that your tree is a standard, single-variety apple tree. If your friends and the expert also agree that all of these green apples are sour, you may use your experience *and* their testimony to reach a conclusion—and to provide evidence to make your argument more convincing to others.

Inductive Logic. In inductive logic, a reasonable conclusion is based on a *sufficient* quantity of accurate and reliable evidence that is selected in a *random* manner to reduce human bias or to take into account variation in the sample. The definition of *sufficient* varies, but generally the number must be large enough to convince your audience that your sample fairly represents the whole subject.

Let's take an example to illustrate inductive reasoning. Suppose you ask a student, one of fifty in a Psychology I class, a question of value: "Is Professor X a good teacher?" If this student says, "Professor X is the worst teacher I've ever had!" what conclusion can you draw? If you avoid taking the class based on a sample of one, you may miss an excellent class. So you decide to gather a *sufficient sample* by polling twenty of the fifty students in the class. But which twenty do you interview? If you ask the first student for a list of students, you may receive the names of twenty other students who also hate the professor. To reduce human or accidental bias, then, you choose a random method for collecting your evidence: As the students leave the class, you give a questionnaire to two out of every five students. If they all fill out the questionnaires, you probably have a *sufficient* and *random* sample.

Claim	Professor X is an excellent psychology teacher
Reason #1:	Professor X is an excellent teacher because she gives stimulating lectures that students rarely miss. *Evidence:* Sixty percent of the students polled said that they rarely missed a lecture. Three students cited Professor X's lecture on "assertiveness" as the best lecture they'd ever heard.
Reason #2:	Professor X is an excellent teacher because she gives tests that encourage learning rather than sheer memorization. *Evidence:* Seventy percent of the students polled said that Professor X's essay tests required thinking and learning rather than memorization. One student said that Professor X's tests always made her think about what she'd read. Another student said he always liked to discuss Professor X's test questions with his classmates and friends.

Finally, if the responses to your questionnaire show that fifteen out of twenty students rate Professor X as an excellent teacher, what *valid conclusion* should you draw? You should not say, categorically, "X is an excellent teacher." Your conclusion must be restricted by your evidence and the method of gathering it: "Seventy-five percent of the students polled in Psychology I believe that Professor X is an excellent teacher."

Most arguments use a shorthand version of the inductive method of reasoning. A writer makes a claim and then supports it with *reasons* and representative *examples* or *data*.

● **APPEAL TO CHARACTER**   An appeal based on your good character as a writer can also be important in argument. (The appeal to character is frequently called the *ethical appeal* because readers make a value judgment about the writer's character.) In a written argument, you show your audience—through your reasonable persona, voice, and tone—that you are a person who abides by moral standards that your audience shares: You have a good reputation, you are honest and trustworthy, and you argue "fairly."

A person's reputation often affects how we react to a claim, but *the argument itself* should also establish the writer's trustworthiness. You don't have to be a Mahatma Gandhi or a Mother Teresa to generate a strong ethical appeal for your claim. Even if your readers have never heard your name before, they will feel confident about your character if you are knowledgeable about your subject, present opposing arguments fairly, and support your own claim with sufficient, reliable evidence.

If your readers have reason to suspect your motives or think that you may have something personal to gain from your argument, you may need to bend over backward to be fair. If you do have something to gain, lay your cards on the table. Declare your vested interest but explain, for example, how your solution would benefit everyone equally. Similarly, don't try to cover up or distort the opponents' arguments; acknowledge the opposition's strong arguments and refute the weak ones.

At the most basic level, your interest in the topic and willingness to work hard can improve your ethical appeal. Readers can sense when a writer cares about his or her subject, when a writer knows something about the topic, about the rhetorical or cultural context, and about the various viewpoints on a topic. Show your readers that you care about the subject, and they will find your arguments more convincing. Show you care by

- using sufficient details and specific, vivid examples.
- including any relevant personal experience you have on the topic.
- including other people's ideas and points of view and by responding to their views with fairness and tact.
- organizing your essay so your main points are easy to find and transitions between ideas are clear and logical.
- revising and proofreading your essay.

Readers know when writers care about their subjects, and they are more willing to listen to new ideas when the writer has worked hard and is personally invested in the topic.

● **APPEAL TO EMOTION**   Appeals to emotion can be tricky because, as we have seen, when emotions come in through the door, reasonableness may fly out the window. Argument emphasizes reason, not emotion. We know, for example, how advertising plays on emotions, by means of loaded or exaggerated language or through images of famous or sexy people. Emotional appeals designed to *deceive* or *frighten* people or to *misrepresent* the virtues of a person, place, or object have no place in rational argument. But emotional appeals that illustrate a truth or movingly depict a reality are legitimate and effective means of convincing readers.

● **COMBINED APPEALS**   Appeals may be used in combination. Writers may appeal to reason and, at the same time, establish trustworthy characters and use legitimate emotional appeals. The following excerpt from Martin Luther King, Jr.'s "Letter from Birmingham Jail" illustrates all three appeals. He appeals to reason, arguing that, historically, civil rights reforms are rarely made without political pressure. He establishes his integrity and good character by treating the opposition (in this case, the Birmingham clergy) with respect and by showing moderation and restraint. Finally, he uses emotional appeals, describing his six-year-old daughter in tears and recalling his own humiliation at being refused a place to sleep. King uses these emotional appeals legitimately; he is not misrepresenting reality or trying to deceive his readers.

> One of the basic points in [the statement by the Birmingham clergy] is that the action that I and my associates have taken in Birmingham is untimely. Some have asked: "Why didn't you give the new city administration time to act?" The only answer that I can give to this query is that the new Birmingham administration must be prodded about as much as the outgoing one, before it will act. We are sadly mistaken if we feel that the election of Albert Boutwell as mayor will bring the millennium to Birmingham. While Mr. Boutwell is a much more gentle person than Mr. Connor, they are both segregationists, dedicated to the maintenance of the status quo. I have hoped that Mr. Boutwell will be reasonable enough to see the futility of massive resistance to desegregation. But he will not see this without pressure from devotees of civil rights. My friends, I must say to you that we have not made a single gain in civil rights without determined legal and nonviolent pressure. Lamentably, it is an historical fact that privileged groups seldom give up their privileges voluntarily. Individuals may see the moral light and voluntarily give up their unjust posture; but, as Reinhold Niebuhr has reminded us, groups tend to be more immoral than individuals.

Appeals to character and reason

Appeal to reason

Evidence

Appeals to character and reason

We know through painful experience that freedom is never voluntarily given by the oppressor; it must be demanded by the oppressed. Frankly, I have yet to engage in a direct-action campaign that was "well timed" in the view of those who have not suffered unduly from the disease of segregation. For years now I have heard the word "Wait!" It rings in the ear of every Negro with piercing familiarity. This "Wait" has almost always meant "Never." We must come to see, with one of our distinguished jurists, that "justice too long delayed is justice denied."

Appeal to emotion

We have waited for more than 340 years for our constitutional and God-given rights. . . . Perhaps it is easy for those who have never felt the stinging darts of segregation to say, "Wait." But when you have seen vicious mobs lynch your mothers and fathers at will and drown your sisters and brothers at whim; when you have seen hate-filled policemen curse, kick, and even kill your black brothers and sisters; when you see the vast majority of your twenty million Negro brothers smothering in

Appeal to emotion

an airtight cage of poverty in the midst of an affluent society; when you suddenly find your tongue twisted and your speech stammering as you seek to explain to your six-year-old daughter why she can't go to the public amusement park that has just been advertised on television, and see tears welling up in her eyes when she is told that Funtown is closed

Appeal to emotion

to colored children . . . when you take a cross-country drive and find it necessary to sleep night after night in the uncomfortable corners of your automobile because no motel will accept you; when you are humiliated day in and day out by nagging signs reading "white" and "colored"; when your first name becomes "nigger," your middle name becomes "boy" (however old you are) and your last name becomes "John" . . . —then

Appeals to character and reason

you will understand why we find it difficult to wait. There comes a time when the cup of endurance runs over, and men are no longer willing to be plunged into the abyss of despair. I hope, sirs, you can understand our legitimate and unavoidable impatience.

ROGERIAN ARGUMENT

Traditional argument assumes that people are most readily convinced or persuaded by a confrontational "debate" on the issue. In a traditional argument, the writer argues reasonably and fairly, but the argument becomes a kind of struggle or "war" as the writer attempts to "defeat" the arguments of the opposition. The purpose of a traditional argument is thus to convince an undecided audience that the writer has "won a fight" and emerged "victorious" over the opposition.

In fact, however, there are many situations in which a less confrontational and less adversarial approach to argument is more effective. Particularly when the issues are highly charged or when the audience that we are trying to persuade is the opposition, writers may more effectively use negotiation rather than confrontation. *Rogerian argument*—named after psychologist Carl Rogers— is a kind of negotiated argument where understanding and compromise replace the traditional, adversarial approach. Rogerian, or *nonthreatening,* argument opens the lines of communication by reducing conflict. When people's beliefs are attacked, they instinctively become defensive and strike back. As a result, the argument becomes polarized: The writer argues for a claim, the reader digs in to defend his or her position, and no one budges.

Crucial to Rogerian argument is the fact that convictions and beliefs are not abstract but reside in people. If people are to agree, they must be sensitive to each other's beliefs. Rogerian argument, therefore, contains a clear appeal to character. While Rogerian argument uses reason and logic, its primary goal is not to "win" the argument but to open the lines of communication. To do that, the writer must be sympathetic to different points of view and willing to modify his or her claims in response to people who hold different viewpoints. Once the reader sees that the writer is open to change, the reader may become more flexible.

Once both sides are more flexible, a compromise position or solution becomes possible. As Rogers says, "This procedure gradually achieves a mutual communication. Mutual communication tends to be pointed toward solving a problem rather than toward attacking a person or group." Rogerian argument, then, imitates not a courtroom debate but the mutual communication that may take place between two people. Whereas traditional argument intends to change the actions or the beliefs of the opposition, Rogerian argument works toward changes *in both sides* as a means of establishing common ground and reaching a solution.

If you choose Rogerian argument, remember that you must actually be willing to change your beliefs. Often, in fact, when you need to use Rogerian argument most, you may be least inclined to use it—simply because you are inflexible on an issue. If you are unwilling to modify your own position, your reader will probably sense your basic insincerity and realize that you are just playing a trick of rhetoric.

Rogerian argument is appropriate in a variety of sensitive or highly controversial situations. You may want to choose Rogerian argument if you are an employer requesting union members to accept a pay cut in order to help the company avoid bankruptcy. Similarly, if you argue to husbands that they should assume responsibility for half the housework, or if you argue to Anglo-Americans that Spanish language and culture should play a larger role in public education, you may want to use a Rogerian strategy. By showing that you empathize with the opposition's position and are willing to compromise, you create a climate for mutual communication.

Rogerian argument makes a claim, considers the opposition, and presents evidence to support the claim, but in addition, it avoids threatening or adversarial language and promotes mutual communication and learning. A Rogerian argument uses the following strategies.

- **Avoiding *a confrontational stance.*** Confrontation threatens your audience and increases their defensiveness. Threat hinders communication.

- **Presenting your *character* as someone who understands and can empathize with the opposition.** Show that you understand by restating the opposing position accurately.
- **Establishing *common ground* with the opposition.** Indicate the beliefs and values that you share.
- **Being willing *to change your views.*** Show where your position is not reasonable and could be modified.
- **Directing your argument toward *a compromise or workable solution.***

Note: An argument does not have to be either entirely adversarial or entirely Rogerian. You may use Rogerian techniques for the most sensitive points in an argument that is otherwise traditional or confrontational.

In his essay "Animal Rights Versus Human Health," biology professor Albert Rosenfeld illustrates several features of Rogerian argument. Rosenfeld argues that animals should be used for medical experiments, but he is aware that the issues are emotional and that his audience is likely to be antagonistic. In these paragraphs, Rosenfeld avoids threatening language, represents the opposition fairly, grants that he is guilty of *speciesism,* and says that he sympathizes with the demand to look for alternatives. He indicates that his position is flexible: Most researchers, he says, are delighted when they can use alternatives. He grants that there is some room for compromise, but he is firm in his position that some animal experimentation is necessary for advancements in medicine.

States opposing position fairly and sympathetically

It is fair to say that millions of animals—probably more rats and mice than any other species—are subjected to experiments that cause them pain, discomfort, and distress, sometimes lots of it over long periods of time. . . . All new forms of medication or surgery are tried out on animals first. Every new substance that is released into the environment, or put on the market, is tested on animals. . . .

States opposing position fairly

In 1975, Australian philosopher Peter Singer wrote his influential book called *Animal Liberation,* in which he accuses us all of "speciesism"—as reprehensible, to him, as racism or sexism. He freely describes the "pain and suffering" inflicted in the "tyranny of human over nonhuman animals" and sharply challenges our biblical license to exercise "dominion over the fish of the sea, and over the fowl of the air, and over every living thing that moveth upon the Earth."

Acknowledges common ground

Well, certainly we are guilty of speciesism. We do act as if we had dominion over other living creatures. But domination also entails some custodial responsibility. And the questions continue to be raised: Do we have the right to abuse animals? To eat them? To hunt them for sport? To keep them imprisoned in zoos—or, for that matter, in our households? Especially to do experiments on these creatures who can't fight back?

Sympathetic to opposing position

Hardly any advance in either human or veterinary medicine—cure, vaccine, operation, drug, therapy—has come about without experiments on animals. . . . I certainly sympathize with the demand that we look for ways to get the information we want without using animals. Most investigators are delighted when they can get their data by means of tissue cultures or computer simulations. But as we look for alternative ways to get information, do we meanwhile just do without?

Suggests compromise position

THE TOULMIN METHOD OF ARGUMENT

In *The Uses of Argument* (1958), British philosopher Stephen Toulmin argued against applying formal logic and the concepts of deduction and induction to written arguments. The six concepts that Toulmin identified are not universal rules but merely guidelines that can be helpful as we analyze the logic of an argument.

- **Data:** The evidence gathered to support a particular claim.
- **Claim:** The overall thesis the writer hopes to prove. This thesis may be a claim of fact or definition, of cause and effect, of value, or of policy.
- **Warrant:** The statement that explains why or how the data support the writer's claim.
- **Backing:** The additional logic or reasoning that, when necessary, supports the warrant.
- **Qualifier:** The short phrases that limit the scope of the claim, such as "typically," "usually," or "on the whole."
- **Exceptions:** Those particular situations in which the writer does not or would not insist on the claim.

● **EXAMPLE OF A TOULMIN ANALYSIS** We can illustrate each of these six concepts using Cathleen A. Cleaver's argument against Internet pornography in her essay, "The Internet: A Clear and Present Danger?" that appears later in this chapter. The relationship of the data, warrant, and claim are shown here.

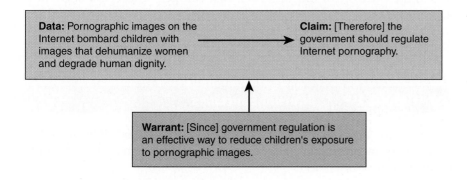

Data: Pornographic images on the Internet bombard children with images that dehumanize women and degrade human dignity. ⟶ **Claim:** [Therefore] the government should regulate Internet pornography.

Warrant: [Since] government regulation is an effective way to reduce children's exposure to pornographic images.

- **Backing:** Government regulation already exists in print, radio, and television media, so it should be extended to the Internet.

- **Qualifier:** *In most cases,* the government should regulate pornography on the Internet. (Cleaver does not actually use a qualifier for her claim. This is a qualifier she might use.)

- **Exceptions:** Government regulations must protect children, but *where children are not involved, regulation may not be as urgent.* (Cleaver implies this exception, since she focuses her argument only on pornography's effect on children.)

● **USING THE TOULMIN MODEL**   Applying the Toulmin model of argument to written texts can help us as readers and writers if we follow a few guidelines. First, the Toulmin model is especially helpful as we critically read texts for their logical strengths and weaknesses. As we become better critical readers, we are likely to make our own arguments more logical and thus more persuasive. Second, as we critically read texts, not all of us find the same warrant statements, because there can be several ways of explaining a logical connection between the data and the stated claim. Third, applying the Toulmin model and using warrants, backing, qualifiers, and exceptions becomes more important when our readers are likely to disagree with the claim.

Just as Rogerian argument tries to reduce conflict in adversarial situations through mutual communication and a strong appeal to character, the Toulmin model helps communicate in adversarial contexts by being especially reasonable and logical. If our readers already agree that pornography on the Internet is a bad thing, we need to give only a few examples and go straight to our claim. But if readers are members of the ACLU or have a strong belief in free speech on the Internet, we need to qualify our claim and make our warrants—the connections between the data and the claim—as explicit and logical as possible. We may also need to state backing for the warrant and note the exceptions where we don't want to press our case. The more antagonistic our readers are, the more we need to be as logical as possible. The Toulmin model is just one approach that can help bolster the logic of our argument.

> ❝ A society which is clamoring for choice [is] filled with many articulate groups, each arguing its own brand of salvation. ❞
> —MARGARET MEAD, ANTHROPOLOGIST

WARMING UP   *Journal Exercises*

The following exercises will help you practice arguing. Read all of the following exercises and then write on the three that interest you most. If another idea occurs to you, write about it.

1 From the following list of "should" statements, choose one that relates to your experience and freewrite for ten minutes. When you finish your freewriting, state a claim and list arguments on both sides of the issue.

- Bicyclists should be subject to regular traffic laws, including DWI.
- The sale of all handguns should be illegal.
- NCAA football should have playoffs.
- High-quality child care should be available to all working parents at public expense.
- Computer literacy courses should be required at the college level.
- Police should live in the neighborhoods they serve.
- Fraternities and sororities should be forbidden to serve alcoholic beverages.
- Students should work for one year between high school and college.
- Businesses should be required to provide free health insurance for all employees.
- Nonmajor courses should be graded pass/fail.

2 Controversial subjects depend as much on the audience as they do on the issue itself. Make a quick list of things you do every day: the kind of clothes you wear, the food you eat, the books you read, the friends you have, the ideas you discuss. For one of these activities, imagine people who might find what you do immoral, illogical, unjust, or unhealthy. What claim might they make about your activity? What reasons or evidence might they use to argue that your activity should be abolished, outlawed, or changed? Write for five minutes arguing *their* point of view.

3 **Writing Across the Curriculum.** Grades are important, but in some courses, they get in the way of learning. Choose an actual course that you have taken and write an open letter to the school administration, arguing for credit/no-credit grading in that particular course. Assume that you intend to submit your letter to the campus newspaper.

4 Arguments for academic or public audiences should focus on a *debatable* claim—that is, a claim about which knowledgeable people might disagree about a certain issue. Sometimes, however, even the notion of what constitutes a "debatable claim" is itself debated. Read and analyze the Doonesbury cartoon reprinted here. What controversies does the cartoon suggest are not really controversies? How does Gary Trudeau use irony to make his point?

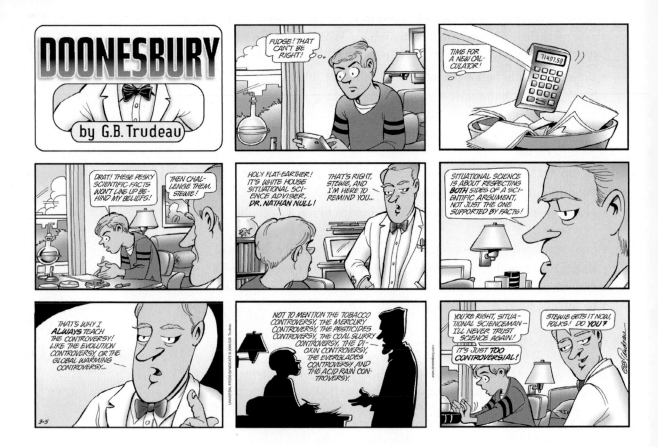

The Internet: A Clear and Present Danger?

Cathleen A. Cleaver

Cathleen Cleaver is a former director of legal studies at the Family Research Council, an organization based in Washington, D.C. She has published extensively on issues relating to children and the Internet, in newspapers and magazines such as USA Today, Newsday, *and the* Congressional Quarterly Researcher. *The following essay was originally a speech given at Boston University as part of a College of Communica-*

tion Great Debate. In this speech, she argues that some industry and government regulation of the Internet is necessary.

- Someone breaks through your firewall and steals proprietary   1
  information from your computer systems. You find out and
  contact a lawyer who says, "Man, you shouldn't have had your
  stuff online." The thief becomes a millionaire using your ideas,
  and you go broke, if laws against copyright violation don't protect
  material on the Internet.

- You visit the Antiques Anonymous Web site and decide to pay   2
  their hefty subscription fee for a year's worth of exclusive estate
  sale previews in their private online monthly magazine. They
  never deliver and, in fact, never intended to—they don't even have
  a magazine. You have no recourse, if laws against fraud don't
  apply to online transactions.

- Bob Guccione decides to branch out into the lucrative child porn   3
  market and creates a Teen Hustler Web site featuring nude adolescents and preteens. You find out and complain, but nothing can
  be done, if child pornography distribution laws don't apply to
  computer transmissions.

- A major computer software vendor who dominates the market   4
  develops his popular office software so that it works only with his
  browser. You're a small browser manufacturer who is completely
  squeezed out of the market, but you have to find a new line of
  work, if antitrust laws don't apply online.

- Finally, a pedophile e-mails your son, misrepresenting himself as a   5
  twelve-year-old named Jenny. They develop an online relationship
  and one day arrange to meet after school, where he intends to rape
  your son. Thankfully, you learn in advance about the meeting and
  go there yourself, where you find a forty-year-old man instead of
  Jenny. You flee to the police, who'll tell you there's nothing they can
  do, if child-stalking laws don't apply to the Internet.

The awesome advances in interactive telecommunication that   6
we've witnessed in just the last few years have changed the way in
which many Americans communicate and interact. No one can doubt
that the Internet is a technological revolution of enormous proportion, with outstanding possibilities for human advancement.

As lead speaker for the affirmative, I'm asked to argue that the In-   7
ternet poses a "clear and present danger," but the Internet, as a whole,
isn't dangerous. In fact, it continues to be a positive and highly beneficial tool, which will undoubtedly improve education, information exchange, and commerce in years to come. In other words, the Internet
will enrich many aspects of our daily life. Thus, instead of defending

...continued The Internet: A Clear and Present Danger?, **Cathleen A. Cleaver**

this rather apocalyptic view of the Internet, I'll attempt to explain why some industry and government regulation of certain aspects of the Internet is necessary—or, stated another way, why people who use the Internet should not be exempt from many of the laws and regulations that govern their conduct elsewhere. My opening illustrations were meant to give examples of some illegal conduct which should not become legal simply because someone uses the Internet. In looking at whether Internet regulation is a good idea, I believe we should consider whether regulation is in the public interest. In order to do that, we have to ask the question: Who is the public? More specifically, does the "public" whose interests we care about tonight include children?

CHILDREN AND THE INTERNET

Dave Barry describes the Internet as a "worldwide network of university, government, business, and private computer systems, run by a thirteen-year-old named Jason." This description draws a smile precisely because we acknowledge the highly advanced computer literacy of our children. Most children demonstrate computer proficiency that far surpasses that of their parents, and many parents know only what their children have taught them about the Internet, which gives new relevance to Wordsworth's insight: "The child is father of the man." In fact, one could go so far as to say that the Internet is as accessible to many children as it is inaccessible to many adults. This technological evolution is new in many ways, not the least of which is its accessibility to children, wholly independent of their parents. 8

When considering what's in the public interest, we must consider the whole public, including children, as individual participants in this new medium. 9

PORNOGRAPHY AND THE INTERNET

This new medium is unique in another way. It provides, through a single avenue, the full spectrum of pornographic depictions, from the more familiar convenience store fare to pornography of such violence and depravity that it surpasses the worst excesses of the normal human imagination. Sites displaying this material are easily accessible, making pornography far more freely available via the Internet than from any other communications medium in the United States. Pornography is the third largest sector of sales on the Internet, generating $1 billion annually. There are an estimated seventy-two thousand pornographic sites on the World Wide Web alone, with approximately thirty-nine new explicit sex sites every day. Indeed, the 10

Washington Post has called the Internet the largest pornography store in the history of mankind.

There is little restriction of pornography-related activity in cyberspace. While there are some porn-related laws, the specter of those laws does not loom large in cyberspace. There's an implicit license there that exists nowhere else with regard to pornography—an environment where people are free to exploit others for profit and be virtually untroubled by legal deterrent. Indeed, if we consider cyberspace to be a little world of its own, it's the type of world for which groups like the ACLU have long fought but, so far, fought in vain.   *11*

I believe it will not remain this way, but until it changes, we should take the opportunity to see what this world looks like, if for no other reason than to reassure ourselves that our decades-old decisions to control pornography were good ones.   *12*

With a few clicks of the mouse, anyone, any child, can get graphic and often violent sexual images—the kind of stuff it used to be difficult to find without exceptional effort and some significant personal risk. Anyone with a computer and a modem can set up public sites featuring the perversion of their choice, whether it's mutilation of female genitals, eroticized urination and defecation, bestiality, or sites featuring depictions of incest. These pictures can be sold for profit, they can be sent to harass others, or posted to shock people. Anyone can describe the fantasy rape and murder of a specific person and display it for all to read. Anyone can meet children in chat rooms or via e-mail and send them pornography and find out where they live. An adult who signs onto an AOL chat room as a thirteen-year-old girl is hit on thirty times within the first half hour.   *13*

All this can be done from the seclusion of the home, with the feeling of near anonymity and with the comfort of knowing that there's little risk of legal sanction.   *14*

The phenomenon of this kind of pornography finding such a welcome home in this new medium presents abundant opportunities for social commentary. What does Internet pornography tell us about human sexuality? Photographs, videos, and virtual games that depict rape and the dehumanization of women in sexual scenes send powerful messages about human dignity and equality. Much of the pornography freely available without restriction on the Internet celebrates unhealthy and antisocial kinds of sexual activity, such as sadomasochism, abuse, and degradation. Of course, by its very nature, pornography encourages voyeurism.   *15*

Beyond the troubling social aspects of unrestricted porn, we face the reality that children are accessing it and that predators are accessing children. We have got to start considering what kind of society we'll have when the next generation learns about human sexuality from what the Internet teaches. What does unrestricted Internet pornography teach children about relationships, about the equality of women? What does it teach little girls about themselves and their worth?   *16*

Opponents of restrictions are fond of saying that it's up to the par- 17
ents to deal with the issue of children's exposure. Well, of course it is,
but placing the burden solely on parents is illogical and ineffective. It's
far easier for a distributor of pornography to control his material than
it is for parents, who must, with the help of software, search for and
find the pornographic sites, which change daily, and then attempt to
block them. Any pornographer who wants to can easily subvert these
efforts, and a recent Internet posting from a teenager wanting to know
how to disable the filtering software on his computer received several
effective answers. Moreover, it goes without saying that the most sophisticated software can only be effective where it's installed, and children will have access to many computers that don't have filtering
software, such as those in libraries, schools, and at neighbors' houses.

INTERNET TRANSACTIONS SHOULD NOT BE EXEMPT

Opponents of legal restrictions often argue simply that the laws just can- 18
not apply in this new medium, but the argument that old laws can't apply
to changing technology just doesn't hold. We saw this argument last in the
early '80s with the advent of the videotape. Then, certain groups tried to
argue that, since you can't view videotapes without a VCR, you can't make
the sale of child porn videos illegal, because, after all, they're just plastic
boxes with magnetic tape inside. Technological change mandates legal
change only insofar as it affects the justification for a law. It just doesn't
make sense that the government may take steps to restrict illegal material
in *every* medium—video, television, radio, the private telephone, *and*
print—but that it may do nothing where people distribute the material by
the Internet. While old laws might need redefinition, the old principles
generally stand firm.

The question of enforcement usually is raised here, and it often comes 19
in the form of: "How are you going to stop people from doing it?" Well,
no law stops people from doing things—a red light at an intersection
doesn't force you to stop but tells you that you should stop and that there
could be legal consequences if you don't. Not everyone who runs a red
light is caught, but that doesn't mean the law is futile. The same concept
holds true for Internet laws. Government efforts to temper harmful conduct online will never be perfect, but that doesn't mean they shouldn't un-
dertake the effort at all.

There's clearly a role for industry to play here. Search engines don't 20
have to run ads for porn sites or prioritize search results to highlight porn.
One new search engine even has sex as the default search term. Internet
service providers can do something about unsolicited e-mail with
hotlinks to porn, and they can and should carefully monitor any chat
rooms designed for kids.

Some charge that industry standards or regulations that restrict ex- *21* plicit pornography will hinder the development of Internet technology. But that is to say that its advancement depends upon unrestricted exhibition of this material, and this cannot be true. The Internet does not belong to pornographers, and it's clearly in the public interest to see that they don't usurp this great new technology. We don't live in a perfect society, and the Internet is merely a reflection of the larger social community. Without some mitigating influences, the strong will exploit the weak, whether a Bill Gates or a child predator.

CONCLUSION: TECHNOLOGY MUST SERVE MAN

To argue that the strength of the Internet is chaos or that our liberty depends *22* upon chaos is to misunderstand not only the Internet but also the fundamental nature of our liberty. It's an illusion to claim social or moral neutrality in the application of technology, even if its development may be neutral. It can be a valuable resource only when placed at the service of humanity and when it promotes our integral development for the benefit of all.

Guiding principles simply cannot be inferred from mere technical effi- *23* ciency or from the usefulness accruing to some at the expense of others. Technology by its very nature requires unconditional respect for the fundamental interests of society.

Internet technology must be at the service of humanity and of our in- *24* alienable rights. It must respect the prerogatives of a civil society, among which is the protection of children.

vo·cab·u·lar·y

In your journal, write the meaning of the italicized words in the following phrases.

- steals *proprietary* information (**1**)
- rather *apocalyptic* view (**7**)
- legal *deterrent* (**11**)
- don't have *filtering* software (**17**)

- the law is *futile* (**19**)
- cannot be *inferred* (**23**)
- usefulness *accruing* to some (**23**)
- respect the *prerogatives* (**24**)

? QUESTIONS FOR WRITING AND DISCUSSION

1. Before you read or reread Cleaver's essay, write down your own thoughts and experiences about pornography on the Internet. Have you run into sites that you find offensive? Should access to such sites be made more difficult? Do you think children should be protected from accessing such

sites—either by accident or on purpose? What do you think are the best method(s) for such regulation: Internet software programs, parental regulation, governmental regulation? Explain.

2. Cleaver begins her essay with several scenarios describing potential abuses and crimes that occur online. Did you find these scenarios effective as a lead-in to her argument? Did they help you focus on her thesis? Should she use fewer scenarios? Why do you think she used all of these examples when only two dealt with child pornography on the Internet?

3. The rhetorical occasion for Cleaver's argument is a debate sponsored by the College of Communication at Boston University. In her essay, can you find evidences (word choice, vocabulary, sentence length, tone, use of evidence, use of appeals) that suggest that her original *genre* was a speech and that her *audience* was college students, college faculty, and members of the community? Cite evidence from the essay showing where Cleaver uses debate elements appropriate for this genre and makes appeals to this audience.

4. Cleaver states her case for government regulation of pornography on the Internet, but who is against regulation, and what are their arguments? What arguments opposing Internet regulation does Cleaver cite? (Are there other opposing arguments that Cleaver does not consider?) How well does Cleaver answer these opposing arguments?

5. Arguing essays make appeals to reason, to character, and to emotion. Find examples of each type of appeal in Cleaver's essay. Which type of appeal does she use most frequently? Which appeals are most or least effective? Does she rely too much on her emotional appeals (see paragraph 13, for example)? For her audience and her context (a debate), should she bolster her rational appeals with more evidence and statistics? Why or why not?

6. Imagine that you are at this debate on the Internet and that your side believes that there should be no or very little regulation of the Internet. What arguments might you make in response to Cleaver? Make a list of the possible pro–con arguments on this topic and explain which ones you will focus on as you respond to Cleaver.

Multigenre Casebook on Web 2.0

Farhad Manjoo, "You Have No Friends"	[Online article]
Sarah Kliff, ". . . And Why I Hate It"	[Magazine article]
"Facebook US Audience Growth"	[Web site]
Emily Nussbaum, from "Say Everything"	[Magazine article]

Larry D. Rosen, "Teens Feel Safe on MySpace"   [Sidebar in journal]

Lily Huang, "Protect the Willfully Ignorant"   [Magazine article]

AdCouncil, "Think Before You Post"   [Public service advertisement]

Simson L. Garfinkel, "Wikipedia and the Meaning of Truth"   [Academic journal article]

James Montgomery, "Can Wikipedia Handle Stephen Colbert's Truthiness?"   [Online article]

Neil L. Waters, "Why You Can't Cite Wikipedia in My Class"   [Academic journal article]

Mark Wilson, "Professors Should Embrace Wikipedia"   [Online article]

Noam Cohen, "Twitter in the Barricádes in Iran: Six Lessons Learned"   [Newspaper article]

The multigenre texts in the casebook represent a snapshot of the ongoing conversation and debate about the purpose and value of Web 2.0 learning and communication styles in both the academic curriculum and in citizens' participation in a democratic society. The articles, essays, blogs, visuals, and graphics in this casebook focus on social networking sites such as MySpace and Facebook, on public wiki sites such as Wikipedia, and on micro-messaging sites such as Twitter. As you read these articles, consider the following questions. Can we define Web 2.0? What common communication technologies or perspectives do all these Web 2.0 sites share? To what degree are Web 2.0 sites replacing traditional print genres? What are the effects of increasing participation in Web 2.0 sites? Do these sites bring increasing democratic participation, a lowering of communication standards, increasing personal communication, decreasing authentic or reliable information, or all of the above? Which of these Web 2.0 sites are passing networking fads and which show promise of staying power?

As you read these texts, maintain a rhetorical perspective: Are these authors making claims of fact or definition, cause-and-effect, value, or policy? Does each document make an argument and consider alternative points of view? (Are some of these texts simply informative without making an argument?) What appeals—to reason, to character, or to emotion—do these authors make? Consider also how these writers construct or address their audience: Who do they think their reader is? What do they believe their readers already know or believe? What strategies do they think will convince or persuade their readers?

Finally, after you have read these texts, consider how the genre of the document—essay or article in a journal or magazine, blog on a Web site, visual, or graphic—affects the argument of the document. Do the visuals or graphics make as strong—or stronger—appeal as the written texts? If your own assignment is to create a multigenre document for a specific audience or if you want to integrate visuals or graphs in your document, consider how each genre will contribute to your overall goal of convincing or persuading your audience.

> 66 The way today's students will do science, politics, journalism, and business next year and a decade from now will be shaped by the skills they acquire in using social media and by the knowledge they gain of the important issues of privacy, identity, community, and the role of citizen media in democracy. 99
> HOWARD RHEINGOLD, AUTHOR OF *SMART MOBS*

> 66 The popularity of Web 2.0 is evidence of a tide of credulity and misinformation that can only be countered by a culture of respect for authenticity and expertise in all scholarly, research, and educational endeavors. 99
> MICHAEL GORMAN, "WEB 2.0: THE SLEEP OF REASON"

You Have No Friends

Farhad Manjoo

At 1:37 a.m. on Jan. 8, Mark Zuckerberg, the 24-year-old founder and 1 CEO of Facebook, posted a message on the company's blog with news of a milestone: The site had just added its 150-millionth member. Facebook now has users on every continent, with half of them logging in at least once a day. "If Facebook were a country, it would be the eighth most populated in the world, just ahead of Japan, Russia and Nigeria," Zuckerberg wrote. This People's Republic of Facebook would also have a terrible population-growth problem. Like most communications networks, Facebook obeys classic network-effects laws: It gets better—more useful, more entertaining—as more people join it, which causes it to grow even faster still. It was just last August that Facebook hit 100 million users. Since then, an average of 374,000 people have signed up every day. At this rate, Facebook will grow to nearly 300 million people by this time next year.

If you're reading this article, there's a good chance you already be- 2 long to Facebook. There's a good chance everyone you know is on Facebook, too. Indeed, there's a good chance you're no longer reading this article because you just switched over to check Facebook. That's fine—this piece is not for you. Instead I'd like to address those readers who aren't on Facebook, especially those of you who've consciously decided to stay away.

Though your ranks dwindle daily, there are many of you. This is 3 understandable—any social movement that becomes so popular so fast engenders skepticism. A year ago, the *New York Observer* interviewed a half-dozen or so disdainful Facebook holdouts. "I don't see how having hundreds or thousands of 'friends' is leading to any kind of substantive friendships," said Cary Goldstein, the director of publicity at Twelve Publishers. "The whole thing seems so weird to me. Now you really have to turn off your computer and just go out to live real life and make real connections with people that way. I don't think it's healthy." I was reminded of a quote from an *Onion* story, "Area Man Constantly Mentioning He Doesn't Own a Television"*:* "I'm not an elitist. It's just that I'd much rather sculpt or write in my journal or read Proust than sit there passively staring at some phosphorescent screen."

Friends—can I call you friends?—it's time to drop the attitude: 4 There is no longer any good reason to avoid Facebook. The site has crossed a threshold—it is now so widely trafficked that it's fast becoming a routine aide to social interaction, like e-mail and antiperspirant.

It's only the most recent of many new technologies that have crossed over this stage. For a long while—from about the late '80s to the late-middle '90s, *Wall Street* to *Jerry Maguire*—carrying a mobile phone seemed like a haughty affectation. But as more people got phones, they became more useful for everyone—and then one day enough people had cell phones that everyone began to assume that you did, too. Your friends stopped prearranging where they would meet up on Saturday night because it was assumed that everyone would call from wherever they were to find out what was going on. From that moment on, it became an affectation *not* to carry a mobile phone; they'd grown so deeply entwined with modern life that the only reason to be without one was to make a statement by abstaining. Facebook is now at that same point—whether or not you intend it, you're saying something by staying away.

I use Facebook every day, and not always to waste time. Most of 5 my extended family lives in South Africa, and though I speak to them occasionally on the phone, Facebook gives me an astonishingly intimate look at their lives—I can see what they did yesterday, what they're doing tomorrow, and what they're doing right now, almost like there's no distance separating us. The same holds true for my job: I live on the West Coast, but I work in an industry centered on the East Coast; Facebook gives me the opportunity to connect with people—to "network," you might say—in a completely natural, unaggressive manner. More than a dozen times, I've contacted sources through Facebook—searching for them there is much easier than searching for a current e-mail or phone number.

In fact, Facebook helped me write this story. The other day I 6 posted a status update asking my Facebook friends to put me in touch with people who've decided against joining. The holdouts I contacted this way weren't haughty—they were nice, reasonable people with entirely rational-sounding explanations for staying off the site. Among the main reasons people cited was that Facebook looked like it required too much work. Chad Retelle, a network systems administrator in Madison, Wis., said he'd seen how his wife—my friend Katie—had taken to the site. But at the same time, it had changed her: "Now she's obligated to spend time maintaining her Facebook page. She's got to check it every morning. I have no desire to do that."

Retelle and other Facebook holdouts also protested that the site 7 presents numerous opportunities for awkwardness—there's the headache of managing which people to friend and which to forget, the fear that one of your friends might post something on your wall that will offend everyone else, the worry that someone will find something about you that you didn't mean to share. Naomi Harris, a magazine photographer in New York, says that, for all that trouble, Facebook

...continued You Have No Friends, **Farhad Manjoo**

seems to offer little in return. "Why?" she asks. "I'm on the computer enough as it is for work. I don't really want to be there for recreation purposes, too. I have no interests in someone from fifth grade contacting me and saying, 'Hey, I sat behind you in class—wanna chat?' "

Finally, I heard what must be the most universal concern about Facebook—*I don't want people knowing my business!* Kate Koppelman is a 23-year-old New Yorker who works in the fashion industry. She was on Facebook all through college, and she concedes that the site has many benefits. And yet, the whole thing creeped her out: "I had friends from back home knowing what was going on with my friends from college—people they had never met—which was weird," she told me. "I found friends knowing things about what was on my 'wall' before I'd had a chance to see it—which was also weird." Koppelman quit Facebook last year. She still uses it by proxy—her roommates look people up for her when she's curious about them—but she says she'll never sign up again. 8

Yet of the many concerns about Facebook, Koppelman's is the most easily addressed. Last year, the site added a series of fine-grained privacy controls that let you choose which friends see what information about you. Your college friends can see one version of your profile, your high-school friends another, and your family yet another; if you want, you can let everyone see essentially nothing about you. 9

Retelle's worry that Facebook demands a lot of work is also somewhat misguided. It's true that some people spend a lot of time on it, but that's because they're having fun there; if you're not, you can simply log in once or twice a week just to accept or reject friends. Even doing nothing and waiting for others to friend you is enough: You're establishing a presence for other people to connect with you, which is the site's main purpose. 10

That brings us to Harris' argument: What's the social utility to Facebook—why should you join? Like with e-mail and cell phones, there are many, and as you begin to use it, you'll notice more and different situations in which it proves helpful. In general, Facebook is a lubricant of social connections. With so many people on it, it's now the best, fastest place online to find and connect with a specific person—think of it as a worldwide directory, or a Wikipedia of people. As a result, people now expect to find you on Facebook—whether they're contacting you for a job or scouting you out for a genius grant. 11

True, you might not want people to be able to follow your life—it's no great loss to you if your long-lost college frenemy can't find you. But what about your old fling, your new fling, your next employer, or that friend-of-a-friend you just met at a party who says he can give you some great tips on your golf swing? Sure, you can trade e-mail ad- 12 dresses or phone numbers, but in many circles Facebook is now the expected way to make these connections. By being on Facebook, you're facilitating such ties; without it, you're missing them and making life difficult for those who went looking for you there.

Skeptics often suggest that online social networks foster intro- 13 verted, anti-social behavior—that we forge virtual connections at the expense of real-life connections. But only someone who's never used Facebook would make that argument. Nobody avoids meeting people in real life by escaping to the Web. In fact, the opposite seems true: Short, continuous, low-content updates about the particulars of your friends' lives—Bob has the flu, Barbara can't believe what just happened on *Mad Men*, Sally and Ned are no longer on speaking terms—deepen your bonds with them. Writer Clive Thompson has explored this phenomenon, what social scientists call "ambient awareness." Following someone through his status updates is not unlike sitting in a room with him and semiconsciously taking note of his body language, Thompson points out. Just as you can sense his mood from the rhythm of his breathing, sighing, and swearing, you can get the broad outlines of his life from short updates, making for a deeper conversation the next time you do meet up.

It's this benefit of Facebook that seems to hook people in the end: 14 Their friendships seem to demand signing up. Last year, Darcy Stockton, a fashion photographer in New York, held nothing back in describing her hatred of Facebook to the *Observer*. "If you have time to network through a site like that, you aren't working enough," she said. "I just don't have the *time* or the *ability* to keep up with yet another social networking site in my free time. I feel there's other things and real experiences I could be having in real life instead of wasting my free time on Facebook."

Stockton now has 250 Facebook friends. In an e-mail, she explained 15 that she'd decided to join the site when her friends migrated over from MySpace. She added, "Thank you for making me eat my words!"

PROFESSIONAL WRITING

. . . And Why I Hate It

Sarah Kliff

The site nurses my worst self-indulgent instincts. Does anyone really care that I love penguins?

I have no idea how many hours of my life I've wasted on Facebook. 1 When I wake up each morning, with my laptop sitting on the edge of my futon, I check it. Before I've thought about brushing my teeth,

I have already seen the photographs of my brother's new apartment in San Francisco and discovered the evidence of my friend's tumultuous breakup: she changed her relationship status from "In a Relationship" to "Single" to "It's Complicated," all while I was sleeping. As best I can figure, since joining the site in 2004 when I was a freshman at Washington University in St. Louis, I've been logging on a dozen times a day. When I should have been studying or working, I found myself instead doing tasks like flipping through 400 photos of myself online, debating whether I wanted the picture where I have food in my hair to be on display to the world. (I decided to leave it: while it's not the most attractive pose, I think it indicates that I am a laid-back, good-humored person.)

I spend an inordinate amount of time like this, worrying about 2 what's in my online profile. When I graduated from college this May, I decided it was time for a Facebook makeover. Looking to present a more "professional" image, I stripped my profile of many of my collegiate interests—you'll no longer know from Facebook that I'm obsessed with penguins—and I purged my membership in questionable Facebook groups such as "Scotland? Sounds more like Hotland" (tamer than it sounds). I know I'm not the only one constantly revamping my cyber-image: according to my Facebook account, 109 of my friends have changed something over the past two days. One friend added "goofy dads" to her interests, and another let it be known that he "falls asleep easily" and "loses things all the time."

What is with all this time we've spent, thinking about ourselves and 3 creating well-planned lists of our interests? Facebook is much worse than e-mail, cell phones, instant messaging and the other devices that keep me constantly connected. It nurses every self-indulgent urge I could possibly have. I hate that Facebook encourages me to home in on each of my idiosyncrasies—that I like running in Central Park, for example, or that my favorite forms of punctuation are the dash and semicolon—and broadcast them to a largely uninterested world. I have a sneaking suspicion that very few people want to know that I am particularly fond of bagels. And no one really cares when I change my Facebook status, a fill-in-the-blank feature where users can let people know what they're up to at any moment. Mine is currently set to "Sarah is trying to write an article about Facebook . . . but is ironically too distracted by Facebook." The network is as much about obsessing over the dull details of my life as it as about connecting with others.

As a recent college graduate, with my friends scattered across the 4 globe, I understand the communicative value of Facebook. Right now, I have 469 "friends"—though I admit many of these virtual relationships are tenuous at best. Still, I would be hard-pressed to give up my four-year-long membership or leave Facebook out of my early morning routine. But who knows what I'm missing out on in the real world while sitting at my laptop, debating whether penguins or bagels are more respectable?

PROFESSIONAL WRITING

Facebook US Audience Growth

FACEBOOK US AUDIENCE GROWTH, LAST 180 DAYS

Looking at Facebook US audience growth over the last 180 days, it's 1 clear that Facebook is seeing massive increases in adoption amongst users 35–65. The fastest growing demographic on Facebook is still women over 55—there are now nearly 1.5 million of them active on Facebook each month.

The biggest growth in terms of absolute new users over the last six 2 month came amongst users 35–44. Over 4 million more US women 35–44 and nearly 3 million more US men 35–44 used Facebook in March 2009 compared to September 2008.

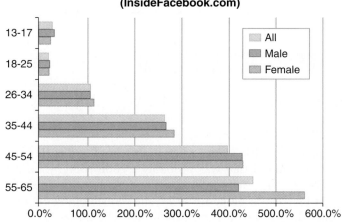

US Facebook Audience Growth, 9/08-3/09
(InsideFacebook.com)

...continued Facebook US Audience Growth, **InsideFacebook.com**

US FACEBOOK USERS BY AGE AND GENDER

With the rapid growth amongst older users, the majority of US Facebook   3
users are now over 25. There are now 6 million users 13–17, 19.5 million
18–25, 13.4 million 26–34, 9.7 million 35–44, 4.6 million 45–54, and 2.8
million over 55. In other words, there are more Facebook users 26–44 than
18–25 today.

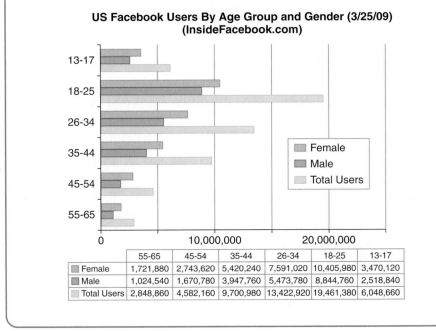

**US Facebook Users By Age Group and Gender (3/25/09)
(InsideFacebook.com)**

	55-65	45-54	35-44	26-34	18-25	13-17
Female	1,721,880	2,743,620	5,420,240	7,591,020	10,405,980	3,470,120
Male	1,024,540	1,670,780	3,947,760	5,473,780	8,844,760	2,518,840
Total Users	2,848,860	4,582,160	9,700,980	13,422,920	19,461,380	6,048,660

PROFESSIONAL WRITING

Say Everything

Emily Nussbaum

I remember very little from junior-high school and high school, and   1
I've always believed that was probably a good thing. Caitlin Oppermann, 17, has spent her adolescence making sure this doesn't happen
to her. At 12, she was blogging; at 14, she was snapping digital photos;
at 15, she edited a documentary about her school marching band. But

right now the high-school senior is most excited about her first "serious project," caitlinoppermann.com. On it, she lists her e-mail and AIM accounts, complains about the school's Web censors, and links to photos and videos. There's nothing racy, but it's the type of information overload that tends to terrify parents. Oppermann's are supportive: "They know me and they know I'm not careless with the power I have on the Internet."

As we talk, I peer into her bedroom. I'm at a café in the West Village, and she is in Kansas City—just like those Ugg girls, who might, for all I know, be linked to her somehow. And as we talk via iChat, her face floats in the corner of my screen, blonde and deadpan. By swiveling her Webcam, she gives me a tour: her walls, each painted a different color of pink; storage lockers; a subway map from last summer, when she came to Manhattan for a Parsons design fellowship. On one wall, I recognize a peace banner I've seen in one of her videos. 2

I ask her about that Xanga, the blog she kept when she was 12. Did she delete it? 3

"It's still out there!" she says. "Xanga, a Blogger, a Facebook, my Flickr account, my Vimeo account. Basically, what I do is sign up for everything. I kind of weed out what I like." I ask if she has a MySpace page, and she laughs and gives me an amused, pixellated grimace. "Unfortunately I do! I was so against MySpace, but I wanted to look at people's pictures. I just really don't like MySpace. 'Cause I think it's just so . . . I don't know if *superficial* is the right word. But plastic. These profiles of people just parading themselves. I kind of have it in for them." 4

Caitlin prefers sites like Noah K Everyday, where a sad-eyed, 26-year-old Brooklyn man has posted a single photo of himself each day since he was 19, a low-tech piece of art that is oddly moving—capturing the way each day brings some small change. Her favorite site is Vimeo, a kind of hipster YouTube. (She's become friends with the site's creator, Jakob Lodwick, and when she visited New York, they went to the Williamsburg short-film festival.) The videos she's posted there are mostly charming slices of life: a "typical day at a school," hula-hooping in Washington Square Park, conversations set to music. Like Oppermann herself, they seem revelatory without being revealing, operating in a space midway between behavior and performance. 5

At 17, Caitlin is conversant with the conventional wisdom about the online world—that it's a sketchy bus station packed with pedophiles. (In fact, that's pretty much the standard response I've gotten when I've spoken about this piece with anyone over 39: "But what about the perverts?" For teenagers, who have grown up laughing at porn pop-ups and the occasional instant message from a skeezy stranger, this is about as logical as the question "How can you move to New York? You'll get mugged!") She argues that when it comes to on- 6

...*continued* Say Everything, **Emily Nussbaum**

line relationships, "you're getting what you're being." All last summer, as she bopped around downtown Manhattan, she met dozens of people she already knew, or who knew her, from online. All of which means that her memories of her time in New York are stored both in her memory, where they will decay, and on her site, where they will not, giving her (and me) an unsettlingly crystalline record of her seventeenth summer.

Caitlin is not the only one squirreling away an archive of her adolescence, accidentally or on purpose. "I have a logger program that can show me drafts of a paper I wrote three years ago," explains Melissa Mooneyham, a graduate of Hunter College. "And if someone says something in instant message, then later on, if you have an argument, you can say, 'No, wait: You said *this* on *this* day at *this* time.'" 7

As for that defunct Xanga, Caitlin read it not long ago. "It was interesting. I just look at my junior-high self, kind of ignorant of what the future holds. And I thought, *You know, I don't think I gave myself enough credit: I'm really witty!*" She pauses and considers. "If I don't delete it, I'm still gonna be there. My generation is going to have all this history; we can document anything so easily. I'm a very sentimental person; I'm sure that has something to do with it." . . . 8

The truth is, we're living in frontier country right now. We can take guesses at the future, but it's hard to gauge the effects of a drug while you're still taking it. What happens when a person who has archived her teens grows up? Will she regret her earlier decisions, or will she love the sturdy bridge she's built to her younger self—not to mention the access to the past lives of friends, enemies, romantic partners? On a more pragmatic level, what does this do when you apply for a job or meet the person you're going to marry? Will employers simply accept that everyone has a few videos of themselves trying to read the Bible while stoned? Will your kids watch those stoner Bible videos when they're 16? Is there a point in the aging process when a person will want to pull back that curtain—or will the MySpace crowd maintain these flexible, cheerfully thick-skinned personae all the way into the nursing home? 9

Right now the big question for anyone of my generation seems to be, endlessly, "Why would anyone do that?" This is not a meaningful question for a 16-year-old. The benefits are obvious: The public life is fun. It's creative. It's where their friends are. It's theater, but it's also community: In this linked, logged world, you have a place to think out loud and be listened to, to meet strangers and go deeper with friends. And, yes, there are all sorts of crappy side effects: the passive-aggressive drama ("you know who you are!"), the shaming outbursts, the 10 chill a person can feel in cyberspace on a particularly bad day. There are lousy side effects of most social changes (see feminism, democracy, the creation of the interstate highway system). But the real question is, as with any revolution, which side are you on?

Teens Feel Safe on MySpace

Larry D. Rosen

Teens Feel Safe on MySpace

More than 80 percent of teens believe the cyber-networking site MySpace is safe. Teens spend an average of two hours a day, five days a week on the site. However, 83 percent of parents of MySpace users worry about online sexual predators.

What Teens Say About MySpace	What Parents of MySpace Users Say
• Typically visit 2 hours a day, 5 days a week	• 38% have not seen their teen's MySpace page
• 7-9% have been approached for a sexual liaison	• 43% don't know how often their teens are on MySpace
• 20% feel MySpace negatively affects school, job, family and friends	• 50% allow their teen to have a computer in the bedroom
• 83% believe MySpace is safe	• 62% have never talked to their teen about MySpace
• 70% would be comfortable showing their parents their MySpace page	• 83% worry about sexual predators on MySpace
• 35% are concerned about sexual predators on MySpace	• 75% worry MySpace fosters social isolation
• 15% are concerned that MySpace fosters social isolation	• 81% worry about their teen meeting online friends in person
• 36% are concerned about meeting online friends in person	• 63% believe there are "quite a few" sexual predators on MySpace
• 46% believe there are "some, but not too many," sexual predators on MySpace	

Source: Larry D. Rosen, "Adolescents in MySpace: Identity Formation, Friendship and Sexual Predators," California State University, Dominguez Hills, June 2006. Chart from Marcia Clemmitt, "Cybersocializing: Are Internet sites like MySpace Potentially Dangerous?" *CQ Researcher* 16(2006), p. 628.

Protect the Willfully Ignorant

Lily Huang

People have learned a lot about one another in the last seven years. *1* Online social networks like Friendster, MySpace and Facebook have helped us farm out information in vast quantities at unprecedented rates. We harvest an astoundingly diverse crop of data by the minute: our favorite music, recent photos, sundry commentary, even activity on the network itself. And we're not the only ones tilling. So are employers, law-enforcement agents, advertisers, unclassified strangers. To the individual user, a network like Facebook is a valuable social space that now poses an increasingly urgent question of privacy, or how best to keep your public plot walled in.

To behavioral economists, this dilemma is part of what makes the *2* phenomenon of online networks an extraordinary social experiment. The economics of privacy is, like anything else, a matter of trade-offs: What is gained and lost by revealing, say, the films you like? How about the real identities of 50 of your Facebook friends? The problem isn't that one trade-off is a more significant compromise of privacy than another. (Facebook's ultracustomized privacy controls take care of that.) The problem is that people can't make informed decisions if they don't know exactly what the trade-offs are. And they've proven that they don't.

The first step to having a true sense of the privacy trade-off you're *3* making on a social network is knowing who gets access to the information you post. In a 2006 study, economists at Carnegie Mellon University tested Facebook users on their familiarity with the network's privacy features. Among users who kept Facebook's default privacy settings, more than half underestimated the number of people who could see at least some portion of their profile, citing a figure in the tens of thousands or less. The correct figure was in the millions.

People also had little idea of what Facebook reserved the right to *4* do with their information. Yes or no questions on the company's privacy policy got as many as 70 percent incorrect answers. Alessandro Acquisti, a professor at CMU and coauthor of the study, attributes these results to the notion of rational ignorance, or "the idea that it is rational to remain ignorant about something. Privacy policies," he says, "are sometimes so long and ambiguous that people rationally say, 'I don't even bother reading it'."

What online networking gaffes do willfully ignorant people make? *5* The most infamous is crossing social spheres—for instance, allowing a compromising weekend photo to be seen by your boss, or even your future boss. Data we make available about ourselves are forms of "economic signaling," says Acquisti. The signal depends on the context in which information is perceived—by friends, colleagues or an unknown future party. On an online network, the signal itself is beyond our control because we don't know and can't predict who will receive it. "We human beings have an innate difficulty in predicting the value of our information," says Acquisti, "[and] how this information can be used in different contexts."

6   Moli, the new social-networking site from Christos Cotsakos, former head of E* Trade, tries to eliminate this problem by letting people keep separate profiles for different spheres. And Facebook now has an exhaustive set of privacy controls that lets you screen your profile, element by element, for various subsets of people in your network. But these methods, Acquisti points out, quickly raise the question of cognitive cost. Moli is only effective if large numbers of people are willing to put in the time and effort to maintain multiple profiles (they haven't) and if, in doing so, they don't make mistakes. To take advantage of Facebook's meticulous controls you have to know the function and implications of each setting: you have to understand every single trade-off. Three-quarters of Facebook users kept privacy settings on default, according to a London study by Sophos, a British information-security firm, in October.

7   Facebook's fine-tuned privacy controls have evolved over several episodes of user outcry since the network's 2004 launch. Founder and CEO Mark Zuckerberg responded swiftly to protest in 2006 over the News Feed and Mini-Feed features, which broadcast user activity. He reports "coding nonstop for two days" to create even more nuanced privacy settings.

8   More choice, though, is not always a good thing. CMU's George Loewenstein has studied the adverse effects of choices that "require expertise that people lack [and] introduce new risks when people want security." He thinks it's possible to strike a balance between too little choice and too much. Car manufacturers, he points out, let consumers pick engine sizes, color and the fabric on the seats, but not the design of the seat belt. "Consumers lack expertise about seat-belt design and don't want to invest time learning about it," he writes. Rather than let people figure out the optimal seat belt for themselves, experts pick a standard.

9   When consumers lack the expertise and clairvoyance to make optimal decisions, responsibility lies with the provider. Networks need to implement stringent default privacy settings, letting users opt into greater exposure from a highly contained circle of contacts, rather than tossing them into the teeming field and letting them build walls for themselves. We'll be grateful for the built-in constraints.

PROFESSIONAL WRITING

Think Before You Post

Ad Council

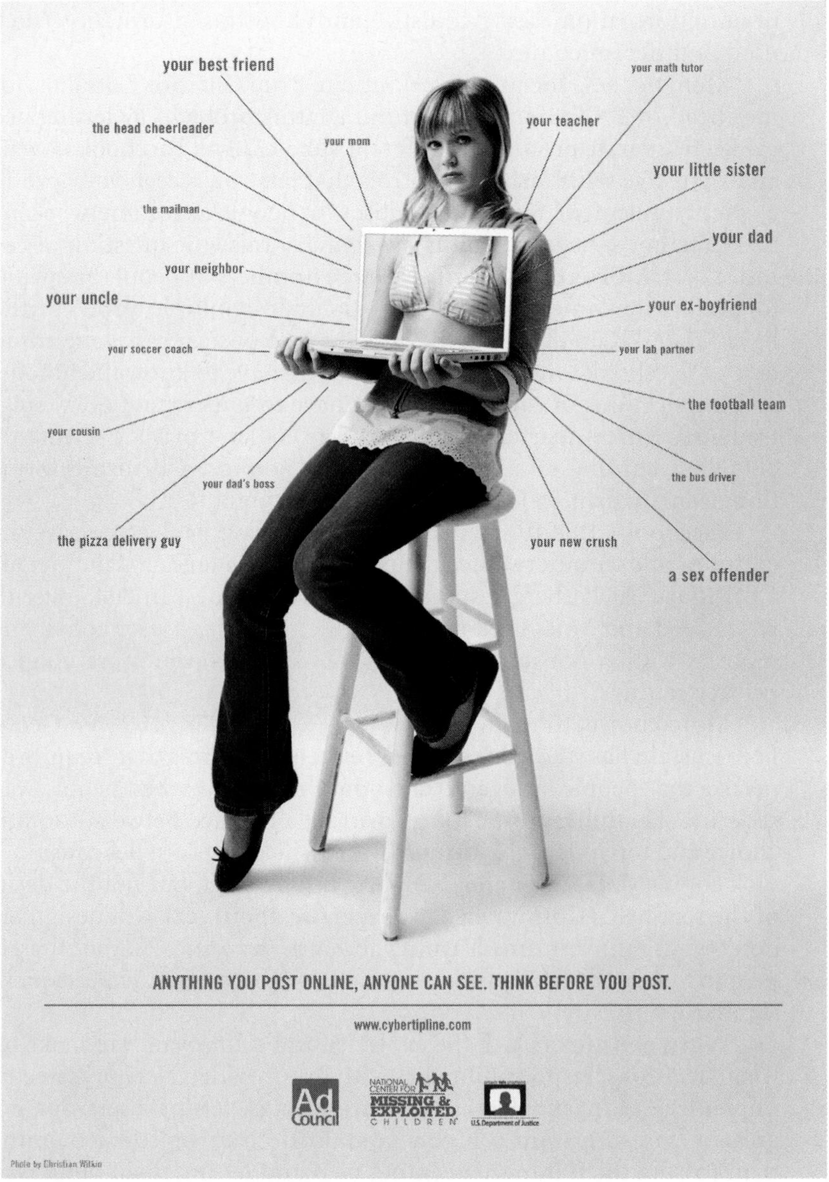
your best friend
your math tutor
the head cheerleader
your mom
your teacher
your little sister
the mailman
your dad
your neighbor
your uncle
your ex-boyfriend
your soccer coach
your lab partner
the football team
your cousin
the bus driver
your dad's boss
the pizza delivery guy
your new crush
a sex offender
ANYTHING YOU POST ONLINE, ANYONE CAN SEE. THINK BEFORE YOU POST.
www.cybertipline.com
Ad Council
NATIONAL CENTER FOR MISSING & EXPLOITED CHILDREN
U.S. Department of Justice
Photo by Christian Witkin

PROFESSIONAL WRITING

Wikipedia and the Meaning of Truth

Simson L. Garfinkel

With little notice from the outside world, the community-written encyclopedia Wikipedia has redefined the commonly accepted use of the word "truth." *1*

Why should we care? Because Wikipedia's articles are the first- or second-ranked results for most Internet searches. Type "iron" into Google, and Wikipedia's article on the element is the top-ranked result; its article on the Iron Cross is also first. Google's search algorithms rank a story in part by how many times it has been linked to; people are linking to Wikipedia articles *a lot*. *2*

This means that the content of these articles really matters. Wikipedia's standards of inclusion—what's in and what's not—affect the work of journalists, who routinely read Wikipedia articles and then repeat the wikiclaims as "background" without bothering to cite them. These standards affect students, whose research on many topics starts (and often ends) with Wikipedia. And since I used Wikipedia to research large parts of this article, these standards are affecting you, dear reader, at this very moment. *3*

Many people, especially academic experts, have argued that Wikipedia's articles can't be trusted, because they are written and edited by volunteers who have never been vetted. Nevertheless, studies have found that the articles are remarkably accurate. The reason is that Wikipedia's community of more than seven million registered users has organically evolved a set of policies and procedures for removing untruths. This also explains Wikipedia's explosive growth: if the stuff in Wikipedia didn't seem "true enough" to most readers, they wouldn't keep coming back to the website. *4*

These policies have become the social contract for Wikipedia's army of apparently insomniac volunteers. Thanks to them, incorrect information generally disappears quite quickly. *5*

So how do the Wikipedians decide what's true and what's not? On what is their epistemology based? *6*

Unlike the laws of mathematics or science, wikitruth isn't based on principles such as consistency or observability. It's not even based on common sense or firsthand experience. Wikipedia has evolved a radically *7*

WIKIPEDIA'S REFERENCE POLICY
en.wikipedia.org/wiki/
Wikipedia:Verifiability

WIKIPEDIA'S "NO ORIGINAL RESEARCH" POLICY
en.wikipedia.org/wiki/Wikipedia:
No_original_research

WIKIPEDIA'S "NEUTRAL POINT OF VIEW" POLICY
en.wikipedia.org/wiki/Wikipedia:
Neutral_point_of_view

WIKIPEDIA'S POLICY ON RELIABILITY OF SOURCES
en.wikipedia.org/wiki/Wikipedia:
Reliable_sources

WIKIPEDIA'S CITATION POLICY
en.wikipedia.org/wiki/Wikipedia:
Citing_sources

different set of epistemological standards—standards that aren't especially surprising given that the site is rooted in a Web-based community, but that should concern those of us who are interested in traditional notions of truth and accuracy. On Wikipedia, objective truth isn't all that important, actually. What makes a fact or statement fit for inclusion is that it appeared in some other publication—ideally, one that is in English and is available free online. "The threshold for inclusion in Wikipedia is verifiability, not truth," states Wikipedia's official policy on the subject.

Verifiability is one of Wikipedia's three core content policies; it 8 was codified back in August 2003. The two others are "no original research" (December 2003) and "neutral point of view," which the Wikipedia project inherited from Nupedia, an earlier volunteer-written Web-based free encyclopedia that existed from March 2000 to September 2003 (Wikipedia's own NPOV policy was codified in December 2001). These policies have made Wikipedia a kind of academic agora where people on both sides of politically charged subjects can rationally discuss their positions, find common ground, and unemotionally document their differences. Wikipedia is successful because these policies have worked.

Unlike Wikipedia's articles, Nupedia's were written and vetted by 9 experts. But few experts were motivated to contribute. Well, some wanted to write about their own research, but Larry Sanger, Nupedia's editor in chief, immediately put an end to that practice.

"I said, 'If it hasn't been vetted by the relevant experts, then basi- 10 cally we are setting ourselves up as a frontline source of new, original information, and we aren't set up to do that,'" Sanger (who is himself, ironically or not, a former philosophy instructor and by training an epistemologist) recalls telling his fellow Nupedians.

With experts barred from writing about their own work and hav- 11 ing no incentive to write about anything else, Nupedia struggled. Then Sanger and Jimmy Wales, Nupedia's founder, decided to try a different policy on a new site, which they launched on January 15, 2001. They adopted the newly invented "wiki" technology, allowing *anybody* to contribute to any article—or create a new one—on any topic, simply by clicking "Edit this page."

Soon the promoters of oddball hypotheses and outlandish ideas 12 were all over Wikipedia, causing the new site's volunteers to spend a good deal of time repairing damage—not all of it the innocent work of the misguided or deluded. (A study recently published in *Communications of the Association for Computing Machinery* found that 11 percent of Wikipedia articles have been vandalized at least once.) But how could Wikipedia's volunteer editors tell if something was true? The solution was to add references and footnotes to the articles, "not in order to help the reader, but in order to establish a point to the satisfaction of the [other] contributors," says Sanger, who left Wikipedia before the verifiability policy was formally adopted. (Sanger and Wales, now the chairman emeritus of the Wikimedia Foundation, fell out about the scale of Sanger's role in the creation of Wikipedia. Today, Sanger is the creator and editor in chief of Citizendium, an alternative to Wikipedia that is intended to address the inadequacy of its "reliability and quality.")

Verifiability is really an appeal to authority—not the authority of *13* truth, but the authority of other publications. Any other publication, really. These days, information that's added to Wikipedia without an appropriate reference is likely to be slapped with a "citation needed" badge by one of Wikipedia's self-appointed editors. Remove the badge and somebody else will put it back. Keep it up and you might find yourself face to face with another kind of authority—one of the English-language Wikipedia's 1,500 administrators, who have the ability to place increasingly restrictive protections on contentious pages when the policies are ignored.

To be fair, Wikipedia's verifiability policy states that "articles should *14* rely on reliable, third-party published sources" that themselves adhere to Wikipedia's NPOV policy. Self-published articles should generally be avoided, and non-English sources are discouraged if English articles are available, because many people who read, write, and edit En.Wikipedia (the English-language version) can read only English. . . .

An interesting thing happens when you try to understand *15* Wikipedia: the deeper you go, the more convoluted it becomes. Consider the verifiability policy. Wikipedia considers the "most reliable sources" to be "peer-reviewed journals and books published in university presses," followed by "university-level textbooks," then magazines, journals, "books published by respected publishing houses," and finally "mainstream newspapers" (but not the opinion pages of newspapers). . . .

So what is Truth? According to Wikipedia's entry on the subject, *16* "the term has no single definition about which the majority of professional philosophers and scholars agree." But in practice, Wikipedia's standard for inclusion has become its de facto standard for truth, and since Wikipedia is the most widely read online reference on the planet, it's the standard of truth that most people are implicitly using when they type a search term into Google or Yahoo. On Wikipedia, truth is received truth: the consensus view of a subject.

That standard is simple: something is true if it was published in a *17* newspaper article, a magazine or journal, or a book published by a university press—or if it appeared on *Dr. Who*.

Can Wikipedia Handle Stephen Colbert's Truthiness?

James Montgomery

"The Colbert Report" is the tongue-in-cheek Comedy Central news 1 show that features the titular humorist spouting off on a variety of political topics in a highly stylized, Bill O'Reilly-esque manner. On Monday's episode, Colbert praised Wikipedia, the online resource that can be read and edited by anyone with access to a computer, for promoting what he termed "Wikiality"—a sort of pseudo-reality that exists when you make something up and enough people agree with you.

"I'm no fan of reality, and I'm no fan of encyclopedias," Colbert 2 opined. "I've said it before: Who is [Encyclopaedia] Britannica to tell me George Washington had slaves? If I want to say George Washington didn't have slaves, that's my right. And now, thanks to Wikipedia, it's also a fact."

While he was speaking, Colbert was also typing away on a laptop 3 computer, apparently editing the Wikipedia entry on George Washington to read, "In conclusion, George Washington did not own slaves."

He also apparently edited the Wiki entry on his own program, re- 4 placing a lengthy section on his reference to Oregon as both "the Canada of California" and "Washington's Mexico" with "Oregon is Idaho's Portugal"—an example, he said, of Wikiality.

"[On Wikipedia], any user can change any entry," he said. "Now 5 'Oregon is Idaho's Portugal' is the opinion I have always held. You can look it up."

Stephen Colbert
Photo: Getty Images/Evan Agostini

The thing is, Colbert was *actually* making the changes—or, at least, 6 someone with the username StephenColbert was. The edits are seen on Wikipedia.com here and here, and they were both made around 6:35 p.m. ET, when "The Colbert Report" tapes in New York.

After making his changes, Colbert encouraged his viewers to spread 7 his concept of Wikiality by changing the site's entries on elephants to reflect the fact that the elephant population in Africa "has tripled in the last six months"—a way, he joked, to disarm environmentalists worldwide.

"What we're doing is bringing democracy to knowledge," he said. 8 "It's time we use the power of our numbers for a real Internet revolution. We're going to stampede across the Web like that giant horde of elephants in Africa. Together we can create a reality we can all agree on—the reality we just agreed on."

PROFESSIONAL WRITING

Why You Can't Cite Wikipedia in My Class

Neil L. Waters

The case for an online opensource encyclopedia is enormously appeal- 1 ing. What's not to like? It gives the originators of entries a means to publish, albeit anonymously, in fields they care deeply about and provides editors the opportunity to improve, add to, and polish them, a capacity not afforded to in-print articles. Above all, open sourcing marshals legions of unpaid, eager, frequently knowledgeable volunteers, whose enormous aggregate labor and energy makes possible the creation of an entity—Wikipedia, which today boasts more than 1.6 million entries in its English edition alone—that would otherwise be far too costly and labor-intensive to see the light of day. In a sense it would have been technologically impossible just a few years ago; open sourcing is democracy in action, and Wikipedia is its most ubiquitous and accessible creation.

Yet I am a historian, schooled in the concept that scholarship re- 2 quires accountability and trained in a discipline in which collaborative research is rare. The idea that the vector-sum products of tens or hundreds of anonymous collaborators could have much value is, to say the least, counterintuitive for most of us in my profession. We don't allow our students to cite printed general encyclopedias, much less opensource ones. Further, while Wikipedia compares favorably with other tertiary sources for articles in the sciences, approximately half of all entries are in some sense historical. Here the qualitative record is much spottier, with reliability decreasing in approximate proportion to distance from "hot topics" in American history [1]. For a Japan historian like me to perceive the positive side of Wikipedia requires an effort of will.

I made that effort after an innocuous series of events briefly and improbably propelled me and the history department at Middlebury College into the national, even international, spotlight. While grading a set of final examinations from my "History of Early Japan" class, I noticed that a half-dozen students had provided incorrect information about two topics—the Shimabara Rebellion of 1637–1638 and the Confucian thinker Ogyu Sorai—on which they were to write brief essays. Moreover, they used virtually identical language in doing so. A quick check on Google propelled me via popularity-driven algorithms to the Wikipedia entries on them, and there, quite plainly, was the erroneous information. To head off similar events in the future, I proposed a policy to the history department it promptly adopted: "(1) Students are responsible for the accuracy of information they provide, and they cannot point to Wikipedia or any similar source that may appear in the future to escape the consequences of errors. (2) Wikipedia is not an acceptable citation, even though it may lead one to a citable source."

The rest, as they say, is history. The Middlebury student newspaper ran a story on the new policy. That story was picked up online by *The Burlington Free Press,* a Vermont newspaper, which ran its own story. I was interviewed, first by Vermont radio and TV stations and newspapers, then by *The New York Times,* the *Asahi Shimbun* in Tokyo, and by radio and TV stations in Australia and throughout the U.S., culminating in a story on NBC Nightly News. Hundreds of other newspapers ran stories without interviews, based primarily on the *Times* article. I received dozens of phone calls, ranging from laudatory to actionably defamatory. A representative of the Wikimedia Foundation (www. wikipedia.org), the board that controls Wikipedia, stated that he agreed with the position taken by the Middlebury history department, noting that Wikipedia states in its guidelines that its contents are not suitable for academic citation, because Wikipedia is, like a print encyclopedia, a tertiary source. I repeated this information in all my subsequent interviews, but clearly the publication of the department's policy had hit a nerve, and many news outlets implied, erroneously, that the department was at war with Wikipedia itself, rather than with the uses to which students were putting it.

In the wake of my allotted 15 minutes of Andy Warhol-promised fame I have tried to figure out what all the fuss was about. There is a great deal of uneasiness about Wikipedia in the U.S., as well as in the rest of the computerized world, and a great deal of passion and energy have been spent in its defense. It is clear to me that the good stuff is related to the bad stuff. Wikipedia owes its incredible growth to open-source editing, which is also the root of its greatest weakness. Dedicated and knowledgeable editors can and do effectively reverse the process of entropy by making entries better over time. Other editors, through ignorance, sloppy research, or, on occasion, malice or zeal, can and do introduce or perpetuate errors in fact or interpretation. The reader never knows whether the last editor was one of this latter group; most editors leave no trace save a whimsical cyber-handle.

Popular entries are less subject to enduring errors, innocent or otherwise, than the seldom-visited ones, because, as I understand it, the frequency of visits by a Wikipedia "policeman" is largely determined, once again, by algorithms that trace the number of hits and move the most popular sites to a higher priority. The same principle, I have come to realize, props up the whole of the Wiki-world. Once a critical mass of hits is reached, Google begins to guide those who consulted it to Wikipedia before all else. A new button on my version of Firefox goes directly to Wikipedia. Preferential access leads to yet more hits, generating a still higher priority in an endless loop of mutual reinforcement.

It seems to me that there is a major downside to the self-reinforcing cycle of popularity. Popularity begets ease of use, and ease of use begets the "democratization" of access to information. But all too often, democratization of access to information is equated with the democratization of the information itself, in the sense that it is subject to a vote. That last mental conflation may have origins that predate Wikipedia and indeed the whole of the Internet.

The quiz show "Family Feud" has been a fixture of daytime television for decades and is worth a quick look. Contestants are not rewarded for guessing the correct answer but rather for guessing the answer that the largest number of people have chosen as the correct answer. The show must tap into some sort of popular desire to democratize information. Validation is not conformity to verifiable facts or weighing of interpretations and evidence but conformity to popular opinion. Expertise plays practically no role at all.

Here is where all but the most hopelessly postmodernist scholars bridle. "Family Feud" is harmless enough, but most of us believe in a real, external world in which facts exist independently of popular opinion, and some interpretations of events, thoroughly grounded in disciplinary rigor and the weight of evidence, are at least more likely to be right than others that are not. I tell my students that Wikipedia is a fine place to search for a paper topic or begin the research process, but it absolutely cannot serve subsequent stages of research. Wikipedia is not the direct heir to "Family Feud," but both seem to share an element of faith—that if enough people agree on something, it is most likely so.

What can be done? The answer depends on the goal. If it is to make 10 Wikipedia a truly authoritative source, suitable for citation, it cannot be done for any general tertiary source, including the *Encyclopaedia Britannica.* For an anonymous open-source encyclopedia, that goal is theoretically, as well as practically, impossible. If the goal is more modest—to make Wikipedia more reliable than it is—then it seems to me that any changes must come at the expense of its open-source nature. Some sort of accountability for editors, as well as for the originators of entries, would be a first step, and that, I think, means that editors must leave a record of their real names. A more rigorous fact-checking system might help, but are there enough volunteers to cover 1.6 million entries, or would checking be in effect reserved for popular entries?

Can one move beyond the world of cut-and-dried facts to check for 11 logical consistency and reasonableness of interpretations in light of what is known about a particular society in a particular historical period? Can it be done without experts? If you rely on experts, do you pay them or depend on their voluntarism?

I suppose I should now go fix the Wikipedia entry for Ogyu Sorai 12 (en.wikipedia .org/wiki/Ogyu_Sorai). I have been waiting since January to see how long it might take for the system to correct it, which has indeed been altered slightly and is rather good overall. But the statement that Ogyu opposed the Tokugawa order is still there and still highly misleading [2]. Somehow the statement that equates the samurai with the lower class in Tokugawa Japan has escaped the editors' attention, though anyone with the slightest contact with Japanese history knows it is wrong. One down, 1.6 million to go.

References

1. Rosenzweig, R. Can history be open source? *Journal of American History 93,* 1 (June 2006), 117–146.

2. Tucker, J. (editor and translator). *Ogyu Sorai's Philosophical Masterworks.* Association for Asian Studies and University of Hawaii Press, Honolulu, 2006, 12–13, 48–51; while Ogyu sought to redefine the sources of Tokugawa legitimacy, his purpose was clearly to strengthen the authority of the Tokugawa shogunate.

PROFESSIONAL WRITING

Professors Should Embrace Wikipedia

Mark Wilson

When the online, anyone-can-edit Wikipedia appeared in 2001, teach- 1 ers, especially college professors, were appalled. The Internet was already an apparently limitless source of nonsense for their students to eagerly consume– now there was a Web site with the appearance of legitimacy and a dead-easy interface that would complete the seduction until all sense of fact, fiction, myth and propaganda blended into a popular culture of pseudointelligence masking the basest ignorance. An *Inside Higher Ed* article just last year on Wikipedia use in the academy drew a huge and passionate response, much of it negative.

Now the English version of Wikipedia has over 2 million articles, 2 and it has been translated into over 250 languages. It has become so massive that you can type virtually any noun into a search engine and the first link will be to a Wikipedia page. After seven years and this exponential growth, Wikipedia can still be edited by anyone at any time. A generation of students was warned away from this information siren, but we know as professors that it is the first place they go to start a research project, look up an unfamiliar term from lecture, or find something disturbing to ask about during the next lecture. In fact, we learned too that Wikipedia is indeed the most convenient repository of information ever invented, and we go there often—if a bit covertly—to get a few questions answered. Its accuracy, at least for science articles, is actually as high as the revered *Encyclopedia Britannica,* as shown by a test published in the journal *Nature.*

It is time for the academic world to recognize Wikipedia for what 3 it has become: a global library open to anyone with an Internet connection and a pressing curiosity. The vision of its founders, Jimmy Wales and Larry Sanger, has become reality, and the librarians were right: the world has not been the same since. If the Web is the greatest information delivery device ever, and Wikipedia is the largest coherent store of information and ideas, then we as teachers and scholars should have been on this train years ago for the benefit of our students, our professions, and that mystical pool of human knowledge.

What Wikipedia too often lacks is academic authority, or at least 4 the perception of it. Most of its thousands of editors are anonymous, sometimes known only by an IP address or a cryptic username. Every article has a "talk" page for discussions of content, bias, and organization. "Revert" wars can rage out of control as one faction battles another over a few words in an article. Sometimes administrators have to step in and lock a page down until tempers cool and the main protagonists lose interest. The very anonymity of the editors is often the source of the problem: how do we know who has an authoritative grasp of the topic?

That is what academics do best. We can quickly sort out scholarly au- 5 thority into complex hierarchies with a quick glance at a vita and a sniff at a publication list. We make many mistakes doing this, of course, but at least our debates are supported with citations and a modicum of civility because we are identifiable and we have our reputations to maintain and friends to keep. Maybe this academic culture can be added to the Wild West of Wikipedia to make it more useful for everyone?

...*continued* Professors Should Embrace Wikipedia, **Mark Wilson**

I propose that all academics with research specialties, no matter how 6 arcane (and nothing is too obscure for Wikipedia), enroll as identifiable editors of Wikipedia. We then watch over a few wikipages of our choosing, adding to them when appropriate, stepping in to resolve disputes when we know something useful. We can add new articles on topics which should be covered, and argue that others should be removed or combined. This is not to displace anonymous editors, many of whom possess vast amounts of valuable information and innovative ideas, but to add our authority and hard-won knowledge to this growing universal library.

The advantages should be obvious. First, it is another outlet for 7 our scholarship, one that may be more likely to be read than many of our journals. Second, we are directly serving our students by improving the source they go to first for information. Third, by identifying ourselves, we can connect with other scholars and interested parties who stumble across our edits and new articles. Everyone wins.

I have been an open Wikipedia editor now for several months. I have 8 enjoyed it immensely. In my teaching I use a "living syllabus" for each course, which is a kind of academic blog. (For example, see my History of Life course online syllabus.) I connect students through links to outside sources of information. Quite often I refer students to Wikipedia articles that are well-sourced and well written. Wikipages that are not so good are easily fixed with a judicious edit or two, and many pages become more useful with the addition of an image from my collection (all donated to the public domain). Since I am open in my editorial identity, I often get questions from around the world about the topics I find most fascinating. I've even made important new connections through my edits to new collaborators and reporters who want more background for a story.

For example, this year I met online a biology professor from Cen- 9 tre College who is interested in the ecology of fish on Great Inagua Island in the Bahamas. He saw my additions and images on that Wikipedia page and had several questions about the island. He invited me to speak at Centre next year about evolution–creation controversies, which is unrelated to the original contact but flowed from our academic conversations. I in turn have been learning much about the island's living ecology I did not know. I've also learned much about the kind of prose that is most effective for a general audience, and I've in turn taught some people how to properly reference ideas and information. In short, I've expanded my teaching.

Wikipedia as we know it will undoubtedly change in the coming 10 years as all technologies do. By involving ourselves directly and in large numbers now, we can help direct that change into ever more useful ways for our students and the public. This is, after all, our sacred charge as teacher-scholars: to educate when and where we can to the greatest effect.

Twitter on the Barricades in Iran: Six Lessons Learned

Noam Cohen

Political revolutions are often closely linked to communication tools. The *1* American Revolution wasn't caused by the proliferation of pamphlets, written to whip colonists into a frenzy against the British. But it sure helped.

Social networking, a distinctly 21st-century phenomenon, has already *2* been credited with aiding protests from the Republic of Georgia to Egypt to Iceland. And Twitter, the newest social-networking tool, has been identified with two mass protests in a matter of months—in Moldova in April and in Iran last week, when hundreds of thousands of people took to the streets to oppose the official results of the presidential election.

But does the label Twitter Revolution, which has been slapped on the *3* two most recent events, oversell the technology? Skeptics note that only a small number of people used Twitter to organize protests in Iran and that other means—individual text messaging, old-fashioned word of mouth and Farsi-language Web sites—were more influential. But Twitter did prove to be a crucial tool in the cat-and-mouse game between the opposition and the government over enlisting world opinion. As the Iranian government restricts journalists' access to events, the protesters have used Twitter's agile communication system to direct the public and journalists alike to video, photographs and written material related to the protests. (As has become established custom on Twitter, users have agreed to mark, or "tag," each of their tweets with the same bit of type—#IranElection—so that users can find them more easily). So maybe there was no Twitter Revolution. But over the last week, we learned a few lessons about the strengths and weaknesses of a technology that is less than three years old and is experiencing explosive growth.

1. TWITTER IS A TOOL AND THUS DIFFICULT TO CENSOR

Twitter aspires to be something different from social-networking sites *4* like Facebook or MySpace: rather than being a vast self-contained world centered on one Web site, Twitter dreams of being a tool that people can use to communicate with each other from a multitude of locations, like e-mail. You do not have to visit the home site to send a message, or tweet. Tweets can originate from text-messaging on a cellphone or even blogging software. Likewise, tweets can be read remotely, whether as text messages or, say, "status updates" on a friend's Facebook page.

Unlike Facebook, which operates solely as a Web site that can be, *5* in a sense, impounded, shutting down Twitter.com does little to stop the offending Twittering. You'd have to shut down the entire service, which is done occasionally for maintenance.

2. TWEETS ARE GENERALLY BANAL, BUT WATCH OUT

"The qualities that make Twitter seem inane and half-baked are what 6 makes it so powerful," says Jonathan Zittrain, a Harvard law professor who is an expert on the Internet. That is, tweets by their nature seem trivial, with little that is original or menacing. Even Twitter accounts seen as promoting the protest movement in Iran are largely a series of links to photographs hosted on other sites or brief updates on strategy. Each update may not be important. Collectively, however, the tweets can create a personality or environment that reflects the emotions of the moment and helps drive opinion.

3. BUYER BEWARE

Nothing on Twitter has been verified. While users can learn from ex- 7 perience to trust a certain Twitter account, it is still a matter of trust. And just as Twitter has helped get out first-hand reports from Tehran, it has also spread inaccurate information, perhaps even disinformation. An article published by the Web site True/Slant highlighted some of the biggest errors on Twitter that were quickly repeated and amplified by bloggers: that three million protested in Tehran last weekend (more like a few hundred thousand); that the opposition candidate Mir Hussein Moussavi was under house arrest (he was being watched); that the president of the election monitoring committee declared the election invalid last Saturday (not so).

4. WATCH YOUR BACK

Not only is it hard to be sure that what appears on Twitter is accurate, 8 but some Twitterers may even be trying to trick you. Like Rick's Cafe, Twitter is thick with discussion of who is really an informant or agent provocateur. One longstanding pro-Moussavi Twitter account, mousavi1388, which has grown to 16,000 followers, recently tweeted, "WARNING: http:// www.mirhoseyn.ir/ & http://www.mirhoseyn.com/ are fake, DONT join.... #IranElection 11:02 AM Jun 16th from web." The implication was that government agents had created those accounts to mislead the public. ABCNews.com announced that Twitter users who said they were repeating ("retweeting") the posts from its reporter, Jim Sciutto, had been fabricating the material to make Mr. Sciutto seem to be backing the government. "I became an unwitting victim," he wrote.

5. TWITTER IS SELF-CORRECTING BUT A MISLEADING GAUGE

For all the democratic traits of Twitter, not all users are equal. A pop- 9 ular, trusted user matters more and, as shown above, can expose others who are suspected of being fakers. In that way, Twitter is a community, with leaders and cliques. Of course, Twitter is a certain kind of community— technology-loving, generally affluent and Western-tilting. In that way, Twitter is a very poor tool for judging popular sentiment in Iran and trying to assess who won the presidential election. Mr. Ahmadinejad, who presumably has some supporters somewhere in Iran, is losing in a North Korean-style landslide on Twitter.

6. TWITTER CAN BE A POTENT TOOL FOR MEDIA CRITICISM

Just as Twitter can rally protesters against governments, its broadcast ability 10 can rally them quickly and efficiently against news outlets. One such spontaneous protest was given the tag #CNNfail, using Internet slang to call out CNN last weekend for failing to have comprehensive coverage of the Iranian protests. This was quickly converted to an e-mail writing campaign. CNN was forced to defend its coverage in print and online.

? QUESTIONS FOR WRITING AND DISCUSSION

1 A key strategy for persuading or convincing your readers is to directly engage them in the topic. For example, Farhad Manjoo in "You Have No Friends" directly addresses his readers in paragraph four: "Friends—can I call you friends?—it's time to drop the attitude: There is no longer any good reason to avoid Facebook." Find two other places in his article where Manjoo directly addresses his readers. Explain why you think this strategy is or is not effective for his readers on Slate.com.

2 In ". . . And Why I Hate It," Sarah Kliff explains the disadvantages of Facebook. What does she dislike about using her Facebook page? Which of her objections has Manjoo already anticipated and responded to? After reading both essays, make your own list of the reasons you both like and dislike Facebook or MySpace.

3 In "Facebook US Audience Growth," which appeared on InsideFacebook.com, analyze the presentation of the graphic information. Do the bar graphs clearly present the information, or would statistical lists, pie charts, or pictures be more effective? What conclusions about this data does the accompanying text provide? What additional or different conclusions or questions might you raise about the significance of this data?

4 For her *New York Magazine* article about Facebook and its users, Emily Nussbaum uses an informal, investigative journalist's style. Does

Nussbaum build an argument or does she just ask questions and let her readers decide for themselves? Cite several passages in this excerpt from Nussbaum's essay to support your answer.

5 In "Protect the Willfully Ignorant," Lily Huang explains how social networking sites like MySpace and Facebook are valuable social spaces that carry a sometimes hidden privacy danger. What are the advantages and disadvantages of these sites and what does Huang recommend be done to increase user's security and privacy? Cite specific passages from the essay to support your answers.

6 Both Larry Rosen's "Teens Feel Safe on MySpace" and the AdCouncil's visual, "Think Before You Post," provide information about privacy issues and attitudes. Which makes the more explicit argument? Explain your choice. In the "Teens Feel Safe on MySpace," what conclusions can you draw about the similarities and differences between teens' and parents' attitudes? Compare specific statistics to support your conclusions.

7 In "Wikipedia and the Meaning of Truth," Simson Garfinkel explains Wikipedia's standards of "truth." He says that "unlike the laws of mathematics or science, wikitruth isn't based on principles such as consistency or observability." So, according to Garfinkel, how *is* truth approximated on Wikipedia? Cite specific passages from the article to support your explanation. When Stephen Colbert (in "Can Wikipedia Handle Stephen Colbert's Truthiness?") claims that "together we can create a reality that we can all agree on," does his experiment support or refute Garfinkel's explanation of how Wikipedia creates truth? Explain your response.

8 Neil Waters in "Why You Can't Cite Wikipedia in My Class" and Mark Wilson in "Professors Should Embrace Wikipedia" represent nearly opposing points of view. According to each author, what are the proper uses and limitations of Wikipedia? Citing examples from both articles, explain what uses of Wikipedia they agree on and then exactly how their recommendations differ.

9 Twitter, like the other Web 2.0 technologies, has definite strengths and weaknesses. In "Twitter on the Barricades in Iran: Six Lessons Learned," what key advantages and disadvantages does Noam Cohen cite about Twitter during the Iranian uprising? How are Twitter's strengths and weaknesses similar to or different from those of Facebook and Wikipedia? Explain.

10 Reread the sidebar quotations by Howard Rheingold and Michael Gorman at the beginning of this Web 2.0 casebook. Citing examples from texts in the casebook and from your own experience, explain which writer (Rheingold or Gorman) has the more accurate judgment about Web 2.0 technologies. (Is there a third opinion or compromise judgment that would be more accurate?)

Arguing: The Writing Process

ASSIGNMENT FOR ARGUING

For this assignment, choose a controversial and debatable topic that catches your interest or relates to your own personal experience. (Avoid ready-made pro–con subjects such as abortion or drugs unless you have personal experience that can bring a fresh perspective to the subject.) Then examine the topic for possible claims of fact or definition, value, cause and effect, or policy. If the claim is debatable, you may have a focus for your arguing assignment. Next, think about your possible audience. Who needs to be convinced about your argument? Who has the power to change the status quo? Are there multiple perspectives or are there multiple stakeholders involved in this issue? Is there a compromise position you should argue for? (How might your understanding of your audience change your claim?) If possible, narrow your audience to a local group that might be influential. Finally, choose a genre or set of genres that best fits your purpose and audience. Use the following grid of possible audiences and genres to help brainstorm combinations of audience and genre that would be most effective for your purpose and topic.

Audience	Possible Genres for Arguing
Personal Audience	Class notes, journal entry, blog, scrapbook, social networking page
Academic Audience	Academic essay, researched argument, examination essay, debate script, forum entry on class site, journal entry, Web site, or multigenre document
Public Audience	Letter to the editor, column, editorial, blog, article, or critique in a newspaper, online site, magazine, newsletter, graphic novel, Web site, or multigenre document

CHOOSING A SUBJECT

If a journal entry suggested a possible subject, do the collecting and shaping strategies. Otherwise, consider the following ideas.

- Review your journal entries from previous chapters and the papers that you have already written for this class. Test these subjects for an arguable claim that you could make, opposing arguments you could

> 66 You can write about anything, and if you write well enough, even the reader with no intrinsic interest in the subject will become involved. 99
>
> —TRACY KIDDER, NOVELIST

consider, and an appropriate audience for an argumentative piece of writing.

- **Writing Across the Curriculum.** Brainstorm possible ideas for argumentative subjects from the other courses you are currently taking or have taken. What controversial issues in psychology, art, philosophy, journalism, biology, nutrition, engineering, physical education, or literature have you discussed in your classes? Ask current or past instructors for possible controversial topics relating to their courses.

- Newspapers and magazines are full of controversial subjects in sports, medicine, law, business, and family. Browse through current issues or online magazines looking for possible subjects. Check news items, editorials, and cartoons. Look for subjects related to your own interests, your job, your leisure activities, or your experiences.

- Interview your friends, family, or classmates. What controversial issues are affecting their lives most directly? What would they most like to change about their lives? What has irritated or angered them most in the recent past?

- **Community Service Learning.** If you are doing a community-service-learning project, consider one of the following possible topics: (1) Which of the agency's activities best meet the goals of the agency? Write an essay to the agency coordinator recommending a reallocation of resources to the most effective activities. (2) How might agency volunteers more usefully serve the agency in future projects? Write to your project coordinator recommending improvements that would better meet the dual goals of academic learning and agency service.

COLLECTING

● **NARROWING AND FOCUSING YOUR CLAIM**   Narrow your subject to a specific topic, and sharpen your focus by applying the "Wh" questions. If your subject is "grades," your responses might be as follows.

SUBJECT: GRADES

- **Who:** College students
- **What:** Letter grades
- **When:** In freshman and sophomore years
- **Where:** Especially in nonmajor courses
- **Why:** What purpose do grades serve in nonmajor courses?

Determine what claim or claims you want to make. Make sure that your claim is *arguable*. (Remember that claims can overlap; an argument may combine several related claims.)

CLAIM OF FACT OR DEFINITION

- Letter grades exist. (not arguable)
- Employers consider grades when hiring. (slightly more arguable, but not very controversial)
- Grades do not measure learning. (very arguable)

CLAIM ABOUT CAUSE OR EFFECT

- Grades create anxiety for students. (not very arguable)
- Grades actually prevent discovery and learning. (arguable)

CLAIM ABOUT VALUE

- Grades are not fair. (not very arguable: "fairness" can usually be determined)
- Grades are bad because they discourage individual initiative. (arguable)
- Grades are good because they give students an incentive to learn. (arguable)

CLAIM ABOUT A SOLUTION OR POLICY

- Grades should be eliminated altogether. (arguable—but difficult)
- Grades should be eliminated in humanities courses. (arguable)
- Grades should change to pass/fail in nonmajor courses. (arguable—and more practical)

Focusing and narrowing your *claim* helps determine what evidence you need to collect. Use your observing, remembering, reading, and investigative skills to gather the evidence. ***Note:*** An argumentative essay should not be a mathematical equation that uses only abstract and impersonal evidence. *Your experience* can be crucial to a successful argumentative essay. Start by doing the *remembering* exercises. Your audience wants to know not only why you are writing on this particular *topic,* but also why the subject is of interest to *you.*

● **REMEMBERING**   Use *freewriting, looping, branching,* or *clustering* to recall experiences, ideas, events, and people who are relevant to your claim. If you are writing about grades, brainstorm about how *your* teachers used grades, how you reacted to specific grades in one specific class, how your friends or parents reacted, and what you felt or thought. These prewriting exercises will help you understand your claim and give you specific examples that you can use for evidence.

ANALYZING STATISTICS

Whether you are evaluating statistical sources in an essay that you are reading or choosing statistical data to use as evidence for a claim in your own essay, use the following questions to help you determine the relevance, validity, and bias of the statistics.

- Who is the author or the group responsible for gathering or presenting the information? Do they have a bias or point of view?
- What is the date of the study or survey? Are the data still relevant?
- For a survey or poll, what is the sample size (number of respondents) and sample selection (demographic group selected)? Is the sample large enough to give reliable results? Is the group randomly selected? Are certain key groups not included?
- Analyze the wording of the questions asked in the poll or survey. Are the questions relatively neutral? Do the questions lead respondents to a certain conclusion?
- Are the conclusions drawn justified by the data? Are the conclusions exaggerated or overgeneralized?

● **OBSERVING**   If possible for your topic, collect data and evidence by observing, firsthand, the facts, values, effects, or possible solutions related to your claim. *Repeated* observation will give you good inductive evidence to support your argument.

● **INVESTIGATING**   For most argumentative essays, some research or investigation is essential. Because it is difficult to imagine all the valid counterarguments, interview friends, classmates, family, coworkers, and authorities on your topic. From the library, gather books and articles that contain arguments in support of your claim. *Note:* As you do research in the library, print out articles or make photocopies of key passages from relevant sources to hand in with your essay. If you cite sources from your research, list them on a Works Cited page following your essay. (See Chapter 13 for the proper format.)

SHAPING

As you plan your organization, reconsider your rhetorical situation. Will the *genre* you have selected (letter, researched essay, letter to the editor, blog, Web site, brochure, PowerPoint presentation) help carry out your *purpose* for your intended audience? Is there a relevant *occasion* (meeting, anniversary, or re-sponse to news item) that your writing might focus on? What is the *cultural, social,* or *political context* for your writing? Finally, reconsider your *audience.* Try imagining one real person who might be among your readers. Is this per-son open-minded and likely to be convinced by your evidence? Does this per-son represent the opposing position? If you have several alternative positions, are there individual people who might represent, in your mind, each of these positions? After reconsidering your rhetorical situation, try the shaping strategies that follow.

● **LIST "PRO" AND "CON" ARGUMENTS**   Either on paper or in a computer file, write out your *claim,* and then list the arguments for your po-sition (pro) and the arguments for the opposing positions (con). After you have made the list, match up arguments by drawing lines, as indicated. (On the computer file, move "Con" column arguments so they appear directly op-posite the corresponding "Pro" column arguments.)

  If some pro and con arguments "match," you will be able to argue against the con and for your claim at the same time. If some arguments do not "match," you will need to consider them separately.

> 66 No one can write decently who is distrustful of the reader's intelligence, or whose attitude is patronizing. 99
> —E. B. WHITE, ESSAYIST

Claim: Grades should be changed to pass/fail in nonmajor courses.

PRO	CON
Grades inhibit learning by putting too much emphasis on competition.	Grades actually promote learning by setting students to study as hard as possible.
Pass/fail grading encourages students to explore nonmajor fields.	Students should be encouraged to compete with majors. They may want to change majors and need to know if they can compete.
Grade competition with majors in the field can be discouraging.	If students don't have traditional grading, they won't take nonmajor courses seriously.
Some students do better without the pressure of grades; they need to find out if they can motivate themselves without grades, but they shouldn't have to risk grades in their major field to discover that.	

● **DRAW CIRCLE OF ALTERNATIVE POSITIONS**   If you are considering multiple alternative positions, put your claim in the middle of a circle and indicate the various positions or stakeholders on the outside of the circle. This diagram will help you identify the most important positions in the debate and will help you organize your writing. The following example is based on the claim that standardized testing in schools should put the students' needs first.

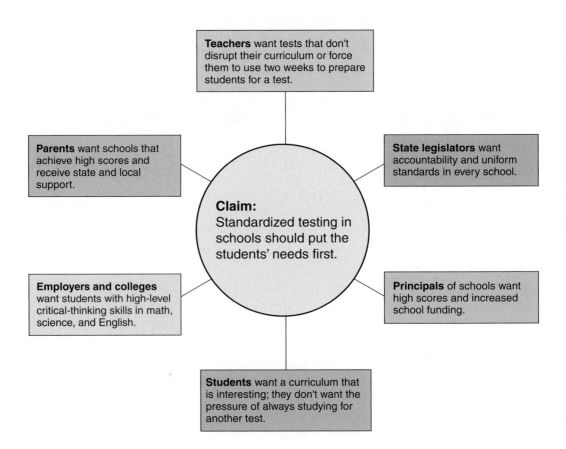

Teachers want tests that don't disrupt their curriculum or force them to use two weeks to prepare students for a test.

Parents want schools that achieve high scores and receive state and local support.

State legislators want accountability and uniform standards in every school.

Claim: Standardized testing in schools should put the students' needs first.

Employers and colleges want students with high-level critical-thinking skills in math, science, and English.

Principals of schools want high scores and increased school funding.

Students want a curriculum that is interesting; they don't want the pressure of always studying for another test.

Once you have a diagram for all the major alternative positions or stakeholders, decide the focus of your argument. For your purpose, audience, and context, you may want to focus just on the different goals of teachers, students, and parents. Or you may want to suggest how teachers, students, and parents should organize and force legislators to change the standardized tests or change how schools are funded based on test results.

● **OUTLINES FOR ARGUMENTS**   For more than two thousand years, writers and speakers have been trying to determine the most effective means to persuade audiences. One of the oldest outlines for a successful argument comes from classical rhetoric. The following six-part outline is intended as a guideline rather than a rigid list. Test this outline; see if it will work for *your* argument.

Introduction: Announces subject; *gets audience's interest and attention;* establishes a trustworthy character for the writer

Narration: Gives *background,* context, statement of problem, or definition

Partition: States thesis or *claim,* outlines or *maps* arguments

Argument: Makes *arguments* and gives *evidence* for the claim or thesis

Refutation: Shows why *opposing arguments* are not true or valid

Conclusion: Summarizes arguments, suggests solution, *ties into the introduction or background*

Most arguments have these features, but not necessarily in this order. Some writers prefer to respond to or refute opposing arguments before giving the arguments in support of their claims. When con and pro arguments match, refuting an argument followed by the argument for your claim may work best. As you organize your own arguments, put your strongest argument last and your weakest argument either first or in the middle.

Because most short argumentative essays contain the introduction, narration, and partition all in a few introductory paragraphs, you may use the following abbreviated outlines for argument.

Outline 1   Introduction (attention getter, background, claim or thesis, map)
Your arguments
Refutation of opposing arguments
Conclusion

Outline 2   Introduction
Refutation of opposing arguments
Your arguments
Conclusion

Outline 3   Introduction
Refutation of first opposing argument that matches your first argument
Refutation of second opposing argument that matches your second argument, and so on
Additional arguments
Conclusion

For Rogerian arguments, you can follow one of the above outlines, but the emphasis, tone, and attitude are different.

Introduction	Attention getter, background Claim (often downplayed to reduce threat) Map (often omitted) Appeal to character (crucial to Rogerian argument)
Opposing arguments	State opposing arguments fairly Show where, how, or when those arguments may be valid; establish common ground
Your arguments	State your position fairly Show where, how, or when your arguments are valid
Resolution	Present compromise position State your solution to the problem, and show its advantages to both sides

● **DEVELOPING ARGUMENTS**   Think of your argument as a series of *because* statements, each supported by evidence, statistics, testimony, expert opinion, data, specific examples from your experience, or a combination of these.

THESIS OR CLAIM: *Grades should be abolished in nonmajor courses.*

Reason 1	Because they may keep a student from attempting a difficult nonmajor course *Statistics, testimony, data, and examples*
Reason 2	Because competition with majors in the field can be discouraging *Statistics, testimony, data, and examples*
Reason 3	Because grades inhibit students' learning in nonmajor fields *Statistics, testimony, data, and examples*

You can develop each reason using a variety of strategies. The following strategies may help you generate additional reasons and examples.

Definition	Define the crucial terms or ideas. (What do you mean by *learning?*)
Comparison	Compare the background, situation, and context with another similar context. (What other schools have tried pass/fail grading for nonmajor courses? How has it worked?)
Process	How does or should a change occur? (How do nonmajors become discouraged? How should a school implement pass/fail in grading?)

These strategies may help you develop an argument coherently and effectively. If several strategies are possible, consider which would be most effective for your audience.

Research Tips ⸺⸺⸺⸺ (GO)

When you draft your arguing essay, don't let your citations or direct quotations overpower your own argument. Two tactics will keep you in control of your argument:

First, always avoid "unidentified flying quotations" by *sandwiching* your quotations. *Introduce* quotations by referring to the author, the source, and/or the author's study. *Follow* quotations with a sentence explaining how the author's evidence supports your argument. For examples, see paragraphs 4 and 5 in the essay by student writer Crystal Sabatke at the end of this chapter.

Second, keep your direct quotations *short*. If possible, reduce a long passage to one sentence and incorporate the quoted material in the flow of your own language. For example, in her essay at the end of this chapter, Sabatke writes,

> According to Ruth Conniff, author of "Big Bad Welfare: Welfare Reform, Politics, and Children," the welfare reform discussion "indicates that what happens to children doesn't matter to Americans, so long as mothers are forced to work" (8).

DRAFTING

You will never really know "enough" about your subject or have "enough" evidence. At some point, however, you must stop collecting and start your draft. The most frequent problem in drafting an argumentative essay is delaying the actual writing too long, until the deadline is too close.

For argumentative essays, start with a working order or sequence and sketch an outline on paper or in your head. Additional examples and appeals to reason, character, or emotion may occur to you as you develop your argument or refute opposing arguments. In addition, if you have done some research, have your notes, photocopies of key data, statistics, quotations, and citations of authorities close at hand. As you write, you will discover that some information or arguments simply don't fit into the flow of your essay. Don't force arguments into your draft if they no longer seem to belong.

PEER RESPONSE

Writer: Before you exchange drafts with a peer reader, provide the following information about your essay.

1. a. Intended audience and genre
    b. Primary claim or thesis
    c. Opposing arguments that you refute
    d. Arguments supporting your claim

2. Write out one or two questions about your draft that you want your reader to answer.

Reader: Read the writer's entire draft. As you reread, answer the following questions.

1. **Arguments.** Without looking at the writer's responses above, describe the essay's (a) target audience, (b) primary claim, (c) opposing arguments that are refuted, (d) arguments supporting the claim. Which of these did you have trouble identifying? What additional pro or con arguments should the writer consider?

2. **Organization.** Identify the following parts of the writer's draft: introduction, narration, partition, argument, refutation, and conclusion. Does the writer need all of these for his or her particular subject and audience? Why or why not? Where could the writer clarify transitions between sections? Explain.

3. **Appeals.** Identify places where the writer appeals to reason, to character, and to emotion. Where could these appeals be stronger? Identify sentences where the writer is overly emotional or illogical (see the section "Revising Fallacies in Logic").

4. **Evidence.** Identify at least one paragraph in which the supporting evidence is strong. Then identify at least one paragraph in which the writer makes assertions without sufficient supporting evidence. What kind of evidence might the writer use—first-hand observation, personal examples, testimony from experts, interviews, statistics, or other? Explain.

5. **Revision plan.** List three key changes that the writer should make during the revision.
6. Answer the writer's questions.

Writer: When your essay is returned, read the comments by your peer reader(s) and do the following.

1. Compare your descriptions of the audience, genre, claim, and pro and con arguments with your reader's descriptions. Where there are differences, clarify your essay.
2. Read all of your peer reader's responses. List revisions that you intend to make in each of the following areas: *audience, genre, arguments, organization, appeals, and supporting evidence.*

REVISING

Argumentation is the most public of the purposes for writing. The rhetorical situation (purpose, audience, genre, occasion, and cultural context) plays a crucial role. As you revise, look at this larger context, not just at phrasing, words, or sentences. Test your argument by having friends or classmates read it. Explain your claim, your focus, and your intended audience, genre, and context. Ask them to look for counterarguments that you have omitted or for weaknesses, omissions, or fallacies in logic. But don't automatically change your draft. Take the advice that makes your overall purpose more effective for your audience.

GUIDELINES FOR REVISION

- **When you finish your draft, reconsider the elements of the rhetorical situation** (writer, purpose, audience, genre, occasion, cultural context). Look at the big picture. What needs changing? What needs to be added? What parts are repetitious or not effective?
- **Ask a class member or friend to read your draft to determine the intended audience for your argument.** See which arguments your reader thinks would not be effective for your audience.

- **Use the Toulmin model to evaluate your essay.** Is your claim clearly stated? Does your claim have a qualifier? Do you note exceptions to your claim? Do you have warrant statements explaining how your data support your reasons and claim?
- **Which of your *because* arguments are most effective?** Least effective? Should you change the outline or structure that you initially chose?
- **Revise your draft to avoid fallacies or errors in reasoning.** Errors in logic create two problems: They can destroy your rational appeal and open your argument to a logical rebuttal, and they lessen your credibility—and thus reduce your appeal to your character. (Review the list of fallacies below.)
- **Support your reasons with evidence: *data, facts, statistics, quotations, observations, testimony, statistics, or specific examples from your experience.*** Check your collecting notes once again for additional evidence to add to your weakest argument. Is there a weak or unsupported argument that you should simply omit?
- **Signal the major arguments and counterarguments in your partition or map.** Between paragraphs, use clear transitions and paragraph hooks.
- **Could your essay be improved by visuals or special formatting?** Reconsider your genre and audience. If visuals might make your essay more effective, do a search on the computer. If you need help formatting your essay, check with a peer, a computer lab assistant, or your instructor.
- **If you cite sources in your essay, check the *accuracy* of your statistics, quotations, and source references.** (See Chapter 13 for the proper format of in-text documentation and the Works Cited page.)
- **Revise sentences to improve conciseness and clarity.**
- **Edit sentences for grammar, punctuation, and spelling.**

● **REVISING FALLACIES IN LOGIC**   Listed below are common fallacies in logic. Reread your draft or your peer's draft and revise as appropriate to eliminate these logical errors.

- **Hasty generalization:** Conclusion not logically justified by sufficient or unbiased evidence. If your friend Mary tells you that Professor Paramecium is a hard grader because he gave her a 36 percent on the first biology test, she is making a hasty generalization. It may be *true*—Prof P. may *be* a difficult grader—but Mary's logic is not valid. She cannot logically draw that conclusion from a sample of one; the rest of the class may have received grades of between 80 and 100.
- **Post hoc ergo propter hoc:** Literally, "after this, therefore because of this." Just because Event B *occurred after* Event A does not mean that

A *necessarily caused* B. You washed your car in the morning, and it rained in the afternoon. Though we joke about how it always rains after we wash the car, there is, of course, no causal relationship between the two events. "I forgot to leave the porch light on when I went out last night, and someone robbed my house": Without further evidence, we cannot assume that the lack of light contributed to the robbery. A more obvious cause might be the back door left unlocked.

- **Genetic fallacy:** Arguing that the origins of a person, object, or institution determine its character, nature, or worth. Like the post hoc fallacy, the genetic fallacy is an error in causal relationships.

  This automobile was made in Detroit. It'll probably fall apart after 10,000 miles.

  He speaks with a funny German accent. He's really stupid, you know.

  He started Celestial Seasonings Herb Teas just to make a quick buck; it's just another phony yuppie product.

  The second half of each statement *may* or *may not* be true; the logical error is in assuming that the origin of something will necessarily determine its worth or quality. Stereotyping is frequently caused by a genetic fallacy.

- **Begging the question:** Loading the conclusion in the claim. Arguing that "pornography should be banned because it corrupts our youth" is a logical claim. However, saying that "filthy and corrupting pornography should be banned" is begging the question: The conclusion that the writer should *prove* (that pornography corrupts) is assumed in the claim. Other examples: "Those useless psychology classes should be dropped from the curriculum"; "Senator Swingle's sexist behavior should be censured by Congress"; "Everyone knows that our ineffective drug control program is a miserable failure." The writers must *prove* that the psychology classes are useless, that Senator Swingle is sexist, and that the drug program is a failure.

- **Circular argument:** A sentence or argument that restates rather than proves. Thus, it goes in a circle: "President Reagan was a great communicator because he had that knack of talking effectively to the people." The terms in the beginning of the sentence (*great communicator*) and the end of the sentence (*talking effectively*) are interchangeable. The sentence ends where it started.

- **Either/or:** An oversimplification that reduces alternatives to only two choices, thereby creating a false dilemma. Statements such as "Love it or leave it" attempt to reduce the alternatives to two. If you don't love your school, your town, or your country, you don't have to leave: A third choice is to change it and make it better. Proposed solutions frequently have an either/or fallacy: "Either we ban boxing or hundreds of young men will be senselessly killed." A third alternative is to change boxing's rules or equipment. "If we don't provide farmers with low-interest loans, they will go bankrupt." Increasing prices for farm products might be a better alternative.

- **Faulty comparison or analogy:** Basing an argument on a comparison of two things, ideas, events, or situations that are similar but not identical. Although comparisons or analogies are often effective in argument, they can hide logical problems. "We can solve the meth problem the same way we reduced the DWI problem: Attack it with increased enforcement and mandatory jail sentences." Although the situations are similar, they are not identical. The DWI solution will not necessarily work for drugs. An analogy is an extended comparison that uses something simple or familiar to explain something complex or less familiar. "Solving a mathematics problem is like baking a cake: You have to take it one step at a time. First, you assemble your ingredients or your known data. . . ." Like baking, solving a problem does involve a process; unlike baking, however, mathematics is more exact. Changing the amount of flour in a recipe by 1 percent will not make the cake fall; changing a numeric value by 1 percent, however, may ruin the whole problem. The point, however, is not to avoid comparisons or analogies. Simply make sure that your conclusions are qualified; acknowledge the *differences* between the two things compared as well as the similarities.

- **Ad hominem (literally, "to the man"):** An attack on the character of the individual or the opponent rather than his or her actual opinions, arguments, or qualifications: "Susan Davidson, the prosecuting attorney, drinks heavily. There's no way she can present an effective case." This is an attack on Ms. Davidson's character rather than an analysis of her legal talents. Her record in court may be excellent.

- **Ad populum (literally, "to the people"):** An emotional appeal to positive concepts (God, mother, country, liberty, democracy, apple pie) or negative concepts (fascism, atheism) rather than a direct discussion of the real issue: "Those senators voting to increase the defense budget are really warmongers at heart." "If you are a true American, you should be for tariffs to protect the garment industry."

- **Red herring:** A diversionary tactic designed to avoid confronting the key issue. *Red herring* refers to the practice of dragging a smelly fish across the trail to divert tracking dogs away from the real quarry. A red herring occurs when writers avoid countering an opposing argument directly: "Of course equal pay for women is an important issue, but I wonder whether women really want to take the responsibility that comes with higher paying jobs. Do they really want the additional stress?" This writer diverts attention away from the argument about equal pay to another issue, stress—thus, a red herring.

POSTSCRIPT ON THE WRITING PROCESS

In your journal, answer the following questions.

1. Describe how your beliefs about your subject changed from the time you decided on your claim to when you revised your essay. What caused the change in your views?

2. What opposing argument was most difficult to counter? Explain how you handled it.

3. Which was your strongest argument? Did you use logical appeals and evidence, or did you rely more on appeals to character or emotion? Explain.

4. How did your writing process for the argumentative essay change from the process for your previous essays? What steps or stages took longer? What stages did you have to go back and rework?

STUDENT WRITING

CRYSTAL SABATKE

Welfare Is Still Necessary for Women and Children in the U.S.

Crystal Sabatke decided to write her arguing essay about changes in the welfare system that require women to work in order to receive certain welfare payments. She decided to focus particularly on readers who believe that welfare mothers will simply become lazy if they don't have to work for the money to support their families. She hopes that "by showing examples of positive welfare stories, I can show that mothers and their children are more important than saving a few cents per dollar." Reproduced below are Sabatke's notes for her audience analysis, her rough draft, the responses to her peer review workshop, and her final, revised draft.

AUDIENCE ANALYSIS: READERS' BELIEFS

My readers will assume that women on welfare who have children can go out and get jobs. That they should get jobs for the betterment of themselves and their children. That when they do get a job, their financial problems will be solved and that welfare will be a thing of the past. In order to shake these assumptions, I believe that emotional appeals should be used. Examples of factual women on welfare in negative situations that prevent them from getting jobs—children, low-income wage jobs, etc.

My readers also believe in the principle of a strong work ethic, the idea that if you work hard, you can achieve the "American Dream." I do feel that I should show how this principle is not applicable in certain situations—ones that my readers probably do not take into strong consideration.

Finally, I feel that my readers blindly value getting jobs more than taking care of children (even though these are the same people who hypocritically focus on family values). I think that family values should be focused on because this is something that is held in high regard by nearly every human being.

Welfare in the United States— Necessity Without Programming

FIRST DRAFT

What defines an American woman? Women in the United States play numerous roles; many are successful executives, mothers, wives, and scholars. Women have broken many barriers throughout U.S. history and have become, in general, a very successful group in society. But what about the women who haven't broken the barriers? What about the women who had children at a young age with a boyfriend or husband who left them alone soon after? What about the women who can't find a job because their education level hinders their prosperity? What about the women who can't seem to find their way above the poverty level and have to seek help from the government?

Throughout the United States, poverty is not abnormal—especially for women and children. With "44.6 percent of the children who lived in [female-headed households] poor in 1994, and almost half of all children who are poor living in female-headed households," (A) doesn't it seem ironic that the government is cutting welfare expenditures for women and children? Many government officials believe that "the welfare system and its recipients are the cause of the problem." (B) What the lawmakers aren't considering, however, is that poverty is essentially the catalyst in a circle of controversy, and that the only way out of the problems is to provide adequate educational opportunities for welfare recipients, along with ample child care programs and options and a sufficient minimum wage for all citizens. The answer is not ending welfare, but dealing with the problems of poverty in a realistic manner.

In contrast to opposing arguments, most women aren't poor and having children because they want more welfare money or because they are lazy, but because they don't have a sufficient education. As Nicholas Zill, a writer for *Public Health Reports,* states, "Girls and boys who become parents while they are still of school age are . . . predominantly those with low test scores and grades, who are disengaged from school or in active conflict with parents, teachers, or school authorities." (C) The government needs to provide for all Americans an education system that works not only for the successful student, but also for the students that are not doing well. Female students, especially, should be educated about birth control and negative outcomes of having children at younger ages. We should not be punishing and impeding children for the mistakes of their parents and the deficiencies of our education system. Welfare is indispensable for uneducated women and their children until a system of education and support can be initiated and proven successful.

For people opposing government assistance of the poor, another popular argument is that welfare needs to be ended in all forms, and women with children need to get jobs. According to Charles Murray, a strong oppressor of the welfare system in America and an advocate of family values, a "strict job program" needs to be established that will force women to "drop out of a welfare program altogether." (D) Essentially, to the opposition, "the welfare-reform discussion indicates that what happens to children doesn't matter to Americans, so long as mothers are forced to work." (E) Unfortunately, however, for women with children who either decide to go into or are forced into the job market, there isn't a child care system that works with mothers to make a "strict job program" successful. The truth is, there is a scarcity of child care options in this country, and the ones that are available are generally out of the price range of a welfare mother. Shouldn't children be put foremost in this debate? If our country is really focused on family values, shouldn't women have the option to stay home and give their children good care even if it means keeping them on welfare? Welfare is essential in providing a means for women to provide not only adequate care for their children, but positive values for their future.

Another category of women on welfare who are quite often overlooked are those mothers who have minimum-wage jobs and who still need government assistance. The current method of getting women into the workplace is the Job Training Partnership Act, or "the Government's biggest training program." (E) According to *The Wall Street Journal,* however, this program, which offers low-wage jobs such as fast food "is a sham" (E) and "actually led to lower wages for poor young women compared with a control group." (E) Once a woman is in the workplace, it is easy to assume that she will be removed from welfare and become an effective member of society. What is not taken into consideration, however, is that a minimum wage can hardly keep up with the needs of a single mother. "The average [welfare] recipient who gets a full-time job . . . makes $6.74 an hour—about $14,000 a year. Daycare for two children can easily cost $12,000."(E) It is obvious that after subtracting child care, this equation leaves a mother with virtually nothing left to provide herself and her children with necessities such as food, clothing, and shelter. The answer is clearly not to simply put women in low-wage-earning jobs. Until Washington can come up with a solution that involves education and child care assistance and has raised the minimum wage enough to support a mother with children, a welfare system still needs to be provided.

The answer is not ending welfare, but providing supplemental programs that can realistically assist a single mother. With the minimum wage being too low, child care costs being impractical, and education programs virtually nonexistent, it is not fair to assume that welfare can be abolished. Of course, there are problems with the current welfare system, but supplemental programming is the only way to effectively change these glitches.

ARGUING ESSAY: PEER-RESPONSE WORKSHEET

To the Writer: Briefly describe the audience for this paper. (Be sure to include your audience's position on the issue you're writing about.) Also note what you want your readers to focus on as they read.

My audience is white, conservative males who are against any welfare. Please comment on my development—and I kind of gave up on my conclusion. How can I make it better?

To the Reader: Answer the following questions.

1. Underline the *claim/thesis.* Is it clear? Make suggestions for improvement.

    Bev: Good thesis. It is clear and placed in a good spot, just after enough background and before the bulk of the paper. However, I would elaborate more on the "realistic manner" either in your thesis sentence or a separate sentence.

Amy: *The thesis is very clear—however, the sentence after it confused me.*

2. Is the claim adequately *focused*—narrow within manageable/defensible limits? Why or why not? Explain.

    Bev: The claim is well focused and clear.

    Amy: *Possibly even too focused. Reads more like an essay map than a thesis.*

3. Do you feel the writer needs to add any *qualifiers* or exceptions in order to avoid overgeneralizing? If yes, explain.

    Bev: You sort of overgeneralize about women on welfare, but not too noticeably. Maybe some statistics concerning these women would help.

    Amy: *Possibly qualify for 2 parent and singles—see paragraph 5.*

4. Does the paper deal with *opposing arguments*? How successful do you feel the paper is in conceding and/or refuting opposing arguments? Explain.

    Bev: Good job of laying out the opposing sides of the argument.

    Amy: *Opposition clearly stated each time and then refuted. No work needed on the ones you have stated. Does not take into consideration two-parent welfare families or singles. Will some of your claims work for them as well?*

5. Does the *evidence* support the reasons? Where is more evidence needed? What kind of evidence is needed?

    Bev: Your use of evidence is effective. However, I would suggest more evidence in the first body paragraph. You only have one quotation—maybe throw another one in there.

    Amy: *More statistics would be helpful, for example, test scores as related to teen pregnancy.*

6. What are *one* or *two* areas that you feel the writer should address *first* in revising this paper? What suggestions can you make for conducting those revisions?

    Bev: Good organization of the paper. You follow a clear layout and it is easy to follow. I would develop your quotations more in paragraph 2. You use good evidence. Just develop it more. In your conclusion, maybe if you tied it into the intro, it would help you out. Restate arguments that you made in the introduction.

    Amy: *The lead paragraph seems to give an essay map but doesn't. Possibly phrase some of the questions to relate to the paragraphs? Conclusion: Instead of summing up what you said, try an analysis of the problem and its solutions.*

7. Return the paper to the writer and discuss your comments.

FINAL DRAFT

Welfare Is Still Necessary for Women and Children in the U.S.

What defines an American woman? Women in the United States play 1 numerous roles; many are successful executives, mothers, wives, and scholars. Women have broken many barriers throughout U.S. history and have become, in general, a very successful group in society. But what about the women who haven't broken the barriers? What about the women who had children at a young age with a boyfriend or husband who left them soon after? What about the women who can't find a job because their education level hinders their prosperity? What about the women who can't seem to find their way above the poverty level and have to seek help from the government?

In the United States, poverty is not abnormal—especially for 2 women and children. With "44.6 percent of the children who lived in [female-headed households] in 1994, and almost half of all children who are poor living in female-headed households," doesn't it seem ironic that the government continues to cut welfare expenditures for women and children? (Wellstone 1). Many government officials believe that "the welfare system and its recipients are the cause of the problem" (Rank 1). What these lawmakers aren't considering, however, is that poverty is essentially the catalyst in a circle of controversy, and that the only way out of the problem is to provide adequate educational opportunities for welfare recipients, ample child care programs and options, and a sufficient minimum wage for all citizens. Until methods such as these are instituted, it is necessary for the government to maintain a supportive welfare system for the women and children of our country.

In refutation of opposing arguments, most women aren't poor 3 and having children because they want more welfare money or because they are lazy, but because they don't have a sufficient education. As Nicholas Zill, a writer for Public Health Reports, states, "Girls and boys who become parents while they are still of school age are . . . predominantly those with low test scores and grades, who are disengaged from school or in active conflict with parents, teachers, or school authorities" (6). Recent studies by the National Center for Health Statistics show that "nearly one in every four children in the U.S. is born to a mother who has not finished high school" (Zill 2). The government needs to provide an educational system that focuses not only on the successful student, but also on the student who is performing poorly.

Because "parent education is linked to children's economic well-being," positive programs need to be created that provide support and alternatives to mainstream education for students who are "high risk" or are not college-bound (Zill 3). Female students, specifically, should be educated about birth control and the negative consequences of having children at younger ages. Until our nation takes active measures to improve the educational system, welfare is necessary to support the children who are born because of the inadequacies of our schools. America should not be punishing and impeding children for the mistakes of their parents and the deficiencies of our school system. Welfare is indispensable for uneducated women and their children until a better system of education and support can be initiated and proven successful.

Another popular argument given by people who oppose welfare *4* is that single women with children should be working, not accepting welfare. According to Charles Murray, a strong critic of the welfare system, we need to institute a "strict job program" that will force women to "drop out of welfare altogether" (285). According to Ruth Conniff, author of "Big Bad Welfare: Welfare Reform Politics and Children," the welfare reform discussion "indicates that what happens to children doesn't matter to Americans, so long as mothers are forced to work" (8). Unfortunately, however, for single women with children who either decide to work or are forced into the job market, there isn't a child care system that could make a "strict job program" successful (Murray 285). With child care costing "about $116 a week for a toddler and $122 for an infant," not only is American day care economically insensitive, but day care options are limited as well (Conniff 8). According to Mark Robert Rank, author of "Winners and Losers in the Welfare Game," the "scarcity of affordable child care for low-income families" makes the current welfare system in this country a "losing game" (1). How can women be expected to get jobs when there aren't sufficient means to care for their children? Ruth Conniff wonders that if our country "is so concerned about family values, wouldn't it make sense to let mothers stay home with their young children?" (8). Welfare is essential to provide means for women to supply not only adequate care for their children but also positive values for their children's future.

Another category of women on welfare who are quite often over- *5* looked are those mothers who have minimum-wage jobs and who still need government assistance. The current method of getting women into the work place is the Job Training Partnership Act, or "the Government's biggest training program" (Conniff 5). According to *The Wall Street Journal,* however, this program—which offers low-wage jobs such as fast-food work—has "actually led to lower wages for poor young women compared with a control group" (Conniff 5). Once a woman is in the workplace, many people assume that she will be removed from welfare and become an independent member of society. What is not considered, however, is that the minimum wage can scarcely keep up with the needs of a single mother. According to a survey done of welfare recipients in Dane County, Wisconsin, "the average [welfare] recipient who gets a full-time job . . . makes $6.74 an hour—about $14,000 a year. Day care for two children can easily cost $12,000" (Conniff 7). It is obvious that after subtracting child care costs, this equation leaves a mother with virtually nothing left to provide herself and her children with necessities such as food, clothing, and shelter—making it necessary to stay on government assistance. Until the minimum wage has been raised to keep up with these strenuous living situations, Washington needs to continue providing welfare to help single mothers and their children survive.

One of the many roles that American women assume is often that 6 of a poverty-stricken single mother. With current education programs that are not effective for "high-risk" women students, with child care costs that are overwhelming, and with a minimum wage so low that it can't keep up with the needs of single mothers, it is not fair to assume that welfare can be abolished. As Michelle Tingling Clement of National Public Radio states, "What [women] truly need is . . . education, skills development . . . and not just any job but jobs that pay living wages with family health benefits and child care" (2). Until programs that can realistically assist women and children are created, welfare is still a definite necessity.

Works Cited

Clement, Michelle T. "Republicans Finalize Welfare Reform Package." *All Things Considered.* Natl. Public Radio, 15 Nov. 1998. Print. Transcript.

Conniff, Ruth. "Big Bad Welfare: Welfare Reform Politics and Children." *The Progressive* 84 (1994): 1–10. Print.

Murray, Charles. "Keeping Priorities Straight on Welfare Reform." *The Aims of Argument.* Ed. Timothy W. Crucius and Carolyn E. Channell. Mountain View, CA: Mayfield, 1998. 285–88. Print.

Rank, Mark Robert. "Winners and Losers in the Welfare Game." Editorial. *St. Louis Post-Dispatch* 15 Sept. 1994: 1–2. Print.

Wellstone, Paul. "If Poverty Is the Question." *The Nation.* The Nation, 4 Apr. 1997. Web. 10 Oct. 1998.

Zill, Nicholas. "Parental Schooling and Children's Health." *Public Health Reports* 111 (1996): 1–10. Print.

QUESTIONS FOR WRITING AND DISCUSSION

1 Sabatke says that her audience consists of white, conservative males who believe that everyone should have a job and no one should be on welfare. Where in her essay does she address this audience? Could she revise her essay to focus on this audience even more specifically? Explain.

2 Read Sabatke's first draft and then the responses by Bev and Amy on the peer-response sheet. Which of Bev's and/or Amy's suggestions do you agree with? What other suggestions might you give Sabatke? Which of the peer-response suggestions does Sabatke take or ignore in her final draft? How might Sabatke have improved her final version even more? Explain.

3 What opposing arguments does Sabatke consider? Choose one of her responses, and explain why you think the counterargument is or is not effective. Think of one additional counterargument that she might consider. Should she address that argument? Why or why not?

4 At what points in her essay should Sabatke give additional evidence? Should she use more statistics about welfare mothers? Should she give 7 a more specific description of the current welfare system? Should she give evidence from case studies of welfare recipients? Explain your choices.

STUDENT WRITING

ERIC BOESE

Standardized Tests: Shouldn't We Be Helping Our Students?

As standardized testing has increased in the nation's high schools in re-cent years, so have the attacks against these tests. Several universities have followed the University of California's lead and deemphasized the SAT test. High school tests, such as the Texas TAAS, California's Stan-ford 9, Minnesota's MJCA, or Colorado's CSAP, have come under fire because they seem to punish the poorer school districts mainly for hav-ing insufficient funds to compete with the wealthy suburban schools. Eric Boese, a student at Colorado State University, decided to write about the problems created by these standardized tests. His purpose, he explains, is to persuade his readers—primarily politicians who set test-ing policies—that "the use of standardized tests in the education system has to be changed."

Over the past few decades our nation's school systems have progressed 1 with leaps and bounds. We have seen improvements in textbooks, technology, teacher resources, and so much more. The opportunities for children to excel going through primary education are enormous, greater now than they have ever been. Still we see so many children being held back. Funds are being used inefficiently, and our priorities have become a little mixed up. I'm talking about what it is that we actually teach in primary schools. Are we teaching students skills and giving them knowledge that will make them better members of society or have we decided that it is more important to teach kids how to do well on tests? The answer to this question you may not like, but it is an answer that we can do something about.

To begin working on a solution, we should first locate the source 2 of the problem. As I have said, everything in the world of education is changing, and I have seen that there is one change in particular that can go a long way towards explaining, and solving, our problem. This change is in the use of standardized tests. They have become a more important and more destructive component of our schools. Of course I'm not suggesting that we throw the tests out, for they can be a vital part of education. I hope to show how the current use of these tests is harming the educational process and show how we can use them in a more productive manner in the future.

Over the last ten years in Texas some interesting things have happened. The first was that, in 1990, an exam called the Texas Assessment of Academic Skills (TAAS) was administered for the first time in a number of schools (Weisman). The test was given in grades three through eight and was used as an exit exam early in school. A lot of stress was placed on this test because it was used to determine the longevity of the careers of teachers and administrators. Their jobs depended on the success of their students in taking the exam. In 1994 George W. Bush, the test's biggest supporter, mandated that it be administered statewide. Over six years, the pass rate of the test increased in all student populations (Weisman). The test appeared to be a huge success.

George W. Bush credited the better scores to the test challenging 4 students to do better. I, however, credit it to how the test changed the way the schools function. An alarming article by Jonathan Weisman reviews just this case. He shows how improvements on the TAAS are not correlated to improvements on other standardized tests that were given to the same students. While the TAAS scores went up, the other scores did nothing. The biggest revelation in his article is when he explains why students raised their test scores on that exam and not on others. What he found was that teachers were teaching them how to take the exam. Student learning was compromised because too much stress was put on teachers to make sure their students scored well. Jonathan Weisman knows this to be true:

> In a study published by the Harvard Civil Rights Project in January, Professors Linda McNeil of Rice University and Angela Valenzuela of the University of Texas delivered a scathing assessment of the TAAS's impact on Texas classrooms, asserting that "behind the rhetoric of the test scores are a growing set of classroom practices in which test-prep activities are usurping a substantive curriculum."

Of course it didn't really take experts to figure this out. Anyone involved in the classrooms of these schools knew that was going on:

> Teachers protested that they were spending eight to ten hours a week in test-preparation drills and that their principals were pressuring them to spend even more. Only 27 percent said they believed the rising TAAS scores reflected increased learning and higher-quality teaching; half said the scores indicated nothing of the sort. (Weisman)

This is a situation that is simply unacceptable. Endorsing tests that have these kinds of side effects is pumping out graduating classes of test takers. It's causing students to become less capable of meeting challenges that will face them in college and in the future. Texas isn't the only place this is taking place, but it is a great example of the way our nation's schools will turn out if we allow the use of these tests to continue to spread.

In Texas there are still other factors that cause the test scores to be 5 misleading. There was legislation that allowed schools to exempt specialed students from taking the test. The number of exemptions increased during the years that the test was administered (Weisman). From this we see that the students aren't even improving as much on the tests as the figures show.

The fact that students score better on this kind of exam reveals 6 nothing about their personal improvements. If used differently, however, the exams could be much more effective in meeting students' needs and less destructive of their education. We could eliminate undue stress on teachers and create better evaluations of students' abilities.

In other places than Texas, standardized tests are being used in *7* counterproductive ways. The biggest problem seems to be that the tests have too much riding on them. In her article "Test Case: Now the Principal's Cheating," Carolyn Kleiner gives some examples of how the stakes of standardized tests have been raised:

> Twenty-eight states now use standard exams to determine gradua-
> tion and 19 to govern student promotion; a growing number also
> dole out performance-based bonuses for schools that show progress
> and threaten intervention, even closure, for those that don't.

Kleiner links the growing importance of the tests to an inevitable side effect, cheating. Of course there are more ways that tests have grown in importance, and yes, more downfalls. The results of standardized tests can have impacts on the jobs of teachers and principals, the money they will make, the reputation of a school or district, and the high school graduation rates. The scores can also affect school funding and various different community issues. People would rather send their children to school somewhere that has a reputation for scoring well on exams and that doesn't have funding problems. In extreme cases, test results can have effects on the property values of residents in a district. George Madaus notes that the test results "don't provide a full picture of a child's—or a school's—accomplishments" and says that "You can't use these tests by themselves to make any decisions" (Kantrowitz et al.). The tests have, however, been used to determine a number of the things above, and as a result, some drawbacks of the tests are that they affect student learning in the classroom, and they cause great stress to students and teachers.

In "Schools for Scandal," Thomas Toch and Betsy Wagner discuss *8* how standardized tests have ultimately led to a problem of educators cheating. The problem of cheating has been one that, until recently, involved students breaking the rules. The new problem we are seeing is that teachers and even principals have started to help their students cheat on some tests. Why would they do this, you ask? It's similar to the situation in Texas—high stakes tests put pressure on them. They are pressured by administrators, principals, and parents alike, all of whom want to see the students get good scores for their own benefit. For parents, good scores are expected, and they see them as being equivalent to their students' doing well in school. In other words, if they see that a school has scored poorly on any given test, they see it as a failure on the part of the school, a further incentive for schools to improve their scores.

It's not something many of us want to hear, but the need for high 9 scores has caused many school officials to encourage cheating as well as raise their school's score by any means possible. "In a national survey of educators in 1990, 1 in 11 teachers reported pressure from administrators to cheat on standardized tests" (Toch and Wagner). On top of the pressures of cheating, there is almost nothing stopping teachers from giving out answers. In most common standardized tests, security monitoring is minimal, answers are available to test givers (who are usually the teachers), and tests are used multiple times. This makes it easy for teachers not only to cheat, but to teach the material that they know will be covered on any given test. Researchers in Colorado found that tests scores dropped dramatically from a first test that teachers had the time to prepare their students for and a very similar test given only a few weeks later. University of Colorado testing expert Lorrie Shepard said, "Teachers are not teaching students skills and concepts. . . . They are teaching specific examples by rote memorization" (Toch and Wagner).

Due to cheating and various other issues, standardized tests reveal 10 less accurate scores each year. In other words, tests are getting worse at what they were designed to do: measure skill levels of students. The reason, Toch and Wagner mention, is that people want high scores. Many tests that challenge students are not being used by schools simply because they yield low scores. The basic skills covered by these tests are inflating scores and forcing teachers to focus on teaching remedial skills and not on the needs of the individual students. In "Education: Is That Your Final Answer?" Jodie Morse gives an example in which the problem is even worse:

> Educators say they have had to dumb down their lessons to teach the often picayune factoids covered by the exams. A study released last month by the University of Virginia found that while some schools had boosted their performance on Virginia's exam, teachers had to curtail field trips, elective courses and even student visits to the bathroom—all in an effort to cram more test prep into the school day. Says the study's author, education professor Daniel Duke: "These schools have become battlefield units."

Causing practices like these to occur in our nation's schools is unjustifiable. The inflation of scores doesn't stop there; tests are being reused to a point where most schools can manage to do very well on them. This creates a false impression of students' skills. The U.S. Department of Education agreed that "with respect to national averages, [school] districts and states are presenting inflated results and misleading the public." How can somebody defend a policy that diminishes the education of students for tests that don't accurately reflect student achievement or, in some cases, even challenge them to think on their own?

So far we have considered some of the many effects of our current *11* testing system. It is equally important to review exactly what materials the tests cover and whether or not they are testing the right things. First of all, 80 percent of standardized tests used in America are produced by corporations (Toch and Wagner). Who says corporations know what should be on these tests in the first place? The relevancy and difficulty of tests are determined by people who have little or no concern for their effects on schools. They are not held accountable for the material covered on their exams and do not feel that security is their concern. Often times, the corporations will make the materials on their tests easier because more schools will buy tests that make themselves look good. In other cases, the corporations simply don't know what to include in their tests for different grade levels. A side effect of corporations writing tests is that they usually recycle their tests and so they rarely "allow schools to return copies of their graded exams to students so they, and their teachers, might learn from their mistakes" (Toch and Wagner). Of the students I surveyed, none claimed that they had ever even learned their own scores on school-mandated standardized tests, and none claimed that they learned anything substantial from the exams that they had taken. On many exams, questions relating to students' advanced-thinking skills are almost nonexistent. Corporations are just not giving tests that are beneficial to students. This is the first change we need to make: either make the corporations answer to a selected group of educational officials or have somebody make tests that have the student in mind.

Along the same lines as above, we need to throw out the tests that are *12* too difficult for students of any particular age group. Only a few people actually oppose this argument. New York State Education Commissioner Richard Mills said that "subjecting 9-year-olds to tests they can't pass is one of the strategies to change things for the better" (Ohanian). I wish somebody would explain this to me. Is this supposed to make students want to work harder because they failed miserably or is it going to discourage them? This may not be an opinion that is held by too many people, but it sure seems to be in some cases. In some states, like Massachusetts for example, students are required to take tests that can last up to 18 hours in order to graduate from high school. We can't expect this much of students who are only 18 years old; not many of them would be able to pass such a test if their classes weren't so focused on preparing them for it, and as we have seen, test preparation often adversely affects student learning.

A level of testing has to be found such that students will be challenged and yet they will not be overwhelmed. Standardized tests should include materials relevant to a student's grade level, some materials that would require the student to explore new ideas, and some questions designed to test a student's advanced-thinking skills. This test would cover materials that would be included in a normal school curriculum and therefore would take up less class time. A teacher could concentrate on students' needs again, and classes could cover more material, explore subjects more deeply and give students the education they deserve. There would be time to do more of what one student claims to love most about school, "getting into great conversations and developing ideas" (Selzer). A test that fits these criteria would give a more accurate evaluation of the student's skills and of the student's potential to succeed in higher-level and college courses. Such a test may not be easy to make, but it would definitely be worth the effort. 13

It's getting harder and harder to see the positive side of using today's standardized tests. Not only are the tests giving inaccurate evaluations of students' skills, but they are causing corruption in our schools and diminishing the opportunities for educational excellence of our students. I've discussed ideas for new tests that could be used, but that is not enough to make up for the disturbances involved with the importance of the tests. It is my opinion that we cannot allow these tests to undermine the current system. First of all, funding should not be determined by scores; it should be determined by need. Taxpayers in any given region would also be able to vote to increase funding for the schools that they support. I mentioned that, in Texas, for teachers and administrators the tests held an additional, personal importance. Determining who holds these positions needs a more personal evaluation than looking at test scores. We need to look at how their students are really improving and the effort they put into their students' education. 14

I'm sure that the public will still have the bias that their students should be getting the best scores, but this is an issue that will have to be faced. They need to be shown that the test scores are a sign for teachers to read to determine the extra attention that some students may require, and this is what the test should be used for. There is no greater purpose for having these tests than for improving education. Many of the problems of the current system will prove to be very difficult to resolve, but any steps towards a new system are ones for the better. 15

It may all sound difficult now, but the state of our schools is in desperate need of change. Pushing for more tests as so many people are doing is not the answer. I urge you to consider how bright children are being discouraged by an unproductive testing system and to be the person who puts the needs of the children first. 16

...continued Standardized Tests: Shouldn't We Be Helping Our Students, **Eric Boese**

Works Cited

Kantrowitz, Barbara, Daniel McGinn, Ellise Pierce, and Erika Check. "When Teachers Are Cheaters." *Newsweek.* Newsweek, 19 June 2000. Web. 15 Apr. 2001.

Kleiner, Carolyn. "Test Case: Now the Principal's Cheating." *U.S. News & World Report.* U.S. News and World Report, 12 June 2000. Web. 10 Apr. 2001.

Morse, Jodie. "Education: Is That Your Final Answer?" *Time.* Time, 19 June 2000. Web. 15 Apr. 2001.

Ohanian, Susan. "Editorials: Standardized Schools." *Nation.* Nation, 18 Sep. 1999. Web. 10 Apr. 2001.

Selzer, Adam. "High-Stakes Testing: It's Backlash Time." *U.S. News and World Report.* U.S. News and World Report, 3 Apr. 2000. Web. 15 Apr. 2001.

Toch, Thomas, and Betsy Wagner. "Schools for Scandal." *U.S. News and World Report.* U.S. News and World Report, 27 Apr. 1992. Web. 10 Apr. 2001.

Weisman, Jonathan. "Only a Test." *New Republic.* New Republic, 10 Apr. 2000. Web. 15 Apr. 2001.

vo·cab·u·lar·y

In your journal, write the meaning of the italicized words in the following phrases.

- determine the *longevity* of the careers of teachers (**3**)
- test-prep activities are *usurping a substantive* curriculum (**4**)
- a further *incentive* (**8**)
- teach the often *picayune factoids* (**10**)
- preparation often *adversely* affects student learning (**12**)

QUESTIONS FOR WRITING AND DISCUSSION

1 In your journal, write three short paragraphs explaining your own experience with standardized tests. First, which tests have you taken, and when did you take them? Next, what was the purpose of the tests—to evaluate you or your school? Finally, describe the effect of these tests on your own education. Did they detract from the regular curriculum? Did they give you motivation and incentive to learn? Did they help you get into college?

2 Eric Boese uses a problem-solving format for his arguing essay. Which paragraphs describe the problems with standardized tests? List these problems. Which paragraphs indicate his solutions? What are his solutions? Is his essay clear or would you give him suggestions for improving his organization? Explain.

3 Boese writes that the intended audience for his essay is politicians who are in favor of increased use of standardized tests. Where does Boese address this audience? Where and how could he make his appeal to this audience even stronger? Write out actual sentences Boese could add to his essay.

4 On the Internet, read more recent articles on standardized testing. Has testing in high schools changed since Boese wrote his essay in 2001? Do more or fewer high schools give mandated tests? Has the quality of the tests improved? Do students and teachers like or dislike these tests? Explain.

After studying the details in this image of the Vietnam War memorial, go to page 550
and read the poem, "Facing It," by Yusef Komunyakaa. What particular lines or images
in Komunyakaa's poem seem to be captured in this photograph?

Responding to Literature

I
n Introduction to Literature class, you and a friend are assigned to work collaboratively on an essay about Eudora Welty's "A Worn Path." You are both interested in how Phoenix Jackson's journey contains images of the phoenix—a mythological bird said to live for five hundred years, after which it burns itself to death and then rises from its ashes to become youthful and beautiful again. You draft your essays separately and then read each other's drafts. At that point, you collaborate on a single essay, combining the best ideas and evidence from your separate drafts. Your collaborative essay shows how Phoenix Jackson is characterized by birdlike images, how she calmly faces images of fire and death on her journey, and how her grandson represents her rebirth.

In a film class, you watch Roman Polanski's *Tess,* an adaptation of Thomas Hardy's novel *Tess of the D'Urbervilles.* You decide to compare the film with the novel, focusing on four key episodes: the "strawberry scene," in which Tess meets Alec; the rape scene at night; the harvesting scene; and the final scene at Stonehenge. On the basis of your comparison, you argue that Polanski's interpretation (and the acting of Nastassia Kinski) retains Hardy's view of Tess as a victim of social and sexist repression.

66 I hungered for new books, new ways of looking and seeing. It was not a matter of believing or disbelieving what I read, but of feeling something new, of being affected by something that made the look of the world different. 99

—RICHARD WRIGHT
AUTHOR OF *BLACK BOY*

66 No one else can read a literary work for us. The benefits of literature can emerge only from creative activity on the part of the reader. 99

—LOUISE ROSENBLATT
AUTHOR OF *LITERATURE AS EXPLORATION*

R ESPONDING TO POEMS AND SHORT STORIES REQUIRES BOTH IMAGINA-
TION AND CRITICAL-READING SKILL. AS READERS, WE ANTICIPATE,
IMAGINE, FEEL, WORRY, ANALYZE, AND QUESTION. A STORY OR POEM IS
LIKE AN EMPTY BALLOON THAT WE INFLATE WITH THE warm breath
of our imagination and experience. Our participation makes us partners with
the author in the artistic recreation.

First, readers must *imagine* and recreate that special world described by the
writer. The first sentences of a short story, for example, throw open a door to a
world that—attractive or repulsive—tempts our curiosity and imagination. Like
Alice in *Alice in Wonderland,* we cannot resist following a white rabbit with pink
eyes who mutters to himself, checks his watch, and then zips down a rabbit hole
and into an imaginary world.

Here are three opening sentences of three very different short stories.

> Young Goodman Brown came forth at sunset into the street at Salem
> village; but put his head back, after crossing the threshold, to exchange
> a parting kiss with his young wife.
>
> —Nathaniel Hawthorne, "Young Goodman Brown"

> As Gregor Samsa awoke one morning from uneasy dreams he found
> himself transformed in his bed into a gigantic insect.
>
> —Franz Kafka, "The Metamorphosis"

> The morning of June 27th was clear and sunny, with the fresh warmth
> of a full-summer day; the flowers were blossoming profusely and the
> grass was green.
>
> —Shirley Jackson, "The Lottery"

Whether our imaginations construct the disturbing image of a "gigantic in-
sect" or the seemingly peaceful picture of a perfect summer day, we actively
recreate each story.

In a similar way, poems invite the reader to participate in actively creating
characters, images, places, feelings, and reflections. Below are lines from several
poems, each creating its own characters, places, images, and themes.

> Because I could not stop for Death—
> He kindly stopped for me—
> The Carriage held but just Ourselves—
> And Immortality.
>
> —Emily Dickinson, "Because I could not stop for Death"

anyone lived in a pretty how town
(with up so floating many bells down)
spring summer autumn winter
he sang his didn't he danced his did.
      —e.e. cummings, "anyone lived in a pretty how town"

Tyger! Tyger! burning bright
In the forests of the night,
What immortal hand or eye
Could frame thy fearful symmetry?
      —William Blake, "The Tyger"

Two roads diverged in a yellow wood,
And sorry I could not travel both
And be one traveler, long I stood
And looked down one as far as I could
To where it bent in the undergrowth
      —Robert Frost, "The Road Not Taken"

Responding to literature also requires that readers *reread*. First, you should reread for yourself—that is, reread to write down your ideas, questions, feelings, and reactions. To heighten your role in re-creating a story or poem, you should note in the margins your questions and responses to main characters, places, metaphors and images, and themes that catch your attention: "Are the names of Hawthorne's characters significant? Is Young Goodman Brown really good? Is his wife, Faith, really faithful?" "Why does Emily Dickinson have her speaker personify Death as the driver of a carriage? Why does her speaker say that 'he *kindly* stopped for me'? What action is taking place?" Don't just underline or highlight passages. Actually *write* your questions and responses in the margins.

Second, you should reread with a writer's eye. In fiction, identify the major and minor characters. Look for conflicts between characters. Mark passages that contain foreshadowing. Pinpoint sentences that reveal the narrative point of view. Use the appropriate critical terms (*character, plot, conflict, point of view, setting, style,* and *theme*) to help you reread with a writer's eye and see how the parts of a story relate to the whole. Similarly, in poetry, look for character, key events, and setting, and *always* pay attention to images and metaphors, to voice and tone, to word choice, and to rhythm and rhyme. Each critical term is a tool—a magnifying glass that helps you understand and interpret the literary work more clearly.

In addition to rereading, responding to literature requires that readers *share* ideas, reactions, and interpretations. Sharing usually begins in small-group or class discussions, but it continues as you explain your interpretation in writing. A work of literature is not a mathematical equation with a single answer. Great literature is worth interpreting precisely because each reader responds differently. The purpose of literature is to encourage you to reflect on your life and the lives of others—to look for new ways of seeing and understanding your world—and ultimately to expand your world. Sharing is crucial to appreciating literature.

> Hawthorne doesn't come right out and say that people become disillusioned by experiencing evil. He shows how it actually happens in the life of young Goodman Brown.

> Shirley Jackson's "The Lottery" helps me see that the notion of human sacrifice and the idea of the human scapegoat still exist in our culture today.

> In "Because I could not stop for Death," Emily Dickinson uses personification and metaphors as vehicles for her own reflection and introspection.

Writing about your responses and sharing them with other readers helps you "reread" your own ideas in order to explain them fully and clearly to other readers.

RESPONDING TO A SHORT STORY

Read and respond to Kate Chopin's "The Story of an Hour." Use your imagination to help create the story as you read. Then *reread* the story, noting in the margin your questions and responses. When you finish rereading and annotating your reactions, write your interpretation of the last line of the story.

PROFESSIONAL WRITING

The Story of an Hour

Kate Chopin

Kate O'Flaherty Chopin (1851–1904) was an American writer whose mother was French and Creole and whose father was Irish. In 1870, she moved from St. Louis to New Orleans with her husband, Oscar Chopin, and over the next ten years she gave birth to five sons. After her husband died in 1882, Chopin returned to St. Louis to begin a new life as a writer. Many of her best stories are about Louisiana people and places, and her most famous novel, The Awakening, *tells the story of Edna, a woman who leaves her marriage and her children to fulfill herself through an artistic career.*

Knowing that Mrs. Mallard was afflicted with a heart trouble, *1*
great care was taken to break to her as gently as possible the news of
her husband's death.

It was her sister Josephine who told her, in broken sentences, *2*
veiled hints that revealed in half concealing. Her husband's friend
Richards was there, too, near her. It was he who had been in the newspaper office when intelligence of the railroad disaster was received,
with Brently Mallard's name leading the list of "killed." He had only
taken the time to assure himself of its truth by a second telegram, and
had hastened to forestall any less careful, less tender friend in bearing
the sad message.

She did not hear the story as many women have heard the same, *3*
with a paralyzed inability to accept its significance. She wept at once,
with sudden, wild abandonment, in her sister's arms. When the storm
of grief had spent itself she went away to her room alone. She would
have no one follow her.

There stood, facing the open window, a comfortable, roomy arm- *4*
chair. Into this she sank, pressed down by a physical exhaustion that
haunted her body and seemed to reach into her soul.

She could see in the open square before her house the tops of trees *5*
that were all aquiver with the new spring life. The delicious breath of
rain was in the air. In the street below a peddler was crying his wares.
The notes of a distant song which someone was singing reached her
faintly, and countless sparrows were twittering in the eaves.

There were patches of blue sky showing here and there through *6*
the clouds that had met and piled one above the other in the west facing her window.

She sat with her head thrown back upon the cushion of the chair *7*
quite motionless, except when a sob came up into her throat and shook
her, as a child who has cried itself to sleep continues to sob in its dreams.

She was young, with a fair, calm face, whose lines bespoke repres- *8*
sion and even a certain strength. But now there was a dull stare in her
eyes, whose gaze was fixed away off yonder on one of those patches of
blue sky. It was not a glance of reflection, but rather indicated a sus-
pension of intelligent thought.

There was something coming to her and she was waiting for it, *9*
fearfully. What was it? She did not know; it was too subtle and elusive
to name. But she felt it, creeping out of the sky, reaching toward her
through the sounds, the scents, the color that filled the air.

Now her bosom rose and fell tumultuously. She was beginning to *10*
recognize this thing that was approaching to possess her, and she was
striving to beat it back with her will—as powerless as her two white
slender hands would have been.

When she abandoned herself a little whispered word escaped her *11*
slightly parted lips. She said it over and over under her breath: "Free, free,

...*continued* The Story of an Hour, **Kate Chopin**

free!" The vacant stare and the look of terror that had followed it went from her eyes. They stayed keen and bright. Her pulses beat fast, and the coursing blood warmed and relaxed every inch of her body.

She did not stop to ask if it were not a monstrous joy that held her. 12 A clear and exalted perception enabled her to dismiss the suggestion as trivial.

She knew that she would weep again when she saw the kind, tender 13 hands folded in death; the face that had never looked save with love upon her, fixed and gray and dead. But she saw beyond that bitter moment a long procession of years to come that would belong to her absolutely. And she opened and spread her arms out to them in welcome.

There would be no one to live for during those coming years; she 14 would live for herself. There would be no powerful will bending her in that blind persistence with which men and women believe they have a right to impose a private will upon a fellow creature. A kind intention or a cruel intention made the act seem no less a crime as she looked upon it in that brief moment of illumination.

And yet she had loved him—sometimes. Often she had not. What did 15 it matter! What could love, the unsolved mystery, count for in face of this possession of self-assertion which she suddenly recognized as the strongest impulse of her being.

"Free! Body and soul free!" she kept whispering.   16

Josephine was kneeling before the closed door with her lips to the 17 keyhole, imploring for admission. "Louise, open the door! I beg; open the door—you will make yourself ill. What are you doing, Louise? For heaven's sake open the door."

"Go away. I am not making myself ill." No; she was drinking in a very 18 elixir of life through that open window.

Her fancy was running riot along those days ahead of her. Spring 19 days, and summer days, and all sorts of days that would be her own. She breathed a quick prayer that life might be long. It was only yesterday she had thought with a shudder that life might be long.

She arose at length and opened the door to her sister's importuni- 20 ties. There was a feverish triumph in her eyes, and she carried herself unwittingly like a goddess of Victory. She clasped her sister's waist, and together they descended the stairs. Richards stood waiting for them at the bottom.

Someone was opening the front door with a latchkey. It was Brently 21 Mallard who entered, a little travel-stained, composedly carrying his grip-sack and umbrella. He had been far from the scene of accident, and did not even know there had been one. He stood amazed at Josephine's piercing cry; at Richards's quick motion to screen him from the view of his wife.

But Richards was too late. 22

When the doctors came they said she had died of heart disease— 23 of joy that kills.

RESPONDING TO A POEM

Read and respond to W. H. Auden's "Musée des Beaux Arts." Begin by examining the painting by Pieter Brueghel, *Landscape with the Fall of Icarus,* reproduced on the next page. Carefully read and reread the poem, comparing it with details in the painting. Then go online to find the description of Daedalus and Icarus described in the Roman poet Ovid's *Metamorphoses.* As you reread Auden's poem, pay particular attention to the detail in the description, to Auden's references to scenes not depicted in the painting, and to the language and word choice.

PROFESSIONAL WRITING

Musée des Beaux Arts

W. H. Auden

In the following poem, W. H. Auden reflects on the art and the theme of Pieter Brueghel's famous painting, Landscape with the Fall of Icarus *(c. 1558). Auden (1907–1973) was born in England, went to school at Oxford, and eventually moved to the United States. Auden describes and interprets Brueghel's vision of the Fall of Icarus, and Brueghel in turn visualizes and interprets the Roman poet Ovid's version of the story of Daedalus and his son, Icarus. In this Greek myth, according to Ovid, Daedalus fashions wings made out of feathers and wax in order to help them escape the island of Crete. Daedalus cautions his son not to fly too near the heat of the sun, but Icarus ignores his father's advice. When Icarus soars too high, the sun melts the wax in his wings, and he plunges into the ocean. In Brueghel's painting, only the white legs of Icarus are visible (in the lower right-hand corner of the painting) as he disappears into the water.*

...continued Musée des Beaux Arts, **W. H. Auden**

Pieter Brueghel, *Landscape with the Fall of Icarus*

About suffering they were never wrong,
The old Masters: how well they understood
Its human position: how it takes place
While someone else is eating or opening a window or just
    walking dully along;
How, when the aged are reverently, passionately waiting   5
For the miraculous birth, there always must be
Children who did not specially want it to happen, skating
On a pond at the edge of the wood:
They never forgot
That even the dreadful martyrdom must run its course   10
Anyhow in a corner, some untidy spot
Where the dogs go on with their doggy life and the
    torturer's horse
Scratches its innocent behind on a tree.
In Brueghel's Icarus, for instance: how everything turns away
Quite leisurely from the disaster; the ploughman may   15
Have heard the splash, the forsaken cry,
But for him it was not an important failure; the sun shone
As it had to on the white legs disappearing into the green
Water, and the expensive delicate ship that must have seen
Something amazing, a boy falling out of the sky,   20
Had somewhere to get to and sailed calmly on.

Techniques for Responding to Literature

As you read and respond to a work of literature, keep the following techniques in mind.

Techniques for Responding to Literature	
Technique	Tips on How to Do It
Understanding the assignment and selecting a possible purpose and audience	Unless stated otherwise in your assignment, your purpose is to *interpret* a work of literature. Your audience will often be other members of your class, including the teacher.
Actively reading, annotating, and discussing the literary work	Remember that literature often contains *highly condensed experiences.* In order to interpret literature, you need to reread patiently both the major events and the seemingly insignificant passages. In discussions, look for the differences between your responses and other readers' ideas.
Focusing your essay on a single, clearly defined interpretation	In your essay, clearly state your *main idea or thesis,* focusing on a single idea or aspect of the piece of literature. *Your thesis should **not** be a statement of fact.* Whether you are explaining, evaluating, or arguing, your interpretation must be clearly stated.
Supporting your interpretation with evidence	Because your readers will probably have different interpretations, you must show which specific characters, events, scenes, conflicts, images, metaphors, or themes prompted your response, and you must use these details to support your interpretation. *Do **not** merely retell the major events of the story or just describe the main images in the poem.* Assume that your readers have already read the story or poem.

WARMING UP   Journal Exercises

Read all of the following questions and then write for five minutes on two or three. These questions should help clarify your perceptions about literature or develop your specific responses to "The Story of an Hour" or to "Musée des Beaux Arts."

1. On your bookshelves or in the library, find a short story or poem that you read at least six months ago. Before you reread it, write down the name of the author and the title of the work. Note when you read it last and describe what you remember about it. Then reread the story or poem. When you finish, write for five minutes, describing what you noticed that you did not notice the last time you read it.

2. Write out the *question* that "The Story of an Hour" seems to ask. What is your answer to this question? What might have been Kate Chopin's answer?

3. The words *heart, joy, free, life,* and *death* appear several times in "The Story of an Hour." Underline these words (or synonyms) each time they appear. Explain how the meaning of each of these words seems to change during the story. Is each word used ironically?

4. Write out a dictionary definition of the word *feminism*. Then write out your own definition. Is Mrs. Mallard a feminist? Is Kate Chopin a feminist? What evidence in the story supports your answers?

5. Kate Chopin's biographer, Per Seyersted, says that Chopin saw that "truth is manifold" and thus preferred not to "take sides or point a moral." Explain how "The Story of an Hour" does or does not illustrate Seyersted's observations.

6. In Ovid's account of the myth of Daedalus and Icarus, the fisherman, shepherd, and plowman are "astonished" as they observe Icarus flying, and Ovid suggests that they might worship Icarus and Daedalus as gods. In what way does Brueghel revise Ovid's account? Explain how and why Brueghel changes this part of the myth.

7. Auden suggests that one theme of Brueghel's painting is that suffering is largely ignored by the general populace. Study Brueghel's painting again. What other themes or ideas are present in the painting that Auden does not mention? Explain another possible interpretation of the painting based on specific images or points of focus in the painting.

8. Auden says that the theme of Brueghel's painting is about suffering, but he also includes a description of "the miraculous birth" and children who "did not specially want it to happen." Does this image distract from Auden's main point, or is the idea of the miraculous birth related to Auden's theme? Explain.

(9) Literature often expresses common themes or tensions, such as the conflict between generations, the individual versus society, appearance versus reality, self-knowledge versus self-deception, and civilization versus nature. Which of these themes are most apparent in "The Story of an Hour" or in "Musée des Beaux Arts"? Explain your choices.

Purposes for Responding to Literature

In responding to literature, you should be guided by the purposes that you have already practiced in previous chapters. As you read a piece of literature and respond in the margin, begin by writing *for yourself.* Your purposes are to observe, feel, remember, understand, and relate the work of literature to your own life: What is happening? What memories does it trigger? How does it make you feel? Why is this passage confusing? Why do you like or dislike this character? Literature has special, personal value. You should write about literature initially in order to discover and understand its importance in your life.

When you write an interpretive essay, however, you are writing *for others.* You are sharing your experience in working with the author as imaginative partners in recreating the work. Your purposes will often be mixed, but an interpretive essay often contains elements of *explaining, evaluating, problem solving,* and *arguing.*

- **Explaining.** Interpretive essays about literature explain the *what, why,* and *how* of a piece of literature. What is the key subject? What is the most important line, event, or character? What are the major conflicts or the key images? What motivates a character? How does a character's world build or unravel? How does a story or poem meet or fail to meet our expectations? How did our interpretations develop? Each of these questions might lead to an interpretive essay that explains the *what, why,* and *how* of your response.
- **Evaluating.** Readers and writers often talk about "appreciating" a work of literature. *Appreciating* means establishing its value or worth. It may mean praising the work's literary virtues; it may mean finding faults or weaknesses. Usually, evaluating essays measure *both strengths and weaknesses,* according to specific criteria. What important standards for literature do you wish to apply? How does the work in question measure up? What kinds of readers might find this story worth reading? An

evaluative essay cites evidence to show why a story is exciting, boring, dramatic, puzzling, vivid, relevant, or memorable.

- **Problem solving.** Writers of interpretive essays occasionally take a problem-solving approach, focusing on how the reader overcomes obstacles in understanding the story or poem, or on how the author solved problems in writing key scenes, choosing images and language, developing character, and creating and resolving conflicts. Particularly if you like to write fiction or poetry yourself, you may wish to take the writer's point of view: how did the writer solve (or fail to solve) problems of image, metaphor, character, setting, plot, or theme?

- **Arguing.** As readers share responses, they may discover that their interpretations diverge sharply from the ideas of other readers. Does "The Story of an Hour" have a feminist theme? Is it about women or about human nature in general? Is the main character admirable, or is she selfish? Is Auden's interpretation of Brueghel's painting faithful to Brueghel's conception, or does Auden impose his interpretation? Is Auden's the only way to interpret Bureghel's painting? In interpretive essays, writers sometimes argue for their beliefs. They present evidence that refutes an opposing or alternate interpretation and supports their own reading.

Most interpretive essays about literature are focused by these purposes, whether used singly or in combination. Writers should *select* the purpose(s) that are most appropriate for the work of literature and their own responses.

RESPONDING TO SHORT FICTION

Begin by noting in the margins your reactions at key points. *Summarize* in your own words what is happening in the story. Write down your *observations* or *reactions* to striking or surprising passages. Ask yourself *questions* about ambiguous or confusing passages.

After you respond initially and make your marginal annotations, use the following basic elements of fiction to help you *analyze how the parts of a short story relate to the whole.* Pay attention to how setting or plot affects the character, or how style and setting affect the theme. Because analysis artificially separates plot, character, and theme, look for ways to *synthesize* the parts: Seeing how these parts relate to each other should suggest an idea, focus, or angle to use in your interpretation.

● **CHARACTER** A short story usually focuses on a *major character*— particularly on how that character faces conflicts, undergoes changes, or reveals himself or herself. *Minor characters* may be flat (one-dimensional), static (unchanging), or stereotyped. To get a start on analyzing character, diagram the *conflicts* between or among characters. Examine characters for motivation: What causes them to behave as they do? Is their behavior affected by *internal* or *external* forces? Do the major characters reveal themselves *directly* (through their thoughts, dialogue, and actions) or *indirectly* (through what other people say, think, or do)?

● **PLOT**   *Plot* is the sequence of events in a story, but it is also the cause-and-effect relationship of one event to another. As you study a story's plot, pay attention to *exposition, foreshadowing, conflict, climax,* and *denouement.* To clarify elements of the plot, draw a time line for the story, listing in chronological order every event—including events that occur before the story opens. *Exposition* describes the initial circumstances and reveals what has happened before the story opens. *Foreshadowing* is an author's hint of what will occur before it happens. *Conflicts* within characters, between characters, and between characters and their environment may explain why one event leads to the next. The *climax* is the high point, the point of no return, or the most dramatic moment in a story. At the climax of a story, readers discover something important about the main character. *Denouement* literally means the "unraveling" of the complications and conflicts at the end of the story. In "The Story of an Hour," climax and denouement occur almost at the same time, in the last lines of the story.

● **NARRATIVE POINT OF VIEW**   Fiction is usually narrated from either the first-person or the third-person point of view.

A *first-person narrator* is a character who tells the story from his or her point of view. A first-person narrator may be a minor or a major character. This character may be relatively *reliable* (trustworthy) or *unreliable* (naive or misleading). Although reliable first-person narrators may invite the reader to identify with their perspectives or predicaments, unreliable narrators may cause readers to be wary of the narrator's naive judgments or unbalanced states of mind.

A *third-person omniscient narrator* is not a character or participant in the story. Omniscient narrators are assumed to know everything about the characters and events. They move through space and time, giving readers necessary information at any point in the story. A *selective omniscient narrator* usually limits his or her focus to a single character's experiences and thoughts, as Kate Chopin focuses on Mrs. Mallard in "The Story of an Hour." One kind of selective omniscient point of view is *stream-of-consciousness narration,* in which the author presents the thoughts, memories, and associations of one character in the story. Omniscient narrators may be *intrusive,* jumping into the story to give their editorial judgments, or they may be *objective,* removing themselves from the action and the minds of the characters. An objective point of view creates the impression that events are being recorded by a camera or acted on a stage.

Reminder: As you reread a story, do not stop with analysis. Do not quit, for example, after you have identified and labeled the point of view. Determine how the point of view affects your reaction to the central character or to your understanding of the theme. How would a different narrative point of view change the story? If a different character told the story, how would that affect the theme?

● **SETTING** *Setting* is the physical place, scene, and time of the story. It also includes the social or historical context of the story. The setting in "The Story of an Hour" is the house and the room in which Mrs. Mallard waits, but it is also the social and historical time frame. *Setting is usually important for what it reveals about the characters, the plot, or the theme of the story.* Does the setting reflect a character's state of mind? Is the environment a source of tension or conflict in the story? Do changes in setting reflect changes in key characters? Do sensory details of sight, touch, smell, hearing, or taste affect or reflect the characters or events? Does the author's portrait of the setting contain images and symbols that help you interpret the story?

● **STYLE** *Style* is a general term that may refer to sentence structure and to figurative language and symbols, as well as to the author's tone or use of irony. *Sentence structure* may be long and complicated or relatively short and simple. Authors may use *figurative language* (Mrs. Mallard is described in "The Story of an Hour" as sobbing, "as a child who has cried itself to sleep continues to sob in its dreams"). A *symbol* is a person, place, thing, or event that suggests or signifies something beyond itself. In "The Story of an Hour," the open window and the new spring life suggest or represent Mrs. Mallard's new freedom. *Tone* is the author's attitude toward the characters, setting, or plot. Tone may be sympathetic, humorous, serious, detached, or critical. *Irony* suggests a double meaning. It occurs when the author or a character says or does one thing but means the opposite or something altogether different. The ending of "The Story of an Hour" is ironic: The doctors say Mrs. Mallard has died "of joy that kills." In fact, she has died of killed joy.

● **THEME** The focus of an interpretive essay is often on the *theme* of a story. In arriving at a theme, ask how the characters, plot, point of view, setting, and style *contribute* to the main ideas or point of the story. The theme of a story depends, within limits, on your reactions as a reader. "The Story of an Hour" is *not* about relationships between sisters, nor is it about medical malpractice. It is an ironic story about love, personal freedom, and death, but what precisely is the *theme*? Does "The Story of an Hour" carry a feminist message, or is it more universally about the repressive power of love? Is Mrs. Mallard to be admired or criticized for her impulse to free herself? Do not trivialize the theme of a story by looking for some simple "moral." In describing the theme, deal with the complexity of life recreated in the story.

The Lesson

Toni Cade Bambara

Toni Cade Bambara (1939-1995) was an activist for the African-American community on many fronts: political, cultural, and literary. She worked for political and social causes in urban communities, taught African-American studies at half a dozen different colleges and universities, and is the author of several collections of short stories and novels, including Gorilla, My Love *(1972),* The Sea Birds Are Still Alive *(1977),* The Salt Eaters *(1980), and* If Blessing Comes *(1987). "The Lesson," which appears in* Gorilla, My Love, *dramatizes the gradual awakening of several children to the political and economic realities of contemporary urban life. As you read the story, pay attention to the narrator, Sylvia. What is the lesson, and what does Sylvia learn?*

Back in the days when everyone was old and stupid or young and foolish and me and Sugar were the only ones just right, this lady moved on our block with nappy hair and proper speech and no makeup. And quite naturally we laughed at her, laughed the way we did at the junk man who went about his business like he was some big-time president and his sorry-ass horse his secretary. And we kinda hated her too, hated the way we did the winos who cluttered up our parks and pissed on our handball walls and stank up our hallways and stairs so you couldn't halfway play hide-and-seek without a goddamn gas mask. Miss Moore was her name. The only woman on the block with no first name. And she was black as hell, cept for her feet, which were fish-white and spooky. And she was always planning these boring-ass things for us to do, us being my cousins, mostly, who lived on the block cause we all moved North the same time and to the same apartment then spread out gradual to breathe. And our parents would yank our heads into some kinda shape and crisp up our clothes so we'd be presentable for travel with Miss Moore, who always looked like she was going to church, though she never did. Which is just one of the things the grownups talked about when they talked behind her back like a dog. But when she came calling with some sachet she'd sewed up or some gingerbread she'd made or some book, why then they'd all be too embarrassed to turn her down and we'd get handed over all spruced up. She'd been to college and said it was only right that she should take responsibility for the young ones' education, and she not even related by marriage or blood. So they'd go for it. Specially Aunt Gretchen. She was the main gofer in the family. You got some ole dumb shit foolishness you want somebody to go for, you send for Aunt Gretchen. She been screwed into the go-along for so long, it's a blood-deep natural thing with her.

Which is how she got saddled with me and Sugar and Junior in the first place while our mothers were in a la-de-da apartment up the block having a good ole time.

So this one day Miss Moore rounds us all up at the mailbox and it's *2* puredee hot and she's knockin herself out about arithmetic. And school suppose to let up in summer I heard, but she don't never let up. And the starch in my pinafore scratching the shit outta me and I'm really hating this nappy-head bitch and her goddamn college degree. I'd much rather go to the pool or to the show where it's cool. So me and Sugar leaning on the mailbox being surly, which is a Miss Moore word. And Flyboy checking out what everybody brought for lunch. And Fat Butt already wasting his peanut-butter-and-jelly sandwich like the pig he is. And Junebug punchin on Q.T.'s arm for potato chips. And Rosie Giraffe shifting from one hip to the other waiting for somebody to step on her foot or ask her if she from Georgia so she can kick ass, preferably Mercedes's. And Miss Moore asking us do we know what money is, like we a bunch of retards. I mean real money, she say, like it's only poker chips or monopoly papers we lay on the grocer. So right away I'm tired of this and say so. And would much rather snatch Sugar and go to the Sunset and terrorize the West Indian kids and take their hair ribbons and their money too. And Miss Moore files that remark away for next week's lesson on brotherhood, I can tell. And finally I say we oughta get to the subway cause it's cooler and besides we might meet some cute boys. Sugar done swiped her mama's lipstick, so we ready.

So we heading down the street and she's boring us silly about what *3* things cost and what our parents make and how much goes for rent and how money ain't divided up right in this country. And then she gets to the part about we all poor and live in the slums, which I don't feature. And I'm ready to speak on that, but she steps out in the street and hails two cabs just like that. Then she hustles half the crew in with her and hands me a five-dollar bill and tells me to calculate 10 percent tip for the driver. And we're off. Me and Sugar and Junebug and Flyboy hangin out the window and hollering to everybody, putting lipstick on each other cause Flyboy a faggot anyway, and making farts with our sweaty armpits. But I'm mostly trying to figure how to spend this money. But they all fascinated with the meter ticking and Junebug starts laying bets as to how much it'll read when Flyboy can't hold his breath no more. Then Sugar lays bets as to how much it'll be when we get there. So I'm stuck. Don't nobody want to go for my plan, which is to jump out at the next light and run off to the first bar-b-que we can find. Then the driver tells us to get the hell out cause we there already. And the meter reads eighty-five cents. And I'm stalling to figure out the tip and Sugar say give him a dime. And I decide he don't need it bad as I do, so later for him. But then he tries to take off with Junebug foot still in the door so we talk about his mama something ferocious. Then we check out that we on Fifth Avenue and everybody dressed up in stockings. One lady in a fur coat, hot as it is. White folks crazy.

"This is the place," Miss Moore say, presenting it to us in the voice   4
she uses at the museum. "Let's look in the windows before we go in."

"Can we steal?" Sugar asks very serious like she's getting the ground   5
rules squared away before she plays. "I beg your pardon," say Miss Moore, and we fall out. So she leads us around the windows of the toy store and me and Sugar screamin, "This is mine, that's mine, I gotta have that, that was made for me, I was born for that," till Big Butt drowns us out.

"Hey, I'm goin to buy that there."   6

"That there? You don't even know what it is, stupid."   7

"I do so," he say punchin on Rosie Giraffe. "It's a microscope."   8

"Whatcha gonna do with a microscope, fool?"   9

"Look at things."   10

"Like what, Ronald?" ask Miss Moore. And Big Butt ain't got the first   11
notion. So here go Miss Moore gabbing about the thousands of bacteria in a drop of water and the somethinorother in a speck of blood and the million and one living things in the air around us is invisible to the naked eye. And what she say that for? Junebug go to town on that "naked" and we rolling. Then Miss Moore ask what it cost. So we all jam into the window smudgin it up and the price tag say $300. So then she ask how long'd take for Big Butt and Junebug to save up their allowances. "Too long," I say. "Yeh," adds Sugar, "outgrown it by that time." And Miss Moore say no, you never outgrow learning instruments. "Why, even medical students and interns and," blah, blah, blah. And we ready to choke Big Butt for bringing it up in the first damn place.

"This here costs four hundred eighty dollars," say Rosie Giraffe. So   12
we pile up all over her to see what she pointin out. My eyes tell me it's a chunk of glass cracked with something heavy, and different-color inks dripped into the splits, then the whole thing put into a oven or something. But for $480 it don't make sense.

"That's a paperweight made of semi-precious stones fused together   13
under tremendous pressure," she explains slowly, with her hands doing the mining and all the factory work.

"So what's a paperweight?" asks Rosie Giraffe.   14

"To weigh paper with, dumbbell," say Flyboy, the wise man from the   15
East.

"Not exactly," say Miss Moore, which is what she say when you warm   16
or way off too. "It's to weigh paper down so it won't scatter and make your desk untidy." So right away me and Sugar curtsy to each other and then to Mercedes who is more the tidy type.

"We don't keep paper on top of the desk in my class," say Junebug,   17
figuring Miss Moore crazy or lyin one.

"At home, then," she say. "Don't you have a calendar and a pencil case 18 and a blotter and a letter-opener on your desk at home where you do your homework?" And she know damn well what our homes look like cause she nosys around in them every chance she gets.

"I don't even have a desk," say Junebug. "Do we?" 19

"No. And I don't get no homework neither," says Big Butt. 20

"And I don't even have a home," say Flyboy like he do at school to 21 keep the white folks off his back and sorry for him. Send this poor kid to camp posters, is his specialty.

"I do," says Mercedes. "I have a box of stationery on my desk and a 22 picture of my cat. My godmother bought the stationery and the desk. There's a big rose on each sheet and the envelopes smell like roses."

"Who wants to know about your smelly-ass stationery," say Rosie 23 Giraffe fore I can get my two cents in.

"It's important to have a work area all your own so that. . . ." 24

"Will you look at this sailboat, please," say Flyboy, cuttin her off and 25 pointin to the thing like it was his. So once again we tumble all over each other to gaze at this magnificent thing in the toy store which is just big enough to maybe sail two kittens across the pond if you strap them to the posts tight. We all start reciting the price tag like we in assembly. "Hand-crafted sailboat of fiberglass at one thousand one hundred ninety-five dollars."

"Unbelievable," I hear myself say and am really stunned. I read it 26 again for myself just in case the group recitation put me in a trance. Same thing. For some reason this pisses me off. We look at Miss Moore and she lookin at us, waiting for I dunno what.

"Who'd pay all that when you can buy a sailboat set for a quarter at 27 Pop's, a tube of glue for a dime, and a ball of string for eight cents? It must have a motor and a whole lot else besides," I say. "My sailboat cost me about fifty cents."

"But will it take water?" say Mercedes with her smart ass. 28

"Took mine to Alley Pond Park once," say Flyboy. "String broke. Lost 29 it. Pity."

"Sailed mine in Central Park and it keeled over and sank. Had to ask 30 my father for another dollar."

"And you got the strap," laugh Big Butt. "The jerk didn't even have a 31 string on it. My old man wailed on his behind."

Little Q.T. was staring hard at the sailboat and you could see he 32 wanted it bad. But he too little and somebody'd just take it from him. So what the hell. "This boat for kids, Miss Moore?"

"Parents silly to buy something like that just to get all broke up," say 33 Rosie Giraffe.

"That much money it should last forever," I figure. 34

"My father'd buy it for me if I wanted it." 35

"Your father, my ass," say Rosie Giraffe getting a chance to finally 36 push Mercedes.

"Must be rich people shop here," say Q.T. 37

"You are a very bright boy," say Flyboy. "What was your first clue?" 38 And he rap him on the head with the back of his knuckles, since Q.T. the only one he could get away with. Though Q.T. liable to come up behind you years later and get his licks in when you half expect it.

"What I want to know is," I says to Miss Moore though I never talk to 39 her, I wouldn't give the bitch that satisfaction, "is how much a real boat costs? I figure a thousand'd get you a yacht any day."

"Why don't you check that out," she says, "and report back to the 40 group?" Which really pains my ass. If you gonna mess up a perfectly good swim day least you could do is have some answers. "Let's go in," she say like she got something up her sleeve. Only she don't lead the way. So me and Sugar turn the corner to where the entrance is, but when we get there I kinda hang back. Not that I'm scared, what's there to be afraid of, just a toy store. But I feel funny, shame. But what I got to be shamed about? Got as much right to go in as anybody. But somehow I can't seem to get hold of the door, so I step away for Sugar to lead. But she hangs back too. And I look at her and she looks at me and this is ridiculous. I mean, damn, I have never ever been shy about doing nothing or going nowhere. But then Mercedes steps up and then Rosie Giraffe and Big Butt crowd in behind and shove, and next thing we all stuffed into the doorway with only Mercedes squeezing past us, smoothing out her jumper and walking right down the aisle. Then the rest of us tumble in like a glued-together jigsaw done all wrong. And people lookin at us. And it's like the time me and Sugar crashed into the Catholic church on a dare. But once we got in there and everything so hushed and holy and the candles and the bowin and the hand-kerchiefs on all the drooping heads, I just couldn't go through with the plan. Which was for me to run up to the altar and do a tap dance while Sugar played the nose flute and messed around in the holy water. And Sugar kept givin me the elbow. Then later teased me so bad I tied her up in the shower and turned it on and locked her in. And she'd be there till this day if Aunt Gretchen hadn't finally figured I was lyin about the boarder takin a shower.

Same thing in the store. We all walkin on tiptoe and hardly touch-in 41 the games and puzzles and things. And I watched Miss Moore who is steady watchin us like she waitin for a sign. Like Mama Drewery watches the sky and sniffs the air and takes note of just how much slant is in the bird formation. Then me and Sugar bump smack into each other, so busy gazing at the toys, 'specially the sailboat. But we don't laugh and go into our fat-lady bump-stomach routine. We just stare at that price tag. Then Sugar run a finger over the whole boat. And I'm jealous and want to hit her. Maybe not her, but I sure want to punch somebody in the mouth.

...continued The Lesson, **Toni Cade Bambara**

"Watcha bring us here for, Miss Moore?"   42

"You sound angry, Sylvia. Are you mad about something?" Givin me   43
one of them grins like she tellin a grown-up joke that never turns out to
be funny. And she's lookin very closely at me like maybe she plannin to
do my portrait from memory. I'm mad, but I won't give her that satisfaction. So I slouch around the store bein very bored and say, "Let's go."

Me and Sugar at the back of the train watchin the tracks whizzin by   44
large then small then gettin gobbled up in the dark. I'm thinkin about this
tricky toy I saw in the store. A clown that somersaults on a bar then does
chin-ups just cause you yank lightly at his leg. Cost $35. I could see me
askin my mother for a $35 birthday clown. "You wanna who that costs
what?" she'd say, cocking her head to the side to get a better view of the
hole in my head. Thirty-five dollars could buy new bunk beds for Junior
and Gretchen's boy. Thirty-five dollars and the whole household could go
visit Granddaddy Nelson in the country. Thirty-five dollars would pay for
the rent and the piano bill too. Who are these people that spend that
much for performing clowns and $1,000 for toy sailboats? What kinda
work they do and how they live and how come we ain't in on it? Where
we are is who we are, Miss Moore always pointin out. But it don't necessarily have to be that way, she always adds then waits for somebody to say
that poor people have to wake up and demand their share of the pie and
don't none of us know what kind of pie she talkin about in the first damn
place. But she ain't so smart cause I still got her four dollars from the taxi
and she sure ain't gettin it. Messin up my day with this shit. Sugar nudges
me in my pocket and winks.

Miss Moore lines us up in front of the mailbox where we started   45
from, seem like years ago, and I got a headache for thinkin so hard. And
we lean all over each other so we can hold up under the draggy-ass lecture she always finishes us off with at the end before we thank her for
borin us to tears. But she just looks at us like she readin tea leaves. Finally
she say, "Well, what did you think of F. A. O. Schwarz?"

Rosie Giraffe mumbles, "White folks crazy."   46

"I'd like to go there again when I get my birthday money," says Mer-   47
cedes, and we shove her out the pack so she has to lean on the mailbox by
herself.

"I'd like a shower. Tiring day," say Flyboy.   48

Then Sugar surprises me by sayin, "You know, Miss Moore, I don't   49
think all of us here put together eat in a year what that sailboat costs." And
Miss Moore lights up like somebody goosed her. "And?" she say, urging
Sugar on. Only I'm standin on her foot so she don't continue.

"Imagine for a minute what kind of society it is in which some peo-   50
ple can spend on a toy what it would cost to feed a family of six or seven.
What do you think?"

"I think," say Sugar pushing me off her feet like she never done be- 51
fore, cause I whip her ass in a minute, "that this is not much of a democracy if you ask me. Equal chance to pursue happiness means an equal
crack at the dough, don't it?" Miss Moore is besides herself and I am dis-
gusted with Sugar's treachery. So I stand on her foot one more time to see
if she'll shove me. She shuts up, and Miss Moore looks at me, sorrowfully
I'm thinkin. And somethin weird is goin on, I can feel it in my chest.

"Anybody else learn anything today?" lookin dead at me. I walk away 52
and Sugar has to run to catch up and don't even seem to notice when I
shrug her arm off my shoulder.

"Well, we got four dollars anyway," she says.   53

"Uh hunh."   54

"We could go to Hascombs and get half a chocolate layer and then go 55
to the Sunset and still have plenty money for potato chips and ice cream
sodas."

"Uh hunh."   56

"Race you to Hascombs," she say.   57

We start down the block and she gets ahead which is O.K. by me 58
cause I'm going to the West End and then over to the Drive to think this
day through. She can run if she want to and even run faster. But ain't nobody gonna beat me at nuthin.

QUESTIONS FOR WRITING AND DISCUSSION

1 Describe one incident when a parent, friend, or family member tried to get
you to do something that you didn't want to do. How did you react? How
was your behavior similar to or different from the reaction of Sylvia, the
narrator in "The Lesson"?

2 Reread the opening sentence of the story. What does the first half of that
sentence reveal about the character of the narrator? Does the rest of the
story confirm that initial impression? Explain.

3 Locate at least one sentence or passage describing the reactions of each of
the following children to the merchandise at F. A. O. Schwarz: Sylvia (the
narrator), Sugar, Flyboy, Mercedes, Big Butt, Junebug, Rosie Giraffe, and
Q.T. How do their reactions to the toys and their prices affect the narrator?
Why does Bambara include all of these children in the story rather than tell
it using just Miss Moore, Sylvia, and Sugar?

➍ Miss Moore is the "teacher" for this "lesson," but what kind of teacher is she, and how do her students react to her? What strategies does she use to help the children learn? Are her methods effective? How do the children react to each other's learning? Does Miss Moore make some mistakes?

➎ What evidence (cite specific sentences) suggests that Sylvia is learning more from this lesson than she wants to? What exactly is she learning? Describe what she might do in the future as a result of what she learns.

➏ Explain how each of the following quotations from Sylvia's thoughts relates to the theme or main idea of "The Lesson":

> White folks crazy.
> I mean, damn, I have never ever been shy about doing nothing or going nowhere.
> If you gonna mess up a perfectly good swim day least you could do is have some answers.
> But ain't nobody gonna beat me at nuthin.

➐ Write two paragraphs comparing and contrasting the "awakenings" of Mrs. Mallard in "The Story of an Hour" and Sylvia in "The Lesson." What—and how—does each character learn? How do they react to what they learn? What do we, as readers, learn?

RESPONDING TO POETRY

Poems often have characters, setting, and point of view, but they also have other features that are important to reading imaginatively and critically. Use the following literary terms to help focus your reading and response to poems.

● **VOICE AND TONE**   The speaker in a poem is not necessarily the same as the author of the poem. When Robert Frost says in "The Road Not Taken," "Two roads diverged in a yellow wood, /And sorry I could not travel both," the "I" in the poem is not directly equivalent to Robert Frost. The "I" represents a speaker faced with this particular choice. *Tone,* the speaker's attitude toward the subject matter, is also important in the poem. A speaker's tone might be happy or sad, delighted or angry, serious or humorous, spontaneous or reflective, straightforward or ironic. In Frost's poem, the speaker's tone is serious and reflective when he says, in conclusion, "I took the one less traveled by, /And that has made all the difference." In Auden's poem, the speaker is a person explaining or interpreting a painting. Phrases such as "how well they understood its human position" or "In Brueghel's Icarus, for instance" reveal the speaker as knowledgeable and perhaps slightly academic. The speaker's tone is serious and reflective: he is praising the virtues of a painting by one of the Old Masters.

- **WORD CHOICE**   In poetry, diction and word choice are especially important. A poet might use academic language and formal phrasing or might use street language or slang. A poet might use short, emphatic words, or longer, more flowing language. Sometimes a poem juxtaposes formal and informal language. Auden deliberately contrasts a more formal diction ("About suffering they were never wrong, /The Old Masters") with more informal and colloquial (spoken) language ("Anyhow in a corner, some untidy spot / Where the dogs go on with their doggy life and the torturer's horse / Scratches its innocent behind on a tree").

- **FIGURES OF SPEECH: SIMILES, METAPHORS, SYMBOLS, PERSONIFICATION**   Figures of speech enable poets to compress experience, to add emotional impact, or to make an experience vivid, dramatic, or memorable. *Simile* is a comparison using *like* or *as:* "My love is like a red, red rose." A *metaphor* creates a direct equivalency without using *like* or *as:* "My love is a red, red rose." William Blake uses metaphor when he writes, "Tyger! Tyger! burning bright / In the forests of the night." The tiger is not literally a burning fire, but the colors of his coat and his potentially violent spirit are directly compared to a fire. A word becomes a *symbol* when it represents something larger or more abstract than its literal meaning. The tiger in Blake's poem becomes a symbol because it represents something larger than itself: the potential for violence and perhaps natural evil in the world. Similarly, readers might argue that Auden uses Icarus to symbolize human suffering in the world. Finally, in *personification,* an abstraction or an inanimate object is given human qualities. Death, in Emily Dickinson's poem, is personified: like the driver of a carriage, it stops to pick up the speaker and carry her on toward eternity.

- **SOUND, RHYME, AND RHYTHM**   Poets often use repetitions of sounds, of rhyming words, and of patterns of stressed (long) and unstressed (short) syllables. Emily Dickinson's poem, "Because I could not stop for death" uses an *iambic* pattern (one short syllable followed by one long syllable) to create a regular rhythm: "Because I could not stop for death— / He kindly stopped for me." Every second and fourth lines end with a rhyming word. William Blake rhymes the first and second lines and uses the *trochaic* pattern (one long syllable followed by one short syllable): "Tyger! Tyger! burning bright / In the forests of the night." In contrast, W. H. Auden uses an open form, without a set rhythm of rhyme. Poets also use patterns or combinations of sounds to reflect the meaning of the poem. *Alliteration* is the repetition of consonant sounds, and *assonance* is the repetition of vowel sounds. "Tyger! Tyger! burning bright" uses the alliteration of the t's and g's in "Tyger! Tyger!" and the repeated b's and r's in "burning bright" to give emphasis and power to the lines. In e. e. cummings's poem, "anyone lived in a pretty how town," cummings repeats the /o/ sound in several successive words to give a smooth, easy flow to the language.

Five Contemporary Poems

Aurora Levins Morales

Born in Puerto Rico in 1954 to a Jewish father and a Puerto Rican mother, Aurora Levins Morales moved with her family to the United States in 1967. She has published a collection of short stories and collaboratively written with her mother, Rosario Morales, a book containing short stories, essays, and poetry, Getting Home Alive *(1986). She currently lives near San Francisco.*

Child of the Americas

I am a child of the Americas,
a light-skinned mestiza of the Caribbean,
a child of many diaspora,[1] born into this continent at a
crossroads.

I am a U.S. Puerto Rican Jew   5
a product of the ghettos of New York I have never known.
An immigrant and the daughter and granddaughter of
immigrants.
I speak English with passion: it's the tongue of my
consciousness,
a flashing knife blade of crystal, my tool, my craft.

I am Caribeña,[2] island grown. Spanish is in my flesh,   10
ripples from my tongue, lodges in my hips:
the language of garlic and mangoes,
the singing in my poetry, the flying gestures of my hands.

I am of Latinoamerica, rooted in the history of my continent:
I speak from that body.
I am not african. Africa is in me, but I cannot return.   15
I am not taína.[3] Taíno is in me, but there is no way back.
I am not european. Europe lives in me, but I have no
home there.

---

[1] **diaspora** "a scattering," referring to the dispersion of Jews from Israel.
[2] **Caribeña** Carribean woman
[3] **taína** a native Indian tribe in Puerto Rico

I am new. History made me. My first language was spanglish.[4]
I was born at the crossroads
and I am whole.   *20*

_____

[4] **spanglish** a mixture of Spanish and English

Gary Soto

Gary Soto was born in Fresno, California, in 1952. Soto is the author of many books of fiction and poetry, including Black Hair *(1985),* Who Will Know Us? *(1990), and* Canto Familiar/Familiar Song *(1994). He currently lives in northern California.*

Black Hair

At eight I was brilliant with my body.
In July, that ring of heat
We all jumped through, I sat in the bleachers
Of Romain Playground, in the lengthening
Shade that rose from our dirty feet.   *5*
The game before us was more than baseball.
It was a figure—Hector Moreno
Quick and hard with turned muscles,
His crouch the one I assumed before an altar
Of worn baseball cards, in my room.   *10*
I came here because I was Mexican, a stick
Of brown light in love with those
Who could do it—the triple and hard slide,
The gloves eating balls into double plays.
What could I do with 50 pounds, my shyness,   *15*
My black torch of hair, about to go out?
Father was dead, his face no longer
Hanging over the table or our sleep,
And mother was the terror of mouths
Twisting hurt by butter knives.   *20*
In the bleachers I was brilliant with my body,
Waving players in and stomping my feet,
Growing sweaty in the presence of white shirts.
I chewed sunflower seeds. I drank water
And bit my arm through the late innings.   *25*
When Hector lined balls into deep
Center, in my mind I rounded the bases

With him, my face flared, my hair lifting
Beautifully, because we were coming home
To the arms of brown people.   *30*

Joy Harjo

A prolific writer of poems and songs, Joy Harjo was born in Tulsa, Oklahoma, in 1951. Her books of poetry include She Had Some Horses *(1983),* The Woman Who Fell From the Sky *(1994), and* How We Became Human: New and Selected Poems *(2002). She has received the Josephine Miles poetry award and the American Indian Distinguished Achievement in the Arts award. She has lived in Colorado, California, and Hawaii.*

Perhaps the World Ends Here

The world begins at a kitchen table. No matter what,
we must eat to live.

The gifts of earth are brought and prepared, set on the
table. So it has been since creation, and it will go on.

We chase chickens or dogs away from it. Babies teethe   *5*
at the corners. They scrape their knees under it.

It is here that children are given instructions on what
it means to be human. We make men at it,
we make women.

At this table we gossip, recall enemies and the ghosts   *10*
of lovers.

Our dreams drink coffee with us as they put their arms
around our children. They laugh with us at our poor
falling-down selves and as we put ourselves back
together once again at the table.   *15*

This table has been a house in the rain, an umbrella
in the sun.

Wars have begun and ended at this table. It is a place
to hide in the shadow of terror. A place to celebrate
the terrible victory.   *20*

We have given birth on this table, and have prepared
our parents for burial here.

At this table we sing with joy, with sorrow.
We pray of suffering and remorse.
We give thanks.   *25*

Perhaps the world will end at the kitchen table,
while we are laughing and crying,
eating of the last sweet bite.

Wislawa Szymborska

*Wislawa Szymborska was born in Poland in 1923. She is the author of
many books of poetry, including two that are translated into English:*
Sounds, Feelings, Thoughts: Seventy Poems by Wislawa Szymborska
(1981) and View with a Grain of Sand: Selected Poems *(1995). She won
the Nobel Prize in Literature in 1996. She currently lives in Cracow.*

End and Beginning
Translated by Joseph Brodsky

After each war
somebody has to clear up
put things in order
by itself it won't happen.

Somebody's got to push   *5*
rubble to the highway shoulder
making way
for the carts filled up with corpses.

Someone might trudge
through muck and ashes,   *10*
sofa springs,
splintered glass
and blood-soaked rugs.

Somebody has to haul
beams for propping a wall,   *15*
another put glass in a window
and hang the door on hinges.

This is not photogenic
and takes years.
All the cameras have left already   *20*
for another war.

Bridges are needed
also new railroad stations.
Tatters turn into sleeves
for rolling up.   *25*

...continued Five Contemporary Poems

Somebody, broom in hand,
still recalls how it was,
Someone whose head was not
torn away listens nodding.
But nearby already   30
begin to bustle those
who'll need persuasion.

Somebody still at times
digs up from under the bushes
some rusty quibble   35
to add it to burning refuse.

Those who knew
what this was all about
must yield to those
who know little   40
or less than little
essentially nothing.

In the grass that has covered
effects in causes
somebody must recline,   45
a stalk of rye in the teeth,
ogling the clouds.

Yusef Komunyakaa

Born in 1947 in Bogalusa, Louisiana, Yusef Komunyakaa served in Vietnam before returning to earn degrees at the University of Colorado, Colorado State University, and the University of California, Irvine. He has published many books of poetry, including Thieves of Paradise *(1998),* Pleasure Dome: New Collected Poems, 1975–1999 *(2001), and* Dien Cai Dau *(1988), in which the poem "Facing It" appears. The photograph of the Vietnam Veterans Memorial at the beginning of this chapter was selected to appear with this poem. After you read the poem, consider how effectively this photograph illustrates the themes and images in the poem.*

Facing It

My black face fades,
hiding inside the black granite.
I said I wouldn't,
dammit: No tears.

I'm stone. I'm flesh.   5
My clouded reflection eyes me
like a bird of prey, the profile of night
slanted against morning. I turn
this way—the stone lets me go.
I turn that way—I'm inside   10
the Vietnam Veterans Memorial
again, depending on the light
to make a difference.
I go down the 58,022 names,
half-expecting to find   15
my own in letters like smoke.
I touch the name Andrew Johnson;
I see the booby trap's white flash.
Names shimmer on a woman's blouse
but when she walks away   20
the names stay on the wall.
Brushstrokes flash, a red bird's
wings cutting across my stare.
The sky. A plane in the sky.
A white vet's image floats   25
closer to me, then his pale eyes
look through mine. I'm a window.
He's lost his right arm
inside the stone. In the black mirror   30
a woman's trying to erase names:
No, she's brushing a boy's hair.

QUESTIONS FOR WRITING AND DISCUSSION

1 In "Child of the Americas," Aurora Levins Morales compares the mixture of languages and cultures within her to geographical mixtures and crossroads. Find several places in the poem where Levins Morales makes this com parison. What kinds of figurative language does she use (simile, metaphor, or image)? Explain how these images help construct one of Levins Morales's themes in the poem.

2 In Greek mythology, Hector was a great Trojan warrior. Hector was killed by Achilles in the Trojan War, but his death was avenged by his brother, Paris. In "Black Hair," how does Gary Soto use the legend of Hector? Which lines suggest references to Hector, and how do these references relate to a theme in the poem?

3 Although Joy Harjo titles her poem, "Perhaps the World Ends Here," the poem is about both beginnings and endings. What images or examples of figurative language illustrate the beginnings, and which refer to endings? In your own words, explain how Harjo does or does not resolve the conflicts between beginnings and endings.

4 Wislawa Szymborska's poem, "End and Beginning," echoes Harjo's theme of beginnings and endings in a poem about the aftermath of war. The end of war, Szymborska says, "is not photogenic / and takes years. / All the cameras have left already / for another war." What images in the poem suggest the hard, dirty, and thankless work required to rebuild a civilization? How do these images fit into Szymborska's overall theme in the poem?

5 In "Facing It," Yusef Komunyakaa contrasts the realities outside the memorial wall with the reflections and images inside the wall. What does Komunyakaa describe that is outside the wall? What does he see in the wall or in the reflections of the wall? What do you think Komunyakaa means when he says of a white vet, "He's lost his right arm / inside the stone"? Explain how these images or reality and reflection help explain a major theme of the poem.

6 Do a comparison and contrast of two of the poems in this chapter. Your purpose is to compare lines, images, figures of speech, and themes in order to show how one poem relates to the other. How do the similarities and differences enhance your reading of one or both of the poems? Possibilities for comparison include the poems by Aurora Levins Morales and Gary Soto, by Harjo and Szymborska, and by Szymborska and Komunyakaa.

Responding to Literature: The Writing Process

ASSIGNMENT FOR RESPONDING TO LITERATURE

Choose one of the poems or short stories from this chapter (or a work of literature assigned in your class), reread and annotate the work, and share your responses with others in the class. Then write an interpretation of the Literary work. Unless stated otherwise in your assignment, assume that you are writing for other members of your class (including the instructor) who have read the work but who may not understand or agree with your interpretation.

Audience	Possible Genres for Responding to Literature
Personal Audience	Class notes, journal entry, blog, scrapbook, social networking page
Academic Audience	Academic analysis, critique, interpretation, journal entry, forum entry on class site, or multigenre document
Public Audience	Literary interpretation, article, or critique in a magazine, newspaper, online site, newsletter, or multigenre document

COLLECTING

In addition to reading, rereading, annotating, and sharing your responses, try the following collecting strategies. Illustrations below are based on an interpretive essay about "The Story of an Hour."

- **Collaborative annotation.** In small groups, choose a work of literature or select a passage that you have already annotated. In the group, read each other's annotations. Then discuss each annotation. Which annotations does your group agree are the best? Have a group recorder record the best annotations.
- **Elements of poetry analysis.** Reread the paragraphs earlier in the chapter on voice and tone, word choice, figures of speech, and sound, rhyme, and rhythm. Focus on the elements that seem most important for the poem you have selected. After you have finished annotating, freewrite a paragraph explaining how these elements work together to create the theme or overall effect of the poem.
- **Elements of fiction analysis.** Reread the paragraphs defining *character, plot, point of view, setting,* and *style.* Choose three of these elements that seem most important in the story that you are reading. Reread the story, annotating for these three elements. Then freewrite a paragraph explaining how these three elements are interrelated or how they explain the theme.
- **Time line.** In your journal, draw a time line for the story. List above the line everything that happens in the story. Below the line, indicate where the story opens, when the major conflicts occur, and where the climax and the denouement occur. For "The Story of an Hour," student writer Karen Ehrhardt drew the following time line.

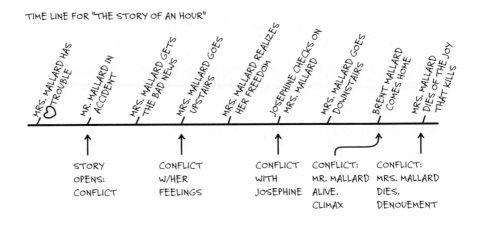

TIME LINE FOR "THE STORY OF AN HOUR"

- **Feature list.** Choose a character trait, repeated image, or idea that you wish to investigate in the poem or story. List, in order of appearance, every word, image, or reference that you find.
- **Scene vision or revision.** Write a scene for this story in which you change some part of it. You may *add* a scene to the beginning, middle, or end of the story. You may *change* a scene in the story. You may write a scene in the story from a different character's point of view. You may change the style of the story for your scene. How, for example, might Toni Cade Bambara have described the opening scene of "The Story of an Hour"?
- **Draw a picture.** For your poem or short story, draw a picture based on images, characters, conflicts, or themes in the work of literature. Student writer Lori Van Sike drew the following picture for "The Story of an

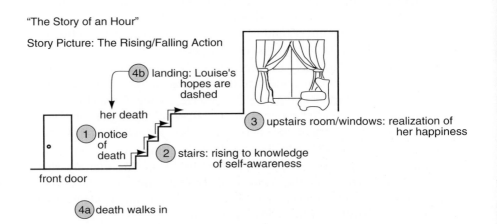

"The Story of an Hour"

Story Picture: The Rising/Falling Action

Hour" that shows how the rising and falling action of the plot parallels Mrs. Mallard's ascent and descent of the stairs.

- **Background investigation.** Investigate the biographical, social, or historical context of the poem or story. Go online or to your library databases to find biographical information or other stories or poems by the same author. How does this background information increase your understanding or appreciation of the poem or story?

- **Character conflict map.** Start with a full page of paper. Draw a main character in the center of the page. Locate the other major characters, internal forces, and external forces (including social, economic, and environmental pressures) in a circle around the main character. Draw a line between each of these peripheral characters or forces and the main character. For his character conflict map for "The Story of an Hour," student writer Darren Marshall used images from his computer program to surround his picture of Mrs. Mallard.

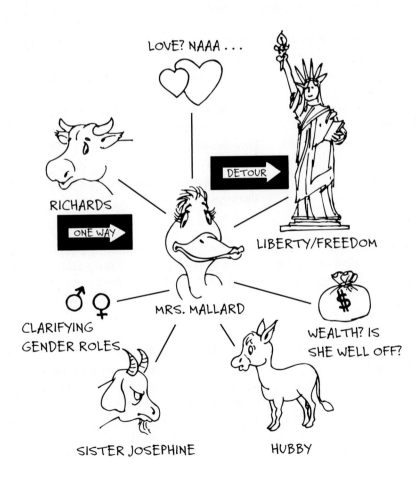

- **Reconsideration of purposes.** What idea, theme, or approach most interests you? Will you be explaining, evaluating, problem solving, or arguing? Are you combining purposes? Do these purposes suggest what kinds of information you might collect?

SHAPING

Test each of the following possible shapes against your ideas for your essay. Use or adapt the shape or shapes that are most appropriate for your own interpretation.

● **EXPLAINING RELATIONSHIPS**   Interpretative essays often analyze how the parts of a poem or story relate to the whole. As you explain these relationships, you should show how key images, lines, or scenes contribute to the overall theme or idea of the poem or story.

Introduction and thesis:	The details and images in the work reveal that the theme is X.
First scene, stanza, or group of lines:	How details and images establish the theme.
Second scene or group of lines:	How details and images relate to or build on previous images and contribute to the theme.
Third scene or group of lines:	How details and images continue building the theme.
Conclusion:	How the author highlights the key images or themes.

● **EVALUATING**   If your response suggests an evaluating purpose, you may wish to set up criteria for an effective poem or short story and then provide evidence showing how this poem or story does or does not measure up to your standards. Using criteria for a story, your essay might use the following outline.

Introduction and thesis:	Story X is highly dramatic.
Criterion 1:	A dramatic short story should focus on a character who changes his or her behavior or beliefs. Judgment and evidence for Criterion 1.
Criterion 2:	A dramatic story must have striking conflicts that lead to a crisis or a predicament. Judgment and evidence for Criterion 2.

| Criterion 3: | A dramatic story should have a theme that makes a controversial point. Judgment and evidence for Criterion 3. |
| Conclusion: | Reinforces thesis. |

● **ARGUING**   During class discussion, you may disagree with another person's response. Your thesis may then take the form, "Although some readers believe this poem or story is about X, the poem or story can also be about Y."

Introduction and thesis:	Although some readers suggest the poem or story is about X, it is really about Y.
Body paragraphs:	State the opposing interpretation and give evidence for that interpretation. Then state your interpretation and give evidence (images, characters, events, points of conflict) supporting your interpretation.
Conclusion:	Clarify and reinforce thesis.

● **INVESTIGATING CHANGES IN INTERPRETATION**   Often, readers *change* interpretations during the course of responding to a piece of literature. Thus, your main point might be, "Although I initially believed X about the poem or story, I gradually realized the theme of the poem or story is Y." If that sentence expresses your main idea, you may wish to organize your essay following the chronology or the steps in the changes in your interpretation.

Introduction and thesis:	Although I initially thought X, I now believe Y.
Body paragraphs:	First step (your original interpretation of the story or poem and supporting evidence).
	Second step (additional or contradictory ideas and evidence that forced you to reconsider your interpretation).
	Third step (your final interpretation and supporting evidence).
Conclusion:	Show how steps lead to thesis.

Note: One strategy you should not use is to simply retell the key parts of a poem or the plot of the story. Your audience has already read the poem or story. They want you to state your interpretation and then use details to show how and why your interpretation is credible. Although you will cite key characters, images, or events in the poem or story, you must explain how or why each of these details support your interpretation.

DRAFTING

To prepare to draft your essay, read through your annotations and gather your collecting and shaping notes. Some writers prefer to write one-sentence statements of their main ideas at the top of the page to keep them focused as they write. Other writers prefer to make rough outlines to follow, based on their adaptations of one of the preceding shaping strategies. When you begin drafting, you may wish to skip your introduction and start with the body of your essay. You can fill in the introduction after you have written a draft.

Once you start writing, keep your momentum going. If you draw a blank, reread what you have already written or look at your notes. If you cannot think of a particular word or are unsure about a spelling, draw a line_____ and keep on writing.

REVISING

Use the following guidelines as you read your classmates' drafts and revise your own essay. Be prepared to make changes in your ideas, organization, and evidence, as well as to fix problems in sentences and word choice.

GUIDELINES FOR REVISION

- **Clarify your main idea or interpretation.** Ask your readers to write, in one sentence, the main point of your interpretation. If their statements do not exactly match your main point, clarify your thesis. Your interpretation (not a statement of fact) should be clearly stated early in your essay.
- **Do not just summarize the poem or story.** Your readers have read the story or poem. Start with your interpretation; cite key images, metaphors, or lines that support your interpretation; and then explain why these images or key words are important.
- **Support each part of your interpretation with references to specific passages from the text.** Do not be satisfied with one piece of evidence. Find as many bits of evidence as possible. The case for your interpretation grows stronger with each additional piece of evidence.
- **Explain how each piece of evidence supports your interpretation.** Do not just cite several pieces of evidence and go on to your next

point. Explain for your readers *how* the evidence supports your interpretation.

- **Define key terms in your essay.** If you are writing about the hero in a story, define what you mean by *hero* or *heroine*. If you are arguing that "The Story of an Hour" has a *feminist* theme, define *feminism*.

- **Signal the major parts of your interpretation.** Let your readers know when you shift to a new point. Use transitions and paragraph hooks at the beginning of body paragraphs.

- **Use the present tense as you describe the events in the story.** If you are describing the end of "The Story of an Hour," write, for example, "Mrs. Mallard descends the stairs and learns the 'good news' about her husband."

- **Quote accurately and cite page numbers for each reference.** Double-check your quotations to make sure they are accurate, word-for-word transcriptions. Following each direct quotation, cite page references as follows:

  In the first sentence, Kate Chopin says, "Mrs. Mallard was afflicted with a heart trouble" (479).

  In "Child of the Americas," the author states the central idea of the poem when she says, "I am of Latinoamerica, rooted in the history of my continent" (line 13).

  Note: The period goes outside the parentheses. See Chapter 13 for correct documentation style.

- **Revise your essay for sentence clarity and conciseness.** Read your essay aloud or have a classmate read it. Reduce unnecessary repetition. Use active verbs. Rework awkward or confusing sentences.

- **Edit your essay.** Check your essay for correct spelling, word choice, punctuation, and grammar.

POSTSCRIPT ON THE WRITING PROCESS

Before you turn in your essay, answer the following questions in your journal.

1. Explain what part of this essay (collecting ideas and evidence, focusing on your interpretation, shaping your essay, drafting, or revising) was most difficult for you. How did you work around the problems?

(Continued)

2. What do you like best about your essay? Refer to specific places in the essay (lead-in, thesis, pieces of evidence, ideas, conclusion). Which specific paragraphs do you like best? Why?

3. What did you learn about the story by writing your interpretation? What do you realize now that you did not understand when you first read the story?

4. If you had two more hours to work on this essay, what would you change? Why?

STUDENT WRITING

GRACE REXROTH

Facing It: Reflections on War

Grace Rexroth was assigned to write an explication of "Facing It," a Vietnam War poem by Yusef Komunyakaa. (This poem appears on page 550 of this chapter.) After reading the poem several times, she noticed that the key images seemed to evoke recurring themes of the painful consequences of the Vietnam War, the war's impact on memory, and the importance of facing the truth and honoring the past. Before you read her essay, read Komunyakaa's poem and take notes on its themes and key images. Decide what "Facing It" means to you before you read Rexroth's essay.

Yusef Komunyakaa's poem, "Facing It," illustrates his difficulty facing the Vietnam Veterans Memorial and the memories of his past as a soldier. The fleeting images he recounts show the tangible aspects of his experience but also mirror his own emotional struggle to reconcile the past with the present moment. In "facing" the memorial, he wrestles with confronting grief and attempting to evade it. The portrayal of his experience illuminates several interconnected themes: the painful consequences of war, its scarring impact upon memory, and the importance of remembering and honoring the past.

Komunyakaa begins his poem by focusing on the tangible stone of the memorial: "My black face fades/hiding inside the black granite" (line 1–2). When he describes his face "fading" into the black granite, it is a physical image as well as a symbolic one. The black granite can be seen as representing the Vietnam War as a whole and Komunyakaa fades into it, connoting the magnitude of the war and the way it consumes him. Yet he is also "hiding" in the granite, focusing on the polished stone as opposed to the meaning of the memorial; he is evading grief and memory. This suggests that it is his first time really "facing" the consequences of the Vietnam War, substantiated by his next lines; "I said I wouldn't/ damnit: No tears/ I'm stone. I'm flesh." He had a preconceived idea of how he would endure this experience: no tears. Komunyakaa is wrestling with himself; the "stone" represents the repression of his memory and emotion, and the "flesh" represents his pain and grief which need an outlet through tears. He would like to be "stone," numb from pain, but must deal with his flesh, his humanity. This is mirrored by his shift in focus between the physical "stone" of the memorial and the "flesh" of the memorial's meaning.

Having given in to tears, Komunyakaa focuses again on the stone 3 of the memorial and his tangible reflection. He says "my clouded reflection eyes me/ like a bird of prey, the profile of night/ slanted against morning" (lines 6–8). His "clouded reflection" could represent his vision, clouded by tears, which means that he is also seeing his "emotional" reflection. His clouded vision may also mean that his visions of the past and the present are distorted, hinting that he feels stranded in a place of emotional and intellectual uncertainty. The idea that it "eyes" him like a "bird of prey" insinuates a sense of fear. He is afraid of his emotions; afraid of being devoured or overcome by grief. He may also be wrestling with the guilt that he survived while so many others died. It is interesting that he then turns away from the memorial saying "the stone lets me go," symbolizing an emotional reprieve (line 9). Yet, he finally turns back to face the stone rather than the reality behind him.

Komunyakaa transitions back to the meaning of the memorial say- 4 ing, "I go down the 58,022 names/ half-expecting to find/ my own in letters like smoke" (lines 14–16). His use of the specific number "58,022" references the fact that each one has meaning; each name represents a life. The idea that he "half-expects" to find his own name connotes the surreal nature of life and death; the absurdity that he is still alive though he took the same risk as those who died. The image of "letters like smoke" suggests that the bare names seem like a ghostly representation of so many vibrant lives.

Finding a specific name, "Andrew Johnson," Komunyakaa is briefly 5 pulled into his violent memories of the war. He sees "the booby trap's white flash," suggesting that he witnessed Johnson's death (line 18). This image is quickly followed by an image of the present; "names shimmer on a woman's blouse/ but when she walks away/ the names stay on the wall" (line19). This juxtaposition depicts Komunyakaa's harsh struggle to deal with the images in his memory and the images of the present. He is desperately trying to reconcile the pain of the past with the odd serenity of the current moment. The image of the woman walking can be construed as an absurd transient image of life amidst the finality of death; she is the vibrancy of life amidst the static dead names.

Komunyakaa returns to focusing on the stone of the memorial, 6 once more seeking a reprieve from his grief. He despondently mentions "a red bird's wings," "the sky," and "a plane in the sky," each a reflection in the black granite mirror of the memorial (lines 22–24). He still cannot turn to face the reality of the life behind him; everything is filtered through the memorial which suggests that he is seeing through his grief. Then, he says "a white vet's image floats/ closer to me, then his pale eyes/ look through mine. I'm a window" (lines 25–27). The fact that Komunyakaa makes the distinction that it is a "white" veteran who moves towards him, further proves that it is Komunyakaa speaking and recognizing the difference between the white veteran's reflection and his own dark image.

The description of the "white vet" is almost ghost-like, seemingly 7 stranded between the speaker's world of memory and the world of the present. The image "his pale eyes/ look through mine" is a symbol of communion, representing the bond of pain and uncertainty shared by veterans. It is interesting that Komunyakaa switches to describing himself as "a window" for the other veteran when he has been viewing the world through the "window" of the memorial. As they look at each other they interact only as reflections in the memorial which adds to the surreal experience of "facing the memorial"—trying to understand life in the midst of death. When Komunyakaa says "he's lost his right arm inside the stone," the reader cannot be certain if the white vet is really handicapped or simply standing at an odd angle (line 28-29). In the memorial, just as in war, everything is blurred and indistinct.

Komunyakaa ends his poem with the image of a woman "trying to 8 erase names" but then qualifies that statement, "No, she's brushing a boy's hair" (lines 30-31). The provocative image of someone trying to erase names could symbolize the country's desire to erase the memory of an unpopular war, perhaps even to shield the public from the pain of its atrocities. The image of the little boy, however, could also represent another generation of young men being groomed for future wars. It is precisely for the benefit of the next generation, Komunyakaa seems to imply, that we must face the consequences of war with truth and integrity. The memorial stands to honor the dead and to remind us that war is waged at a precious cost. Komunyakaa is "facing" the memorial, suggesting that we all *must* face the past to create a better future.

QUESTIONS FOR WRITING AND DISCUSSION

1 If you read and took notes on Komunyakaa's poem before you read Rexroth's explication of "Facing It," explain how your interpretation of the poem was similar to but also different from Rexroth's explication. Cite specific images or passages from the poem to illustrate the similarities and differences between your reading and Rexroth's explication of the poem.

2 At the end of the first paragraph of her explication, Rexroth identifies three key themes that she found in the poem. What are those themes? In which paragraphs does she illustrate each of these themes? Explain your choices.

3 Rexroth supports her explication of the themes in this poem by analyzing key passages and images. Reread her essay and *list* the specific images that she comments on. Then compare your list with the poem. Does Rexroth refer to or analyze every key image or relevant passage? Are there other images that she might also analyze? Explain.

4 Does Rexroth interpret Komunyakaa's poem as a war protest poem or as a poem that honors the sacrifices of war? Does Rexroth do both at the same time? Reread Rexroth's final paragraph and explain, as clearly as you can, how she handles this ambiguous or contradictory portrayal of war.

STUDENT WRITING

PAT RUSSELL

Death: The Final Freedom

Following a class discussion of the feminist theme in Kate Chopin's "The Story of an Hour," Pat Russell wrote in his journal, "Is the story a feminist one? No. It is not just about feminism but about how people stifle their own needs and desires to accommodate those of their mate." In his essay, Russell argues that the traditional feminist reading limits the universal theme of the story. As you read his essay, see if you are persuaded by his argument.

The poor treatment of women and their struggle for an individual *1* identity make up a major underlying theme of Kate Chopin's stories. Although many regard Chopin's "The Story of an Hour" as a feminist story, today a more universal interpretation is appropriate. This story is not about the oppression of a woman, but about how people strive to maintain the

...continued Death: The Final Freedom, ***Pat Russell***

normality and security of their relationships by suppressing their own individual wants and needs.

Evidence in favor of the feminist argument begins with the period the story was written in, sometime around the turn of the century. Society prevented women from coming out of the household. Most women weren't allowed to run a business, and for that matter, they couldn't even vote. Their most important jobs were wife and mother. This background sets the tone for the main character's life. In the beginning we are told Mrs. Mallard has a "fair, calm face whose lines be-spoke repression" (Chopin 414). There is also evidence that suggests her husband is ignorant of her ideas and forceful with his own. Chopin writes: "There would be no powerful will bending her in that blind persistence with which men and women believe they have a right to impose a private will upon a fellow creature" (415). In addition, Mrs. Mallard is described early as fearful and powerless, and later as a triumphant "goddess of Victory," indicating her rebirth. These citations suggest that this is a feminist story, but this label limits the meaning behind the story.

Many people who are unhappy with their marriages either fail to recognize their unhappiness or refuse to accept responsibility for it. I feel sorry for those who don't recognize their unhappiness. However, it is pathetic to see someone such as Mrs. Mallard hold onto a relationship simply because she doesn't know how to let go. "And yet she had loved him—sometimes. Often she had not" (415). She continuously fell in and out of love with her husband until he "died," at which point she told herself that love didn't matter compared to the self-assertion "which she suddenly recognized as the strongest impulse of her being" (415). It is as if she has waited for all of her life for this moment; she prays for a long life, when only the day before she dreaded it. She weeps for him but at the same time compares her husband to a criminal, a man whom she has lived her life for, never once thinking of herself. But now "there would be no one to live for during those coming years; she would live for herself" (415). She is lucky in that she feels "free." Her emotional suppression is over, and she will no longer have anyone to blame for her unhappiness.

It is important not only to try to interpret the author's intended meaning of the story, but also to think about what message "The Story of an Hour" has for us today. As a feminist story, the lesson "The Story of an Hour" teaches is one-dimensional. Interpreting it as a story about the struggle of all people opens up the possibility of teaching others that selfishness and selflessness are both good, when used in moderation. In Mrs. Mallard's case, correcting this balance becomes a matter of life and death. In the face of her suppressor, her desperation for freedom forces her to choose death.

Work Cited

Chopin, Kate. "The Story of an Hour." *The Awakening and Selected Stories.* New York: Penguin, 1984. 413–16. Print.

QUESTIONS FOR WRITING AND DISCUSSION

1. With what parts of Russell's interpretation do you agree? What additional evidence from the story might Russell cite in support of his interpretation? What ideas or sentences might you challenge? What evidence from the story might refute those statements?

2. Write out your definition of *feminism*. Where does or should Russell explain his definition? How should Russell clarify his definition?

3. Write out Russell's main idea or thesis. Explain why his thesis is an interpretation and not just a statement of fact.

4. What shaping strategy does Russell use to organize his essay?

5. Write out two other possible titles for Russell's essay. Explain why your alternate titles are (or are not) better than Russell's title.

PEARSON
mycomplab

For additional writing, reading, and research resources, go to http://www.mycomplab.com

MAP EVOLUTION EVOLVING

How a controversial entry in Wikipedia has changed over time

The entry for evolution on Wikipedia, the Internet encyclopedia that anyone can edit, was altered 2,081 times by 68 editors between December 2001 and last October. IBM's Watson Research Center produced this image, which tracks the transformation. Each vertical line is a new version; each color is a different editor.

1 DECEMBER 3, 2001
The initial version of evolution, 526 words long, is posted by someone with the user name "Dmerrill." It offers links to pages for creationism and intelligent design but makes no mention of controversy.

2 JULY 13, 2002
An anonymous user redefines evolution as "a controversial theory some scientists present as a scientific explanation." Within two hours, it is changed to read "the commonly accepted scientific theory."

3 OCTOBER 1, 2002
"Graft," shown in yellowish green, makes his debut. He will create 79 edits over three years and spend hours hashing out the content on discussion pages with pro- and antievolution editors. A biology grad student at Harvard University, Graft has edited more than 250 Wikipedia entries.

4 AUGUST 9, 2004
A black line occurs whenever the entire entry is deleted by a vandal. (Entries are also defaced with nonsense or vulgarities.) Editing Wikipedia has become such a popular pastime that, even with more than 1 million entries, about half of all vandalisms are corrected within five minutes.

5 MARCH 29, 2005
The entry reaches its longest point, 5,611 words. That evening, 888 words are excised, causing a

clifflike drop in the graph. The deleted text, a cynical passage about creationists, was cut by proevolution editors who insist on a neutral point of view.

6 SEPTEMBER 19, 2005
A week before the intelligent design trial in Dover, Pennsylvania, begins, an edit war erupts when "Jlefler" writes that "a strong scientific and layman community advocate creationism." The phrase is removed or reapplied eight times in one hour, leaving a narrow yellow zigzag.

Map courtesy of:
Frank Van Ham, Fernanda Viegas, and Martin Wattenberg,
Visual Communication Lab,
IBM Research

In a Web 2.0 environment where users regularly modify site content, researchers need to take extra care in evaluating the source of any information. This graphic shows how the Wikipedia entry on evolution changed over time. See Journal Entry 1 on page 580, which asks you to analyze these changes.

Researching

I n your biology class, you study the Human Genome Project. You discover that this 13-year research project mapped the 20,000–25,000 genes in human DNA. Among the uses of this research are new tests that can predict one's likelihood to contract specific diseases. Though such testing seems like a good thing, you also wonder about its effects—especially since many new commercial ventures offer genetic testing directly to consumers. How will the reliability of these tests be regulated? How would knowing that one is predisposed to an incurable disease affect one's mental well-being? Might these predispositions be used against people by employers or insurers? These questions lead you to investigate the ethical and social implications of genetic testing. You hope that this work will help those interested in having these tests to do so in informed ways—and perhaps encourage further public conversation about the implications of this emerging technology.

After spending two months in France living with a family and trying to understand their dinner conversation, you wonder why you—and other Americans—know so little about foreign languages. After reflecting on your inadequate background in French language and culture, you decide to investigate the current state of foreign-language studies in the United States. During your research, you begin to wonder if Americans know very little about foreign languages and cultures simply because foreign language are rarely required of students either in high school or in college. You decide to study the current state of foreign-language studies and perhaps to demonstrate a need for a consistent foreign-language requirement in public schools. You hope to persuade more students to study foreign languages and encourage some schools to revise their requirements.

> **"** Research is formalized curiosity. It is poking and prying with a purpose. **"**
> —ZORA NEALE HURSTON, NOVELIST AND FOLKLORE RESEARCHER

> **"** You know when you think about writing a book, you think it is overwhelming. But, actually, you break it down into tiny little tasks any moron could do. **"**
> —ANNIE DILLARD, NATURALIST, AUTHOR, *PILGRIM AT TINKER CREEK*

ALTHOUGH STARTING A RESEARCH PROJECT SOUNDS DIFFICULT AND COMPLICATED, RESEARCH IS REALLY A NATURAL AND ENJOYABLE PART OF OUR EVERYDAY EXPERIENCE, BOTH OUTSIDE AND INSIDE COLLEGE CLASSROOMS. FOR EXAMPLE, WE PRIDE OURSELVES ON BEING GOOD CONSUMERS—whether we're window-shopping for a good bargain, finding the best used car, asking co-workers for tips on the best new restaurant in town, or reading up on a new diet. But being a good "consumer" applies to the ways that we interact with information as well. The old saying "Let the buyer beware" applies not only to products we buy, but to information and arguments we "buy" as well. This chapter can help you become better information consumers and users.

The techniques discussed in the previous chapters of this book all involve forms of research. There are specific occasions, however, when you need to do a more thorough job of learning about a topic in order to build a more substantial piece of writing that carefully documents the supporting information. At that point, your initial interest in a topic becomes a set of research questions—questions that you seek to answer by reading a large variety of sources and/or doing sustained and deliberate field research.

Completing a systematic research project requires you to achieve what is often called "information literacy"—the ability to use disciplined methods to find, evaluate, and utilize the wide array of information sources available to you. Four specific skills discussed in this chapter will help you to become information literate.

1. You will need to learn skills for *collecting ideas and information* in the library, on the Internet, and from field research. While many schools have orientations or workshops run by the library, the techniques in this chapter can help you to practice those skills.

2. You will need skills for *critically evaluating* the information you find or generate. The glut of information available on any given topic is a mixed blessing. You need skills that can help you decide which sources are the most reliable, relevant, and useful for your own research. You'll also need to analyze each source for its point of view and potential biases.

3. You will need skills for *smoothly integrating* the information you find into your own writing, introducing the author and source and indicating to your readers how or why that information is relevant to your point. This is important because you are taking information out of its original context; you want your reader to be clear about why *you* are including this information.

4. Finally, you will need skills for *documenting your sources* in the body of your paper and in a Works Cited (MLA) or References (APA) page. Documenting sources not only allows you to give credit where it is due,

but leaves a path for your readers to check the validity of your information or learn more from your sources.

As should be clear by now, a sustained research project takes a good deal of time, planning, reflection, and evaluation and documentation of sources. This chapter outlines the key tasks in this disciplined and reflective process, such as:

- developing a research topic, question, and plan;
- locating, evaluating, and keeping track of your sources of information;
- shaping information to fit your purpose, audience, and genre;
- continually revising your ideas *and* your writing; and
- documenting the sources of your information.

As with other writing assignments presented in this text, the processes for completing a research project are recursive. That is, doing research is not as simple as following a linear set of steps. You will often need to stop and retrace your steps, revise your research question, collect new information, or revise parts of your paper during the writing process. To illustrate the various stages in one writer's process of completing a research project, you will find student writer Kate McNerny's notes, drafts, and documentation interspersed throughout this chapter. At the end of this chapter, you will find the end product of all that work, her paper entitled "Foreign Language Study: An American Necessity," which illustrates important features and forms of a source-based paper in Modern Language Association style.

Techniques for Researching

Since research projects differ from other writing both in process and in the end product—and because much of the writing you do in college will involve research—you need techniques specific to this important form of writing. Here are some of the most important techniques to keep in mind.

Techniques for Researching

Technique	Tips on How to Do It
Use purpose, occasion, audience, genre, and context as your guides for writing.	Remember that research is just a method of collecting and documenting ideas and evidence. The rhetorical situation still directs your writing. *Continued*

> If I find **10,000** ways something won't work, I haven't failed. I am not discouraged, because every wrong attempt discarded is another step forward.
>
> THOMAS EDISON, INVENTOR

Technique	Tips on How to Do It
	Consider not only what *you* are trying to learn, but the final product you want to produce, what you are trying to accomplish, and what readers might already believe, know, or need to know before they read your essay.
Find the most reliable and relevant sources about your subject.	Instead of trying to reinvent the wheel, discover what other people know and then build on it. Ask what you and your readers need to know in order to understand the specific topic, and what sources are most likely to supply that information in the most credible way.
Critically evaluate your sources for accuracy, reliability, and bias.	Consider the author's expertise, the place of publication, possible biases of the author. Be especially careful about Internet sources; though they can be reliable, they often represent people or organizations with a pronounced bias or give inaccurate or misleading information.
Use sources to make *your* point.	As you gather information, you may revise your thesis in light of what you learn, but don't let the tail wag the dog: Don't allow your sources to control you or your paper. Keep your purpose and audience in mind, choosing the pieces of information that are most applicable to your own rhetorical situation.
Document your sources, both in the text and at the end of the paper.	As you are trying to build your own case, citing reliable sources can help you to show the credibility of your information. To document sources effectively, be sure to include in-text citations as you incorporate materials into your draft. Including in-text citations as you write and having electronic or paper copies of each article you use can help you avoid inadvertent plagiarism.

USING PURPOSE, AUDIENCE, AND GENRE AS GUIDES

As you begin your research, you aren't looking for just any information you can find on a given topic; you are looking for information that can help you to illustrate that topic for a specific purpose, for a particular group of readers, and with a particular genre in mind. For this reason, even before you start writing, thinking about your purpose, audience, and genre can help you to find the sources that will support your project.

● **KNOW YOUR PURPOSE**   Like any other kind of writing, researched papers have a *purpose*. Reporting, explaining, evaluating, problem solving, and arguing are all purposes for research papers. Keeping an eye on purpose can guide you to the types of information that are most relevant to your area of investigation. Purposes may appear in combinations, as in a paper that summarizes current research and then proposes a solution to a problem. One of the ways that you will decide whether a source of information is worth reading and including in your list of sources is whether the piece is directly relevant to the goals of your paper. For example, not all articles about foreign languages were useful to Kate McNerny as she did her research; she was specifically seeking information about how foreign language is taught and the effects of knowing (or not knowing) a foreign language. A quick glance at her Works Cited list on page 647 shows how each chosen source supports that purpose.

● **ACCOMMODATE YOUR AUDIENCE**   Research papers have a defined *audience,* too. If you write a senior research paper in your major, you will write for a professor and for a community of people knowledgeable about your field. If you are a legal assistant or a junior attorney in a law firm, a superior may ask you to research a specific legal precedent and present that research in the most concise form possible. If you work for a manufacturer, a manager may assign you a research report on the sales and strategies of a competitor and ask you to use appropriate graphs and charts. For these reasons, you will need to consider your audience both as you research and as you write. The subject you choose, the kind of research you do, the documentation format, the vocabulary and style you use all should be appropriate for your selected audience. As you locate information through your reading or generate information through field research, you should continually ask yourself whether that information is likely to be important for the actual readers by considering the likely questions that they will have. And as you begin to write, thinking about your audience will help you to choose an organization, form, and style that your audience will find appropriate.

● **CONSIDER YOUR GENRE**   Finally, you must consider what *genre* (particular kind of writing) for presenting your information best fits your purpose and meets the expectations of your audience. If you are researching advances in sports medicine for an audience of experts, you need to use a genre (article, pamphlet, PowerPoint presentation) used by experts in the field. If your paper is an academic article, you may have an abstract at the beginning, a section reviewing and evaluating current research and methodologies, subsections for each of your main points, diagrams and charts for illustration, and an appendix with supplementary materials. If, however, you are writing primarily for jogging enthusiasts, your research-based paper may look more like an informal essay or take the form of a Web site or blog. The student essay by Kate McNerny at the end of this chapter illustrates one typical genre. Her argument is meant to convince stakeholders in the debate about foreign language study, including students, parents, and school administrators, so she chooses to present the argument in ways that are both scholarly and relevant to the needs of this audience.

FINDING THE BEST SOURCES: CURRENCY, RELIABILITY, AND RELEVANCE

It goes without saying that you want the "best" sources that you can find. But what makes something one of the "best" sources? In fact, the "best sources" are those that connect most clearly to your topic but also work for your particular purpose, for your particular audience, and for the particular genre you choose. Within these guidelines of purpose, audience, and genre, you need to judge your sources by three key criteria: currency, reliability, and relevance.

1. By **currency,** we mean that the piece is recent enough to take into account the most up-to-date data and findings of experts.
2. By **reliability**, we mean that the research presented is credible, both because of the qualifications of its author and because of the methods that author has used to collect his or her research.
3. By **relevance**, we mean the degree to which the piece serves your purpose, audience, and genre.

For example, a rich and detailed study of the structure of DNA by a noted biologist might provide current and reliable information on the topic of genetic engineering, and might inform *you* about the topic; but if it does not illuminate the ethical questions you are examining for your paper, you should choose not to include it.

PLANNING YOUR RESEARCH

As you can tell by now, good research requires time, patience, and adaptability. As you begin, it is important to *readjust your inner clock.* Initially, you'll think that you're not making much progress. However, once you readjust your inner clock, set more modest goals, and content yourself with a slower but more persistent pace, you've won half the battle. You also should realize that research is a messy process; you will continually be asking new questions, finding new focal points, and adding and removing source material. If you come to expect those complications in the early stages of the process, you'll feel less frustrated when you reach a dead end and also readier to appreciate valuable information when you discover it. However—and this is a *big* however—**planning is still an important part of successful research processes**. Being *adaptable* is not the same thing as being *disorganized*. In order to do productive searches, you need to begin by developing focused research questions. Focused questions center on the information you will need to write credibly on your topic.

For example, as a future history teacher, you become interested in possibilities for teaching history using contemporary methods that focus on more than just memorizing facts and taking tests. You would like to present these ideas to other students in your major as a type of guide to teaching techniques. To prepare for your research, you do the following brainstorming:

I might begin by finding out how history classes are taught in various settings. I could find that out in a number of ways. I could:

- Interview students, set up focus groups, or distribute a survey about their experience in high school
- Visit high schools and sit in on some classes and maybe interview teachers
- Look for education journals that discuss current techniques, especially using the ERIC (the Education Resources Information Center) database
- Use my own memories of high school history classes
- Write about my own interest in history, and what most intrigues me—then create a lesson plan that I might like myself
- Look at the types of standardized tests that are used
- See if there are any new media sources—videos, graphic novels, wikis, blogs, etc.—that might interest students more than the conventional teaching method
- Watch *The History Channel* to see how they make history more appealing

Strategies like these will direct you toward important information, as well as the potential sources of that information.

WARMING UP   Journal Exercises

Following the model of the scenario above, consider the following rhetorical situations, and brainstorm types of research you might do in order to complete such a research project.

1 You are an engineering major who believes that the public does not have enough knowledge about the inherent problems of biofuels. You want to write an article for a publication such as *Discover Magazine* to inform them about these problems, but need to present the information in a way that is understandable to the general public. What kinds of research would be best for this rhetorical situation?

2 You are a nursing major, and believe that nurses have an obligation to help communities to better understand how to prepare for a possible pandemic. You believe that a lack of understanding of how viruses are spread is a serious problem and would keep the public from behaving in responsible ways should a pandemic occur. You would like to produce both an informational pamphlet that could be distributed in doctor's offices and a Web site for further information. What kinds of research might you do to (1) find out what the public perceptions/misperceptions are and (2) find accurate information and translate it into understandable terms?

MAINTAINING YOUR VOICE AND PURPOSE: EFFECTIVELY INCORPORATING SOURCES

Completing an effective research project is not only about finding reliable and relevant sources; it is also about how you *use* those sources. The reading you do informs your ideas and positions on a topic. But what sources you *do* choose to cite should be the most relevant, credible, and useful to your discussion—whether they support your position or not.

Including reliable and relevant information shows that you are informed on the subject, offering background information and summarizing what people are (or are not) saying on the subject to capture the various points of view. But sometimes, in the process of including the ideas of others, our own voice can be muted and our own purposes can be de-emphasized. If you start stringing together passages from your sources, you'll be summarizing rather than doing research. You'll be letting the sources tell you what to think, what information is important, or what conclusions to reach. *Write your own paper; don't let your sources write it for you.* It is crucial that you use your sources to make *your* point and that *your* voice still emerges in your writing. You will need to decide how best to incorporate information from your sources in each given case—that is, when it is best to quote, paraphrase, or summarize a source. For more on quotation, paraphrasing, and summary, see Chapter 5 (Reading) as well as the Writing Processes section below.

To better understand ways to effectively incorporate sources, read the following two examples. In the first, the writer (who is arguing for the need to develop better teaching methods for high school history classes) simply reports information. In the second, the writer incorporates the information in ways that serve her own purposes.

Mere Summary: According to Rothcart, history classes are not interactive enough. History classes are too focused upon factual information like names and dates. Students benefit instead by critical thinking. Rothcart presents a great many examples to illustrate this fact. One of his examples shows that students tend to forget all the information once a test is past (Rothcart 2007).

Incorporating Information for the Writer's Purpose: One of the reasons history curricula and teaching methods must be revised is because students are simply not retaining information—a point that is illustrated by Rothcart's recent study. Teaching methods need to *reflect* that fully understanding history requires critical thinking skills, skills that Rothcart also finds lacking when memorization is stressed (Rothcart 2007). In my own observations of high school curricula and interviews with high school students, I found that methods based on memorization and multiple-choice testing still dominate most school systems.

Note how in the second example, the information from Rothcart is put in the context of the writer's own purpose and audience. The researched information meshes with the writer's own primary information and argument about the need to change the way history courses are taught.

DOCUMENTING YOUR SOURCES

Documenting your sources is another important part of writing a research paper. The documentation process takes place in three stages:

1. **You must keep careful notes as you collect information.** The note-taking process includes two parts: (1) recording the bibliographic information you will need to document your sources later, and (2) digesting the specific information from each piece that is relevant to your topic, purpose, and audience. This will help you incorporate this information into your own paper as you draft.

2. **As you incorporate source material into your own argument during the writing process, you must include in-text citations to identify that source for your readers.** The in-text citations also signal to your readers that further information can be found at the end of your paper.

3. **At the end of the paper, you should include a list of Works Cited (MLA) or References (APA) that provides your readers with the information they will need to find that source for themselves.** If your readers want more information, or if they doubt a fact or statistic, your documentation enables them to track down the sources. *Note:* Decide on the documentation format (usually MLA or APA style) before you begin your research as you will need to know what relevant bibliographical information to record in your notes.

Research Processes

ASSIGNMENT FOR RESEARCHING

Choose a subject that strongly interests you, about which both you *and a specific audience* would like to learn more. It may be a subject that you have already written about in this course. **Remember that your research plan should go beyond finding information "on your topic," and should consider the purpose, audience, and genre in which you will write.** Consider using library resources (both paper and online), primary research (such as questionnaires, interviews, or field studies), electronic sources (Web sites, blogs, wikis, organizational databases), and unpublished sources of information. Be sure to check with your instructor for suggested length, appropriate number or kinds of sources, and additional format requirements. And plan for the documentation style appropriate for your subject, purpose, and audience.

Audience	Possible Purposes and Genres for Researched Writing
Personal Audience	• A blog on your own experiences with languages on a trip abroad in order to collect others' similar experiences • A journal describing your own experiences with standardized testing under No Child Left Behind meant to show teachers the pressures on students it creates • A personal essay that combines research on attention deficit disorder with your own experiences with the disorder, which you hope will help others in similar situations

Academic Audience	• A humanities-based essay that joins the debate among ethicists about the effects of technology on our lives
	• A social sciences study based on survey information about student attitudes toward plagiarism
	• A natural sciences study of the effects of industry on a local creek, based on field research and published studies of water pollution
	• A study that explores the challenges of start-up ventures, based on recent legislation regulating business operations and meant for other students in the Entrepreneurship program at your college
Public Audience	• A wiki, or an entry in an existing wiki, about your own use of a genetic testing service in order to correct erroneous public opinions
	• A Facebook page that attempts to encourage young people to pay more attention to current political debates
	• A letter to the editor arguing that standardized testing is important for teacher accountability
	• A report for your local community on why public spaces for recreation are needed to revitalize the community
	• A Web site outlining alternative energies for consumers searching for a new car

CHOOSING A SUBJECT

As should be clear by now, you and your research project will be spending a good deal of time together. Think about the difference between spending time with someone you really like, and spending time with someone whom you find dull or uninteresting. In the first case, time goes by quickly and you're happy for each occasion; in the second case, time drags and you have little energy. Choose your topic carefully—find one that really interests you—and the research project will be enjoyable and productive.

- You've likely already generated a good many potential topics in your journal. So you can start by rereading your journal entries for possible research subjects. Even a personal entry may suggest an idea. If you wrote about how you fainted in the gym during aerobics or weight training, you might research the potential dangers of exercising in high heat and humidity or sitting in a sauna after hard exercise. If you wrote a journal entry about a friend's drinking problem, you might like to read more about the causes and treatments of alcoholism.

- You might also re-read other essays that you have written to see if they might be enriched by more sustained research. If your observing essay, for example, was about a tattoo parlor that you visited, use that essay as the starting point for further investigation and research. Whom could you interview to find out more about tattooing? What is the history of tattooing? Why is it becoming more popular? What controversies surround its use? What resources does your library have? What sites can you find on the Internet? You might also use a topic from your remembering, reading, or investigating essays as a starting place for additional reading and research, or consider how writing you've done in other classes might be a starting point for additional research.

- **Writing Across the Curriculum.** Topics you are studying in other classes might suggest possible issues in which you and others in that area of study might have an interest.

Build on what you already know and what already interests you rather than launching into an entirely unknown subject. Also consider the rhetorical situation (purpose, audience, and genre) of your project.

● **NARROWING AND FOCUSING YOUR SUBJECT**   Once you have a tentative idea, you'll need to narrow it, focus it, or otherwise limit the subject to make it appropriate for your audience and context. The topic of alcoholism, while a fine subject, is too general to help you develop a research plan. Focus on a particular research question: "Do beer commercials on television contribute to alcoholism?" "Are there really positive effects of drinking moderate amounts of alcohol?" "What methods does Alcoholics Anonymous use to help people?" "Have DWI laws actually reduced the number of fatal automobile accidents?"

Your research question will eventually lead to a *thesis statement* that you will demonstrate in your research essay. Though you won't really be sure about your thesis until you've completed at least some of your research, it can be useful to start with a working thesis or hypothesis. For example, a tentative thesis might look something like this: "Although some studies show a definite link between consuming moderate amounts of red wine and reduced incidence of heart disease, the negative effects of alcohol consumption far outweigh the potential benefits." Then you'll need to see if the research supports that initial hypothesis. It's important that you be willing to change your mind as the research warrants it. But having a working version of your thesis will help you to tell whether you research question is still too broad (you can't begin to read everything about it in just a few weeks) or too narrow (in two weeks, you can't find enough information about that question). Two techniques may help narrow and focus your subject.

1. **Think about your *purpose* and *audience.*** The best way to focus your paper is to reflect on your purpose: What kinds of claims do you want to make about your topic? (If necessary, review the claims of fact, cause

and effect, value, and policy outlined in Chapter 11, "Arguing.") As you collect articles, think about the kinds of claims you might want to make about your topic.

Claims of Fact: Are makers of hard liquor being discriminated against by not being allowed to advertise on TV? Is alcoholism a disease or just an addiction?

Claims of Cause and Effect: Does TV advertising increase alcohol consumption or just affect the brands that are consumed? Can students who are "recreational" drinkers become alcoholics? Do recovery programs like Alcoholics Anonymous really work?

Claims of Value: Does beer have any nutritional value? Are microbrews really made better or are they fresher than beers from larger breweries?

Claims of Policy: Do age-based drinking laws really work? Should liquor consumption be banned at campus sporting events? At dorms, fraternities, and sororities? At any campus function? Should makers of hard liquor be allowed to advertise on television?

Asking questions about your potential audience may also help you find a focus for your essay. If you are writing for a local audience, consider what they believe and what they might be interested in. Is the topic of alcohol regulation controversial? Who are your readers? What are they likely to believe about this issue? Profile your audience and brainstorm how you can connect your research question to those particular readers.

2. **Use *question analysis*.** The who, what, when, where, and why questions that you use to focus your topic are the same questions that reference librarians use to help you focus your research in the library.

Who:	What group of people is interested or affected?
What:	How are key terms defined? What academic discipline is involved?
When:	What is the period or time span?
Where:	What continent, country, state, or town is involved?
Why:	What are possible effects or implications?

Answering these questions—by yourself, in a group, or with a reference librarian—may suggest new angles, new avenues for research, or subtopics that could lead to a focus for your research paper. As you narrow your topic, you are narrowing and focusing the range of your research in the library.

Student writer Kate McNerny, brainstorming with another class member, applied these questions to her subject about foreign-language study and came up with key questions about school language requirements that led to her more focused argument. As a result of her question analysis, McNerny decided to discuss both language and culture, to focus on current conditions, and to recommend that secondary schools require foreign languages. *In any research, however, what you look for and what you find are always different. You will need to modify your focus as you read and learn.*

WARMING UP   Journal Exercises

Do at least one of the following journal exercises to help get yourself into a research frame of mind or to discover a possible research subject.

1. Look again at the illustration at the beginning of this chapter that graphically "maps" how the debate about evolution developed on the Wikipedia site through revisions to the evolution entry. Then look at the language education screen shot from Wikipedia that shows how the entry on that topic has been revised. Assume that you become interested in the ways that Wikipedia, despite its credibility problems, tracks public debates and changing public opinions. First, learn as much as you can

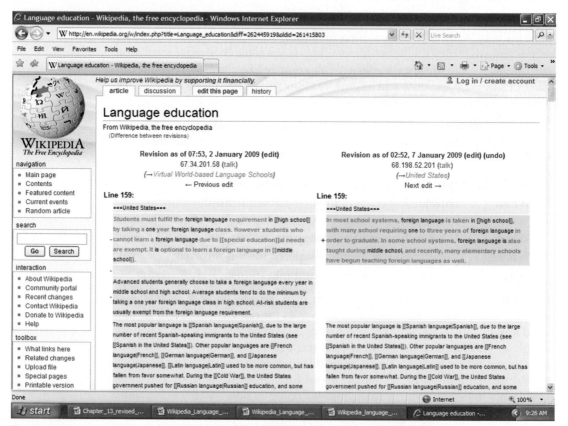

The language education entry on Wikipedia, showing the January 2 and January 7 revisions of line 159.

about the history and mission of Wikipedia. Then, choose a few topics that interest you. Find the Wikipedia entry for that topic, and click on the "history" tab at the top of the page. Following the instructions there, trace the way that the debate on that topic has developed and see if you can find any trends on particularly controversial topics, in the reliability and tone of the entries, in the ways that biases or political beliefs influence the entries, and so on.

2 Choose a topic that you are considering for your research project, and find one credible scholarly article that was published very recently—this year if possible. Check the works cited or reference page to see what sources were cited by that author. Starting with the most recent, locate sources that seem closest to your own topic and check their reference pages as well. Record trends in the research on this topic: names of authors who seem to be most often cited, key terms that are important (look especially at titles and abstracts), and any other information you can glean from a quick skimming. Then use this information to help set up your own research plan and search terms. Be prepared to explain in class what other relevant books, articles, or Web sites you found using this research method and how you located them.

3 **Writing Across the Curriculum.** Sit down with a family member, friend, or classmate. On a sheet of paper, write down the subject of the most interesting course that you are currently taking. Hand the sheet of paper to that person and ask him or her to write down questions for an interview designed to find out *why* you like this course and *what* you like best about it. Then have that person interview you and record your responses. At the end of the interview, discuss your responses. What ideas could you research in order to explain to your interviewer what is interesting about this subject?

4 **Writing Across the Curriculum.** Keep a notebook in your pocket consistently for at least three days. Each time you hear a debate on television, run across a controversial story in the newspaper or on the Internet, hear people debating a topic in a class, around campus, or in social settings, etc., jot down the topic of that debate. Decide which topics seem to you most important, most interesting, and most relevant to your own interests and area of study. If you hear two people discussing the need for alternative energies and you are a marketing major, you might consider studying how such new products might be sold; if you are a biology major, you might consider studying their true environmental impact; if you are a philosophy major, you might study the ethics of using potential food sources for energy purposes. Try to connect whatever topics you find most interesting to areas of study within your own major or discipline—or one that you are considering.

DEVELOPING A RESEARCH STRATEGY

With a computer and the Internet, it is easy to find books, articles, and Web sites that somehow relate to your topic. It is more difficult, however, to determine which sources are credible and appropriate for your audience and purpose. To do so, you need methods for locating the types of information you are seeking and methods for evaluating the sources that you find. Some of those methods apply to all types of sources; others are more specialized depending on the type of source you are seeking or evaluating. You also need to consider the types of sources that exist, and how to choose among them (and combine them) in ways that best serve your own purposes, audience, and genre.

Because a researched essay involves an extended examination of your topic, your audience will expect you to support your thesis and conclusions with substantial and convincing evidence: background information, facts, statistics, descriptions, and other results of interviews and research. And because researched essays are often meant for scholarly purposes and audiences, this type of writing frequently has some strict conventions and expectations that help readers to check the validity of your argument. Supporting sources are cited in the text and included in a Works Cited (MLA) or References (APA) page at the end of the paper. In that sense, a research paper is like a scientific experiment. **The audience of a researched paper will expect to be able to trace your whole experiment—to see what ideas and evidence you worked with, where you found them, and how you used them in your paper.** Therefore, if you are writing for an academic or professional audience, you may want to search specialized databases and indexes such as *Academic Search Premier* and subject indexes such as *Architectural Index, AGRICOLA, Art Abstracts, Biological Abstracts, ERIC, MEDLINE, PsycINFO,* or *Sociological Abstracts.* To find the databases that are most appropriate for specific disciplines or topics, you can consult your reference librarian or faculty members in that discipline.

If, on the other hand, you are taking on a research project that is meant for a popular audience, your research strategy might be somewhat different. For example, if your goal is to determine how direct-to-consumer genetic testing sites market their products to consumers, much of your research might be performed by examining the Web sites of those companies and/or by reading trade journals from the medical profession or marketing firms. In this case, your strategy might be to do a combination of primary research (direct analysis of the sites, interviews with potential users, an experiment in which you show some of the sites to individuals and gauge their reaction) and reading statements about genetic testing by medical practitioners and organizations. You could also read the opinions of experts in medical ethics. If you bring those three sets of sources together, you can develop a strategy that will allow you to summarize previous opinions on this topic *and* add your own analysis of this marketing technique and its ethical implications.

If you examine Kate McNerny's Works Cited list at the end of this chapter, and note the way that she used each of these sources in the paper itself, you can reconstruct the strategy and thought process she used in her research. Note how she included popular sources such as *U.S. News and World Report*, journals from the fields of education and language education, information from business trade publications like *HR Focus* and *Occupational Outlook,* and information from organizational Web sites such as *Foreign Language Study Abroad Service*. Each of these sources had a specific purpose in Kate's study, showing how each discipline or field has approached the question of language education. As Kate performed her research, she asked two key questions: What questions do I need to answer to write credibly on this topic? What sources of information are most likely to answer these questions? To answer the question about the public's perception of foreign language study, *U.S. News and World* report fits the bill; to consider public policy, *Congressional Quarterly Weekly Report* is most apt.

COLLECTING AND NOTETAKING

Once you have developed and focused your topic and have developed a strategy for beginning your research (which will continue to evolve), the process of informing yourself about that focused topic begins. This is the longest part of the process, and so requires a great deal of patience and organization. This process will proceed over a period of weeks, so it is important that you be conscientious about keeping good notes. Keep in mind that without care, a great deal of time and effort might be wasted, as you will need to go back and recover lost information, search for the materials you'll need for proper documentation, and re-read many of the materials you've collected. Most importantly, if you don't keep careful notes, your own thinking about the topic is less likely to develop productively. Your notes should thus record information you will need for documentation as well as provide a running log of the ways that your thoughts on the topic progress.

● **RECORD BIBLIOGRAPHIC INFORMATION**   While you will not complete your Works Cited or References page until you are in the final stages of writing, selecting a documentation style before you begin is crucial as you then will know what bibliographic information you will need to collect. If you are writing a paper for the humanities, follow the Modern Language Association (MLA) style set forth in the *MLA Handbook for Writers of Research Papers* (7th ed., 2009). If you are writing a paper in the behavioral sciences, use the American Psychological Association (APA) style as described in the *Publication*

Information for a Bibliographic Record

Author(s), if Known	Bergentoft, Rune
Full title and full subtitle of the source *In the case of a book, include the title/subtitle as it appears on the title page; if you are using only one section or chapter, list that title as well.* *In the case of a periodical, list both the title of the specific article and the full title of the journal.*	"Foreign Language Instruction: A Comparative Perspective" *The Annals of the American Academy of Political and Social Science*
Publisher, city/state/country of publication *In the case of a book, list the place and publisher.* *In the case of an electronic publication in a database, list the database name.* *In the case of a Web site, list the sponsoring organization or individual who maintains the site.* *For nonstable online sources, list the URL (you can cut and paste this into your bibliographic file and even make it a hyperlink).*	*Sage Journals Online*
Dates of publication and access *In the case of a journal, list the volume, issue, and date of publication (sometimes the precise date, sometimes the month or season of publication).* *In the case of an electronic source, the date of last revision, usually listed at the bottom of a Web page, and the date you accessed the information.* *The medium (print, Web, DVD, etc.) in which you accessed the source, and the date for accessing Web sources.*	Volume 532 Issue 1 March 1994 Web, Apr. 24, 2003

Beginning and ending page numbers (if available)	Pages 8–34
With a book, list the page numbers of the portion that you are citing or referencing.	
With a journal article, list the page numbers of the entire article.	
If the article is electronic, record page numbers only if they are stable (as in a PDF) or the page numbers from the print source are identified.	

Manual of the American Psychological Association (6th ed., 2009). This chapter illustrates both the MLA and APA styles.

Though methods of documenting each type of source have specific guidelines (see the overview later in this chapter), there are specific pieces of information that you will need in all cases. Setting up your filing system in advance helps you to record that information as you do your research. As you find and select a likely source of information, be sure to record the information as shown in the chart above (either on paper or electronically).

Tip: **In some cases, it may be useful to photocopy or download important sources for later rereading and reference.** Make sure that your copies clearly show authors, titles, and page numbers. (For some research projects, your instructor may request photocopies of every source you paraphrase or quote.)

● NOTE THE SOURCE'S RELEVANCE, RELIABILITY, AND CURRENCY
Keeping in mind that you want to base your own argument on credible sources, it is important to articulate the reasons a particular source is reliable (and why your audience will consider it so) while you take notes. Jot down the reasons you find this source reliable, based on some of the techniques that follow in this chapter for evaluating sources. You might also note any potential biases in the source. Though there are slightly different criteria for evaluating each kind of source, these are questions that you can ask that apply to all sources of information.*

---

*These criteria are adapted from guidelines designed by Elizabeth E. Kirk, the library instruction coordinator for the Milton S. Eisenhower Library at Johns Hopkins University, and are available at http://www.library.jhu.edu/researchhelp/general/evaluating.

- **Authorship.** Who is the author? Is the author well known? Are the author's credentials or biographical information available on the Internet or elsewhere? Does the author have a reason to be biased? The less you know about the author, the more cautious you need to be about using the source. *If you decide to use a document by a questionable authority, indicate exactly what you know or don't know about the author's credentials.*

- **Publishing organization.** Does the site indicate the organization responsible for the text? Is it published in a "refereed" journal (a journal whose articles are chosen and edited by other experts in the field)? Is there information about the publication, or in the case of an electronic publication, the organization, Webmaster, or designer of the page? Is this organization recognized in its field? *If you know the source is not authoritative or has a commercial basis, indicate the organization's identity if you quote from the site.*

- **Point of view or bias.** Every document or text has a point of view or bias—but some biases may mean that the site's information is not reliable or accurate. Does the author or the organization have a commercial, political, philosophical, religious, environmental, or even scientific agenda? Is the organization selling something? *When you use a source with highly selective or biased information or perspectives, indicate the author's probable bias or agenda when you cite the text.*

- **Reliability and knowledge of the literature.** Reliable sources refer to other texts available or published in that discipline or field. Look for documents that have in-text citations or references to other sources, a fair and reasonable appraisal of alternative points of view, and a bibliography. *Any source that has no references to other key works may simply be one writer's opinion and/or may contain erroneous information. If you have reason to believe the source is not reliable or accurate, find another source.*

● **SUMMARIZE PERTINENT SOURCE MATERIAL** Once you have selected a reliable, relevant source and recorded the bibliographic information, it is important to make some notes that will remind you what specific information you expect to use from this source. You can do this in a number of ways.

When an article is particularly central to your topic, consider annotating the article or parts of it that are applicable to your own topic, purpose, and audience. By making notes in the margin (either on paper or by using the reviewing function of your word processing program), you can later find the parts of the source that you expect to use and can recall how those parts of the source relate to your topic and serve your purpose. For example, when Kate McNerny was reading Rune Bergentoft's article, she made notes in the margin of page 18.

Annotating an Article

18   THE ANNALS OF THE AMERICAN ACADEMY

Note that the length of lessons varies by country.

THE INCIDENCE
OF LANGUAGE STUDY

The length of a foreign language lesson varies between 35 minutes, in the United Kingdom, and 60 minutes, in Italy. In general, these differences should be kept in mind when the number of lessons devoted to the teaching of a foreign language is compared across countries. In our study, however, the periods of varying length have been converted into clock hours.

Most countries require foreign language. I wonder if this has changed since the time of this study.

From the academic year 1992-93 onward, the study of at least one foreign language is obligatory in all the countries examined, with the exception of Japan. Several countries require knowledge of two foreign languages for entry to the upper secondary school; in the Netherlands, the requirement is three foreign languages. In a number of countries, there is currently a debate on whether the study of a second foreign language should be made obligatory.

Other countries are having this debate too.

The number of students enrolled in third languages differs by country. In the Netherlands, it is a high of 85 percent; in Finland, 77 percent of upper secondary students study a third foreign language. In other countries, the percentage is very much lower. It is interesting to find that, although the study of a foreign language in Japan is optional, as much as 98 percent of the students there take a foreign language.

I wonder why Japanese students make this choice without being required to do so. What motivates them? That might be worth examining

The fact that the study of a foreign language is obligatory does not necessarily mean that 100 percent of an age group is engaged in foreign language study. Some countries report 98 or 99 percent to indicate that ex-

The requirement doesn't seem to apply to all. I wonder how the decisions are made.

ceptions are made. Russia reports about 80 percent.

A large proportion of that foreign language study is devoted to English. Table 2 and Figures 3A and 3B and 4A and 4B indicate the percentage of students in each country studying particular foreign languages in primary and secondary schools.

It seems clear that except for German in France and French in Spain, only a small percentage of students in European countries study languages other than English. It is also noteworthy that there is a small set of students enrolled in a large number of language classes.

HOME LANGUAGES

The data available show that the percentage of students with a home language other than an official language of the country where they reside varies considerably from one country to another (see Table 3). Sweden reports 12 percent; the Netherlands, about 5 percent; and Norway, 4 percent. In Scotland, less than 1 percent of the students enrolled in obligatory schooling report having a home language other than English. The number of home languages ranges from about 25 in the Netherlands to nearly 200 in the United Kingdom; not all of them are taught in school. Sweden reports 126, of which 95 are taught in school. Few students in the Netherlands—about 5 percent—are offered teaching in their home language in the obligatory school. By contrast, the corresponding figure for Sweden is 57 percent and for Norway, 71 percent.

(text continues on page 25)

English seems to be dominant. I wonder if that is why Americans don't feel they need a foreign language.

The problem I am examining seems to be similar in other countries; I might look for a more recent study of this to check if this has changed.

What is the influence of having an "official language"? Does that discourage foreign language study?

Some of these statistics might be useful.

Even if you don't annotate the article extensively, you should include a brief summary of the source's thesis, its method of argument, the key information and evidence presented, and when appropriate, some particularly apt quotations (see next item). For example, Kate McNerny might have chosen to summarize some of the relevant information from the Bergentoft article as follows:

On page 18ff, Bergentoft's essay puts the issue of foreign language study into an international context. Even when students in other countries are required to study a foreign language, it seems that English is the dominant choice. This might suggest why Americans feel less of a need to study foreign language. Why is it that in Japan, 96% of students choose to study a foreign language without being required to do so? What effect does that have on my possible thesis? Are requirements the real answer? *Note to self:* It would be useful to find if there have been any changes since this 1994 study was published.

● **NOTE KEY QUOTATIONS**   As you read, you will likely find some lines that capture some facet of your topic in particularly compelling ways. Either annotate the article in the margin by noting that you may want to include this quotation, or cut and paste that quotation into your notes (along with the page number and a clear note that this is a direct quotation, so as to avoid plagiarism). You might add a brief description about how you intend to use that quotation. For example, Kate McNerny used the following quotation in her piece. The note section looked like this:

From Bergentoft, page 18: "The fact that the study of a foreign language is obligatory does not necessarily mean that 100 percent of an age group is engaged in foreign language study." I could use this direct quotation to show that requirements do not always translate into full participation in foreign language study. *Note to self:* I might consider not only the requirements, but how they are put into practice.

● **SYNTHESIZE SOURCES IN YOUR NOTES**   The process of collecting sources provides an important chance for you to further focus your own argument. After reading and summarizing each new piece, take a moment to jot down your thoughts about what you have learned from this piece, **and how it corroborates, contradicts, or expands upon the ideas in other sources you have read**. This is one of the portions of the process that is "recursive"— that is, you may need to keep returning to your notes on previous sources and adding new insights and information you have found. By cross-referencing the pieces you read, you will start to see how the various sources of information speak to one another, and how you can start to synthesize them with each other to see the bigger picture. So, for example, after Kate McNerny read Bergentoft's article, she then read another piece, this one by Marion E. Hines. In that essay, she found a quotation from a Department of Education Study called "Goals 2000." She went back to her previous notes from Bergentoft, and added this:

> *From Bergentoft, page 18:* "The fact that the study of a foreign language is obligatory does not necessarily mean that 100 percent of an age group is engaged in foreign language study." I could use this quotation to show that requirements do not always translate into full participation in foreign language study. *Note to self:* I might consider not only the requirements, but how they are put into practice.
>
> I could compare this with the implementation of the Department of Education's statement in "Goals 2000": "All of our people, not just a few, must be able to think for a living, adapt to changing environments, and understand the world around them" (qtd in Hines). Hines shows how despite this directive, schools still prioritize math and reading for most students, and so don't feel that the goals were being taken seriously (pp. 18–20). I should illustrate how policies are important, but also that they need to be funded and put into effect on the local level to have an impact.

By putting together these two sources, McNerny is able to correlate the situation in other countries with that at home, and also able to raise two other important issues: How well are policies and goals put into effect? Are foreign languages seen as less important than math and science?

● **RETHINK AND REVISE YOUR HYPOTHESIS OR WORKING THESIS**
It can be very useful for you to pause as you are doing your research to see how new pieces of information are affecting your original hypothesis. If you make this a regular part of your notetaking, you will have a rich resource as you start the writing processes of shaping and drafting your paper. As you continue to learn more, you are likely to continuously revise your thesis.

CHOOSING AND EVALUATING SOURCES

Once you have prepared for the collecting process by setting up a system something like the one above, it's time to start filling those files with rich information. Although you may begin your search in the reference section, via

> ❝ Knowledge is of two kinds. We know a subject ourselves, or we know where we can find information upon it. ❞
> —SAMUEL JOHNSON, FROM BOSWELL'S *LIFE OF JOHNSON*

the library's online catalog, or on the open Web environment, as you narrow and focus your topic or draft sections of your paper, you may come back and recheck the basic references, the online catalog, the periodical indexes, or bibliographies. Along the way, you might also turn to *informal contacts* with friends or acquaintances. Friends, family members, business associates, or teachers may be able to suggest key questions or give you some sources. The bottom line: be nimble by asking lots of questions and pondering who or what might provide the answers you need.

What follows outlines the types of sources that are useful for most research projects and gives you some advice on how to use and evaluate each type of source for its relevance, reliability for your topic, and rhetorical situation.

● **PRIMARY AND SECONDARY SOURCES**   Research sources fall into two general categories: primary and secondary. Some sources—accounts of scientific experiments, transcripts of speeches or lectures, questionnaires, interviews, private documents—are known as *primary sources.* They are original, firsthand information, "straight from the horse's mouth." Secondhand reports, analyses, and descriptions based on primary sources are known as *secondary sources.* Secondary sources may contain the same information, but they are once-removed. For example, a lecture or experiment by an expert in food irradiation is a primary source; the newspaper report of that lecture or experiment is a secondary source.

The distinction between primary and secondary sources is important for several reasons. The first reason concerns reliability. Secondary sources may contain errors. The newspaper account, for example, may misquote the expert or misrepresent the experiment. If possible, therefore, find the primary source—a copy of the actual lecture or a published article about the experiment.

One reason for using primary sources is to make your researched document more persuasive through an appeal to character (see Chapter 11, "Arguing"). If you can cite the original source—or even show how some secondary accounts distorted the original experiment—you will gain your readers' trust and faith. Not only does uncovering the primary data make your research more accurate, but your additional effort makes all your data and arguments more credible. So, for example, if you were to cite a newspaper article (a secondary source) that discussed the latest report from the World Health Organization on alcohol consumption, you might also seek out, read, and analyze relevant parts of that report itself, so as to add more depth to the journalistic report—and in some cases, show the shortcomings of the news story. *Unpublished public documents,* such as deeds, wills, surveyors' maps, and environmental impact statements, may contain a wealth of information. *Notes from classes, public lectures,* or *television programs* are also useful sources.

Although the library is an important source of both primary and secondary information, in some types of research projects, it can be useful for you to use another kind of primary source: field research or information that you have generated on your own. This kind of information can be developed through a number of processes:

- *Phone calls* and *letters* to experts, government agencies, or businesses may yield background information, statistics, or quotations.
- *Experiments* can help you to test out your hypothesis or the claims made by others in a controlled environment.
- *Interviews* (discussed in Chapter 7, Investigating) can be an excellent source of primary information.
- *Focus groups* gather small groups to discuss a few specific questions to see what opinions emerge. It is often worthwhile to use audio or video recording to capture the responses.
- *User tests,* a type of focus group, generate information on how well a product, a set of instructions, or some technology works.
- *Case studies* test a general premise by analyzing a particular situation or set of situations. For example, if you are a business student, you might collect information about the practices of two entrepreneurs in setting up their businesses and compare them.
- *Ethnographies* are similar to case studies, but they take a more holistic approach to your observation of a culture. Both case studies and ethnographies involve the methods discussed in Chapter 3 ("Observing").
- *Surveys* can help you to see general trends and correlate various social practices by posing a series of written questions to a specific group (discussed in Chapter 7, Investigating).

While many types of research benefit by primary source information—both that you find and that you generate yourself—nearly *all* research projects require you to do **secondary research**. Even if you are developing your own primary research methodologies or analyzing primary source documents, it is very unlikely that you will be the first one to do so. A careful researcher will investigate how others have done related research, imitate or slightly revise those methods, compare their own results with those of previous studies, and account for those differences. In other cases, secondary research represents the bulk—or even the full spectrum—of your research, either because the topic is not one that lends itself to primary research or because you do not have the resources or the ability to generate new information in a reliable way. What follows outlines some of the main categories of secondary research sources and provides some methods of evaluating them. This process of critically evaluating sources also involves many of the techniques discussed in the Reading chapter as well as the techniques discussed below in the section on collecting information.

● **BACKGROUND INFORMATION AND GENERAL REFERENCE**   Before you begin more comprehensive searches for information, you may need an overview of your subject that can be obtained through specific types of secondary sources known as "General Reference" materials. Though many people associate encyclopedias with their grade-school "research"—when they copied passages out of *The World Book* or *Collier's Encyclopedia*—encyclopedias are an excellent source of basic information and terminology that may help you focus, narrow, and define your subject. General and specialized encyclopedias (including online encyclopedias and wikis such as Wikipedia, which are discussed in the section on Open Web sources below), dictionaries, almanacs, or biographies can supply information that can help you develop search terms for deeper research. In addition to the general encyclopedias, there are hundreds of references—one or two might just save you hours of research in the library and lead you directly to key facts or important information on your topic. *Use them as background reading, however, not as major sources.*

If you need basic definitions, facts, figures, or statistics, reference sources are very convenient. The standard college dictionary or thesaurus is a start, but the *Oxford English Dictionary,* known as the *OED,* or *Webster's Third New International Dictionary of the English Language* may help you find deeper meanings and nuances for key ideas or definitions. There are also many specialized dictionaries for scientific terms, slang words, symbols, and a host of other specialized reference materials for basic facts, figures, or statistics such as the *World Almanac,* the *Book of Facts,* or the *Statistical Abstracts of the United States.* If your subject is a person, look at *Who's Who in America,* or check one of the references that indexes collections of biographies. *Biography and Genealogy Master Index* and *Biographical Dictionaries* reference more than three million biographical sketches.

The *librarian* is often the most valuable resource for your research. At some point during your research in the library, probably after you have a focused topic and have collected some sources, talk to a reference librarian. For many writers, asking for help can be really intimidating. To make the process of asking for help as painless—and productive—as possible, try to have some focused questions prepared: "Hi, I'm Kate McNerny. I'm doing a research project for my college writing course. My topic is foreign-language study in the United States. I'm trying to find information about the current state of foreign-language study in the United States and collect some arguments for increasing requirements in secondary schools and colleges. Here's what I've found so far [explain what you've done]. What additional reference books, Web sites, indexes, dictionaries, or bibliographies might help me in my research?" The resulting conversation may be the most productive five minutes of your entire library research. After you've talked to the librarian once, it will be easier to return and ask a question when you hit a snag.

● **THE 21ST CENTURY LIBRARY: PHYSICAL AND ONLINE SOURCES**
After gaining a global understanding of your topic and noting related concepts and search terms, your search for more in-depth information begins. This almost always involves library resources. But what we call a "library" has changed

a great deal over the past few decades. While the physical space that contains books, journals, and library staff is still an instrumental research location, what we call a library now also includes the electronic databases that enrich the physical offerings.

As you begin collecting information, acquaint yourself with both versions of the library. If you have not already done so, inquire at the information desk about library tours or walk through the library with a friend or classmate. Locate the *reference section;* the *online catalog* for books and articles; the *indexes* for newspapers, journals, and magazines; the *microfilm room;* the *stacks;* and the *government documents* section.

Just as it is a good idea to acquaint yourself with the physical library, it is also important that you acquaint yourself with the online offerings of your institution. The online library has become integrated with the physical one, making it easier for you to locate books, articles, and government documents relevant to your topic that are still offered in paper versions. You can find the library call numbers and locations of sources. You can determine if a source is available or checked out and get an abstract or a short description of a source. For some systems, you can print out or cut and paste the bibliographical information right into your research filing system.

● **ONLINE DATABASE SOURCES**   You will likely find that your library provides access to many different bibliographic databases, which allow you to search efficiently and in many cases retrieve full text of periodical articles and other research materials. EBSCO Academic Search Premier, LexisNexis Academic, and InfoTrac are popular databases that span academic disciplines. Other databases such as ERIC, which focuses on education topics, or PsycINFO for psychology, specialize in materials from a particular discipline. FirstSearch and similar services allow you to search multiple databases at once for the information you need.

When McNerny started her search in her library's online databases, she chose EBSCO Academic Search Premier. After looking at the abstract and the full text of an article by Marion Hines, she decided to email them to herself. Once she had them in electronic form, she reasoned, she could refer to them whenever necessary, search them electronically, and retain an electronic record of the information necessary for completing her bibliographical entry. She could also print them if she liked. The electronic bibliographic record of the Hines article appears on page 594.

While library databases usually turn up relatively reliable sources, it is still important for you to evaluate the source using criteria that can help you determine the point of view, currency, and relevance to your project. If you were to find the full text of the Hines article cited on the next page, you could download the piece. The first page provides a great deal of information that you can use to evaluate the source.

Drawing on the citation information, a search of the publication and organizational site, and the biographical information provided, you can do an

The online bibliographic record for the Hines article.

1. Author and title of article
2. Key bibliographic information needed for the citation
3. Other key words that might be helpful in searching databases
4. The URL at which the article can be found
5. The name of the database
6. Link to Paul Simon's book, *The Tongue-Tied American*

Evaluating a Journal Article

Questions to Ask About Journal Articles	Kate McNerny's Notes
Who is the author? What can you determine about this individual or group?	Hines is the president of a chapter of Delta Kappa Gamma and an assistant professor of Foreign languages. She has also served as a curriculum director in a school system and is a member of many professional organizations.
What is the publication or publisher? What is its purpose?	According to its Web site, the mission of The Delta Kappa Gamma Society International is to "promote professional and personal growth of women educators and excellence in education." The Bulletin "is a professional journal containing articles submitted by members. It keeps members apprised of current educational issues and concerns."
What point of view or biases might that purpose suggest?	While this organization is geared toward women educators, it also is devoted to scholarly publication, and so is less likely to have any specific gender biases. There are none evident in the article itself. However, it is clearly an advocacy organization for educators, so it takes the point of view of teachers.
Does the article draw on serious research, citing literature from the field, or just opinions?	The Reference page includes a number of other authoritative sources including primary sources such as government publications and previous publications by Hines.
How accurate and reliable is the information in the article?	The accuracy can be checked by comparison with other studies and by tracing the sources on the reference page.

The Delta Kappa Gamma Bulletin   15

Foreign Language Curriculum Concerns in Times of Conflict

Marion E. Hines

A Congressional committee on intelligence has declared language as the single greatest limitation in the intelligence community; yet, United States foreign language programs are faced with the paradox of having to justify budgets, prove relevance, and resist marginalization. This article discusses federal intervention to encourage reform in foreign language education in times of conflict, and argues that globalization and national security dictate the inclusion of foreign language study in the core curricula of American schools, colleges and universities.

The United States' chronically weak language resources and lack of linguistic preparedness are invariably exposed when events such as the war in Iraq and the September 11 terror strikes threaten the balance of power, peace or détente in global affairs. In order to regain or maintain a competitive edge, the government offers grants to encourage the restructuring of

Marion E. Hines, Ph.D., president of Delta Chapter, Washington, D.C., is an assistant professor in the Department of Modern Languages and Linguistics at Howard University. Dr. Hines is a former curriculum director of foreign language education in the District of Columbia Public Schools. Her professional memberships include the American Council on the Teaching of Foreign Languages, the Modern Language Association, the American Association of Teachers of French, and the College Language Association.

curriculum, to 'retool' educators, and to infuse new technologies. The efforts have been heroic, but they have not succeeded in correcting the overall problem.

The United States has never adopted a language policy. This has led government and school officials as well as the general public to fall back on reactive instead of proactive decision-making in times of crisis. Paul Simon, former Senator from Illinois and author of the now-classic *The Tongue-Tied American: Confronting the Foreign Language Crisis* states, "In every national crisis from the Cold War through Vietnam, Desert Storm, Bosnia and Kosovo, our nation has lamented its foreign language shortfalls. But then, the crisis 'goes away' and we return to business as usual. One of the messages of September

Continued

Questions to Ask about Journal Articles	Kate McNerny's Notes
How current is the article?	The article was published in 2003 and references works from 2002, so it is relatively current. However, since educational policies change frequently, it is important to see if there are any new government documents on the topic or responses to Hines' work.
Does the information fit my own purpose and audience? How?	This piece suggests that foreign language study is somehow relegated to a lower priority than math and science. This might provide another point of comparison. Also, since Bergentoft discusses international policies on foreign language education, I can compare U.S. policy with that in other countries.

evaluation of the article's reliability and currency by answering the questions below. You can also start to consider its relevance to your topic and how this piece relates to others you have found.

QUESTIONS FOR EVALUATING JOURNAL SOURCES

- Who is the author? What can you determine about this individual or group?
- What is the publication or publisher? What is its purpose?
- What point of view or biases might that purpose suggest?
- Does the article draw on serious research, citing literature from the field, or just opinions?
- How accurate and reliable is the information in the article?
- How current is the article?
- Does the information fit my own purpose and audience? How?

As this set of questions and the evaluation on page 595 suggest, the evaluation and notetaking process you use as you find library database sources accomplishes several things. It helps familiarize you with each source, it helps you better understand the key organization and publishing sites for information on your topic (especially if you pay attention to the reference pages), and it helps the conversation on the topic that you are trying to enter come into focus as you compare the various sources you find. The process, then, is cumulative and recursive—each new piece of information can help you consider that which you have already found and that which you might look for to further your research.

● **OPEN WEB SOURCES**   It is no longer sufficient to refer to the Internet or worldwide web as a single entity. Those terms really just refer to information that can be accessed through an open Web search engine such as Google. But

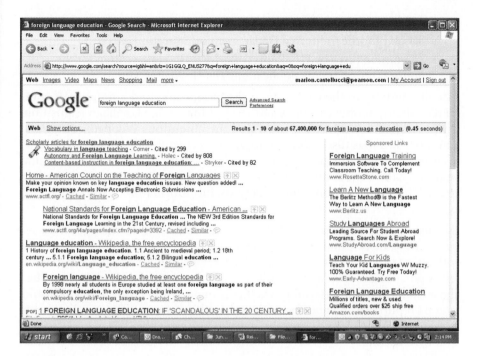

how and where you find this information—through a Web search engine—is less crucial than the work you must do to choose among the items that those searches turn up.

Using a Search Engine   The first problem we face when doing a search on the open Web is the sheer mass of data that unfocused searches can yield. The second problem is the mixture of source types that an open Web search can produce. A single Google search may turn up scholarly sources, commercial sites, blogs, wikis, personal pages, and Facebook pages. This means that you will need to be especially vigilant as you evaluate the reliability and relevance of the sources you find.

For example, you might do a Google search on "foreign language education," and the first screen that will show up of the 67 million hits would look like the one shown above. On this one screen, you will find a number of source types. You are offered the following:

- a link for "scholarly sources" on the topic;
- a statement by the American Council on the Teaching of Foreign Language;
- a paper on the "scandalous" nature of American foreign language policy from the Stanford University Web site, authored by Leon Panetta, currently the CIA director, but previously the assistant to the Director

of the Department of Health, Education, and Welfare and Distinguished Scholar for the California Department of Education.

- an opinion piece by U.S. Representative Rush Holt, written for the political liberal online publication, *The Huffington Post*.

Also, if you look to the right side of the page, you'd find a number of commercial sites that offer products and services for foreign language acquisition; if you scrolled down further, you'd find the ubiquitous Wikipedia entry and a number of blogs discussing the topic, with contributors ranging from experts to those with an axe to grind. Evaluating which sources (if any) would be useful can be quite difficult. But if you overlook these sources altogether, you might also miss some potentially useful information. That's why your evaluation process is crucial.

Evaluating Web Sources   Choosing relevant sources from the open Web requires the same care and attention that is required of judging library sources—with an extra dose of patience and diligence. Creating the most focused search terms possible can help a great deal. The active notetaking activities described above can help you to determine whether a source you are considering really fits your own purpose and audience. Discarding those sources that are not directly relevant will pay dividends later as you try to bring together this material within your own writing.

There are also some particular challenges with evaluating Web sources for reliability. For example, we are often unable to judge the context of the information without looking a bit deeper. When we read an article in the *New York Times,* for example, we can expect a certain level of accuracy and reliability that comes from the editorial process; conversely, when we read an article in a supermarket tabloid, we know we should expect very little accuracy. We know not to quote a tabloid article about diet supplements when we are writing an academic paper about health and nutrition. Even on television, we know when we're watching *CNN News* and when we're seeing an infomercial. On the Internet, however, we may have very few context cues to help us judge what we're reading.

All of this is not to suggest, then, that open Web sources are to be wholly avoided. There are excellent resources that can be useful and authoritative. If you adapt the source evaluation techniques discussed in this chapter to Web sites and blogs as well, you can distinguish between those that are appropriate to serious research, and those that are best discarded. Here are some questions to ask about those types of sources.

QUESTIONS FOR EVALUATING OPEN WEB SOURCES

- Who is the author and/or sponsoring organization? What can you determine about this individual or group?
- What is the purpose of the site? What biases might that purpose suggest?

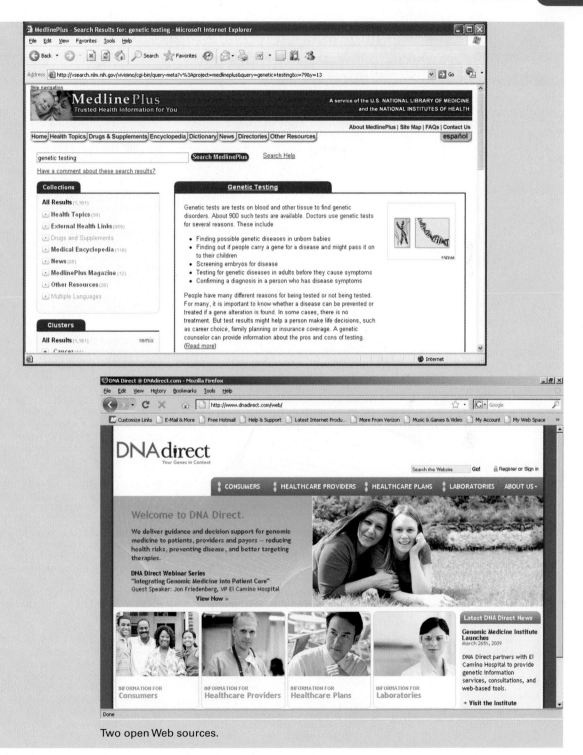

Two open Web sources.

Evaluating Open Web Sources

Questions for Evaluating Open Web Sources	Notes on Medline Plus	Notes on DNA Direct
Who is the author and/or sponsoring organization? What can you determine about this individual or group?	This government site is directed by Dr. Donald A.B. Lindberg, Director, National Library of Medicine. It is sponsored by the National Institutes of Health.	This is a commercial site that states its goal as bringing "the power of personalized medicine to patients, consumers and healthcare professionals" through genetic testing. The board of directors includes more business people than medical professionals.
What is the purpose of the site? What biases might that purpose suggest?	The site "brings together authoritative information from NLM, the National Institutes of Health (NIH), and other government agencies and health-related organizations" and gives "easy access to medical journal articles." The site notes that "there is no advertising on this site, nor does MedlinePlus endorse any company or product."	While it has a Standards page that lists the ways that it helps consumers make decisions about genetic testing, it also has some features that are clearly designed to make its product attractive to customers.
Is the site presented in an authoritative and thoughtful way? Does it draw upon serious research or just opinions?	It provides information "from the world's largest medical library, the National Library of Medicine." And "extensive information from the National Institutes of Health and other trusted sources on over 750 diseases and conditions."	The site makes claims on its Standards page to select only scientifically valid tests supported by the literature. But it also discusses its marketing standards, and much of the site's literature is press releases, news stories, and customer testimonies. It also features many photos that seem more like marketing than serious information for my purposes.
How current is the information?	The site is updated daily.	The site was last updated in 2008, and many of the links are from 2003–2008.
Does the information fit my own purpose and audience? How?	The site provides up-to-date information on genetic testing and links to scholarly data (in readable form) about the latest research on the topic. It can help me to determine the value and dangers of genetic testing directly to consumers.	Since the site is largely about helping consumers make informed decisions about whether to be tested, it could be useful to demonstrate the uses of genetic testing that consumers consider. It is less useful for detailed scientific information on genetic testing.
Is this site reliable and relevant to my project?	This site is useful because of its authoritative sources and the way it attempts to make complex information understandable. It does not seem to be selling anything, though it takes the perspective of medical professionals and scientists with a stake in advancing their field. Overall, it should provide worthwhile information.	It is not reliable as a source of unbiased information on the topic of genetic testing, but I could analyze this and other sites to show how genetic testing is marketed to consumers. That can help to show both the potential benefits and the need for caution when science and business are allied.

- Is the site presented in an authoritative and thoughtful way? Does it draw upon serious research or just opinions?
- How current is the information?
- Does the information fit my own purpose and audience? How?

Consider, for example, two sites you might find on genetic testing, Medline Plus and DNA Direct. Using the evaluation questions above, you could evaluate these sources as shown on page 600.

Evaluating Web 2.0 Sources   The challenges of evaluating open Web sources is increased by the Web 2.0 world in which we live. In Web 2.0, Internet users not only *seek* information, but regularly *post* information to the Web. The most obvious examples of this interactive Web are wikis and blogs, both of which consist of a constant stream of postings by all types of individuals, from top-notch experts to novices, from those who value objective research to those with their own agendas—and those who just like to subvert the process. We have already seen several examples of how wikis work in this chapter.

Another source of information that has driven the Web 2.0 movement is blogs. While blogs began as open, and often personal, journals, they are now sites of public debate. As such, blogs are useful sites for gauging public opinion; at the same time, they require the same critical eye that you would use on any type of Web site, and then some. As part of the Web 2.0 movement, they offer a voice to anyone who wishes to post, without regard to the expertise of the author (though many blog authors *are* experts) and without the refereeing and editing process of published journals. For that reason, you should consider not only what blogs to select, but how to use them. Using a blog to show the wide range of opinions on a topic can be useful; citing information from them as authoritative (as with wikis) is usually not advisable, unless you then go to the primary sources of information. When evaluating a blog, you should ask these questions.

QUESTIONS FOR EVALUATING BLOGS

- Who is the author and/or sponsoring organization? What kinds of people tend to contribute to this blog?
- What is the purpose of the site? What biases might that purpose suggest?
- Does the owner of the blog manage and vet the postings? Does he/she provide commentary from an expert position?
- How current are the postings? How active is the blog? Is there an archive of past postings?
- Does the information fit my own purpose and audience? How?
- Is this site reliable and relevant to my project?

Some blogs are maintained by experts who provide running commentary on the ideas that are discussed on the site. For example, *Bilingual Talk* is a blog

Evaluating a Blog

Questions for Evaluating Blogs	Kate McNerny's Notes on Bilingual Talk Blog
Who is the author and/or sponsoring organization? What kinds of people tend to contribute to this blog?	The author is an expert in multilingual education with an M.A. in education from Berkeley and experience in teaching and educational administration.
What is the purpose of the site? What biases might that purpose suggest?	The site seems to be devoted to promoting multilingual education in the U.S., to monitoring news and policy changes, and to inviting comments and discussion about those changes.
Does the owner of the blog manage and vet the postings? Does he/she provide commentary from an expert position?	Yes, Ms. Sanchez posts news stories and comments upon them, then invites responses.
How current are the postings? How active is the blog? Is there an archive of past postings?	The last posting was two months ago, so it seems a bit spotty. The blog does not seem particularly active, with 0 comments to some postings and only a handful to others. Yes, there is an archive dating back to 2006, but there are often few postings.
Does the information fit my own purpose and audience? How?	The links to the news and policy articles can be useful, though I may need to trace them to the primary source information. Since the comments are so spotty, it will give me less information about public opinion.
Is this site reliable and relevant to my project?	Many of the news articles might be applicable, but since the site is more about English language learners than about native U.S. citizens learning a foreign language, it is not as directly relevant as other sources.

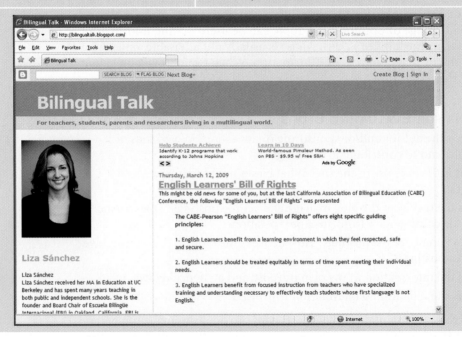

site that is maintained by Liza Sánchez, the founder and Board Chair of *Escuela Bilingüe Internacional* (EBI) in Oakland, California (see page 602). Sanchez is an expert on foreign language education who received her MA in Education at UC Berkeley and who has taught in both public and independent schools. The blog posts news and information on foreign language education (including links to full stories) "for teachers, students, parents and researchers living in a multilingual world" and invites comments from readers.

As a researcher like Kate McNerny, you could use this information in a number of ways. You could read the opinions of Sánchez in light of the other information on the topic you have found, and make note of the reader's comments. You could follow the links she posts, many of which provide an overview of public policy and opinion on multilingual education. But if you want to take full advantage of a blog, and if you start early enough, you could post your own comments and queries to the site as a way of gathering more primary source information—giving you access to ideas and opinions from readers from all over the country (or all over the world, in some cases). You can learn a great deal about public opinion in this way.

When evaluating blogs, you will need to pay special attention to who is contributing to these sources. In many cases, those who would visit and contribute to such a site already have a specific point of view or bias; in this case, it is likely that most of the visitors will already be in favor of multilingual education. That doesn't necessarily mean that the information is not useful, but it does mean that you'll need to acknowledge the likely biases when you assess the information and again when you incorporate it into your own draft.

In sum, you should treat open Web sources with a healthy skepticism. While it would be shortsighted to ignore the information available via the Web, it is also important that you contextualize that which you find within a variety of other, more authoritative sources. If you combine open Web information with library sources and primary information, you will likely have well-rounded and innovative research. And if you use open Web sources much like you treat reference sources—as a starting point that you will use to drive other research—they can be quite useful.

Writing Processes

Once you've collected information for your research paper, you may feel overwhelmed by the task of shaping it into a coherent form. You can take control of your data, however, by reconsidering your purpose and thesis. Reread the notes you've been collecting, especially those that have attempted to synthesize your sources, and revise your working thesis.

Think about the project globally and decide how the various pieces of what you've collected can fit together into the argument you now feel compelled to make about your topic, to your audience, and in a particular genre. The goal is to find an organizational structure that will make sense to your readers.

SHAPING

To shape the materials you have collected into a draft, you might begin by answering the following questions:

QUESTIONS FOR SHAPING YOUR RESEARCHED PAPER

Narrowed topic or question:	What aspect of your subject is most interesting to you now?
Research:	Does your research display a variety of perspectives and types of sources? Do you have enough solid research to help support your claim? If not, what more do you need and how will you search for it?
Purpose:	Is your purpose primarily to inform, explain, evaluate, describe a problem and propose a solution, or argue a claim? If your purpose is argumentative, is your claim debatable?
Working thesis:	After the research you have done, what thesis, claim, or proposal do you want to impress upon your readers? Is your claim arguable? If not, should you adjust it?
Audience:	Analyze your audience. How can you interest them in your subject? What aspects of your collected data are most appropriate for your audience?
Genre:	What genre will work best for your assignment or your purpose and audience? Will graphics and images be appropriate for this genre and audience?

66 Writing is the hardest work in the world not involving heavy lifting. 99
—PETE HAMILL, JOURNALIST

These questions will help you to pinpoint problems you may be having with the project, help you identify solutions, and increase the likelihood of your success. As you shape, draft, and revise your research paper, you may continue to refocus your topic and question, refine your thesis, or revise your sense of audience. At this point, you may also decide to search for a bit more information, if your claim isn't fully supportable with what you have.

● **PLAN**   Your next step is to design some order, sequence, plan, or outline for your research paper. Forcing yourself to immediately write an outline, however, simply may not work. You should have an idea from your previous papers about how your writing process works best, but if you're stuck, feeling frustrated, or overwhelmed, try several of the following strategies.

- *Review strategies for shaping* that are appropriate for your particular purpose. If you are arguing for a certain claim, reread the shaping strategies discussed in Chapter 11. If you are evaluating something or analyzing a problem and proposing a solution, review the strategies discussed in Chapter 9 or 10.
- *Explain to a friend or classmate your purpose, audience, and working thesis.* Then try to explain how you might proceed.
- *Try freewriting, looping, or clustering* to develop a plan.
- *Reread the notes you made to summarize the various sources you found and look for recurring trends.*
- *Take a break.* Let your ideas simmer for a while. Go for a walk. Work on assignments for another course. Go jogging or swimming. Let your mind run on automatic pilot for a while—the information and ideas in your mind may begin organizing themselves into an initial "sketch outline" without your conscious effort.
- *Try branching or treeing your main ideas.* On paper or at the chalkboard, begin with your topic and draw the trunk and main branches of your topics. Try to explain your sketch or chalkboard drawing to someone.

Think of these activities as a circle: Begin at any point, work in either direction, and repeat them as necessary. When something starts to work, stay with it for a while. If you start to block or become frustrated, go on to the next activity.

● **WORKING OUTLINE**   If the shaping activities helped you discover a basic design or plan, translate it into a working outline. If not, you may need to begin drafting in order to *discover* an outline—sometimes the shape of your piece becomes clearer as you write. Kate McNerny decided to follow a pattern for writing an argument. Although she modified it considerably to change her purpose to problem solving, the sketch outline helped her organize her ideas and source material so she could begin drafting.

I. Introduction: Comments—quotations from informal survey—why people feel they don't need to know a foreign language.

Mention study on misconceptions of school-aged children about Russian children.

II. Narration: Foreign-language studies' position in other countries as opposed to U.S.

Mention "Official English" here?

Include example of European requirements?

Statistics on how many Americans are actually competent in another language.

Mention bills to require a state language?

U.S. position in world as far as power, trade.

III. Partition: American students should be required to study a foreign language throughout the six years of junior and senior high school. To increase number of students studying foreign language, we need changes in administrators and teachers, changes in students, and changes in state and national policies.

IV. Arguments: An increase in number of students studying foreign languages would:

Help to improve diplomatic relations with other countries—peace cannot be achieved without this.

Change Americans' attitudes toward foreigners and change foreigners' attitudes toward Americans.

Facilitate international trade and other business.

Increase jobs for students abroad and at home.

Without requirement, no incentive for many students.

V. Refutation: Not necessary because other countries can speak English. (This is more an argument against learning a language, not against a requirement.)

Not essential for quality education.

As requirement, would detract from other important subjects.

Not enough federal, state, or local money to change number of foreign-language courses offered.

VI. Conclusion: Call for action on part of federal government.

Contrary to popular belief, we are not an isolated country.

A required study of languages will bring us one step closer to global understanding and peace.

DRAFTING

At this point, some of the most difficult work is behind you. Congratulate yourself—there aren't many people who know as much as you do right now about your subject. You are an authority: You have information, statistics, statements, ideas from other writers and researchers, and your own experiences and observations at your fingertips. You also have a variety of materials to keep you going: annotated articles, summaries, syntheses that show the connections between sources, and consistent attempts to formulate and re-formulate your thesis. It is now time to articulate your own position on the topic by drafting your own piece of writing.

While drafting a researched project has many similarities to the drafting processes discussed throughout this book, the key difference is the need to successfully incorporate the ideas of others toward your own ends. Effective use of sources requires both creativity and scrupulous honesty. On the one hand, you want to use other people's information and ideas when and where they serve *your* purpose and *your* ideas. On the other hand, the sources you cite or quote must be used *fairly* and *honestly*. You must quote accurately, cite your sources in your text, and document those sources accurately. And you must give credit for other writers' ideas and information.

This honest incorporation of sources into your draft can come in two stages. First, after you have written your first draft, you might go back and compare what you have written to the notes you have taken. Consider where in that draft the claims you are making or information you are presenting has come from one of your sources, and add an in-text citation. In some cases, that information or claim may draw upon more than one source.

Also, as you re-read your draft, you should ask what claims you are making need further support in order to be credible. When you find a claim that needs support, follow two steps. First, look back over your notes and annotated articles to see if you have the evidence you need to support that claim; if so, add in a summary, paraphrase, or quotation from that source, along with an in-text citation. If you can't find enough support for your claim, you have two options.

1. If you believe that the claim is credible and important to your argument, do another search for information that will help you to support the claim.
2. If the claim seems tangential to your argument or is not supported by the evidence you have, you may need to revise or discard that claim.

Though this process might seem inefficient, it is not; quite to the contrary, this is the part of the drafting process that will allow you to build on only the premises that have strong support and help you to follow the information to viable conclusions.

● **WHAT SOURCES TO CITE**   Since you have learned a great deal about your topic through your research, it is natural that as you draft, some information will come naturally from your head. But if this information got into

> 66 Writing a book is not as tough as it is to haul 35 people around the country and sweat like a horse five nights a week. 99
>
> —BETTE MIDLER, SINGER, ACTOR, AUTHOR

your head through the research of some other individual, it is important that you give due credit and that you use the authority of that source to support your own argument. So what sources do you need to cite? You must cite a source for any fact or bit of information that is not *general knowledge*. Obviously, what is "general knowledge" varies from one writer and audience to another. **As a rule, however, document any information or fact that you did not know before you began your research.** You may know, for example, that America spends more money on defense than it does on education. However, if you state that the defense budget for the previous year is greater than the total amount spent on education for the past forty years, then cite the source for that fact.

Knowing when you must cite a source for an idea, however, can be tricky. You do not need to indicate a source for *your* ideas, of course. But if you find a source that agrees with your idea, or if you suspect that your idea may be related to ideas from a particular source, cite that source. A citation gives your idea additional credibility: You show your reader that another authority shares your perception.

● **AVOIDING PLAGIARISM**   Considering the amount of time that you have spent reading and studying your topic, it can be hard to distinguish the genesis of an idea—and that can lead to unintentionally forgetting to acknowledge your source. So in the drafting stage and in the revision process, you should be especially vigilant about avoiding plagiarism. Plagiarism occurs when we use the language, ideas, or visual materials from another person or text without acknowledging the source—even unintentionally. Use the following guidelines to avoid plagiarism.

- Do not use language, ideas, or graphics from any essay, text, or visual image that you find *online*, in the *library,* or from *commercial sources* without acknowledging the source.

- Do not use language, ideas, or visuals from *any other student's essay* without acknowledging the source.

Students who plagiarize typically fail the course and face disciplinary action by the college or university.

Sometimes, however, students create problems by rushing or by not knowing how to quote or paraphrase accurately and fairly. You can avoid this *inadvertent* plagiarism by quoting accurately from your sources, by paraphrasing using your own words, and by citing your sources accurately.

Let's assume that you are working with the following passage, taken from the opening paragraph of an article by Marion E. Hines, "Foreign Language Curriculum Concerns in Times of Conflict," which appeared in the *Delta Kappa Gamma Bulletin* in 2003:

Original: The United States' chronically weak language resources and lack of linguistic preparedness are invariably exposed when events such as the war in Iraq and the September 11 terror strikes threaten the balance of power, peace or detente in global affairs. In order to regain or maintain a competitive edge, the government offers grants to encourage the restructuring of curriculum, to "retool" educators, and to infuse new technologies. The efforts have been heroic, but they have not succeeded in correcting the overall problem.

Plagiarism: Every college needs to require a foreign language, in part because we need to communicate better in times of crisis. Events such as the war in Iraq and the terror strikes of September 11 have exposed our lack of linguistic preparedness. Better knowledge of foreign languages would help us communicate with people from different cultures or religions.

Explanation: This writer uses several phrases lifted directly from the source (see highlighted text) without using quotation marks or acknowledging the source.

Proper Citation: Every college needs to require a foreign language in part because we need to communicate better in times of crisis. Marion E. Hines, an assistant professor in modern languages and linguistics at Howard University, argues that "the United States' chronically weak language resources and lack of linguistic preparedness" result in our inability to communicate with people from different cultures or religions (15).

Explanation: In this passage, the writer cites the author before introducing the quotation, uses quotation marks for words and phrases that appear in the article, and uses the proper citation format at the end of the sentence. This article by Marion E. Hines would also be cited in the Works Cited or References page at the end of the essay.

As you take notes and write your drafts, practice using proper citation practices. If at any point you have a question about how to cite your sources accurately, recheck the sections in this chapter or ask your instructor.

● **HOW TO CITE SOURCES IN YOUR TEXT**   Knowing *what* to cite and how to distinguish your ideas from those of others is the first step. But you also need to know *how* to cite your sources in a form that your audience will recognize and be able to use easily. In the text of your paper, you will usually need to cite your sources according to either the Modern Language Association (MLA) style or the American Psychological Association (APA) style. Remember: Choose either the MLA style or the APA style and stick with it. Don't mix styles.

According to the MLA style, the in-text citation contains the author and page number of your source (Torres 50). No comma appears between author and page number. (If the author is unknown, identify the title and page number of your source. Italicize book titles; place quotation marks around article titles.)

According to the APA style, the in-text citation contains author and date (Torres, 1996). Use a comma between author and date. If you are quoting, include a page number after the author and date (Torres, 1996, p. 50). Use a *p.* (or *pp.* for more than one page) before the page number(s).

The in-text citation (either MLA or APA) refers readers to the end of your paper, where you give complete information about each source in a "Works Cited" (MLA) or "References" (APA) list. For illustration purposes, the following examples use MLA style. See the "Documenting Sources" section (pp. 613–634) for examples of both APA and MLA styles.

● **IDENTIFY CITED REFERENCES (MLA STYLE)** Once you have decided that a fact, a paraphrase, or a direct quotation contributes to your thesis and will make a strong impression on your reader, use the following guidelines for in-text citation.

- **Identify in the text the persons or source for the fact, paraphrased idea, or quotation.**

As two foreign-language teachers noted, "Like it or not, we are members of a world community consisting of hundreds of nations, and our fates are closely intertwined" (Long and Long 366).

Note: The parentheses and the period *follow* the final quotation marks.

- **If you cite the author in your sentence, the parentheses will contain only the page reference.**

According to Paul Simon, former member of the President's Commission on Foreign Language, the United States should erect a sign at each port of entry that reads, "WELCOME TO THE UNITED STATES—WE CANNOT SPEAK YOUR LANGUAGE" (1).

- **Use block format (beginning on a new line, indented one inch from the left margin, and double-spaced) for quotations of five lines or more.**

Educator Gerald Unks points out two instances in which a lack of language proficiency caused companies to initiate fatal marketing programs.

> When Pepsi-Cola went after the Chinese market, "Come Alive with Pepsi" was translated into Chinese in Taiwan as "Pepsi Brings Your Ancestors Back from the Dead." No Sale! General Motors sought to sell its Nova in South America, oblivious to the fact that "No va" in Spanish means "It doesn't go." (24)

Note: In block quotations, the final punctuation mark comes *before* the parentheses, and no quotation marks are used to set off the cited material.

- **Vary your introductions to quotations.**

Educator Gerald Unks claims that "only 15 percent of American high school students study a foreign language. Only 8 percent of our colleges require credit in a foreign language for admission (down from 34 percent in 1966)" (24).

The problem is that high school students are not taking foreign languages, and most colleges no longer require a foreign language for admission: "Only 15 percent of American high school students study a foreign language. Only 8 percent of our colleges require credit in a foreign language for admission (down from 34 percent in 1966)" (Unks 24).

- **Edit quotations when necessary to condense or clarify.** Use ellipsis marks, which are three points preceded and followed by a space (. . .), if you omit words from the middle of a quoted sentence.

As two foreign language teachers noted, "We are members of a world community . . . and our fates are closely intertwined" (Long and Long 366).

> If you omit words from the end of a quoted sentence or omit sentences from a long quoted passage, place a period after the last word quoted before the omission; follow it with ellipsis marks—for a total of four periods. Be sure that you have a complete sentence both before and after the four points.

Paul Simon advises us that our nation's lack of language proficiency may have been a partial cause of our disastrous policies in Vietnam:

> Vietnam and the Middle East have taught us that our security position is not solely a matter of dealing with the Warsaw Pact countries or the giants among the nations. Before our heavy intervention in Vietnam, fewer than five American-born experts on Vietnam, Cambodia, or Laos . . . could speak with ease one of the languages of that area. . . . What if—a big if—we had had . . . a mere twenty Americans who spoke Vietnamese fluently, who understood their culture, aspirations, and political history? Maybe, just maybe, we would have avoided that conflict. (9)

Note: The first line is indented an additional half-inch because in the source the quotation begins a new paragraph.

> In some cases you may want to change the wording of a quotation or add explanatory words of your own to clarify your quotation. If you do so, clearly indicate your changes or additions by placing them within square brackets.

As Simon suggests, if only a few Americans knew Vietnamese, then "maybe, just maybe, we would have avoided [the Vietnam War]" (9).

REVISING

You have been revising your research essay since the first day of the project. You thought about several subjects, for example, but you chose only one. You started with a focus but revised it as you thought, read, and wrote more. You tested and synthesized ideas and continually revised your working thesis as you learned more. Now, however, you have a complete draft to revise, and that too requires a few steps in order to make the process as effective and efficient as possible.

First, assess the adequacy of the content: If there is something missing in your data, be willing to track down the information. If a favorite source or quotation no longer seems relevant, have the courage to delete it. If the evidence for one side of an argument appears stronger than you initially thought, change your position and your thesis. *Being willing to make such changes is not a sign of poor research and writing. Often, in fact, it demonstrates that you have become more knowledgeable and sophisticated about your subject.*

Then, think about the overall organization of the paper. You might, for example, just skim the beginnings of sections and paragraphs to see if they are in a reasonable and coherent order. If an example on page 4 would work better as a lead-in for the whole paper, reorder your material accordingly. You might even try to reverse engineer a new outline. If the outline you create from the draft seems to have gaps or rough transitions, try to re-organize or fill in gaps in the logic.

After you have gotten the structure and evidence of the paper in place (which might take a few revising sessions), it's time to move on to matters of style. Using techniques that you've been discussing in this course, check to see if each paragraph is a coherent unit, if sentences are precise and clear, and if your word choices are appropriate to the audience and purpose.

After you have finished your first revision, ask friends or classmates to give you their responses. Accept their criticism gracefully, but ask them to explain *why* they think certain changes would help. Would they help to make your purposes clearer? Would they be more appropriate for your audience? Don't be intimidated and feel that you must make every change that readers suggest. You must make the final decisions.

GUIDELINES FOR REVISION

- **Revise in Stages:** Don't try to multi-task; it is more efficient and effective to complete one revision task at a time, beginning with large issues such as organization and working your way down to careful editing.

* **Check that each claim you have made is supported:** Read the draft, pausing each time you are making a claim, and be sure that there is adequate evidence to make that claim credible. If possible, ask a classmate to try to locate unsupported claims as well.

* **Check that the types of supporting evidence you have included are appropriate to your audience, purpose, and genre:** Remember that the amount and type of information required of an academic paper might be very different than that of a Web site or pamphlet, and that some audiences value specific kinds of information (statistics, quotations, etc.) more than others.

* **Check to be sure that each piece of information is properly cited:** Using the guidelines in this chapter, be sure that all information gathered from sources has an in-text citation that corresponds with the Works Cited or Reference list.

* **Consider the tone, style, and grammar of your paper:** Revise any sentences or word choices that are not consistent with your purpose, audience, and genre or your document.

* **Review the Works Cited and References page carefully:** There are very strict rules for properly citing sources in both MLA and APA style; if you are unsure of those rules, use the guidelines in this chapter as a reference.

DOCUMENTING SOURCES

Both the MLA and APA documentation styles require citation of sources in the text of your paper, followed by a Works Cited (MLA style) or References (APA style) list at the end of your paper. Use footnotes only for content or supplementary notes that explain a point covered in the text or offer additional information. *Note:* MLA in-text documentation and Works Cited documentation are explained here. See pages 627–634 for APA in-text documentation and References format.

● **IN-TEXT DOCUMENTATION: MLA STYLE** In the MLA style, give the author's name and the page numbers in parentheses following your use of a fact, paraphrase, or direct quotation from a source. These in-text citations then refer your readers to the complete documentation of the source in a Works Cited or Works Consulted list at the end of the paper. As you cite your sources in the text, use the following guidelines.

If you cite the author in the text, indicate only the page number in parentheses.

According to Vicki Galloway, Project Director for the American Council on the Teaching of Foreign Languages, a student's horizons will not be broadened by "grammar lectures and manipulative classroom exercises" (33).

If the author is unknown, use a short version of the title in the parentheses.

Most students do not realize that their SAT and ACT scores increase with every year that they study a foreign language (*Knowing Other Languages*).

If the source is unpublished, cite the name or title used in your Works Cited.

In an informal interview, one university administrator noted that funding of foreign-language study has steadily decreased over the past ten years (Meyers).

If the source is from the Internet or the Web, use the author, or if there is no author, use the title. Include page or paragraph numbers if provided (as, for example, in a PDF document).

Many Web sites now provide detailed information about how to plan a study-abroad semester or year (*Foreign Language*).

If your bibliography contains more than one work by an author, cite the author, a short title, and page numbers. The following examples show various ways of citing a reference to Paul Simon, *The Tongue-Tied American.*

In *The Tongue-Tied American*, Simon explains that students can earn a doctorate degree in the United States without ever studying a foreign language (2).

As Simon notes, "It is even possible to earn a doctorate here without studying any foreign language" (*Tongue-Tied* 2).

In the United States, one can earn a doctorate degree without studying a single foreign language (Simon, *Tongue-Tied* 2).

Note: Use a comma between author and title, but not between title and page number.

If a source has two or three authors, cite all authors' names in the text or in the parentheses.

A recent study sampling 536 secondary schools revealed that 91 percent did not require foreign-language credits for graduation (Ranwez and Rodgers 98).

Note: If there are three authors, use commas to separate them, e.g., (Ranwez, Rogers, and Smith 98).

If a source has more than three authors, you may either list all authors' names, separated by commas, or simply give the name of the author listed first followed by the abbreviation *et al.,* meaning "and others."

> Teachers should integrate the study of history, culture, politics, literature, and religion of a particular region with the study of language (Berryman et al. 96).

If you cite several volumes from the same source, precede the page number with the volume number and a colon, as indicated.

> Language and grammar can be taught with real-life contexts or scenarios (Valdman 3:82).

Note: If you cite only one volume of a multivolume work, you need not list the volume number in your in-text citation, but you must list it in your Works Cited.

If you are citing a quotation or information that is itself cited in another source, use the abbreviation *qtd. in* for "quoted in" to indicate that you have used an indirect source for your information or quotation. (If possible, however, check the original source.)

> As Sue Berryman and her colleagues explain, "The course is developed as a world tour during which time the students take a vicarious trip . . . to become saturated in every aspect of a particular area of the globe" (qtd. in Simon 96).

If you cite two or more authors as sources for a fact, idea, or plan, separate the citations with a semicolon, as follows.

> Most recently, two prominent foreign language educators have published plans to coordinate foreign-language studies (Lambert 9–19; Lange 70–96).

Content or Supplementary Notes You may include footnotes or endnotes in your paper if you have an important idea, a comment on your text, or additional information or sources *that would interrupt the flow of your ideas in the text.* During her research, for example, McNerny read about the movement to make English the "official language" of the United States. She didn't want to digress in her paper, so she described the controversy in a supplementary endnote. Here is a first draft of that note.

> 1. Several states currently have bills before their legislatures to make English the "official language." Proponents of these bills argue that immigrants need incentives to learn English. Many opponents from ethnic and civil rights groups believe these bills are racist (McBee 64). If Americans

were all educated in foreign languages, these bills would be unnecessary. Americans' ignorance and fear of foreign languages are probably a reason that these bills are so popular.

● **WORKS CITED LIST: MLA STYLE** After you have revised your essay and are certain that you will not change any in-text documentation, you are ready to write your list of sources. Depending on what you include, it will be one of the following:

- A Works Cited list (only those works actually cited in your essay)
- A Works Consulted list (works cited and works you read)
- A Selected Bibliography (works cited and the most important other works)
- An Annotated List of Works Cited (works cited, followed by a short description and evaluation of each source)

A Works Cited list alphabetically orders, by author's last name, all published and unpublished sources cited in your research paper. Each citation indicates the medium of publication of the source you consulted, such as print, Web, DVD, television, and so on. If the author is unknown, alphabetize by the first word (excluding *A, An,* or *The*) of the title. Use the following abbreviations for missing information other than an unknown author:

n.p. (no place of publication)
n.p. (no publisher given)
n.d. (no date of publication given)
n. pag. (no pagination in source)

The first line of each citation begins at the left margin, and succeeding lines are indented one-half inch. Double-space the entire Works Cited list.

Following are examples of MLA-style entries in a Works Cited list, organized by kind of source. Use the citations as models for your own Works Cited list. For additional information and examples, see *MLA Handbook for Writers of Research Papers* (7th ed., 2009).

Note: In your essay or manuscript, citations of titles of articles, poems, and short stories should be surrounded by quotation marks ("The Story of an Hour"). Titles of books, plays, novels, magazines, journals, or collections should be italicized (*Caramelo, National Geographic*); note that new MLA guidelines suggest italics instead of underlining.

Print Periodicals: MLA Style

For all articles published in print periodicals, give the author's name, the title of the article, and the name of the publication. For newspapers and magazines, add complete dates and inclusive page numbers. Use the first page

Citing an Article in a Periodical

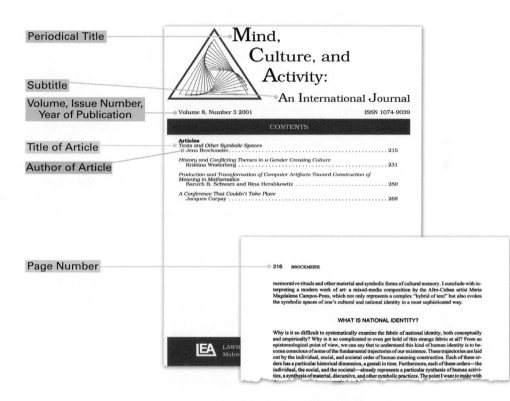

Periodical Title

Subtitle

Volume, Issue Number, Year of Publication

Title of Article

Author of Article

Page Number

MLA

Works Cited Format

Brockmeier, Jens. "Texts and Other Symbolic Spaces." *Mind, Culture, and Activity: An International Journal* 8.3 (2001): 215-30. Print.

In-Text Citation

Educational psychologist Jens Brockmeier defines national identity as "a synthesis of material, discursive, and other symbolic practices" (216).

APA

References Page Format

Brockmeier, J. (2001). Texts and other symbolic spaces. *Mind, Culture, and Activity: An International Journal, 8*, 215-230.

In-Text Citation

Educational psychologist Jens Brockmeier (2001) defines national identity as "a synthesis of material, discursive, and other symbolic practices" (p. 216).

number and a plus sign if an article is not printed on consecutive pages. For all professional journals, add volume numbers, issue numbers, years of publication, and inclusive page numbers. Add *Print* as the medium of access for articles in printed periodicals. See page 623 for articles you access on the Web or in online databases.

Article in a Weekly or Biweekly Magazine

Hersh, Seymour M. "Chain of Command." *New Yorker* 17 May 2004: 38–43. Print.

Article in a Monthly or Bimonthly Magazine

Appenzeller, Tim. "The End of Cheap Oil." *National Geographic* June 2004:
    80–109. Print.

Morrison, Ann M., Randall P. White, and Ellen Van Velsor. "Executive Women:
    Substance Plus Style." *Psychology Today* Aug. 1987: 18+. Print.

Article in a Scholarly Journal

According to the newest MLA guidelines, all entries for scholarly publications such as professional journals should now include the volume, issue, year of publication, page numbers (when available), and the medium of access. For an illustration of a scholarly journal article and its citation, see page 617.

Brodkey, Linda. "Writing Ethnographic Narratives." *Written Communication* 9.1
    (1987): 25–50. Print.

Swope, Christopher. "Panel OKs Bill to Make English Official Government
    Language." *Congressional Quarterly Weekly Report* 54.1 (1996): 2128–29. Print.

(For page numbers over 100, use only two digits for the final page citation: 2128–29.)

Article in a Newspaper

Omit the introductory article (*New York Times* instead of *The New York Times*). If the masthead indicates an edition (late ed.), include it in your entry. Newspaper articles do not usually appear on consecutive pages, so indicate the page number on which the article begins and then put a plus sign + to indicate that the article continues on later pages. Indicate section numbers (A, B, C) when appropriate.

Harmon, Amy. "In New Tests for Fetal Defects, Agonizing Choices for Parents."
    New York Times 20 June 2004, natl. ed.: A1+. Print.

Unsigned Article in a Newspaper

"A Jet Crash That Defies Resolution." *Los Angeles Times* 5 Sept. 2001: A1. Print.

Op Ed Piece

Fish, Stanley. "When Principles Get in the Way." *New York Times* 26 Dec 1996, late
    ed.: A27. Print.

Published Interview

Palin, Sarah. Interview by Katie Couric. *CBS Evening News.* CBS, New York. 30
    Sept. 2008. Television.

Citing a Book

FREAKONOMICS

A ROGUE ECONOMIST EXPLORES
THE HIDDEN SIDE OF EVERYTHING

"Prepare to be dazzled."
— Malcolm Gladwell, author of *The Tipping Point* and *Blink*

NEW YORK
TIMES
BESTSELLER

STEVEN D. LI
STEPHEN J.

FREAKONOMICS

A Rogue Economist
Explores the Hidden
Side of Everything

Steven D. Levitt
and
Stephen J. Dubner

William Morrow
An imprint of HarperCollinsPublishers

Title
Subtitle

Authors

Publisher's Imprint
Publisher

The gang that Venkatesh had fallen in with was one of about a hundred branches—franchises, really—of a larger Black Disciples organization. J. T., the college-educated leader of his franchise, reported to a central leadership of about twenty men that was called, without irony, the board of directors. (At the same time that white suburbanites were studiously mimicking black rappers' ghetto culture, black ghetto criminals were studiously mimicking the suburbanites' dads' corp-think.) J. T. paid the board of directors nearly 20 percent of his revenues for the right to sell crack in a designated twelve-square-block area. The rest of the money was his to distribute as he saw fit.

Three officers reported directly to J. T.: an enforcer (who ensured the gang members' safety), a treasurer (who watched over the gang's

99

Page Number

Date of Publication   Place of Publication

FREAKONOMICS. Copyright © 2005 by Steven D. Levitt and Stephen J. Dubner.
All rights reserved. Printed in the United States of America. No part of this book may be used or reproduced in any manner whatsoever without written permission except in the case of brief quotations embodied in critical articles and reviews. For information address HarperCollins Publishers Inc., 10 East 53rd Street, New York, NY 10022.

HarperCollins books may be purchased for educational, business, or sales promotional use. For information please write: Special Markets Department, HarperCollins Publishers Inc., 10 East 53rd Street, New York, NY 10022.

FIRST EDITION

MLA

Works Cited Format
Levitt, Steven D., and Stephen J. Dubner. *Freakonomics: A Rogue Economist Explores the Hidden Side of Everything.* New York: William Morrow-Harper, 2005. Print.

In-Text Citation
The authors of one recent bestseller claim that "if you were to hold a McDonald's organizational chart and a Black Disciples org chart side by side, you could hardly tell the difference" (Levitt and Dubner 99).

APA

References Format
Levitt, S. D., & Dubner, S. J. (2005). *Freakonomics: A rogue economist explores the hidden side of everything.* New York, NY: William Morrow-Harper.

In-Text Citation
The authors of one recent bestseller claim that "if you were to hold a McDonald's organizational chart and a Black Disciples org chart side by side, you could hardly tell the difference" (Levitt & Dubner, 2005, p. 99).

Unsigned Editorial in a Newspaper

"A Primary Choice: Mark Green." Editorial. *New York Times* 2 Sept. 2001, sec. 5: 8.
Print.

Review

Rosen, Charles, and Henri Zerner. "Scenes from the American Dream." Rev. of
Norman Rockwell: Pictures for the American People by Maureen Hart
Hennessey and Anne Knutson. *New York Review of Books* 8 Oct. 2000:
16–20. Print.

Print Books: MLA Style

Order the information as follows, omitting information that does not apply. For
an illustration of a book and its citation, see page 619.

Author's Last Name, First Name. "Title of Article or Part of Book." *Title of Book.*
Ed. or Trans. Name. Edition. Number of volumes. Place of Publication: Name
of Publisher, date of publication. Publication Medium [Print].

Book by One Author

Cisneros, Sandra. *Caramelo*. New York: Random, 2002. Print.

(The names of well-known publishers are often shortened to the first key
word. Thus, "Houghton Mifflin Co." becomes "Houghton," and "Harcourt Brace
Jovanovich, Inc." becomes simply "Harcourt.")

Two or More Works by Same Author

Morrison, Toni. *Jazz*. New York: Knopf, 1992. Print.

--- *Song of Solomon*. New York: Knopf, 1977. Print.

Book with Two or Three Authors

Dernado, John, and Emmanuel Rongieras d'Usseau. *Allez, Viens!* Austin: Holt,
2003. Print.

Padilla, Amando M., Halford H. Fairchild, and Concepcion M. Valadez. *Foreign
Language Education*. Newbury Park: Sage, 1990. Print.

Book with More Than Three Authors

Abrams, M. H., et al. *Norton Anthology of English Literature*. 7th ed. New York:
Norton, 2000. Print.

Unknown or Anonymous Author

Encyclopedia of White-Collar Crime. Westport: Greenwood, 2007. Print.

Book with an Author and an Editor

Austen, Jane. *Pride and Prejudice*. Ed. Mark Schorer. Boston: Houghton, 1956.
Print.

Edited Book

Myers, Linda, ed. *Approaches to Computer Writing Classrooms*. Albany: State U of
New York P, 1993. Print.

(The words University and Press are commonly shortened to U and P wherever
they appear in citations.)

Translation

Allende, Isabel. *Paula*. Trans. Margaret Sayers Peden. New York: Harper, 1996.
Print.

Article or Chapter in an Edited Book

Sophocles. *Electra*. Trans. David Grene. *Greek Tragedies*. Ed. David Grene and
Richmond Lattimore. Vol. 2. Chicago: U of Chicago P, 1960. 45–109. Print.

Work in More Than One Volume

Morrison, Samuel Eliot, and Henry Steele Commager. *The Growth of the American
Republic*. 2 vols. New York: Oxford UP, 1941. Print.

Work in an Anthology

Chopin, Kate. "The Awakening." *Harper Single-Volume American Literature*. Ed.
Donald McQuade et al. 3rd ed. New York: Longman, 1999. Print.

Encyclopedia or Dictionary Entry

"Don Giovanni." *The Encyclopedia Americana*. 2004 ed. Print.

Government Document by Known Author

Juhnke, Gerald A. *Addressing School Violence: Practical Strategies & Interventions*.
ERIC Counseling and Student Services Clearinghouse. Greensboro: GPO,
2001. Print.

Government Document by Unknown Author

United States. Maternal and Child Health Bureau. *Babies Sleep Safest on Their
Backs: Reduce the Risk of Sudden Infant Death Syndrome (SIDS)*. Bethesda:
GPO, 2001. Print.

(*GPO* stands for "Government Printing Office.")

Unpublished Dissertation

Burnham, William A. "Peregrine Falcon Egg Variation, Incubation, and Population
Recovery Strategy." Diss. Colorado State U, 1984. Print.

Pamphlet

Guide to Raptors. Denver: Center for Raptor Research, 2003. Print.

Citing a Work from an Online Subscription Database

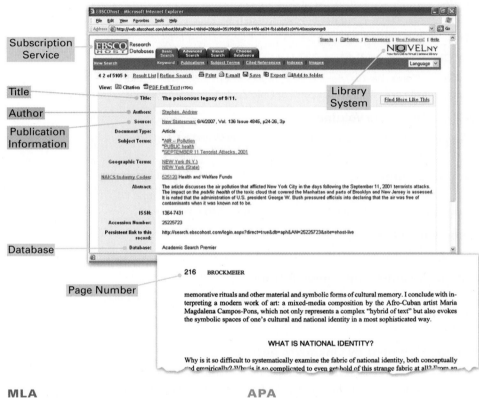

Subscription Service

Title

Author

Publication Information

Library System

Database

Page Number

MLA

Works Cited Format

Stephen, Andrew. "The Poisonous Legacy of 9/11." *New Statesman* 4 June 2007: 24-26. *Academic Search Premier.* Web. 20 June 2007.

In-Text Citation

Journalist Andrew Stephen reports that 10,000 people have so far filed court claims alleging that they were exposed to toxic substances after the attack on the World Trade Center (24).

APA

References Format

Stephen, A. (2007 June 4) The poisonous legacy of 9/11. *New Statesman:* 24-26.

In-Text Citation

Journalist Andrew Stephen (2007) reports that 10,000 people have so far filed court claims alleging that they were exposed to toxic substances after the attack on the World Trade Center.

Web Sources: MLA Style

As more and more sources are available online, the seventh edition of the *MLA Handbook for Writers of Research Papers* (2009) has made some adjustments, asking you to identify sources you access on the open Web and in online databases using Web as the medium of publication. It has also suggested that URLs are no longer required, though writers are encouraged to include a URL when the citation information is not adequate to allow readers to easily find the source. The current abbreviated basic features of an Internet citation, given below, appear in complete form on the MLA home page at http://www.mla.org; the Purdue Online Writing Lab also provides some useful information on the new MLA guidelines at http://owl.english.purdue.edu/owl/. Use the specific citations following this list as models for your own citations. For additional examples, consult the MLA home page or the most recent edition of the *MLA Handbook for Writers of Research Papers.*

1. Name of author, editor, translator, director, performer, if known
2. Title of article, short story, poem, or short work in quotation marks, or title of a longer work, such as a book, in italics
3. Publication information for any print version of the source if known
4. Title of periodical, database, scholarly project, or Web site (italicized), or for a site with no title, a description such as *home page*
5. Name of the editor of the project or database (if available)
6. The name of any organization sponsoring the Web site
7. Date of electronic publication, update, or posting
8. Medium of access (in these cases, Web) and date when researcher accessed the source or site
9. Electronic address or URL only if the citation does not provide adequate information for readers to access the site.

Web Site

American Medical Association. Home page. Apr. 2007. Web. 12 May 2007.

Document from a Web Site

Trapp, Douglas. "Faces of the Uninsured." *American Medical Association.* AMA, 28 Sept. 2009. Web. 25 Oct., 2009.

Scholarly Project Web Site

Labyrinth: Resources for Medieval Studies. Georgetown U, 2005. Web. 20 June 2009.

(If the online source includes paragraph numbers instead of page numbers, use *par.* with the number.)

Magazine Article

Smith, Dakota. "Black Women Ignore Many of Media's Beauty Ideals." *Women's E-News.* Women's eNews, 17 June 2004. Web. 4 June 2007.

Anonymous Magazine Article

"The First Private Rocket Ship Soars into Space." *USNews.com.* US News & World Report, 22 June 2004. Web. 6 June 2007.

Article from an Online Subscription Database

To cite online material from a database to which a library subscribes, first give the print publication information. Then complete the citation by giving the name of the database (italicized), the medium of access (in this case, Web) and the date of access. See page 622 for an illustration of an online database source and its citation.

Hines, Marion E. "Foreign Language Curriculum Concerns in Times of Conflict." *Delta Kappa Gamma Bulletin* 70.1 (2003): 15–21. *Academic Search Premier.* Web. 14 Feb. 2009.

Newspaper Article

Safire, William. "The Great Cash Cow." Editorial. *New York Times.* New York Times, 23 June 2004. Web. 25 June 2004.

Newspaper Editorial

Regan, Tom. "The New Political Correctness and the GOP." Editorial. *Christian Science Monitor.* Christian Science Monitor, 2 Feb. 1999. Web. 3 Feb. 1999.

Unsigned Newspaper Editorial

"A Primary Choice: Mark Green." Editorial. *New York Times.* New York Times, 2 Sept. 2001. Web. 3 Oct. 2009.

Letter to the Editor

Fuld, Leonard. Letter. *New York Times.* New York Times, 4 Sept. 2001. Web. 6 Sept. 2001.

Review

Iovine, Julie V. "Hi, Honey, I'm at the Airport." Rev. of *The Terminal*, dir. Steven Spielberg. *New York Times.* New York Times, 9 May 2004. Web. 9 June 2009.

E-book

Adams, Henry. *The Education of Henry Adams.* Boston: Houghton, 1918. *Bartleby.com.* Bartleby, 1999. Web. 17 June 2009.

Poem

Wheatley, Phillis. "On Being Brought from Africa to America." *Poems on Various Subjects, Religious and Moral.* Philadelphia, 1786. *Electronic Text Center.* U of Virginia Lib., Nov. 2006. Web. 4 June 2008. <http://etext.lib.virginia.edu/toc/modeng/public/WhePoem.html>.

Podcast

Brody, Jane. "Health Update." Podcast. *New York Times*. New York Times, 4 June
2007. Web. 14 May 2007.

Blog

Baron, Dennis. "Semantic State of the Union." Blog posting. *Web of Language*.
N.p., 24 Jan. 2007. Web. 6 May 2007.
<http://webtools.uiuc.edu/blog/view?blogId=25>.

Archived Listserv Posting

Anson, Chris. "Plagiarism Essay." Online posting. *Council of Writing Program
Administrators*. Council of Writing Program Administrators, 27 Feb. 2007.
Web. 13 May 2007.

Usenet Posting

Benenson, Fred. "Free Thesis Project Released Today." Online posting.
Freeculture. N.p., 5 May 2007. Web. 15 May 2007.

Posting to a Discussion List

Mitchell, Kerri. "Composition Philosophies and Rhetoric." Online posting.
Syllabase Discussion Group. Colorado State U, 24 Sept. 2003. Web. 17 Jan.
2008. <http//writing.colostate.edu/Syllabase/classroom/communication
/discussion/display_message.asp?MessageID=23726>.

Synchronous Communications (MOOs, MUDs)

Grigar, Dene. Online defense of dissertation "Penelopeia: The Making of Penelope
in Homer's Story and Beyond." *LinguaMOO*. U of Texas, 25 July 1995. Web.
25 July 1995. <telnet://lingua.utdallas.edu:8888>.

E-Mail Communication

Gogela, Anne. "RE: Teaching British Literature Survey." Message to the author.
30 May 2004. E-mail.

Map

Map of the Battlefield of Gettysburg. Map. New York: H. H. Lloyd, 1864. *Map
Collections 1500–2004. American Memory*. Lib. of Congress, 2 May 2007.
Web. 15 May 2007. <http://hdl.loc.gov/loc.gmd/g3824g.cw0333000>.

Other Sources: MLA Style

Film

The Terminal. Dir. Steven Spielberg. Perf. Tom Hanks and Catherine Zeta-Jones.
Dreamworks, 2004. DVD.

Recording

Carey, Mariah. "Hero." *Music Box*. Columbia, 1993. CD.

Television or Radio Program

"Not Quite Dead." Narr. Mike Wallace. *Sixty Minutes*. CBS. WCBS, New York,
13 Apr. 1997. Television.

Performance

Clapton, Eric. EnergySolutions Arena, Salt Lake City. 8 Mar. 2007. Performance.

Letter

McCarthy, Cormac. Letter to the author. 22 Feb. 2008. TS.

TS stands for "typescript."

Lecture or Speech

Evans, Pierre. "Colorado Raptors." U of Colorado, Boulder. 17 Sept. 2008. Lecture.

(In this case, it is best to avoid using the in-text citation by mentioning the
speaker's name in the text. If the title is unknown, omit it.)

Personal Interview

Miller, J. Philip. Personal interview. 19 Mar. 2009.

Personal Survey

Morgan Library Interlibrary Loan Questionnaire. Personal survey. 15 March 2008.

Cartoon

Roberts, Victoria. Cartoon. *New Yorker*. New Yorker, 13 Jan. 1997. Web. 3 Dec.
2008.

Advertisement

Give the name of the product or company followed by the label
Advertisement, not underlined or in italics. Follow with the usual publication information.

Escape Hybrid by Ford. Advertisement. *National Geographic* May 2004: 2.
Print.

Painting, Sculpture, or Photograph

Indicate the artist's name first, followed by the title, the date of composition,
and the medium. List the museum or collection, the owner if indicated, and the city.

Marc, Franz. *Deer in the Forest II*. 1914. Oil on canvas. Staatliche Kunsthalle,
Karlsruhe.

Vermeer van Delft, Jan. *The Astronomer*. 1668. Musée du Louvre, Paris. *Louvre*.
Web. 3 Jan. 2009.

Publication on CD-ROM, Diskette, or Magnetic Tape

"World War II." *Encarta*. Seattle: Microsoft, 1999. CD-ROM.

Godwin, M. E. "An Obituary to Affirmative Action and a Call for Self-Reliance."
CD-ROM. *ERIC*. SilverPlatter. Oct. 1992.

● **IN-TEXT DOCUMENTATION: APA STYLE** In APA style, give the author's name and date when you use a summary or paraphrase. If you quote material directly, give the author's name, the date, and the page number. (Use *p.* for one page and *pp.* for more than one page.) These citations will direct your reader to your References list, where you give complete bibliographical information. As you cite your sources, use the following guidelines.

If you do not name the author in the text, give the author and date in parentheses at the end of the citation. If you are specifically citing a quotation or a part of a source, indicate the page with *p.* (for one page) or *pp.* (for more than one page).

> A recent study of elementary school students studying a foreign language showed that participants from bilingual households "invariably scored higher than participants from English-speaking only households" (Cortes, 2002, p. 320).

If you cite the author in the text, indicate the date in parentheses immediately following the author's name, and cite the page number in parentheses following the quotation.

> According to Vicki Galloway (1984), a student's horizons will not be broadened by "grammar lectures and manipulative classroom exercises" (p. 33).

If you include a long direct quotation (40 or more words), indent the passage one-half inch from the left margin. Omit the enclosing direct quotation marks. Place the period at the end of the passage, not after the parentheses that include the page reference.

> In an article explaining the strategic value of foreign language study, Hines (2003) argues that our response has been inadequate:
>> The United States' chronically weak language resources and lack of linguistic preparedness are invariably exposed when events such as the war in Iraq and the September 11 terror strikes threaten the balance of power, peace or détente in global affairs. (15)

If you are paraphrasing or summarizing material (no direct quotations), you may omit the page number.

> According to Coxe (1984), many top American businesspeople agree that students who combine some business or economics training with fluency in Japanese have unlimited job possibilities.

Note: Although the APA style manual says that writers may omit page citation for summaries and paraphrases, check with your instructor before you omit page references.

If you have previously cited the author and date of a study, you may omit the date.

> In addition, Coxe points out that many top American businesspeople agree that students who combine some business or economics training with fluency in Japanese have unlimited job possibilities.

If the work has two to five authors, cite all authors in your text or in parentheses in the first reference.

Note: In your text, write "Frith and Mueller"; in a parenthetical citation, use an ampersand "(Frith & Mueller)."

> Frith and Mueller (2003) cite another recent example of foreign-language ignorance in marketing. When the California Milk Processor Board wanted an ad agency to translate the "Got Milk?" campaign into Spanish, the unfortunate translation came out as "Are you lactating?" (p. 33).

> Two researchers cited another recent example of foreign language ignorance in marketing. When the California Milk Processor Board wanted an ad agency to translate the "Got Milk?" campaign into Spanish, the unfortunate translation came out as "Are you lactating?" (Frith & Mueller, 2003, p. 33).

For subsequent citations, cite both names each time if a work has two authors. If a work has three to five authors, give the last name of the first author followed by *et al.* Include the year for the first citation within a paragraph.

> Shedivy et al. (2004) found similar results.

If a work has six or more authors, use only the last name of the first author and the abbreviation *et al.* followed by the date.

> Teachers should integrate the study of history, culture, politics, literature, and religion of a particular region with the study of language (Berryman et al., 1988).

If a work has no author, give the first few words of the title (italicized, if a book or report, or in quotes, if an article or chapter) and the year.

> Most students in the United States would be surprised to learn that the Russian government sponsored rock concerts (A Day in the Life, 1988).

If the source is from the Internet or the Web, use the author, or if there is no author, use the title.

> Many Web sites now provide detailed information about how to plan a study-abroad semester or year (Foreign Language, 2004).

If the author is a corporation, cite the full name of the company in the first reference.

> Foreign-language study must be accompanied by in-depth understanding and experience of culture (University of Maryland, 1990).

If the source is an unpublished personal communication (e-mail, letter, memo, interview, phone conversation), provide an in-text citation, but do not include the source in your "References" list.

> As Professor Devlin explained, "Foreign-language study encourages students to see their own language and culture from a fresh perspective" (personal interview, September 21, 2003).

If you are citing a government document, give the originating agency, its abbreviation (if any), the year of publication, and (if you include a direct quotation) the page number.

> Newcomers to a foreign culture should "pay attention to their health as well as their grammar. What the natives regularly eat may be dangerous to a foreigner's constitution" (Department of Health and Human Services [DHHS], 1989, p. 64).

If your citation refers to several sources, list the authors and dates in alphabetical order.

> Several studies (Frith & Mueller, 2003; Hines, 2002; Simon, 1980) have documented severe deficiencies in Americans' foreign-language preparation.

● **REFERENCES LIST: APA STYLE** If you are using APA style, you should make a separate list, titled References (no underlining or quotation marks), that appears after your text but before any appendixes. Include only sources actually used in preparing your essay. List the sources cited in your text *alphabetically,* by author's last name. Use only *initials* for authors' first and middle names. If the author is unknown, alphabetize by the first word in the title (but not *A, An,* or *The*). In titles, capitalize only the first word, proper names, and the first word following a colon. As in MLA reference style, begin the first line of each reference flush left and indent subsequent lines one-half inch. Double-space the entire References list. The APA recommends using italics for titles of books, journals, and other documents.

Following are samples of APA-style reference list entries. For additional information and examples, consult the *Publication Manual of the American Psychological Association* (6th ed., 2010).

Periodicals: APA Style

The following examples illustrate how to list articles in magazines and periodicals according to APA style.

Note: Do *not* underline or italicize or put quotation marks around titles of articles. Do italicize titles of magazines or periodicals. Italicize the volume number for magazines, if there is one, and omit the *p.* or *pp.* before any page numbers. If an article is not printed on continuous pages, give all page numbers, separated by commas.

Article in a Weekly or Biweekly Magazine

Hersh, S. M. (2004, May 17). Chain of command. *The New Yorker,* 38–43.

Article in a Monthly or Bimonthly Magazine

Dunbar, D. (1997, February). White noise. *Travel and Leisure, 27,* 106–110, 150–158.

Unsigned Article in a Magazine

E-commerce takes off. (2004, 15–21 May). *The Economist, 371,* 9.

Article in a Journal with Continuous Pagination

Italicize the volume number and do not include pp. Also, APA style requires repeating all number digits: Write 2552–2555. If the article has a DOI, include it (see page 633).

Sady, S. P. (1986). Prolonged exercise augments plasma triglyceride clearance. *Journal of the American Medical Association, 256,* 2552–2555.

Article in a Journal That Paginates Each Issue Separately

Italicize the volume number followed by the issue number (not italicized) in parentheses. If the article has a DOI, include it (see page 633).

Brodkey, L. (1987). Writing ethnographic narratives. *Written Communication, 9*(1), 25–50.

Article in a Newspaper

Use p. or pp. before newspaper section and page numbers.

Harmon, A. (2004, June 20). In new tests for fetal defects, agonizing choices for parents. *New York Times,* p. A1.

Unsigned Article in a Newspaper

A jet crash that defies resolution. (2001, September 5). *Los Angeles Times,* pp. A1, A7.

Op Ed Piece

Fish, S. (1996, December 26). When principles get in the way. *New York Times,* p. A27.

Unsigned Editorial

European summit of uncertainty. (1994, January 7). [Editorial]. *Los Angeles Times,* p. B6.

Books: APA Style

A Book by One Author

Cisneros, S. (2002). *Caramelo.* New York, NY: Random.

Book by Several Authors

For books with up to six authors, use last names followed by initials and an ampersand (&) before the name of the last author. For books with more than six authors, use last name and initial of the first author followed by "et al."

Conklin, N. F., & Lourie, M. A. (1983). *A host of tongues: Language communities in the United States.* New York, NY: Free Press.

Corbett, P. J., Myers, N., & Tate, G. (2000). *The writing teacher's sourcebook* (4th ed.) New York, NY: McGraw-Hill.

Additional Books by Same Author

List the author's name for all entries. Note that in-text citations are distinguished by copyright year. In the case of two works by the same author with the same copyright date, assign the dates letters *a, b* according to their alphabetical arrangement.

Morrison, T. (1977). *Song of Solomon.* New York, NY: Knopf.

Morrison, T. (1992). *Jazz.* New York, NY: Knopf

Unknown or Anonymous Author

Encyclopedia of white-collar crime. (2007). Westport, CT: Greenwood Publishing Group.

Book with an Author and an Editor

Austen, J. (1956). *Pride and prejudice* (M. Schorer, Ed.). Boston, MA: Houghton Mifflin.

Note: APA style usually uses the full name of publishing companies.

Work in an Anthology

Chopin, K. (1989). The story of an hour. In E. V. Roberts & H. E. Jacobs (Eds.), *Literature: An introduction to reading and writing* (pp. 304–306). Englewood Cliffs, NJ: Prentice Hall.

Note: Titles of poems, short stories, essays, or articles in a book are not underlined or italicized or put in quotation marks. Only the title of the anthology is underlined or italicized.

Translation

Lefranc, J. R. (1976). *A treatise on probability* (R. W. Mateau & D. Trilling, Trans.). New York, NY: Macmillan. (Original work published 1952)

Article or Chapter in an Edited Book

Sophocles. (1960). *Electra* (D. Grene, Trans.). In D. Grene & R. Lattimore (Eds.), *Greek tragedies* (Vol. 2, pp. 45–109). Chicago, IL: University of Chicago Press.

Government Document: Known Author

Machenthun, K. M. (1973). *Toward a cleaner aquatic environment.* Environmental Protection Agency. Office of Air and Water Programs. Washington, DC: U.S. Government Printing Office.

Government Document: Unknown Author

Maternal and Child Health Bureau. (2001). *Babies sleep safest on their backs: Reduce the risk of sudden infant death syndrome (SIDS)*. Bethesda, MD: U.S. Government Printing Office.

Dissertation (Published)

Wagner, E. (1988). On-board automatic aid and advisory for pilots of control-impaired aircraft. *Dissertation Abstracts International, 49*(8), 3310. (UMI No. AAd88-21885)

Electronic and Internet Sources: APA Style

The World Wide Web and the Internet are still changing, so even the latest APA guidelines, available in the sixth edition of the *Publication Manual of the American Psychological Association* (July 2010), may continue to change. See section 7 of the APA manual for the latest information on citing electronic sources. The basic features of an electronic or Internet citation, given in abbreviated form below, are available for downloading from the APA home page at http://www.apa.org/journals/webref.html. Use the specific citations following this list as models for your own citations.

1. Name of author (if given)
2. Title of article (with APA capitalization rules)
3. Title of periodical or electronic text (italicized)
4. Volume number and/or pages (if any)
5. If information is retrieved from an electronic database (e.g., ABI/FORM, PsycInfo, Electric Library, Academic Universe), give the print information only or the publication's home page URL, if known.
6. When a digital object identifier (DOI) is available, include it instead of the URL.
7. Use the words "Retrieved" (include date here only if the publication is undated) "from" (give the URL). Use the words "Available from" to indicate that the URL leads to information on how to obtain the cited material rather than the complete address of the material itself.

8. Do not use angle brackets around URL.
9. If citation ends with the URL, do not end URL with a period.

Note: APA style does not cite personal communications such as e-mail in a reference list. Cite such references in the text only. Also, you may vary the in-text citation by mentioning the name of the author(s) or the work in your text, in which case you need only cite the date parenthetically.

Article in a Journal with DOI Assigned

Jackson, B., et al. (2007, May). Does harboring hostility hurt? *Health Psychology,*
    26(3), 333–340. doi: 10.1037/0278-6133.26.3.333

Article in a Journal with No DOI Assigned

Brockmeier, J. (2001).Texts and other symbolic spaces. *Mind, Culture, and Activity:*
    An International Journal, 8, 215-230. Retrieved from
    http://lchc.ucsd.edu/mca/Journal/index.html

Article in an Internet-Only Journal

Twyman, M., Harries, C., & Harvey, N. (2006, January). Learning to use and assess
    advice about risk. *Forum: Qualitative Social Research, 7*(1), Article 22.
    Retrieved from http://www.qualitative-research.net

Article in a Newspaper

Greenhouse, L. (2004, June 25). Justices, in 5–4 vote, raise doubts on sentencing
    rules. *New York Times.* Retrieved June 27, 2004, from http://www.nytimes
    .com

Work from an Online Subscription Database

Hines, M. E. (2003, Fall). Foreign language curriculum concerns in times of conflict.
    Delta Kappa Gamma Bulletin, 70, 15–22.

Message Posted to an Online Forum

Etter, B. (2001, August 24). Composition, philosophies, and rhetoric. Message
    posted to http://writing.colostate.edu/SyllaBase/classroom/communication
    / discussion/display_message.asp?MessageID=16232

Blog

Cambridge, B. (2007, April 24). ACT survey conclusion-more grammar instruction.
    NCTE Literacy Education Updates. Retrieved May 6, 2007, from http://
    ncteblog.blogspot.com

Other Sources: APA Style

In the APA system, unpublished personal communications (e-mail, letter, interview, memo, etc.) do not appear in the References list. Do, however, cite personal communications in your text. (See "In-Text Documentation: APA Style.")

Review

Rosen, C., & Zerner, H. (2000, October 8). Scenes from the American dream [Review of the book *Norman Rockwell: Pictures for the American people*]. *New York Review of Books,* 16–20.

Published Interview

Lamm, R. (1995, November 30). Governments face tough times [Interview with Baun, R.]. *Coloradoan,* p. B9.

Film

Spielberg, S. (Director). (2004). *The terminal* [Motion Picture]. United States: Dreamworks.

Recording

Carey, M. (1993). Hero. On *Music box* [CD]. New York, NY: Columbia Records.

Television or Radio Program

Bogdonich, R. (Producer). (1997, April 13). *Sixty minutes.* New York, NY: WCBS.

STUDENT WRITING

KATE MCNERNY

Foreign Language Study: An American Necessity

Kate McNerny's purpose was to persuade students, administrators, and ordinary citizens that learning the language and culture of a foreign country is important, both to people as individuals and to America as a nation. In this paper, she uses interviews, library research, research on the Internet, and her own experience to alert her readers to the seriousness of the problem and to recommended a solution. She argues the American schools should require students to study at least one foreign language during junior and senior high school. McNerny follows the MLA style for in-text documentation, supplementary notes, and the Works Cited list. The marginal annotations highlight key features of her research paper.

Kate McNerny

Professor Thomas

English 101

6 May 2003

Foreign-Language Study:

An American Necessity

"Why should I learn a foreign language—everyone speaks English!" "I would never use another language—I never plan to leave the United States." "I had a hard enough time learning English!" These are only a few of the excuses people have given for opposing foreign-language studies, and unfortunately they represent the ideas of more than a few American citizens. In possibly the most multicultural nation in the world, it is ironic that so many people—who themselves have come from foreign cultures and foreign languages—should want to remain isolated from international languages and cultures. A recent indication of the backlash against foreign languages came when the House of Representatives passed legislation recommending that English should be the official language of the U.S. Government.[1] In addition, twenty-three states already have Official English laws on the books (Swope 2128; Torres 51). Because these attitudes are so widespread, we need a national policy supporting foreign-language study in elementary and secondary schools. If we are to continue to develop as a people and a nation, we must be able to communicate with and understand the cultures of people from countries around the globe.

Historically, Americans' attitudes toward foreign languages have swayed from positive to negative, depending on current

McNerny 1

/double space

/double space

/double space

1"

½"

½"

1"   1"

1"

For her lead-in, McNerny uses quotations she collected in her informal survey.

McNerny first states her thesis for this problem-solving essay: "We need a national policy supporting foreign-language study." McNerny presents historical background on the problem.

(Proportions shown in this paper are adjusted to fit space limitations of this book. Follow actual dimensions discussed and your instructor's directions.)

McNerny 2

events around the world. Theodore Huebener's study *Why Johnny Should Learn Foreign Languages* shows how attitudes reflect the times. In 1940, in an isolationist period before World War II, a committee of the American Youth Commission issued a report labeling foreign-language studies as "useless and time-consuming" (Huebener 13). An even more appalling statement came from a group of Harvard scholars. They suggested that "foreign language study is useful primarily in strengthening the student's English. . . . For the average student, there is no real need at all to learn a foreign language" (Huebener 14). With such attitudes, it is no wonder that students and administrators ignored foreign language programs during the 1940s and 1950s.[2] Through the years, each international crisis has brought a renewed interest in foreign languages. Just as the advent of Sputnik in the late 1950s was followed by a surge of interest in learning foreign languages, the terrorist attacks of September 11, 2001 have created more interest in languages less commonly taught in the United States (Hines 20).

Despite some occasional surges of interest, however, foreign-language study still holds the weakest position of any major subject in American secondary schools. A recent study of foreign-language programs reports that "only 15 percent of American high school students study a foreign language. Only 8 percent of [American] colleges require credit in a foreign language for admission (down from 34 percent in 1966)" (Unks 24). Because available programs at the junior and senior high school level are generally limited in variety

---

Ellipsis points indicate material omitted from the source.

The superscript number refers the reader to the "Notes" page for McNerny's comment on the history of the problem.

Square brackets in quoted material indicate a word added by McNerny to clarify the sentence.

McNerny 3

and scope, only a small percentage of those students who take a foreign language ever become fluent in it. A 1984

"Let me put this in terms you'll understand. First, you'll have to tell me what language you're speaking."

study that sampled 536 secondary schools revealed that most offered a foreign language, but 91 percent did not require foreign-language credits for graduation (Ranwez and Rodgers 98). In contrast, most European countries require all students to learn at least one and often two foreign languages. Norway, Spain, France, Sweden, Italy, England, Germany, and Finland all require at least one foreign language. According to Rune Bergentoft, currently a Mellon Fellow at the National Foreign Language Center, "Several [European] countries require knowledge of two foreign languages for entry to the upper

McNerny included the cartoon at this point to illustrate Americans' stubborn ignorance of foreign language.

In-text citation for a source with two authors. Note also how McNerny makes use of key statistics, a powerful form of evidence.

Noting Bergentoft's qualifications adds reliability to the quotation that follows.

McNerny 4

secondary school; in the Netherlands, the requirement is three foreign languages" (18).

The United States cannot continue to lag behind other countries in language capability. As two foreign-language researchers noted, "We are members of a world community consisting of hundreds of nations, and our fates are closely intertwined" (Long and Long 366). It is time to change attitudes and to recognize that in order to successfully interact with its "world community," the United States must drastically change its foreign-language practices and policies. American students should be encouraged to start their language studies in elementary school and required to study at least one foreign language during their six years of junior and senior high school.

How do we encourage more students to study a foreign language in our elementary and secondary schools? The solution requires changes on the part of administrators and teachers, changes in the attitudes and experiences of students themselves, and changes in our state and national foreign language policies.

School administrators across the country often oppose the idea of requiring foreign languages because they cannot see the contribution these studies make to the overall goals of the schools' curriculum. In a recent survey, New Jersey secondary school administrators "rated social studies objectives as contributing most to the attainment of high priority goals, and foreign language as contributing least" (Koppel 437). These administrators fail to realize that language studies can add a valuable dimension to a social studies program. Educators can use a combined program to

McNerny restates her thesis, using more specific language: "American students should be . . . required to study at least one foreign language during . . . junior and senior high school."

*McNerny's **essay map**: The solution requires changes by administrators, by students, and by national policymakers.*

*Notice **punctuation** for in-text citation: Source appears in parentheses after the quotation marks but before the period.*

McNerny 5

emphasize a global perspective in language and cultural studies. "The world looks and sounds different when one is 'standing in the shoes' of another, speaking another language, or recognizing another's point of view based on an alternative set of values" (Bragaw 37). This global awareness is crucial in our increasingly interdependent world.

Likewise, teachers need to continue to make changes in their foreign-language courses to attract more students. More and more primary and secondary language courses already focus on cultural issues more than grammar, but now they need to use all the computer, on-line, and Internet resources currently available to attract and motivate their students. Linguist Mark Warschauer, in a preface to papers collected at a conference on Global Networking in Foreign Language Learning, asserts that "foreign language learners can communicate rapidly and inexpensively with other learners or speakers of the target language around the world. With the World Wide Web, learners can access a broad array of authentic foreign language materials . . . or they can develop and publish their own materials to share with others across the classroom or across the globe" (ix). Teachers need to make use of the Internet's communication possibilities to help motivate and interest their students.

Of course, students themselves need motivation in order to enroll in foreign-language classes. Many students simply fail to see why they will ever need to use a foreign language. I used to belong to that group. I remember my mom always telling me, "Take French classes. Learn how to speak French so you can visit your cousins in

This use of a direct quotation supports McNerny's point in a compelling way.

McNerny shows how new technologies can make foreign language learning more valuable in current times.

McNerny's transition helps the reader see why she will now discuss a related topic—student motivation.

Though most of McNerny's essay is based on library research, here she adds personal experience to illustrate the need.

Note how McNerny uses open Web sources as evidence that many useful programs already exist.

France someday." At the time, during junior high, I did take French classes for a while, but then dropped them when my schedule became "too busy." Then, as my mom had promised, I got the opportunity to visit my cousins in France. For some reason, the fact that I couldn't speak French didn't really hit me—until I stepped off the train at Gare du Nord in Paris and couldn't find the relative who was supposed to meet me. After frantically searching the entire station several times, I had to break down and ask for help. At the information desk, a few completely butchered French phrases escaped my lips—only to be received by an unimpressed, unresponsive station attendant. He muttered something about dumb Americans. Then, with a wave of his hand, he gestured toward some unknown destination. I did survive that painful ordeal, but I vowed I wouldn't embarrass myself—and other Americans—again.

Another way to change students' attitudes is to encourage them to participate in exchange programs or study-abroad programs.[3] Again, the Internet and the World Wide Web offer students and their teachers immediate access to a variety of exchange and study-abroad programs. The World Wide Web has hundreds of sites related to foreign-language study that can help both teachers and students. The International House World Organization, at http://www. international-house.org, is "a worldwide network of language schools sharing a common commitment to the highest standards of teaching and training" (*International*). Students wishing to find out about exchange and study-abroad programs should browse the Web, perhaps beginning at a site such as the *Foreign Language Study Abroad Service* at http://www.netpoint.net/~flsas. The Foreign Language Study Abroad Service was started in 1971 and is, according to its home page, "the oldest study abroad service in the U.S." (*Foreign*).

Study-abroad programs and exchange programs help students learn the language, but just as important, they enable students to learn about different cultures. In his resource book, *Teaching Culture*, H. Ned Seelye, Director of Bilingual-Bicultural Education for the State of Illinois, cites just one of many cultural lessons that American students—and tourists—need to learn:

> At a New Year's Eve celebration in an exclusive Guatemalan hotel, one American was overheard telling another, "You see all these people? They're all my wife's relatives. And every damn one of them has kissed me tonight. If another Guatemalan man hugs and kisses me I'll punch him right in the face!" The irritated American was disturbed by two things: the extended kinship patterns of the group and the *abrazo de ano neuvo* as executed by the men (he did not complain of the female abrazos). Both customs—close family ties that extend to distant relatives and the abrazo given as a greeting or sign of affection devoid of sexual overtures—elicited hostility in the American who was bored by unintelligible language and depressed by nostalgia and alcohol. (85)

1" (marginal annotation)

In order to prevent such linguistic and cultural misunderstandings, more and more Americans should take advantage of study-abroad

McNerny introduces the author, the title of the book, and the author's credentials to lend authority to the quoted passage.

At the end of the quotation, McNerny cites only the page number, since she has already introduced the author. The page number follows the period in indented block quotations.

McNerny does not end her paragraph with a quotation; instead, she keeps her own voice primary by relating it to her own purpose.

McNerny 8

and exchange programs that will acquaint them with a variety of
cultures and languages.

Note how McNerny appeals to another portion of her audience— businesspeople.

Finally, in order to coordinate our schools' foreign-language
studies, America needs changes in our state and national
foreign-language policies to ensure that every child will receive some
basic instruction in foreign languages and culture. Changes in our
foreign-language requirements would not only promote cultural
understanding but also would strengthen U.S. international relations
in business and diplomacy. International trade is continually
increasing in the United States and has created a demand for
businesspeople competent in foreign languages. Many top American
businesspeople agree that students who combine some business or
economics training with fluency in Japanese have unlimited job
possibilities (Coxe). Company executives simply cannot expect to
make efficient, sound decisions in their international markets without
understanding and speaking the language of the country they are
dealing with (Huebener 45). Educator Gerald Unks points out two
instances in which a lack of language proficiency caused companies
to initiate fatal marketing programs:

These specific examples illustrate how important foreign language proficiency can be for businesses, appealing to this audience.

> When Pepsi-Cola went after the Chinese market, "Come
> Alive With Pepsi" was translated into Chinese in Taiwan
> as "Pepsi Brings Your Ancestors Back from the Dead." No
> Sale! General Motors sought to sell its Nova in South
> America oblivious to the fact that "No va" in Spanish
> means "It doesn't go." (24)

Another recent example of foreign-language ignorance in
marketing occurred when the California Milk Association

McNerny 9

wanted an ad agency to translate the "Got Milk?" campaign into Spanish. The unfortunate translation initially came out as "Are you lactating?" (Frith and Mueller 33). These examples illustrate that business people need thorough competence in, not just a rudimentary knowledge of, foreign languages.

Finally, proficiency in foreign languages and cultures is important not only for business and trade overseas, but also for jobs in America. Required foreign-language study would help our future citizens understand and appreciate our multicultural heritage—and help them become employable. Verada Bluford, writing in *Occupational Outlook Quarterly*, argues that as our country "becomes more involved in foreign trade, tourism, and international cooperative ventures, the number of jobs open to fluent speakers of a foreign language increases" (25). Bluford explains that there are "language-centered jobs" such as teaching, translating, and interpreting, but there are also "language-related jobs," such as jobs in marketing and finance, engineering, airlines, banking, and government, where language skills are necessary. These "language-related jobs" will go to students who have language skills in addition to some other skill (Bluford 26). A foreign-language requirement, whether mandated by each state or by Congress, would make all Americans better citizens of the world and their own country.

The need for required language study in the United States is urgent. Some states already require schools to introduce children to some foreign language during their grade school years (Kuo). For example, North Carolina, Arkansas, Louisiana, Arizona, and Oklahoma already have laws, and Oregon has a proposed law that

Before quoting from Bluford, McNerny names the author and the journal from which the article is taken.

McNerny begins her conclusion, citing precedents and calling for state and federal administrators to support a foreign-language requirement.

McNerny 10

will require all tenth-graders to know a language other than English (Kuo). Since some individual schools and states realize the benefits of foreign-language requirements, Congress should guide all the states and formulate a national foreign-language policy that would make all our schools more like the European model.

In this paragraph, McNerny addresses potential reader questions about whether her plan is feasible.

Although the ideas and the plans for a national policy exist, often the funds do not. Some funds can be diverted from within school districts, but the federal government must take some initiative. The current administration spends endless time and money subsidizing business interests and propping up weak foreign economies. Since foreign-language knowledge contributes strongly to success in both these areas, however, it would be practical for the administration also to support expansion of language studies. Instead, it continues to reduce funding for special programs, including language studies centers and international teaching facilities (Unks 25). Realistically, a foreign-language requirement in junior and senior high school cannot be initiated without the support of both local school districts and the federal government. Americans must acknowledge the fact that they are not isolated from the rest of the world. Successful interaction in the "world community" depends on our ability, as a nation, to effectively communicate with and understand people from other countries. Understanding, communication, and world peace cannot be achieved without cultural awareness and foreign-language proficiency.

McNerny ends with an appeal to the reader's emotions—a desire for a peaceful world.

½"
McNerny 11

1"
Notes

1. Americans not only hesitate to take a foreign language but also seem bent on keeping foreign languages officially "out of sight." The debate over "official English" has spilled over into the workplace, in the form of "English-only" rules in business. Robert Brady, writing in *HR Focus*, reviews the two sides of the English-only debate: "Advocates of English-only rules argue that a single language promotes good organizational communications, ensures workplace safety, improves service to the English-speaking customer base, and avoids discrimination." On the other side, Brady says, opponents believe that requiring employees to speak English goes against the melting-pot heritage of our country—and may violate Title VII of the Civil Rights Act. Many opponents from ethnic and civil rights groups believe these bills and rules are racist (McBee 64). Americans' ignorance of foreign languages (and the fear that ignorance breeds) is an important cause of the popularity of both the "official English" laws and the "English-only" rules.

2. One of the most disturbing facts is that although Huebener's study was done in 1961, very little has changed in over forty years. Except for slight changes in statistics, dates, and names of wars, Americans have remained strikingly insular in their attitudes toward foreign languages and foreigners.

3. Recent figures on study-abroad programs illustrate the huge gap between the number of foreign students who study in the United States and U.S. students who study abroad. In an article on language learning and study abroad, Barbara Freed gives the following figures: "Close to half a million international students

1"

1"   1"

Content notes are placed on a separate page and double-spaced. Indent the first line of each numbered note one-half inch.

In her notes, McNerny includes her ideas about "English-only" and "official English," which would have been digressive in the text of her paper.

In this footnote, McNerny puts statistics that didn't seem to fit in the flow of her paragraph but are relevant to study-abroad programs.

McNerny 12

came to the United States to study in 1993–94 [while] approximately 71,000 American undergraduates participated in study abroad programs" (3). That means that nearly ten times more foreign students study English in the United States than American students study foreign languages abroad.

1"

1"   1"

1"

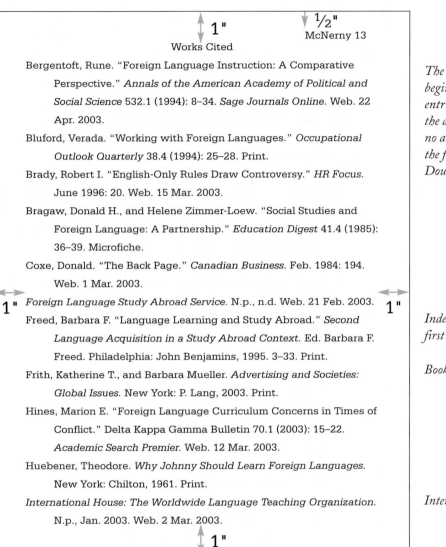

Works Cited

Bergentoft, Rune. "Foreign Language Instruction: A Comparative Perspective." *Annals of the American Academy of Political and Social Science* 532.1 (1994): 8–34. *Sage Journals Online.* Web. 22 Apr. 2003.

Bluford, Verada. "Working with Foreign Languages." *Occupational Outlook Quarterly* 38.4 (1994): 25–28. Print.

Brady, Robert I. "English-Only Rules Draw Controversy." *HR Focus.* June 1996: 20. Web. 15 Mar. 2003.

Bragaw, Donald H., and Helene Zimmer-Loew. "Social Studies and Foreign Language: A Partnership." *Education Digest* 41.4 (1985): 36–39. Microfiche.

Coxe, Donald. "The Back Page." *Canadian Business.* Feb. 1984: 194. Web. 1 Mar. 2003.

Foreign Language Study Abroad Service. N.p., n.d. Web. 21 Feb. 2003.

Freed, Barbara F. "Language Learning and Study Abroad." *Second Language Acquisition in a Study Abroad Context.* Ed. Barbara F. Freed. Philadelphia: John Benjamins, 1995. 3–33. Print.

Frith, Katherine T., and Barbara Mueller. *Advertising and Societies: Global Issues.* New York: P. Lang, 2003. Print.

Hines, Marion E. "Foreign Language Curriculum Concerns in Times of Conflict." Delta Kappa Gamma Bulletin 70.1 (2003): 15–22. *Academic Search Premier.* Web. 12 Mar. 2003.

Huebener, Theodore. *Why Johnny Should Learn Foreign Languages.* New York: Chilton, 1961. Print.

International House: The Worldwide Language Teaching Organization. N.p., Jan. 2003. Web. 2 Mar. 2003.

The "Works Cited" list begins a new page. List the entries alphabetically by the author's last name. If no author is given, list by the first word in the title. Double-space all lines.

Indent five spaces after first line of each entry.

Book

Internet Web page

Works Cited

Article from a journal

Koppel, Irene E. "The Perceived Contribution of a Foreign Language to High Priority Education Goals." *Foreign Language Annals* 15.6 (1982): 435–39. *ERIC.* Web. 1 Mar. 2003.

Kuo, Fidelius. "Foreign Language Proposal in Washington State Worthy." *Northwest Asian Weekly.* Northwest Asian Weekly, 9 Dec. 1994: 4. Web. 3 Apr. 2003.

For inclusive page numbers over 100, use only the last two digits in the second number (366–68).

Long, Delbert H., and Roberta A. Long. "Toward the Promotion of Foreign Language Study and Global Understanding." *Education* 105.4 (1985): 366–68. *ERIC.* Web. 22 Mar. 2003.

McBee, Susanna. "A War over Words." *US News.com.* US News & World Report, 6 Oct. 1986. Web. 19 Mar. 2003.

Ranwez, Alain D., and Judy Rogers. "The Status of Foreign Languages and International Studies: An Assessment in Colorado." *Foreign Language Annals* 17.2 (1984): 97–102. *ERIC.* Web. 1 Mar. 2003.

Seelye, H. Ned. *Teaching Culture: Strategies for Foreign Language Educators.* Skokie: National Textbook, 1974. Print.

Swope, Christopher. "Panel OKs Bill to Make English Official Government Language." *Congressional Quarterly Weekly Report* 54.30 (1996): 2128–29. *Academic Search Premier.* Web. 3 Mar. 2003.

Torres, Joseph. "The Language Crusade." *Hispanic.* 9.6 (1996): 50–54. Print.

Article from a monthly magazine

Unks, Gerald. "The Perils of Our Single-Language Policy." *Education Digest* 41.2 (1985). Microfiche.

Warschauer, Mark. Preface. *Telecollaboration in Foreign Language Learning.* Ed. Mark Warschauer. Honolulu: Second Language Teaching and Curriculum Center, 1996. Print.

1"   1"   1"

Appendix: Writing Under Pressure

The main chapters of this text describe purposes for writing and strategies for collecting, shaping, drafting, and revising an essay. These chapters assume that you have several days or even weeks to write your paper. They work on the premise that you have time to read model essays, time to think about ideas for your topic, and time to prewrite, write several drafts, and receive feedback from other members of your class. Much college writing, however, occurs on midterm or final examinations, when you may have only fifteen to twenty minutes to complete the whole process of writing. When you must produce a "final" draft in a few short minutes, your writing process may need drastic modification.

A typical examination has some objective questions (true/false, multiple-choice, definition, short-answer) followed by an essay question or two. For example, with just twenty-five minutes left in your Western Civilization midterm, you might finish the last multiple-choice question, turn the page, and read the following essay question.

> Erich Maria Remarque's *All Quiet on the Western Front* has been hailed by critics the world over as the "twentieth century's definitive novel on war." What does Remarque's novel tell us about the historical, ideological, national, social, and human significance of twentieth-century warfare? Draw on specific illustrations from the novel, but base your observations on your wider perspective on Western civilization. Good luck!

Overwhelmed by panic, you find the blood drains from your face and your fingers feel icy. You now have twenty-two minutes to write on the "historical, ideological, national, social, and human significance of twentieth-century warfare." Do you have to explain everything about modern warfare? Must you use specific examples from the novel? Good luck, indeed! Everything you remembered about the novel has now vanished. Bravely, you pick up your pen and start recounting the main events of the novel, hoping to show the instructor at least that you read it.

You can survive such an essay examination, but you need to prepare yourself emotionally and intellectually. Following is some advice from senior English majors who have taken dozens of essay examinations in their four years of college. These seniors answer the question, "What advice would you give to students who are preparing to take an essay examination?"

> Even though I'm an English major, I'm perfectly petrified of writing impromptu essays. My advice is to calm yourself. Read the question.

Study key words and concepts. Before beginning an essay question, write a brief, informal outline. This will organize your ideas and help you remember them as well. Take a deep breath and write. I would also recommend *rereading* the question while you are writing, to keep you on track.

The first step is to know the material. Then, before you begin, read the instructions. Know what the teacher expects. Then try to organize your thoughts into a small list—preferably a list that will become your main paragraphs. Don't babble to fill space. Teachers hate reading nonsense. Reread what you've written often. This will ensure that you won't repeat yourself. Proofread at the end.

Organization is important but difficult in a pressure situation. Well-organized essays do have a tendency to impress the professor, sometimes more than information-packed essays. Organize your notes and thoughts about those notes as you study (not necessarily in a chronological order, but rather in a comprehensible order). Good luck.

Read the question carefully.

Get your thoughts in order.

Write what the question asks, not what you wish it asked.

Don't ramble.

Give textual facts or specific examples.

Summarize with a clear, understandable closing.

Proofread.

Keep calm. Your life doesn't depend on one test.

My advice would be first to learn how to consciously relax and practice writing frequently. *Practice!!!* It's important to practice writing as much as possible in any place possible, because the more writing you do, the better and easier it becomes. Also, your belief that it *can* be done is critical!

Know the information that you will be tested on well enough so that you can ask yourself tough and well-formed questions in preparation. You should be able to predict what essay questions your professor will ask, at least generally. I always go to the test file or ask friends for sample essay questions that I can practice on. Then I practice writing on different areas of the material.

The common threads in these excerpts of advice are to know your audience, analyze key terms in the question, make a sketch outline, know the material, practice writing before the test, and proofread when you finish writing. Knowing how to read the question and practicing your writing before the test will help you relax and do your best.

KNOW YOUR AUDIENCE

Teachers expect you to answer a question exactly as it is asked, not just to give the information that you know. Because teachers must read dozens of essays, they are impressed by clear organization and specific detail. As one senior says, teachers hate babble because they cannot follow the thread of your argument. Although they demand specific examples and facts from the text, they want you to explain how these examples *relate* to the overall question. In a pile of two hundred history exams graded by one professor, margins featured comments like "Reread the question. This doesn't answer the question." "What is your main point? State your main point clearly." "Give more specific illustrations and examples." Keep this teacher in mind as you write your next essay response.

ANALYZE KEY TERMS

Understanding the key terms in the question is crucial to writing an essay under pressure. Teachers expect you to respond to *their* specific question, not just to write down information. They want you to use your writing to *think* about the topic—to analyze and synthesize the information. In short, they want you to make sense of the information. Following are key terms that indicate teachers' expectations and suggest how to organize your answer.

Discuss: A general instruction that means "write about." If the question says *discuss,* look for other key words to focus your response.

Describe: Give sensory details or particulars about a topic. Often, however, this general instruction simply means "discuss."

Analyze: Divide a topic into its parts, and show how the parts are related to each other and to the topic as a whole.

Synthesize: Show how the parts relate to the whole or how the parts make sense together.

Explain: Show relationships between specific examples and general principles. Explain what (define), explain why (causes/effects), and/or explain how (analyze process).

Define: Explain what something is. As appropriate, give a formal definition, describe it, analyze its parts or function, describe what it is not, and/or compare and contrast it with similar events or ideas.

Compare: Explain similarities and (often) differences. Draw conclusions from the observed similarities and differences.

Contrast: Explain key differences. Draw conclusions from the observed differences.

Illustrate: Provide specific examples of an idea or process.

Trace: Give the sequence or chronological order of key events or ideas.

Evaluate: Determine the value or worth of an idea, thing, process, person, or event. Set up criteria and provide evidence to support your judgments.

Solve: Explain your solution; show how it fixes the problem, why it is better than other alternatives, and why it is feasible.

Argue: Present both sides of a controversial issue, showing why the opposing position should not be believed or accepted and why your position should be accepted. Give evidence to support your position.

Interpret: Offer your understanding of the meaning and significance of an idea, event, person, process, or work of art. Support your understanding with specific examples or details.

MAKE A SKETCH OUTLINE

The key terms in a question should not only focus your thinking but also suggest how to organize your response. Use the key terms to make a sketch outline of your response. You may not regularly use an outline when you have more time to write an essay, but the time pressure requires that you revise your normal writing process.

Assume that you have twenty-five minutes to read and respond to the following question from a history examination. Read the instructions carefully, note the key terms, and make a brief outline to guide your writing. Answer *one* of the following. Draw on the reading for your answer. (25 pts)

1. Define globalization, then explain both the advantages and disadvantages of globalization for both modern and third-world countries. Based on your explanation, argue for or against globalization as a means of improving the standard of living in both modern and third-world countries.

2. Explain the arguments that the United Nations does and does not play a positive role in international relations (discuss and illustrate both sides of the argument). Then take a stand—citing the evidence for your position.

Let's assume that because you know more about the United Nations, you choose the second question. First, you should identify and underline key words in the question. The subject for your essay is the *United Nations* and its role in *international relations*. You need to *explain* the reasons why the UN does or does not have a positive effect on international relations. You will need to *discuss* and *illustrate* (give specific examples of) both sides of the controversy. Finally, you need to *take a stand* (argue) for your belief, citing *evidence* (specific examples from recent history) of how the UN has or has not helped to resolve international tensions.

Based on your rereading and annotation of the key words of the question, make a quick outline or list, perhaps as follows.

I. Reasons (with examples) why some believe the UN is effective

   A. Reason 1 + example

II. Reasons (with examples) why some believe the UN is not effective

   A. Reason 1 + example

   B. Reason 2 + example

III. Reasons why you believe the UN is effective

   Refer to reasons and examples cited in I, above, but explain why these reasons and examples outweigh the reasons cited in II, above.

With this sketch outline as your guide, jot down reasons and examples that you intend to use, and then start writing. Your outline will make sure that you cover all the main points of the question, and it will keep your essay organized as you concentrate on remembering specific reasons and examples.

WARMING UP   Journal Exercise

For practice, analyze at least one question from two of the following subject areas. First, underline key terms. Then, in your journal explain what these terms ask you to do. Finally, sketch an outline to help organize your response. If you are not familiar with the topics, check a dictionary or Google the key terms. (Do not write the essay.)

Biology
- Describe the process by which artificial insulin was first produced.
- What is reverse transcriptase and how was it used in genetic engineering?
- Humans—at least most of us—walk on two legs as opposed to four. How might you account for this using a Darwinian, Lamarckian, and Theistic model?

History
- Discuss the significant political developments in the English colonies in the first half of the eighteenth century.
- Account for the end of the Salem witchcraft delusion, and discuss the consequences of the outbreak for Salem Village.

Human Development
- Discuss evidence for nature versus nurture effects in human development.
- Contrast Piaget's, Vygotsky's, and Whorf's ideas on connections between language and thought.

Humanities
- How and why did early Christian culture dominate the Roman Empire? In terms of art and architecture, discuss specific ways in which the early Christians transformed or abolished the Greco-Roman legacy.

Literature
- Aristotle wrote that a tragedy must contain certain elements, such as a protagonist of high estate, recognition, and reversal, and should also evoke pity and fear in the audience. Which of the following best fits Aristotle's definition: *Hamlet, Death of a Salesman,* or *The Old Man and the Sea*? Explain your choice.

Philosophy
- On the basis of what we have studied in this class, define *philosophy*. Taking your major subject of study (for example, biology, history, literature), discuss three philosophical problems that arise in this field.
- Write an essay explaining the following statement. Be clear in your explanation and use specific examples. "Egoism allows for prudent altruism."

Political Science
- Evaluate the achievements of the current administration's policy in Africa.
- Analyze the role of force in the contemporary international system.

Psychology
- Contrast Freud's and Erikson's stage theories of personality.
- What is meant by triangulation of measurement (multiple methodology)?

KNOW THE MATERIAL

It goes without saying that you must know the material in order to explain the concepts and give specific examples or facts from the text. But what is the best way to review the material so that you can recall examples under pressure? The following three study tactics will improve your recall.

First, read your text actively. Do not just mark key passages in yellow high lighter. Write marginal notes to yourself. Write key concepts in the margin. Ask questions. Make connections between an idea in one paragraph and something you read earlier. Make connections between what you read in the text and what you heard in class.

Second, do not depend only on your reading and class discussion. Join or form a study group that meets regularly to review course material. Each person in the group should prepare some question for review. Explaining key ideas to a friend is an excellent way to learn the material yourself.

Finally, use your writing to help you remember. Do not just read the book and your notes and head off for the test. Instead, review your notes, *close* your notebook, and write down as much as you can remember. Review the assigned chapters in the text, close the book, and write out what you remember. If you can write answers to questions with the book closed, you know you're ready for an essay examination.

WARMING UP   **Journal Exercise**

Get out the class notes and textbook for a course that you are currently taking. Annotate your notes with summary comments and questions. In the margins, write out the key ideas that the lecture covered. Then write out questions that you still have about the material. Open your textbook for that class. Annotate the margins of the chapter that you are currently reading. Write summary comments about important material. Write questions in the margins about material that you do not understand. Note places in the text that the instructor also covered in class.

PRACTICE WRITING

As several of the senior English majors suggested, practicing short essays *before* an examination will make you feel comfortable with the material and reduce your panic. A coach once noted that while every athlete wants to win, only the true winners are willing to *prepare* to win. The same is true of writing an examination. Successful writers have already completed 80 percent of the writing process *before* they walk into an examination. They have written notes in the margins of their notebooks and textbooks. They have discussed the subject with other students. They have closed the book and written out key definitions. They have prepared questions and practiced answering them. Once they read a question, they are prepared to write out their "final" drafts.

WARMING UP   **Journal Exercise**

For an upcoming examination in one of your other courses, write out three possible essay questions that your instructor might ask. For each question, underline the key words, and make a sketch outline of your response. Set your watch or timer for fifteen minutes, and actually write out your response to *one* of your questions.

PROOFREAD AND EDIT

In your normal writing process, you can put aside your draft for several days and proofread and edit it later. When you are writing under pressure, however, you need to save three or four minutes at the end to review what you have written. Often, you may be out of time before you have finished writing what you wanted to say about the question. At this point, one effective strategy is to draw a line at the end of what you have written, write "Out of Time," and then write one or two quick sentences explaining what you planned to say: "If I had more time, I would explain how the UN's image has become more positive following the crises in Israel and Iraq." Then use your remaining two or three minutes to reread what you have written, making sure that your ideas are clear and that you have written in complete sentences and used correct spelling and punctuation. If you don't know how to spell a word, at least write "sp?" next to a word to show that you think it is spelled incorrectly.

SAMPLE ESSAY QUESTIONS AND RESPONSES

The following are sample essay questions, students' responses, and instructors' comments and grades.

HISTORY 100: WESTERN CIVILIZATION
Examination II over Chapter 12, class lectures, and Victor Hugo's *The Hunchback of Notre Dame*

Essay I (25 Points)

What was the fifteenth-century view of "science" as described in *The Hunchback*? How did this view tend to inhibit Claud Frollo in his experiments in his closet in the cathedral?

ANSWER 1

An excellent response. Your focus an superstition and heresy along with the specific examples of the roasted mouse, the "Philosopher's Stone," and La Esmeralda's goat illustrate the fifteenth-century view of science and its inhibiting effect. Grade: A

The fifteenth-century view of "science" was characterized by superstition and heresy. In *The Hunchback of Notre Dame*, for example, we see superstition operating when the king's physician states that a gunshot wound can be cured by the application of a roasted mouse. Claud Frollo, a high-ranking church official, has a thirst for knowledge, but unfortunately it pushes beyond the limits of knowledge permitted by the church. When he works in his closet on the art of alchemy and searches for the "Philosopher's Stone" (gold), he is guilty of heresy. Frollo has read and mastered the arts and sciences of the university and of the church, and he wants to know more. He knows that if he presses into the "Black Arts," the Devil will take his soul. And indeed, the "Devil" of passion does. Frollo feels inhibited because many of the experiments he has performed have made him guilty of heresy and witchcraft in the eyes of the church. And this seems to be the case in almost anything "new" or out of the ordinary. La Esmeralda, for instance, is declared "guilty" of witchcraft for the training of her goat. Her goat appears to have been possessed by the Devil himself, when, in fact, all the girl is guilty of is training the goat to do a few simple tricks. All in all, the fifteenth-century view of "science" was one not of favor, but of oppression and fear. Thankfully, the Renaissance came along!

ANSWER 2

The fifteenth-century view of science was that according to the Bible, God was the creator of all, and as to scientific theory, the subject was moot. No one was a believer in the scientific method—however, we do find some science going on in Claud Frollo's closet, alchemy. At that time he was trying to create gold by mixing different elements together. Though alchemy seems to be the only science of that time period, people who practiced it kept it to themselves. We even find King Louis IX coming to Frollo, disguised, to dabble in a little of the science himself. At this time people were rejecting the theory of the Earth revolving around the sun because, as a religious ordeal, God created the Earth and man, and they are the center of all things, so there were no questions to be answered by science, because the answer was God.

Give more examples from the novel and show how the fifteenth-century view actually inhibited Frollo. Otherwise, generally good response. (Why was creating the Earth such a religious "ordeal"?) Grade: B

ANSWER 3

According to *The Hunchback of Notre Dame*, the view of "science" in the fifteenth century was basically alchemy, that is, being able to turn base metals into gold. Everything else that we would regard as scientific today was regarded as sorcery or magic in the fifteenth century. What inhibited Claud Frollo in his experiments of turning base metals into gold was that, according to the laws of alchemy, one needed "The Philosopher's Stone" to complete the experiment, and Claud Frollo was unable to find this particular stone.

Needs more specific illustrations from the novel. Frollo is inhibited by his lack of scientific method and the censure of the church. Underline title of novel: The Hunchback of Notre Dame. Grade: C

ANSWER 4

During the period that the *Hunchback* took place, the attitude toward science was one of fear. Because the setting was in the medieval world, the people were afraid to admit to doing some things that were not being done by a majority of people. The overall view during that period was to keep one's own self out of trouble. The fright may be the result of the public executions which were perhaps Claud Frollo's deterrent in admitting to performing acts of science which others are uneducated in. Claud Frollo was outnumbered in the area of wanting to be "educated" and he kept to himself because he feared the people. He was in a position that didn't give him the power to try and overcome people's attitude of fear toward science. If he tried, he risked his life.

State your ideas more clearly. Your response doesn't answer the question. Very limited in your examples of science. Grade: D

BIOLOGY 220: ECOLOGY
FINAL EXAMINATION

Essay II (20 Points)

Water running down a mountainside erodes its channel and carries with it considerable material. What is the basic source of the energy used by the water to do this work? How is the energy used by water to do this work related to the energy used by life in the stream ecosystem?

ANSWER 1

Good response. Clear focus on the hydrologic cycle, photosynthesis, and solar energy and the source of energy for both the stream and its ecosystems. Grade: A

The process begins with the hydrologic cycle. The sun radiates down and forces evaporation. This H_2O gas condenses and forms rain or snow, which precipitates back to earth. If the precipitation falls on a mountain, it will eventually run down the hillside and erode its channel. (Some water will evaporate without running down the hill.) The energy used by water to do its work relates directly to the energy used by life in the stream system. The sun is an energy input. It is the source of energy for stream life just as it is the source of energy for the water. Through photosynthesis, the energy absorbed by the stream is used by higher and higher trophic levels. So the sun is the energy source for both running water and the life in the stream. It all starts with solar energy.

ANSWER 2

Very clear explanation of the hydrologic cycle, but response doesn't explain how source of energy for the stream ecosystem is related, through photosynthesis, to solar energy. Grade: B

Ultimately, the sun is the basic source of energy that allows water to do the work it does. Solar power runs the hydrologic cycle, which is where water gets its energy. Heat evaporates water and allows molecules to rise in the atmosphere, where it condenses in clouds. Above the ground, but still under the effects of gravity, water has potential energy at this point. When enough condensation occurs, water drops back to the ground, changing potential energy to kinetic energy, which is how water works on mountainsides to move materials. As water moves materials, it brings into streams a great deal of organic matter, which is utilized by a number of heterotrophic organisms. That is the original source of energy for the ecosystems and also how energy used by water is related to the energy that is used by life in streams.

ANSWER 3

The actual energy to move the water down the mountains is gravitational pull from the center of the earth. The stream's "growth" from the beginning of the mountain-top to the base starts out with being a heterotrophic system. This is because usually there is not enough light to bring about photosynthesis for the plants and in turn help other organisms' survival, so the streams use outside resources for energy. Once the stream gets bigger (by meeting up with another stream), it is autotrophic. It can produce its own energy sources. When the water reaches the base and becomes very large, it falls back to a heterotrophic system because the water has become too deep for light to penetrate and help with photosynthesis.

Reread the question. The basic source of energy is solar power. You almost discover the answer when you discuss photosynthesis, but after that, you get off track again. Grade: C—

Credits

by permission of Random House, Inc. **Aurora Levins Morales,** "Child of the Americas," from *Getting Home Alive* by Aurora Levins Morales and Rosario Morales, © 1986 Firebrand Books. Ann Arbor, MI. Used with permission. **Wislawa Szymborska,** "The End and The Beginning," from *View With A Grain Of Sand.* English translation by Stanislaw Baranczak and Clare Cabanagh. Copyright © 1995 Harcourt, Inc. Reprinted by permission of the publisher. "On 'A Worn Path'," by Julia MacMillan & Brett MacFadden. Reprinted with permission. **Pat Russell,** "Death—The Final Freedom." Student essay reprinted with permission. **W.H. Auden,** "Musee des Beaux Arts." Copyright 1940 and renewed 1968 by W.H. Auden from *Collected Poems* by W.H. Auden. Used by permission of Random House, Inc. "The Lesson," by Toni Cade Bambara from *Gorilla, My Love.* Copyright © 1972 by Toni Cade Bambara. Used by permission of Random House, Inc. **Joy Harjo,** "Perhaps the World Ends Here," from *The Woman Who Feel From the Sky.* Copyright © 1994 by Joy Harjo. Used by permission of W. W. Norton & Company, Inc. **Yusef Komunyakaa,** "Facing It," from *Pleasure Dome: New and Collected Poems.* Copyright © 2001 by Yusef Komunyyakka and reprinted by permission of Wesleyan University Press. **Kate McNerny,** "Foreign Language Study: An American Necessity." Student essay reprinted with permission. **Friedman, Thomas I.** *The World Is Flat: A Brief History of the Twenty-First Century.* New York: Farrar, 2004. **Bergentoft,** "Foreign Language Instruction: A Comparative Perspective." *The Annals of the American Academy of Political and Social Science.* 1994, 532: 8-34. Reprinted by Permission of SAGE Publications. Screen shots courtesy of EBSCO Information Services. From *The Delta Kappa Gamma Bulletin.* Reprinted by permission. Reprinted by permission of Google™. U.S. National Library of Medicine & National Institutes of Health and DNA Direct. Courtesy of DNA Direct. Screen shot courtesy of Liza Sanchez, from Bilingual Talk. **Susan Kruglinski,** "Map Evolution Evolving: A Very Public Online Fracas," *Discover Magazine,* Vol. 27, No. 07, July 2007. Copyright © EBSCO Information Services. Reprinted by permission. Citing a periodical (journal cover) *Mind, Culture and Activity: An International Journal,* 8 (2001): 215-30. Citing a work from an online database, EBSCO, Stephen, Andrew, "The Poisonous Legacy of 9/11." *New Statesman* 24 June 2007: 24-26. *Academic Search Premier.* EBSCO. New York Public Library. 20 June 2007. http://www.epnet.com/

Image Credits

2 Mark Shasha **3** Franz Pfluegl\Shutterstock **7** Frank & Ernst, reprinted by permission of Newspaper Enterprise Association, Inc. **14** Mona Lisa by Dennis Wiemar © Layne Kennedy/Corbis **15** Photos.com **44** Diether Endlicher\AP Wide World Photos **45** Courtesy of www.istockphoto.com **47a** Monet, Claude (1840–1926), "Impression, Sunrise" 1872. Oil on canvas, 48 x 63 cm. Painted in Le Havre, France. © Estate of Claude Monet/ARS Artists Rights Society, NY. **47b** Corbis-NY **52a** Stephen Reid **52b** Stephen Reid **61** Alabama Tourism Department **64** © The New Yorker Collection 1976, from cartoonbank.com. All Rights Reserved. **83** George H. H. Huey\Corbis-NY **86** Garcia Bavi **127** Photos.com **141** "Day and Night" by M. C. Escher. © 1997 Cordon Art-Baarn-Holland. All rights reserved. **149** Lucy Reading-Ikkanda iStockphoto **155a** Getty Images **155b** Lew Robertson\iStockphoto **155c** Diane Diederich\iStockphoto **155d** Getty Images **155e** Miles Sherrill\iStockphoto **155f** Shutterstock **155g** Edyta Pawlowska\ Shutterstock **155h** DivaNir4a\iStockphoto **156a** Ryan McVay\Getty Images, Inc. Photodisc/Royalty Free **156b** Shutterstock **156c** Getty Images **156e** Edyta Pawlowska\Shutterstock **156f** iStockphoto **157a** Getty Images **157b** iStockphoto **157c** Feng Yu\Shutterstock **182** Courtesy www.adbusters.org **183** Courtesy of www.istock-photo.com **188a** Courtesy of the Library of Congress **188b** Courtesy of the Library of Congress **190** © Robert C. Kauffmann/Swim Ink 2,LLC / Corbis. All Rights Reserved. **191** Jim Goldberg\ Magnum Photos, Inc. **192** M. Spencer Green\AP Wide World Photos **193b** Getty Images, Inc. **196a** © Corbis **196b** AP Wide World Photos **196c** Brad Roberts **198** Courtesy www.adbusters.org **201** © The New Yorker Collection 2005, Robert Mankoff from cartoonbank.com. All Rights Reserved. **202a** Alfred Eisenstaedt, V-J Day: Sailor Kissing Girl (1945). Life Magazine. © 1945 TimePix **202b** © (Photographer)/ Corbis. All Rights Reserved. **203** © The New Yorker Collection 2000, Peter Mueller from cartoonbank.com. All Rights Reserved. **213** Printed by permission of the Norman Rockwell Family Agency, Copyright © 1960 the Norman Rockwell Family Entities. **216** AP Wide World Photos **218** Sal Veder\AP Wide World Photos **230** Susan Van Etten\PhotoEdit Inc. **237** Eliza Snow\Shutterstock **244** AP Photo/Paul Sakuma **247** Jane Reed\Harvard University **285** Courtesy of www.istockphoto.com **316** Erich Lessing\Art Resource, N.Y. **338** Grant Wood , American 1891–1942, "American Gothic," 1930. Oil on beaver board. 30 11/16" x 25 11/16" (78 x 65.3 cm). Unframed. Friends of American Art Collection. 1930.934. The Art Institute of Chicago. Photography © The Art Institute of Chicago. All Rights reserved by the Estate of Nan Wood Graham/Licensed by VAGA, New York, NY. **392** © UNICEF/HQ89-0052/Gilles Vauclair **404** © The New Yorker Collection 2004, Bruce Eric Kaplan from cartoonbank.com. All Rights Reserved. **410** © The New Yorker Collection 1987, James Stevenson from cartoonbank.com. All Rights Reserved. **438** Everett Collection **456** Doonesbury © 2006 G.B. Trudeau. Reprinted by permission of Universal Press Syndicate. All rights reserved. **480** Getty Images **522** Steve Raymer\Corbis-NY **523** Courtesy of www.istockphoto.com **566** Courtesy of International Business Machines Corporation. Unauthorized use not permitted. **567** Courtesy of www.istockphoto.com **637** www.CartoonStock.com **567** Courtesy of www.istockphoto.com **H-47** © The New Yorker Collection 1987, Michael Maslin from cartoonbank.com. All Rights Reserved.

Index

A

Abbey, Edward, 318
Academic audience. *See* Genres
"Active and Passive Euthanasia," 442
Active reading. *See* Critical reading
Ad hominem fallacy, 422, 504
Ad populum fallacy, 504
Advertisements, citing, 626
Agreeing/disagreeing, 168–169. *See also* Arguing
Alejandrez, Daniel "Nene," 86, 102–105
Allen, Gregory, 68
Alliteration, 545–546
"All's Not Well in Land of 'The Lion King,'" 354–356
Alter, Jonathan, 192
"'American Gothic,' Pitchfork Perfect," 338, 345–347
Analogy, 70–71, 269, 504
Analysis. *See also* Causal analysis; Visuals, analyzing
    of audience, 22–23
    by criteria, 364–365, 417–418
    in expository writing, 286
    for responding to literature, 553
    of rhetorical situation, 25–26
    for shaping responses, 168
    of statistics, 494
    transitional words for, 270
"…And Why I Hate It," 467–469
"Animal Rights and Beyond," 318
"Animal Rights Versus Human Health," 452–453
Annotating texts, 163
"Anorexia Nervosa," 315, 317, 319, 334–336
Anthologies, citing, 621
"anyone lived in a pretty how town," 525, 546
APA style, 609, 610, 629–634
Appeals, 186, 197–199, 446–450
Arguing
    appeals for written argument, 446–450
    circle of alternative positions for, 496
    claims for written argument, 442–446
    developing arguments, 498–499
    essay genre conventions, 24
    listing "pro" and "con" arguments, 495
    outlines for arguments, 497–498
    as purpose of writing, 17, 534
    reporting versus, 270
    in research papers, 605–606
    responding to literature, 534, 557
    Rogerian argument, 450–453
    roles played in, 441
    techniques for, 440–442
    Toulmin method, 453–454
    writing process and, 491–505

"Argument Culture, The," 403–407
Aristotle, 189
Artworks, 344–347, 626
"Athletes and Education," 34–37
Attitude for writing, positive, 7–8
Atwood, Margaret, 7, 127, 142–145
Auden, W. H., 529–530, 544–545
Audience
    analysis of, 22–23
    for analyzing visuals, 211
    for arguing, 491
    critical rereading for, 131
    for descriptive writing, 63
    for designing visuals, 212
    essay examples, 26–29
    for evaluations, 364
    for expository writing, 287, 309, 312
    for investigative writing, 239, 259, 270
    narrowing and focusing the subject for, 578–579
    for problem solving, 387, 410
    purposes for writing based on, 20
    for reading and responding, 159
    reexamining before drafting, 72
    for research papers, 569–571, 576–579, 582, 604
    for responding to literature, 553
    as rhetorical situation element, 17
    for summary/response essay, 171
    for visual design, 200
    for writing about memories, 107
Authors, citing, 620, 631

B

Background investigation, 555
Bambara, Toni Cade, 15, 314–315, 537–543
Barrie, John, 393–395
Bartholomae, David, 129
"Beauty," 94–100, 114
"Because I could not stop for Death," 524, 545
Begging the question, 503
Bellow, Saul, 91
Berry, Wendell, 393
Berthoff, Ann, 65
Bibliographic records, 583–586
Biographical sketch, 243–246
Bird, Caroline, 444–445
"Black Hair," 547–548
Blake, William, 525, 545–546
Blakely, Chris, 325–333
Blixen, Karen, 49
Blogs, 8–9, 601–603, 625, 633
Body paragraphs, 320–321

I-1

Boese, Eric, 513–520
Books, citing, 619, 620–621, 631–632
"Borrowers Can Be Choosy," 370–378
Bovard, Juli, 114, 121–124
"Boy's Desire, The," 92–93, 114
Brainstorming, 108
Branching, 311, 493
Brochure genre, 25
Brodsky, Joseph, 549–550
Brosseau, Nancie, 315, 317, 319, 334–336
Browe, Sonja H., 177, 179–180
Burroughs, William, 52
Butler, Carolyn Kleiner, 217–220
Byron, Lord, 323

C
Cameron, Chris, 365
"Can Citizen Journalism Pick Up the Pieces?" 422–428
"Can Wikipedia Handle Stephen Colbert's Truthiness," 480–481
Canada, Geoffrey, 389–391
Carlyle, Thomas, 127
Cartoons, citing, 626
"Casebook on Responses to Climate Change," 136–157
Causal analysis
    for evaluations, 366
    in expository writing, 288, 292–294, 315, 317
    for problem solving, 417
    questions for, 311
Cause and effect, claims of, 443–444, 493, 579
Cause-and-effect fallacies, 323–324
Cause-and-effect relationships, 292
"César Chávez Saved My Life," 86, 102–105
Character, appeals to, 198, 448–449
Characters in short fiction, 535, 555
Chávez, César, 86, 183
"Child of the Americas," 546–547
Chopin, Kate, 526–529, 535, 536
Chronological order
    in descriptive writing, 68
    for evaluations, 366
    in expository writing, 315
    in investigative writing, 268
    for problem solving, 418
    transitional words for, 115, 270
    for writing about memories, 90, 110
Circle of alternative positions, 496
Circular argument, 503
Citing sources. See Documenting sources
Claims. See also Thesis or main idea
    for arguing, 441, 442–446, 492–494
    of cause and effect, 443–444, 493
    circle of alternative positions for, 496
    for evaluations, 341
    evaluations versus, 340
    of fact or definition, 442–443, 493
    listing "pro" and "con" arguments, 495
    narrowing and focusing, 492–493, 578–579
    for research papers, 578–579

about solutions or policies, 445–446, 493
as thesis for arguing, 441
about value, 444–445, 493
about visual's significance, 185
Classification, 269, 313, 323
Cleaver, Cathleen A., 453–454, 456–461
"Climate Repair Manual, A," 148–150
Climax, 535
Closed questions, 266
Clustering, 108, 109, 493
Cohen, Noam, 487–489
Coherence in body paragraphs, 320
Coleridge, Samuel Taylor, 189
Colgrave, Sukie, 288
Collaborative annotation, 553
Collecting, methods of
    analyzing statistics, 494
    for analyzing visuals, 213
    answering questions, 66, 310–311
    for arguing, 492–494
    asking questions, 261–263
    brainstorming, 108
    branching, 311
    citing sources, 264
    clustering, 108, 109
    for descriptive writing, 65–66
    double-entry notes, 66
    for evaluations, 362–364
    for expository writing, 310–312
    field research, 264–267, 364
    freewriting, 66
    investigating, 312, 363–364, 415, 494
    for investigative writing, 261–267
    looping, 108–109
    narrowing and focusing claims, 492–493, 578–579
    noting key quotations, 588
    observing, 311, 362–363, 414, 494
    overview, 31
    for problem solving, 411–415
    reading, 312, 363, 415
    reading log, 163–164
    recording bibliographic information, 583–586
    remembering, 312, 363, 414, 493
    in researching, 583–589
    for responding to literature, 553–556
    sketching, 65–66
    summarizing, 263–264, 586–588
    synthesizing sources, 588–589
    text annotation, 163
    for writing about memories, 108–109
"College Is a Waste of Time and Money," 444–445
"Coming Home," 217–220
Commercial products or services, evaluating, 343–344
Community-service learning, 260–261
Comparison/contrast, 68–69, 110–111, 268–270, 365–366, 504
Composition of visuals, 185, 187, 188
Conclusions, 71, 114, 269, 323, 367, 606
Conflict, 535

Connections, making for memories, 89
Conrad, Joseph, 45, 70
Context
    analyzing visuals in, 186, 191–195
    critical rereading for, 131
    essay examples, 26–29
    as rhetorical situation element, 18
    social or cultural, 18, 89, 215–217, 287, 387
Contrast. *See* Comparison/contrast
Cook, Jessica, 429–436
Coward, Noel, 360
Credibility, appeals to, 198
Criteria, 340, 341
Criteria analysis, 364–365, 417–418
Critical reading. *See also* Summary/response essays
    as active reading, 128
    for analyzing visuals, 213
    annotating texts, 163
    class discussion guidelines, 132–133
    in collecting, 312
    defined, 130
    double-entry log for, 130
    for evaluations, 363
    importance of skills in, 128
    for problem solving, 415
    reading, defined, 128
    rereading guide, 130–132
    in researching, 570
    responding to an essay, 138–141
    strategies for, 130–132
    summarizing an essay, 137–138
    writing process and, 159–173
Cross, Donna Woolfolk, 314
Crouch, Dennis, 240
Cultural or social context, 18, 89, 215–217, 287, 387
cummings, e. e., 525, 546
Currency of sources, 572, 585–586

D

"Damnation of a Canyon, The," 318
Dargis, Manohla, 348–350
Databases, online, 593–596, 633
"Death and Justice," 318–319
"Death: The Final Freedom," 563–565
Declaration of Independence, 41–42
Definition
    claims of, 442–443, 493
    in descriptive writing, 69–70
    in expository writing, 287, 288–290, 312–313
    extended, 289
    formal, parts of, 288–289
    questions for, 310
    in responding to literature, 559
    revising, 323
Denouement, 535
Descriptive process analysis, 290, 291–292
Descriptive writing. *See* Observing
Devlin, Dudley Erskine, 159–162

Dialogue, in writing about memories, 113–114
Dickinson, Emily, 524, 545
Dictionaries, citing, 621
Didion, Joan, 261
Digital publications, citing, 626
Dillard, Annie, 45, 567
Dinesen, Isak, 49
Direct quotation, 165–166, 499
Discussion list postings, citing, 625
Dissertations, citing, 621, 632
Doctorow, E. L., 48
Documenting sources
    APA style, 610, 626–634
    in investigative writing, 264
    mixing APA and MLA styles, avoiding, 609
    MLA style, 610–611, 613–626
    recording bibliographic information, 583–586
    sources requiring citation, 607–608
    stages of, 575–576
    summarizing source material, 586–588
    in-text citation, 264, 570, 609–611, 613–615, 627–629
Dominant idea. *See* Thesis or main idea
Double-entry log, 9, 130
Double-entry notes, 66
Drafting
    in analyzing visuals, 220
    arguments, 499, 501
    creating a draft, 72
    described, 31–32
    in descriptive writing, 72
    evaluations, 368–369
    in expository writing, 321
    in investigative writing, 269–270
    in problem solving, 418
    research papers, 607–611
    in responding to literature, 558
    summary/response essays, 170–171
    in writing about memories, 114–115
Drew, Elizabeth, 440
Drews, Frank, 240
"Drivers on Cell Phones Are as Bad as Drunks," 240
Duster, Troy, 395, 399–400

E

Edison, Thomas, 569
Edited books, citing, 621, 632
Editorials, citing, 618, 620, 624, 630
Ehrenreich, Barbara, 133–141
Einstein, Albert, 91
Either/or fallacy, 421, 503–504
E-mail, 25, 625
Emotion, appeals to, 197, 449
"Empty Windows," 82–84
Encyclopedias, citing, 621
"End and Beginning," 549–550
Endnotes (MLA style), 615–616
Energy for writing, tips for, 7–8
Escher, M. C., 141

Essay exams. *See* Pressure, writing under
Essay map, 319
Evaluating
    artworks, 344–347
    blogs, 601–603
    commercial products or services, 343–344
    criteria for, 340
    journal articles, 595–596
    online database sources, 263, 593, 595–596
    open Web sources, 263, 598–603
    performances, 347–350
    possible solutions to problems, 413
    for problem solving subject, 410–411
    purpose of, 340
    as purpose of writing, 17, 533–534
    responding to literature, 533–534, 556–557
    techniques for, 340–343
    writing process and, 360–370
"Evaluating a Web Site," 351–354
Evidence
    in argumentation, 441
    audience and, 22
    critical rereading for, 132
    for evaluations, 340, 341
    in expository writing, 288
    for responding to literature, 531, 558–559
    supporting responses, 139, 171
Example, in expository writing, 313–314
Exams. *See* Pressure, writing under
Explaining. *See also* Expository writing
    causal analysis for, 292–294
    definition for, 287, 288–290
    figurative expressions for, 289–290
    process analysis for, 287, 290–292
    as purpose of writing, 17, 286, 533
    research tips for, 313
    responding to literature, 533, 556
    techniques for, 287–288
    writing process and, 308–324
Exposition, 535
Expository writing. *See also* Explaining
    collecting for, 310–312
    genres for, 309
    purpose of, 286
    revising, 321–324
    shaping, 312–321
    subject for, 309–310
Expressing, as purpose of writing, 17
Extended definitions, 289

F
"Facebook US Audience Growth," 469–470
"Face to Face," 243–246
"Facing It," 522, 550–551
"Facing It: Reflections on War," 560–562
Fact, claims of, 442–443, 493, 579
Fahnestock, Jeanne, 339
Fallacies in logic, 421–422, 502–504

Feature list, 554
Field research, 263, 264–267, 364
"50 Things You Can Do," 155–157
Figurative expressions, 289–290
Films, citing, 625, 634
First person, 90, 535
Fist Stick Knife Gun, 389–391
Fitzgerald, F. Scott, 269
Fletcher, Lawrence, 226–234
Flower, Linda, 20, 137
Focal point of visuals, 187, 188
Footnotes (MLA style), 615
"Foreign Language Study," 634–648
Foreshadowing, 535
Formal definition. *See* Definition
Fornes, Maria Irene, 8
Forster, E. M., 15
Forum postings, citing, 633
Freewriting, 5, 19, 22, 25, 66, 108–109, 493
Freire, Paulo, 138
Frost, Robert, 87, 525, 544
Fuentes, Carlos, 89
Furnish, Dale, 67–68

G
Gaines, Ernest J., 72
Garfinkel, Simson L., 477–479
Gates, Henry Louis, Jr., 246–248
Generalization, hasty, 502
General Reference materials, 592
Genres
    for analyzing visuals, 211
    for arguing, 491
    audience and, 22, 63
    choosing appropriately, 17–18
    common, conventions for, 24–25
    critical rereading for, 131
    defined, 17
    for descriptive writing, 63
    for designing visuals, 212
    for evaluations, 360, 364
    for expository writing, 287, 309, 312
    for investigative writing, 239, 259, 270
    for problem solving, 410, 415–416
    for reading and responding, 159
    for research papers, 569–570, 571–572, 576–577, 604
    for responding to literature, 553
    for service-learning projects, 260–261
    for summary/response essays, 171
    of visuals, analyzing, 186, 195–196
    for writing about memories, 109, 110
"Gimme an A (I Insist!)," 242–243
Goldberger, Paul, 51
Goldman, Albert, 68–69
Goodman, Ellen, 215–217, 612
Gorman, Michael, 463
Government documents, citing, 621, 632

H

Hairston, Maxine, 31
Hamill, Pete, 604
Harjo, Joy, 548–549
Harris, Sidney, 69–70
Hasty generalization, 502
Hawthorne, Nathaniel, 524
Hemingway, Ernest, 3, 272
"Henry Louis Gates Jr. Will Now Take Your Questions," 246–248
Hightower, Jim, 395, 401
Hoffman, Gregory, 110, 114
Hoffman, Roy, 11–13
"Hollywood Indian, The," 272–279
"Homeless and Their Children, The," 251–257, 268–269
Horton, Sarah, 183
Houston, Jeanne Wakatsuke, 92
"How Male and Female Students Use Language Differently,"
        176–177, 302–307
"How to Take Control of Your Credit Cards," 296–300
Howard, Rebecca Moore, 393–395
Huang, Lily, 474–475
Hurston, Zora Neale, 567

I

Iambic pattern, 545
"I'm O.K., but You're Not," 28–29, 318
Images, 48, 111, 316
Impression: Sunrise, 47
Inductive logic, 446, 447–448
Internet
        blogs, 8–9, 601–603, 625, 633
        citing sources (APA style), 632–633
        citing sources (MLA style), 623–625
        evaluations using, 363–364
        online databases, 593–594
        open Web sources, 263, 596–603
        research tips for, 263
"Internet, The: A Clear and Present Danger," 453–454, 456–461
Interpreting, for shaping responses, 169
Interviewing, 246–248, 264–265, 415
Interviews, citing, 618, 626, 634
Introductions, 71, 114, 269, 317–319, 367, 605
Inverted pyramid, 267–268
Investigating
        in collecting, 312, 494
        for evaluations, 363–364
        for problem solving, 415
        purpose of, 238
        for responding to literature, 555, 557
Investigative writing
        brief report with graphics, 232–233
        field research for, 263, 264–267
        interviewing, 246–248, 264–265
        profile of a person, 243–246
        report on research study, 239–242
        research tips for, 263
        techniques for, 238–239
        "Wh" questions for, 239, 267–268, 270

writing process, 258–272
"IPCC Fourth Assessment, The," 146–147
"Is Deborah Tannen Convincing?" 177, 179–180

J

Jackson, Shirley, 524
Jefferson, Thomas, 41
Johnson, Samuel, 589
Jong, Erica, 75
Journal, 8–13, 72
Journal articles, evaluating, 595–596
Journalistic reports. *See* Investigative writing; Reporting
Judgment, 341

K

Kafka, Franz, 524
Kammen, Daniel M., 150–155
Kidder, Tracy, 309, 491
King, Martin Luther, Jr., 449–450
Kingsolver, Barbara, 5
Kliff, Sarah, 467–469
Klockeman, Courtney, 379–383
Koch, Edward, 318–319
Koester, Jennifer, 176, 177–179
Komunyakaa, Yusef, 522, 550–551
Kozol, Jonathan, 251–257, 268–269, 292–293
Kress, Gunther, 17
Kushner, David, 243–246, 264

L

Laboratory report genre, 24
Language, critical rereading for, 132
Larsen, Elizabeth, 249–251, 268, 269
Lazarus, Margaret, 354–356
Lead-in, for expository writing, 317–319
Lectures, citing, 626
Lee, Andrea, 90–91, 110, 114
Lessing, Doris, 3
"Lesson, The," 537–543
"Letter from Birmingham Jail," 449–450
Letters, citing, 626
"Letter to America," 127, 142–145
"Letter to Margaret Atwood," 173–176
Letter-to-the-editor genre, 25
Lewis, Karyn M., 223–225, 317
Library, 263, 363–364, 592–593
Lippmann, Walter, 237, 439
Listserv postings, citing, 625
Lives of a Cell, The, 291–292
Logic, errors in, 421–422, 502–504
Looping, 108–109, 493
Loos, Anita, 106
"Lottery, The," 524
Lynch, Patrick, 183

M

Macke, Jennifer, 76–81
Magazines. *See* Periodicals

Main idea. *See* Thesis or main idea
Malamud, Bernard, 72
Manjoo, Farhad, 464–467
Mannes, Marya, 339
Maps, citing, 625
Márquez, Gabriel Garcia, 6, 114
Maynard, Joyce, 87
McNerny, Kate, 583, 634–648
Mediaspeak, 314
Meininger, Linda, 370–378
Memories. *See* Remembering
"Metamorphosis, The," 524
Metaphor, 70, 269, 545
Midler, Bette, 607
Miller, Carolyn, 18
Milton, John, 439
"Miss Clairol's 'Does She... Or Doesn't She?'" 205–210
Mitchell, William, 183
Mitford, Jessica, 318
MLA Handbook for Writers of Research Papers, 583
MLA style, 609, 610–611, 613–626
Momaday, N. Scott, 91
Montgomery, James, 480–481
Moore, Abigail Sullivan, 242–243
Moraga, Cherrie, 267
Morales, Aurora Levins, 546–547
Morrison, Toni, 91, 114
Mowat, Farley, 290–291
Muir, John, 50–51
Multigenre Casebook on Web 2.0, 462–489
"Multiracialness," 295–296
Murray, Donald, 9, 19
"Musée des Beaux Arts," 529–530, 544–545
"My Friend Michelle, an Alcoholic," 280–283
Myths about writing, 3–5

N

Nabokov, Vladimir, 368
Narratives, 89, 90, 187, 188–189, 535–536
Necessary and sufficient causes, 292
Neeld, Elizabeth Cowan, 312
Nestle, Marion, 395, 396–397
"New Regulations and You," 429–436
Newspapers, citing, 618, 620, 624, 630, 633
Niebuhr, Reinhold, 393
Nonthreatening (Rogerian) argument, 450–453
Nussbaum, Emily, 470–473

O

Objects, observing, 51–52
O'Brien, Edna, 4
Observing
    for analyzing visuals, 213
    in collecting, 311, 494
    before drafting, 72
    effectively, 46–47
    for evaluations, 362–363
    objects, 51–52

people, 49–50
places, 50–51
for problem solving, 414
sensory details, 46, 48, 89
techniques for writing about observations, 48–49
what is not there, 48
for writing about memories, 89
writing process and, 63–75
Occasion, 17, 89, 131
"One Thing to Do About Food," 395–401
"On Keeping a Journal," 11–13
Online databases, 593–596, 633
"On Writing 'Athletes and Education,'" 38–40
Open questions, 265–266
Open Web sources, 263, 596–603
Orman, Suze, 296–300
Orwell, George, 111
"Out of the Picture on the Abortion Ban," 215–217
Outlines, 169–170, 416–417, 497–498, 606, A-4–5

P

Pamphlets, citing, 621
Paragraph hooks, 319–320
Paraphrase, 165, 166
Past tense, 90
Performances, 347–350, 626
"Perhaps the World Ends Here," 548–549
Periodicals
    APA style citation, 629–630
    journal article evaluation, 595–596
    MLA style citation, 616–618, 620
    online, APA style citation, 633
    online, MLA style citation, 624
"Permanent Tracings," 76–81
Persona, 112–113, 269
Personal audience. *See* Genres
Personal essay genre, 24
"Personality Pill, The," 317–318
Personification, 545
Petrie, Neil H., 34–40
Petrosky, Anthony, 129
Petry, Todd, 114, 118–120
Picture, drawing for literature, 554–555
Place of publication, 18
Place to write, tips for, 6–7
Plagiarism, avoiding, 165, 166, 608–609
Plato, 446
Plot, in short fiction, 535
Plug-In Drug, The: Television, Children, and the Family, 444
Podcasts, citing, 625
Poetry, 529–530, 544–552, 553, 624
Policies, claims about, 445–446, 493, 579
Pollan, Michael, 395, 397–399
Porter, Katherine Anne, 341
Post hoc fallacies, 323–324, 502–503
Posting to electronic forums, 25
Prescriptive process analysis, 290–291
Present tense, 90, 559

Pressure, writing under, A-1–11
  analyzing key terms, A-3–4
  knowing the material, A-2, A-6–7
  knowing your audience, A-3
  making a sketch outline, A-4–5
  overview, A-1–3
  practicing for, A-2, A-7
  proofreading and editing, A-8
  sample questions and responses, A-8–11
Primary sources, 590–591
"Pro" and "con" arguments, listing, 495
Problem solving
  answering objections, 414
  convincing your readers, 387, 389–391, 413–414
  demonstrating a problem exists, 387, 388–389, 411–412
  discovering possible solutions, 412–413
  evaluating possible solutions, 413
  listing step for implementation, 414
  mapping effects of a problem, 412
  patterns for, 416–417
  proposing a solution, 17, 387, 389–391, 412–413
  as purpose of writing, 534
  responding to literature, 534
  techniques for, 386–388
  writing process and, 409–421
Process analysis, 287, 290–292, 310, 315
"Professors Should Embrace Wikipedia," 484–486
Profile of a person, 243–246
"Progress or Not," 192
Proofreading essay exams, A-8
"Protect the Willfully Ignorant," 474–475
Proust, Marcel, 47
Public audience. *See* Genres
Publication Manual of the American Psychological Association, 583, 585
Purpose for visual design, 200
Purposes for writing
  audience analysis and, 22–23
  audience-based, 20
  combinations of, 20–21
  critical rereading for, 131
  defined, 17
  essay examples, 26–29
  expository writing, 286
  genre choices and, 24–25
  incorporating sources and, 574–575
  investigative writing, 270
  narrowing and focusing the subject, 578–579
  reexamining before drafting, 72
  research papers, 569–570, 571, 578–579, 604
  responding to literature, 533–534, 556
  subject and thesis relationship to, 21
  subject-based, 20, 21
  summary/response essays, 171
  writer-based, 19–20

Q

Quammen, David, 318

Questionnaires, 265–267, 415
Quotation, 165–166, 239, 499, 559, 588

R

Rachels, James, 442
Radio programs, citing, 626, 634
Ralli, Tania, 193, 194–195
Ransom, Elizabeth, 395, 399–400
Raymond, James C., 48
Reading. *See* Critical reading
Reading log, 163–164
Reason, appeals to, 197, 446–448
Recordings, citing, 625, 634
"Red Chevy, The," 114, 121–124
Red herring fallacy, 504
"Red Light for Scofflaws, A," 388–389
Reference librarian, 263, 592
Reference sources, 592
References list (APA), 610, 629
Reflecting, for shaping responses, 169
Relevance and reliability of sources, 572, 585–586
Remembering
  for analyzing visuals, 213
  in collecting, 312, 493
  for evaluations, 363
  events, 92–93
  people, 91
  places, 92
  for problem solving, 414
  techniques for writing about memories, 88–91
  writing process and, 106–117
Reporting. *See also* Investigative writing
  arguing versus, 270
  brief report with graphics, 232–233
  as purpose of writing, 17
  on research study, 239–242
Research papers. *See also* Documenting sources
  audience, 571
  avoiding plagiarism, 608–609
  genres, 571–572
  purpose of, 571, 574–575
  voice in, 574–575
  writing process, 603–613
Research review genre, 24
Research study, report on, 239–242
Researching. *See also* Research papers; Sources
  choosing and evaluating sources, 589–603
  collecting and notetaking, 583–589
  for evaluations, 363–364
  field research, 263, 264–267, 364
  finding the best sources, 572
  planning for, 572–573
  for problem solving, 415
  skills needed for, 568–569
  strategies for, 582–583
  techniques for, 569–570
  tips for, 263, 313, 367, 499

Responding to literature
  critical-reading skills required for, 524
  imagination required for, 524–525
  poetry, 529–530, 544–552
  purposes for, 533–534
  rereading required for, 525
  sharing required for, 525–526
  short fiction, 526–529, 534–544
  techniques for, 531
  writing process and, 552–560
"Response to Deborah Tannen's Essay, A," 176, 177–179
Responses
  to essays, 138–141
  to opposing points of view, 441
Reviews, citing, 620, 624, 634
Revising
  in analyzing visuals, 220–222
  arguments, 501–504
  described, 32
  in descriptive writing, 72–75
  distance and objectivity for, 72–74
  editing versus, 32
  evaluations, 369–370
  in expository writing, 321–324
  fallacies in logic, 502–504
  in investigative writing, 270–272
  in problem solving, 419–421
  research papers, 612–613
  in responding to literature, 558–559
  summary/response essays, 171–173
  in writing about memories, 115–117
Rexroth, Grace, 560–562
Rheingold, Howard, 463
Rhetorical appeals, 186, 197–199, 446–450
Rhetorical situation, 16–19, 25–26, 130, 341, 441. *See also specific
  elements*
Rhyme, 545–546
Rhythm, 545–546
Richard, Paul, 338, 345–347
Richman, Adam, 422–428
Richman, Phyllis C., 342, 364
Rico, Gabriele Lusser, 285
"Rise of Renewable Energy, The," 150–155
Rituals, writing, 3, 5–11
"Road Not Taken, The," 525, 544
Rodriguez, Richard, 92–93, 110, 114
Rogerian argument, 450–453
Rogers, Carl, 451
Rosen, Charles, 214–215
Rosen, Larry D., 473
Rosenblatt, Louise, 523
Rosenfeld, Albert, 452–453
Russell, Pat, 563–565

S

Sabatke, Crystal, 505–512
Sagan, Carl, 70–71
Sale, Roger, 285

Sánchez, Liza, 603
Sandwiching quotations, 499
"Say Everything," 470–473
Schaef, Anne Wilson, 445–446
Schlosser, Eric, 395, 396
Schnoor, Jerald L., 146–147
Scholarly journals, citing, 618, 630, 633
Scientific method, 446
Scudder, Samuel H., 53–56, 66, 71
Search engines, using, 597–598
Secondary sources, 590, 591
Secor, Marie, 339
Sedaris, David, 355, 356–359
Selected Bibliography (MLA), 616
Setting for short fiction, 536
Shange, Ntozake, 8
Shaping
  analogy for, 70–71, 269
  for analyzing visuals, 214–220
  arguments, 494–499
  body paragraphs, 320–321
  causal analysis for, 288, 292–294, 311, 315, 317, 366, 417
  chronological order for, 68, 90, 110, 115, 268, 270, 315, 366, 418
  circle of alternative positions for, 496
  classification for, 269, 313
  comparison/contrast for, 68–69, 110–111, 268–270, 365–366, 504
  conclusions, 71, 114, 269, 323, 367, 606
  criteria analysis for, 364–365, 417–418
  definition for, 69–70, 287, 288–290, 310, 312–313
  described, 31
  for descriptive writing, 66–71
  developing arguments, 498–499
  dialogue, 113–114
  essay map for, 319
  for evaluations, 364–367
  example for, 313–314
  for expository writing, 312–321
  genre for, 109
  images for, 111
  introductions, 71, 114, 269, 317–319, 367, 605
  inverted pyramid for, 267–268
  for investigative writing, 267–269
  lead-in, 317–319
  listing "pro" and "con" arguments, 495
  logical analysis for, 168
  metaphor for, 70, 269
  organization strategies for, 68–71
  outlines for, 169–170, 416–417, 497–498
  persona, 112–113, 269
  for problem solving, 415–418
  process analysis for, 287, 290–292, 310, 315
  questions for, 66–67, 109, 604
  research papers, 604–606
  for responding to literature, 556–557
  responses, 164, 167–169
  simile for, 70, 269

spatial order for, 67–68
summaries, 164–167, 169–170
titles, 71, 114, 239, 269, 366–367
voice and tone, 111–112, 269, 314–315, 574–575
for writing about memories, 109–114
Shaw, George Bernard, 387
Short fiction, responding to, 526–529, 534–544, 553
"Should Educators Use Commercial Services to Combat Plagiarism?" 393–395
Simile, 70, 269, 545
Singer, Peter, 395, 400
Sketch outline, A-4–5
Sketching, for collecting, 65–66
"Slumdog Millionaire," 348–350
Smith, Lillian, 237
Social networking online, texts on, 464–476, 487–489
Social or cultural context, 18, 89, 215–217, 287, 387
Solutions, claims about, 445–446, 493
"Some Don't Like Their Blues at All," 223–225, 317
Soto, Gary, 547–548
Sound, in responding to poetry, 545–546
Sources. *See also* Documenting sources
    background information, 591–592
    blogs, 601–603
    evaluating, 263, 593, 595–596, 598, 600–603
    General Reference materials, 592
    journal articles, 595–596
    online databases, 593–596
    open Web, 263, 596–603
    primary and secondary, 590–591
Spatial order, 67–68
Speeches, citing, 626
Spirit of the Valley, 288
Stafford, William, 31
"Standardized Tests: Shouldn't We Be Helping Our Students," 513–520
Statistics, analyzing, 494
Steinbeck, John, 67
Steinem, Gloria, 6
Stix, Gary, 148–150
Stone, Bridgid, 280–283
"Story of an Hour, The," 526–529, 535, 536
Strain, Lauren, 272–279
Strayer, David, 239
"Struggle to Be an All-American Girl, The," 27–28, 317
Style, 132, 536
Subject
    for analyzing visuals, 212
    for arguing, 491–492
    audience–subject relationship, 23
    for descriptive writing, 63–65
    for evaluations, 361–362
    for expository writing, 309–310
    for investigative writing, 259–260
    narrowing and focusing, 578–579
    for problem solving, 410–411
    purpose and, 20, 21
    for research papers, 577–578

for summary/response essay, 159
for writing about memories, 107
Summarizing, 137–138, 166–167, 239, 263–264, 575, 586–588
Summary/response essays
    avoiding plagiarism, 165, 166
    drafting, 170–171
    outlines for, 169–170
    response shaping, 164, 167–169
    revising, 171–173
    summary shaping, 164–167, 169–170
"Surfin' the Louvre," 249–251, 268, 269
Surveys, citing, 626
Swift, Dean C., 173–176
Symbols in poetry, 545
Synchronous communications, citing, 625
Synthesizing sources, 588–589
Szymborska, Wislawa, 549–550

T
"Take This Fish and Look at It," 53–56
Tannen, Deborah, 127, 176–177, 302–307, 403–407
"Teach Diversity—with a Smile," 133, 134–136, 137–138, 139–141
"Teaching Tolerance in America," 159–162
"Teens Feel Safe on MySpace," 473
Television programs, citing, 626, 634
Tense, 90, 559
Text, visuals with, 186, 189–191, 200
Text message genre, 25
Texts. *See also* Critical reading
    analyzing and responding to, 138–139
    annotating, 163
    defined, 128
Themes, 187, 189, 536
Thesis or main idea. *See also* Claims
    comparing with conclusion, 323
    critical rereading for, 131
    for evaluations, 341
    for expository writing, 319
    for investigative writing, 239
    for narratives of memories, 89, 90
    purpose for writing related to, 21
    reexamining before drafting, 72
    for research papers, 589, 604
    for responding to literature, 531
    of responses, 139
    rethinking and revising, 589
"Think before You Post," 476
Third-person omniscient narrator, 535–536
Thomas, Lewis, 291–292
Thurber, James, 112–114
Time line, 553–554
Time of day to write, 6–7
Titles, 71, 114, 239, 269, 366–367, 584
"To Dispel Fears of Live Burial," 318
"Today's Special," 356–359
Tollett, John, 351–354
Tone and voice, 111–112, 269, 314–315, 544–545, 574–575

Tools for writing, selecting, 6–7
Topic sentence, 320
Toufexis, Anastasia, 317–318
Toulmin, Stephen, 453
Toulmin method of argument, 453–454
"Trailing History," 58–61
Transitional words, 115, 270, 319–320, 324
Translations, citing, 621, 631
"Triple Self-Portrait," 214–215
Trippett, Frank, 388–389
Twain, Mark, 31, 115
Tweet genre, 25
Twitchell, James, 205–210, 319–321
"Twitter on the Barricades in Iran," 487–489
"Tyger, The," 525, 545–546

U

Unity in body paragraphs, 320
Usenet postings, citing, 625
Uses of Argument, The, 453

V

Value, claims about, 444–445, 493, 579
Vidal, Gore, 3
Visuals, analyzing
        composition, 185, 187, 188
        in context, 186, 191–195
        defined, 185
        focal point, 187, 188
        genre, 186, 195–196
        narrative, 187, 188–189
        processes for, 211–223
        rhetorical appeals, 186, 197–199
        social context as focus of, 215–217
        story as focus of, 217–220
        synthesizing your analysis, 185, 198–199
        techniques for, 185–186
        text with, 186, 189–191
        themes, 187, 189
        visual as focus of, 214–215
Visuals, designing, 199–200, 211–223
Vogel, Scott, 58–61
Voice and tone, 111–112, 269, 314–315, 544–545,
        574–575
"Vulgar Propriety," 379–383

W

Walker, Alice, 94–100, 110, 114, 238
Waters, Neil L., 481–484
Weaver, Constance, 127
Web, the. *See* Internet
Web 2.0 sources, evaluating, 601
Weekly, Kurt, 111–112, 114

"Weight Loss 101 for the Adult Fitness Program," 226–234
"Welfare Is Still Necessary for Women and Children in the U.S.,"
        505–512
Welty, Eudora, 31
"Wh" questions, 239, 267–268, 270, 411–412, 579
When Society Becomes an Addict, 445–446
White, E. B., 287, 289–290, 495
White, Stephen, 82–84
"White Lies: White-Collar Crime in America," 325–333
"Who's a Looter," 193, 194–195
"Why You Can't Cite Wikipedia in My Class," 481–484
Wikipedia, texts on, 477–486
"Wikipedia and the Meaning of Truth," 477–479
Wiley, Jennifer, 199
Williams, Robin, 351–354
Williams, Sherley Anne, 20, 367
Wilson, Mark, 484–486
"Wind Catcher, The," 114, 118–120
Winn, Marie, 444
Wong, Elizabeth, 27–28, 317
Word choice, in responding to poetry, 545
Works Cited list (MLA), 610, 616
Works Consulted list (MLA), 616
Wright, Richard, 523
Writer, 16–17, 23
Writer-based purposes, 19–20
Write-to-learn journal entries, 9–10
Writing courses, benefits of, 4–5
Writing journal entries, 9, 10
Writing process. *See also specific dimensions*
        for analyzing and designing visuals, 211–223
        arguing and, 491–505
        critical reading and, 159–173
        in Declaration of Independence, 41–42
        dimensions of, 30–33
        evaluating and, 360–370
        explaining and, 308–324
        finding yours, 33
        investigative writing and, 258–272
        observing and, 63–75
        problem solving and, 409–421
        recursive nature of, 32
        remembering and, 106–117
        research papers and, 603–613
        responding to literature and, 552–560

Y

"You Have No Friends," 464–467
"Young Goodman Brown," 524

Z

Zerner, Henri, 214–215
Zoellner, Robert, 28–29, 318